ALSO BY HAYDEN HERRERA

Matisse: A Portrait

Frida: A Biography of Frida Kahlo

Frida Kahlo: The Paintings

Mary Frank

ARSHILE GORKY

ARSHILE GORKY

His Life and Work

✻

HAYDEN HERRERA

Farrar, Straus and Giroux

New York

Farrar, Straus and Giroux
19 Union Square West, New York 10003

Copyright © 2003 by Hayden Herrera
All rights reserved
Distributed in Canada by Douglas & McIntyre Ltd.
Printed in the United States of America
First edition, 2003

Library of Congress Cataloging-in-Publication Data
Herrera, Hayden.
    Arshile Gorky, his life and work / Hayden Herrera.—1st ed.
        p.   cm.
    Includes bibliographical references and index.
    ISBN 0-374-11323-8 (hc : alk. paper)
        1. Gorky, Arshile, 1904–1948. 2. Painters—United States—Biography.
    I. Gorky, Arshile, 1904–1948.   II. Title.

ND237.G613 H47 2003
759.13—dc21
[B]
                                                                    2002033881

Designed by Jonathan D. Lippincott

www.fsgbooks.com

1   3   5   7   9   10   8   6   4   2

For Desmond

Contents

✳

Prologue 3

PART I
1. Charahan Surp Nishan 9
2. Armenians in Ottoman Turkey 12
3. Khorkom 16
4. Boyhood 30
5. The Departure of Sedrak Adoian 38
6. Akhtamar 40

PART II
7. To Van 47
8. The American Mission at Van 53
9. Massacres 57
10. The Siege of Van 66
11. Our Fatherland 76

PART III
12. Flight into Russia 83
13. Yerevan 89
14. Famine 96

PART IV
15. Watertown and Providence 107
16. The Young Master 116

PART V

17. The Early Years in New York 127
18. Apprentice to the Masters 136
19. Teaching 144
20. *The Artist and His Mother* 151
21. *Portrait of Myself and My Imaginary Wife* 158
22. The Cafeteria People 170
23. Copy Art and Imitate Nature 180

PART VI

24. Another Cup of Coffee, Another Piece of Pie 197
25. Fervent Scrutinizer 209
26. Exhibitions 215
27. Marny George 228
28. Corinne 239
29. Lyrical Man 247

PART VII

30. The Artists' Union and the American Abstract Artists 255
31. The Newark Airport Murals 264
32. "Deeper and Purer Work" 281
33. Armenian Portraits 292
34. The End of the Decade 301
35. A Language for All to Understand 313

PART VIII

36. Mougouch 321
37. Cohabitation 329
38. San Francisco 337
39. Marriage 350
40. *Garden in Sochi* 358
41. Camouflage 365

PART IX

42. Surrealists in Exile 379
43. *Waterfall* 393

PART X

44. Virginia 413
45. *The Leaf of the Artichoke Is an Owl* 427
46. Cutting Down the Raphaels 440
47. November and December in New York 458

PART XI

48. Roxbury 469
49. The Eye-Spring 474
50. Fearfully Linked with the Sun 481

PART XII

51. Sherman 493
52. Phoenix 502
53. A Tree Cut Down 510
54. The Sky Miner's Haul 518
55. Third Virginia Summer 522

PART XIII

56. Gorky and the Surrealists 535
57. Castine 544

PART XIV

58. The Glass House 555
59. Show at Julien Levy 562
60. No More Ploughs 577
61. Peeled Onion 583
62. Darkness Spreads over My Soul 600

PART XV

63. Aftermath 619
64. Fame 626

Notes 635
Selected Bibliography 715
Acknowledgments 729
Index 731

❊ PROLOGUE ❊

Gorky, 1946

In an old barn fixed up to serve as a studio, Arshile Gorky backed away from the canvas on his easel. Cigarette dangling from the side of his mouth, he scrutinized the thin black lines that wove into and around plumes of transparent color. His enormous brown eyes seemed to interrogate them. He stepped forward and, with his sign painter's brush full of turpentine-thinned oil paint, he drew the tip across the upper part of his canvas to make another shape. With a different, broader brush he added a burst of red and worked it smooth so that it glowed like an ember. In the last year his paintings had become spare. Some critics said they were too spare, too much like drawings. But simplicity was what Gorky wanted now, just a few continuous lines and three or four colors to create a grouping of forms.

For years he had painted and repainted his canvases so many times that the pigment built up like a sculptural relief. "Try to lift it!" he would say to friends, knowing that they would stagger under the weight. His shapes always looked as though they were about to metamorphose, so he changed them just a little, hoping to find exactitude. "I don't like that word, 'finish,'" he once said. "When something is finished, that means it's dead, doesn't it? I believe in everlastingness. I never finish a painting—I just stop working on it for a while . . . The thing to do is to always keep starting to paint, never finish painting."

After years of apprenticing himself to the great masters of the School of Paris, Gorky, now in his midforties, knew that he could make masterpieces. His hand moved with a precision and ease braced with tension.

He was under pressure to produce paintings for his forthcoming show at the Julien Levy Gallery on Fifty-seventh Street in Manhattan, but that was not what created the tension. It was internal, fueled by his search for a way to make a good painting. "It would be a sad thing for an artist if he knew how to paint—so sad," he said. "An artist paints because it is a challenge to him—it is like trying to twist the devil."

Gorky's previous show, ten months earlier, in March 1945, had been his first gallery exhibition in a decade. The Surrealist poet and critic André Breton had hailed him as "the eye-spring . . . the first painter to whom the secret has been completely revealed!" Gorky's art, Breton said, plumbed the depths of the subconscious, the "spring" of the soul. The prominent critic Clement Greenberg had faulted Gorky for being seduced by Surrealist charm, but two years later Greenberg would deem Gorky "the equal of any painter of his own generation anywhere."

Back and forth Gorky went, looking and painting, looking and painting. He hardly glanced through the window at the snow that smoothed the curves of the Connecticut hills. The only sound was the occasional snap of the wood stove he had just installed. He loved the morning ritual of building a fire, and he had pushed as many logs into the stove's belly as would fit. Although the barn was warm, he did not take off his dark knitted wool cap or his red-and-black-checked lumberman's jacket—his habitual painting attire. Perhaps the heat made him think back to fires in his family's oven, a cylindrical hole dug into the earth floor of a mud brick house on the south shore of Lake Van in Turkish Armenia.

On his canvas, interlocking forms stretched upward. They looked like bodies, bones, flowers. They quivered with energy like flames. The shapes Gorky invented could be many things. "I never put a face on an image," he often said, but he admitted that his forms had definite meanings to him and that the sensitive viewer was free to invent his or her own meanings—meanings that would probably resonate with his own.

Gorky's concentration was fierce and total. When his work was going well nothing could pull him away from it. He smelled smoke. "My cigarette," he thought, and kept on painting. Then he saw flames licking up the chimney pipe. The chimney was close to a wooden beam and it had no heat shield around it. Soon the flames reached the ceiling. Gorky picked up a bucket and ran to get water from the landlady's house on the top of the hill. He went up and down the hill fetching water, but the fire would not be put out. On one of these trips to the house his landlady asked what he was doing. "Studio on fire," he murmured. She called the fire department, and the volunteer fire brigade arrived along with Gorky's friends and neighbors, the writer Malcolm Cowley and the painter Peter Blume. Help came too late. As the blaze consumed the barn, Gorky dashed inside, closing the door behind him. He had to be dragged out of the smoke-filled interior. Instead of saving his paintings, he brought out a hammer, a screwdriver, a box of charcoal, and a photograph of his mother and himself at the age of about twelve taken in 1912 in the city of Van. He lay on the ground and wept. Cowley remembered: "Gorky just kept banging his forehead on the ground, banging, banging and saying his whole life's work was in there, that he had lost everything he'd ever done."

In New York City, the day after the fire, Gorky met his wife, Mougouch, who had been visiting her parents in Washington. His voice over the telephone had sounded so hollow that she expected him to be a wreck. Instead he was excited and happy. He told her that the painting that had been on the easel was still burning in his head. He could paint it again. His lost paintings were not lost because they were inside him. He felt it was a kind of rebirth.

The studio fire in 1946 was the first in a series of calamities that would, two and a half years later, fell Gorky's spirit for good. For Gorky these calamities were a return to origins: his life began and ended with misfortunes. The great bridge of years in between brought us one of the most voluptuous and astringent painterly intelligences of this century.

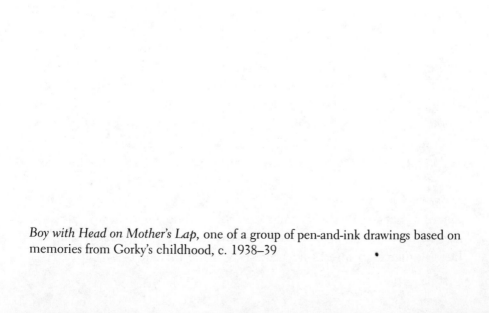

PART I

Boy with Head on Mother's Lap, one of a group of pen-and-ink drawings based on memories from Gorky's childhood, c. 1938–39

1

Charahan Surp Nishan

꧁

On a summer night in 1903 near the shore of Lake Van in Turkish Armenia, the Der Marderosian family gathered in their ancient monastery church, Charahan Surp Nishan. Arshile Gorky's grandmother, the widow Hamaspiur, had brought the family together to hold a vigil for her youngest son, sixteen-year-old Nishan, who had vanished several days before. She suspected that he had been abducted by Kurds, for he had fallen in love with a Kurdish girl whose brother took offense. Widow Hamaspiur knew that Armenians who erred in any way were fair game for Turkish or Kurdish brutality. Only five years earlier, her husband, Sarkis Der Marderosian, the last of a long line of Armenian apostolic priests, had been nailed to the door of the church where he served in Van City.

Gorky's mother, Shushan, may have joined her mother and her five siblings at this vigil. Perhaps Shushan brought her children to the vigil too—her daughters, Akabi and Satenik, and her tiny son, Vosdanig, who a year or so later would be renamed Manouk and a quarter of a century after that, in America, would change his name to Arshile Gorky.

As the Der Marderosian family sat on the carpet-covered floor beneath the smoke-blackened dome of the tiny stone church, the faint flicker of incense candles lit their solemn faces. The summer heat, the darkness outside, and the binding mood of apprehension made the square room seem close. Finally, over the murmur of their prayers came the sound of a thud against the heavy wooden church doors. Hamaspiur Der Marderosian rose to open them. On the threshold lay her favorite

son's body. It was covered with dagger wounds and his clothes were
soaked in blood.

Centuries of living as a subject minority in Ottoman Turkey had
given the Armenian people, once known for their rugged independence,
a fatalistic passivity, but Hamaspiur did not follow her countrymen's
habit of accepting fate. Instead she clenched her fists and wept. Months
went by and each day the force with which she rejected God's will grew.
She paced back and forth inside the church dedicated to the fifth-
century saint Yeghisheh, whose power to cure madness gave Charahan
Surp Nishan its name: Holy Sign of the Demon Seizer. In her fury,
Hamaspiur resembled the insane people who used to be chained to a pil-
lar near Saint Yeghisheh's relics until their screams were spent and the
devils within them were expelled. No such miracle would cure her grief.
Her endless pacing took her out into the graveyard, past her husband's
gravestone, where she could look over the ever-changing surface of Lake
Van, a lake so vast it has been called an inland sea. Hamaspiur Der
Marderosian beat her hands and forehead against the church doors and
cried, "Why, oh God, did you take him?" There was no answer except,
her family said, in recurrent nightmares, and that answer gave no solace:
"Beat not on my doors," said the voice of God. Having been warned in a
dream that his mother's blasphemy would bring a curse on her family,
her eldest son, Moses, tried to silence her. But Hamaspiur's grief was beyond even her son's remonstrations.

To revenge herself against God, Hamaspiur set Charahan Surp Nishan on fire. Only the wooden parts of the structure, the altar, and other
accoutrements burned. Most of the church was built of stone and remained intact. The local villagers were horrified at what Hamaspiur had
done. With this act of sacrilege, the Der Marderosians' official ties to the
church were severed. Hamaspiur left the walled monastery complex to
spend the last six years of her life in a monastery in the mountain village
of Ermerur. Charahan Surp Nishan and its lands were rented to a priest
and fell into decay.

Arshile Gorky would look back with admiration at his grandmother's
rebellious spirit. As a grown man, he had a passion for fire. "I think our
lives flow like a molten lava," he said. The hot light of embers and flames
glows in many of his paintings and drawings. For Gorky no celebration
was complete without a bonfire, and every fire he built had to be a con-
flagration. But, according to family legend, Hamaspiur's fire had brought

a curse on her descendants. Though he left religion as a young man, Gorky was superstitious, and he felt that curse. He told friends that his mother used to call him "the black one, the unlucky one who will come to a no-good end." The fatalistic attitude with which he bore life's sufferings astonished those close to him.

This fatalism showed up during the Great Depression when poverty, neglect, and the struggles associated with being an artist nearly overwhelmed him: Gorky would shrug his shoulders and say that to suffer for art was his destiny. Discussing thought versus feeling in art with friends at the Waldorf Cafeteria in New York in the 1930s, Gorky startled them by suddenly interjecting: "The story of Christ is misunderstood. In my ancient country we saw the story differently. The figure of Christ was that of a man of fate, not a man of tragedy who gives his life to save us. In my country the son is a man of fate. It is the fate of the son to kill his father, but Christ's father was God and Christ couldn't kill God." His companions assumed that Gorky was talking about his compulsion to be loyal to father Picasso. Gorky could not kill off his artistic progenitor; he had to follow as a worthy disciple. "I am not a man burdened by art but necessarily doing what I must do," Gorky said. "I am, therefore, not a tragic hero like Christ but I am a man of fate."

2

Armenians in Ottoman Turkey

⚘

Gorky regaled his friends with stories of his idyllic childhood. His first ten years must have held many delights: a strong and lively boy, he was his mother's only son. Although he was a member of a Christian minority in a Muslim world, Gorky's early years were shielded from some of the harshness of being an Armenian in Ottoman Turkey.

Situated in the northeast corner of Asia Minor, Armenia has a history of successive invasions and brief periods of political independence. In *The Decline and Fall of the Roman Empire*, Edward Gibbon describes Armenia as a "theater of perpetual war." Since ancient times the plentiful natural resources of Armenia's vast highland plateau, with its volcanic earth and alluvial valleys, have made Armenia prey to the rapacity of neighboring peoples. But the principal cause of its turbulent history has been its strategic position as a trading route between East and West.

In the ninth century BC this land was ruled by Urartian kings, one of whom established his capital at what is now the city of Van. During the next centuries, Assyrians, Medes, and Persians invaded. Then some time between the eighth and the fifth centuries BC, the Armenians, an Indo-European people thought to have migrated eastward possibly from central or south central Europe, appeared on the plateau. They conquered and assimilated the various indigenous peoples. From the second century BC to the fifth century AD the Armenians had a united kingdom. Around 301, when King Tiridates III converted to Christianity and forced his people to follow suit, Armenia became the first Christian nation. Throughout subsequent invasions by Greeks, Romans, Persians,

Arabs, Seljuks, Mongols, Tartars, and finally the Ottoman Turks, the Armenian apostolic church was the central force that preserved Armenian cultural identity.

In the late ninth century, after an Arab caliph conferred the title of "prince of princes" on an Armenian noble named Ashot Bagratuni and recognized him as king, Armenia once again became an independent kingdom. The century and a half of Armenian sovereignty that followed was a period of cultural flowering. Several schools of manuscript painting flourished and splendid churches were constructed. One of them was Gorky's favorite, the Church of the Holy Cross on the island of Akhtamar in Lake Van. The magnificent churches in the city of Ani were built during this period as well. But independence ended in 1045 when the Armenian plateau came under Byzantine rule. Then in 1064 Seljuk Turks appeared in the Van area, overthrew Byzantine control, and ushered in a period of turbulence and cultural decline. When the Mongols overran the area in 1236 and appropriated the Armenians' hereditary grazing lands, the Armenian ruling class disappeared.

A modicum of relief came to the Armenians with the Ottoman Turks' conquest of Constantinople in the mid-fifteenth century. As the Ottomans spread their power to the east, they brought order and religious tolerance. Non-Muslim subjects were organized into *millets* (religious communities), which were virtually autonomous and which preserved religious and national homogeneity. The Armenian *millet*, for example, was ruled by the authority of the patriarch of the apostolic church at Constantinople. As long as taxes were paid, the Armenians in the eastern *vilayets*, or provinces, were free to go about their business as farmers and traders. Armenians in Constantinople achieved positions of great wealth and power in banks, businesses, and intellectual institutions. Yet Armenians were not allowed to bear arms or to join the army, and they were not equal before the law. Their disputes were handled in Muslim courts in which Christian testimony was not accepted and only Muslim witnesses were allowed. Thus if an Armenian was robbed or injured by a Muslim, he or she had virtually no legal recourse.

During the nineteenth century, when the Turkish Empire became so bankrupt and weak that it earned the description "sick man of Europe," all these disparities were exacerbated. Humiliated by the disintegration of the empire in the Balkans and the Middle East and infuriated by European powers vying for its control (and demanding reforms in the treatment of Armenians), the Ottoman government in Constantinople became more and more repressive. An English vice-consul from Van reported in 1883 on the "utter corruption and ineptitude" of the Turkish authorities, who were known as "birds of prey." Van's governor spent his time collecting bribes, and the courts of justice were "engines for extorting money from litigants for the benefit of officials." Dr. Clarence D. Ussher, an American missionary stationed in Van beginning in 1900, told the story of a Turkish robber who, while robbing an Armenian home, impaled his eye on a nail. He went to court and demanded that the Armenian he had robbed have one of his eyes gouged out. The judge imposed this penalty.

The Turkish governors of the eastern provinces allowed, even encouraged, the Kurds, a nomadic people who had entered the Armenian plateau in the fifteenth and sixteenth centuries, to rob, exploit, and expropriate Armenian villagers. As a result, in Van province many villages, including Gorky's mother's native Vosdan, had become almost entirely Kurdish. Being Muslim, Kurds could bear arms while Armenians could not, and in return for a tax, the Turks gave the Kurds the right to quarter themselves and their herds during the winter in Armenian homes and at the Armenians' expense. In some villages the Armenians and the Kurds lived in harmony: the Armenians were the farmers and the Kurds the herdsmen. Indeed, members of Gorky's family spoke Kurdish and had Kurdish friends. But in many villages the Kurds' acts of robbery, arson, vandalism, abduction, rape, and murder were a constant source of misery to Armenians. In 1877 Kurdish rampages prompted a special correspondent for the *Times* of London to write: "I have not seen one Christian village which has not been abandoned in consequence of the cruelties committed on the inhabitants. All have been ransacked, many burnt, upwards of 5,000 Christians in the Van district have fled to Russian territory, and women and children are wandering about naked." In 1891, when Sultan Abdul Hamid II enlisted the Kurds in cavalry units called Hamidiye, modeled on those of the Russian Cossacks, he gave them license to rob and kill Armenians.

In the last four decades of the nineteenth century, as Armenians learned about Western ideas of liberty through increasing contact with Europeans, Russians, and Americans, an Armenian national consciousness developed. The loyal *millet* finally grew restive and formed revolutionary societies, the three principal ones being the Armenakan Party established in Van in 1885, the more radical Hunchak Party founded in Geneva in 1887, and the Dashnak Party formed in Russia in 1890. All three groups advocated reform and self-determination for Armenians. The Hunchaks went further: they wanted to create an autonomous Armenian state. Van, where Gorky was born and raised and where Armenians were in the majority, was a center of Armenian unrest.

In 1895 and 1896 Sultan Abdul Hamid II ordered the annihilation of Turkey's Armenian population. The massacres that took place followed such a set pattern (the murder, rape, looting, and burning began and ended each day with a bugle call) that there is no question that they were planned by the government in Constantinople. Somewhere between 100,000 and 300,000 Armenians were killed; about a half million were left homeless. In Van City Armenian revolutionaries resisted the massacres, saving the inhabitants from mass murder, but Armenian villages on or near the lake were looted and burned.

The massacres of the mid-1890s did nothing to dampen the Armenian nationalist zeal. Nor did they end the systematic persecution and impoverishment of the Armenians. Armenian lands and possessions continued to be stolen by Kurds and by illegal taxation that forced Armenians into debt to Turks and Kurds. The pace of emigration picked up. Armenians went to Russia, Syria, and other parts of the world. About 2,500 Armenians fled to America in 1896 and 1897, and in 1898 nearly 2,000 more joined them. Typically a young male would be smuggled out of Turkey and, once established in America, would start sending money and eventually steamship tickets to the family he had left behind. Two of Gorky's paternal uncles, Krikor and Misak Adoian, left for America in 1896. Neither was able to earn enough money to bring over other family members. Misak died of tuberculosis, probably caused by miserable living conditions. When Krikor returned to Armenia, neighbors noticed that he was still wearing the same clothes that he'd worn when he left.

3

Khorkom

⚒

How much butchery
has the moon's hard eye
seen, and with its frozen heart
passed by?
—Verse from "Lake of Van" by Raffi

During the massacres of 1895–96, there were brutal deaths on both sides of Gorky's family. Many of the men in the village of Khorkom—where Gorky's father's family lived—were rounded up, given the option to convert to Islam, and, when they refused, shot. Gorky's father may have been away when this happened, but one of Gorky's paternal uncles was found dead under a pile of corpses. On Gorky's mother's side of the family, there was an even crueler death. Gorky's younger sister, Vartoosh Mooradian, told her son, Karlen, the story. In 1894, when her mother, Shushan, was fourteen, a typical age for an Armenian girl to wed, she married Tomas Prudian, a guerilla from Shadakh (now called Catak), a village twelve miles south of her home in Vosdan.

Sixteen-year-old Shushan was in her house tending her two baby daughters, Sima and Akabi, on the evening of June 3, 1896, when she heard a pounding at the door. Rising to open it, she was met by two Turks who burst into the room, pushing her husband ahead of them. Tomas Prudian's hands were bound. Shouting "Christian dog!" the Turks threw him to the floor. One Turk took hold of Shushan so that she could not rush to her husband's side. The other took out his knife and began to flay Prudian. Before he died they lifted him to his feet and pushed his wife against his blood-soaked body, forcing her face against his. One of his murderers pulled Shushan's eyelids up so that she would be forced to watch her husband's suffering. As Shushan and her husband exchanged their last words, the other Turk cut Prudian's throat from ear to ear.

According to Gorky's nephew Karlen Mooradian, the Turks then vanished, leaving Shushan in a state of hysteria. Very likely they would have raped her, for the defilement of Christian women was customary. When Shushan's neighbors, including a priest in the traditional black robe with a peaked hood, came to offer help they found Shushan on the floor weeping and shielding her babies. Before dawn the following day, Shushan and her children were put on a horse and sent back to Vosdan.

What Vartoosh Mooradian told her son, Karlen, may be an exaggeration—Vartoosh, like Gorky, was inventive about the facts of their family's past. Shushan and Tomas Prudian's granddaughter Liberty Miller said that Prudian was killed in November 1895, when the Turkish army held the women and children of Shadakh hostage, thereby forcing the men to come down from the hills and surrender their weapons. Prudian and all his male relatives were lined up in front of the family home and shot.

In 1899, three years after her husband was murdered and one year after her father was killed, nineteen-year-old Shushan married a thirty-six-year-old widower named Sedrak Adoian and moved five miles southeast to his family farm at Khorkom, a primitive village of some one hundred low mud brick houses, intermingled with poplar trees and set at the foot of the Taurus Mountains, where the Khoshab River flows into Lake Van's southeast shore. Travelers wax poetic in describing Lake Van's luminous blues, sometimes suffused with turquoise, purple, pink, and many, many other colors. Because Lake Van is full of soda and is seven times saltier than the ocean, the water looks pigmented and it turns milky where it beats against the shore. Although the lake has no outlet, several rivers run down from the surrounding mountains, and there are fish called *darekh* to be caught where the fresh water enters.

Fertile fields divided by irrigation ditches stretch out from Khorkom on three sides, and a vast array of wild flowers grow beside the small canals and in any fields left uncultivated. Although the Armenian tableland has little rainfall, Armenian farmers were known for their industry and for their agricultural skills. The rich soil of Khorkom's vegetable gar-

dens was irrigated by water from the Shamiram canal, an ancient irrigation system built by the Urartians that flows to this day. The land around
Khorkom was much greener in the years before 1915, when the Armenians were driven out and their homes taken over by Kurds, who, being
a nomadic people, did not have the Armenian gift for cultivation. The
shore was lined with fields and orchards, but even before 1915 the hills
and mountains had long since been deforested. One of the striking
things about traveling in eastern Turkey is how few trees there are. Their
absence gives a majestic openness and clarity of shape to the vast expanses of dry yellowish earth. Convinced that Van was the most beautiful
place in the world, Gorky subscribed to the well-known Armenian
proverb "Van in this life, paradise in the next."

Gorky's father and his family raised wheat, sheep, and goats. For
farmwork the Adoians had four water buffalo, four oxen, and seven
horses. The family orchards produced apples, apricots, pears, and wal-
nuts. There were melon fields and vineyards as well. Sedrak Adoian was
also a carpenter and a trader who transported poplar lumber across Lake
Van and sold it at Adeljivas on the lake's north shore. The boats used for
such transport were about thirty-five feet long with a single mast from the
top of which hung a triangular sail. If there was no wind they were propelled by oars. Like most other peasant families, the Adoians were self-
sufficient: they took any surplus produce to Van City to exchange it for
cloth, sugar, and shoes.

Sedrak Adoian's offspring by Shushan saw him as a prosperous man,
the wealthiest farmer in their village, but they were small children when
he left for America in 1906, and they probably exaggerated their father's
wealth and prominence. Gorky's older sister Saten (she was always called
by the diminutive Satenik or Satenig) wrote: "None of us remember our
father at all, we just know he was a wealthy trader. We were always with
our mother, a very beautiful woman with black hair and deepset eyes."
Satenik recalled that her mother had "two women who did housework,
baked bread, etc., and seven men tending the sheep and other farm
tasks."

Shushan's second marriage was arranged by her brother Moses. As
was customary in Armenia, she had no say in the matter. Often a bride
did not meet the groom until the marriage ceremony. The Adoians probably met the Der Maderosians during a pilgrimage to Charahan Surp
Nishan. Shushan's brothers may have thought that their sister had no

hope of marrying someone of her own class and from her own village: she had already been married, she had two daughters under the age of five, and at nineteen, she was no longer considered young. In addition, she had lived through trauma, perhaps even a dishonoring rape.

With her oval face, her delicate mouth, her huge, finely shaped dark eyes beneath high-arched eyebrows, Shushan was beautiful. And Sedrak, from the evidence of photographs, was handsome. His long, rather stern face had a powerful bone structure—square jaw, jutting chin, long nose, high forehead. His dark sad eyes were very like Gorky's, but his features were more regular and more chiseled than his son's. Sedrak was six foot four, and Shushan was five foot eight: all they had in common, wrote their grandson Karlen Mooradian, was their tall stature.

When the marriage was arranged the families agreed that Shushan would keep only one of her daughters. She chose to keep three-year-old Akabi and she took four-year-old Sima to the American Mission orphanage in Van City. As the English traveler H.F.B. Lynch wrote in his vivid account of his travels in Armenia in the late nineteenth century: "It often happens that a widow, about to marry again, will bring her young child to the feet of the missionaries, beseeching them to bring it up and educate it in her place, as their monument—for so she puts it—before God." After the massacres of 1895–96, the American missionaries in Turkey set up numerous orphanages to care for the children of murdered parents. These orphanages also looked after the children of widowed mothers who could not support their offspring or who wanted to remarry.

In 1896, the same year Tomas Prudian was murdered, Sedrak Adoian had lost his wife, Lusi Amirkhanian. Like Shushan, Sedrak had two children—a son, Hagop, and a daughter, Oughaper. When Shushan moved into Sedrak's family home, her father-in-law, Manouk Adoian, was the head of the extended family. His wife, Nanig, was alive, but little is known about her: her daughter, Yeghus (who herself had a daughter and two grandsons), was the most powerful woman in the family. Besides his older sister, Yeghus, Sedrak had a younger brother, Krikor, who had two sons.

As the new bride in the household, Shushan was at the low end of the family totem pole. According to Armenian custom, a bride was forbidden to speak to her elders unless spoken to. The silence lasted until the birth of her first child and sometimes longer, depending on the locality. One American missionary noted that the bride "was the slave of the household. She was not supposed to speak aloud until the next son brought home his wife to the patriarchal roof and the last bride whispered for the rest of her life, at least in the presence of her father-in-law." Shushan would have been given all the most humble chores—washing her father-in-law's feet before he retired, filling a clay pitcher with water from the village spring. Other duties of a newlywed Armenian woman included sweeping the house, taking lunch to the men in the field, and at night placing a jug of water on the fire so that the women in the household had warm water for the preparation of bread. If she was working in the fields, her baby was brought for her to suckle, or she might keep it in a cradle placed in the shade of a tree so that she could nurse it when it cried. After they were weaned, her children were the responsibility of her mother-in-law, who had the final say in their rearing. In the Adoian household Yeghus played the mother-in-law role.

Shushan and Sedrak Adoian had three children, Gorky and two girls. None of their birth dates are absolutely certain. Gorky's older sister, Satenik, said that she was "not much older than Gorky" and gave her birth date as 1901. His younger sister, Vartoosh, is said to have been born in 1906. (The manifest of the ship that brought her and Gorky to America in February 1920 said she was sixteen, which would put her birth date in 1904.) This vagueness about birth dates is understandable given that Armenian farmers lived according to the calendar of the seasons and of religious holidays, not according to the calendar of numbered days. Birthdays were not celebrated by Armenian families from Van, but the birth of a male child was marked in the Adoian family by planting a poplar tree. When the sapling grew large enough the boy's name and date of birth were carved on it. Gorky is said to have loved his tree and cared for it with pride. His 1936 recollection of the calendars used at Lent in his Khorkom home gives an idea of the Armenian villagers' notion of time: "The walls of the house were made of clay blocks, deprived of all detail, with a roof of rude timber. . . . In the ceiling was a round aperture to permit the emission of smoke. Over it was placed a wooden cross from which was suspended by a string an onion into which seven feathers had been plunged. As each Sunday elapsed, a feather was removed, thus denoting the passage of Time."

The usual date given for Gorky's birth is the one he himself put down in 1939 when he applied for United States citizenship papers: April 15, 1904. The ship's manifest gave his date of birth as 1903, the same year given by his half brother, Hagop, when he registered Gorky with the Rhode Island superintendent of schools. Later, when Gorky enrolled at New York's National Academy of Design in 1925, he gave his date of birth as April 1902 and the place as Kazan, Russia. In 1942 Gorky wrote to Dorothy Miller, curator at the Museum of Modern Art, that he was born on October 25, 1904, at Tiflis. No doubt he chose October 25 because that is Picasso's birthday. When he felt that it was an advantage to be younger, he said he was born in 1905. A sculptor friend once observed that "Gorky was always older than us around 1935. I was pretty surprised to find him getting younger than me in 1942."

Gorky transformed his biography with the same impulse for poetic invention with which he transformed both what he saw in nature and what he saw in the art of the past—thus a cloud could become a peasant woman, a portrait by Cézanne could become a self-portrait by Gorky. If, as I suspect, Gorky was born at the turn of the century, it might have been pride that made him change his age. When he arrived in the United States in 1920 and entered the Providence school system, he spoke no English. He would therefore have been placed, along with other recent Armenian immigrants, in a class of much younger students. Very likely the nineteen- or twenty-year-old Gorky decided to drop a few years from his age.

Gorky was both secretive and fantastical about his childhood. His nephew Karlen Mooradian felt that Gorky's fable making was a way of escaping the curse placed on the family by his grandmother's setting fire to the ancestral church. The traumas Gorky endured during the Armenian genocide of 1915 were another reason for his obfuscation and his invention of an idyllic childhood in the Russian Caucasus. Studies of Armenians who lived through the massacres show that many recalled their early lives in glowing terms. Gorky's widow, Agnes Fielding, who prefers to be called "Mougouch," the nickname Gorky gave her, says that he never talked about the horrible events of his youth and that he hated being asked for specific information about his past (or about anything else). Instead, like many holocaust survivors, he turned his youth into a myth. That myth would become the chief subject of his art.

When Gorky was born he was, like all Armenian children, swaddled and placed in a wooden cradle anchored to posts supporting the roof. Most Armenian parents lined the cradle with warm sand covered with a cloth. The sand that became wet from urine was removed and more was added as needed. Young children were called upon to pull a rope attached to the cradle to make the cradle rock. Gorky was named Vosdanig—"Little Vosdan," a fairly common Armenian name—probably after his mother's hometown. When he was about four and his father's father died, he was, according to Armenian tradition, given his grandfather's name, Manouk (or Manoug), which means "infant" or young one. Though Gorky disliked the name, Manouk is what he was called as a youth, and people who knew him then always used that name.

Given the paucity of information about Gorky's early childhood, we must reconstruct his first years by knowing about the place he lived and about the customs of Armenian villagers. Although life returned to "normal" after the massacres of 1895–96, the shores of Lake Van were no paradise during the early years of the twentieth century. Sedrak Adoian may have been a well-to-do trader and farmer, but most Armenian farmers were heavily in debt. The more a farmer planted the more he was taxed, with the result that in the years before World War I many farmers refused to till their fields at all. Van Armenians were generally malnourished, and in 1904, when Van's wheat crop failed and the Turkish authorities stockpiled what little grain there was, many Armenians died of starvation. Having witnessed such suffering at an early age, Gorky had a permanent horror of poverty. Years later when he was walking through Union Square with his young sister-in-law, Esther Magruder, and she commented on the poverty of the vendors manning their stalls, Gorky became vehement: "These people aren't poor! I know what poor is! When you have an empty belly and there is no hope of filling it, that's poverty!"

The growth of secret societies opposed to Turkish and Kurdish tyranny continued in the early twentieth century. The guerilla fighters infiltrated the peasantry, and by 1904 there were over one thousand Armenian insurgents in the mountains around Van, Bitlis, and Sasun. That year the socialist and atheist Dashnaks took over the island of Akhtamar in Lake Van not far from Khorkom. A few years later the head of the American Mission at Van reported that Khorkom "has suffered perhaps more than any other [village] from the baleful influence of Tashnagist [Dashnak] infidelity." In April 1908, Turkish soldiers raided an Armenian arms depot in the Church of Saint Gregory on Varag Mountain northeast of Van City, but Armenian revolutionaries fought them off. The next day, the Turks attacked the Armenians of Van City with clubs, daggers, and pistols. According to the missionary doctor Clarence D. Ussher, a hundred Armenian merchants in the bazaar were slaughtered. Others were tortured and mutilated. Two English travelers, the brothers Noel and Harold Buxton (the former was an Anglican minister and the latter a member of Parliament) likewise bore witness to the bloodshed. They reported that the houses in the Armenian sections of Van City were pillaged and burned and that Armenians, even young children, were butchered. "In some cases horseshoes were riveted on to men's feet; wild cats were attached to the bare bodies of men and of women so that they might tear the flesh with their claws; many were soaked in oil, and burnt alive in the streets."

Armenians took refuge in the American Mission compound, yet even the walled American compound was not safe. During the night the Turks attacked the school where Shushan Adoian's teenage daughter, Sima, was a boarder. A number of students vanished. No doubt, according to custom, the prettiest girls were abducted and given to Turks. When news of the massacre reached the villages around the lake, the people were terrified. What Shushan learned was that Sima had died. Years later Satenik maintained that Sima had died of a broken heart. Perhaps "broken heart" was a euphemism for other brutality. Of her oldest half sister's death, Satenik recalled: "My mother never talked about her. She couldn't bring herself to mention her."

The conflict spread to the outlying villages as the Turkish militia searched Armenian houses for arms caches. The searches were cruel. Villagers were robbed, raped, and beaten. If a farmer could not produce hidden arms he was punished with the *bastinado*, which consisted of beating the soles of the feet until they swelled and burst open, often leaving the victim crippled for life. The Adoian home was a safehouse for revolutionaries. Strange men would arrive in the middle of the night. "They had faces like wolves," recalled Akabi, whose job it was to give them food and send them on their way. During the weapons searches, Gorky's father's oldest son, Hagop, who belonged to the Dashnak Party, got into a skirmish with Turkish soldiers. As Hagop told the story, he "pulled the Turkish Pasha from his horse, then fled to the mountains and thence to America by way of Cairo."

The hostilities raged until July, when the Ittihad ve Terakke Jemieti

(Committee of Union and Progress), a group that combined army officers and Young Turk reformers, overthrew the regime of Abdul Hamid II
and restored the constitution of 1876. All Turkish subjects, including Armenians, were now guaranteed civil and religious liberties, including the
freedom to travel and to emigrate. Armenians and other minorities could
serve in the army and they were represented in the parliament. With the
lifting of travel restrictions, and prompted by the military draft, over
three thousand Armenians emigrated to America in the twelve months
that followed the Young Turk revolution. Most left their villages in
wagon caravans headed for the Black Sea. Departure day was a big event.
Women sewed valuables and good-luck amulets into the departing men's
clothes. The trip, which took several weeks, was dangerous, for caravans
traveling through mountain roads were prey to Kurdish brigands.

The Young Turk revolution of 1908 was a moment of high hope for
both Christian and Muslim citizens of the Ottoman Empire. "Liberty,
equality, and fraternity" became the motto of the new constitutional government. At what was called "daybreak in Turkey," Armenians and Turks
rejoiced together in the streets of Constantinople. Even in the eastern
provinces, Armenians believed that a new era of security and harmony
had begun. Hundreds of Armenians returned from Russia to their homeland in eastern Turkey. Armenians and Turks may not have danced together in the streets of Van as they had in Constantinople, but the mood
had changed. Upon his return to Van in 1908 after a year's furlough in
the United States, Dr. Ussher noted that when the Armenians lined
Van's streets to greet him, men on horseback fired pistols in the air. "Before our furlough," the doctor observed, "even the possession of a
weapon by an Armenian was sufficient to cause his imprisonment under
a life sentence. The revolution had changed all that."

But daybreak soon dimmed. Internal dissension, foreign wars, and the
growth of a nationalistic ideology brought a counterreaction. Humiliated
by the defeat of the Ottoman army in the Balkan wars (1908–12) and by
the loss of Albania, Bulgaria, Bosnia and Herzegovina, and Crete, the
Turks grew hostile to their subject minorities. As early as spring 1909, a
coup perpetrated by the former sultan Abdul Hamid led to the massacre
of some twenty-five thousand Armenians in Adana and the surrounding
villages in Cilicia. There were attacks in other parts of Turkey as well: in
Van City a late spring snowstorm thwarted plans for a massacre. A January 1913 coup brought the dictatorial triumvirate of the Enver, Talaat,

and Djemal pashas to power. Now life became even more unbearable for Armenians and further massacres were planned.

During Gorky's childhood, living conditions in villages like Khorkom were primitive. There was little communication with the outside world: other than horseback or two-wheeled wooden carts pulled by oxen or donkeys, there was no means of transportation. Villagers lived in roughly constructed, thick-walled, one-story houses made of mud bricks (or in some towns of stone). The houses were like dark underground burrows. Floors were of earth, and ceilings were made of branches and mud. To preserve heat, windows were few and small. Usually they were covered not with glass but with oiled paper. The Adoians' home was an exception: it had glazed windows flanking the door.

Village houses were so close together that you could walk from one to another on top of flat roofs that were covered with turf or with tiles. In summer women repaired to their roofs to sew, gossip, and set fruit out to dry. At the edges of their roofs they built walls of prickly branches to keep goats away from the fruit. Years later when Gorky wished to describe someone as discombobulated, he would call on one of his favorite Armenian expressions: "He has goats on his roof."

In the icy winter months, which lasted from October to April, the snowdrifts piled so high that the livestock had to be kept inside. Sharing a house with animals helped to keep the family warm. The best and warmest room in the house was next to the stable. In the middle of this room's packed earth floor was the *tonir*, or oven, the traditional centerpiece of the Armenian home. The *tonir* consisted of a ceramic cylinder sunk three to five feet into the earth floor—literally a hole in the ground. It was fueled with *tezeks*, or sundried bricks of cow dung and straw. In autumn each family built an approximately ten-foot-tall hollow, beehive-shape pile of *tezeks* just outside the house. Directly above the *tonir* was an opening in the roof to draw out the smoke. From the outside, the chimney above the opening looked like a large mushroom. It was in the central room with its *tonir* that the family received guests. Here also, in the cold winter months, the whole family slept. They lay with their feet near the *tonir*, their bodies radiating out like spokes.

The *tonir* burned continuously. On its clay walls women baked flat, round, unleavened pitalike bread called *lavash*, which was baked until it was dry enough to be stored. When it was time to eat it was softened with water. Not only was the *tonir* used for cooking, it was the heart and emblem of family life. In Armenian villages, when a bride entered her new home for the first time she brought incense from her father's house to burn in her in-laws' *tonir*. She blessed and kissed the *tonir* and, accompanied by her husband, walked around it three times. A departing family member would kiss the *tonir* and take embers from it to light the fire in his or her new home. Like earth and water, the fire in the *tonir* was revered and linked with the female principle. It figures in many Armenian idiomatic expressions. To take only two examples, "May your smoke not be extinguished" meant "May your family life continue." "My smoke has died down" meant "I experienced a calamity." During the February festival called Diarendas (which some scholars believe was originally dedicated to the fire and sun god Mihr, or Mithra), villagers made bonfires and danced around them. Sometimes they built one huge communal bonfire in the churchyard and danced around that. In most villages the principal celebrants were the recently married men and women— dancing was a fertility rite. Others who danced around the fire were new mothers hoping to preserve their children from evil and sickness and childless women hoping to become fertile. Men in need of purification leapt over the fire. When the villagers returned to their homes they carried candles and lit braziers on their roofs, and the leaping and circling continued.

At night the Adoian family sat around the *tonir* on rugs laid over the earth floor. On really cold nights the women would put embers in a brazier, which consisted of an earthenware or iron pot with four legs and with a screen over its opening. They would spread a heavy quilt or a carpet over this heat box and family members would sit in a circle with their feet tucked under the communal covering. Yeghus would place a tray of dried fruit and cheese on top of the *tonir* and, as they ate, the family would tell stories, knit, play cards, and drink coffee. Akabi would be asked to sing, and Shushan, too, had a soft and beautiful voice. On winter evenings, itinerant storytellers and minstrels traveled from home to home entertaining the housebound villagers with sad Armenian folk songs or with recitations of poems and stories, sometimes to the accompaniment of Armenian instruments, including the *saz*, the *tar*, and the *kemancha*. Listening to the stories and songs around the *tonir*, the children dozed off with their heads in their mother's skirts. The stories and songs would, years later, find their way into Gorky's paintings, giving his art its peculiar, rather eastern atmosphere and its melancholy tinge:

> I tell stories to myself, often, while I paint, often nothing to do with the painting. Have you ever listened to a child telling that this is a house and this is a man and this is the cow in the sunlight . . . while his crayon wanders in an apparently meaningless scrawl all over the paper? My stories are often from my childhood. My mother told me many stories while I pressed my face into her long apron with my eyes closed. She had a long white apron like the one in her portrait, and another embroidered one. Her stories and the embroidery on her apron got confused in my mind with my eyes closed. All my life her stories and her embroidery keep unraveling pictures in my memory.

The sparse furnishings of Armenian houses usually consisted of a spinning wheel, a loom, a dowry chest, storage cupboards, and a number of earthenware jugs for water and other provisions. Each family member had a woolen mattress and a comforter. There were no chairs or beds, but there were rugs and cushions to sit on. Meals were served from a pot or a tray placed over the *tonir* or, in more prosperous houses, on a separate tray placed on a low stool. Forks were a rarity. Most people ate with a wooden spoon or they simply scooped up their food with a folded *lavash*. The villagers' diet was meager, consisting mainly of millet and other grains, tea, goat's milk, vegetables, fruits, bread, *madzoon* (yogurt), sharp-tasting dry sheep's milk cheese, and the occasional egg. Fish and lamb were luxuries. When the men were working in the fields, lunch was brought to them by a son or by one of the wives (usually the newest wife to enter the family). At home, wives ate only after their husbands had been served and had finished eating. Boys ate with the women until they were somewhere between seven and twelve.

Gorky's aunt Yeghus, whom the children called grandma and who was the oldest woman in the family aside from Gorky's grandmother, presided over domestic matters. She supervised food preparation, the making of cloth and clothes, and child rearing. It was she who assigned chores to her brothers' wives and offspring. In Armenian families older sisters do much of the work of caring for younger children, and Gorky's sister Akabi—a strong, warm, and cheerful girl—took care of him.

Yeghus would have been the person who kept the keys to the pantry, or *maran*, where the food that had been gathered and prepared during the warm months was stored. Layers of apples were preserved in sand contained in a large pot. Pears were hung from the ceiling on strings. Grapes could be kept fresh until Easter if they were put up in a jar full of grape molasses. Cooked meats (sometimes pounded dry) and salted fish were stored in anticipation of the winter months as well.

Because he was a boy, Gorky probably had an easier childhood than his sisters did. Although he was too young to help much with the farmwork, he is said to have carried water and bread to the field-workers. He sometimes accompanied his mother to the water mill where wheat was ground into flour, a memory that stayed with him always and that he returned to in his art. Village boys also pulled weeds, cut and carried wood, and removed stones from the freshly plowed fields, piling them up as cairns to encourage fertility. By the time they reached puberty boys also helped with the harvesting and threshing. One of Gorky's favorite chores was to care for the horses at the end of the day. He had a favorite horse named Asdgh, or Star, named after the white star on its forehead. He also had a sheepdog named Zango. Years later he would tell friends about riding up into the mountains with the shepherds to tend the family's sheep.

Gorky must have been his grandfather Manouk's favorite, for the old man, who was exceedingly fond of apricots, designated Gorky as his apricot gatherer. For the rest of his life Gorky associated apricots, which are native to Armenia, with moments of happiness in Khorkom. He called them "those flirts of the sun," and he painted their cleaved and downy lusciousness, even the feeling of their scent, into his abstract paintings of the 1940s. Indeed, one of his 1944 canvases is named *Scent of Apricots on the Fields*.

Another thing that he associated with Khorkom was the plow. It, too, became a subject in his art. Farming methods were primitive, and it took an enormous amount of time to produce enough food for the long winters. Peasants used two kinds of hand-carved wooden plows. One was an *aror*, or scratch plow made of a tree branch. The other was the *gutan* used for wet or heavy soil. It usually had wheels, a metal share, a coulter, and a moldboard (Fig. 45). If a plow was stolen by Kurds, a farmer could be ruined. At New Year in some parts of Armenia farm women drew pictures of their tools on the outside walls of their houses, and the image of the plowshare had the place of honor on the front door.

At plowing time, neighbors shared water buffalo or teams of oxen. An American consular report from 1910 described the farmers' process: "Each furrow is turned so slowly that the amount turned per day would not equal a few hours plowing with an up-to-date plow and a strong team of horses." For the Armenian peasant, farming was a religious ritual ruled by ancient traditions. Farmers cast their seed to form a cross: the first handful was for God, the second for the poor, the third for the birds, and the fourth for themselves. The men did the sowing and the plowing; they, after all, were the bearers of seed.

All his life Gorky shared with his fellow Armenians a devotion to the land. In America he would remember the pleasure he took in watching his family fields being tilled, and he would long to recover such simple, earthbound rituals. His fondness for whittling and assembling miniature Armenian plows was a way of holding on to his agrarian childhood. Even when he was drawing in the fields of Virginia near the end of his life, he thought back to the beauty of Armenian plows, and what emerged on his paper were abstract shapes informed by those memories. Gorky's series of paintings entitled *The Plough and the Song* (1947) makes the same connection between human and agricultural fertility that was made by the farmers of his youth. In a letter written in 1938 he asked Vartoosh and her husband to sing the Armenian farmers' song *"Kasheh gutan ari yar vaile"* ("Pull the plow, O come my sweetheart!"). Not long before his death, he told a newspaper interviewer how much he missed the field-workers' songs. "And there are no more plows," he said. "I love a plow more than anything else on a farm."

4

Boyhood

✣

According to family legend, Shushan Adoian, whose name means "lily," was a sensitive, poetic woman who used to sing to herself as she wandered in the family orchard. It seems that Shushan aspired to live on a higher spiritual plane than did most Armenian farmers' wives. Krikor's son Ado Adoian recalled that "she was a lover of nature, far more so than any other of the Khorkom ladies. She loved to rise very early in the morning and walk in our orchards. And Gorky's mother was particularly attached to a rose bush directly in front of our house. . . . [She] loved to sit beneath the rose bush and [listen to] the nightingales. She was a modest lady, very kind, who loved to be in nature. She influenced Gorky in that respect."

Shushan had high ambitions for her only son. She wanted him to be a *vartabed*, which can mean a teacher or a priest, or more simply a master at some trade. As the last-born male in a family that boasted a long line of priests, Gorky was expected to excel. (The "Der" before Armenian names like Der Marderosian signifies that the person comes from a priest's family.) To his wife in the 1940s, Gorky would recall his discomfort when his mother made him sit on a marble bench in a garden and "have thoughts." Since Khorkom had no marble benches, Gorky was fabricating—a marble bench is like a marble pedestal. She would sit him down and lecture to him about the beauty of nature and about the importance of developing his mind, his younger sister remembered. "You must be educated," Shushan insisted. "Learn your lessons perfectly for you must become a teacher to your people! In such a manner do I expect you to become a poet."

As a grown man Gorky worshiped the memory of his mother, and in the 1920s and 1930s he would immortalize her in drawings and paintings in which she looks like an icon of the Holy Mother. All his life he liked to tell stories about her. So did his sister Vartoosh. She maintained that Shushan taught them to read Grabar, the classic Armenian used only by scholars and in church services. This seems unlikely, for Shushan was herself illiterate, as was her husband, Sedrak. But every night at bedtime Shushan made sure that her children kneeled facing east and crossed themselves before and after saying the Hail Mary. Years later Gorky told his wife about his terror when he listened to his mother praying after he had gone to bed. "Her prayers were so ardent that Gorky and Vartoosh hid beneath the bedclothes to protect themselves from visions of devils and angels," wrote Mougouch in a letter to a friend in 1949. Shushan's hopes for Gorky reemerged in his perfectionism and fear of failure. "If he did not create significantly," Vartoosh said, he felt he would be "unworthy of being remembered. Because mother . . . had come from a great family in Vosdan. And so she wanted Gorky, as the last man, to continue in that way." Gorky never forgot being left by his mother standing in front of the mural of the Last Judgment with its good white angels and evil black angels. Seeing himself as a dark being, this grandson of a priest feared damnation. At an early age the seeds of his determination to prove that he was good and worthwhile were planted deep in his heart.

Sometimes Gorky accompanied his mother to the spring to fetch water. On the way, they passed the family vegetable garden, a place that in the late 1930s and early 1940s would inspire a pivotal series of paintings entitled *Garden in Sochi*. Gorky's sister Satenik Avedisian recalled: "The Turks used to come there to sit. It was a lovely place. Full of pear trees. It was on a high slope and looked down onto the lake of Van." The garden had a magic rock on which Gorky's mother and the other village women rubbed their bare breasts in the hope of becoming more fertile. Here also was a long-dead pine called a *pshad* tree, which spread out along the ground for about thirty meters. Considered holy, it was called the tree of the cross or the tree of wish fulfillment. Satenik remembered the time when men digging around the holy tree discovered an illuminated Bible, which prompted Krikor to stop the digging because he was afraid that the Turkish authorities might become suspicious. Perhaps they would suspect the Armenians of burying a cache of arms.

The holy tree was covered with strips of cloth that villagers had torn off their clothing and tied to the barren branches in the hope that this offering would answer their wishes, cure their illnesses, and bring beautiful wives to their sons and handsome husbands to their daughters. With a mixture of pagan and Christian belief, passersby placed candles around the holy tree's base. Such trees, covered with cloth strips can still be seen in certain parts of Turkey, but I could not find the Adoian family's tree — it probably went up in flames when, in April 1915, the Turks torched all the villages of the valley.

At dawn and dusk the Adoians attended Surp Vardan, Khorkom's small, domed, cross-shaped church. Dressed in cassocks, Gorky and the other boys held candles and sang the long drawn-out, dissonant notes of antiphonal church songs. The priest, Der Hagop, Gorky's cousin Ado recalled, was "not overly literary but a pleasant man." Ado also recalled that even at school the children received religious training: "Ours was a church country and so they also taught us to memorize psalms in school and our teacher, Sahak, a believer, would take us to church. But if it was late or early morning, we went to church with our grandmothers and read or recited excerpts from the ancient Armenian fathers to aid the clerics in the services." On one occasion during Gorky's boyhood, the church served as a theater and all the villagers turned out to see the Russian Armenian actor Hovhannes Zarifian and the Armenian poet Hovhannes Toumanian (1869–1923), whose songs and poems Gorky would come to love. When this illustrious pair stopped in Khorkom on their way to Akhtamar and Van City, and performed a play called *Tearful Shepherd*, it was the first formal theater piece the Khorkom villagers had ever seen.

After church Gorky and his friends would raid the church's apple trees. "And we stole the finest smelling apples from the priest's orchard, filled our pockets with them and took the long way to Vart Badrik," Ado recalled. They would sit on the beach facing the island of Akhtamar and devour their loot. Gorky believed that one sense affected another, that smells as well as sights formed part of his visual memory: the scent of apples, apricots, wheat fields, freshly turned earth, manure, and smoke from the *tonirs*. As a result, some of Gorky's paintings are so sensuous you can almost smell them.

Gorky would throw any uneaten apples into the lake. "His thoughts," Ado said, "were that the Lake Van fish would appreciate those apples, love them greatly, and therefore when the fishermen came the following morning they would be graced with numerous fish." When he had apples to spare, Gorky played a game called *boral*, meaning "shouting spring." This involved whittling chips of wood, inserting them around the circumference of an apple, then suspending the toy over an irrigation ditch so that the current made it spin like a waterwheel. If the water flowed too slowly, he could speed it up by building a dam. The goal was to make the apple spin fast enough to kick up a splash with a swooshing sound.

The promontory of Vart Badrik, which stretches about a quarter of a mile out from Khorkom's shore and ends in a steep grassy hill rising some thirty feet above the water, was the best place to swim. After swimming Gorky and his friends would climb the hill and enter a ruined chapel that contained the tomb of Vart Badrik, a medieval prince and hero. Pretending to be priests, they would stand by the stone altar and recite passages from Daniel, Ezekiel, and Mark. They meant no disrespect by their mimicry. "All of us were believing youngsters," Ado Adoian affirmed. "Even the walls of an Armenian church were holy to us. Each lad would spit on a piece of stone, touch that stone with a finger and then touch the wall in turn with the same finger."

Ado remembered that scattered in the grass near the shrine were medieval carved stones, some of which had been taken by villagers to use as gravestones in the nearby cemetery. No sign of these stone slabs, or *khatchkars*, remains today; a few large stones lying in the grass may or may not be rubble from the destroyed shrine. Gorky loved the *khatchkars'* elaborate low-relief carvings, most of which depicted the cross as the tree of life. He used to run his fingers over the designs, marveling at their delicacy. His lifelong friend Yenovk Der Hagopian recalled: "In Khorkom, we would go together to the shrine of Vart Badrik and become thrilled by the *khatchkars* all around it. . . . We were always so amazed. Neither I nor he had any advanced ideas about art at such an early age, naturally. At that time, all we knew was that they were beautiful and we would go there and touch them with our hands." Recognizing Gorky and Yenovk's enthusiasm for the *khatchkars*, their parents showed them miniatures in family Bibles. This was the earliest education in the visual arts that these two future artists received.

There were other pleasures on the promontory of Vart Badrik. "In summer," said Ado, "we picked the numerous antaram, small four-leaf yellow flowers." Turtles provided another diversion. Large turtles crawled out of the lake and climbed the grassy hill to lay their eggs. The boys would stand on the turtles' backs and beat their shells to make them lay eggs. These they would take to their mothers and grandmothers, who believed that turtle eggs made hair silky.

The Khorkom school was a one-room mud brick structure attached to the church. It had four grades, all taught at once by two teachers, Ohan and Sahak. Each child had a slate and a piece of chalk, and each sat ramrod straight on his or her straw mat laid on the dirt floor. After fourth grade, children from Khorkom went to the school attached to the slightly larger church in the neighboring village of Koshk, just up the Khoshab River. Khorkom also had a tiny library, which had to be kept secret from the Turks: it was here that those villagers who were literate could read liberal-minded newspapers from Van and Tiflis. Ideas of freedom inculcated by these papers gave Khorkom the reputation of being among the more progressive villages in Van. One of Gorky's childhood acquaintances recalled: "During the winter days in our house . . . the teacher used to read aloud in his free time. People listened to the writings of Toumanian, Aghayan, Raffi, Issahakian, and other writers, books and stories. During those gatherings the village shepherd Nohrabed Alexander told wonderful stories from the forty Klhkani Teveri and at the end, he sang and chanted with his beautiful voice those marvelous songs."

According to Vartoosh, when Shushan first delivered her son to the Khorkom school she said to his teacher: "Do what you will with him, but make him a *varbed*." Her instructions followed Armenian tradition: a mother turning her child over to the teacher says, "Let his flesh be yours and his bones be left to us," meaning "You may beat him to make him learn, but do not break any bones." At school Gorky studied drawing, writing, and vernacular Armenian, but schoolwork did not interest him, and, hoping that the teacher would leave him alone, he sat in the back of the classroom quietly whittling or drawing on his slate and pretending to be stupid. One day, noticing Gorky bent over his slate, the teacher demanded to see it. What he saw was a drawing of a savage dog fight. "What miracle is this, my boy? Surely you will become a painter!" Gorky stammered: "I don't know what I'll become, but I love to draw."

Gorky maintained that he drew constantly from the time he was three and that he began painting at age seven. "His hand would even move and draw while he was asleep," Akabi recalled. Satenik remembered her five-year-old brother finding a dead *darekh* and drawing the fish over and over again in the sand. Even as a boy Gorky drew on any handy surface. He once angered his teacher by drawing angels' wings in the church's Bible. When he insisted on drawing and making things with his penknife rather than studying, Shushan referred to her son's soul as "black."

Many of Gorky's boyhood drawings were of animals. He drew, for example, storks standing on one leg. These birds, so revered in Armenia, may have been the source for the numerous semiabstract images of birds in Gorky's adult paintings. When as a boy he drew buffalo, he tried to make them as realistic as possible. "Whose buffalo is this?" he asked his cousin as he showed him one of his drawings. When Ado gave the correct name of the buffalo's owner, Gorky demanded, "How do you know?" and Ado said that he had recognized the particular buffalo "by his straight and sharp horns."

Gorky was also skilled at modeling soldiers and animals out of yellow clay called *gaghchi* that he found on the lake's shore. With these figurines he orchestrated historic battles and his companions cheered as the Armenian army moved toward victory. An expert whittler, he carved shepherd's flutes for his friends and one adorned with a man's head for himself. Among Gorky's other childhood talents were cutting butterfly and tortoise shapes out of walnut leaves and painting Easter eggs with pigments made out of yolks, crushed flowers, green plants, and apple or pear juice mixed with peels.

Gorky's boyhood exploits survive only in a few fragments told and retold by his sisters and by Ado. What Gorky remembered of his childhood he wove into fantastic stories, thus creating a tapestry that concealed the truth even as it fed his art with another kind of truth. A series of ink drawings from the late 1930s evokes Gorky's nostalgia for his Khorkom childhood. In one of them he drew himself as a small boy looking up at his parents, who appear twice, both times as a devoted couple. Another shows a small, dreamy boy with his head in his mother's lap (p. 7). She sits bolt upright in a chair and stares straight ahead at a cameo portrait of a man who looks like Sedrak. Other memory images depict Khorkom's agrarian life: a small boy holds the hand of one of several barefoot farm women carrying sacks of grain; a boy who must be Gorky is seated on a horse, probaby Asdgh, with his doting mother standing nearby.

Much larger than his companions, Gorky had huge hands and feet and his long, fluid strides earned him the nickname Ukht, or Camel. "Though but a year older than I," Ado said, "it required two ordinary steps to equal one of his." Several tales of Gorky's childhood tell of his physical prowess. All his life he would take pride in his strong and well-coordinated body. As a boy he enjoyed demonstrating his athletic skills by playing a team game called *kiyokhk*. One team formed a circle around a log that represented a castle. The other team ran around the circle trying to break through in order to capture the castle. Being taller, stronger, quicker, and more skilled than his companions, Gorky captured the castle so quickly that no one else on his team had a chance to try. His fellow players would beg him to give them a few runs at the castle, but Gorky would insist that the game be played seriously: "One should play hard, hard, so I must strike the castle."

Gorky also swam farther and faster than anybody else and he was the best at gathering eggs from the rookeries in the tops of Khorkom's poplar trees. To protect his head, he invented a special hat made of twigs and long, thorny branches, but the angry rooks pecked at him anyway. Gorky would hit anyone who attempted to steal stork eggs, for storks, a boon to farmers because they killed the snakes in the wheat fields, were considered sacred. In the late afternoons Gorky would sometimes borrow a fisherman's boat and row into the reeds to search for eggs laid by small black birds with white foreheads called *gonju*. Unable to fly, these birds would dart out of the water, emitting peculiar shrieks. Once when his companions put some chicks into the boat, Gorky carefully put them back, saying, "Let the chicks grow."

Gorky was probably older than his school friends: he may have started school late since he did not talk until he was six. He was thought to be backward, and the village children called him "the mute." In later life, Gorky delighted in telling friends about his inability to speak. Until he was six, he said, he spoke only with the birds.

Gorky and his sisters told various stories about his first words. One is that Sedrak and Krikor were having one of their usual arguments about money and Gorky burst out with: "Money, money, money! That's all you talk about, money!" Another story tells of his mother's taking him to a precipice and telling him that unless he spoke she would jump. As she moved toward the edge he cried, "Mother!" Various reports insist that he learned under the tutelage of Yeghus's son, his thirteen-year-old cousin Kevork Kondakian, who was hired to be his tutor. Gorky told his wife that the tutor took him up on the roof of their house and commanded, "Now jump!" And Gorky said his first words: 'No, I won't!' "

The cause of Gorky's delayed language development is not known. Kevork Kondakian attributed it to Krikor's violent and abusive behavior. Whatever the cause, whether trauma or an early version of the depression that would plague Gorky as an adult, his stubborn silence allowed Gorky to develop a private world. Since he couldn't talk, he observed, and since not being able to converse meant that he could not easily check his observations against those of others, his private world grew rich in fantasy.

5

The Departure of Sedrak Adoian

꒰꒱

In 1906, just about the time Gorky learned to talk, Sedrak Adoian left for America. Very likely his brother Krikor went with him; Sedrak's oldest son, Hagop, a member of the Dashnak Party, had left earlier. No doubt Gorky's father emigrated in the hope of growing rich, but he may also have owed taxes or been in trouble with the Turkish authorities. It is thought that he was an Armenian nationalist, possibly even a member of one of the revolutionary societies. If so, he risked imprisonment, which almost always meant the cruelest forms of torture.

Most Armenians traveling to America between 1899 and 1910 were farmers or laborers. Forty percent belonged to the "skilled" or "professional" classes. When they arrived in the New World the Armenians sought work in the industrial Northeast, and many furthered their education. Usually they sent money back to their wives, but it was often confiscated by their extended family. Shushan may have received some money from Sedrak, but her position in the family was low, and her money may have been appropriated by Yeghus, by Krikor's wife, Baidzar, or by Gorky's aging grandmother — in Armenian villages, such household economic matters were ruled by ancient and rigid family codes.

With the Adoian men gone, the farmwork became the women's responsibility. Although they hired a cousin named Rus Adoian to help with the plowing, Shushan had to rise early and go to work in the fields. She and Baidzar carried on their husbands' battles, fighting over money and over who performed what chores. Shushan felt that Baidzar was lazy. Baidzar probably thought that Shushan put on airs. Eventually Baidzar took her family and her mother-in-law and moved to Van City. Their departure must have brought a moment of peace, but Krikor soon returned from America, persuaded his mother to sign over the deeds of the Khorkom property to him, and forced Shushan and her children to move out of the family house and into a smaller one. Krikor's younger son, Azad, recalled: "They [Sedrak's family] were poorer than us and Sedrak was lazy."

As the years went by, Shushan and her children felt abandoned by Sedrak. There was something shameful about his failure to send the money and the steamship tickets that would have enabled them to join him in America. Part of the problem was the depressed American economy. In the difficult years of 1907 and 1912–14 many Armenians were jobless and could not save anything to send home. Another difficulty was that Hagop Adoian had always been jealous of his father's family by his second marriage. Now that Sedrak was dependent on him, Hagop made no effort to see that money was sent to his stepmother and his half siblings. And Sedrak Adoian was too weak a man to insist.

With Hagop's help, Sedrak eventually found employment as a foundry worker in Providence. A photograph taken by a professional photographer in 1910 (perhaps to be sent home to his family in Van) shows the forty-seven-year-old Sedrak wearing a tie, a white shirt, and a three-piece suit that looks a little worn (Fig. 48). For the photograph he has carefully placed a chain with a watch or a medal hanging from his lapel. In an enormous, elaborately carved chair, he sits rigidly upright, trying, it would seem, to look like a proud, prosperous, and determined citizen of the New World.

Sedrak Adoian's three younger children turned his departure from Van into a legend. They remembered that he placed them on a horse, led them to the shore of Lake Van, and gave them hard-boiled eggs to eat. After presenting Gorky with a pair of red slippers, he galloped off along the edge of the lake, disappearing into the mist. Exactly what happened is not known, for, as Gorky's widow, Mougouch, wrote to Gorky's first biographer, Ethel Schwabacher, "The father indeed disappeared when he [Gorky] was three or five. Gorky had a thousand childhoods, ten fictitious brothers about whom he wove the most delightful stories and I must say as the wish and fact were so hopelessly and charmingly tangled, it seems a shame that now they are to be put straight."

6

Akhtamar

❊

On certain religious holidays Shushan and her children would walk six or seven miles to Charahan Surp Nishan. Other pilgrims traveled on horses or donkeys. "They gave us a room in the tower," Satenik recalled. "Those were very happy times." Sheep were sacrificed and cooked over open fires. Musicians played, pilgrims prayed and sang, and men danced arm in arm. The Adoians also made pilgrimages to the much larger and more important monastery of Narek (now destroyed), a medieval center of manuscript illumination southwest of Khorkom.

At the time of the harvest festival Shushan and her children would walk down to the Vart Badrik promontory, board the sailboat that Sedrak had used to carry lumber, and sail to the island of Akhtamar, seven miles offshore. Although Akhtamar was no longer a fully functioning monastery after the anticlerical Dashnaks (one of whom is said to have been Gorky's maternal uncle Aharon) took it over in 1904, the revolutionaries did not oppose the villagers' yearly pilgrimages.

Gorky would have known the legend about how the island got its name, a story immortalized in a sixteen-verse poem titled "Akhtamar" by Hovhannes Toumanian. In the legend, a young man from Khorkom swims out each night to the island of Akhtamar, his way guided by a fire on the island's shore lit by his love, Tamar. Angered by this courtship, some boys from the island put out her fire. Toumanian's poem ends with these verses:

And Tamar's lover,
swimming, is lost in the dark.
The wind lifts his sighs.
Akh! Tamar, he calls.

Under the steep rocks
in the frightening darkness
where the wild sea shouts
Akh! Tamar, he cries.

In the morning the waters,
rippled only now, and calm,
wash him ashore.
On his cold lips two words
are frozen forever,
"Akh! Tamar"
the island's new name.

On this small, rocky island stands one of the most beautiful churches in eastern Turkey. Built between 915 and 921 out of dark reddish-brown blocks of soft volcanic stone called tufa, the domed cruciform Church of the Holy Cross is small but majestic (Fig. 44). King Gagik Ardsruni, who commissioned it during this period of Armenian cultural efflorescence, was clearly proud of its exquisite proportions: he had a portrait of himself wearing a halo and holding a miniature version of the church carved in relief on the church's western facade. The king's robe, embroidered with birds encircled by interlaced plant tendrils, must have remained in Gorky's mind. In the 1930s and early 1940s he would place birdlike creatures inside rounded shapes in two series of paintings that looked back to his early years.

The four apses in the church's tall interior have faded frescoes depicting the apostles and scenes from the life of Christ. The images of the Virgin and the crucified Christ clearly impressed Gorky, for echoes of them appear in *The Artist and His Mother, Portrait of Myself and My Imaginary Wife,* and other paintings from the 1930s. Gorky's fantastical imagination—his invention of abstract, hybrid forms that seem creature-like in their animation—was surely nourished by Akhtamar's most extraordinary feature, the relief carving on the church's exterior. Girdling the church is an ornamental band with local fauna and fabulous beasts interwoven in an elaborate vine scroll. Below is a frieze with scenes from the Old and New Testaments, plus various Armenian saints, angels, and seraphs and some wonderful grotesques. The carved figures have huge eyes with dark holes to indicate the iris and the pupil. These eyes predict the large dark eyes in Gorky's so-called Armenian portraits of the 1930s. The Virgin and Child on the side of the church facing Khorkom (Fig. 46) would (along with a 1912 photograph) form the basis of Gorky's Madonna-like portraits of his mother. Saint Theodore and Saint Serge, both on horseback and both wielding lances with which to kill, respectively, a dragon and a panther, may have been somewhere in the depths of Gorky's mind when he painted what appears to be an armored equestrian in the *Betrothal* series of 1947.

Behind the church among the trees stand *khatchkars*, worn with age. Some of the crosses carved on them have bifurcated bases, a motif that might be a source for the dark vertical band with a lobed bottom in Gorky's *Garden in Sochi* series. Since this series was based on his family's vegetable garden with its so-called tree of the cross, it is not surprising that Gorky would have combined the tree in his father's garden with the treelike crosses seen on Armenian *khatchkars*.

After Sedrak Adoian left for America in 1906, Shushan's life changed for the worse, and it became worse still after Krikor returned, assumed the role of paterfamilias, and lent support to his wife's antagonism. Apparently Sedrak Adoian was still not sending enough money and Krikor and Baidzar resented having to help support Shushan and her children. The position of fourteen-year-old Akabi (who was not an Adoian but a Prudian) was so unpleasant that, to get her away from Krikor's tyranny, Shushan allowed her brother-in-law to marry Akabi off to a cousin from Shadakh named Mkrdich Amerian. The wedding took place in Khorkom on February 10, 1910. Akabi's daughter, Liberty Miller, said: "They married my mother off as soon as she was able. She didn't see him until they got to the altar." According to Armenian tradition, bride and bridegroom joined hands and touched foreheads. The priest placed a wreath on each of their heads. Gorky's two portraits of Akabi painted around 1937 both depict his half sister crowned with a wreath. Vartoosh remembered being showered with almond candies at Akabi's wedding. Shushan was miserable. Soon after their wedding Akabi and Mkrdich (also spelled Muggerdich or Mgrditch) went to live in Van City.

The following summer Gorky visited his maternal uncles Moses and Aharon in the mountain village of Ermerur, where his grandmother had moved after setting fire to her family church. Most likely Shushan accompanied her children on this visit, which may have been prompted by her mother's illness. In any case, Gorky would always remember Hamaspiur Der Marderosian's funeral that summer—the candles, the wailing women, the body lying in state. His 1947 painting *The Orators* may embody his memories of the ceremony.

When the family returned to Khorkom, Shushan's relationship with Krikor and Baidzar became even more hostile. Egged on by Baidzar, Krikor had terrible battles with his sister-in-law. Letters of remonstration from Sedrak were to no avail. These fights ended with Krikor beating Shushan. On one occasion he struck her so hard that she fell on a stone just outside the door. Either the blow or the fall is said to have caused internal bleeding. Gorky was witness to many such beatings, and later in his life, his own physical violence would destroy at least two relationships with women.

Finally, in the fall of 1910, Shushan could no longer tolerate her brother-in-law's temper. Encouraged by her brother Aharon, who ran the carpentry shop at Van's American Mission, she gathered up her children and went to live in Van City. Leaving his village was a terrible wrench for Gorky. He missed his cousins and he missed the farm. Kevork Kondakian recalled: "When he left the house with his mother and lost the horse and dog, he felt very, very bad." Years later, when Gorky was filling out a questionnaire from New York's Museum of Modern Art, he answered the question "What in your ancestry, nationality, or background do you consider relevant to an understanding of your art?" this way: "Perhaps the fact that I was taken away from my little village when I was five [more like ten] years old yet all my vital memories are of these first years. These were the days when I smelled the bread, I saw my first red poppy, the moon, the innocent seeing. Since then these memories have become iconography, the shapes even the colors: millstone, red earth, yellow wheatfield, apricots etc."

PART II

Self-portrait, study for *The Artist and His Mother*, c. 1936

7

To Van

※

In September 1910, leaving Krikor and Yeghus in possession of the farm, Shushan and her three youngest children traveled from Khorkom to the city of Van on a primitive horse-drawn cart with wooden wheels of the type that are used in rural Van to this day. Krikor allowed his sister-in-law to take only a few essentials: quilts, a rug, cooking utensils, and clothes. The trip of some twenty miles took the better part of two days and was dangerous: the government made no effort to stop Kurds who descended from the hills to rob and murder Armenians. During these years, the American missionary hospital in Van treated numerous Armenians with bullet wounds inflicted by Kurds.

The Adoians followed a dirt road that led northeast along the lake's shore. Across the water the snow-covered cone of Mount Sipan must have made their progress seem slow: the extinct volcano spread over so much of the horizon that it looked more or less the same size even as they drew closer to Van. Finally they left the lake behind, crossed a wide, treeless plain, and traversed the green and sparsely inhabited Shamiram section of Van. In the distance they saw the mighty crenellated walls that enclosed the old city. Ahead and to their left stood the Tabriz Gate, the old city's principal entrance. Towering over the old city and forming its back wall was the famous Rock of Van, also called Castle Rock. About three hundred and fifty feet high and about a mile long, this stone cliff rises straight up out of the fertile plain. With the tombs of ancient Urartian kings, an Ottoman citadel, and serrated walls crowning its highest ridge, the rock looks like a recumbent dinosaur. Carved on its vertical face are cuneiform inscriptions—proud testaments to Urartian rulers' achievements. According to the classic Armenian epic *David of Sasun*, the giant Pkr Mher split the Rock of Van with his lightning sword, then entered it with his fire colt, Kurkik. The giant and his horse will continue to live in the rock until evil is gone from this world. In Gorky's time, Castle Rock was a military zone and the townspeople were not allowed to climb it.

Passing through the Tabriz Gate just under the rock, the Adoians entered the walled city, which covered an area of about a square mile. They headed south and found themselves in a lively metropolis deemed one of the most beautiful towns in eastern Turkey. After the primitive mud brick houses of Khorkom, the mosques, minarets, churches, government buildings, and crowded bazaar must have filled Gorky and his sisters with awe. The narrow, unpaved streets were lined with flat-roofed houses two or three stories tall, most built of mud bricks plastered with a mixture of mud and straw and set on stone foundations. Windows were few and placed high up, and the grander houses had second-story porches or enclosed belvederes and roofs with deep overhangs.

The streets were full of pedestrians, men on horseback, and from time to time camels carrying imported goods to the bazaar. Many men wore the fez. Others wore turbans. Some were dressed in Oriental robes, a few in European attire. Both Turkish and Armenian women covered their heads with veils or large scarves. Some Turkish women wore the burka, which covers the body from head to foot. To Gorky, used to living among Khorkom's fifty or so Armenian peasant families, Van must have seemed frighteningly full of Turks. It was in fact the one large town in Asia Minor in which Armenians outnumbered Turks.

Henry Morgenthau, the American ambassador to Turkey, wrote that when he visited Van in the fall of 1914 it was "one of the most peaceful and happy and prosperous communities in the Turkish Empire." He felt that compared with other parts of Turkey, and thanks to governor Tahsin Pasha's favorable attitude toward Armenians, "the Moslem yoke" rested lightly on the Armenians of Van. Armenians, Turks, and Kurds had relatively good relations, Morgenthau said. Other observers were less sanguine. H.F.B. Lynch, for example, saw Van as a "tinderbox." The town swarmed with secret police and was full of corrupt and ignorant government officials. Fear and suspicion, he said, were written on every face: "One may assert without exaggeration that life is quite intolerable for an inhabitant of this paradise of Van." Elizabeth Barrows, an American missionary who arrived in Van in 1900 and later married Clarence Ussher, wrote in a letter home that, though Van was beautiful and "very pleasant," it was also sad because so many houses had been left in ruins after the massacres of 1895–96. "It makes my heart bleed to ride through street after street of ruined homes and to think of the suffering the people have [endured] and are enduring."

Having come to live in the walled city a few months before her mother and her half siblings, the newlywed Akabi was able to find for them a room in an Armenian home on Galjunts Street in a Turkish section of the old town. Although the room had several windows facing the street, it was hot and the children often had fevers. The advantage of the Adoians' new home was that it was close to where Akabi lived with her husband, Mkrdich Amerian, and his mother and aunt. It was also not far from the home of Shushan's younger sister, Yeva, who had been a political activist ever since her girlhood in Vosdan. Shushan often took her children to visit Akabi, who, with a group of other Armenian women, was busy weaving a large rug for one of the city's churches. Watching Akabi weave would be an important memory for Gorky. In New York he would often gaze in admiration at the Oriental carpets displayed in the Metropolitan Museum, and he owned at least one book on carpets. Textile patterns were part of his aesthetic formation: they would feed the inventiveness of his semiabstract forms.

The first months in Van were difficult. Sedrak sent money but not enough, and Shushan took in sewing to supplement the family's income. Gorky missed the relative freedom of his life in Khorkom. During the five years he lived in Van City his happiest times were the summers when he returned to Khorkom.

Gorky and Satenik attended the Husisayeen School, an institution with some three hundred pupils, founded in the mid-nineteenth century; its name indicates that it was dedicated to Jesus. The curriculum in the Armenian schools of Van consisted of the Armenian language, religion and literature, plus math, science, geography, history, and the Turkish and French languages. Lynch reported that the Turkish authorities sometimes censored the reading material available to Armenian students. Milton and Shakespeare were suspect. A Bible in modern Armenian was allowed. He saw a copy of Xenophon's *Anabasis* in which the name of Armenia had been removed from a map. Gymnastics, too, were prohibited in Armenian schools: the Turks feared that sports might be the equivalent of military training.

Since Gorky had to pass through Turkish quarters on his way to and from school, his mother accompanied him to keep him out of danger. Wariness was a quality that Armenians encouraged in their children: to be trusting was to be foolishly vulnerable. For Gorky, the short walk to school was full of visual interest. All kinds of objects were displayed at the bazaar, and he and his mother would stop to watch the artisans at work in their stalls. Van was famous for its Armenian silversmiths, who made jewelry, headdresses, belts, boxes, and daggers and decorated them using a method called nielloing, in which intricate designs engraved in the silver's surface are filled with an amalgam of silver, copper, lead, and sulfur, and in which the designs show up as black lines in the silver's surface.

During the two months that the Adoians lived on Galjunts Street in the walled city, Shushan grew increasingly unhappy with their cramped quarters and with the dangers of living in a Turkish section. In November 1910, with the help of money sent by Sedrak, she moved her family to Aikesdan, an area of some ten square miles stretching eastward from the Tabriz Gate (Fig. 51). With its broader streets and its houses surrounded by walled gardens, orchards, and vineyards, Aikesdan was much less congested than the walled city. The house that the Adoian family rented was a modest one on Chaghli Street in the southeast section of Aikesdan, between Norashen and Arakh, two heavily populated Armenian quarters. Shushan must have felt connected to her new neighborhood: her father, Sarkis Der Marderosian, had served as priest in the Arakh church, the largest church in Aikesdan, and his murder in 1898 had made him a martyr to local Armenians, who were therefore well disposed to his daughter and grandchildren. Living among Armenians gave Gorky more freedom to roam, but even in Aikesdan there was constant danger. When he returned home late from exploring the harbor, Shushan was frightened. "Mother begged him not to go," Vartoosh remembered, "because there were Turks who might harm him."

Like most other streets in Aikesdan, Chaghli Street had irrigation ditches running on either side. These made the orchards and gardens extraordinarily lush. Following Chaghli Street to its end, Gorky and his sisters discovered a vast plain sloping up toward the Varag range. It was full of wildflowers, especially the blue *gunerzuk,* which Armenians think of as their national flower. Here also were fields of cucumbers and watermelons, and sometimes the Adoian children went beyond the tilled fields to gather flowers, rhubarb, and *sint,* a green plant that Shushan cooked with eggs. One section of the Varag plain was called Urpat Arn, or Friday Stream, because sweethearts strolled there on Friday evenings. Gorky and his friends loved to tease them. Given Armenian reserve and the high value set on a girl's virginity, one cannot imagine that there was much to spy on.

Every morning at five the Armenians of Aikesdan were woken by the *zhamhar,* or time caller, who knocked on their doors with a stick and cried, "Waken for church." Feeding the time caller was a duty shared by all churchgoers. The *zhamhar* was a guest at the Adoians' house about once a month, and the first family member to arise would give him bread. Since the Adoian children were in school from dawn to dusk and attended religious services at school, they went to church with their mother only on Sundays and on religious holidays.

Easter is the Armenians' most important holiday. Children were given a new outfit to wear, and villagers celebrated with feasts, egg fights, and exchanges of visits. To prepare, they boiled eggs in water with onionskins so that the eggs turned deep reddish brown. The egg fights consisted of competitors tapping the tips of their eggs together; the person whose egg did not crack won the loser's cracked egg. Gorky painted such beautiful Easter eggs that friends and neighbors commissioned him to paint theirs. His decorative motifs included flowers, birds, and trees—all subjects that would reappear in his painting. With the money he earned from painting eggs he bought paper and pencils, thus initiating a long habit of spending his earnings on art supplies instead of on things that his mother (and later his first wife) considered necessities. After taking their painted eggs to have them blessed in church, the Adoians celebrated by eating Easter eggs for dinner.

With his mother, Gorky visited various churches in and around the city—certain churches were attended at certain holidays. In September, to commemorate the apparition of the cross in 653, worshipers came from near and far to the eleventh-century church at Varag Mountain, east of Aikesdan. Gorky is said to have been greatly impressed by the monastery's splendid collection of medieval illuminated manuscripts.

Along with *khatchkars* and handwoven carpets, the calendar pages of these manuscripts, with their rich purples and reds and yellows and their exquisite birds and plant/animal hybrids, lodged themselves in Gorky's imagination (Fig. 52). The tendency of his line to erupt into little, pointed sproutlike shapes, and his line's elegant but tense sinuosity, must have been informed by the medieval illuminators' elaborate interlaces. The manuscript painters' fondness for vertically stacked decorative elements seems also to have affected Gorky's approach to composition. He surely admired as well the crisp energy of the monks' calligraphy: it helped to form his concept of how a mark on paper should look.

The library where Gorky supposedly saw the medieval manuscripts is now a farm building. Its manuscript collection was burned during the Turkish siege of Van in 1915. In the ruined library's dark, dirty interior a Kurdish farmer has stored one of those primitive wooden plows that Gorky so loved. The plow looks as though it has not been used for years.

8

The American Mission at Van

Although Shushan was reluctant to send her children to a Protestant establishment, when the Adoians moved to Aikesdan her brother Aharon, who ran the carpentry shop at the nearby American Mission, persuaded her to send her children to the missionary school. Should there be another massacre, they would be safer inside the American Mission compound. The mission, founded by the Congregational Church of America in 1871, consisted of a group of buildings intermingled with trees and enclosed by a high mud wall. The principal edifice in the compound was a handsome church with tall arched windows, a gable roof over the nave, and an attached bell tower. No doubt this American-style church looked peculiar to Armenians accustomed to flat-roofed, dark, fortress-like churches. The compound also had a three-story hospital built under the guidance of Dr. Ussher (Fig. 53), two large school buildings, two smaller school buildings, a lace-making school (organized to help the mission's orphans earn a living), a dispensary, and several ample residences for the missionaries.

Early on, the American missions in Turkey learned that it was inadvisable to interfere with the spiritual life of the Turks: the missionaries therefore concerned themselves primarily with the needs and sufferings of the Armenians. After the massacres of 1895–96 the American Mission at Van was home to four or five hundred Armenian orphans, among them Gorky's half sister Sima. By the time Gorky arrived in Van, the orphans had been moved to the German Mission.

Boys entered the school at seven and were usually finished by age eighteen. The curriculum emphasized Bible training, but it made no attempt to inculcate Protestant beliefs. The missionaries taught music, Armenian, Turkish, English, mathematics, and history. There was also a visiting drawing teacher named B. Hohannes Baghdasarian. As in Van's Armenian schools, the Turkish government censored books and gymnastics were forbidden.

Gorky remained an inattentive scholar who frequently got into mischief. Arshag Mooradian, a fellow student at the missionary school, recalled: "He wasn't so good in mathematics. He had a few problems. What he did all day? He had a stick and a knife. He used to carve it all day." Shushan fretted over her son's indifference to schoolwork. She tried to get Arshag to intervene: "Help Manoug!" she begged. "Please, help Manoug at school." Vartoosh said that Gorky astonished one of his teachers when he made an exact copy of a map on the blackboard. Another area in which Gorky excelled was carpentry. In the shop run by his uncle Aharon and overseen by Ernest A. Yarrow, superintendent of the boys school and a graduate of Wesleyan College, he learned to make plows, saddles, and furniture.

In 1912 Gorky and his mother rode in a horse-drawn cart along Aikedan's main street and entered the old city by the Tabriz Gate. Gorky had not been inside the city walls since visiting Akabi when her son Gurken was born the year before. The reason for the trip was to have a photograph taken to send to Sedrak Adoian in America. The result was a heartwrenching portrait of two people who, for all their touching efforts to appear to be comfortably off, look like victims (Fig. 47). The face of the thirty-two-year-old Shushan is a mask of numb despair. Perhaps because she had never been photographed before, she does not arrange her face to give it a flattering angle or expression. Gorky, at her side, appears slightly embarrassed at being roped into posing with his mother. He holds a tiny bouquet of flowers, no doubt plunked into his hand by the photographer. In this very first photograph of him he does not look eight, but at least twelve.

The faces of both mother and child have the look of a plea. The purpose of the photograph was probably to remind Sedrak Adoian of his responsibilities to his wife and children. Shushan appears as the soul of propriety in her flowered apron and her *yazma* (shawl). Gorky in his Chesterfield coat (Shushan dressed him better than she dressed his sisters) and with his handkerchief in his pocket looks like an obedient son.

There is a passivity in both figures' postures that seems to go beyond the immobility that posing for long exposures required. It is as if fatalism had slowed Gorky and his mother to a standstill.

Even in Aikesdan with its gardens and its proximity to the Varag plain, Gorky pined for Khorkom. His longing intensified on the day his uncle Krikor turned up riding Astgh and bringing fruits and vegetables from the Khorkom garden. Satenik recalled: "Gorky was so incredibly happy. Gorky took it by the reins and he brought it into our garden, in the city, and he led it back and forth, back and forth." Gorky wept that night and said he wanted to go home to Khorkom.

In late summer, when school was closed and the missionaries fled the city heat for their summer retreat in Artemid, many residents of Van went to visit relatives in outlying villages. Sometimes Akabi would take Gorky with her when she visited her mother-in-law in Shadakh, but most of each summer Gorky spent in Khorkom, where he stayed long enough to help with the harvest. During these months he and his cousins enjoyed all their usual pursuits: swimming, whittling, stealing turtle and rook eggs, sleeping outside in hammocks. Gorky was still the biggest boy and the leader of his group. Although he was full of energy and fun, he was also prone to outbursts of anger. Gorky's good friend Yenovk Der Hagopian said: "He was very temperamental. Since we were little, he'd get mad. He could hurt you. He was stronger than I. Couple of times he did hurt me and once I came home with red eyes, crying." For weeks Yenovk avoided Gorky. Then one day while swimming he felt something tugging at his leg, and Gorky's head popped up from under the water: "If you don't talk to me, I'll drown you!" Gorky said. With that threat, their friendship resumed, and Yenovk remained a great friend for the rest of Gorky's life.

At the end of the summer the thought of returning to Van and to school made Gorky miserable. When it was time to go he vanished. After calling and searching, his mother and sisters finally found Gorky crouched behind a wall, hugging the sheepdog, Zango. "Oh, Zango. Lucky, lucky Zango!" he was saying. "You don't have to go to school. I wish I was a dog."

The political climate in Van province during the years Gorky spent in Aikesdan (1910–15) grew increasingly grim. In 1911 the Turkish garrison in the city of Van grew from eight to thirty-two regiments, and there were frequent threats of massacre. Caravans of Armenians fleeing their homeland could be seen moving across the mountains between Van and the Black Sea. Akabi's husband, Mkrdich, was among them when he left for America in 1911. The American Missionary Reports for 1912–13 tell of the persecution of Armenians and of the Turkish authorities looking the other way. On September 18, 1912, Dr. Ussher wrote to Dr. James L. Barton at the headquarters of the American Board of Commissioners for Foreign Missions in Boston: "The trend toward reaction is showing itself in frequent plunderings and murders." He reported that the roads were unsafe, that the villagers' cattle were often "carried off." A month later he wrote that unless he could get the Muslims in touch with Christianity, there would be "bloodshed beside which the massacres of 1896 will seem insignificant."

The viewpoint of the dictatorial triumvirate of Enver Pasha, minister of war, Talaat Pasha, minister of the interior, and Djemal Pasha, military governor of Constantinople became more and more racist and national-istic. "Turkey for the Turks" was their cry. Anything that got in the way of their goal to unite Turks in all of Asia into a pan-Turkic empire had to be eliminated. The Armenians were just such an obstacle. Persecutions in-tensified and Armenians were full of foreboding. An eclipse of the sun in 1914 was a thrilling event for Gorky and Vartoosh, who watched it through smoke-blackened glass to protect their eyes. The streets of Aikes-dan were crowded with people. Some were excited. Many were full of dread, for they saw the eclipse as an omen of disaster.

9

Massacres

On August 2, 1914, two days before the outbreak of World War I, Turkey signed a secret agreement: if Russia, in support of Serbia, entered the war against Austria and Germany, Turkey would join the Central Powers. On August 3, 1914, Turkey began to mobilize. The day after Germany declared war on Russia, martial law was proclaimed in Van. On August 4 soldiers with fixed bayonets stood outside the marketplace of the walled city while procurement agents took the Armenian merchants' stock of sugar, kerosene, petroleum, soap, rice, raisins, grain oil, copper, canvas, and leather. Large containers were placed on street corners, and the residents of Van were required to contribute their quotas of milk. Although goods were demanded of Turks as well, the burden of requisitioning fell more heavily on the Armenians. Turkish officers appropriated the Armenians' cattle and all their wheat was reserved for the army.

Meanwhile, conscription took Armenian farmers away from their fields and Armenian merchants from their shops. On October 7, the American missionary Grace Higley Knapp reported that there was no fuel available and the city was full of Hamidiyes—those mounted Kurdish troops modeled on the Cossacks. In early August 1914, Dr. Ussher was returning to Van from a meeting at Harput when he witnessed the forced conscription of Armenian field workers. He saw troops of recruits parched with thirst. He saw an Armenian woman's house in flames and learned that when the Turkish recruiters came to her village and were told that her son was out cutting wood, they called him a deserter and torched her home. "In Van we found conscription going on and the people in panic," wrote Dr. Ussher. "The drafted men had been told to bring five days rations with them, but had not been given time to provide themselves with these rations, and came to the city starving. On my professional rounds I often passed recruiting stations and would see these men drawn up in line, standing for hours in the scorching sun, while officers entered on registration blanks all statistics required by the Prussian government of its army. Many fainted where they stood from hunger and exhaustion."

Gorky's aunt Yeva was part of a resistance group headed by Levon Pasha Shagoyan, a legendary character who later led a group of villagers from Khorkom to Iraq and founded a village there. Occasionally Shagoyan stayed at Shushan's house (he is said to have been a distant relative), and Gorky heard the adults talking in anxious voices. His awareness of danger was sharpened by his mother's prayers. Always vehement in her exhortations of God, Shushan now prayed for safety. "In Aikesdan," Vartoosh remembered, "we prayed before going to sleep. We stood, first Mummy, then Gorky, Satenik and I, and looked to the east, *Aghotaran*. We only prayed that God give peace, that war shouldn't happen, and God guard our lives. Mummy said this aloud and we made the cross and knelt."

In late October the Turkish fleet bombarded Russian Black Sea installations, and the Ottoman Empire entered the war on the side of Germany. In December, full of imperialist ambitions to march beyond Russia, through Afghanistan, and on to India, Enver Pasha led the ninety-five thousand underfed and poorly equipped soldiers of the Ottoman Third Army eastward, where they were defeated at the Russian military base of Sarikamish. Within two weeks 80 percent of his troops were dead. Entire divisions were later found frozen like statues. Forced to retreat, Enver Pasha blamed his humiliation on the Armenians in the volunteer regiments of the Russian army, whom he accused of treason.

The Committee of Union and Progress (as the Turkish governing body was called) decided to seize the moment and wipe out the Armenian population of Turkey while the Western powers were too preoccupied with war to intervene. The decision appears to have been taken a month or so after Enver Pasha's defeat. By the end of February 1915, Armenian government officials and employees were dismissed. Armenian military officers were imprisoned and soldiers were disarmed and enrolled in labor battalions in which they were treated like pack animals.

Ambassador Henry Morgenthau wrote: "Army supplies of all kinds were loaded on their backs, and, stumbling under the burdens and driven by the whips and bayonets of the Turks, they were forced to drag their weary bodies into the mountains of the Caucasus. Sometimes they would have to plough their way, burdened in this fashion, almost waist-high through snow. They had to spend practically all their time in the open, sleeping on the bare ground. . . . They were given only scraps of food; if they fell sick they were left where they had dropped." With time the government became more forthright in its extermination procedures: Armenian soldiers were rounded up and taken to secret places where they were slaughtered. It was not long before Armenians in the eastern provinces learned what was happening to Armenian soldiers, and the atmosphere of dread intensified.

That winter refugees from the area of Baskale, south of Lake Van, poured into Van City, telling tales of horror. During a Russian retreat the Turks had herded the Armenians from their pillaged and burned villages, killed all the males over ten, and raped the women. Young girls were abducted and given to Muslims as wives. Onnig Mukhitarian, in his memoir of Van during this period, said, "Good-looking women and girls were brought to the Shamiram Turkish ward in Van . . . to be auctioned off. . . . Some ten thousand Armenians were massacred at this time."

The Turkish army was finally defeated on the Persian front as well. When, after his failed expedition in Persia, Jevdet Bey, the new governor of Van, returned to Van in mid-February 1915, he, like his brother-in-law Enver Pasha, blamed his military reversals on the Armenian volunteer units of the Russian army. With this as a pretext, he began a reign of terror in the Armenian villages. The wife of the head of the American Mission at Van wrote on May 29, 1915, to her husband, who was in the United States: "Several times during the winter we heard that Jevdet Pasha was urging massacre of Christians on the Van Turks, but many were much opposed saying, 'we must live with these Christians afterward.' When he appeared in Van all felt sure it meant trouble, but no one knew just what form it would take."

Governor Jevdet Bey was tall and handsome, with intense black eyes and a black mustache. He was exquisitely groomed and dressed, charming and correct in his manners, but he was widely known to have tortured and murdered Armenians in diabolical ways. He branded people to death, crushed testes, and placed cats in a victim's pants—this torture by scratching became known as *"le supplice des chats"* (the cat punishment). He was most famous for a punishment he favored when posted at Baskale. There he had horseshoes nailed to his victims' feet and made the shod men dance until they collapsed. For the invention of this entertainment, he became known as "the Iron Marshal from Baskale."

When Jevdet returned defeated from the Persian front in February, he brought with him a personal regiment of four hundred known as the *lez* and also called the "Butcher Regiment" because it was composed of Turkish convicts. This brought the number of Turkish soldiers in Van to about four thousand. Upon his return, Armenian notables, including Bishop Yeznig, welcomed him with assurances of loyalty. For all the apparent cordiality, in late February and March Jevdet's persecution of Armenians increased. Armenian leaders and clergymen patrolled the streets to prevent skirmishes that Jevdet could use as an excuse for massacre. If an Armenian was offended by some outrage on the part of a Turk or Kurd, he or she was told to turn the other cheek. Nevertheless there were confrontations and reprisals. One that young Gorky could easily have witnessed occurred early in April at the square in Norashen, near the Adoian home. Turkish police shot and killed a young Armenian, then opened fire indiscriminately at passersby, some of whom were schoolchildren. A fourteen-year-old Armenian schoolboy—a contemporary of Gorky's—was killed.

Through the spring the Turkish police intensified their systematic harassment of Armenians. The terror spread all over the province and erupted in other parts of Turkish Armenia as well. Groups of policemen would ride into Armenian towns and villages searching for arms. If arms were not produced they would apply the *bastinado*. As Y. K. Rushdouni reported in a June 7, 1915, letter from Van published in the *Manchester Guardian*: "It became evident that the government was bent on the systematic destruction of the Armenian population. A feeling of despondency seized hold of all."

In Van City, tension heightened when it became evident that Turkish reinforcements were pouring into the area and that Turkish soldiers were digging a line of trenches around the Armenian quarters at Aikesdan. The Armenians responded by digging trenches of their own, building and reinforcing walls, and setting up eight *teerks*, or strongholds, most of which were fortified houses. By noon on April 17, the Armenian defense command had soldiers manning their posts on a round-the-clock alert.

All traffic and communication between Aikesdan and the walled city stopped. The following day the Turkish police forcibly occupied the Armenian schools attached to the churches of Haykavank and Arakh. Between April 17 and April 20, Armenians living in districts immediately adjoining Turkish quarters or in mixed neighborhoods evacuated their homes and moved to the center of Aikesdan to be within the two-square-mile area protected by the Armenian defense line. Between four and six thousand Armenians, among them the Adoians, found refuge in the American Mission. Others moved into the German compound or were placed in private homes. Because the foreign missions flew their national flags, it was thought that they would not be attacked. For everyone's safety, the American missionaries remained neutral and did not allow armed Armenians to enter their compound.

Elizabeth Barrows, now married to Dr. Ussher, wrote in her diary that on the evening of April 17, "neighbors began to bring beds, carpets, boxes and wheat (because they thought our premises safe). Next day streams of people poured through our gate with household effects. By the next morning, Monday, seventy extra people were living here." Soon five thousand refugees filled the church, the schools, the lace-making house, the carpentry shop, wagon sheds, hen houses, and the laundry. In addition, they put up makeshift dwellings and tents. Many families were placed in the missionaries' own homes. Clarence and Elizabeth Ussher, for example, gave shelter to one hundred Armenians. "Our premises are a sight," Elizabeth Ussher wrote on May 8. "Every available covered spot is crowded with families with little bedding, cribs, crying babies, and many sick from exposure, lack of food and fear." Housing and feeding the refugees was a huge problem. Some brought cattle; others were so poor they came empty-handed.

Not long after his return from the front, Jevdet demanded that the Armenian leaders provide four thousand Armenian soldiers to the Turkish army. Knowing that Armenians serving in the Turkish army were being disarmed, forced into hard labor, and killed, the Armenians demurred. They offered Jevdet four hundred soldiers and said they would pay the exemption fee for the remaining thirty-six hundred men. Jevdet insisted on four thousand or nothing, so the Armenians kept stalling. A snowstorm during Holy Week postponed negotiations. Dr. Ussher and Ernest Yarrow tried to mediate with Jevdet on the Armenians' behalf, but Jevdet was not swayed: "They must obey or I will break them;" he said. "I will start massacres again at Shadakh first and then at Van. If the rebels dare to shoot one bullet that will be a signal for me to attack the city."

During one of Dr. Ussher's meetings with Jevdet, the governor said he wanted to billet fifty Turkish soldiers with cannon and supplies in the American Mission compound. Since this would have violated the mission's neutral status, Dr. Ussher told Jevdet that he needed to consult with his colleagues. Having done so, Dr. Ussher suggested that Jevdet send only five to ten soldiers. The issue had not been resolved when trouble broke out between Turks and Armenians at Shadakh. Upon learning that the head of the Armenian school there had been arrested and was to be executed, the Armenians surrounded the government building and demanded his release. On April 14 there were armed clashes between Armenians and Turks.

Jevdet, who may in fact have instigated this conflict to create a pretext for massacre, now made one of those vicious and deceitful decisions for which he was known. He invited four Armenian notables and four prominent Turks to go to Shadakh to restore peace. The Armenian contingent included the much-loved Dashnak leader Ishkhan, who was one of the few Armenians in Van who knew about military tactics. On Friday, April 16, the first evening of the twenty-four-hour journey, a feast was prepared for the eight-man delegation at which all four Armenians were murdered. The next day Jevdet summoned Vramian, Aram, and several other Dashnak leaders to his office. Vramian went and was arrested, sent with an escort to Constantinople, and murdered along the way. As he rode in his carriage to meet Jevdet, Aram was warned about the fate of his friend, and he turned back.

News of Ishkhan's death and Vramian's arrest (it was not immediately known that he had been killed) both heightened the Armenians' anxiety and galvanized their fighting spirit. Hmayag Manoogian, an eyewitness at Van, said: "Everybody, whether old or young, male or female, partisan or neutral, reactionary or revolutionary, felt, with an explosive force, that there could be no other choice than armed resistance." Another eyewitness, Onnig Mukhitarian, remembered the mixture of panic, despair, exaltation, and resolve as the people of Aikesdan poured into the streets in the hours after Vramian's arrest: "Shop doors are being locked and muffled preparations are being started in cellars. Groups of young men, stripped for action, cross the streets and orchards; when they meet they whisper a few words and hurry on."

Efforts were still being made to register five hundred of the four thousand soldiers Jevdet Bey demanded. On April 19, when Bishop Yeznig went to talk with Jevdet, he found the governor truculent and cold. The Armenians at Shadakh and in the Haiyotz Dzor valley (where Khorkom lay) had revolted, Jevdet said. They would be punished. "Either the Turks or the Armenians are to survive," he announced. "This land will belong exclusively to either Moslems or Christians." That was the bishop's last meeting with Jevdet. On Dr. Ussher's final visit he overheard the governor's orders to the colonel of the *lez*: "Go to Shadakh and wipe out its people." Jevdet then turned to the American doctor and, holding his hand below his knee, said: "I won't leave one, not one so high." No sooner had Dr. Ussher left than Jevdet sent his Butcher Regiment, mounted and armed with guns and daggers, not to Shadakh as he had said but to Haiyotz Dzor. Six villages in that valley were destroyed, among them Khorkom.

The destruction of the villages in the province of Van had actually been going on for several days. The massacres, rapes, and torchings started in the north. Ambassador Morgenthau wrote: "On April 15th, about 500 young Armenian men of Akantz were mustered to hear an order of the Sultan; at sunset they were marched outside the town and every man shot in cold blood. This procedure was repeated in about eighty Armenian villages in the district north of Lake Van, and in three days 24,000 Armenians were murdered in this atrocious fashion." News of the burning of villages in the Haiyotz Dzor valley and other villages on the south side of the lake on April 19 reached Aikesdan the same day. Ussher reported: "We have absolute proof that fifty-five thousand people were killed." The women and children and property were divided among the Turks.

Another eyewitness account comes from the Cuban-born Venezuelan mercenary General Rafael de Nogales, who, in the third week of April, was making his way toward the city of Van to take over the command of the siege for the Turkish army. At Adeljivas on the north shore of the lake, where Gorky's father used to sail to sell his lumber, Nogales saw Muslims stabbing Christian artisans and then forcing the wounded men's wives, mothers, and daughters to drag the men's bodies out of the shops and onto the street, where a crowd of Kurds and Turks robbed them and finished them off. When Nogales ordered the attackers' leader to desist, he was told they were carrying out orders from the governor to "exterminate all Armenian males of twelve years of age and over." Sailing from Adeljivas to Van, Nogales stopped at Ahktamar, where he discovered monks' corpses "huddled on the threshold and atrium of the sanctuary." Their killers, a detachment of Turkish policemen, stood nearby. At Artemid on April 21 the night sky was lit by flames from the burning church. Coming closer, Nogales smelled scorched flesh and saw the bodies of Armenians near and in the church. The next day Elizabeth Ussher noted that Artemid was still burning and that 150 Armenians had been killed there.

Refugees, mostly old men, women, and children, arriving from the Haiyotz Dzor valley and from villages around the lake described the carnage to the inhabitants of Van. Dr. Ussher summed up what he learned this way: "Where they [the Turkish soldiers] saw a mother nursing her babe they shot through the babe and the mother's breast and arm. They would gallop into a crowd of fleeing women and children, draw their daggers, and rip up the unfortunate creatures. I forebear to describe the wounds brought to me to repair." Shushan and her children must have felt desperate about the fate of family members in Khorkom and Vosdan.

That these massacres were part of a carefully organized plan to exterminate Armenians in Ottoman Turkey and not, as the Turks claimed, a reaction to an uprising of the Armenians at Van is clear. In his postwar report on what happened in Van, Ibrahim Arvas, a Turkish deputy to parliament from Van, said: "Ittihad [the Committee of Union and Progress] was underhandedly instigating the [Turkish] people, prodding them to hurl themselves upon the Armenians." Although Turkish authorities used the so-called Armenian rebellion to justify their decision to kill and deport the Armenian population of the eastern provinces, the Van massacres began *after* the start of deportations and massacres of Armenians in Cilicia. In Ambassador Morgenthau's view there was little question that Jevdet Bey "came to Van with definite instructions to exterminate all Armenians in this province." When on April 19 Jevdet gave his soldiers orders to massacre and burn the Armenian villages around Lake Van, he warned: "The Armenians must be exterminated. If any Moslem protect a Christian, first, his house shall be burned, then the Christian killed before his eyes, then his family and himself."

The procedure that Turkish soldiers used to wipe out Armenians all over Turkey was to gather together the handful of men that had not been conscripted into the army, march them out of town, and shoot them. Next the beautiful women were given to Muslims. Other women were beaten, stripped naked, raped, abducted, and murdered. Some killings were particularly vicious. For example, a Turk would slash the belly of a pregnant woman and pick the fetus out with the end of his sword. Ernest Yarrow told of babies yanked from the arms of their mothers and dashed to the ground or strangled. Finally the village would be plundered and burned. Anyone left alive was deported. In the spring of 1915 long lines of Armenians stretched over the countryside as they plodded southward through the dry land toward the Syrian desert. Refugees were repeatedly robbed, both by the guards escorting them and by bands of Kurds, who descended from the hills and carried off the young women. The Armenians' clothes were stolen, they were starved, and even when they passed a river, they were forbidden to drink. Many committed suicide by throwing themselves in rivers or wells. Others were forced to leave their babies or parents on the side of the road to die. When the survivors of these death marches finally reached the camps at Der el Zor in Syria, they continued to be mistreated, and many died of starvation and disease.

10

The Siege of Van

Before dawn on April 20 a group of Armenian women from Varag were seized by Turkish soldiers as they tried to slip through the Turkish defense line and enter Aikesdan. Two armed Armenian men rushed to their defense and were shot dead. Elizabeth Ussher's diary entry for April 20 says, "This occurred in front of the German compound; so many were eyewitnesses that the trouble was initiated by the Turks. Although the *vali* [governor] calls it a rebellion, it is really an effort to protect the lives and the homes of the Armenians." The missionaries may have been biased in favor of the Armenians, but the report of an officer attached to the Turkish War Office supports the view that the Armenians at Van took up arms as a response to Turkish provocation. Austrian vice field marshal Pomiankowski described the Van uprising as an act of "desperation on the part of the Armenians who saw that the general slaughter had begun."

However it happened, this skirmish triggered full-scale war. The Turks opened fire first on the Armenian quarters of Aikesdan and then on the Armenian sections of the walled city. Bullets flew in all directions and cannons boomed out from the heights of the Rock of Van. Several Armenians were killed by flying bullets and shells that burst at the tops of poplar trees, scattering shrapnel. "There was panic in the streets," wrote Mukhitarian. "Most were praying, frozen in fear, some were stamping their feet in uncontrolled despair; yet others were crying hurrahs as young men made their way through swarms of people to man their positions and face the enemy."

The Armenians faced nearly impossible odds. The Turks had some five thousand well-equipped soldiers, plus cannons, hand grenades, inflammable liquids, and bombs. The Armenian defenders numbered only about fifteen hundred men, of whom only a fifth had any training (Fig. 55). Their arsenal consisted of a mere 101 rifles, 90 Mauser pistols, many of them antiquated, 120 revolvers, and a small supply of bullets and gunpowder.

The day the siege began, Jevdet Bey wrote to Bishop Yeznig saying that the insurrection at Shadahk had spread to the city of Van and that all of Haiyotz Dzor, Artschak, and part of Timar had been "punished." His men, he said, had already burned much of the north part of Aikesdan and taken an area near Ararkh. He had ordered them to bombard the old city until nothing was left but a "pile of ruins." Jevdet worked quickly. Even the minarets of mosques became stations for Turkish gunners. In the evening of the first day of the siege, burning houses were seen all over Van. "The fires burned throughout the night of the first day of fighting," Mukhitarian recalled. "Tongues of fire piercing through dense clouds of smoke cast an eerie light over the city." For Gorky this was a new kind of fire, not fire as the center of family life: fire as destroyer.

Later that evening the Turkish artillery attacks on Aikesdan came to an abrupt stop. During half an hour of silence all that could be heard was the crackle of burning houses and the distant thunder of cannon falling on the old city. The Armenians asked themselves, could the Turks have given up the idea of overrunning Aikesdan? Then the rattle of artillery fire resumed, and people closed their eyes and plugged their ears. The noise convinced the Armenians that the Turks were about to invade their streets and massacre every Christian in sight. But the Armenian combatants countered this intimidation by singing patriotic songs.

General Nogales, who arrived in Van City on April 22, two days after the hostilities had begun, recalled his first meeting with Jevdet Bey. As the Latin American soldier of fortune and the Turkish governor sat on Castle Rock watching houses burning in the old city some three hundred feet below, explosions rattled their teacups. In moments when the firing died down, Nogales heard the cry of ravens doing battle with dogs over Turkish and Armenian corpses. Yet over the next days a mood of camaraderie and defiance prevailed behind the Armenian lines. If the Armenians could not win, at least they could die with honor. In his memoir of the siege of Van, Haig Gossoian recalled: "Three days of successful resistance were sufficient to eradicate the tendency to servile fear and to cowardice which six centuries of unparalleled persecution had implanted in them. On the fourth day, they were eager to sacrifice their life, ready to assist in any way possible."

The Aikesdan Armenians set up a provisional government and organized various committees to take care of such things as munitions, food distribution, and law and order. A code of law was instituted: the Armenian defenders were to keep clean, avoid alcohol, tell the truth, and not insult the religion of the enemy. Everyone set to work, male and female, young and old. Boys served as messengers between defense positions. Unarmed men (for there were not enough guns to go around) dug trenches and dodged bullets as they rebuilt walls. The supply committee gathered and distributed whatever supplies the Armenians had been able to keep after the Turkish requisitions. A munitions shop was set up to recast spent bullets and pack cartridges with gunpowder from unexploded Turkish shells. Although it is probable that, like their neighbors, the Adoians took refuge in the American compound during the three days that preceded the siege, Vartoosh told Karlen that they left Chaghli Street only after the hostilities broke out. "Our section became a battlefront," she recalled. "The men were fighting in the area and they moved us. Akabi came too, her little boy, Gurken, and Mummy." As the Adoians made their way to the American Mission, cannon shells came from all directions and the noise was deafening: "The entire region was at war and we were in great fear." At the American compound they moved into what Vartoosh called "the building of the American missionaries." Perhaps she meant the church or a school building. "It was a huge place," she said. "Gorky was with the men running about. They took ammunition to the soldiers, carried supplies."

During occasional pauses in the Turkish artillery fire, the Adoians would return to their house to see if it was still standing and to gather food from the garden. "We had even planted flowers," Vartoosh said, "and I remember once that I went and brought a big bunch of flowers from our home." Since Shushan had not been able to carry much with her when she evacuated her home, she made frequent trips back to Chaghli Street. These trips worried her children, who knew the danger of venturing beyond the two-mile area protected by the Armenian defense lines.

If, as Vartoosh maintained, Gorky was a runner carrying food and ammunition to the soldiers, then he must have been at least fourteen at the time: many boys of that age served as messengers to the front. Perhaps he joined the scout troop organized the previous year by Dr. Ussher's fourteen-year-old son, Neville. Besides helping to keep the mission clean, the scouts gathered bullets, protected the mission against fire, kept various buildings supplied with water, carried the wounded on stretchers to the American hospital, and reported on the sick. They also collected bottles, sterilized them, and filled them with milk to be distributed to babies and to sick people outside the mission. One of the scouts' more dramatic moments was recalled by Dr. Ussher in his memoir. Neville and another scout were hunting for unspent Turkish bullets when Neville jumped into a large hole and stepped on something soft, which made a noise. It turned out to be a small child. A mother had placed her two babies in the hole to protect them from a cold wind; then she had lain down beside them and died. Bearers had carried her away, but in the darkness they did not see her children, who were too weak to call for help. Neville and his cohort used their staffs and their own coats to make a litter on which to carry the babies to the hospital.

There are many stories of the courage of Armenian youngsters during the defense of Van. Extolling the bravery of the defenders, Ambassador Morgenthau, for one, took note of the "ardour and energy of the Armenian children." Boys helped by defusing Turkish cannonballs as soon as they fell. The balls exploded from fifteen to thirty-five seconds after being fired, and the boys would hear a blast, watch for the ball's landing, then douse it with water. This was a risky sport and at least four boys died at it. The cannonballs and spent bullets, delivered to the munitions shop, were reused to make new amunition.

Some Armenian children became heroes. One fourteen-year-old boy wrapped himself in a kerosene-soaked quilt and raced through flying bullets to the door of the enemy-occupied French consulate. There he set the quilt on fire and ran back behind the Armenian lines. When another boy was shot in the leg after he dashed out and torched a Turkish stronghold, a girl of about twelve risked her life to pull him back to safety. Onnig Mukhitarian recalled a seventeen-year-old orphan girl, a beggar named Sevo (meaning "swarthy"): "A fiery amazon with flying black tresses, totally indifferent to danger, she would rush from one post to another carrying messages, or, with a pistol slung from her shoulder, she would spy on the enemy, or substitute for a wounded fighter until replaced." The boys in a school band braved bullets in order to shore up the fighting men's morale with Armenian military tunes and patriotic songs like the national anthem and the "Marseillaise."

Jevdet Bey was amazed and enraged by the audacity of the Armenian defense. Putting aside the political differences that had divided them so bitterly in the past, the Armenians had an esprit de corps that seemed to make them invincible. Since they had little ammunition, they had to make every bullet count. "The resistance of the Armenians was terrific and their valor worthy of all praise," said General Nogales. "Each house was a fortress that had to be conquered separately." The civilians caught this fighting spirit. "Everybody did his or her best," another eyewitness, Y. K. Rushdouni, reported. "While the shrapnel was raining upon Van, the Armenian children were playing soldiers in the streets."

Moments of despair alternated with moments of triumph. One of the triumphant moments came on the second day of the siege when the Armenian fire brigade dug a tunnel to the British consulate, which was occupied by Turks and which held a strategic position on Aikesdan's main crossroads. Using a handmade pump, the Armenians soaked the consulate's substructure with kerosene and set it on fire. Another great success came on April 23 when the Armenian trench diggers dug a tunnel some five hundred paces long and placed dynamite under the huge enemy barracks just northeast of the Armenian defense lines. Buried too deep in the earth, the dynamite failed to explode, but bales of hay in the basement caught fire that night and the barracks went up in flames. When the Turks fled their burning buildings, the Armenians would retrieve the food and ammunition left behind. "These conflagrations," wrote Mukhitarian, "lifted morale, especially among the noncombatants. At night they created a holiday spirit of joviality; people sang and danced while the band trumpeted tunes of victory. The death toll on both sides depended on whom you were talking to, Armenians or Turks.

While the Armenians in the city were holding out against the Turkish army in April and early May, villages in the province of Van continued to be systematically plundered and burned. Elizabeth Ussher's May 8 letter to friends in America (based on her daily diary entries) said the "tragedy is too awful to describe. It is nothing but wholesale and systematic massacre of as many as possible. . . . It is evident now that there was a well laid plan of the government to wipe out all the villages of the vilayet and then crush the city rebels. Before the trouble began here many outlying villages had been burned and their inhabitants either killed or driven away.

As the villages were destroyed, their inhabitants fled to Aikesdan. On April 25 over ten thousand peasants from about sixteen villages flooded Aikesdan's streets and orchards. Many of the women and children had been wounded when the men were shot. Male babies had their throats cut. Some women arrived naked, having been stripped by Turkish soldiers. The refugees had no food or bedding and a measles epidemic had broken out among them. Dr. Ussher described the arrival of the survivors this way: "Sunday morning, April 25, at about four o'clock, there was a loud and prolonged pounding and knocking at the great double-leaved wooden gate of our compound." In his bathrobe and slippers the doctor went to see who was there. Outside, he discovered several hundred people from Haiyotz Dzor, over a hundred of whom were wounded and begged to be admitted to the American hospital. "Many of them were most horribly mutilated, little babies shattered—!" One can only imagine the horror of an adolescent boy like Gorky witnessing the arrival of people he knew, perhaps even family members, from Khorkom.

From the twenty-fifth of April on a steady stream of refugees entered Aikesdan. Many children who arrived had lost their parents or been separated from them in the chaos. Mothers despaired over the children they had abandoned on their trek, unable to carry more than one or two children. One morning a weeping and shivering five- or six-year-old girl and her two-year-old brother were found huddled against the American Mission's gate. Walking barefoot through snow, the girl had carried her brother on her back for seven miles. Elizabeth Ussher wrote: "Their mother who had two other children to bring had left them and they wandered on alone following the others as best they could. They spent the night on the plain alone and why they didn't freeze I can't see for the baby had absolutely nothing on him but a short ragged cotton shirt and the night was cold. Their hands and feet were blistered and sore and they were so hungry that we couldn't get a word from them until they had had a bath, a warm breakfast and clean clothes to comfort them."

In the first days of the siege, the refugees had to slip through the lines, but starting on May 9, the Turkish militia began to drive groups of ten to one hundred refugees into Aikesdan. Soon the refugees numbered fifteen thousand. Many died of starvation and exposure shortly after their arrival, and as the days went by, pneumonia, dysentery, typhoid, and smallpox also took their toll. The newcomers, Mukhitarian recalled, were "utterly despondent," and "the insidious venom of hopelessness, vacillation and doubt reached into the ranks of our defenders." The refugees kept coming. Jevdet Bey knew that the Armenians would soon use up their meager food supply. He would break the Armenian resistance with famine. "No more horrible spectacle can be imagined than the sight of these refugee skeletons dressed in tattered garb," wrote Mukhitarian. "They had just lost their homes, their everything; they had seen their father, brother, or son murdered; their sisters and mothers ravished. Some, unable to comprehend such inhumanity, had lost their minds; others had been numbed by the experience; forlorn and sullen, they showed no interest in life and lacked all self-respect. Still others told of their experiences in an impersonal manner, as if telling of ancient happenings." Years later Gorky would tell tales of his childhood as if it were an "ancient happening," but he never revealed the truth about what he saw during the siege of Van.

Realizing that they could not hold out much longer, the Armenian defense command sent a number of messengers to the Russian border to inform the Russian army and its Armenian volunteer regiments of their predicament. On April 27 Dr. Ussher and Ernest Yarrow wrote: "To Americans, or any foreign Consul. International troubles in Van. Government threatens to bombard American premises. Inform American government American lives in danger." They had the message sewn into a messenger's clothing and dispatched him. No one knew whether any of the messages got through. The defenders set their hopes on their knowledge that the Russian army and several regiments of Armenian volunteers were moving in the direction of Van.

On May 8 the Armenians of Aikesdan saw flames on Varag Mountain. Everyone knew what this meant: the monastery with its famous library was burning. Neighboring villages were in flames as well. The American compound was on a slight rise and had a view over the plain to the mountain, so Gorky and others who had taken refuge at the mission could see the fires. When the Armenian defenses at Varag collapsed, five thousand people fled from Varag and Shoushantz village to Aikesdan and the mood of defeatism spread. Elizabeth Ussher wrote: "In some cases the villagers fought as long as their ammunition lasted, then fled with the women who could follow leaving the women with little children to be killed or insulted by the Turks. These abandoned ones who survived are the last to straggle in after sometimes a week of wandering and hiding in the mountains. Many have been stripped of all but one ragged garment and in a few cases come in absolutely nude. Some are so badly wounded (several women were stabbed in the back) that they died soon after reaching us. All are hungry, footsore and sick from exposure and fear." On May 13 she wrote that another group of refugees had arrived and there was no bread for at least eight hundred of them.

The attacks of Turkish artillery continued, some five hundred shells each day. If an Armenian barricade was destroyed and couldn't be rebuilt until after dark, soldiers fought in hand-to-hand battle. Occasionally the Turks burst through the Armenian lines and rushed through the streets and orchards of Aikesdan. Although the American Mission was supposed to be exempt from Turkish attack because of its neutral status and because it was plainly marked by the American and Red Cross flags, those who had sought haven there knew that at any moment Jevdet might defy international law. Indeed, soon after Nogales arrived in Van he discovered two loaded cannons pointed at the American compound. When Nogales called Jevdet Bey's attention to this, the governor pretended it was an error and ordered the guns aimed in another direction. The American Mission was especially vulnerable to artillery fire from Turkish barracks just to the north and south. Dr. Ussher recalled: "So central was our position with regard to the opposing forces that Turkish bullets flew constantly across our premises, peppering our walls and falling like hailstones on our roofs. Several of our refugees had already been wounded within our gates." Grace Knapp said that in the first week of the siege three cannonballs fell on the American compound and thirteen people were wounded by bullets, one fatally. She wrote: "We became so used to the pop-pop-pop of rifles and booming of cannon that we paid little attention to them in the daytime, but the fierce fusillades at night were rather nerve-racking."

Dr. Ussher sent a message to Jevdet to ask his soldiers to respect the neutrality of the mission. His request was answered with two cannonballs, one of which landed on Ussher's porch but did not explode. The other exploded against a wall. Jevdet also replied in writing. He said that armed men had been seen entering and leaving the American Mission and that he was about to attack the Armenian trenches just southeast of the mission. If a single shot was fired from those trenches, he would be "regretfully compelled" to destroy the American Mission. Bullets and cannonballs continued to explode in the mission compound. During a mid-May lull in the fighting, Shushan sent Gorky to Chaghli Street to get some vegetables from her garden. Gorky found the empty house riddled with bullet holes. The porch had been destroyed by cannon fire. He gathered as much produce from the garden as he could carry and then picked a bouquet of roses for his mother.

By the fourth week of the siege, the outlook seemed hopeless. Food and ammunition were running out. Many Armenian soldiers had been killed or were too badly wounded to fight. The American hospital was overcrowded. Dr. Ussher was the only doctor, the supply of medicine was nearly exhausted, and an epidemic threatened. Refugees were given bread tickets and waited in line at the public bakeries for a ration of bread that Knapp described as "barely sufficient to sustain life" (Fig. 54). The only hope was that the Russian army would come to the rescue.

On the evening of Friday, May 14, the missionaries were gathered as usual to plan, pray, and sing hymns when one of them standing at a third-story window caught sight of boats sailing away from Van. "We became a 'city all gone up to the roof tops,' wondering and surmising," Knapp recalled. Looking through field glasses, the American missionaries discovered that the boats carried Turkish women and children. The following morning they saw more boats leaving the port, and carts, pack animals, and carriages full of Turkish families were moving out of the city and clogging the road leading southwest to Artemid and Vosdan.

Late in the afternoon, after the white sails had vanished, the Turkish artillery fire resumed, fiercer and louder than ever. Jevdet Bey now turned his cannons on the American flag flying over the mission compound. There was, said Dr. Ussher, an "uncanny shriek, rising to a crescendo which can never be forgotten." A shell exploded in the hospital yard. Another brought down the Red Cross flag. Five more burst in quick succession, one in Ernest Yarrow's garden. Others tore holes in the boys and girls schools' roofs and in the roof of one of the missionary residences. After seven cannons had exploded there was silence. The following morning the bombardment began again. From the mission compound's upper stories people watched as spurts of dust and smoke from explosions came closer and closer. Soon cannonballs were again landing all over the compound. One killed a small Armenian girl. Thirty-six shells fell in the American Mission that day, causing panic and despair among the compound's four to six thousand refugees. Jevdet Bey was having his revenge.

On Sunday afternoon, May 16, the sound of artillery fire ceased. Dr. Ussher went to the attic of what was left of his house and looked with binoculars at the Turkish barracks in Varag plain. In the barracks' court-yard he saw soldiers hoisting a cannon onto the back of a large mule. Packhorses, cattle, and sheep were being driven into the courtyard. An hour or so later the packhorses began to leave. Now he felt certain that the Turks, having been warned that the Russian army was on its way, were in retreat. Looking north, Dr. Ussher saw the Turkish stronghold at Toprak Kale Hill in flames. Word came that the Armenian defenders had taken Toprak Kale and that the Turks had fled.

11

Our Fatherland

Once reconnoitering parties ascertained that it was safe to venture forth, the Armenians of Aikesdan headed for the old city. At the Tabriz Gate they were met by survivors who told them that very few of the old city's residents had been killed. Elizabeth Ussher rode to the walled city with her husband and Grace Knapp: "Our beautiful Van except in the small defended Armenian area, is in utter ruin," she reported. "We rode between burning houses. Sometimes the smoke and cinders almost blinded us. The Armenian defenders climbed the Rock of Van, took down the Turkish flag, and raised the tricolor Armenian flag. Haig Gossoian, who had been a leader of the defense in the old city, recalled: "The castle rock, the symbol, since time immemorial, of the durability of our people, at last was in our hands again."

At midnight on that first day of liberation the Armenians set fire to the Turkish barracks. "The whole city was awake, singing and rejoicing all night," Knapp recalled. "A magnificent blaze it made," said Dr. Ussher, "and in the light of that the people danced and laughed and sang, almost crazed by the sudden reaction of joy at the very hour when their last hope seemed gone." In what Gossoian described as a "night of orgy, of saturnalia," the Armenians proceeded to take and burn other Turkish strongholds and government buildings. "It would require the brush of genius," wrote Mukhitarian, "to put on canvas the crimson hue of the clouds caused by the burning of the Turkish military and administrative buildings . . . [and] the overpowering feeling of elation and vengeance."

As the Armenians who had been isolated in Aikesdan's protected area explored the ruined city and beyond, their euphoria frequently turned to anguish. Searching the burned-out houses, they found friends with their throats cut. Wells were filled with mutilated bodies. Noravank church was burning. Inside were the charred corpses of Armenians who had gone there to seek refuge. In the Turkish prison at the foot of Castle Rock they discovered that before the Turks fled from Van they had set the Turkish inmates free and killed all the Armenian prisoners. They learned also that the Armenian sailors who had carried the fleeing Turkish families across the lake had been ordered to dig trenches that soon served as their graves. As the American missionary nurse Grisell McLaren traveled near the town of Tatvan on the lake's west shore, she came upon a group of about fifty Armenian women and children whose husbands had been killed by Turks retreating toward Bitlis. "The Armenians," she said, "have a peculiar way of telling their troubles or showing their grief by singing, or chanting, or wailing, or a combination of all three, and this was the noise we heard. As they sat there on the hillside rocking back and forth wringing their hands, we heard the women and children repeating over and over after the manner of their race, the stories of the awful massacre that had taken place in their village the day before."

Now that the Armenians saw the tales of barbarity confirmed, they wanted revenge. On May 17 their rage precipitated a two-day rampage. They looted and burned the Turkish quarters. Where they found survivors they sometimes killed them, but they spared the women and children, whom they escorted to the American Mission. Aware of the looting and destruction, the Armenian leaders and the American missionaries looked the other way. During these days of chaos, the Armenians who had taken refuge in the American compound began to leave. Gorky and his mother and sisters returned to their battered home. Since their neighborhood had been a battle zone, much of it was rubble.

Word came that the Russian army and the Legion of Ararat, which comprised four units of Armenian volunteers, was fighting its way toward Van. As the troops approached the city, the townspeople went out to greet them. The first to arrive was the Armenian general Dro mounted on an enormous dark horse and followed by volunteers wearing high boots and Russian hats and carrying rifles with fixed bayonets on their shoulders. The armed and uniformed defenders of Van advanced in formation, singing a military march. The bells of the Armenian churches, which had been silenced by Ottoman decree for so many years, rang out. Behind the soldiers came the clergy dressed in richly ornamented robes. Then came the delirious populace laughing, praying, weeping, and shouting hurrahs as they waved embroidered banners and welcomed the volunteers with bread and salt. The students of the Normal School and members of its band took up their positions around a little homemade cannon that was the pride of the munitions committee. The cannon thundered and the band played:

> Our Fatherland, for centuries
> Subdued and fettered,
> By the sacred blood of her valiant sons
> Shall again be free.

General Dro gave a short speech. His soldiers fired five salvos, which were answered with ten. Cannons abandoned by the Turks on top of Castle Rock boomed as everyone proceeded to the base of the rock and entered the old city by the northwest gate. Soon the Russian flag waved beside the Armenian tricolor from the height of the rock.

The following day, May 18, some four thousand soldiers constituting the main body of the Russian army arrived, led by white-bearded General Nikolaev. The Castle Rock cannons fired more salutes. The keys of Van were laid at the general's feet. The Armenian defenders lined the broad avenue leading to Aikesdan and, wrote Elizabeth Ussher, "as the troops rode through, flowers were thrown at them and cheers and songs filled the air. . . . The Russians had come!"

General Nikolaev appointed Aram Manukian, coordinator of the defense of Van, as governor of the new Republic of Van. A provisional government was organized. There was hope that the Russian army would liberate western Armenia, meaning the Armenian provinces in eastern Turkey, and that the region might become an autonomous republic under Russian protection. On May 21 Aram, as the new governor called himself, issued an appeal for support to his fellow citizens. The advance of the Russian army, he said, "marks the end of centuries of thraldom and political persecution. We are today celebrating the fruition of the creative and constructive spirit of the Armenian people."

The Armenians of Aikesdan, including the Adoians, were repairing their houses, but the old city was, as Dr. Ussher put it, "a mass of charred ruins which no one attempted to restore." In Aikesdan, schools, businesses, and churches reopened. The town was full of Russian soldiers who set up camp next to the American Mission. In the evenings nearby residents could hear them singing around their campfires. Gorky was entranced. The Russian soldiers came to the orchard behind the Adoians' house to pick fruit. "They didn't bother us," Vartoosh recalled. "They spoke Russian and used sign language. We understood what they wanted." Various notables and intellectuals from Russia arrived, among them the poet Hovhannes Toumanian, who had stopped in Khorkom to perform a play a few years before. Another visitor was Tolstoy's daughter, who came to help the refugees. During the month and a half of Russian occupation, Gorky learned a few Russian phrases and songs that would later help him pass himself off as a Russian.

Meanwhile the Russian army and the Armenian volunteers were pursuing Turks southwest toward Bitlis, where they hoped to prevent the slaughter of a hundred thousand Armenians. (They failed. The men were massacred and the rest of the city's Armenian population was sent on a death march toward the Syrian desert.) As the Russians advanced, they discovered villages and rivers full of corpses. They collected and cremated the bodies, and their tally indicated that fifty-five thousand Armenians had been killed in Van. The head of the German Mission at Van described traveling from Van City to Artemid after the Turkish retreat. What he wrote could, no doubt, apply to Khorkom and other villages southeast of Van as well: "The greater part of it is nothing now but a heap of ruins. . . . All uncannily still. Our glance swept over the magnificent valley of Haiotz Tzor. . . . everywhere in the villages one sees blackened and ruined houses."

While the Russians held the terrain around Van, some intrepid Armenians who had taken refuge in Aikesdan returned to their villages to rebuild their homes. Gorky's uncle Aharon was one of them. Near the ruins of Charahan Surp Nishan he found and buried the bodies of the two small sons of his brother, Moses. In Khorkom, Uncle Krikor, Aunt Yeghus, her daughter, and her daughter's two sons had been killed. Rus, the cousin who had worked on the Adoians' farm, was found dead with his five children.

In newly liberated Van, jubilation was tempered by hunger. The supply of wheat remained low and the flour mills were mostly in disrepair. Dysentery and typhus spread in the city. Hundreds died, including, on

July 14, Elizabeth Ussher. Dr. Ussher, Mr. and Mrs. Yarrow, and several other American missionaries nearly succumbed to typhus as well. Yet the people of Van were in safety compared with those in the other eastern provinces. In these summer months the Armenian population of Turkey was deported or massacred. Calling the Armenian self-defense during the siege of Van a "rebellion" or a "revolution," the Turkish government used it as an excuse to wipe out as many as one and a half million people, almost the entire Armenian population of Turkish Armenia.

❋ PART III ❋

Khatchkar at Etchmiadzin

12

Flight into Russia

While the Van Armenians were going about the work of reconstruction and dreaming of an autonomous Armenia, the Russian army advancing toward Bitlis was met with a fierce Turkish counteroffensive. Threatened with encirclement, the army was forced to retreat eastward toward the Caucasus. On June 31 the Russian military ordered the Armenians in Van to evacuate the city and to move toward the Russian border with the retreating army. The Armenians were to take refuge in Russian Armenia, which had been part of the Russian Empire since 1827. Within three days the city emptied. The Armenians gathered up whatever provisions they could carry, buried their valuables, and set fire to their grain fields so that they would not feed the advancing Turkish army. Some departing families set fire to their homes as well: better destroyed than possessed by the Turks. They then began a 150-mile trek over rugged mountains. A few had carts, horses, donkeys, oxen, and buffalo, but most traveled on foot. "Many," said Clarence Ussher, "carried everything they owned on their own backs."

Vartoosh remembered the Armenians' panic when they were awoken at dawn by the town crier banging on their doors and yelling "Retreat!" The streets filled with people wondering how to proceed. "We took nothing but a few days supply of bread. And Mother had a little money," Vartoosh said. Believing that they would return, they buried their belongings. At dawn they walked to Deramair church, just outside the city of Van. "We entered, prayed. All the people would enter in a line, pray, and come out, and then we continued on the march. There was

nothing but parched earth when we left Van. The Armenian comman-
dos placed those who could not walk on caravans. But all of us walked."

News of the retreat spread from village to village, and there was much
weeping as caravan after caravan headed toward Russia. The roads were
bad and progress was slow. Russian officers hurried the refugees along,
determined to get through the mountain pass just north of Lake Van
while the Russian Armenian volunteers were still able to hold back the
Turks and Kurds. All day the sound of footsteps rumbled over the hot,
dry land. A long yellowish dust cloud swirled above the 250,000 refugees
escaping toward the border. At night, when the travelers stopped to rest,
they built cooking fires, and the darkness was filled with the cries of children who had become separated from their parents and of parents who
had lost their children.

The Adoian family followed the multitude moving north along the
lake's east shore. Before they left the Van area, Akabi recalled, they encountered a hailstorm, and Gorky opened an umbrella to protect his
family. "We walked day and night with little rest," said Vartoosh. "We had
no food to speak of. If mother found anything she would give it to Gorky
because you take more care of a boy than girls and he was the only boy
and he was very thin. My mother always worried about him. He was her
favorite." With her four-year-old son, Gurken, strapped to her back,
Akabi had trouble keeping up with the others. According to Vartoosh, fellow refugees walking nearby advised, "Leave him behind!" But Akabi
said, "No. I'll carry him. I'm not leaving him." Akabi remembered it differently. She said that it was her mother who told her to abandon her
son. During the flight from Van the Adoians passed hundreds of children
and sick people left to die by the side of the road.

When they reached the Bend-i-mahi River and the Muradiye waterfall at the northeast arm of the lake, they stopped on the far bank.
Shushan sent Vartoosh to fill a jug with water for the journey. They
waited, but Vartoosh did not return. Searching and calling, they finally
found the nine-year-old girl lost and in tears. After this, Shushan tied her
children to her with a rope.

On the long trek in the fierce summer heat across rough, arid, often
mountainous land, some forty thousand Armenians died of hunger, exhaustion, disease, and Kurdish depredations. Many were killed at the
Bergri pass, two days' journey by foot from Van City and just beyond
the Muradiye waterfall. Dr. Ussher's memoir says that before he and the

other missionaries left Van City they knew that they had no time to lose, for the Armenian volunteers near Bergri were being driven eastward and could not hold open the line of retreat into Russia for long. At sunset on the second day of their journey, the missionaries heard guns in the distance as they were skirting the northeastern branch of the lake. They left the lake behind and forded the Bend-i-mahi. The river was in flood, and G. C. Raynolds, head of Van's American Mission, reported that one refugee saw his entire family except one boy swept away by the current. The Russian Red Cross doctors lifted exhausted children onto horses and carried them across the river. At night they rode back and forth along the line of stumbling travelers, lighting the roughest sections of the road with lanterns.

The American missionaries reached Bergri on August 5, two days after leaving Van. Grace Knapp wrote: "We forded a wide and deep river, then entered a narrow valley, from the mountains commanding which Kurds suddenly began to fire down on the Red Cross caravan and the thousands of foot travelers. One man in an ambulance was killed, others wounded. The drivers of ambulances and litters whipped up their horses to a mad gallop. It was a race for life." Desperate to escape but hemmed in between the hills and the Bend-i-mahi River, the refugees threw their baggage off their carts to lighten their loads. The crowd surged in panic, and entire families were pushed into the river. Dr. Ussher wrote: "Hundreds threw themselves over the precipice into the river to escape the worse fate of falling into the hands of the Kurds. Fathers and mothers killed their own children to save them from the Turks. But thousands struggled on panting, gasping, for mile after mile. . . . It seemed an eternity of horror." Gorky's cousins the Melikians, who had returned to Khorkom after the siege of Van, must have reached the pass at Bergri about the same time as the American missionaries. Arax Melikian recalled that at Bergri a Kurd tried to steal her mother's bracelet but it wouldn't come off. Just as the Kurd was about to cut off her mother's hand, Arax's younger sister, Mariam, screamed. Another Kurd unsheathed his dagger, but at that moment both men were distracted by the call of a cohort, and they abandoned their prey. Dr. Ussher estimated that about seven thousand Armenians died that day at Bergri.

It seems likely that the Adoians left Van on August 1, which probably meant that they traveled safely through the Bergri pass on August 3, two days before the American missionaries and at a time when the volunteers still controlled the pass. Vartoosh said: "Walking night and day for eight days, our shoes were all gone. We clambered over hills and fields. We slept at night a little bit but we had to wake very early to set off because the people who left after us were all killed on the field of Bergri." One can only imagine Gorky's terror as the man of his family, unable to protect his mother and sisters from the threat of the Kurds who lay in wait for the Armenian caravans.

The refugees traveled to Bayazid, then crossed the Taparez mountain range. Shouts and curses filled the air as people struggled to keep pack animals moving upwards on steep slopes full of ditches and boulders. A cloud of soft volcanic dirt almost blocked the sun. On a mountain pass the refugees were alarmed by a banging and a strange roar, which turned out to be a cream-colored, chauffeur-driven touring car with two Russian officers in the back seat. It was the first automobile that most of the Armenians had ever seen.

In the foothills of Mount Ararat, their hunger was relieved when they passed a building where bread was being baked and distributed. Thirst was still a problem. "Springs were far apart," wrote Dr. Ussher, "and such crowds would gather round one of these, after plodding half a day through the dust under the scorching sun, that few had a chance fully to slake their thirst. Waters became polluted and disease spread. Many thousands died of dysentery soon after reaching Russia." The Adoians were resourceful. "We lacked water, so we would dig in the ground in search of moisture," recalled Vartoosh. A group of Yezidis, a tribal people who even today live in tents in these mountains, were selling ice. With some of the money that she had brought from home (Akabi said that her mother had the equivalent of three hundred dollars), Shushan bought some ice to soothe her children's parched mouths. "The plain was full of pea-like plants which we picked and ate," Vartoosh said. "When the moon came at night we had to walk. Our shoes were no more. We ate grass when we found it."

After winding up and down mountain roads and passing through what looked like a lunar landscape full of strangely shaped outcroppings of pitted brown volcanic rock, the Adoians caught sight of that symbol of Armenian perseverance, the snow-capped peak of Mount Ararat. "We entered the Ararat plain," Vartoosh said. "Oh, we were spellbound by its great size when we were passing it on our march. It was the first time we had seen such a high mountain, and we were so joyous. We had read about it in school but hadn't seen it." On the eighth night the Adoian family reached Igdir on the Turkish side of the Arax River. Sick and exhausted, Shushan collapsed in front of a shop. Then they heard a familiar voice. "Akabi, Akabi! Is that you?" The voice belonged to Simon Kachaturian, a cousin of Akabi's husband. The man was dressed in his Armenian soldier's uniform, and when he saw their pitiful state he brought them bread and a bucket of water. Gorky and Akabi purchased several pounds of flour and a melon that turned out to be rotten. Desperate for food, Akabi stole some cheese.

During these days some 270,000 exhausted, thirsty, and hungry refugees poured through this border town. Most of them slept in the peach, apricot, and apple orchards that still lie on Igdir's outskirts. The Armenian and Russian residents gave the Adoians hot tea, and an Armenian family gave them permission to sleep in their orchard. They stayed two days at Igdir, baking bread, bathing, and washing clothes. But the refugees living in the orchards fell ill, and in the next two months hundreds died each day from exposure, hunger, dysentery, and typhus.

Since the town was growing crowded with the arrival of more and more refugees, the Adoians were ordered to continue their journey. With a file of other refugees, they moved north to the Arax River, where Russian volunteers guided them across into Russian Armenia. Now they walked across the vast dry plain below Ararat. It was, said Dr. Ussher, "filled with a shifting multitude overflowing the horizon, wandering aimlessly hither and thither; starving, wailing like lost and hungry children." Finally they reached Etchmiadzin, the Armenians' holy city and the seat of the Catholicos, the supreme head of the Armenian Church. Here they lived for two or three weeks in the churchyard of the great cathedral. Since they had no bedding or blankets they slept on the ground with a crowd of other refugees. The city's churches, monastery buildings, schools, courtyards, and poplar groves were overflowing with refugees not only from Van but from the provinces of Bitlis and Erzerum. Although the church did its best to feed the hungry, cholera and other diseases spread. "People turned black and died," said Vartoosh. Some two hundred refugees died each day. Their bodies were piled on carts and buried in mass graves.

Akabi developed a fever. The family was afraid she might have typhus. Gorky's maternal aunts Yeva and Nevart, who had also made the trek from Van, both died of cholera. After weeks of discomfort and fear,

Gorky announced, "We have to leave this place." Shushan told him to hire a cart and a driver, and on September 1 the Adoian family left Etchmiadzin and drove thirteen miles east across a flat, boulder-strewn plain that H.F.B. Lynch describes as having once been the bed of an inland sea. The bleakness was relieved here and there by streams bordered by poplars and by the occasional church and village. Nearing Yerevan, the Adoians passed cotton and rice fields. When they finally climbed the low orchard-covered hills that ring the city and crossed the Hrazdan River to Yerevan, the world turned from ocher-gray to green.

13

Yerevan

❊

After the journey of some two hours from Etchmiadzin to Yerevan, the cart dropped the Adoian family off beside the steps of Surp Sarkis church on the banks of the Hrazdan River. "We got to the doorway and just sat there," Vartoosh recalled.

Ringed with gardens, vineyards, and orchards, the town lay north of Ararat and south of the somewhat less mighty Mount Alagoz. Ernest Yarrow compared Yerevan's setting to the Garden of Eden. Indeed there were many who believed Yerevan was the place where Noah settled after the floodwaters subsided. When the Adoians arrived, Yerevan had a population of about fifty thousand. With the influx of Armenian refugees from the eastern provinces of Turkey, the town swelled to a city of five hundred thousand. Whitish dust blew up from the narrow, now heavily traveled, unpaved streets, causing numerous cases of the eye disease trachoma.

For several days the Adoians slept near the door of Surp Sarkis church. "Mother and Akabi left us there and searched Yerevan for a room," Vartoosh recalled. In November 1915, after moving from one room to another, they found a permanent home, a humble one, at 18 Katanovsky Street, a two-story building near Surp Boghos Bedros (the Church of Saints Paul and Peter). The Adoians rented a room on the first floor; their landlady lived on the second floor. The church gave them ration books, and they joined a long line of refugees waiting for bread. Jobs were scarce, so they stood in the main square each morning and waited to be hired as day laborers in the surrounding countryside.

"They put us on carts and drove us out," Vartoosh said. "We used to pick grapes. You were allowed to eat as much as you wanted but you couldn't take any home with you." When the grape harvest was over the Adoians found work in a factory canning fruit and vegetables. Later Shushan worked in one of the Russian cotton factories, and Akabi, who had learned rug weaving in Van, repaired rugs.

Gorky attended the boys' division of the Temagan Seminary attached to Surp Sarkis, the only Armenian secondary school in Yerevan. Satenik and Vartoosh went to the much smaller girls' division. Although the refugee children received only about two hours of schooling a day, Gorky learned to speak and write Caucasian Armenian, which was quite different from the dialect used in Van. In time, Caucasian Armenian became his habitual language. He also learned a few words of Russian. Vartoosh, who worshiped her brother, said: "Gorky was one of the most brilliant students in his class." Although he was certainly brilliant, he never did well in school. As in Khorkom, he sat in the back of the class and whittled. A fellow student recalled how furious this made their teacher. "Why don't you at least pay attention? You might learn something," the teacher said, fuming. Gorky just sat there shaking his head.

Before the Russian Revolution of 1917, the Russian government gave the refugees a regular allowance. Knowing that it was insufficient, American missionaries from Van, including Dr. Raynolds, Dr. Ussher, and Ernest and Jane Yarrow formed the American Relief Committee in 1916. After school, Gorky worked at various jobs, some of them attached to this organization. To provide employment and income for refugees, the missionaries, with Yarrow in charge, set up shops for rug weaving, tailoring, sandal and wool making, the knitting of socks, carpentry, and forging. Women were paid less than men: it was thought that women needed less financial support because the American Relief Committee gave fifteen rubles a month to some fifteen to twenty thousand fatherless children, many of whom, like Gorky, had been pupils at the American Missionary School in Van. Ernest Yarrow was particularly moved by the misery of the Armenian widows and the grown girls, for whom it was almost impossible to find work. Yarrow said that in the year since their arrival in Yerevan, the refugees had contracted "horrible scourges." Typhus, dysentery, and cholera killed about 20 percent of them.

For a while Shushan had a job as assistant in an orphanage pantry.

Whatever food she could find she gave to her children. As a result, she became anemic and her health deteriorated until she could no longer work. Gorky did odd jobs for the orphanage that Dr. Raynolds set up in 1917 to care for Armenian children who had lost one parent or both in the genocide. It was at the orphanage that Gorky was reunited with his cousins Ado and Azad Adoian, whom he had lost track of since the summer before the massacres. Sometimes Gorky was able to bring home bread that he saved from his meals at the orphanage. He also worked in the American Relief Committee's carpentry shop run by his uncle Aharon.

In the evenings, to supplement the family's income, Gorky and Vartoosh carved traditional women's combs out of ox and bull antlers that they bought from street vendors. Gorky was skillful at sawing and filing the bone to make the combs' teeth. He earned additional money by doing odd jobs such as running errands for shops or taking milk to market. Like many other adolescent boys, he was not always efficient: often he lost track of what he had been told to do and he had to be sent out again. Perhaps what distracted him was a store selling art supplies. "He made good money, and spent it generously too, on paper, pencils, crayons," Vartoosh said. "You see he loved to draw, and he drew all the time. Mother did not think much of Gorky's art and thought he was wasting entirely too much time and especially money on foolishness. But Gorky continued sketching on anything he could conveniently get hold of."

For the first few months, Shushan cherished hopes that the Russians would occupy eastern Anatolia so the Armenians could go home. In September 1915 the Russian army and the Armenian volunteers did retake Van, and by spring 1916 they were in control of the rest of the Armenian plateau. But the Russians planned to populate this land with Russian peasants and Cossacks, not to create an Armenian state. In the same year, Count Vorontsov-Dashkov, governor of Transcaucasia and a man sympathetic to the Armenians, was replaced, and the Russian authorities suddenly ordered the demobilization of the Armenian volunteer units; Armenian volunteers were made part of the regular Russian army. Armenian civic activity was forbidden, and Armenian newspapers were suppressed. Perhaps more painful to the Adoian family, a law was passed that forbade Turkish Armenian refugees to return to their homeland. Although this law was reversed during the first phase of the Russian Revolution in the spring of 1917, and although some 150,000 Armenians attempted to resettle in western Armenia, many, including Shushan Adoian, were by this time too poor or too sick to make the journey.

In October 1916 Mkrdich Amerian came to Yerevan to collect his wife, Akabi, and their son, Gurken. He brought money that Sedrak Adoian had given him to pay for Shushan and her three younger children's passage to America, but the amount was enough for only one ticket. Vartoosh recalled: "Mother would not think of leaving Armenia. She never loved my father. She said she would not go." Her husband's failure over a period of eight years to save enough money to bring his whole family to the United States must have filled Shushan with despair and rage. She decided that Satenik should travel with Akabi, but Satenik did not want to leave home. The parting was traumatic. In later years Satenik would ask her own daughter, "Why did my mother reject me? Why did she send me away?"

On October 9 Shushan, Gorky, and Vartoosh went to the train station to see off Akabi, Satenik, Gurken, and Mkrdich. According to Vartoosh, her mother "just sat under the wall and dropped not a single tear. Then when we came home, mother felt extremely terrible and began to cry." Shushan surely knew she would never see her elder daughters again.

After her daughters' and grandson's departure, Shushan resumed work at the orphanage, and now Vartoosh, too, started a job there making beds and sewing numbers on the orphans' shirts and stockings. Shushan's employment did not last long. A deep depression kept her at home. She left her floor unswept and her roof in disrepair, and she did not even bother to light her *tonir*. When the Melikian family arrived in Yerevan from Etchmiadzin, they were shocked by her misery. Arax Melikian and her mother, Azniv, visited Shushan and found her "in a very bare room with earthen floor, and just some rags there, and she was sitting in a corner on those rags. . . . She was sitting there very quiet, very sad."

After the first year in Yerevan, there were few happy moments for the Adoians. Hunger was the theme of their lives. Vartoosh remembered a rare day when, after a gathering at their landlady's apartment, this kindly woman gave Vartoosh some money for bread and Vartoosh bought as much as she could carry. "I put it all on my head and took the bread and brought it home. We had been hungry. Mother and Gorky got so happy. Now we had bread for a few days. It gave us hope."

In addition to working at the carpentry shop, Gorky apprenticed once or twice a week as a typesetter in a state-run printing press on Astafian Street, near Yerevan's main square. His cousin Ado found work there too. While employed at the printing shop, Gorky learned bookbinding, and he took home pages to bind with Vartoosh's help. "We had a little frame," his sister recalled, "and I sewed the pages together. Mother was ill. We made a little money that way. While we worked, we talked about everything." The print shop was a meeting place for a group of intellectuals, many of them from Van, who published an underground newspaper, which called for the restoration to Armenians of their homeland. Gorky served as the newspaper's typesetter. His exposure to radical ideas at the Yerevan printing shop, together with the socialist thinking of the revolutionary leaders he had encountered in Van, probably formed the basis of his future political beliefs in America. The print shop helped to develop his reverence for books as well. Gorky would borrow books and, said Vartoosh, "he was always carrying books in his pockets. History and literature and art." This habit continued into his adulthood: many New York acquaintances remember that when they happened to meet Gorky on the street he would pull an art book out of his pocket and use it to illustrate some point.

In 1917 the political situation in Russian Armenia and the Caucasus became increasingly unstable. The Russian army suffered severe defeats in Europe and food shortages helped to spark the February-March Revolution, which drove Czar Nicholas II from the throne. A liberal provisional government led by Kerensky was established, and soviets, or councils of workers, peasants, and soldiers, were set up all over Transcaucasia. Armenians welcomed the establishment of the new regime, believing assurances that the government would create an autonomous Armenia under Russian protection.

During the October Revolution, when the Bolsheviks replaced Russia's provisional government with Bolshevik commissars, the Armenians remained loyal to the provisional government. They felt that their only hope for an autonomous Armenia lay in the restoration of a democratic Russia. As it turned out, they were right not to trust the Bolsheviks. By the end of 1917, Lenin withdrew the Russian army from Turkey, and Russia began to negotiate a separate peace with Germany. The Treaty of Brest-Litovsk signed by the Bolsheviks and Germany early in 1918 dashed hopes for a western Armenia administered as an autonomous region under Russian protection. The treaty gave Turkey Kars, Ardahan, and Batum, as well as the eastern provinces that Russia had occupied during World War I.

With the Russian retreat from Turkey late in 1917, many more Turkish Armenians fled to the Caucasus, and the economic situation in Russian Armenia worsened. According to the American Missionary Report for September 1917, 250,000 refugees, most of them from Van, were packed into various towns and villages. After the October Revolution, government aid to the refugees ceased. And after March 1918, when the American consul at Tiflis ordered all Americans to leave Russia immediately, help from the American Relief Committee was sporadic.

In May 1918 Turks invaded and took Alexandropol, northeast of Yerevan, massacred Armenians there and in other towns, and then marched on and encircled Yerevan itself. On May 24 they were defeated by a defending force that included women and old men. This victory saved Armenia from being wiped off the map. When the independent Republic of Armenia was declared at Tiflis on May 28, 1918, the Armenians were left with a small autonomous state that comprised the district around Lake Sevan, parts of Sharur, Yerevan, Etchmiadzin, and Alexandropol. On June 2 the news of the Turkish defeat and withdrawal from Yerevan was confirmed. At the Treaty of Batum on June 14, all the land that was assigned to Armenia was forty-five hundred rocky, landlocked square miles. Of the 700,000 people living in the new Republic of Armenia, 300,000 were destitute refugees. Among them were the Adoians.

The glory of the newly autonomous nation was short-lived. The republic was thrown into turmoil by a civil war between the Dashnak-led government and the Armenian Communists. During this time of near anarchy, political and racial relations between the various peoples deteriorated. In Yerevan the Armenians and Tartars fought each other. Armed bands attacked in broad daylight, and it was unsafe to travel outside the city. In October 1918, when Turkey surrendered to the Allies and the armistice was declared, these events brought some psychological, but no material, relief to the Armenians. Azad Adoian described the chaos: "Armenia turned, supposedly, into an independent country. They broke off links with the Russians. In what is now called Freedom Square, they pulled up their Mausers, broke into shops, burned them, looted them, took money and ran. Armenian against Armenian. There in the square was a small cinema. They killed a man and just took his money. It wasn't politics, just robbery!" The Armenian republic lasted from spring 1918 to the winter of 1920, when the Armenians, to protect themselves from the Turks, ceded Armenia to the Soviets. At that point the Red Army moved in and Armenia became a Soviet republic.

14

Famine

꙲

In August 1918, Gorky's uncle Aharon told his sister that, because of the danger of civil war, she and her children should flee Yerevan for Tiflis. Shushan tied their belongings into a bundle and they left. At this point Gorky must have been seventeen or eighteen for, according to Vartoosh, he still had one more year of secondary school to complete, and the average age at graduation was eighteen or nineteen. The Adoian family walked north toward the Georgian capital. In those days, the hundred-mile trip took thirteen hours by train, but traveling by train was not an option—the line between Yerevan and Tiflis went through territory occupied by the Turks. By foot, the trip probably would have taken the better part of a week. Shushan, Gorky, and Vartoosh went first to Kanaker, a town on a hill outside of Yerevan. From there they took the northern route. Eight miles out of Yerevan, at a tiny village called Shahab, their journey came to an end. Shushan was too weak from malnutrition to continue. "When she became ill," Vartoosh recalled, "all responsibility fell on Gorky."

In Shahab, a wheat-growing village with only one street, the Adoians found shelter in a one-room mud hut. To support Shushan, Vartoosh found work as a maid and Gorky used what little money remained to buy a donkey with which he carried wheat from Shahab to sell in Yerevan and grapes from Yerevan to sell in Shahab. To supplement their diet, Vartoosh and Shushan would glean any grain left in the wheat fields after the threshing. As winter approached, food became scarcer, Shushan grew sicker, and the donkey died. In the bitter cold of December 1918, Gorky said to his sister, "Vartoosh, we must take mother to Yerevan." The return to Yerevan was a terrible struggle, for Shushan was almost too weak to walk. The roads were full of other sufferers, starving women and bands of parentless children wandering in search of food. It was not unusual to find corpses lying by the side of the road.

Upon reaching Yerevan, they discovered that their former landlady on Katanovsky Street had rented out their rooms, so they moved into a half-ruined room in an abandoned building in the old section of town. Gorky tried to put his mother in a government hospital, but, claiming that she had a husband in America and was not really in need, the officials refused her admittance. In a rage, Gorky argued to no avail that they never received money from their father.

There was a deadly famine in the winter of 1918–19—the coldest winter in Yerevan's memory. People froze in the streets. The settled population of Armenia went hungry; the refugees starved. In Yerevan's marketplace farmers shook their sticks at the women and children whose hunger drew them too close to the food stalls. Supplies were cut off by civil war and by the Turkish blockade. Lack of food, fuel, medicine, and shelter caused riots and epidemics. In and around Yerevan half a million refugees roamed the land in search of food and found shelter in caves and dugouts. They ate grass and roots when they could find them. Sometimes they were reduced to gnawing on human bones. A newspaper reported: "The populace is feeding upon the bodies of cats and dogs. There have even been cases when a starving mother had eaten the kidney or the liver from the corpse of her own child. . . . The skeleton-like women and children rummage in the refuse heaps for moldered shoes and, after cooking them for three days, eat them." Another 20 percent of Armenia's population, or approximately two hundred thousand people, died that winter of cholera, typhus, and dysentery. On March 17, 1919, the American missionaries, who had returned to Yerevan, sent a message to the United States: "No bread anywhere. Government has not a pound. Forty-five thousand in Erevan without bread. Orphanages and troops all through Erevan in terrible condition. Another week will score ten thousand lives lost. For heaven's sake hurry!" When the news of this suffering reached the American people, the expression "starving Armenians" gained currency. A generation of American children was told to finish what was on their plate and to "think of the starving Armenians." It was a phrase that Gorky would come to loathe; to him, being a refugee, being part of a starving mass, was a source of shame.

After moving into the crumbling room in the old section of Yerevan, Gorky and Vartoosh searched for work. "Mother could not work," Vartoosh recalled. "There was no food and she was starving and her stomach swelled up and she was very weak. And when the winter got worse the ceiling of our room began to leak, and so each morning before Gorky and I went to work we would lift mother up and put her in the window so that she would not get wet from the leaking roof. By evening we would return and mother was the same way." In the famine of that winter, even the wild grasses were gone from the outskirts of Yerevan. Gorky and Vartoosh saved food from their lunches—an egg or a piece of bread—to give to Shushan, but she would insist that they eat it themselves.

Early in the morning on March 20, 1919, Gorky and Vartoosh placed their mother in the window. Since she was too weak to hold a pencil, Shushan asked Gorky to take dictation of a letter she wanted to send his father. With his sister at his side, Gorky sat on the dusty floor. His mother said, "Vosdanik, write that I can never leave Armenia, that I will never come to America." Then, Vartoosh recalled, "Suddenly she stopped speaking. Gorky looked up and said, 'mother, mother.' And he rushed to her. And suddenly she starved to death in our arms. She was age thirty-nine. Her head fell on Gorky."

Gorky ran to the house of Krikor Moudoyan, who had been one of his teachers in Van. Krikor contacted city officials, and a cart came and took Shushan away. Gorky and Vartoosh did not accompany their mother's body. Along with others who had died that day, she was buried in a common grave. Vartoosh said, "I don't know if there was a proper burial. I don't know which cemetery she is buried in." Gorky always wished his mother could have been buried in Van because, as Vartoosh put it, "that was the earth she loved the most." When he spoke about his mother's death to friends in America, Gorky gave various causes for it. Sometimes he agreed with Vartoosh that she had died of starvation. Other times, perhaps out of shame that he had failed her, he said Shushan had died of a dog bite.

In the days that followed, Gorky and Vartoosh were taken in by their uncle Aharon, whose wife had also died during that terrible winter.

American relief supplies finally arrived in the Caucasus, and Vartoosh was given a bag of flour and a twenty-pound bag of rice. The American missionaries gave Gorky and Vartoosh work in the orphanage. Kertzo Dickran Der Garabedian, a family friend from the Khorkom days, kept an eye on Gorky and Vartoosh, as well. Both he and their uncle Aharon thought that Gorky and Vartoosh should go live with their father and sisters in America. Dickran suggested that they join him and a group of several Armenian families who were planning to emigrate. He offered to take them as far as Constantinople, where they could find passage to the New World.

Gorky decided that they should go, but preparations for departure were not easy. Their father sent three hundred dollars, but, Vartoosh said, the Dashnak government officials refused to release it on the grounds that Gorky and Vartoosh were underage. They also needed travel permits. To secure them, Gorky went to the office of General Dro, leader of the Armenian volunteer troops who had helped to liberate Van after the 1915 siege. Preoccupied with defending Armenia from Kemalist Turks, a territorial dispute with the Azeris, and a minor war with the Republic of Georgia, General Dro did not take kindly to a young man of draft age asking for exit papers. According to Vartoosh, Dro accused Gorky of betraying his country and hit him with his Mauser.

Finally Dickran secured Gorky and Vartoosh's papers. He also obtained a letter of reference from Dr. Ussher for the various members of the traveling party. The letter was addressed to the American consulate in Tiflis: "The bearers, Dickran Der Garabedian, Manoug Adoian, and Nazlu Shaghoian are worthy Armenians of good character and ability, personally known to me. Any assistance to them in reaching their relatives in America will be appreciated and will not be misplaced. C. D. Ussher."

On May 19, 1919, two months after their mother died, Vartoosh and Gorky boarded a train for Tiflis. The group with whom they were traveling included Dickran and his wife, the wife of the Vanetzi resistance fighter Levon Pasha Shagoyan (also spelled Shaghoian), and Mariam Melikian. During their weeks in Tiflis, a European-style city with broad avenues and grand houses, Gorky and Vartoosh were stunned by the wealth, the plentiful food, and the availability of all kinds of merchandise in the shops. Vartoosh maintained that in Tiflis Gorky was able to see Georgian medieval art and that it was during this period that he decided to become an artist. No doubt he saw ancient Georgian churches, and he may have seen illuminated manuscripts and other paintings. But, as a destitute refugee from Van, he would not have had access to the wealthy and cultured Armenian community of Tiflis—a city in which Armenians outnumbered Georgians. Since Gorky was unable to speak Georgian or Russian, he gravitated to his fellow Armenian refugees. At the American Mission he ran into one of his teachers from Van, and he wept as he told this man about his mother's death. The teacher took Gorky and Vartoosh in and gave them food and clothing.

From Tiflis, again accompanied by Dickran, Gorky and Vartoosh made their way by rail west across Georgia to Batum on the Black Sea. They spent three weeks sleeping on the floor of a large warehouse at the dock. It was crowded with other Armenians waiting for transport. Finally, with the rest of their party, they boarded a merchant ship bound for Constantinople. During the eight-hundred-mile voyage, they stopped at every port, but it is unlikely that Gorky and Vartoosh would have wanted to disembark in Turkish cities like Trebizond and Samsun, where numerous Armenians had been massacred only a few years earlier.

Their excitement must have been great as their ship turned south, passed the Symplegades rocks, and entered the straits of the Bosphorus. With Europe on the right and Asia on the left, and with fortresses and palaces lining the shores, they approached Constantinople. The city's splendor was even more astonishing than that of Tiflis—palace after palace, one more fairy tale–like in its opulence than the last, Byzantine churches, splendid mosques with sparkling domes and minarets, graceful bridges, and ferry landings and parks. And Constantinople was still a relatively cosmopolitan city. Although many Armenians had been killed in 1915, especially the elite and the intellectuals, the presence of foreign embassies had saved as many as a hundred thousand Constantinople Armenians from deportation and massacre.

When Gorky and Vartoosh disembarked in Constantinople in September 1919, they went with a group of Armenian refugees to Uskudar, a section on the Asian side of the Bosphorus. Near the Haydar Pasha railroad station and not far from the Galata Bridge, the Armenian residents of Constantinople had set up a refugee camp consisting of tents and a soup kitchen. After getting settled in the camp, and with Dickran's help, they made efforts to contact Sedrak Adoian so that the three hundred dollars he had sent to Yerevan could be redirected to Constantinople.

Gorky and Vartoosh went to the American Ministry of Relief to request their money, but it was not immediately available. Instead they were given food: baked beans and condensed milk, a novelty that Vartoosh remembered fifty years later.

One of the Armenian relief workers at the tent colony, a wealthy woman doctor named Vergine Kelekian, took an interest in Gorky and Vartoosh. Her husband, Sedrak, was a cashier at the Ottoman State Bank and her son, Hampartzoum, worked for a shipping company. No doubt these connections helped in the complex transactions of securing the money Gorky's father had sent and in purchasing steamship passage to America. Vergine Kelekian took Vartoosh to live with her in the Bebek section of Constantinople, but Gorky preferred to stay in the tent colony, where he was enjoying the companionship of other young men from Van: two of his friends were Yenovk Der Hagopian's older brother, Parsegh, and Krikor Moudoyan, his former teacher from Van and the man he had run to when his mother died. Gorky was free to explore the city as he liked, for Constantinople was under Allied occupation and relatively safe. At night he and his friends played music and sang. He encouraged his sister to stay with the Kelekians. "I can find ways to take care of myself," he reassured her, and he did find work at a cobbler's shop. With his friends from Van, he often visited Vartoosh in Bebek. It was probably the Kelekians who took Gorky and Vartoosh to see Constantinople's architectural monuments. "We saw Haghia Sophia from the outside only," Vartoosh said, "because at that time it still remained a mosque, and I remember Gorky smiled when learning that its dome had been built by the Armenian architect Trdat of Ani." He also admired the buildings designed by Sinan, the great sixteenth-century Armenian architect who had served under Sultan Suleyman the Magnificent.

As autumn progressed, the weather turned cold and life in the refugee tents became uncomfortable. Still no word came from Sedrak Adoian. Toward the end of his five-month stay in Constantinople, Gorky moved in with the Kelekians. He amused his hosts by imitating the various regional Armenian dialects that he had heard in the refugee camp. Eventually, when Mkrdich and Akabi Amerian sent money, Hampartzoum Kelekian obtained exit papers and passage on a merchant ship. On January 25, 1920, Vartoosh and Gorky said good-bye to the Kelekians and, together with Dickran and his wife, boarded a ship bound for Athens. It tied up at Athens for one night, but they remained on board.

The next day they continued on to the Greek port of Patras, where their boat docked for fifteen days. Gorky made friends with a Greek girl who was on her way to Chicago. Together they ventured ashore. "They would go and pick flowers," Vartoosh recalled.

On February 9 Gorky and Vartoosh boarded an Italian ship bound for New York called the *President Wilson.* Their fellow passengers in steerage were mostly Armenians and Greeks. When the boat stopped for one day at Naples, Gorky and Vartoosh debarked and bought oranges and lemons. "They were selling silly necklaces and Gorky bought one for me in Naples," Vartoosh said. In Naples they were required to take a medical examination that included a test for trachoma. Dickran failed the eye test and was detained in Naples for medical treatment. During the Atlantic crossing Gorky and the Greek girl (who shared no common language) strolled up and down the deck and sat close to the side of the ship watching the sea.

The immigrants from steerage class were out on deck watching the New York skyline on February 26, 1920, when the *President Wilson* sailed up the Verrazano Narrows and into Upper New York Bay. Suddenly a cry went up: "Liberty!" The Statue of Liberty was there on the port side. "My heart was banging against that rail!" Vartoosh recalled. "We just stood there, holding hands. We were both crying." The ship berthed at a New York pier and the immigrants were ferried across to Ellis Island. The ship's manifest of alien passengers presented upon arrival to the U.S. Immigration Office listed Gorky's first name as "Manouk" and Vartoosh's as "Vartanouche." Their ages were given as seventeen and sixteen. They waited in a long line outside the massive red-brick processing center. Once inside the building they were told to leave their belongings in the baggage hall and go upstairs to the immense Registry Room, where thousands of anxious non-English-speaking immigrants were questioned and examined. Gorky and Vartoosh were given numbers and told to wait. The processing took three days, during which time Gorky and Vartoosh slept in separate men's and women's dormitories. "They examined Gorky and put a chalk cross mark on his back and took him into another room," Vartoosh recalled. "I became very scared. There was an Armenian man there, a translator, and he said, 'Don't be frightened, it isn't anything. He looks a little frail, is slender of build. They think he may be ill.' " (Actually a cross written on an immigrant's clothing meant that he or she was suspected of being mentally unstable; Ellis

Island had a code: "I" for an eye problem, etc.) Gorky was told to go into one of the holding pens with wire walls at the edge of the hall. Doctors listened to his chest, checked for tuberculosis, and peered into his eyes to see if they were infected with trachoma. The medical examiners found nothing wrong. He passed the literacy test as well.

Finally Gorky and Vartoosh were given boarding cards and told that they should wait downstairs until their names were announced. They followed the file of successfully registered immigrants moving toward the "Kissing Room," the place where new arrivals greeted family members who had entered the United States before them. Akabi's husband, Mkrdich Amerian, and her daughter's godfather, Voskian, an old friend from Van, had come from Watertown, Massachusetts, to fetch them. Hagop Adoian had come down from Providence to meet them, too, but for reasons unknown their father was not there. It had been decided that Gorky and Vartoosh would first go to live with their older sisters in Watertown. With these three men to vouch for them, Gorky and Vartoosh entered the United States.

Upset by the rush of people and automobiles, Gorky made his way with his family to Grand Central Station, where Akabi was waiting. At the sight of them she burst into tears and laughter. Once they were all settled on the train to Boston, Akabi took from her bag a mysterious packet wrapped in silver foil. It held a strange but delicious food that the Adoians had never tasted: observing their curiosity and pleasure, Akabi began to laugh again. "That is called chocolate," she said. From Boston they took a bus or trolley to Watertown. They had finally arrived at their new home.

PART IV

Gorky painting in the backyard of his sister Akabi Amerian's house in Watertown, 1923

15

Watertown and Providence

It is hard to imagine what Gorky and Vartoosh felt when they first saw Watertown, a manufacturing center on the Charles River with gable-roofed clapboard houses set in small yards. Twenty years later Gorky remarked that he was amazed to find that a barking dog sounded the same in America as in Armenia. For a century the town had been a magnet for immigrants, most recently Armenians. Most of them were men who, like Sedrak, had left their wives and children behind with the intention of either saving enough money to bring them over or returning to the homeland wealthy. In general, Armenians did well, for they were conscientious, abstemious, and ambitious and had a strong work ethic. Moreover, they had one of the highest literacy rates among immigrant groups—all but 2 percent could read. The annual earnings of the Armenian worker in America, $454, were higher than those of most other immigrant groups except for the Eastern European Jews, Slovenians, and northern Italians. Yet the average Armenian earned $1.62 a day, whereas nonimmigrant workers earned a daily wage of $3.60. As early as 1915 over 46 percent of Boston and New York's working Armenians were in the artisan and shopkeeping category. When Gorky arrived in Watertown in 1920, many Armenians had started small businesses, and by the time he left five years later Armenians owned at least fifteen markets. One of them, the Star Market, opened in 1916 and was so successful that there were soon Star Markets all over New England.

Most of Watertown's Armenians lived in the East End, an area called "Little Armenia" that is thought to be the oldest continuing large con-

centration of Armenians in America. Having abandoned hope of returning to their homeland after the 1915–16 genocide, Armenian men tried
to bring over any surviving family members they could locate. Bachelors
and widowers looking for Armenian wives made arrangements through
intermediaries or traveled to foreign countries such as Syria, Iran, and
Lebanon where Turkish Armenians had taken refuge: intermarriage was
frowned on in the Armenian community.

Armenians in Watertown found jobs at factories such as the Walker &
Pratt Stove Company or they worked at the foundry, the Aetna Mills, or
the stockyard. Watertown's most important employer of Armenian immigrants was the Hood Rubber Company, housed in a sprawling brick
building on Arsenal Street. It was here that Akabi's and Satenik's husbands, Mkrdich Amerian and Sarkis Avedisian, and later Satenik, Gorky,
and Vartoosh worked. Hood Rubber produced rubber footwear, rubber
gloves, tires, floor tiles, and battery boxes. In the early 1920s its workforce
consisted of some ten thousand men and women. Turnover was low, for
Hood Rubber was considered an excellent place to work. During the
labor unrest of the 1920s, when American-born employees organized
lockouts, threatened to strike, and demanded the expulsion of all foreign-
born employees (because immigrants were willing to work for low
wages), the company continued to hire Armenians.

Many of East Watertown's houses were inhabited by several families.
Such was the case at Akabi's place on Coolidge Hill Avenue, where Akabi's and Satenik's families lived along with a number of male boarders.
Since she had come to America in 1916, Akabi, now twenty-four, had
given birth to a daughter, Azaduhi (called Liberty), and a son, Thomas.
Her son Gurken, born in Van and now called Jimmy, was nine years old
when Gorky and Vartoosh arrived in Watertown. Satenik, now nineteen,
had married Sarkis Avedisian in March 1919. Family legend has it that
her marriage took place on the very day her mother died in Yerevan and
that, as she walked down the aisle, a candle carried by a young page set
her veil on fire. One of the wedding guests pulled the veil from her head
in time, but the fire was seen as a bad omen connected to the family
curse. When Gorky and Vartoosh first entered Akabi's home, Satenik did
not come downstairs. She was lying in bed facing the wall and weeping
over a recent miscarriage. In the next few years she gave birth to two
daughters, Shushik and Varsik (called Florence and Lillian). With all

these children and adults living under one roof, it must have seemed almost like the Old Country.

After Gorky and Vartoosh had stayed a month in Watertown, Akabi felt that her house was overcrowded and sent her younger siblings off to see their father in Providence. Sedrak Adoian lived at 207 Pond Street with his son Hagop and daughter-in-law, Heghine Najarian, an Armenian from Kharpert. Hagop, who was about thirty-five in 1920, was a giant of a man, cold and with a fierce temper. The hardships he had borne in Turkey remained with him: besides Armenian-language newspapers, the only reading materials in Hagop's house were books on the Armenian massacres, which he is said to have read over and over again. "There was a meanness in him," remembered Satenik's daughter Liberty. "A real Adoian with a stubborn streak. He probably raised his hand. You could see that from his children, maybe his wife too. A lot of Armenian men were that way. The women had to be submissive. His wife, Heghine, was meek and mild." Heghine was four feet tall, good-natured, and the mother of four children. Since Hagop was the homeowner and it was he who had paid for his father's passage to America, he was the head of the household.

When Gorky and Vartoosh arrived in Providence, the fifty-seven-year-old Sedrak Adoian was still an impressive-looking man with a long, hard, somewhat sad face, blue eyes, large ears, a long nose, and a powerful jaw. According to his grandson George, even after he came to the United States Sedrak always slept with his clothes on and with a hatchet under his pillow. Hagop's older son, Charles, remembered his grandfather making his weekly trip to buy a quarter of a pound of tea at the tea shop where Charles was a clerk. Charles noticed a deep cut on his grandfather's hand and offered to take him to the hospital. "No," said Sedrak, "I urinate on it two or three times a day and that's what heals my hand up."

For Gorky and Vartoosh, the first meeting with Sedrak Adoian after twelve years of separation was a shock. Gorky barely remembered what his father looked like and Vartoosh, having been an infant when her father left, did not remember him at all. During their years in Yerevan, Gorky and Vartoosh had learned to speak in the eastern Armenian dialect. Their father spoke the dialect used in Van and he had trouble understanding them. When asked what her first impressions of her father were, Vartoosh replied: "We knew he was our father, but when you don't see him for twelve years, you don't have the same feelings right away that you would had you grown up with him. . . . Then when you are introduced, they say, 'This is your father.' It is a strange feeling. Gorky stayed with him in Providence, but I returned to Watertown to stay with Akabi. But Gorky visited often."

Hagop and Sedrak worked at the Iron Winding Company foundry in Cranston, near Providence. Sedrak was a grinder; Hagop was a caster. The work was backbreaking, hot, smelly, and dangerous. When they came home they smoked their narghile (hookah) pipes, which had long tubes leading from a tall bottle to a mouthpiece. At each inhalation, bubbles rose in the glass bottle. Sedrak's grandchildren remember him as an affectionate and jolly man who told stories about the Old Country, about long journeys on a white horse, and about Armenians murdered by Turks. Sometimes they sang. Hagop had a good tenor voice and he sang Armenian songs that filled Sedrak with nostalgia.

Gorky disliked Providence and he disliked the job his father and Hagop found for him at the Iron Winding Company. Being a foundry worker was not his idea of what he wanted in the New World. When his old friend Arshag Mooradian (who had been a fellow student at the American Mission School in Van) turned up in Providence that spring, he found Gorky unable to work because of a burn on his foot that probably came from a foundry accident. Hagop, too, had frequent burns caused by drops of molten iron that spilled as he poured it into molds. In spite of his injury, Gorky was hungry for adventure. "Arshag. Let's go and look around the city," he said. When they passed a store window displaying a large painting of a shepherd, Gorky said, "You see that? I am going to be a painter one day, better than that!"

That spring Gorky attended the Old Beacon Street School. Entering as a non-English-speaking immigrant was a humbling experience, especially as Armenians were the objects of pity. Gorky told his wife, Agnes Magruder (Mougouch), that after a church service the minister said to him, "Oh you, young man, where are you from?" When Gorky replied, "Armenia," the minister said, "Oh, one of the starving Armenians." After spending the summer in Watertown, he was back in Providence in the autumn of 1920, again living with his father and Hagop, who had moved to 22 Cranston Street. From January to June of 1921 Gorky went to Bridgeham Junior High School. Later he would tell people that when he first came to America he studied engineering for three and a half years at

Brown University. On other occasions he said that he had attended the Rhode Island School of Design. No doubt he invented this more prestigious educational background for himself to further his career. Americans, in his view, respected name brands. But his fabrication may also have come from his need to forget his traumatic youth and from the shame he felt at being a refugee and a foundry worker's son.

Gorky began to reinvent his biography early. It seems plausible that when the six-foot-two, twenty-year-old Armenian turned up in January 1921 at Bridgeham Junior High School, he was mortified at being placed in a class with twelve-year-olds and decided to permanently change his age. Along with other older foreign pupils he would have been the butt of jokes. Perhaps Gorky was reminded of being made fun of by village boys in Khorkom for not being able to talk. In any case, he was, and remained, too vulnerable a person to tolerate being teased: even in later life he often thought he was being laughed at when he wasn't.

As he struggled with junior high school, Gorky was harboring ideas about what he wanted to do with his life. Although it is clear that his interest in art was growing, apart from a few anecdotes told by family and friends, little is known about his first attempts to paint with oils on canvas. Perhaps he was drawn to art as an escape from the practical demands of his life; perhaps painting was an opening into a world in which imagination could banish unhappy realities. In addition, being an artist could give him entry into a privileged world that was not delimited by American economic and class distinctions. In this world—the art world—mastery brought prestige regardless of birth or wealth.

Gorky's decision to become an artist was reinforced by his friendship with Mischa Reznikoff, a small, lively Ukrainian-born art student at the Rhode Island School of Design, with whom Gorky went to cowboy movies every week. Reznikoff recalled: "At that time he was drawing Caucasian mountains and sunsets, very unlike what he was doing later. What he remembered of his old country. He told me he came from the Caucasus. He was just a beginner, his sentimental period. He always talked of himself as being a Russian rather than an Armenian. I knew that [he wasn't Russian]—because when you asked him in Russian, he couldn't speak it."

Gorky's father and half brother were not pleased with Gorky's artistic ambitions. There were terrible fights. "Gorky and Hagop did not get along," said Hagop's son George Adoian. "My father and grandfather worked fourteen hours a day. They wanted Gorky to work like anybody else. Gorky said no, he wanted to go to the Roger Williams Park and draw pictures and paint." One day Gorky came home with a bouquet of roses for Heghine. When his sister-in-law asked him where he had found them and he told her he'd picked them in Roger Williams Park, she cried: "Don't bring them! Don't bring them! They'll arrest you!" The idea of a young man wasting his time painting flowers in a park infuriated Hagop, but it amused Hagop's daughters. As Gorky became more and more convinced that he was born to be an artist, he began to put on artist's airs. George Adoian recalled: "My sisters, Lucille and Dawn, would see him. Gorky dressed up like Jesus Christ and came walking down the street. He was wearing a long beard and a cape. They thought it was funny and they burst into a fit of laughter." Another witness to Gorky's youthful role playing said that everybody teased him: "Hey, Manouk, they said—you gonna be an artist or something?" For Gorky, the traditional burdens of the romantic artist—incomprehension and derision—began at home, and he seems to have embraced them as a birthright.

Gorky spent his second summer in America, the summer of 1921, in Watertown with his sisters. Akabi and her family now lived at 86 Dexter Avenue in a two-family house with a second-story porch looking over the back yard. Akabi rented out the ground floor and with her extended family she lived on the second floor. Like Sedrak and Hagop, Gorky's brothers-in-law thought that he should get a job, but his sisters supported his artistic ambitions. According to his cousin Kevork Kondakian, who had been Gorky's tutor in Khorkom, "His sisters were taking care of him just like a child. Especially Vartoosh loved him like he was a seven-year-old. The only brother they had, so they gave him everything he needs. He wanted to do nothing else but art. He had to go after that like a fever. Vartoosh gave him money, everything. The courage to do anything he wants."

After work Akabi (Fig. 57) and Gorky would sit on her front porch while she talked and he drew. He gave his older sister some of his early paintings—family portraits and copies of paintings in the Boston Museum of Fine Arts. One was a copy of a portrait (probably by Van Dyck) of a Spanish grandee with a lace collar and a pointed beard. Many years later the paintings were badly damaged in a fire that Akabi believed was another manifestation of the curse. When she was cleaning up after the fire, she threw a dozen or so blackened canvases into the garbage. Gorky was furious. He would not give Akabi any more paintings, he said. "See if I care!" said the cheerful Akabi. "I love you anyway."

The area of Watertown where the Adoians lived was full of refugees from Van. "We had Vanetzi picnics, a big crowd," said one of Akabi's lodgers, a man named Kooligian. Gorky liked being surrounded as in Khorkom by so many family members. He loved his nieces and nephews and he called them *mougouch* (or *mogooch*), an Armenian term of endearment that would later become his second wife's nickname. Akabi's daughter Liberty, who was three when Gorky first arrived in Watertown, said: "I loved him dearly. He was very warm, very loving. We called him Manoug, not Uncle or anything like that. He was handsome. . . . He loved to sing Armenian songs and loved to joke."

In the fall of 1921 Gorky returned to Providence and attended the Technical High School, which offered courses in such subjects as car mechanics, engineering, and electrical work. According to Vartoosh, Gorky also had some kind of gainful employment. Although most of the school's curriculum did not interest Gorky, it did include art classes, and Gorky's art teachers saw his talent and hung his pictures on the walls. The pressure on Gorky to give up art and join his father and half brother at the foundry remained extreme. So did Gorky's resistance to his father, which only increased when Sedrak began to court an Armenian woman from Van named Akabi Sarafian. Over the protests of both sons, the sixty-year-old Sedrak finally married late in 1923. What Hagop disapproved of was that Akabi Sarafian already had two children by a previous marriage—more mouths to feed. From Gorky's point of view, his father's courtship was a strike against his mother's sacred memory. Gorky tried to dissuade his father: "Father, you're old already. Why do you want to get married?" But Sedrak was in love, and he answered: "My son, if I get a boil on my back, I can't say, 'Vartoosh, Satenik, look at my back.' But if I had a wife, I'd say, 'Look here.' "

By the time his father remarried, Gorky was no longer living in Rhode Island. The fights with his brother had grown intolerable. Hagop resented Gorky because he felt their father indulged him. "Anything Gorky wanted his father would give him," George Adoian remembered. "After Gorky moved to New York, he would write to his father and ask him for money or shoes from Brockton." Mostly Gorky and Hagop fought about money, about Gorky's paying his fair share. Gorky and

Hagop's fights were also political. "My father had a hot temper," said George Adoian. "He was going to shoot my aunt because of a political argument. My father was very violent about Armenian politics. He was a Dashnak. Gorky was strictly pro-Russian. Gorky and my father got into a dispute and Gorky moved to Watertown." In the years to come Gorky saw his half brother and father only occasionally. As he made his way in the world, he pulled away from them. He pretended that his father was dead, that he had ridden away along the shore of Lake Van never to be heard of again.

Living in Watertown's "Little Armenia" with his sisters and their families was not much more conducive to making art than living in Providence had been. Gorky's brothers-in-law finally persuaded him join them at the Hood Rubber Company. Inside Hood Rubber's immense, well-lit rooms men with bow ties and rolled-up shirtsleeves and women with flapper-style bobbed hair worked long hours in the moist heat full of chemical fumes. Gorky's job was to transport the frames on which shoe soles were carried. During lunch breaks he escaped to the open air and privacy of the factory's roof, where he took to drawing in chalk on the black roof tiles. A floor supervisor named Shirley covered for him, warning him when it was time to get back to work. One day when he failed to return from a break on time and was discovered drawing on the roof, the foreman warned him not to go up there anymore. Gorky paid no heed and was caught again. Vartoosh said he was fired after two months for drawing on the shoe frames. Freed from factory work, Gorky took odd jobs such as washing dishes in cafeterias in order to contribute to the family income and to buy drawing supplies and a small paint box. Thus equipped, he stationed himself on the banks of the Charles River and proceeded to draw and paint.

When in November 1923 Gorky's boyhood friend Yenovk Der Hagopian turned up in Watertown, his reunion with Gorky was an emotional one. "He was astonished by me, I was astonished by him. He stared at me, I stared at him." Hagopian, a neophyte painter, a musician, and soon a worker at the Hood Rubber Company, remembered that Gorky liked to paint in the thick of human activity. Once he led the way to a busy intersection on Arsenal Street and announced: "I'm going to paint this. Let's start here." Aghast by Gorky's audacity, Yenovk cautioned: "Manouk, are you crazy, many people pass by here." But Gorky still had his leader's personality. "I don't care, let's go," he said. "All right," Yenovk agreed. "You do it." Gorky unfolded his easel and began to paint. Yenovk had an easel too, but he placed it low in the tall grass where he thought he could not be seen. "Then one car stopped, two cars," Yenovk said, "then half a dozen cars stopped to watch him. Here was a unique person, tall and with a beard and whiskers, painting out there." To Yenovk's horror, a policeman appeared. "Hey, where do you come from?" the officer asked. Gorky kept his eyes on his work. Finally he answered: "I come from heaven. Where do you think I come from? I'm a man like you." Gorky kept on painting, and the policeman warned: "Don't get too wise or I'll take you in." When the policeman went to call the police station from a phone booth, Gorky and Yenovk decided to decamp. On Dexter Avenue Gorky set up his easel again, and another police car pulled up beside him. This time Gorky gathered up his belongings and began to walk. The police car cruised slowly beside him. The policeman asked to see Gorky's picture, and Gorky held the canvas so close to the officer's face that all the man saw was a blur. "You know," the policeman said, "I'm not that ignorant. You have to give me more distance to see it." Having seen Gorky's painting from a proper distance, he told Gorky that it was beautiful. But why, he asked, didn't Gorky go to the golf course to paint? "It's a beautiful place," said the officer. "Sergeant, I'm from Watertown too," said Gorky. "I work in Hood Rubber. I know the golf course. I know every angle in Watertown, so I'm not a stranger. But this is a very nice, interesting spot and I felt like painting it. Is there any crime in that?" The policeman had the last word: "Only if you stop traffic."

16

The Young Master

At some point in 1922 Gorky briefly attended the Scott Carbee art school in Boston. A 1946 letter to Gorky from Norris C. Baker, a former Scott Carbee student, tells us why Gorky's attendance at the school was cut short: "One day we had a very young girl model, you worked feverishly on your oil painting, you caught the childlike character and soul on your canvas—Carbee did not come near you until the end of the class and then he castigated you & told you if you couldn't paint the way he wanted you to you needn't come to his classes—you calmly took the canvas and smashed it all to hell, packed your paints & left—I never remember seeing you at the classes again."

In the winter of 1922 Gorky enrolled in Boston's New School of Design (later called the New England School of Design) at 248 Boylston Street, across from the Boston Public Gardens. Founded in 1913, the school was directed by Douglas John Connah, a portrait painter and illustrator. It offered a two-year course in drawing, painting, and design. Gorky enrolled in night classes. During his two years of attendance he educated himself in the history of art by devouring books and by visiting museums, especially the Isabella Stewart Gardener Museum and the Boston Museum of Fine Arts. To learn oil painting technique, he made copies of works by old masters such as Frans Hals.

Katherine Murphy, a fellow student at the New School of Design, remembered Gorky as being much older than the other students. He was, she said, "very attractive," "gangly," and possessed of "some fire." She recalled that Gorky washed dishes in a restaurant in exchange for meals.

One dishwashing job was at the Hayes Bickford, about a block from the school. He also worked at odd jobs like touching up old portraits for a Charles Street art dealer and making posters for the Majestic Theater at 219 Tremont Street. The Majestic's chief function was to serve as a try-out house for plays headed for Broadway, but it also featured vaudeville (it is very likely that Gorky saw the Marx Brothers perform *I'll Say She Is* there in 1923). Between acts at the Majestic Gorky deployed a skill he had honed by copying presidential portraits at the Boston Museum of Fine Arts: he went onstage and drew pictures of American presidents on a blackboard, one a minute.

In Boston, Vartoosh recalled, "his whole mind revolved around art." His family continued to feel that he was wasting time instead of seeking a steady job. Vartoosh was the one family member who completely approved of her brother's career choice. When on June 8, 1923, she married Gorky's old friend from Aikesdan Moorad Mooradian and moved to her new home on Watertown's Templeton Drive, Gorky must have felt a mixture of loss and relief. Moorad was handsome and kind and he spoke good English, having joined the American army during World War I (Fig. 58). But the Adoians did not approve of him. He was from Shadakh, not from the shores of Lake Van, and he was only a laborer at Hood Rubber. When her family argued against her choice of a husband, Vartoosh dug in her heels. According to Akabi's daughter Liberty Miller, "Vartoosh wouldn't listen to anyone. She'd sit and brush her long black hair to one side and sigh. 'I love him. I love him.' Then she eloped." Later she was given a proper Armenian wedding at Akabi's house. Kooligian, the lodger, recalled: "We sang and danced a lot that night. It was a regular Armenian wedding party. Oh, Manoug [Gorky] was in good form. He had a good voice and was such a good dancer. Akabi begged, 'Don't jump so hard. You're gonna bring the house down.'" Liberty remembers Gorky trying to teach her godfather, Voskian, a certain dance: "He'd had a couple of drinks. He was very jovial, got along with everybody. He said, 'Put your leg back! Put your leg back!' But his legs were long and Voskian's were short." Another time he passed out after drinking raki and trying to teach Vartoosh to waltz. When he came to he insisted on playing leapfrog, which was fine for him as he soared over his friends' and family's crouching bodies, but less fun for the shorter party guests, who tumbled when they tried to scale Gorky.

Although Gorky loved his younger sister, he was distancing himself from her too. "Gorky had other ideas about his career and the people he wanted to meet," says painter Will Barnet. "He was already trying to move into higher circles, to change his class, to get out of the ghetto. He was laying the groundwork for assimilation so that he would be free to do what he wanted to do." As Gorky became part of a new circle of friends whom he met through art school, he kept his Armenian background hidden. His rejection of the Armenian community increased when he ran up a bill for drinks at an Armenian club in the building that published the newspaper *Hairenik*, and, being penniless, he offered the manager one of his paintings to settle his bill. Furious, the manager put his foot through the canvas, smashed the frame, and growled that artists who painted naked women were no better than brothel keepers.

About the time he entered the New School of Design, Gorky made a major break with his Armenian origins by changing his name. Until 1932, when he settled on the spelling "Arshile Gorky," Gorky wrote his name in various ways: Archele or Archel, and sometimes Gorki. Vartoosh told Karlen Mooradian that Gorky changed his name because he feared he might not meet the high standards that his mother had imposed on him as a boy. "He said to me, 'Vartoosh dear, when I have made significant contributions, then at that time I will proclaim to the world my Armenian race.'" In fact, the name change was typical of Armenian immigrants during this period. Often immigration officials, unable to pronounce an Armenian name, invented a new one. For an upwardly mobile artist, the name Arshile Gorky was preferable to Vosdanik or Manouk Adoian. Moreover, Gorky always felt that the Russians had saved Armenia: they had rescued the population of Van City in 1915, and when Russian Armenia became a Soviet republic in 1920, the Russians fostered its development into a modern country. The proud young Gorky hid his poverty as well as his origins from his friends. Ethel M. Cooke, the drawing teacher at the New School of Design, said: "He told us he was Russian, he'd been in a Russian concentration camp or some kind of camp. I didn't get the story straight. He didn't seem to need money. Perhaps he came with some kind of scholarship. We all thought he had training. He was so accomplished."

Friends remember that Gorky first considered taking a more American-sounding name. He played with the possibility of calling himself Archie Gunn or Archie Colt, an idea that must have come from seeing cowboy movies. "Arshile" is thought to be a version of Achilles, but many Armenian names begin with "Ar." Most likely he chose the name Gorky, which he may have known means "bitter" in Russian, because he admired the Russian writer Maxim Gorky, who had worked for the Armenian Relief Organization after the massacres of World War I and in 1916 coedited the first anthology of Armenian poetry published in Russian translation. Gorky went so far as to tell his art school friends that he was Maxim Gorky's nephew. This falsehood sometimes failed to convince, especially when people realized that Gorky couldn't speak Russian or when they knew that Maxim Gorky was a nom de plume: Gorky's given name was Alexei Peshkov. On one occasion the New School of Design's director, Douglas John Connah, introduced Gorky as Maxim Gorky's nephew to a friend of the author, and the friend's befuddlement caused everyone considerable chagrin.

For all his bravado and his invention of a charismatic personality, Gorky was full of self-doubt. The pressure on him to succeed was enormous and, like most young people, he had a tendency to inflated hopes followed by plummets into despair. He would later tell his wife that during his Boston years he had thought of suicide. Once he swam out into the Charles River with the intention of drowning, but then he remembered "What about painting?" and swam back to shore as quickly as he could. In Boston Gorky worked long hours and taught himself to paint. "You have to be strong enough to plow to be able to paint," he told Ethel Cooke. Years later he wrote: "Had I known that painting was so exhausting I should not have chosen it as a career. But, no matter, it must have been my destiny. I must have been born to it." His professors were amazed at his talent, and in spring 1924 he was made a part-time assistant instructor in the life-drawing class. The job bolstered his confidence. Vartoosh remembered that when Gorky began teaching art he said, "Vartoosh, think how happy Mother would be now that I am a teacher."

According to Ethel Cooke, the school's faculty was especially impressed by Gorky's drawing: "It was noticeable right away that he could draw and knew what he was about and he just got ahead by leaps and bounds and we were all quite proud of him." Although his astonishing natural facility may have been nurtured by drawing lessons in the schools he attended in Turkish and Russian Armenia and Providence, Gorky was essentially self-taught. His formal art training would consist of two years of study in Boston and one in New York. But mainly he learned by copying and by being what Meyer Schapiro called a "fervent scrutinizer" of paintings. Stuart Davis, who became a close friend of Gorky's at the end of the 1920s, remembered that around 1930 Gorky showed him a portfolio of drawings from his New School of Design years. The drawings were done, Davis recalled, "in the orthodox life-and-portrait-class style. But his genuine talent was clearly expressed within the framework of ideas required in such studies, and I found them stimulating, distinguished." In Ethel Cooke's opinion, Gorky's drawings were as good as John Singer Sargent's, and, she noted, Sargent was an artist whom Gorky greatly admired. Indeed, Gorky used to carry a book on Sargent under his arm: "I imagine he slept with it under his pillow. He was that sort of a student." It is possible that Gorky met Sargent. Connah was using Sargent's former Boston studio, and when Sargent returned to Boston to work on murals, he not only visited the New School of Design but also welcomed its students in his studio. Sometime in the 1940s Gorky told his wife that Sargent had given him his paintbrushes.

Gorky was popular at the New School of Design. Among his close friends was the director's son, Jack. With Jack Connah, Ethel Cooke, and an Irishman named Frank Cronin, he used to take long walks and visit exhibitions. Ethel Cooke remembered: "We'd have these wonderful talks about art and how they [artists] lived. We'd all go out to eat together in Boston. It was a wonderful life." Gorky and Jack Connah, who at six foot seven towered over even Gorky, were, she said, very concerned with physical fitness, and they made a point of swimming and other forms of exercise. Gorky also kept fit by running along the Charles.

Gorky's dedication to painting apparently left no time for women. Indeed, when he first arrived at the New School of Design he told someone that he hated women. One day a girl in his painting class placed her easel so close to his that each time she turned she brushed against Gorky. Brought up in a culture in which relations between the sexes were extremely reserved, Gorky was horrified by such forwardness in American women. He marched into Ethel Cooke's office and said: "Miss Cooke! Can't you make Helen behave?"

"Oh, what's she doing now?" asked the drawing teacher.

"Well, she rubs into me."

From Gorky's Boston years comes his first *Self-Portrait* (c. 1923–24) (Fig. 67), which he may have painted during his afternoon portrait class. The small group of students included Katherine Murphy, who recalled that during class Gorky would "relax, walking back and forth with intricate dance steps, telling his long fanciful delightful tales of his boyhood in Russia." The first *Self-Portrait* reveals Gorky's skill at the loose, slashing brushwork favored by the Munich School and derived from seventeenth-century Dutch painters such as Frans Hals. American exemplars of this style were Frank Duveneck and William Merritt Chase. Douglas Connah had formerly been the proprietor of the New York School of Art (also called the Chase School), where Robert Henri, that master of the bravura flourish, was a popular teacher.

As in all of his subsequent self-portraits, in this first one Gorky clearly identifies himself as an artist, complete with smock and ascot. Already his hairline curves back at the temples, giving his face the shape of a palette, a motif that he would emphasize in later portraits and a shape that recurs often in his abstract paintings of the 1930s. Keen-eyed and determined, he is emphatically not a starving Armenian—his face in this *Self-Portrait* is much fuller than that of the gaunt man in contemporary photographs. Nor does he have that dark, hooded look about his eyes that, in photographs, makes him look Armenian. The man in this portrait could more easily be named Ivan or Maxim than Vosdanik or Manouk. This is the face of an artist who has made up his mind to attach himself to the mainstream of Western tradition.

A few months later Gorky posed for a photograph that shows him playing the young master again—this time accompanied by friends (Fig. 61). Ethel Cooke said the photograph was taken on a Sunday after he had been working on a portrait of her, now lost. The three friends ranged around him are Ethel, a model named Miss Lisle, and a man whom Karlen Mooradian identifies as an artist friend from Van called Felix Chooligan. Gorky is clearly the dominant figure. His long, pale, clean-shaven face with its intelligent, shadowed eyes appears to be that of a man of at least twenty-four. His right hand is posed, rather self-consciously, on his right knee: later photographs suggest that Gorky was well aware that his enormous, long-fingered hands were an asset. He holds up his left hand in the rhetorical gesture of a teacher among students.

Gorky's growing confidence led to another contretemps between him and the police. Often he set up his easel in the Boston Public Gardens and the Boston Common, and one day in 1924 he decided to paint the rush-hour crowds entering the Park Street subway station at the end of the Common. When he was accused of blocking traffic, Gorky told the officer that he was an American and an artist and he had a right to paint there. The result of this escapade was *Park Street Church*, signed "Gorky, Arshele," one of the first appearances of his pseudonym (Fig. 62). "During noon recesses," Katherine Murphy recalled, "Gorky used to sketch outdoors and one dull day, Gorky painted a small panel of the Park Street Church. A parishioner passing by offered Gorky five dollars for the painting if he would make his figures more distinct and less like peasants. Naturally Gorky was furious and returned to the school enraged but sorry that he had not sold the little oil for $5.00 and offering it at that price. So I gave him $10.00 for the little oil and $10.00 was quite a sum to me then."

For this small painting Gorky turned to an Impressionist style almost half a century after Impressionism's first flowering. This was a natural thing for a young Boston painter to do. Impressionism was still popular in the United States, and especially so in Boston, where paintings by Monet, Renoir, Sisley, Pissarro, and Degas were very much available both on the walls of the Boston Museum and in publications. New England contemporaries like Ernest Lawson and John Twachtman had developed a heavier, more matter-of-fact idiom that suited Gorky. ("Your Twachtman," Gorky said in 1926, "painted a waterfall that was a waterfall in any country, as Whistler's mother was anyone's mother. He caught the universal idea of art."

Unlike the French Impressionists' small, feathery flecks of color, which atomize structure and make volumes seem permeated by air and light, Gorky's heavier, more patterned brush strokes do not dissolve the structure of Park Street Church. Instead a sense of firm material reality is sustained; the play of light is merely an overlay. Gorky would never lose touch with immediate, tactile reality—both the reality of what his eyes saw and the reality of paint on canvas. Even in his most abstract paintings, shapes and colors have the feel of lived experience, of nature observed.

Park Street Church's odd, tender colors predict Gorky's later, highly personal use of color, which, though informed by Picasso and Miró, seems to come from a path or place different from School of Paris painting. Whereas Parisian painting takes off from color harmonies of Western tradition since the Renaissance, Gorky's color appears to be connected with Armenia. A glowing streetlight suggests that when he worked on this painting Gorky extended his lunch hour into the late afternoon in order to capture Boston's urban bustle as people on their way home from work dash into subway kiosks under a slow, crepuscular light.

Late in 1924 Gorky decided to leave Boston. He had been offered a teaching position at the New York City branch of the New School of Design, opened in 1923 by Connah. One reason for going, Vartoosh said, was his dissatisfaction with the art climate in Boston. New York was the liveliest art center in America, and he hoped that his work would find a more enthusiastic reception there. More important, Gorky needed to reinvent himself in a new milieu. When he said good-bye to his fellow teachers and students at the New School of Design, he shook Katherine Murphy's hand and said: "I shall be a great artist or if not, a great crook."

Naturally, his family disapproved. "They all thought that he should work in a factory, that he couldn't live from art," Vartoosh recalled. Perhaps they knew they were losing him. Akabi, like Vartoosh, would now mother Gorky from a distance: when she knew he was penniless, she sent him packages of paints.

Gorky boarded a train for New York City, where he would, after a year of struggling with the old masters and with Impressionism, apprentice himself to the next high moment in the modernist tradition, Cézanne. He would study and teach and worship the art he saw in museums and, with great single-mindedness, create the character that befitted a painter named Arshile Gorky. In Manhattan he grew a beard that made him look like Jesus or, if not Jesus, certainly a suffering genius. Artists are artificers—great crooks. For Gorky, youthful fakery was one element in the crucible of self-invention. With time he would fill out and even burst beyond the disguises he assumed.

PART V

Gorky clowning with his students, 1926

17

The Early Years in New York

❈

The young man on the train to New York was an extraordinary mixture of sophistication and naïveté, of braggadocio and shyness. His ambition was outsized, his skills well-honed. He had a reasonable command of English, yet his speech had, one friend observed, "an Anatolian turn to it." He left out definite and indefinite articles and he transformed words the way he transformed shapes: his malapropisms sounded like metaphors. Stuart Davis recalled the intelligence and passion with which Gorky talked about ideas, especially art ideas. But he never forgot Gorky's "complex personal jive." It was, he said, "no mere matter of a simple foreign accent, although that was present, but an earthquake-like effect on sentence structure and a savagely perverse use of words to mean something they didn't. He was completely conscious of this bizarre linguistic collation, and on occasion messed it up still more in company where he thought it would be effective strategy."

Gorky began life in New York in a rooftop studio lent to him by someone called Sigurd Skon. In September 1926 he lived on West Fiftieth Street, and sometime later that year or early the next he moved into a studio on Sixth Avenue at Fifty-seventh Street. This was probably the studio he shared for about a year and a half with his friend Stergis M. Stergis, a Greek-born art student whom he met in the mid-1920s. In 1928, when Stergis told him that he was planning to leave New York, Gorky found a studio of his own on the second floor of 47a Sullivan Street on the corner of Washington Square South.

Lined with brownstone buildings that had been divided into apartments, Sullivan Street was in the midst of New York's Greenwich Village community of painters, critics, and writers. Gorky could walk to the Whitney Studio Club, which the sculptor Gertrude Vanderbilt Whitney had founded in 1914 in her house on West Eighth Street. The Whitney Studio regularly bought and exhibited work by living Americans whom the art establishment ignored. Even more important for Gorky's artistic formation was the Gallery of Living Art, housed until 1942 in the New York University Library, only a few steps from Gorky's door. It displayed Albert E. Gallatin's collection of modern art and was, together with the Whitney, a favorite haunt of New York's nascent avant-garde. Gorky is said to have memorized all of Gallatin's pictures, and many of the collection's paintings—works like Miró's *Dog Barking at the Moon*, André Masson's *Cockfight*, and Picasso's 1906 *Self-Portrait* (Figs. 91 and 6)—are echoed in Gorky's paintings from the late 1920s and the 1930s.

Living in Greenwich Village suited Gorky during this period of inventing himself as a nationless, classless bohemian. As Stuart Davis put it (perhaps a little snidely): "At the right time he was in the right place. In the Bohemian twenties he inhabited a studio on Sullivan Street in Greenwich Village. The year of the Wall Street Crash he moved to Union Square, where he remained throughout the decade of demonstrations, artists' unions, and government projects." Gorky's bohemian disguise consisted of a long black overcoat, a red scarf, and either a proletarian-looking wool knit cap or, on days when he wanted to look prosperous or gangsterlike, a black felt hat tilted forward over his eyes. When he escaped the confinement of his one-room studio by strolling or sitting in Washington Square, he was often the target of jeers from a group of street urchins from neighboring tenement buildings. He countered by befriending the youngsters and giving them drawing lessons using chalk on pavement. Of a favorite pupil, Gorky would say, "This one draws just like Uccello. . . . These are the authentic artists. . . . When we try to do that we have a very difficult time, but for them it is very easy." A few years later, when he grew a beard, the neighborhood children would shout at him: "Take 'em off, Murphy, we know ya!"

Gorky's Sullivan Street studio overlooking Washington Square was furnished with secondhand tables and easels, and he set up still lifes all around the studio. "He had twenty or thirty settings over there, and a canvas in front of each one," Stergis said. "He started painting kind of an assembly line. When I went to say good-bye to him, the fruit and vegetables had rotted, but he was still painting from one of them." What Raphael Soyer, the social realist painter, remembered about the Sullivan Street studio was the beautifully arranged still life objects on a small wooden table. They looked, Soyer said, like a "wonderful kind of painting . . . it was unnecessary to paint it. A musical instrument, a guitar, sheets of music. . . . It was a work of art in itself." Stuart Davis was struck by the huge amount of art supplies Gorky had managed to acquire — "A massive easel of foreign make, great quantities of canvases of large size, hundreds of tubes of the most expensive colors, dozens of palettes covered with huge piles of paint, forests of fine brushes, bolts of linen for paint rags, and carboys of oil and turpentine." Adding to the atmosphere were several plaster casts and a stringed musical instrument. "The question of how he acquired this truly impressive stockpile and kept it replenished was raised from time to time, but no really clear picture of the feat was ever arrived at." Mariam Davis, the Armenian-born wife of Stuart Davis's brother Wyatt, offered a clue to the mystery: Gorky's rent and painting materials, she said, were paid for by "a Jewish woman that he sort of liked named Mrs. Moscowitz." Who this benefactor was is not known; neither is her relationship to Gorky.

On January 9, 1925, Gorky was admitted to the National Academy of Design on 109th Street and Cathedral Parkway. He was a day student in a life-drawing class taught by the realist painter Charles Hawthorne. When he registered he gave his address as 1680 Broadway, and for his date and place of birth he said April 1902 in Kazan, Russia. For reasons unknown, he abandoned this school after exactly one month. Written in red ink on the file card that records his attendance at the school are the words "2/9 left." Even while he attended class at the National Academy, he also enrolled and began to teach at the New York branch of Connah's New School of Design at 1680 Broadway, the address he had listed as his own. The school had eleven teachers and offered courses in drawing, illustration, commercial illustration, costume design, fashion, and interior decoration. No doubt the tuition of seventy-five dollars per term was waived, since Gorky served as a class monitor. In 1926, when the New School of Design moved to 145 East Fifty-seventh Street, Gorky was still registered.

Mark Rothko (then called Rothkowitz) probably met Gorky in 1925, the year Rothko enrolled at the New School of Design. Rothko recalled: "Gorky came down from Boston with Mr. Connah. Gorky was the monitor in the class in which I was enrolled. . . . Gorky was head of the class, in charge of it. He taught, as well as saw to it that the students were on good behavior. And he expected good performance. He was strict. Perhaps I shouldn't say this, but Gorky was overcharged with supervision." Rothko, a Russian Jew born in 1903 in Dvinsk, had experienced horrors of his own before coming to America in 1913. Being close to Gorky in age, he had a difficult time accepting Gorky's overzealous leadership, and the two men did not strike up a friendship. As the years passed, Gorky continued to treat Rothko as a subordinate, not as a colleague. Once when Rothko visited his studio, he found himself obediently taking out Gorky's garbage. "I'm afraid I still thought of him as my class monitor," Rothko explained.

Rothko remembered that Gorky admired Frans Hals, whose work he copied in the Metropolitan Museum. *Lady in the Window* (c. 1925–26) is a copy after Hals's *Malle Babbe*, probably the Metropolitan's version. But Gorky may have studied it at home in reproduction, for the image is reversed right to left as if he had looked at it in an engraving or a flipped photograph. Besides Hals, he also liked Adolphe Monticelli, a nineteenth-century Italian Impressionist who built up landscapes out of thick dabs of bright color, thus creating an all-over pattern of strokes. These artists were not, Rothko said, necessarily Gorky's favorites; they were simply painters whose works were available for viewing by students, "and it was part of his job to lecture to us and expound on the techniques used by the artists hanging in the Metropolitan." Rothko also recalled that Gorky had "considerable talent" for sculpture, which he worked at during class, and that when Gorky spoke of his childhood, it was "difficult to tell where reality ended and imagination began. . . . He had a wild, poetic imagination, . . . always expounding about the unique beauties and poetry of the place of his birth." Like many other of Gorky's acquaintances, Rothko saw Gorky as a melancholy man for whom art was the "single greatest source of happiness" and "rather like an obsession."

In October 1925 Gorky registered to study at the Grand Central School of Art, which had opened the year before and was housed on the seventh floor above the Grand Central Terminal. (To get there you took an elevator at track 29.) By 1926 the school had over eight hundred students, making it one of the largest art schools in the city. The school's director, Edmund Greacen, a distinguished American Impressionist working in the tradition of William Merritt Chase, recognized Gorky's exceptional talents and soon made him drawing instructor for the evening antique class, which consisted of drawing from plaster casts. Eleven months later Gorky was appointed a full member of the faculty in the department of painting and drawing. He taught the antique class as well as classes in still life and "life drawing and painting."

One of his first teachers at the Grand Central School was the Russian-born Nicolai Ivanovich Fechin, a realist whose portraits enjoyed a certain success in America after he showed at the Carnegie Institute in 1910. Fechin painted the sitter's head in lucid detail and made the rest of the figure an opportunity for virtuoso brush handling. His use of thick globs and patches of paint and his habit of leaving knobs of thickened pigment on the canvas surface were traits that Gorky would adopt a few years later. Stergis recalled: "Gorky thought Fechin was one of the greatest painters. He had wonderful technique. I have a portrait here [by Gorky]. You'd think it was by Fechin."

A Grand Central School catalog, probably from the 1926–27 season, lists Gorky as an instructor and says that "Archele Gorky" was a member of the Allied Artists of America and that he had been represented in many exhibitions. The latter claim must be a white lie—Gorky is not known to have participated in any shows until 1930. The catalog goes on to give Gorky's birthplace as Nizhni Novgorod, Russia, and to say that he had studied at the School of Nizhni Novgorod and later at the Académie Julien in Paris under Albert Paul Laurens, a teacher with a strict academic point of view. (Vartoosh sometimes covered for Gorky by saying that he had gone to Paris on his way from Turkey to America, but the truth is that Gorky never went to France.)

During his first months in New York, Gorky continued to paint in the freely brushed, heavily pigmented manner that he had learned in Boston and that was encouraged by Fechin. One example is *Portrait of George Yphantis* (c. 1926–27), made during one of Gorky's frequent visits to Watertown. Gorky and Yphantis, who had been a fellow student at the New School of Design, visited the Boston Museum together, where they talked at length about portrait painting. "Realizing that there were limits to what could be conveyed by words and theory, Gorky proposed to me that he paint an oil portrait of myself, and for my benefit at a single sitting. Accordingly we met on the next Saturday morning at the studio of the New England School of Design for this purpose. It had been arranged that I provide all necessary materials, and that the portrait remain my property permanently." The result of this demonstration was a portrait that reveals Gorky's skill at capturing a likeness while at the same time keeping his surface lively so that the portrait's interest goes beyond mere representation.

On a Watertown visit he painted Akabi's daughter Liberty, who remembers that she was about nine years old when he asked her to put on her red coat with a gray fur collar and said, "Sit down. I'm going to paint you." Liberty sat on a plain wooden chair and Gorky went to work, all the while carrying on a conversation with John Hussian (Mariam Melikian's husband) and Yenovk Der Hagopian. "Manouk, I'm getting tired," Liberty complained. "Sit still. Sit still!" he commanded. "Well, I'm tired." "Just a little bit more. It'll be over soon," Gorky insisted, and he finished that same afternoon. Liberty was surprised to see that he had made her blue eyes brown. Perhaps he thought brown eyes were more typically Armenian. She remembers Gorky's disapproval when he discovered that she and a cousin were taking ballroom dancing lessons. "What are you doing?" he protested to Akabi. "Raising whores for New York City?" That was the end of his nieces' dance lessons.

As these anecdotes suggest, Gorky's move to New York was not the total break with his Armenian background that has sometimes been imagined. In the early 1930s he spent a good part of the summer months with his sisters in Watertown, and he often went there for holidays as well. Satenik remembered that when he came for Christmas in 1933 he was very thin and there were holes in his shoes, but when she tried to fatten him up by cooking elaborate Armenian dishes, he was annoyed. It was a ridiculous waste of time to eat three meals a day, he said. Satenik sent Gorky, her husband, Sarkis, and a relative named Armenag off to buy a Christmas tree, and, typically for Gorky, who loved excess, they came back with a tree that was much too large for the living room. "We lived on the second floor," Satenik recalled. "I see Gorky just dangling from the roof of that porch with one hand, holding up the tree with the other. Armenag pulling. When they got it through the top window they couldn't get it to stand up. They went off and this time they came back with the most enormous nails. They hammered in about twenty of those nails. We had a new carpet! Then it was too high for the ceiling so they had to cut off the top of the tree."

During one visit Gorky took Satenik's daughter Varsik to the Boston Museum of Fine Arts. "At eleven you are self-conscious," Varsik Avedisian explained. "He was different. To me he looked like something from out of the blue. . . . He had on this tweed jacket and I think with leather patches at the elbow. He carried a little sketchbook with him and I felt so proud." During the ten-minute walk to the streetcar Gorky held his niece's hand and walked so fast she had to trot to keep up. "We got on the streetcar to go to Boston and he would stand up hanging onto the strap and looking around and everybody was looking at him wondering what kind of animal was this." Waiting at Harvard Square to transfer to another train, Gorky sketched bystanders, and Varsik had to nudge him when their streetcar came. At the museum Gorky stood before certain paintings for what seemed like an hour. "He would stand maybe fifteen feet away and look at it and praise things that I didn't even notice until he said something— little minute details, something you would think was insignificant and he would say how beautiful it was and he would make it beautiful to me, too. We looked at the old masters, Van Dyck. He loved El Greco."

Gorky also visited his father and Hagop at Hagop's Rhode Island farm. There he rode, helped with the farmwork, and played with his nieces and nephews. On visits to Niagara Falls, where his maternal uncles Moses and Aharon had settled in a tiny apartment above a grocery store, he could vent his anger at his father's abandonment of his mother and subsequent remarriage. Moses had been in the United States since 1908 and Aharon had come in 1926, bringing his wife and Moses' wife as well. When Gorky and Aharon were first reunited they embraced with such enthusiasm that they slipped and tumbled down a snowy hill, clutching each other and laughing all the way. Later they drank raki and danced so wildly that they made the walls shake.

In his early years in New York Gorky tried to make a living by painting society portraits. Ethel Cooke recalled: "The Ferragil Gallery was on Fifty-seventh Street then. A man named Purdy got Gorky to do portraits of these society dames. He did a few of them. I think they offered $1,500 a portrait. It was quite a price." Making conventional portraits was for Gorky an onerous task. "They aren't pretty, Miss Cooke, and I can't make them pretty and they all fall in love with me," he complained. Gorky was far too uncompromising to fill the bill as a society portraitist. Stergis recounted:

Knoedler Galleries, I think it was, commissioned him to paint five portraits of different women. The cheapest one, I think, was

$1,500 or $2,000 to $3,000. At the time they gave him a very nice studio. He painted one of the women. The most beautiful portrait! She had a black velvet dress with green sash thrown over, from one shoulder down. Very beautiful!

At the unveiling they had a lot of family friends. The husband remarked to Gorky, taking him aside, "Would you mind to tone down the lips?"

He had a beautiful spot on the lips. Gorky threw up his hands. He started swearing in Russian. He pulled the canvas down. And of course, the result? They had advanced a thousand dollars, which he had spent for canvases and so on. He was eating for a change. That money was gone. He never got the balance of it. He had no place to go. I said, "Arshile come to my place, until you find another place."

He moved in with me. He only finished one painting, and that was the unhappy ending of it. He didn't do the rest. The gallery didn't want nothing to do with him.

When Haroutune Hazarian, an Armenian collector friend of Gorky's, brought an Armenian painter named Panos Terlemezian to Gorky's studio, Gorky showed them a portrait of a woman that he had slashed with a knife. "Look. I was going to get a thousand dollars for this painting. She like it; I don't like it! So, I'm going to destroy it!" Knowing how much Gorky needed the money, Hazarian admired his intransigence. From the beginning, Gorky was an exacting critic of his own work: according to Stergis, during the year and a half that Gorky lived with him they both hauled batches of their unsatisfactory paintings to the incinerator "because we got tired of all those canvases."

On September 15, 1926, the day Gorky became a full-fledged member of the Grand Central School of Art's faculty, an interview with him headlined "Fetish of Antique Stifles Art Here, Says Gorky Kin" appeared in the *New York Evening Post*. Full of pronouncements, it is the expression of a young man enjoying to the hilt the role of maestro. When the interviewer visited his West Fiftieth Street studio, Gorky told him the usual fibs about his age and nationality: the article said that Gorky came from "one of Russia's greatest artist families, for he is a cousin of the famous writer, Maxim Gorky. . . . The young Russian hears occasionally from his famous cousin, Maxim, who is now in Venice, treating a cardiac ailment and writing."

The *Post's* reporter quoted Gorky as blaming the neglect of American modernism on America's infatuation with old masters and famous names. "Americans," he said, "follow the 'smart,' with the result that the young New York artist has less opportunity to exhibit his work than a comparable artist in Europe." In Gorky's studio the interviewer saw "a still-life study of a few glass objects and some fruit" on the easel, and propped around the room were many other still lifes, portraits, and landscapes that revealed a "facile, talented hand." When the interviewer pointed out that the bustle of New York's skyscrapers had not affected his art, Gorky said, "Art is not in New York you see; art is in you. Atmosphere is not something New York has, it is also in you. . . . Art is always universal." Gorky made it clear to the reporter that modern art was "the greatest the world has known" and that the dismissal of artists like Cézanne, Matisse, and Picasso was crazy. "These men," he said, "are greater artists than the old masters. Cézanne is the greatest artist, shall I say, that has lived."

18

Apprentice to the Masters

୪୫

When Gorky set about to paint a still life or a landscape in 1926 and 1927, "Papa Cézanne" was at his side or inside his head. In the morning he would study reproductions of Cézanne's landscapes, then, after scaring away intrusive onlookers, set up his easel in Central Park (Fig. 63). When the light was gone, he'd go home to compare his landscape with those by Cézanne. Gorky made no attempt to hide what he took from Cézanne. The Master of Aix would remain a touchstone: even in Gorky's abstract drawings of the 1940s, the handling of forms in space recalls Cézanne's way of inviting the eye to move back and forth between the canvas as a frankly acknowledged surface and the illusion of depth.

A 1926 painting of nudes (signed "A. Gorky") shows a Cézannesque search for structural underpinnings as it unites three figures at different levels of depth—a Rodin sculpture in the foreground, a female model in the middle ground, and a shadowy figure of a male in the background (Fig. 66). The visual links between the shapes of these figures suggest a fascination with Cézanne's stress on linear continuities across the canvas surface between objects that are at different spatial depths. Moreover, the idea of painting a sculpture recalls Cézanne's still lifes in which Puget's sculpture of Cupid appears. The recollections of Stergis, who owned this early painting, throw light on its subject matter:

> I have a painting he did at the Metropolitan Museum of a Rodin statue, *The Poet and the Model*. The Rodin Gallery was right at the main entrance. . . . He set up his easel, had to pick up his be-

longings and take them to the locker at four o'clock. Well, he forgot the time. The guards got annoyed. "Either stop at the right time and pick up all those things or we won't let you in!"

So he goes and buys himself an alarm clock. He was quite a character. Tall, long hair. He used long brushes—one of those thirty-inch-long brushes. He put paint on canvas and walked back again. People were attracted and stood around watching him instead of going to the gallery. There was quite a crowd over there, every day, when he was painting. Finally, at four o'clock the alarm clock would go off! And then he'd take the stuff to store.

Several of Gorky's Cézannesque landscapes, still lifes, and portraits appear to be based on reproductions in Julius Meier-Graefe's *Paul Cézanne*, published in 1923, a copy of which Gorky owned. (At some point he also acquired Roger Fry's *Cézanne: A Study of His Development*, published in London in 1927.) Others were inspired by reproductions in *Cahiers d'Art*, which Christian Zervos began to publish in Paris in 1926 and which, through the 1930s, formed the most important source for young American modernists eager to know what was happening in Europe. In addition, Gorky could have seen a few original Cézannes in the Boston Museum, at the Metropolitan, and at Manhattan galleries such as Durand-Ruel, Reinhardt, and Wildenstein.

The still lifes of 1926 and 1927 show Gorky following Cézanne's lead by tipping a plate of fruit up toward the picture plane so that it does not sit on the table in proper perspective. Another way of flattening space and creating surface-depth tension that he learned from Cézanne was to make the space around objects as vital as the objects themselves. To do this, he built up forms out of Cézannesque patches of color that both define objects and impress themselves on the spectator as actual strokes of pigment on the canvas surface. The brush strokes in Gorky's 1926–27 paintings are often laid on one next to the other in a parallel pattern that unites, for example, a road, some shrubbery, and the sky (Fig. 1).

Like a newly arrived immigrant carefully adapting himself to the social mores of his new world, Gorky was respectful and circumspect in his early Cézanne imitations. In *Pears, Peaches, Pitcher* (Fig. 2), for example, the touchings and overlappings of fruits is exquisitely calibrated, but unlike Cézanne's apples, Gorky's peaches and pears do not seem to jitter with excitement where they interconnect. It must have been one of these

Cézanne impersonations that Gorky showed Mischa Reznikoff when they first got together in New York. Reznikoff recalled: "I went to New York Public Library and here is Gorky, standing up there on the steps. I was small and he was very tall. He was wearing a Burberry coat down to his ankles." Gorky insisted that Reznikoff come immediately to his Sullivan Street studio. "Mischa," he said, "I painted an apple. The walls of the studio are bulging! I am afraid the studio is going to collapse! It's such a strong apple." The two painters made their way downtown to Gorky's studio, and Reznikoff was disappointed by Gorky's apple: "It's 16 by 20, a little canvas, an apple in the middle . . . It was well painted but it didn't bulge the walls of the studio or anything like that. It was his imagination, you see!"

The walls did not "bulge" because Gorky, trying too hard to find himself by seeing through Cézanne's eyes, made everything too perfect. Cézanne, on the other hand, had the genius to make a few elements seem just a little off or a little awkward and unfinished. A contemporaneous photograph shows Gorky in his studio painting one of his still life setups. Perhaps part of Gorky's problem was that he arranged the objects with such care that when it came time to paint them there was little room left for invention. Nevertheless, the Cézannesque still lifes are an impressive achievement: Gorky's ability to get the feel of European painting was extraordinary for a young painter in these years when most American modernism had a distinctly provincial character. It was especially extraordinary given the fact that Gorky had been exposed to European art for only five years.

As Gorky gained confidence during his three-year apprenticeship to Cézanne, his brushwork became looser and less systematic. Taking his cue from Cézanne's late watercolors, he often left much of the white canvas showing so that light seems to permeate his landscapes. *Still Life with Skull* (c. 1927–28) (Fig. 76), probably prompted by the reproduction of Cézanne's *Boy with a Skull* in Meier-Graefe's *Paul Cézanne*, has none of the ironic calm with which Cézanne approached the *vanitas* theme. Brushwork is agitated and the skull and crossbones seem to fight their way free of smothering fabric. After a year or so Gorky had entered so fully into Cézanne's head that he could speak the Frenchman's language while keeping the tenor of his own voice. *Still Life* (c. 1928) (Fig. 3) shows Gorky moving away from Cézanne in the direction of Cubism, which, according to then-popular formalist theories, was the next logical step in the history of art. Fruit, a jug, and a white tablecloth are painted in a more abstract and cursory manner than in earlier still lifes. The objects, especially the cloth, begin to take off and become animate, semiabstract shapes. Gorky opened the contour of a pear so that its color seems to drain out into the greenish blue ground. This example of Cézanne's *passage* predicts the way that in Gorky's subsequent still lifes objects meld into one another, thus flattening space.

In his self-portraits Gorky not only borrowed Cézanne's formal methods but also projected his identity onto that of his idol. His second *Self-Portrait* (c. 1926–27) (Fig. 68), for example, is modeled on Cézanne's self-portraits, probably *Self-Portrait with Beret* (c. 1900), reproduced in Meier-Graefe's book. As in the Cézanne, the loosely painted blue background seems to press in on the figure's contours. Also reminiscent of Cézanne is the way the firm black line that moves down Gorky's face and across his shoulder turns the negative space between figure and house into a positive shape.

If Gorky had presented himself as the masterly apprentice in the *Self-Portrait* he painted in Boston in 1924, he was now the artist "burdened by fate." As he said, his destiny was to suffer for art, and his burden was to catch up and fall in step with the flow of art history—a flow that he saw as a dialectical progress that culminated in Cézanne and then Cubism. But there was another aspect of his burden as well. In 1927, on one of his visits to his sisters in Watertown, he gave a talk at a fund-raising fair sponsored by a left-wing Armenian organization called Harachtimagan. The money the fair made was intended to aid Armenians in Soviet Armenia. Vartoosh remembered that in his speech her brother said: "The grief and suffering of the Armenian people has plowed a furrow across their brow." (In the Armenian idiomatic expression, *jagadakir* means destiny written on the forehead.) In his portrait Gorky has furrows between his eyebrows and there are indications of worry lines on his forehead. At twenty-six or twenty-seven, his *jagadakir* lay heavy upon him.

That weight was expressed also in a poem called "Thirst" that Gorky published in the November 1926 issue of the *Grand Central School of Art Quarterly.* In fact, the poem is not his own. It was written by the Armenian poet Siamanto, who in 1911 wrote a series of poems based on the 1909 massacre of the Armenian population at Adana. Just as Gorky borrowed other masters' painting styles, on several occasions he resorted to borrowing poems and writings by other people in order to express his own feelings. As a painter, the borrowings were a way of inventing himself by mastering the art of the past; his plagiarisms, on the other hand, were prompted by feelings of inadequacy. He wanted to present himself as a person who wrote poetry as well as painted, but his command of the English language was poor. "Thirst" is what Gorky would have said had he been able to write in English. The poem is full of the melancholy that, along with Gorky's enthusiasm and humor, many of his friends say was his salient trait:

> My soul listening to the death of
>   the twilight.
> Kneeling on the far-away soil of
>   suffering, my soul is drinking
>   the wounds of twilight and of
>   the ground; and within, it feels
>   the raining dawn of tears.
> And all the stars of slaughtered
>   lives, so like to eyes grown dim,
>   in the pools of my heart this
>   evening are dying of despair
>   and of waiting.
> And the ghost of all the dead to-
>   night will wait for the dawn
>   with mine eyes and my soul,
>   perhaps to satisfy their thirst
>   for life, a drop of light will fall
>   upon them from on high.

The "slaughtered lives" of Gorky's youth remained all the more central to his experience because they were unacknowledged.

In the 1926–27 *Self-Portrait* Gorky not only painted in the manner of Cézanne; he appeared to want to *be* Cézanne. This is true also of a third self-portrait, of around 1927, on the back of which he wrote: "Self-Portrait at the age of 9. 1913" (Fig. 69). It shows a wistful boy who is clearly European, not Armenian: it is as if Gorky's wish to join Western tradition made him reinvent his boyhood in terms of what he imagined Cézanne might have looked like as a child. Although he holds a small bouquet, the child bears no resemblance to the boy in the famous 1912 photograph of Gorky and his mother, which formed the basis of two versions of *The Artist and His Mother,* said to have been started at about this time (Figs. 4 and 5). Indeed, as Jim Jordan observes in his catalogue raisonné of Gorky's paintings, Gorky's *Self-Portrait at the Age of Nine* is modeled on Cézanne's *Louis Guillaume* (c. 1882). But in the Gorky the boy's head nearly fills the small canvas, so that the relationship of figure to viewer is more intimate. Cézanne's portrait is acerbic and cool. Gorky's is plaintive. It looks forward and back at the same time: into this sad, knowing youth, Gorky projected all his longing for his lost childhood and all his ambition for his future.

In his last Cézannesque *Self-Portrait* (c. 1928) (Fig. 70), Gorky found himself as a fiercely dedicated *poète maudit.* The contrast between Gorky here and in the 1926–27 self-portrait brings to mind the impression Gorky made in real life. As art critic Harold Rosenberg told it: "Gorky tried out a variety of roles in the social comedy of the Young Master: for a while he wore a coat with a fur collar and passed as a successful European portrait painter. At other times, he raised a huge beard and played the lone bohemian." In the 1928 *Self-Portrait* Gorky does not yet have a beard but he is definitely bohemian. He has put aside his jacket and tie. His shirt is open at the neck, his vest unbuttoned. Now he looks tougher, even a little belligerent, recalling the truculent expression that Cézanne occasionally gave himself in self-portraits. This is the Arshile Gorky whom some friends found arrogant and, as Rothko observed, "overcharged with supervision." He is the artist as spiritual leader, the man who pursues his ideals and is not seduced by commercial success. A real artist, Gorky said in his 1926 newspaper interview, "cares not what he sells any more than where he is. If a painting of mine suits me, it is right. If it does not please me, I care not if all the great masters should approve it or the dealers buy it. They would be wrong. How could there be anything fine in my painting unless I put it there and see it?"

By 1928, when he painted his fifth *Self-Portrait* (Fig. 71), Gorky had moved from Cézanne to Matisse and had raised a full but neatly trimmed beard. "I am painting myself, looking in a mirror," Gorky explained to a disapproving friend. "When I finish, it's going to be one of the best portraits in New York!" The portrait is modeled on Matisse's 1906 *Self-Portrait* (Fig. 72) in which the Frenchman sports a beard and wears a striped boatnecked fisherman's shirt. Only a few of the stripes are carried over into Gorky's self-portrait, and the colors he chose have nothing to do with French tradition. For Gorky, it must have been a happy coincidence that Matisse's hairline, receding in two backward loops, resembled his own. But, possibly because Matisse's face was not exotic or fierce enough to suit his purposes, Gorky overlaid Matisse's self-portrait with elements from self-portraits by Gauguin and Van Gogh. As in Gauguin's *Self-Portrait* of 1889, he twisted one of his eyes to a demonic angle. His glaring eyes express the uncompromising single-mindedness that he felt was the artist's prerogative, and they bring to mind an anecdote about Gorky's opening his studio door a crack when an acquaintance dropped by while he was working. "Are you mad?" Gorky snapped as he shut the door in the man's face. Gorky refused to be distracted. "He worked like a madman," Reznikoff said.

The wary, wounded, angry look that we see in Gorky's self-portraits may have something to do with thwarted love. In the second half of the 1920s Gorky fell in love with and wanted to marry a young woman called Nancy. Noting Gorky's poverty, her father put a stop to the relationship. All that we know about the liaison comes from Stergis's memory:

> Nancy was brunette, light brown hair. American girl. She was his sweetheart. They were very much in love. Her father was a retired captain on a big liner. She lived on Staten Island but her father wouldn't let her see him. It was quite a pathetic thing! Gorky never used to want her to be alone. That was his first love. She used to come and visit him, meet him in New York. We used to take her back to Staten Island, leave her a few blocks away from her home. . . . I have a portrait he didn't finish of her with a violin.

Having lost Nancy, and with his studio mate, Stergis, gone, Gorky was lonely and depressed. Perhaps it was around this time that Vartoosh turned up bringing her friend Shnorig Avedissian, who remembered: "It was winter. He had a scarf tied around his neck. His place was cold. When he opened the door he was quite yellow. We took him by surprise." Gorky's first reaction was anger: "Why did you come all the way here in this cold?" he asked Vartoosh. Shnorig kept her distance. "He was the kind of a person, you couldn't fool around," she recalled. He was too sick to paint and he had, in any case, run out of pigments. Vartoosh made her brother lie down on the dilapidated sofa, which consisted only of a wooden board covered with cloth. She rubbed liniment into Gorky's neck and cooked him a pot of *tanabour*, a soup of barley and vegetables thickened with yogurt. Not wanting to leave him alone, Vartoosh and Shnorig spent the night on his studio floor. When the color came back into his face, Shnorig dared to chat with Gorky about the strange art she saw on the walls. Looking perhaps at some reproduction or at one of his drawings that he had hung upside down in order to study its abstract qualities, she teased: "Gorky, did you put that up right? Is it upside down? What is it supposed to be?"

"*Toun inch kides?* What do you know? Keep quiet!"

"Gorky, this looks pretty good."

"If you want that, I'll give it to you."

"I don't want those crazy things. I wouldn't hang them in my bathroom!"

"My drawings will be valuable one day and you'll regret not taking it."

19

Teaching

𝄇

The Grand Central School of Art was divided into two camps, for and against Gorky. "There were, in fact, wars among the students over him," said Revington Arthur, who studied with Gorky for three years, starting about 1927. The students who persevered in his class were the ones who were attracted to modernism. "Gorky was always speaking about Cézanne, so we looked at the book by Meier-Graefe." Gorky also informed his students about Cubism, still considered a radical style in spite of having been introduced to New Yorkers in the 1913 Armory Show. He showed his students how Cubism came out of Cézanne and how Picasso and Braque, beginning around 1907, had changed the notion of space by replacing traditional perspective with a vision that fragmented the object as it approached it from all sides and within a duration of time.

Hans Burkhardt, who began to study with Gorky at Grand Central and continued to study with him privately in the 1930s, saw Gorky as a teacher who, though clearly devoted to modernism, did not impose any particular style. To allow a student to find his or her own language, Gorky would sometimes give no criticism for several weeks. "Why don't you help me?" Burkhardt once said to Gorky, and Gorky replied, "Look, I'll help you when you really need it. But I'll let you do it your own way first." Revington Arthur saw Gorky's undoctrinaire teaching in a different light: "He cared nothing at all about what you were doing. The way you learned was to follow him around and learn from what he did. That is absolutely the best teaching in the world . . . As it should be with any artist, Gorky's own work was absolutely the first and most important thing. The students were very secondary."

Gorky's students remember his theatrical presence: his lean, dark good looks and olive pallor, his moustache, and his long black hair flying as he strode from easel to easel. The first evening of Gorky's life-drawing class, he warned his students: "Don't think you are all going to be artists. Perhaps one out of 50,000 succeeds, so don't be disappointed if you don't." Gorky's passion was inspirational. As his student Max Schnitzler put it: "He threw himself all over. But he was a force, a power, a giant." He could be funny, too. Revington Arthur recalled Gorky's amusement with Cézanne's painting of a donkey rearing as it encounters a group of women sitting in the woods: "But Gorky wouldn't laugh. He had a very curious tooth formation . . . His teeth were spaced very far apart."

Gorky would bring records of Armenian music to class and ask his students to interpret the sounds visually. Once he invited a Hungarian violinist to come and play so that his students would put more feeling into their drawings. One pupil recalled that Gorky used to sing and dance Armenian dances. His physical grace and the pleasure he took in it flowed into his own paintings' rhythms, for his art was deeply connected to his sensations. Touch, Gorky believed, should come into play in painting. As he explained to Schnitzler: "Form, form, form must be touched."

When Revington Arthur joined Gorky's drawing and painting class it met five afternoons a week, and there were four or five students in attendance. "You signed up for a class like Gorky's for a week or two weeks, maybe a month. And if you liked it you stayed and if you didn't like it you left. Most people left." Herluf Svenningsen, who took Gorky's antique class in 1928, remembered about twenty students working from casts of antique sculptures. They met three nights a week, and tuition was fifteen to twenty-five dollars a month. Helen Austin was the only woman in a group of five or six Grand Central students who also worked with Gorky on weekends. Gorky called her "Sis," and after class he often joined her and her husband, Nathaniel, for dinner at Richard's, a basement restaurant off Fourth Street. Gorky was, she said, "ascetic, scrupulous, neat, naïve." Sometime around 1927 she acquired his *Self-Portrait at the Age of Nine,* and it was in that year that Gorky made a fine Cézannesque portrait of her that remained in her collection for decades. When she saw something in his studio that was, as she put it, "not tied down," she would ask if she could have it, and Gorky would pause and say, "Yeah, sure, Sis."

"In order to paint," Gorky advised, "you've got to draw more than ten years because painting is no more than drawing with paint." He would insist that his students make "skatch after skatch" so that the hand would learn to follow the promptings of the mind and eye. It should also follow the promptings of feeling. "The trouble nowadays," Gorky wrote to his niece Liberty in the 1930s, "is that the teacher will say to the children, 'I want you to draw a straight line.' But if you cannot draw a straight line, then draw a crooked line because that is what you know. . . . Draw whatever you feel. If you draw a horse which looks funny to others, that is all right because to you that is what the horse looks like." Similarly, Gorky told a private pupil, Ethel Schwabacher (who was Ethel Kramer until she married in 1935): "Paint what you love." He might also have advised her to paint what she imagined. Once when she and Gorky were drawing in Central Park, Gorky discovered the shape of a tomato in the foliage of a tree that Ethel was in the process of rendering, and he proceeded to add the suggestion of a tomato to Ethel's drawing. Another time she was painting a peacock and Gorky advised her to paint out the bird's head and tail, leaving only the body as an abstract shape. His mind traveled from object to analogy to metaphor, from shape to symbol to abstract form, and he wanted his student to have that kind of mental fluency.

Gorky did not want his students to draw in a tight or niggardly way. Once he reprimanded an overly careful pupil: "If you're going to stand around and look at that painting much longer, take a knife and slash it up!" The painter Walter Murch, who studied with Gorky at Grand Central until 1928 and after that took private lessons with him for about two years, said that Gorky prescribed a particular size of paper, about fourteen by eighteen inches. He made his class begin with a lead pencil and later move on to charcoal. Murch's first drawing was a highly realistic nude to which Gorky gave a pitying look. "Never more draw like that," he said. He told Murch not to use a pencil in such an academic way: the medium itself must be a vehicle for expression.

Gorky demonstrated his criticisms by making a separate drawing or by drawing on students' drawings. He would come over, take a pencil, and, Revington Arthur recalled, "in a few seconds would just show you how this thing was done." Ethel Schwabacher remembered Gorky setting up still lifes for her to draw: "I would draw, and then he would draw over it, and say, 'Well don't you see, it might be this way or that way.' And then, he was a very wonderful-looking person, very tall, about six foot four, and had very dark eyes, and very romantic and beautiful, and he would say, 'Permit me,' and he would lean over, and 'Permit me' meant, Would you let him draw on your work. And so of course my attitude was that this would be a marvelous way to learn." Gorky's verbal instructions were usually cryptic: he said, "It goes this way. . . . it comes that way, it goes in, it comes out." Sometimes, Schwabacher recalled, after the "Permit me," Gorky would take Ethel's brush and "paint the whole painting." Once when Gorky finished a small still life that Ethel had begun, he insisted on saying it was hers. She knew it wasn't, but "the result of it was that I was able to see how his mind worked on various problems."

Not all of Gorky's students were so malleable. The abstract painter Alice Trumbull Mason remembered Gorky coming up to the woman whose easel flanked hers, looking at the highly conventional painting on the woman's easel, and sweeping the brush out of her hand in order to paint a fish on top of her figure's head. The result was a storm of tears. Mina Metzger, who from 1934 to 1935 shared private lessons with Ethel Schwabacher three afternoons a week from one to four, earned from Gorky the nickname of "Maestro" because she would not let Gorky touch her work. "So he would tell her how to make a little more black, a little more white, a little more red, and put it on with this kind of a stroke," Schwabacher recalled. "He would practically do it, but only using words. And then at times he . . . would say, 'Ethel, mix a color for me to put on my painting.' He would paint in the same room, and we would all work together."

Gorky emphasized relationships of line and shape. Modeling was unimportant—indeed, detrimental. When Mischa Reznikoff studied one of Gorky's portraits, Gorky advised him to look not at the figure but at the loosely painted background—presumably this was a way to focus on form rather than subject matter. And he advised Raphael Soyer to remove the highlight from the hair in a portrait Soyer was making of Gorky. "You know, this disturbs the painting," Gorky said. "If you just make the shape of the hair and omit the shine, not try to make the texture of the hair but rather give its shape and color, it will then play a stronger part in the picture." Besides giving verbal advice and drawing on his students' drawings to illustrate his ideas, Gorky also taught by example. In 1926 he took a palette knife and a twenty-by-twelve-inch canvas and in three hours painted a still life of fruit and a vase of tulips as part of a classroom demonstration. Shortly thereafter it was purchased for a hundred dollars by the tobacco merchant Nathan I. Bijur, a student and patron who frequently included Gorky in his family lunches.

"Look to nature," Gorky said. "Everything you need is there." But artists were to look at nature selectively: he told Hans Burkhardt to look at a small part of an object and use it as a stimulus to creation. When he took his students on drawing outings to Central Park, to the Bronx, and to the Manhattan docks, Gorky would scrutinize a potential motif and, with a wave of his hand in the direction of a cluster of trees or rocks, he would exclaim: "All wrong!" meaning that nature itself could be badly composed. He and the students sometimes took the ferry to Staten Island and set up their easels in the meadows. A series of snapshots taken by his student Nathan Graber shows Gorky "horsing around" with his class on a grassy hill (p. 125). He leapfrogs high over one young man's shoulders, fiddles with a pretty female student's hair, and mugs for the camera wearing an inside-out jacket and a broad-brimmed felt hat. These are among the rare photographs taken of Gorky smiling and looking happy.

Mina Metzger recollected her first meeting with Gorky in 1929 or 1930. She was visiting the Grand Central School of Art when "there came into the room a tall, dark, much bearded and melancholy but alive-looking young man . . . One of the first things I heard [him say] was 'everything is in space.'" He also said that color cannot make a bad drawing good: "Color does not count, you may use any color—drawing is everything." But it was what Gorky said about the masters of the past that taught Mina Metzger the most. "He seemed to know not only about how they constructed their paintings, but what lived in their very souls. . . . While working he would suddenly stop and say: 'Come, let us get some inspiration,' and he would pick up some book with reproductions of paintings which some great master left to us and create again what thought and heart had gone into these."

Often, after working in his studio for several hours with Schwabacher and Metzger, Gorky would take them to a museum, usually the Metropolitan. He also took students to the Museum of Modern Art after it opened in November 1929 and to the Frick, which opened to the public in 1935. No doubt he accompanied them to the Gallatin Collection as well. At the Metropolitan or the Frick, Gorky would demonstrate how an abstract composition lay beneath the arrangement of figures and objects. To find the abstraction within realism he would focus on small details such as the folds in drapery, the curve of a neck, or the shapes of fingers. Sometimes he would make a telescope with his hands to see a part instead of the whole or to separate an object from its context. In her 1957 monograph on Gorky, Schwabacher wrote that Gorky was best at clarifying his ideas when standing directly in front of a painting in a museum. Once, for example, when she was working on a flower still life, Gorky suggested that they go to the Metropolitan to look at an Oriental carpet in a Vermeer. "Some days later," Schwabacher said, "I met him accidentally in front of this very painting. He was standing there, intent, solitary, sad . . . There was tenderness, cruelty and eagerness in his glance; he was communicative rather than responsive." Almost without pausing to say hello, Gorky turned to the Vermeer and pointed out the leaf design in the rug, a detail that occupied only a few inches of the painting. As they moved through the galleries, Gorky swooped down on paintings "like some great bird" of prey. As he stood close to a canvas, "his hand moved forward with an instinctive gesture as if he held a brush and was about to continue work." He did not talk like an art historian. "He would say 'beautiful' or something like that," Schwabacher recalled. "Or one time he said to me, 'Well, Ingres distorts more than Picasso.' " His words were not what mattered most. "It was where he stopped, in front of what." Often Gorky had his students study paintings by drawing them. "And he would expect the drawing to convey the weight and solemnity of the original painting." In the hall of medieval armor Gorky exclaimed, "What shapes!" and began to draw. When he was satisfied, they continued on to look at Coptic embroideries. "Better than Matisse," Gorky pronounced. Before they left, he bought postcards to use in those moments when he needed, in his words, "to get some inspiration."

As he gained experience, Gorky attracted increasing numbers of private pupils, who came to his studio in the afternoons or on weekends. After he stopped teaching at the Grand Central School in 1931, these private classes were his chief source of income. When Mina Metzger came to discuss studying with Gorky in the early 1930s and asked how much it would cost, he replied: "I don't think you can afford it." She inquired again, and this time Gorky said ten dollars. She agreed to pay that amount, but when she left and Gorky looked out his window and saw her Daimler waiting by the curb, he wished he had asked for more.

Recognizing his poverty, as well as the aesthetic value of his work, some students bought his paintings. But Gorky frequently gave things away. Hans Burkhardt recalled: "One day I arrived there and there was a big pile of Gorky's paintings lying in the hallway. He tore them all up. You could have picked up most of his early works—they were just lying around." Once Burkhardt came in time to rescue some of them and Gorky was pleased to see that his student appreciated his work. "He was extremely poor, often going without food to buy a brush or a tube of paint. Many times he would offer me a beautiful painting for ten or twenty dollars, so that he might have money for his rent. And often I would bring in sacks of food and put them in the kitchen without a word. I know he appreciated it, but his pride kept him from ever saying anything about it."

Gorky was fond of his students and they doted on him, but, like many other artists, he found teaching draining and he resented the time it took away from painting. The painter Saul Schary, who first met Gorky when he came to Schary's exhibition opening in 1927, recalled that occasionally Gorky's private students would be late in paying for their classes or would buy a picture and then forget to pay the monthly installments. "They'd bother the hell out of him and take up his time in the studio and then not pay him even though they were wealthy."

In the 1940s, Gorky used to return from an occasional afternoon of escorting Ethel Schwabacher and Mina Metzger to the Metropolitan Museum in a state of high indignation. He would tell his wife how he had made some observation about a painting and one of the women had told him that he had said something quite different about it the week before. "Why are you trying to sell me back my own words?" he would answer with a snort. Nor did he like it when Mina and Ethel tried to make sense of what he was saying. What was important in both his visual and his verbal communications was the poetry and flux, not fixed or literal meaning. For all his exasperation, teaching helped sharpen Gorky's perceptions and shape his philosophy of art. Moreover, it gave him a position and prestige—he was fulfilling his mother's hopes for his career.

20

The Artist and His Mother

※

Gorky's two versions of *The Artist and His Mother* are thought to have been begun around 1926, the year he became a member of the Grand Central School of Art's faculty and came under the influence of Cézanne. Painter Saul Schary, however, said that he saw Gorky start one of the two versions around 1933 or 1934. Both canvases are sixty by fifty inches, large by the standard of Gorky's early work. The version in the National Gallery of Art in Washington is less resolved in terms of the arrangement of the figures in space and thus appears to be the earliest conception. But it was finished last. Gorky still worked on it occasionally in the early 1940s. A November 1942 letter from his wife to her mother said: "He is working like mad making new studies of the portrait of himself and his mother." The other painting, now in the Whitney Museum of American Art, is one of Gorky's best-known and most-loved works. It is signed and dated "A. Gorky/26–29." Probably it was finished around 1936. More than any of his other works, these two self-portraits of Gorky as a boy standing beside his mother tap all the artist's reservoir of sorrow.

If Gorky really began these double portraits in 1926, he must have scraped away and overpainted most of what he first did. While there is, in the image of Gorky's mother, something of the hauteur and the remoteness of Cézanne's portraits of Mme Cézanne, and although Shushan's face is simplified into a Cézannesque oval, this pair of portraits belongs less to Gorky's Cézanne-inspired period of 1926–28 than to the 1930s, when Gorky became obsessed with the precise contours of Ingres and when Picasso was his hero. The pencil drawing on which the National

Gallery version is based is dated 1934 and shows a brilliant assimilation of Picasso's Ingres-inspired drawings from around 1920. Whatever their dates, both versions of *The Artist and His Mother* evolved over many years. It is as if painting, scraping, repainting these canvases was Gorky's way of holding his mother in his memory and coming to terms with her loss.

Both portraits are based on the 1912 photograph of Gorky and his mother taken in Van and sent to Gorky's father in America (Fig. 47). Willem de Kooning remembered Gorky's attachment to this image: "It was kind of painful to him. There was something sad about it, as if he didn't make it or something." No doubt the photograph gave Gorky both comfort and pain: the comfort of remembering his mother's love and the pain of having failed to keep her from starvation. Sedrak Adoian must have given the photograph to Akabi, for it hung in her house next to the 1910 photograph of Sedrak seated in a carved wooden chair. When he decided to paint his mother's portrait, Gorky asked Akabi if he could borrow the photograph. "That's the only picture I have of Mother. I don't want to lose it," Akabi said, and Gorky promised to return it. Now that he was launched on his career, he could remedy his father's desertion and pay his mother the tribute she deserved.

In these two double portraits Shushan Adoian looks more dead than alive. Floating within the dark contours formed by her shawl, her head seems to have no solid substance. Especially in the National Gallery version, her face has been scraped away so many times that it appears evanescent—it is as if she were fading out of the picture. Mother and child belong to different spheres. She resides in a spirit land; he belongs to the world of the living. Compared with her smooth, dematerialized face, the rest of the painting is full of vigorous strokes that suggest the artist's immediate presence.

As in all of his other portraits, Gorky gave great emphasis to the eyes. Plaintive yet fatalistic, the eyes of both mother and son bore into us with an immense sadness. Shushan's grief brings to mind popular prints of the traditional personification of Armenia—a woman sitting weeping amid the ruins of the medieval Armenian city of Ani. The historian Richard G. Hovannisian describes this Armenian feeling of loss when he writes that, for decades after the massacres and deportations, Armenian poets "could speak of nothing but the longing for a home, a mother, and some love. In the 1930s to be an Armenian orphan in Fresno, in Paris, in Bourju-Hammoud meant to be an outcast from world and nation." Gorky's portraits speak of this longing. The eyes of both mother and son are orphaned eyes, eyes too deadened with suffering to ask for help. Once directed through the photographer's lens to the abandoning husband and father, their gazes seem to ask us to bear witness to the anguish of an entire people.

In the photograph mother and son pose in front of a painted architectural backdrop set up in the photographer's studio. The fact that the backdrop was a fiction accounts in part for the ambiguous, dreamlike relationship of the figures to space. The window in the architectural backdrop was simply a dark rectangle. Gorky gave the window more emphasis: it is blood red in the Washington portrait and in the Whitney's portrait it is a bleak khaki gray. In both portraits Gorky widened the window so that it both separates and joins him and his mother. It also sets off his mother's pale face like a cloth of honor in a Flemish Renaissance painting of the Virgin. Certainly the enlarged window improves the composition, and Gorky clearly appreciated the spatial tensions created by the discontinuous line of the windowsill. As in a Cézanne still life in which the line that defines the edge of a tabletop changes level after it disappears behind some object like a jug, so in Gorky's two double portraits the line that defines the sill is higher to the right of his mother's head than it is to the left. The window's apparent lack of transparency makes it seem as blank and flat as Shushan's eyes, which are open yet unseeing, like the depthless eyes of the dead. Gorky's window is the opposite of the open windows seen so often in Matisse's paintings: Matisse let inside and outside join; the space in Gorky's *The Artist and His Mother* portrays a closed, sepulchral world.

Although the two portraits invoke a whole tradition of Mary imagery, the closest parallel is the relief of the Virgin and Child carved on the outside of the Church of the Holy Cross at Akhtamar (Fig. 46). In both the sculpture and the double portraits the woman's hieratic frontality gives her a regal presence. The way the Virgin's veil is attached to her collar in the relief is similar to the way Gorky's mother's shawl meets the collar of her apron. At Akhtamar the Madonna's delicately carved lips create a slightly off-center black shadow very like the shadow between Shushan's lips in the Whitney painting. In the relief the large dark circles drilled into the stone to stand for both pupil and iris may have been the source for Gorky's way of combining pupil and iris into one dark orb. The eyes in Gorky's portraits are penetrating but they are also like holes.

In the 1912 photograph (and in the squared-up drawing), Shushan wears a flower-print cotton apron—the apron that years later he would mistakenly describe as embroidered when he told his dealer about lying with his face in his mother's lap while she told him stories. In the pair of portraits, Gorky eliminated the flowers. They would not have suited Shushan's enthroned Madonna pose, and they would have given this ghostly image too worldly a specificity. The white apron also suggests her purity: the name Shushan means lily, which, in turn, connotes the Madonna's unblemished virginity. Gorky also made his mother's apron longer so that it is cut off by the canvas's lower edge. As a result, she looms up before us, a ghost rising to the mind's surface from the dark well of memory. Shushan ascends like the Queen of Heaven, timeless and absolute as an icon. Gorky bearing his gift of flowers is the humble adorer, or perhaps his mother's protective angel.

It is not surprising that references to Christian iconography should appear in Gorky's art. Though he was not a believer, his devout mother made sure he had a religious upbringing. Moreover, the only paintings he saw as a child were Bible illustrations and wall paintings in churches. Gorky's only known outright religious image is a lost *Deposition* (c. 1929) reproduced in the Grand Central School's 1930 catalog. Although it is Cézannesque in style, the arrangement of Christ and the three Marys appears to be taken from a fifteenth- or sixteenth-century source. He may have produced a few other paintings of Christian scenes. "The very first painting I ever saw by Gorky could have been in the Renaissance," Revington Arthur recalled. It was "a head framed by a door looking out over a landscape . . . And then there was one of a crucifixion."

Saul Schary said that when he observed Gorky beginning what was probably the National Gallery version of *The Artist and His Mother*, Gorky laid in the figure of the mother and then struggled with the placement of the figure of himself. He got the head right, but the feet were cut off by the bottom of the canvas. When he started by laying in the feet, the head went out of the top. Finally Schary blocked in the figure so that both ends fit. It is certainly true that the spatial relationships are odd: Gorky seems to be both beside and behind his mother, and his head is enormous in proportion to his body. It is as if Gorky exaggerated the distortion that resulted from the photographer's slightly elevated vantage point. Yet, given the fact that the drawing for the National Gallery version is expertly overlaid with a numbered grid so that the image could be transferred to canvas, Schary's story seems exaggerated. The omission of Shushan's feet in both the drawing and the paintings is not the result of Gorky's supposed inability to fit them in: they are missing because he wanted his mother to seem to rise up into the canvas like an apparition.

All dressed up in a double-breasted chesterfield coat, Gorky dutifully takes his father's place at his mother's side, but their relationship is stiff. In the photograph, the drawing, and the National Gallery painting, his feet point forward. By contrast, in the more refined, psychologically complex Whitney version Gorky's feet point away from his mother, as if he would, if he could, walk away. For all his resistance, Gorky's head inclines slightly in his mother's direction, ever close but always separate and thus condemned to yearning. Shrinking from contact with his mother, the boy holds his arm tight against his body; his hand is partially clenched. All the tension that this twelve-year-old boy feels about physical intimacy with his mother is expressed in the attraction and repulsion of folds. Where her sleeve swells out in his direction, Gorky's sleeve contracts and becomes concave. The place where the mother's and son's sleeves touch (in the National Gallery version) or pull apart (in the Whitney version) is, in its own way, as charged as the famous space between God's and Adam's hands in Michelangelo's Sistine Chapel ceiling. In the Whitney's *The Artist and His Mother*, a channel of space separates mother and son, and, because Gorky made the gray that fills this space into a positive shape in itself, the separateness is all the more emphatic. The feeling of separation that resonates in the gray space between mother and son would continue to reverberate in late abstract paintings such as *The Limit* (1947) (Fig. 173), in which a gray expanse evokes immense spaces that are both empty and full of longing.

The reds, pinks, and oranges in the National Gallery's *The Artist and His Mother* are replaced in the Whitney version by pale, moonlight colors. White as a shroud, Gorky's mother's apron is traversed by a patch of swift pink strokes—similarly in the National Gallery's portrait Shushan's lap is covered with reddish pink strokes. It is as if this area were particularly alive for Gorky, as if he were reliving the warmth of pressing his cheek into his mother's apron. The Whitney painting's several tones of gray may record the tones of the black-and-white photograph that served as model. But the grays are also like the colors of memory worn thin by the passage of time. Flattened, abstracted shapes that anticipate the biomorphic forms in Gorky's later paintings float to the surface, making mother and son seem disembodied—again like memories.

The surfaces of both versions of *The Artist and His Mother* show signs of endless reworking. Some parts are scraped porcelain-smooth so that no brush strokes are visible. Other sections, those painted last—possibly even overpainted in the 1940s—are loosely brushed or scumbled. Over a period of several years, Saul Schary watched Gorky put on layer after layer of pigment with soft sable or camel brushes, then scrape the canvas down with a razor to get a "fine egg-shell finish." Gorky himself was "scrupulously clean and tidy," Schary observed, and he scrubbed the oak floor of his studio every week until it was white. Indeed, Gorky had an acute sensitivity to the quality of surfaces. The sculptor Isamu Noguchi, who met Gorky in 1936 and became a close friend, recalled: "He was a perfectionist certainly, and that's the reason he was a great painter . . . He was always scrubbing his floor. He felt that scrubbing his floor was a very important part of his meditation, a part of a preparation of painting, that he had to go through this ceremony before he could paint, and so everything had to be ship-shape."

After he scraped his canvas he would hold it over the bathtub and wipe off the paint flecks with a damp rag. Then he would paint—very often the same colors that had been there before—then scrape and sand over and over again. The many-layered surface gained depth and richness: "The surface of the paint was beautiful," said de Kooning. "It's like metaphysical. The idea of the surface—it's like a place. Like the surface of Vermeer. You are living someplace."

Gorky's smooth surfaces were an homage to Ingres, whose youthful self-portrait hung in reproduction in his studio as a standard against which to measure his own work. Friends recall that the book in his pocket was often a book about Ingres, and if you ran into him he would take it out and expound on Ingres's genius. His ambition was to learn to draw like Ingres. When the abstract painter Vaclav Vytlacil asked why as an abstractionist he kept making these Ingres-like drawings, he came back with, "Just in case! In case the art market drops!" He loved to visit Ingres's paintings in the Metropolitan, and when Ingres's portrait of Mme d'Haussonville was purchased in 1927 by the Frick Collection, Gorky was enthralled. He also loved the immaculate chilliness of portraits by the Italian Mannerist Bronzino, several of whose portraits were represented in his collection of reproductions. He owned reproductions of portraits by John Singleton Copley as well: clearly Gorky was attracted to paintings in which the contours are so fearfully precise that the forms they define become flat and rise to the picture surface like elements in an abstraction. Gorky's delight in flat shapes that seem to detach from the larger shapes of which they form a part recalls also his love of Paolo Uccello, especially of Uccello's *Rout of San Romano* (in London's National Gallery), a reproduction of which hung on his wall. Other prints in his collection are of Renaissance portraits and Madonnas, and there are as well numerous works by his chosen modernist heroes—Cézanne, Matisse, Picasso, Braque, and Miró.

One of his Picasso reproductions was a 1906 *Self-Portrait* that Gorky knew firsthand from his frequent visits to the Gallatin Collection (Fig. 6). This youthful image of Picasso was key to Gorky's transformation of the boy he saw in the 1912 photograph. Picasso's huge, dark Iberian eyes, his looping hairline and overlarge ear, the intentionally stiff position of the arms, and the clumsy, fistlike right hand are all echoed in the depiction of Gorky in *The Artist and His Mother.*

One final source for the pair of double portraits was Fayum mummy portraits. Gorky loved these late Egyptian portraits of the dead, which were placed on the outside of cloth-wrapped mummies, and he owned a reproduction of the Metropolitan Museum's Fayum portrait of a young man with curly black hair and huge dark eyes. Like such a portrait, Gorky's mother's face has a peculiar mixture of intensity and deathly withdrawal. In his 1936 essay about his Newark Airport murals, Gorky said the Fayum portrait painters "operated upon the dead so that the dead might live forever—never to die!" He painted his mother to give her life after death.

21

Portrait of Myself and
My Imaginary Wife

✼

Around 1927 Gorky fell in love with Blanche Becker, one of his students at the Grand Central School of Art. Like most of Gorky's other girl-friends, she was beautiful (she modeled for Lord and Taylor department store); she was a decade younger than he was, and, as the daughter of Orthodox Russian Jewish immigrants who lived in Woodbine, New Jersey, she came from a very different background. With her long, wavy brown hair, pale blue eyes, and sensuous lips, Blanche was, her daughter Alma Perry says, "half Rita Hayworth and half Tallulah Bankhead." Gorky asked Blanche to marry him, but, says Alma, although "she was enthralled by Gorky and wanted to marry him, she felt he was dangerous. She was a shy person, but she was a real flapper. She said Gorky was too passionate, and then my father who was a photographer entered the picture, and Gorky threatened to have my father killed if he pursued my mother. My mother picked my father instead of Gorky because Gorky frightened her with his wild emotions. But Gorky was her real love. He remained the ghost in the family."

Gorky gave Blanche Becker several paintings. One was a small Cézannesque still life of a ginger pot and fruit. Another was a kind of joint effort like the still life he made with Ethel Schwabacher. "My mother painted, and Gorky came and painted over her shoulder." Blanche also posed nude for him. Sometime in the 1930s, when their relationship was over, her brother burned the drawings Gorky had given her because he thought they were indecent.

One evening in 1929 as Gorky and Mischa Reznikoff were preparing to leave the Grand Central School of Art, Gorky passed the door of the life-drawing studio and noticed a young model with delicate features—a high forehead, narrow nostrils, full, vulnerable-looking lips, and a strong chin and jawline very like his mother's. Also like Shushan was the hint of melancholy about her large brown eyes. The model's real name was Sirun Mussikian—Sirun means beautiful in Armenian—but she called herself Ruth March French. Sirun also modeled at the National Academy of Design and the Art Students League, and it was at the latter institution that painter Mercedes Carles (later Mercedes Matter) spotted Sirun and Gorky together: "Gorky used to come and sit in the league's cafeteria and talk and argue. Maybe he came there because he was having a love affair with a model. The model was beautiful with dark hair, a slender figure."

Joseph Solman, a student at the National Academy from 1926 to 1929, remembers seeing Gorky, whom he had not yet met, waiting for Sirun to come downstairs after finishing her modeling session. "He waited downstairs in the academy's dark hallway. Sometimes he stood under a profile portrait of Claude Monet by Sargent. Gorky put his collar up and his moustache drooped down to his chin—he had such a dramatic effect. The students knew he was waiting for the model. She had dark hair and high cheekbones. All the students in the life class thought she was such a beautiful girl, and naturally there was a magical aura about her because she was reading *My Life* by Isadora Duncan." Sirun had a look that particularly appealed to Gorky: "He kept describing her as 'the wild horse,'" Stuart Davis's wife, Roselle, remembered. She called him a "Beverly Hills Rasputin."

At his first encounter with Sirun, Gorky took note of her high-bred energy, and he set out to tame it. With the confidence of a popular teacher with whom many of the female students were infatuated, he walked into the Grand Central School of Art life class, stopped at a student's easel, and pronounced, "Here you have a beautiful white Arabian horse! And you make a mess of dirty socks." When class was over, Sirun thanked Gorky for the compliment. "Oh that's nothing," said Gorky. He invited her to have a cup of coffee and to join him and Mischa Reznikoff and Reznikoff's girlfriend for dinner the following night. Sirun recalled their first meeting: "He saw me from the doorway. He came up to me. I was on my way home. When he learned that I was Armenian and had been born in Van, it was crazy, as though he was absolutely possessed . . .

It was like the sun had risen after a million years. I was good-looking and quite shy. I fulfilled everything he wanted in a woman."

Sirun was nineteen when she met Gorky. He was probably twenty-eight or -nine. Having immigrated to the United States with her family in 1914 at the age of four, she escaped the siege of Van City and the massacres of 1915. Her childhood was miserable, nonetheless. When her parents divorced, her mother left Sirun and her sister with their insane and abusive father, who, when Sirun was twelve, tried to kill her: "I was sitting on a twin bed opposite him," Sirun recalled. "He shot me and I got up and he shot me again! He said that life was so awful that he really wanted me to have no part of it."

According to Mischa Reznikoff's story, early in their courtship Sirun surprised the innocent and puritanical Gorky by inviting herself to his studio and then, at the end of the evening, telling him that it was too late for her to go home. "Why don't you just stay over here?" said Gorky, who was used to having Vartoosh spend the night. "You sleep on the bed and I'll stay on the rocking chair." The same thing happened the next night—he offered her his bed without him in it. Sirun was perplexed: "Why would I go to a man's studio if I was not going to spend the night with him?" That second night she must have been more forward, but her advances were repulsed. At three in the morning Mischa Reznikoff heard a knock on his door. He opened the door to find a distraught Gorky "looking like Jesus Christ." "Mischa, I'm in love with this girl, Ruth. She asked me to come to bed with her." After a pause Gorky said, "I bit her!"

Gorky clearly needed counseling. "Look here, Gorky," said Mischa, "some girls like to be treated rough and some like to be treated very gentle, delicate-like." Gorky looked miserable, but when he noticed Reznikoff's drawing pad on the table, his eyes lit up: "Well, draw some positions," he said. Mischa drew and explained various sexual postures while Gorky watched in silent fascination. Suddenly he pointed to a thigh in one of the drawings of entwined couples and said, "Pardon me, Mischa, but that line is not very well constructed." With this, Mischa told Gorky to go home.

During the last months of 1929 and the first few months of 1930, Sirun (or Ruth, as Gorky called her) lived with Gorky. Now their principal problem was poverty. When the Depression hit in October 1929 and people stopped buying paintings, Gorky became increasingly anxious.

"He'd get moody at times and he'd worry about money and then he'd worry about selling his work," said Sirun. Sometime in 1931 he stopped teaching at Grand Central, apparently because enrollment had dropped. He still had his private students. When they came to his studio Gorky would insist that Sirun hide in the bedroom. Once when Gorky went out on an errand, an inquisitive student peeked into his bedroom and was shocked to find a woman lying on the master's bed. Though Gorky disapproved, Sirun continued to model for a dollar an hour. With the money she earned, she bought their groceries. Gorky paid the monthly rent of seventy-five dollars. Even with a fire in the cast-iron wood stove, the studio was cold. Their small bedroom was "miserable," Sirun said, but Gorky didn't care. "He didn't even see it, didn't even feel it. Nothing affected him. I don't think he even knew what he ate. Perhaps if he was eating Armenian food he'd know if it was good. But otherwise, he didn't know if something was crappy or not." When he was still teaching at Grand Central, Gorky earned two hundred dollars a month, but he spent half of it on art supplies. Sirun recalled his profligacy: "He used to squeeze the stuff out of the tube by the mile! Nothing was going to make him stop. Nothing! He bought all colors. He talked a lot about ochre; yellow ochre was a favorite. He used them all. Sometimes straight and put them on just with a palette knife as thick as can be, and other times, he was very delicate. He could no more have not painted than he could have stopped breathing."

To make ends meet, Gorky worked harder than ever. "He was always at that easel. We never had any fun. He often would paint at night," Sirun recalled. Gorky's total focus on his work left little room for a full relationship with a woman: "He had no sense of another person. He didn't want to take the time." He did try to educate Sirun about art, informing her about Cézanne's dictum that nature could be reduced to the cylinder, the sphere, and the cube. "He explained everything to me about his work . . . He really did want to share." He also talked to Sirun about his childhood and about his mother. "He talked about her gentleness—a wonderful mother image. He really appreciated her. He loved her. I think probably every woman that he painted looked like his mother."

Gorky and Sirun rose early, and she went to work while he painted. In the late afternoon or evening, they took long walks and, if Gorky's work was finished for the day, they often joined Stuart and Roselle Davis at an Armenian restaurant. They retired at eleven or twelve. Gorky was habitually tired, Sirun said, and his frequent despondency was difficult for her to cope with. "His life was certainly a struggle," she observed, remembering that Gorky liked to quote one of his Russian idols, either Lenin or Maxim Gorky, saying "Life is a struggle."

Although Sirun said Gorky did not demand it of her, she felt like his servant: "I washed his brushes . . . It was a big thing, a routine. . . . There wasn't much housework." Sirun also served Gorky as model. She lay on a roll-up daybed with her head propped on two pillows. Sometimes she modeled for his students, such as Nathan Bijur, as well. "I posed for both of them, and Gorky was painting a huge nude. He also did a beautiful head of me . . . I sat for twenty-five minutes, then rested for five." But Gorky would tease her, quoting from Cézanne: "Women should be like cabbages. When they sit still they should not move." Gorky's large *Reclining Nude* (1929) (Fig. 81) shows a woman who must be Sirun posing with her arms folded behind her head and one hip thrust up in the fertility goddess posture taken by many of Matisse's odalisques. But Gorky was more prudish than the Frenchman. He brought Sirun's bent upper leg down so that her thigh hides her sex. Years later Sirun told Gorky scholar Melvin Lader that when Gorky painted her nude he based his composition on Velázquez. If that is true, then Gorky reinterpreted Velázquez's *Rokbey Venus* through the eyes of Matisse. Gorky's *Portrait of a Woman* (c.1928), based on Matisse's glum portrait of his mistress and model Henriette in *Woman with a Veil* (1927), must be the portrait of Sirun that she called a "beautiful head."

Besides lack of money and Gorky's single-minded passion for painting, problems arose in Gorky and Sirun's relationship from his insistence that the women he loved adapt to his ideal. Roselle Davis recalled that Gorky put Sirun "on a pedestal and she didn't care very much about being on a pedestal. She wanted to be treated as a woman. . . . It just seemed that his love for this girl was not so much his love of her as a human being as it was love of her image, her physical image, and so there were constantly conflicts between them." Gorky always chose women of extreme beauty, but he did not want real closeness with them. Perhaps because Armenian village families slept in one room, the overt expression of sexual feeling was repressed, and even displays of physical affection between mother and child were frowned on. Sirun said: "In a woman he wanted something pleasant to look at like a statue but never to interfere in his mind or soul. Someone he could take sustenance from or worship but never give and take. Never. Never!" This projection of an image onto a woman brings to mind something that Gorky's second wife, Agnes Magruder (known as Mougouch after she married Gorky), noted about Gorky's friendship with the Surrealist André Breton. Gorky, she wrote in a letter to a friend, related to Breton as *"the poet,* in the huge beautiful god-like sense of that word. All of Gorky's relationships were like this, when I knew him anyway—Woman, Friend, Patron, Dealer, Poet—they were the primitive, archetypal symbols. That was the difficulty, and an increasingly frightening one to cope with: after a time other people's personalities and necessities would obtrude, and would annoy and distress him."

Gorky told Yenovk Der Hagopian that Sirun was the only woman besides his mother who met his ideal. Like his mother, he said, Sirun descended from a family of Vanetzi priests. Given Gorky's way of distancing women by idealizing them, and given the high standards he imposed on women—standards set by his veneration of his mother—it is not surprising that Gorky had sexual inhibitions. He was inexperienced, insecure, and modest. He was also squeamish: the more earthy and visceral aspects of women's sexuality did not appeal to him. When his sexual performance worried him he would seek Stuart Davis's advice. But no lessons in "technique" could make Sirun happy. She remembered:

> You know, sex wasn't even particularly important to Gorky. I never felt that it was. It was all in his head. It was all romanticism . . . Something no woman probably ever told you about him was that he said making love to a woman was as much as working an eight-hour day. You can imagine how that made a woman feel! You thought that at the back of his mind, even while having intercourse, he was thinking, "Oh my goodness, all my strength is going! I should save it up for painting." I never forgot that. It was so odd that he would equate this marvelous love expression with a hard day's work.

Another of Gorky and Sirun's problems was that he wanted her to be Armenian, whereas, having had an unhappy childhood, she wanted to forget her Armenian past and be completely American. He tried to teach her Armenian and he took her to Armenian movies, but he was disappointed when she was less moved by the loss of their homeland than he was. "He didn't want any part of my American life . . . I have never known anyone more Armenian than Gorky," she said. "He was very conscious of the past, their marvelous quality, their martyrdom . . . He loved the look of the Armenian people. He loved their eyes. 'There's real soul there!' You can't bear to look at a white person after you've looked at a black person . . . He loved New York, but he thought America was vulgar. Everything was vulgar to Gorky. That was his favorite word. He really was living in Armenia in Greenwich Village."

Sirun wondered why such a passionate Armenian had changed his name. Gorky told her that when he was a boy he had met Maxim Gorky and that Gorky had given him his name. She knew that was a lie. His motive for pretending to be Russian, she said, was opportunism. "He felt he could get where he wanted to go being a Russian. Russian was very fashionable then."

Having found an Armenian sweetheart, he was eager to show her off to his family, but not to his father, whose existence he kept secret from her. In 1929 he took Sirun to visit Hagop Adoian's farm in Norwood, Rhode Island. His niece Lucille remembered that "they slept in our room. He took her everywhere, gallivanting, during the day and stayed almost a week." When Gorky and Sirun visited Akabi in the summer of 1930, they shocked his oldest sister by sleeping without clothes. "They were very lovey-dovey," Akabi's daughter Liberty recalls. "Gorky was holding her hand, squeezing her, and giggling like someone really in love." In Watertown Gorky painted during the day. At night, during family gatherings, there was much arguing over politics. Vartoosh and Moorad were vehement Communists; Akabi and Satenik and their husbands were not. "His relatives, they scrapped and screamed about politics," Sirun recalled. "He really didn't have that much interest."

A 1930 photograph taken in Vartoosh and Moorad Mooradian's backyard on Templeton Parkway in Watertown shows Gorky with his arms around both his sister and his girlfriend (Fig. 80). Fine-featured and not as recognizably Armenian as either of her companions, Sirun smiles at the camera. But she looks less comfortable than Vartoosh at being pressed against Gorky's side to pose for the snapshot, and she uses her right arm to make a wedge. She was, in fact, too independent, too American for Gorky. His prudish and authoritarian behavior toward women is exemplified in a story that Vartoosh told about the occasion of this photograph.

Vartoosh had recently had a marcel wave, and her short hair was crimped in the fashion of the late 1920s. Since Gorky disapproved of anything artificial or sexually provocative, he was displeased by his sister's new hairdo. "What have you turned into?" he asked, and he slipped away, filled a pail with water, and when he returned said: "Vartoosh, will you come here and see what this is?" Unsuspecting, Vartoosh obeyed and Gorky lowered her head and poured water over it. "From now on you will never make your hair like that," he commanded. Vartoosh let her hair grow long and never again went to a hairdresser for anything but a trim.

Entranced by Sirun's Armenian background, Gorky went with her to visit her mother in Lowell, Massachusetts. There he discovered that Sirun's father had been committed to a Watertown mental asylum. Unbeknownst to Sirun, who refused to talk to Gorky about her father, Gorky went to see Mr. Mussikian and found out that he had been a distinguished bacteriologist at the University of Chicago. "I have met the greatest man!" he later raved to Sirun. She was horrified. She had not seen her father since he had shot her when she was twelve. In spite of her resistance, Gorky organized a reunion, and Vartoosh and Moorad drove them to the asylum. "My father was cold and indifferent. He was very disappointed because I wasn't in college."

That summer in Watertown Gorky kept trying to persuade Sirun to sign papers to have her father released. Vartoosh witnessed the conflict: "She refused to sign. They fought. He said she was heartless and godless." The battles raged on. Gorky's "wild horse" was untamable. Having witnessed familial violence as a child, Gorky resorted to chasing Sirun around the kitchen table with a butcher knife. As Sirun came to identify Gorky with her abusive father, their bond frayed. She knew that Gorky loved her and she thought that he wanted to marry her, but his love turned tyrannical: "Had he been a little more patient with me—I was neurotic and needed love and affection and security so badly. I met a man like Gorky who isn't going to give that, doesn't know how to give that. . . . The only way he could deal with me was to get hysterical and hit me and threaten suicide."

Needing to escape from Gorky as she had escaped from her father, Sirun took refuge with her sister in Buffalo, but "there he was on the doorstep the next day." Back in New York, Gorky became ever more controlling. "He threatened to commit suicide all the time. If I didn't come and be a good girl, he'd kill himself." Gorky's deep-seated insecurity turned into a kind of paranoia. "It was just awful. He was so possessive, so jealous . . . He was so violent, so obsessive, so frightened that I would get away, because he felt I was the only Armenian woman that he could find that he could love." Sirun discovered that when she left the studio Gorky followed her. Once in an effort to escape she told him she was going out in the neighborhood for a few hours. Instead she jumped on an uptown bus. Her relief at being away from him did not last long: glancing out the bus's rear window she spotted Gorky in the middle of the street running after the bus and nearly catching up with it at every red light. Another time, after following Sirun all over the city, Gorky caught up with her on Riverside Drive. He ordered her to come home with him, and when she refused he said he would drown himself. When this ploy failed to make her comply, he rushed off in the direction of the Hudson River.

The memory amused Sirun. "He was such a romantic!" she said. But at the time his violence terrified her. After one fight Sirun took refuge with Mariam Davis. "She was a beautiful girl, just beautiful," Davis recalled. "They lived together for a while and then he . . . it was a little tough on her and she left. I think he beat Ruth up before she left him. One night Ruth came and saw us at night and she was crying. Next thing I knew, she was gone."

Sirun began to see Fernando Félix, a Mexican guitarist whom she had known in Los Angeles. One day when she had fled Gorky's studio after yet another quarrel, Gorky rummaged through her belongings and discovered a letter from Félix. The return address was near Cooper Union. Gorky raced downtown and burst in on the lovers. Félix fled. Gorky exploded. "He came and dragged me out by my hair. I tried to get away from him. He hit me very badly once in the face and he knocked me down." Now Sirun left Gorky for good. "You can hit me or call the cops," she said, "but I'm never coming back to you."

Thirty-two years later she looked back on her liaison with Gorky. Had he not hit her in the face, she said, she might not have been able to free herself from him. Though she felt she loved him, he was more than she could handle: "I was so young and ignorant and so concerned with my own feelings and problems that much of his genius and talent escaped me, although I always knew he was a great artist. I think it was one of Picasso's wives that said that living with Picasso was like living with a monument. One had the same feeling with Gorky." Sirun refused to play handmaiden to Gorky's tortured genius: "I just didn't feel that I wanted to sacrifice myself." He was like Oedipus, she said: "Tragedy seemed to stalk him everywhere . . . If he had been a little wiser, if I had been a little wiser, things would have been different."

After Sirun's final departure, Gorky went to see the Armenian-born sculptor Raoul Hague and wept. Hague recalled Gorky's despairing account of his Mexican rival (whom Hague remembered as being José Limon): "Gorky found her in a hotel on Broadway. He broke the door down and picked her up by the wrists. She was either naked or in a negligee. He put her in a taxi and took her down to his studio. After that she would not stand for it. That was the end." Gorky also sought solace by confiding in Yenovk Der Hagopian. "He came to Watertown," Hagopian recalled. "He was starving. We sat at Belmont View near the big pond or by the Charles River. Talk, talk, talk. Never talked about art. Only about the love affair. We came home at two o'clock in the morning. Brokenhearted. He was broken!" Dreading the emptiness of his studio now that Sirun was gone, Gorky begged Yenovk to come and live with him. Back in New York, he tried to pull his life together. The many different versions of his *Nighttime, Enigma, and Nostalgia* drawing series suggest the cavernous solitude he felt as he looked back on his months of struggle and love.

The distance that Gorky put between himself and the women in his life is suggested in the small but poignant *Portrait of Myself and My Imaginary Wife* (c. 1933–34) (Fig. 23). Here he depicted the ideal Armenian spouse, a modest and devoted accompaniment to her husband. With her darkly shadowed eyes, she bears some resemblance to Gorky's sisters. But the Armenian eyes are superimposed on a type derived from Picasso's neoclassical women of the 1920s, and the idealized wife looks back also to the passive plenitude of Corot's women. As in *The Artist and His Mother*, Gorky pulls away from the woman he adores. Like the mother and son in that portrait, the man and woman are side by side but appear to be in separate spatial spheres. The woman's position is especially unclear: her right shoulder overlaps Gorky's, but because her head is smaller in scale she seems to hover just behind him, like a muse whispering in his ear. With her soft, maternal comeliness, she embodies all of Gorky's yearning for his homeland and his wish to find a wife who could bring back the happiness of his youth and restore the tight-knit family structure he had experienced in childhood. Mina Metzger wrote: "Arshile lived alone in the early 1930s and was often lonely. He said his one wish was to have a wife, a couple of children, live in the country and be able to paint—that is not too much to ask, is it?"

Gorky's blindness to Sirun's reality and his attempt to reinvent her as the perfect Armenian woman seem to be encapsulated in this double portrait in which Gorky keeps his imaginary wife at bay. Eyes downcast, he turns away from her and meditates on some inner vision. To turn and look at the actual woman might distract him from his reverie—his vision might vanish. A few years later a brief first marriage would collapse because once again he tried and failed to mold a woman according to his ideal.

Portrait of Myself and My Imaginary Wife is informative on another count as well. Gorky's head is bent forward and to the side like that of the crucified Christ. His severe, sorrowing features bring to mind Jesus' harshly angular face on medieval carved wooden crosses. The shape and tilt of his head and the way it looks disconnected from his body are also very close to the head of the crucified Christ painted in the northern apse of the Church of the Holy Cross at Akhtamar. In addition, Gorky's greenish pallor brings to mind the livid flesh of Matthias Grünewald's Isenheim altarpiece (1510–15), a painting he greatly admired. If Gorky presented himself as Jesus, then the imaginary wife might be one of the Mary figures mourning at the base of the cross, but, as far as Gorky is concerned, her presence cannot ease the martyr's pain.

As we have seen, Gorky was not reluctant to associate himself with Christ's sufferings, and strangers sometimes saw him as a look-alike for Jesus. Mariam Davis recalled a time at the Metropolitan Museum when Gorky was approached by a woman who asked, "Are you Jesus Christ?" (Drawing himself up to his full height, Gorky said, "No, Madam. I am Arshile Gorky.") A similar mix-up occurred when he and a group of friends were out rowing at Orchard Beach and suddenly the sky grew stormy. All the rowers rushed toward shore, including Gorky, who, proud of his virile physique, was rowing with his shirt off. Seeing him framed by glowering clouds and with his bare chest and his beard, people on the shore panicked. "They felt that they had seen Christ on the water," Roselle Davis said. "And he really was quite exciting to look at because, there again, minus his shirt, he was aware of the figure he cut." When Gorky went home to Watertown with the beard he grew in 1928, the local children pursued him down Dexter Avenue, yelling "Hey! Here comes Jesus Christ!" To Satenik's question "Gorky, why do you have a beard?" Gorky answered, "I want to paint myself as Christ, with long hair and a beard." Gorky shared with his countrymen a heritage of martyrdom: the way his head hangs to one side in *Portrait of Myself and My Imaginary Wife* may recall the bowed heads of Armenians hung on public gallows, photographs of which he surely knew. Gorky never lost the feeling of being cast out, exiled, a martyr for art, just as his grandfather had been a martyr for the church and many friends and family members had been martyrs for their country. He called himself "a man of fate," but he painted himself as the Man of Sorrows.

22

The Cafeteria People

꓃

During the Depression decade, Manhattan's downtown avant-garde coalesced into a bohemia. De Kooning's friend the poet and critic Edwin Denby looked back at that time from the vantage point of the mid-1950s: "The difference that strikes me between downtown then and now is that then everybody drank coffee and nobody had shows." Concurring, sculptor David Smith said artists "drank coffee and hung around together in New York like expatriates." Of their alienation he observed, "One did not feel disowned—only ignored and much alone, with a vague pressure from authority that art couldn't be made here." If the establishment neglected them, the artists were very much aware of one another, and their camaraderie was a bulwark against public indifference. Poverty, politics, and modernist aesthetics brought artists together intellectually while the Artists' Union, the WPA Federal Arts Project, and the American Abstract Artists group brought them together on a more practical level. Lee Krasner, the painter and wife of Jackson Pollock, described the downtown milieu this way: "In the late 1930s the 'art scene' consisted of a rather intimate group of painters and their friends . . . One knew who was painting and what their work was about. We didn't know this through galleries, since almost none of us had anywhere we could show, and the galleries weren't interested in showing our kind of painting . . . We would meet at a bar or we might visit each other's studio from time to time and talk . . . The focus was on French painting."

With each year of residence in Manhattan, Gorky enlarged his circle of artist friends, most of whom lived in or near Greenwich Village.

Around 1929, possibly through Sirun Mussikian, he met Raoul Hague, who, having been born in Constantinople, where until 1915 an Armenian elite dominated intellectual and economic life, had a habit of teasing Gorky about the "thick-headed mountaineers from Van" who migrated to Constantinople to work as porters on the docks. Gorky was not amused. "They are innocent people," he said, "they are pure people. They are not stupid." And, to Hague's discomfort, Gorky began to weep. Sparring was an important ingredient of Gorky and Hague's friendship. "They really cut each other up," recalled Willem de Kooning. "They used to argue in Armenian like two old time Armenians in Armenia. They had terrific fantasies, like folklore, and used it against each other. Very mean and cutting too. But it never bothered Gorky." Except when it did.

One small circle within the downtown art world comprised Russian painters, among them John Graham, Alexander Vasilieff, Mischa Resnikoff, and the charismatic David Burliuk. Burliuk (born in the Ukraine in 1882) was the perfect bohemian. He went around Manhattan wearing exotic vests, a long-tailed Prince Albert, one pendant earring, and a tall silk hat. To complete the picture, he sometimes painted a bird or a flower on his cheek. Warm, enthusiastic, passionate about modern art and about his own genius, Burliuk was given to pronouncements like "I am the father of Russian Futurism." Having been a prominent member of the Russian avant-garde, he knew European modernism at first hand. Naturally he drew people to him, and his studio became a meeting place for artists.

Around 1929, through John Graham (born Ivan Dabrowsky in Kiev in 1887), Gorky met Stuart Davis, who in turn introduced Gorky to his brother, the photographer Wyatt Davis. Wyatt lived with his wife, Mariam, on the corner of Fourteenth Street and Seventh Avenue. "The reason Gorky came around to our house," she says, "was because I was an Armenian and he could have a free meal. He used to dance around the living room. His voice was a baritone, a full voice. When I knew him he said he was a Russian count. He liked playing games. After a while, when he found out I didn't believe him and that I was Armenian and came from a little town like him, he admitted that he was Armenian. He talked very little about Armenia." On one occasion Gorky amazed and terrified the Davises and their friends by doing his version of a Russian or Armenian sword dance. He pushed the table aside, picked up two carving knives, and began to sway and sing. As his voice grew louder and his gestures wilder, he leapt in the air, swirling the knives around him and slapping them on his thighs. The artist Charles Mattox recalled: "He was nicking himself. Blood spurted all over the place. He was slipping and dancing in his own blood." Mariam's memory was more prosaic: "We had a couple of daggers and he tried to dance with daggers and he got them all dull."

Around 1930, because she thought Gorky was lonely, Mina Metzger's daughter Rook McCulloch introduced him to the science professor Alexander Sandow and to his wife Helen. "When he came I was sick in bed with the flu," Helen Sandow recalls, "and Gorky was so modest that he barely looked at me. He couldn't. I don't suppose in Armenia men come to visit a woman who is in bed even if she is with her husband. He stayed a while and then he and my husband hit it off very well. Although my husband was a biophysicist, he was interested in drawing and painting, and he and Gorky talked constantly about art and went to museums together."

Of Russian Jewish extraction, Helen Sandow was lovely and slender with very dark hair. Gorky told her she looked like Akabi. But at first he kept his Armenian origins a secret, pretending as usual to be Russian. Helen Sandow recalls: "I introduced him to some Russian friends and they said, He's not Russian. He couldn't speak Russian. So I asked him, and he said, no, he was Georgian. In those days it was elegant to be Georgian, not Armenian. In those days you didn't dare admit to being Armenian. It was practically confessing you were starving." When she asked Gorky if it was true that he was related to Maxim Gorky, he said: "No. They keep asking me, so I say yes." In the end Gorky confided to the Sandows that he was Armenian, and he entertained them by cooking Armenian shashlik and dancing Armenian dances. "I remember him dancing and saying, 'I'm going to live to be eighty!'" On the other hand, when Gorky brought Vartoosh to meet the Sandows, he told them she was his cousin. Helen Sandow attributes this deception to the Mooradians' outspoken Stalinism. "Gorky was very careful. He was afraid to be identified as an Armenian—of being thought of as a Communist Armenian. Gorky brought to our house a famous Armenian Communist who came to this country for a month. His name was Nazarbekian." (Avetis Nazarbekian was an Armenian revolutionary who with his wife, Maro, cofounded the Hunchak Party. He stayed at Gorky's studio in 1934.)

Gorky enjoyed listening to Helen play the piano, and, though he knew little about music, he had definite tastes—he liked Bach and Mozart, but not Chopin and Beethoven, whose work he found nerve-wracking. When he stayed for supper, he would sit at the kitchen table sketching while Helen cooked. Once when she came near he covered his paper with his hand so that she could not see what he was drawing. Later she saw that he had drawn her lower body nude.

Before Gorky left the Sandows on their first evening together, he invited them to come to his studio. Having heard Gorky cast aspersions on all modern American painters except Stuart Davis, Helen said to her husband, "He'd better be good." He was. "When we got to his studio his work hit you between the eyes. We were speechless with delight and awe." Almost every evening for the next two years Gorky would turn up at the Sandows's East 10th Street apartment and Helen would invite him to stay for dinner. She did not realize that he needed those dinners until one day he gave them a lithograph to express his gratitude. "Two years later he came and said could we buy a painting. Although my husband was an instructor at New York University making forty dollars a week, he immediately said yes. I knew all we had in the bank was three hundred dollars. Gorky said, 'Well, come to my studio. We'll pick a painting.' We didn't pick. He picked. He said, 'This is the painting you are going to buy.' I loathed the painting at first sight. It was the only one I didn't want to buy." Gorky chose for the Sandows a Cubist abstraction with a pipe that is clearly influenced by the flat planes and muted colors of Stuart Davis's *Eggbeater* series of 1929. The price was one hundred dollars, because that was the amount of money he needed at the time.

Helen Sandow was amazed at the facility with which Gorky drew. It was, she said, "like seeing a baby born with all its arms and legs, just the way it had to be. He never had to change a line." Once the Sandows ran into Gorky at one of his favorite painting sites, a rock outcropping in Central Park near Sixty-sixth Street and Fifth Avenue. "Arshile! What are you doing?" asked Alexander Sandow. "Skatching," said Gorky. They walked over to the drawing on Gorky's easel and Helen Sandow exclaimed about its beauty: "He said, 'You like it?' I said, 'I *love* it.' He said, 'Take it, it's yours,' and he wrote on it, 'To my friends Helen and Sandy.' I spent my time urging him to paint realistically. 'This is how you should paint now,' I said. 'Then everyone would know what a great painter you are, and later, when you have made a reputation, you can paint any way you like.' He never took my advice. He painted the way he felt."

Around 1930 John Graham, who loved to introduce his friends to one another, brought David Smith and his wife Dorothy Dehner to Gorky's studio. "These are two talented American artists," Graham announced. Although he was not much older than Smith and Dehner, who were both students at the Art Students League, Gorky played the role of the master. "They don't look like artists to me," he said. "They look like college kids." With that he turned away, and while his back was turned, Smith propped two small paintings that he had brought with him against the wall. When Gorky saw them he somberly avowed, "Well, he is not without talent." After this inauspicious beginning, a close friendship did not evolve. "We were friends with him in a way, though it was difficult to penetrate the front that he presented to the world," Dehner recalled. The painter Rosalind Bengelsdorf Browne remembered Gorky and David Smith having "big battles" and Gorky calling Smith a "German sausage-maker." Another story has it that Smith was once so exasperated with Gorky's arrogance that he threatened to hit him and chased him down the street, yelling "You f—ing little rug peddler!" They must have been on friendly terms some of the time because a few years later, as they sat in a cafeteria drinking coffee and eating pastry, Gorky, Smith, and Graham hatched a plan to make a joint painting. Finally they agreed on a limited palette, various shades of brown—raw sienna, burnt sienna, and raw umber. "The painting never came to pass," said Dehner. "Graham said it was Gorky's fault and Gorky said it was Graham's."

Gorky was notoriously dismissive of other people's art. It was as though he had no idea what should and shouldn't be said—at least he pretended to have no idea. In Bengelsdorf's view, Gorky "loved to create an uproar. And he was very open about his dislike of an artist. I mean he would go to an artist's opening and crucify him. Sometimes we were embarrassed because he'd talk in a very loud voice." At exhibition openings he'd say, "Very beautiful walls" or "The frames are terrific." De Kooning remembered him coming up to an artist who was having an opening and giving such exaggerated praise that it was clear that he was being sarcastic. "My," he'd say in a loud voice. "What faces! What expressions!" De Kooning recognized Gorky's rudeness but loved him anyway. "He didn't care," said de Kooning. Gorky had "no feelings, socially."

When Gorky and de Kooning became friends, de Kooning was a commercial artist and neophyte painter in his midtwenties who had left

Holland as a stowaway and come to New York in 1921. Gorky and de Kooning are said to have met at the opening of John Graham's 1929 exhibition at the Valentine Dudensing Gallery. De Kooning had a better story. He said he had been wanting to get to know Gorky, but Gorky kept rebuffing his overtures. First they met at a party at Mischa Reznikoff's apartment. Gorky was talking to Graham when he noticed a handsome blue-eyed man of medium height. He approached him and said, "You talk like a truck driver." De Kooning answered, "Well, be careful, otherwise I'll take on the ways of a truck driver and beat you up." Gorky said: "That's silly, I'm much taller than you are." Thrusting his long arms with his enormous hands in front of de Kooning's face, he warned, "Look how long my arms are!" For the moment, de Kooning didn't want to have anything more to do with this belligerent giant.

The next time de Kooning encountered Gorky at a party, he quickly thumbed through an art magazine to find a reproduction that might serve as a conversation opener. He took the magazine over to Gorky, but Gorky turned him away with a dismissive gesture. At yet another artists' gathering de Kooning tried to join a conversation between Gorky and Stuart Davis. He told them that he had just discovered a wonderful painter at the Metropolitan Museum—Nicolas Poussin. Pretending to have never heard of Poussin, Gorky and Davis played de Kooning along. Finally Davis, who talked out of the corner of his mouth like a gangster in a Hollywood movie, said, "Well, I don't know. Sounds like a foreigner to me," and to his chagrin de Kooning realized that Poussin was someone that the other two had known about for years.

De Kooning did not give up. One day he ran into Gorky and, in his thick Dutch accent, said, "Nice to see you again." This time Gorky was cordial, so de Kooning took heart: "Some day, if you don't mind, I'd like to come to your studio." "Why don't you come right now?" Gorky offered. "So we went to his place," de Kooning remembered. "I was very taken with it. It had a marvelous atmosphere. It was immaculately clean. I was terribly impressed. All this work and strong paintings. Enormous amount of paints, brushes, all in order. An enormous number of postcards of other paintings." For a brief period de Kooning became something of a Gorky acolyte: "I attached myself to him." He saw that Gorky had a deep instinctual knowledge of painting. "He understood everything and had insight . . . He got the point."

By 1929, possibly through Burliuk or possibly by chance at a mu-

seum, Gorky had met John Graham. Highly respected as a critic, cos-
mopolite, connoisseur, and a painter who had exhibited in Paris and
knew such Parisian luminaries as Picasso, Graham was a central figure
in New York's vanguard art world. During the 1930s Gorky and Graham
could often be seen walking and talking, the one a gigantic Armenian
mountain man with huge melancholy eyes and long locks of black hair
that constantly fell over his high forehead, the other an aristocratic Russian of medium height, lean, and bald, with a trim moustache and eyes
so intense that they drove his thoughts home like nails (Fig. 99). Both
were careful about how they dressed. Gorky got himself up like an artist,
whereas the dandyish Graham was apt to dress in three-piece Saville
Row suits, a bow tie, a dark homburg, a perfectly tailored dark coat. His
scarf was gray—probably English cashmere; Gorky's was long, hand-
knitted, and red. Graham sometimes sported a lavender silk faille vest
and he had a liking for expensive gloves. De Kooning remembered Graham marching in a May Day parade, waving his hands encased in beige
chamois gloves and crying "We want bread!"

During the 1930s Gorky and Graham stood by each other in important ways: art dealer Julien Levy recalled that Gorky came to his gallery
in the winter of 1932 to urge him to look at Graham's work, and it was
Graham who suggested that Levy look at a portfolio of Gorky's drawings.
When Gorky went to discuss his work with Levy, his drawing portfolio
just happened to be already in Levy's back office, where, the secretary reported, he frequently "forgot" it. Gorky confessed, "I always expect you
will have opened it and discovered masterpieces."

Both Gorky and Graham had a vast and deep knowledge of art and
both had a propensity to assume the role of teacher. Not surprisingly,
their friendship had thorny moments. The young painter Jacob Kainen,
who in the midthirties visited Gorky's studio several times in the company of Graham, recalled that "Graham was the magus and critical father; aside from his superior social and educational level he was eighteen
or nineteen years [more like thirteen] older than Gorky . . . Gorky
wanted his mentor's approval but it never came. Certainly they admired
each other . . . but some wounding reservation, perhaps unspoken, was
implicit in their relationship." Gorky and Graham would talk behind
each other's back, and then, at their next meeting, they would embrace
and exclaim, "We mustn't talk this way about one another!"

Gorky was usually deferential to Graham. Occasionally he would rebel. On one studio visit, Graham arrived with a book on Gothic stone sculpture, placed it on Gorky's drawing table, and motioned to Gorky and Kainen to stand on either side as he slowly turned the pages. "After a while," said Kainen, "he stopped commenting and began asking for our opinions, curtly, like a professor with advanced students." Annoyed at being treated like a student, Gorky turned away and said, "I like the wall in back of the sculpture better than the sculpture. The sculpture seems routine."

"We were the cafeteria people," said de Kooning, recalling Graham's circle and their gatherings at coffee shops in the Depression decade. In this underground group, de Kooning once identified Graham, Gorky, and Stuart Davis as "the Three Musketeers." They were recognized as "the three outstanding modern artists." In December 1931 Graham wrote to his friend and patron the art collector Duncan Phillips: "Stuart Davis, Gorky and myself have formed a group and something original, purely American is coming out from under our brushes." Downtown in avant-garde circles this trio may have held the promise of American art's renewal, but uptown in the establishment world of galleries and museums they were hardly known at all.

Over endless cups of coffee and during studio visits, Gorky and Graham came to share many ideas about art and the creative process. Their vibrant interchange is reflected in numerous artistic parallels. Graham may have been Gorky's mentor in the articulation of intellectual matters, but Gorky had an instinctive knowledge of painting that surpassed Graham's, and he was the superior painter. In the 1930s, when Gorky and Graham were watching *Cahiers d'Art* in order to catch up with the latest inventions of Picasso, Gorky was able to make Picasso his own, whereas Graham seemed always to be speaking, albeit fluently, a borrowed language. Despite all Graham's talk about "spontaneous gestures" and "automatic écriture," so helpful for Gorky and others in the New York School, Graham could not act on the freedoms he himself proposed. As a result his paintings look rigid—constructions arranged with a sure hand and a powerful intellect, but not impelled from within. From the evidence of the work, the influence went back and forth, but mostly Graham followed Gorky. De Kooning learned from both, but in relation to the portraits that Gorky, Graham, and de Kooning produced in the late 1930s and early 1940s, it appears that Graham took from de Kooning ideas that de Kooning had adopted from Gorky. All three artists took their cues from Picasso, and all three venerated Uccello and especially Ingres.

John Graham's book *System and Dialectics of Art*, published in New York and Paris in 1937, was widely read in vanguard circles. A defense of modernism, it was set up as a series of questions and answers that resound with the high-voltage idealism that electrified conversations between artists gathered at lunch counters, studios, park benches, and in WPA payday lines. All the combustive issues of the Depression years are bandied about in the book—ideas that would form an important part of a theoretical substructure on which the New York School could build. Graham spoke about the Freudian unconscious, Jungian primordial memories, Marxist politics, Surrealism, Picasso's ascendancy, the role of creativity and tradition, the artist's relationship to society, the neglected artist as martyr, and the importance of flatness and spontaneity in painting. Above all, he extolled the primacy of abstract art as the logical culmination of art history. Graham's tone is relentlessly declamatory: pronouncements were necessary in an era when abstract art was attacked on the left by the social realists, who said it was the irrelevant and elitist product of bourgeois decadence, and on the right by the regionalists, who saw it as the effete creation of corrupt city dwellers. There were even some cognoscenti who considered abstraction to be old hat: Alfred H. Barr, director of the Museum of Modern Art, was predicting a return to figuration, and neither the Modern nor the Whitney showed many American artists working in an abstract vein.

"I can find the source of almost *all* of Gorky's erratic dictums in Graham," Gorky's second wife, Mougouch, once said. "They thought the same way." The Armenian and the Russian shared the same distrust of rational thinking: knowledge comes through intuition, they believed. Facts were humdrum. Vision was what counted. The ideas flowed both ways: both were brilliant talkers, but Graham could write and Gorky could not. As advocates for abstract art they were equally passionate. Subject matter they deemed unimportant—it was the emotion that lay behind the image that mattered. And both believed that art should take nature as its starting point and move in the direction of abstraction. Any objects would do as a jumping-off point. Gorky once proposed that a group of artists take a piece of string and a light bulb and see what they could make of it. In 1942 Graham said that his 1941 painting *Studio* started as a realistic interior with a few items of furniture and that "every subse-

Fig. 1. *Staten Island,* 1927–28

Fig. 2. *Pears, Peaches, Pitcher,* c. 1926–27

Fig. 3. *Still Life,* c. 1928

Fig. 4. *The Artist and His Mother*, c. 1926–42

Fig. 5. *The Artist and His Mother,* c. 1926–36

Fig. 6. Pablo Picasso, *Self-Portrait,* 1906

Fig. 7. *Portrait of the Artist and His Mother,* c. 1936

Fig. 8. *Composition with Vegetables,*
c. 1928–29

Fig. 9. *Still Life,* 1929

Fig. 10. Pablo Picasso,
Musical Instrument, 1923

Fig. 11. *Still Life,* 1929

Fig. 12. *Still Life with Palette*, c. 1930

Fig. 13. *Still Life (Harmony)*, c. 1931

Fig. 14. *Still Life*, c. 1930–31

Fig. 15. *Blue Figure in Chair*, c. 1931

Fig. 16. *Organization*, 1933–36

Fig. 17. Pablo Picasso, *Painter and Model*, 1928

Fig. 18. Gorky at work on *Organization* in studio at 36 Union Square, c. 1935

Fig. 19. *Still Life on Table*, c. 1936–37

Fig. 20. *Painting*, 1936–37

Fig. 21. *Composition*,
1936–37

Fig. 22. *Organization*
No. 2, 1936–37

Fig. 23. *Portrait of Myself and My Imaginary Wife*, 1933–34

Fig. 24. *Portrait of Ahko*, c. 1937

Fig. 25. *Portrait of Vartoosh,*
1933–34

Fig. 26. Vartoosh and
Karlen in Gorky's
studio at 36 Union
Square, 1936

Fig. 27. *Self-Portrait*, c. 1937

Fig. 28. *Self-Portrait*, c. 1936–37

Fig. 29. *Mechanics of Flying*, Newark Airport, 1936

Fig. 30. Pablo Picasso, *Three Musicians*, 1921

Fig. 31. *Image in Khorkom*, c. 1936

Fig. 32. *Image in Khorkom*, 1936

Fig. 33. *Khorkom*, c. 1937–38

Fig. 34. *After Khorkom*, c. 1937

Fig. 35. *Enigmatic Combat*, c. 1937

(*above*) Fig. 36. *Summer in Sochi, Black Sea,* 1936

(*left*) Fig. 37. *Apricots,* c. 1938

Fig. 38. *Untitled (Women Dancing),* mid-1930s

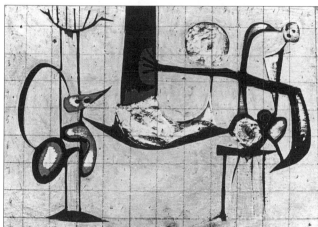

(*above*) Fig. 39. *Argula,* c. 1938–39

(*left*) Fig. 40. *Untitled,* c. 1939–40

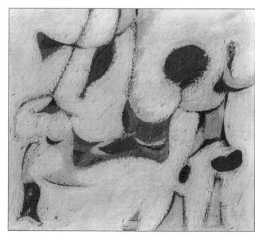

Fig. 41. *Composition,* c. 1939–41

Fig. 42. *Garden in Sochi*, c. 1941

Fig. 43. Joan Miró, *Personages Attracted by the Form of a Mountain*, 1936

quent painting of this subject became a further abstraction or summation of the phenomena observed." Gorky's creative process was not nearly as systematic. His powers of invention were so active that he transformed nature as soon as (or even before) he made the first mark.

Neither man set great store by originality. Both were firm in their respect for the unbroken chain of tradition that culminated, they believed, in Picasso. Both believed that art should uncover the depths of the subconscious, yet both insisted on an aesthetic discipline that required knowledge and control. Although they were sometimes critical of Surrealism, the revolutionary art movement that took over Paris beginning in the mid-1920s, both men were influenced by Surrealist thinking and both were imbued with a Surrealist attraction to enigma and to the drama and pain of sex. The Surrealist idea of disassociation was central to their method. Writing about his Newark Airport murals in 1936, Gorky called the procedure of taking an object or part of an object and presenting it out of context "the poetic elevation of the object." In the case of the murals, he took airplanes and other aeronautical objects, detached them from their normal contexts, and broke them down into basic parts, or, as Gorky put it, he performed an "operation" on the object. Graham likewise used the word *operate* in connection with the process of abstraction. Only painting, he said, "operates in space alone."

Like the third Musketeer, Stuart Davis, Gorky and Graham also believed in keeping pictures flat, and they embraced the concept of "negative space" given currency by the German émigré Hans Hofmann, who, like Graham, was a crucial transmitter of European modernism. "In a perfect composition shapes excluded and shapes included are equally important," Graham wrote. Ingres worshipers that they were, Gorky and Graham emphasized the importance of drawing and edges. The organization of forms should, Graham said, be "final and infallible" and "the edge of paint where one color meets the other ought to be absolutely spontaneous and final." Recognizing the obsessive exactitude of Gorky's contours, Graham said Gorky had "the curse of great taste." Yet Gorky and Graham were also concerned with sensuous, free, painterly handling—the importance of touch and of leaving evidence of process. Combining precision and spontaneity was a tall order but one that Gorky accepted, as can be seen by the endlessly reworked contours in his 1930s paintings.

23

Copy Art and Imitate Nature

Around 1937, when some loosely brushed paintings by Picasso were exhibited in New York, artists at the opening kidded Gorky: "Just when you've gotten Picasso's clean edge, he starts to run over." Gorky came back with "If he drips, I drip." Raphael Soyer recalled that "in those days it was common to scoff at Arshile," who was known as the "Picasso of Washington Square." When in 1932 Julien Levy refused to give Gorky a show because he found the work "too Picassoid," Gorky explained, "I was *with* Cézanne for a long time and now, naturally, I am *with* Picasso." Levy promised a show "someday, when you are *with* Gorky."

In the 1930s Gorky's forthright adoption of other artists' modes was so empathetic and at the same time so impelled by his own creative intelligence that he transformed his sources by inventing his own characteristic shapes, colors, and turns of line. He made the borrowed personal: to Gorky, making art was "making confession." His works thus have an intimacy, a connection with the most vulnerable aspects of his inner life—something that is usually lacking in his European models. The more one examines Gorky's early works, the more they appear like Gorkys rather than like Picassos. Moreover, his unabashed borrowings can be seen as forward-looking: for an American to be influenced by Picasso in the heyday of American Scene painting was, art historian Meyer Schapiro points out, "an act of originality."

To Gorky, originality was suspect. When people complained that he was derivative, he would agree: "Yes, Cézanne is my father, Picasso is my mother." He insisted that he had a right to learn by imitating his parents.

The abstract painter John Ferren told Gorky that paintings like his could be seen all over Paris: "They call them Picassiettes—plates of Picasso." Gorky countered: "Reflection of Picasso is necessary on almost a moral basis." To his friend the painter Balcomb Greene, he explained: "I feel Picasso running in my fingertips."

One of Gorky's favorite sayings was "Copy art and imitate nature." Mougouch remembers him saying "People make such a thing about originality. Look at the people who are original! There's nothing left of them ten years later!" To a young abstract painter whom he had just finished wowing with his aesthetic theories, Gorky declared: "The only difference between us is that I saw those issues of *Cahiers d'Art* before you did." When Jacob Kainen presented himself to pose for a portrait at Gorky's studio in 1934, Gorky went into his storage room and pulled out *Still Life with Skull*. "What does this look like?" he asked. "Cézanne," Kainen replied. "Right," said Gorky. He then pulled out *The Antique Cast* (c. 1928–29), and Kainen's identifying its source as Matisse pleased him.

Gorky's ambition, which was enormous, was to absorb, and then add to, art history. His approach seems to belong to a pre-Romantic era, a time when less value was placed on originality. Indeed, his attitude toward past masters recalls the Renaissance system of apprenticeship or even the Chinese insistence on learning to paint in the manner of an established earlier master. Gorky actually saw only a few original works by his School of Paris heroes. His main access to their works was in black-and-white reproductions in *Cahiers d'Art*. Thus when he adopted, for example, Braque's or Picasso's Synthetic Cubism, he added his own feeling for color and his own highly sensuous way of applying paint to the canvas.

However much he believed in apprenticeship, Gorky's susceptibility to influence sometimes made him anxious: In 1939, when he was struggling to free himself from Picasso with the help of Miró, he visited the great Picasso show that Alfred Barr had organized at the Museum of Modern Art. In front of Picasso's *Seated Woman* (1927), he sat for an hour with his head resting on his hand like Rodin's *Thinker*. He was transfixed also by Picasso's *The Three Musicians* (1921). Turning away from the painting, he said to Mina Metzger, "He is a devil."

Harold Rosenberg posited the idea of Gorky's "deliberate rejection of originality." Repeating a story told to him by de Kooning, Rosenberg wrote that when Gorky first visited de Kooning's studio, he exclaimed, "Aha, so you have ideas of your own." "Somehow," de Kooning said, "that didn't seem so good." Years later de Kooning would express dismay at Gorky's dependence on earlier masters. He could not see why this man who knew so much and who had such a sense of authority needed to be reverent. "He could be overcome by any authorities," de Kooning said. "Somebody like André Breton . . . He was impressed . . . by leaders."

Perhaps as an uprooted immigrant from a place that had been wiped off the map, Gorky chose to root himself in European culture because it offered him a structure to replace the highly structured society in which he was reared. He told his friend the painter Saul Schary that the slowness with which he found his own painterly voice was related to the slowness with which he developed language as a child. And he explained his reasons for following in the footsteps of the great masters: "In the old days you went into an artist's studio, and you worked under him. Inevitably you came out painting like him. Nowadays, you don't work in an artist's studio, but inevitably you do adopt a master of your own and you work as an apprentice to that man." Perhaps also, Gorky's mother's high ambitions for him played a role in his prolonged apprenticeship. Instead of taking his place in a long line of priests, as she had wished, he would take his place in the long line of art history. It was imperative that he excel, for art was his destiny. "The son is always killing the father," Gorky said. But in his case the father was art, and he could not kill what he loved. This inhibition might explain Gorky's difficulty in pushing beyond what he learned from others. "Since I, as a son, cannot kill my father—that is my past, the past of art—then I have to die because I am born to art and cannot deny my father and cannot murder him."

Gorky's development retraced the path from Cézanne to Cubism, but he did not go straight from Cézanne to Picasso. As we have seen, in 1928 he had a brief moment of infatuation with Matisse. Beside his Matissean *Self-Portrait* wearing a sailor shirt, he produced several portraits and still lifes inspired by Matisse that year. In *Still Life with Flowers* and *Still Life*, for example, he holds on to Cézanne's structure while opting for a painterly luxuriance that brings to mind the exuberant brush handling and emotionally charged color of Matisse's Fauve years. Matisse was very much in evidence in New York at the time. He had several one-person exhibitions and was represented in numerous group shows. *Cahiers d'Art* frequently reproduced his paintings, and Gorky could also study his work in his own large collection of Matisse reproductions, which he probably purchased at Fourth Avenue stalls or at Joe Kling's art store. For all his devotion to Matisse, Gorky followed his own sensibility when he transformed flowers and fruit into voluptuous, semiabstract shapes that predict the orificelike circles and ovals with dots in their centers that inhabit his abstractions in the 1930s and 1940s.

After playing Matisse, Gorky moved on in 1928 to a painterly Cubism that combines Cézannesque structure with paint handling that reflects his passion for Braque's lusciously painted still lifes of the 1920s (Fig. 79). Like most American Cubists, he was not interested in emulating Cubism's early analytic phase of around 1910 to 1911. In 1928 works like *Still Life* and *Still Life with Pears* (Fig. 78) Gorky loosened his brushwork and fattened his paint surface. But his feeling for color diverges from the color sensibility associated with the School of Paris. Slightly off shades—olives, ochres, aubergines, fleshy pinks, and various browns—have the scent of the East, the mud walls, flowers and fruits, the carpets and manuscript illuminations that Gorky knew as a boy in Van.

The objects in the Braque-inspired still lifes of 1928 and early 1929 slowly take on a metamorphic energy. Shapes begin to allude to mysterious realities other than the actual objects that they represent. In *Still Life with Horse* (1928) (Fig. 77), for example, Gorky made the back of a chair look like the profile of a horse. This kind of ambiguous, hybrid image, the seeing one thing within the shape of another, would soon become central to his work. From now on, Gorky's vision focused on the potential of an object for change: what he saw with his eyes was immediately transformed by what the Surrealist poet André Breton would call Gorky's "limitless play of analogies."

After modeling his work on Braque's painterly still lifes from the 1920s, Gorky moved to Synthetic Cubism—a style that Picasso and Braque developed in 1913 and that took flat, usually geometric shapes resembling cut-out papers and put them together to form the image of an object. At first, in works like *Composition with Vegetables* (c. 1928–29) (Fig. 8), he kept his objects whole and painted them with lush strokes just as he had in his Braque-inspired still lifes. But he has begun to set the objects before an abstract arrangement of flat, rectilinear planes that come straight out of his knowledge of Picasso's Synthetic

Cubism. Also, the fruits and vegetables become more and more creature-like—a pitcher handle suggests an ear, the top of the pitcher looks like an eye. But all this animation is held in check by the way the color planes anchor shapes to the canvas's framing edge.

Two of Gorky's most evocative Cubist still lifes from 1929 (Figs. 9 and 11) are dominated by a large, richly textured white shape that has been seen as a precursor to the so-called boot shape that is the central motif in the *Garden in Sochi* series of the late 1930s and early 1940s. The curving contour of this bootlike shape turns it into a "biomorph"— one of those protozoan creatures that populate Miró's and Masson's work of the 1920s and whose presence in Gorky's canvases creates a feeling of mysterious drama. In one of the still lifes Gorky even gave the creature an eye. It is as though a fruit or tablecloth fold from a still life of the previous year had metamorphosed into a live being.

In both these still lifes from 1929 Gorky borrowed the idea, seen in Picasso's two paintings of *Seated Woman* from 1926 and 1927, of portraying a single head as if it were viewed from several vantage points, so that two interlocked profiles can be read as looking either this way or that, depending on whether a form is seen as positive or negative. Thus, the white, bootlike biomorph's left profile interlocks with what looks like a human profile facing right. Gorky clearly enjoyed the way the interlocking profiles create a play between the object and its shadow and the way the interlocking of positive and negative shapes adds tension to the shifting of planes within a shallow space. But his approach is not as witty as Picasso's. As Jim Jordan notes, Gorky was not interested in the playfulness of the collage aesthetic that he found in Synthetic Cubism.

The larger of Gorky's two 1929 still lifes is based on Picasso's *Musical Instrument* (Fig. 10), also called *Mandolin and Music Stand*, of 1923. Gorky appropriated Picasso's curvilinear Cubism with its free-form shapes and emulated also Picasso's somber colors and rich paint surface. Following the examples of both Braque and Picasso (and perhaps remembering the pigment sprinkled with sand with which he decorated Easter eggs as a boy), he added sand to his pigment. As a result, textures as well as colors—various shades of brown plus black and white—serve to differentiate shapes. Looking at how Gorky transformed his source in Picasso, we see that the central white biomorph in the larger of Gorky's pair of still lifes takes off from the lobed shape that appears behind and to the left of the mandolin in Picasso's *Musical Instrument*. Gorky also borrowed Picasso's trefoil shape, and the narrow, dark shape to the right of Picasso's trefoil becomes, in the Gorky, a curving brown form that can (because Gorky added the suggestion of a Punchinello nose and chin) be read as a profile facing right. In general, Gorky arranged his shapes so that they orient themselves on horizontal and vertical axes, whereas Picasso's shapes are more free-floating. This makes Gorky's still lifes flatter and more abstract than Picasso's.

Both of Gorky's 1929 still lifes have a warm brown ground—brown was an elegant color, he told Sirun Mussikian about this time. In the smaller painting he added a few bright hues to the symphony in browns—his mixture of blue, red, and green, plus black and white recalls the full-blown and almost harsh colors of certain Synthetic Cubist Picassos. But the ochre of the large shape with a red circle—a shape that is Gorky's version of that favorite Cubist motif the clay pipe—shows Gorky moving into his own personal color range.

The smaller of the two still lifes in which the white "boot" motif predominates has three small areas where a part of a colored plane is etched with a series of parallel black lines. These striations create frets where they appear on the neck of the mandolin. Elsewhere their function seems to be entirely decorative. Gorky went on in 1930 and 1931 to use these parallel black lines as a way of enriching his surface in a series of five or six Cubist still lifes. His source was of course Picasso, who often used striated areas in his Cubist still lifes of the early 1920s. A more immediate source could have been the black stripes in some of Stuart Davis's *Eggbeater* paintings. Indeed, the device was taken up in the early 1930s by a number of other Americans, including Graham, who, like Gorky, watched every move Picasso made.

The easiest to decipher of Gorky's various striated Cubist still lifes is *Still Life with Palette* (c.1930) (Fig. 12). Here a white palette and pitcher set on a red tabletop are surrounded by a cluster of abstract shapes. Gorky has begun to loosen up Synthetic Cubism by adding more curving lines and rocking rhythms. His shapes become increasingly animistic. For example the pitcher's opening looks like an eye; the eye makes the spout into a beak and the handle into a bird's wing. Gorky may not in this instance have intended the pitcher to look like a bird, but in the next years many of his abstractions take on a clearly avian form.

In a group of paintings from the early 1930s, Gorky took the palette in *Still Life with Palette* and reinvented it as a free form. Biomorphs threaten to disrupt Cubist order as they wriggle free from interlocking planes and peer out through eyes that are dots or circles. In *Abstraction with Palette* (c. 1930) and in *Blue Figure in Chair* (c. 1931) (Fig. 15), the palette becomes the merged anatomy of an embracing couple. Both paintings combine sources in Picasso's 1915 *Harlequin* and *Three Musicians* (Fig. 30) with ideas taken from Picasso's interlocked, positive/negative heads seen in both versions of *Seated Woman*. Gorky's 1931 lithograph *The Kiss* and the drawings made in connection with it are variations on the same composition. Gorky told friends that the print's imagery represented the painter and model making love.

In later works the protean palette turns into buttocks, heart, breasts, head, and even a belly. A much-striated *Still Life* (c. 1931) (Fig. 13), also called *Harmony*, that Gorky gave his sister Vartoosh turns the palette into that familiar Surrealist icon the womblike C shape with a seed placed in the opening as if it were a birth canal. In Surrealism the C shape usually alludes to female anatomy—the vulva or womb. Sometimes the Surrealists made the C into a devouring mouth with teeth, a *vagina dentata* denoting the seductive but dangerous female. With this in mind, we might read Gorky's striated still life as a highly abstracted image of a man and a woman. The palette and the shapes metamorphosed from the palette have a similar anthropomorphism in another striated *Still Life* (c. 1930–31) (Fig. 14), a painting that may be Gorky's first response to Picasso's 1928 *Painter and Model* (Fig. 17), which he saw when he baby-sat for the children of the collector Sidney Janis and his wife, Harriet, and which may depict a male on the right and a female on the left.

In several of Gorky's paintings from 1931, most notably *Sunset in Central Park*, Miró momentarily supersedes Picasso as the dominant influence. *Sunset in Central Park*'s yellow background recalls the bright yellow grounds in many of Miró's paintings of the 1920s, and Gorky's whimsical biomorphic creatures—a bird in the sky and what may be a dog in the lower right corner—are distinctly Miróesque. Indeed, the dog seems to have been lifted from Miró's *Dog Barking at the Moon* (1926), a painting that Gorky often admired after it was acquired by the Gallery of Living Art in 1929.

For the next several years Gorky went back and forth between Miró and Picasso, following Picasso more closely but softening that master's severity with lilting rhythms inspired by Miró. And all the while Ingres was never far from his heart: much of his energy was focused on his two great Ingres-inspired portraits of *The Artist and His Mother*. What he learned from Cubism he applied to these two double portraits. Conversely, ideas explored in the portraits—ideas about finding the perfect edge, about making colors resound with feeling, and about painting and repainting until the image answered to some powerful experience buried deep within—were brought to bear on his Cubist abstractions. As a result, Gorky's abstractions became more vibrant, personal, and original as the decade moved on.

While Gorky was casting about in his paintings for a language that could voice his feelings, he also explored all different styles and methods in his drawings. He drew incessantly and on any handy surface: "I'm certain if he had worn a white shirt instead of a sweater, very worn out at the elbows," said his first wife, Marny George, "he would have had it completely covered with drawings in no time." "Always keeping my hand in," Gorky would explain, but the truth was that he had a deep, visceral passion for making lines flow from his hand onto paper. He amazed friends by whipping out a Rembrandt or a Matisse on a cafeteria napkin. Raoul Hague had a blackboard in his studio on which his artist friends used to draw. "One guy used to draw women's calves, sort of erotic. Gorky would say, 'That's crazy. Wipe it!' And then he'd draw a profile of a Greek head, just three lines." De Kooning loved to watch Gorky's enormous and "very beautiful hands" at work. Gorky would take out his pocketknife and sharpen his pencils until the leads were half an inch long. "I use this like a surgeon's tool," he told de Kooning. "Now," he explained as his pencil went back to the paper, "I am going to take the light out."

Some early drawings show Gorky rehearsing borrowed styles, especially those of Ingres, Picasso, and Matisse. "He loved all of Matisse's linear drawings," Mougouch recalled, "and there are many drawings on big sheets of paper in which Gorky almost never took the pen off the paper. This was Gorky doing a Matisse. It was part of Gorky's training himself in line." Jacob Kainen remembered an evening at Stewart's Cafeteria around 1936 when Gorky boasted that he could imitate the style of any modern master, including Picasso, Matisse, and Braque. "How about Ingres?" asked Mischa Reznikoff. Gorky looked miserable. "Ingres had his own delicate line," he answered. "At times I resent him . . . but oh, how I would like to draw like Ingres." Gorky's worship of Ingres, seen for example in his pencil *Self-Portrait* from the mid-1930s (Fig. 101), was informed by Picasso's homage to Ingres in portrait drawings such as the one of Ambroise Vollard from 1915.

Between 1931 and 1934 Gorky searched for and found his personal vocabulary of form in a group of drawings that can be divided into five principal themes. These themes, as set forth in 1995 in an extraordinary exhibition at the Princeton University Art Museum, were: Cubist Standing Figure, Column with Objects, Ecorché, Image in Khorkom, and Nighttime, Enigma, and Nostalgia. (Although Gorky occasionally named a drawing when it entered a collection, in the 1930s he left his drawings untitled.) Seeing the drawings arranged according to theme in the exhibition and its accompanying catalog revealed the extremely painstaking nature of Gorky's search for perfection. As a series developed, he made tiny alterations in value relationships, shapes, density of shading, types of mark making, and the materials used. In the process he evolved the kinds of shapes and lines that would characterize his work for the rest of his life.

Although the exact chronology of Gorky's drawings is not known, he seems to have begun by using a pencil to work out a semiabstract grouping of forms that occupied most of his sheet of paper. In later versions—often in pen and ink and sometimes wash—he frequently left a border of blank paper to frame the image. Having arrived at his basic scheme, he might trace its outlines onto one or more sheets of paper so that one drawing became the template for several variations.

This method recalls the way Gorky often reworked his paintings of the 1930s by keeping the same general composition but changing the colors. It also anticipates his habit of working in series in the 1940s. If the process seems unspontaneous, one could say that Gorky chose discipline in order to give his powers of invention free play. He was like a Renaissance master painting the Virgin a little differently for each successive commission.

Yet there is something fearfully careful, constricted, perhaps even repressed in many of the early drawings. This quality seems to come out of the same urge that made Gorky excessively fastidious. The drawings themselves pose the question: Why would a man so impassioned by art making be unwilling to let himself go and freely enjoy the process of invention? Harold Rosenberg uses the word *niggling* to describe the way Gorky pursued perfection "stroke by measured stroke." In Gorky's work of the 1930s, Rosenberg says, "meticulousness reaches the point of obsession." In the end, it is Gorky's obsessive carefulness—his avoidance of bravura flourishes—that gives these early drawings their peculiar strength and tension.

The *Cubist Standing Figure* series began with a semiabstract female nude (Fig. 84) based on several 1928–29 Picasso drawings, including Picasso's group of semiabstract female figures on the beach reproduced in the 1929 issue of *Cahiers d'Art*. Gorky's image was based also on Picasso's small oil entitled *Dinard—Design for a Monument*, which Gorky saw in Gallatin's Museum of Living Art in the early 1930s, as well as on Picasso's *Figure au bord de la mer*, which he studied in his copy of the catalog of a Picasso show at the Galérie George Petit in Paris. As the *Cubist Standing Figure* sequence unfolds, the figure and the shapes out of which it is constructed become more abstract. The two-lobed shape that refers to buttocks in the first version shifts around and duplicates itself so that it becomes a palette, a pelvis, or a heart. Like the C shape that stands for a female in the *Still Life* (c. 1931) Gorky gave to Vartoosh, this double-lobed form often has a small circle between its lobes—almost certainly a reference to an orifice.

The transformative powers of Gorky's imagination are brilliantly displayed in several 1932 drawings of seated male nudes. In one he took off from the shapes he saw in a plaster cast of an écorché attributed to Michelangelo and transformed musculature into a swirl of shapes. Certain groups of muscles on the man's back and right shoulder turn into birds, and just below the birds the muscles form a face that recalls José Clemente Orozco's stylized Mexican Indian faces. Although these shapes most likely emerged in the process of drawing, Gorky must have seen them and decided to allow them to stay. In another écorché drawing, c.1931 (Fig. 85), calf muscles turn into a bird, the écorché itself has a bird head, and the line of the écorché's backbone continues upward and becomes a rope from which the écorché dangles. The image imparts a feeling of despair, as if Gorky empathized with the flayed hanged man. Years later he said he had spent a lifetime becoming like a peeled onion, hypersensitive to every emotional nuance.

A similar melancholy pervades the largest of Gorky's drawing series, *Nighttime, Enigma, and Nostalgia* (c.1931–33) (Figs. 86 and 87). In this group Gorky adapted the Surrealist notion of psychic automatism, a visual equivalent of literary free association whereby the artist, hoping to gain access to the unconscious, lets his hand move over paper or canvas in an improvisatory manner without conscious control. The principal motif in the *Nighttime, Enigma, and Nostalgia* series is a configuration of cursive lines set within a trapezoid. (In some versions the trapezoid is combined with other clearly delimited spaces enclosing images.) The meandering lines inside the trapezoid look improvisatory, but, like Miró, who drew light pencil lines to guide even his most spontaneous squiggles, Gorky kept his drawing under absolute control. The very notion of spontaneity is contradicted by the way Gorky repeated the same composition in some fifty versions of *Nighttime, Enigma, and Nostalgia*. As he explored all possible permutations of this theme, he made new decisions about which parts of his linear web should be filled in with crosshatching, thus becoming positive shapes, and which shapes should be left the white of the paper.

Gorky's attraction to the look of automatism—he was too vigilant an artist to actually practice it—has various sources, among them André Masson. Unlike Miró, Masson seems to have actually let his hand follow his impulse. In works like *Metamorphosis* (1929) and *Cock Fight* (1930) (Fig. 91), Masson whipped his line like a cowboy whirling his lasso. Later he filled in certain loops and meanders to create biomorphic shapes and creatures. The swooping lines in Gorky's *Nighttime, Enigma, and Nostalgia* also recall the maze of lines in Picasso's 1927 etching *Painter with a Model Knitting*. Yet another source was Picasso's surrealizing works of the late 1920s and early 1930s—especially *Seated Woman* (1927) and the *Crucifixion* drawings of the same year. Max Ernst's meandering line in *The Kiss* (1927) and in *Night of Love* (1928), both reproduced in 1928 in *Cahiers d'Art*, is still another likely source for Gorky's *Nighttime, Enigma, and Nostalgia*. Ernst's apparently automatist line, full of lobes punctuated by eyes, shares with Gorky's drawings the feeling that enigma is suffused with erotic insinuation.

The subject of the *Nighttime, Enigma, and Nostalgia* series seems to be a confrontation between two wrestling biomorphs—a recumbent open-mouthed, wide-eyed female on the right and an E-shaped male on the left—enclosed in a trapezoidal space. I read the scene as a drama of sexual aggression recalling Masson's scenes of combat (often sexual) in which biomorphic creatures have at each other. The shapes struggling in the nocturnal gloom might be a sad rumination on the enigma—to

Gorky—of sex and procreation and on Gorky's recent struggles with Sirun Mussikian. Indeed, John Graham's description of Picasso's art is a fitting description of the *Nighttime, Enigma, and Nostalgia* series. In Picasso, Graham wrote, "cosmic form-beings of all time consort and separate, yearn for each other in fateful lassitude, thirst in hope and abandon." Gorky's biomorphs in *Nighttime, Enigma, and Nostalgia* certainly do "consort," but, as in Gorky's *Portrait of the Artist and His Imaginary Wife*, one has the feeling that the yearning will never be satisfied.

In some versions of *Nighttime, Enigma, and Nostalgia* three elements are added—a bust, a skeletal fish, and a rectangle divided in two by a diagonal. All three are derived from Giorgio de Chirico's *The Fatal Temple* (1913) (Fig. 88), which Gorky would have seen as early as 1927 at the Museum of Living Art. If the principal motif is indeed coupling biomorphs, then the bust and the skeletal fish might combine with them to create a cycle of life.

As Gorky kept working on his drawing series in the early 1930s, his handling became more fluent, various, and expressive. Taking for his starting point Picasso's crosshatched drawings, he explored every possibility of crosshatching he could think of. He experimented also with techniques such as spreading a veil of ink wash around and sometimes over shapes, and he introduced brown ink in one marvelously rich and comparatively loose drawing in which shapes cut loose from the set pattern of the *Nighttime, Enigma, and Nostalgia* series and move in the direction of the freer and more sensuous *Khorkom* series (c. 1933–6) (Figs. 89 and 90). To enhance his drawings' texture and to give them the look of age, he sometimes erased and scraped the paper or rubbed it with a damp cloth. Gorky treated the paper surface as if it were a sensitive material like skin. Sometimes he even washed his drawings under the bathtub faucet. On one occasion he forgot that he had not used indelible ink, and when he took a wet sponge to the drawing, the image vanished. Elaine de Kooning recalled his reaction: "Horrified at first, he shrugged his shoulders characteristically and said: 'Oh well, I didn't like it anyway,' and immediately began another."

Mougouch says that Gorky destroyed drawings that did not satisfy him. He would strew them around the studio and then sweep them out the door. Thus the drawings that remained in his portfolios must have had something in them that Gorky valued or that he felt merited further study. One of Gorky's letters to Mougouch (May 31, 1941) gives a picture of the Gorky drawings destined for the trash basket: "This morning after you left I was in the midst of arranging my drawings—and there were quantities spread all over the floor, Mr. Bernard Davis came in; he had hardly crossed the doorstep before he cried out, without ever stopping to wish me good morning or good day 'Hey! What are you doing? Walking over your drawings? There are mines of gold in them; how wasteful you are!' "

According to the Gorky myth promulgated by Ethel Schwabacher, Gorky made so many drawings in the early years of the Depression because he could not afford paints and canvas. In fact, the catalogue raisonné of Gorky's paintings lists some forty oil paintings for the first three years of the 1930s. Also, we know from Stuart Davis that Gorky's studio was full of art materials. Had Gorky wanted to paint more and draw less, he certainly would have found a way. Probably he felt that working in series with pen and ink or pencil on paper was the best way to delve deeply into certain art problems, such as the melding of Surrealism into Cubism or the relationship of line to shape and of surface to depth.

His focus on drawing series during the first years of the decade might also have been a way of keeping anxiety and depression at bay. He was lonely after the loss of Sirun, and his loneliness was compounded when on May 10, 1932, he saw off Vartoosh and Moorad when they sailed for Europe en route to Armenia. (The couple set out full of hopes for a better life under Stalin, but during their two years in Soviet Armenia they found life to be so miserable that they returned to America.) Gorky was also worried about money and saddened by the misery he witnessed during the Depression—the homeless wrapped in newspapers lying outside his door or the jobless with their hollow, deadened eyes sitting in Union Square. He confirmed that he intended the *Nighttime, Enigma, and Nostalgia* drawings to evoke melancholy. When one of the series was acquired by the Museum of Modern Art in 1941 and Gorky was asked to fill out a questionnaire about it, he responded to the museum's queries "Was a specific model used? Has the subject any special personal, topical or symbolic significance?" with these words: "Wounded birds, poverty and one whole week of rain."

Perhaps he was referring to a wounded bird that he saw in the pond at the south end of Central Park. The sculptor Reuben Nakian (an American of Armenian origin) told the story:

> Gorky and I were in Central Park, sitting on a bench at the lake there. And there were pigeons around, and one of them was hurt and was about to drown. And we were watching as a man from a nearby peanut stand waded in the water to rescue it. So, when it was over, Gorky turned to me and said, "My god, I felt the agony you had." You know, I was worried and felt we should run and save it, jump in the water, when we saw the other man doing it. But I didn't say a word and just sat there, and he felt my alarm just as though he had the ability to feel right through me. He had that uncanny, that mystic quality, an amazing ability to perceive things deep down inside.

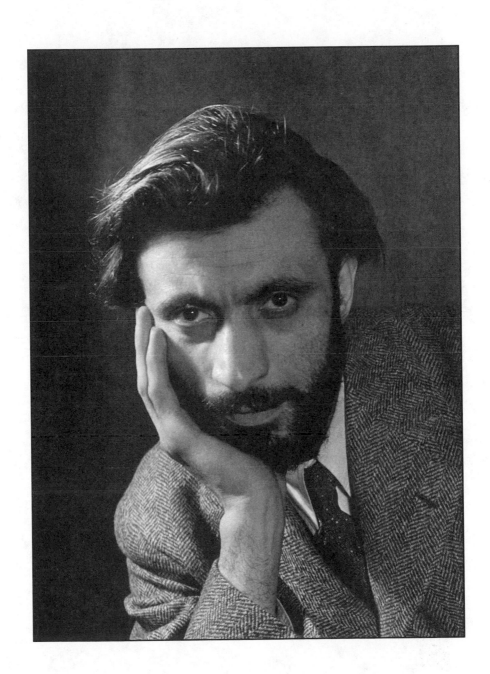

PART VI

Gorky posing for Wyatt Davis, c. 1930

24

Another Cup of Coffee,
Another Piece of Pie

᪆

In 1930, with the help of two hundred dollars that Vartoosh had received from an insurance settlement, Gorky moved from Washington Square to a much larger studio at 36 Union Square, a three-story building whose entrance was on Sixteenth Street. As Stuart Davis and Harold Rosenberg noted, Gorky seemed to move with the times: in the bohemian twenties the Village was the center of intellectual ferment, and during the Depression years Union Square was a lively place to be. The Garment Workers' Union and Tammany Hall were off Union Square on Seventeenth Street, and the square itself was the site of soapbox orations, political demonstrations, and May Day parades. Many artist friends were neighbors: Raphael Soyer lived across the square, and Raoul Hague, Stuart Davis, and Jacob Kainen all lived on Fourteenth Street. Balcomb Greene, whose studio was on East Seventeenth Street but who had not yet met Gorky, happened to witness Gorky's moving in: "His moving was symbolic. The previous painter to occupy the immense studio facing on 16th Street was an academic craftsman who had pulled his battered belongings into a hall room, letting this gigantic Modern sweep into his quarters. Gorky swept in with his bolts of canvas, his mountain of an easel, his cases of pigments, his stentorian commands to the movers, his indifference to me crowding past in the hallway."

The entrance to Gorky's new home was on the north side of Sixteenth Street, the first door on the left walking east from Union Square. On the ground-floor corner of his building was a lunch counter. Stuart Davis recalled that the stairs leading up to Gorky's studio were "ventilated by the aromas of a grease kitchen on the ground floor and a civil-war-type dentist's parlor to the left." A flight of marble steps led from the entrance lobby to a landing off of which was an apartment occupied by a woman who performed electrolysis. Climbing another flight of dimly lit and dusty stairs, these narrower and made of wood, you came to the second floor. Turning left down a dark hall, you passed a door that led to the Russian painter Alexander Vasilieff's corner studio. At the end of the hall, on the left, was a door with "A. Gorky" hand-painted in small letters.

Opening the door, you would find yourself in a small, dark hallway. In the 1930s, when landlords were artists' scourges, Gorky painted this hallway black so that if someone knocked he could open his door just a crack and not be seen. In a storeroom off the hallway Gorky kept hundreds of neatly stacked canvases. He knew just where to locate each of his old paintings should he feel inclined—as he often did—to rework them. From the hallway you entered a high-ceilinged studio about thirty foot square and always freshly painted in white (Figs. 18, 82, and 83). At its far end was a bathroom, a tiny kitchen in an alcove, and two bedrooms. Gorky's bedroom looked north over low, flat roofs of brownstones. In warm weather it was possible to climb out its window onto the fire escape and down onto the tar roof just below.

From the pressed-tin ceiling in Gorky's studio hung an electric cord with a single bulb at its end. Stuart Davis, exaggerating like all great storytellers, wrote that the studio was "pitch black at high noon, in spite of a sizable side-light let into the one wall which allowed it to be called a studio. Like all such skylight affairs, it was heavily sanded and etched by filth on the outside, and the few quantums of light that survived the struggle to penetrate it reeled to the floor one meter inside." The studio had two windows facing Sixteenth Street and an enormous window looking north to the red brick garment workers' building, which cast a pink light on Gorky's walls. On the sill of the large window stood Gorky's collection of vases, bottles, and medical flasks—vessels he liked for their shapes. Close by was his worktable and his mighty easel with its attached photographer's lamp.

The room was immaculate and sparsely furnished. Gorky loved heavy furniture with solid, thick legs, and he spent hours stripping the paint off it. One example was the round oak pedestal dining table on which he arranged still lifes for students to paint. There was also a model stand, a daybed, and three straight-backed chairs, but not one comfortable place to sit. More important to Gorky than his furnishings were the reproductions that hung on his studio walls. Sometimes he turned them sideways or hung them upside down so that he could study them as abstract form. Although he generally did not hang his own paintings in his home, many visitors remember seeing *The Artist and His Mother*, either on an easel or on the wall.

Gorky did not like clutter, but his shelves were full of art books, and on the worktable there was a profusion of art materials: numerous Grumbacher or Winsor and Newton brushes of all sizes stood in pottery vases, their bristles all perfectly clean. "He had gorgeous brushes," de Kooning said. "He went out of his mind with all those different types of brushes. 'Now I know,' he would say. And I finally found brushes in his studio I didn't even know about. But he wouldn't tell me. I didn't ask him because he would say, 'O, some store.' Yes that was the way he was." On Gorky's palette, pigments were squeezed out in neat mounds. He bought the best-quality paints. His favorite brand was Le Fevre because he said it was less slick, but he also used Winsor and Newton and Rembrandt oil pigments. The painter Elaine Fried, who was de Kooning's girlfriend beginning in 1937 and who would marry de Kooning in 1943, was astonished at Gorky's supplies: "You had the feeling about Gorky that if he got his hands on some money he'd say, 'Well, I'll buy paint while I've got the money because I can always get food.' "

Everyone who visited Gorky's studio was amazed by its order and by the scrubbed parquet floor. Gorky was fastidious in his personal habits as well. "He was terrifically clean," said de Kooning. "He even scraped his feet and he was just merciless to others about smell. He used to call people with dogs 'lousy advertising agency people with dogs.' " Every weekend Gorky stripped to the waist, pushed his furniture first to one side and then to the other, and got down on his knees to wash his studio floor with a huge scrubbing brush and a box of powdered soap. The floor became bleached almost to a sand color. Gorky's friend and patron Margaret Osborn remembered that the floor had the same ascetic quality that emanated from Gorky himself, "a spareness, that did not so much reject materialism, as have no need of it." She caught the feeling of Gorky's studio: "It had a most solitary character, that of a place immensely removed from ordinary life. . . . It was his, to an extraordinary degree, there he was in a sense a monarch. In a city as nomadic as New York, this man from a country of strong traditions, had made, not without struggle and loneliness, a kingdom, taken to himself that corner, set his stamp on it."

As the economic crisis worsened after the October 1929 stock market crash, the situation for artists became desperate. Collectors stopped buying, galleries closed, and museums cut their budgets. As Suzanne La Follette wrote in the *Nation*: "The impoverished artist, like the impoverished bond salesman or the down-and-out worker, gets along as best he can from day to day, and never knows when the morrow will find him wholly destitute." President Hoover kept assuring the public that everything would be better soon, but the Depression only deepened. By March 1930 four million people were jobless. The following year unemployment doubled, and by 1933 some fifteen million Americans were out of work—over one quarter of the American labor force.

Gorky had always had, Ethel Schwabacher noted, an "obsessive need to keep poverty at bay." During the Depression his own hunger and the suffering he witnessed—breadlines, Hoovervilles, and the death from malnutrition of his friend and former student Nick Mayne—took him back to the kind of destitution he wished to forget. "Gorky described it as the bleakest, most spirit-crushing period of his life and spoke with bitterness of the futility of such paralyzing poverty for the artist," Mougouch wrote. "He often said that, if a human being managed to emerge from such a period, it could not be as a whole man and that there was no recovery from the blows and wounds of such a struggle to survive. You will see much of this obsessive agony in some of the painting in the storehouse and I think I can say that SURVIVAL was the meaning and flavor of those days—to him."

Almost everyone who knew Gorky during the Depression saw his poverty. Ethel Schwabacher said that every time the doorbell rang "he would almost tremble, because he thought it was his landlord coming to get the rent, which he didn't usually have . . . He actually didn't have enough money to eat and paint simultaneously. He would go down and get a doughnut and some coffee from a shop downstairs on his corner, and when he came to lunch, which he did fairly often at my house, I always had the feeling that he was afraid to eat because he thought maybe it didn't look dignified to be hungry. So he ate very sparingly. And I thought the best thing I could do was to overlook it, and not make any comment about it." Gorky was frequently reduced to borrowing money. Gaston de Havenon, who met him in 1932 through Gorky's patron Bernard Davis, recalled that Gorky never complained about being broke but that he occasionally asked to borrow twenty-five dollars for art materials. He would give de Havenon a drawing to keep as collateral: "After paying back his debt, I tried to give him back the drawing and he always tell me to keep it as a souvenir, which I did." Friends and students tried to think up ways to help Gorky without offending his pride. Saul Schary remarked: "He was not the kind of guy you could give money to. He wouldn't take a handout. So I cooked up the idea of doing a portrait of him and asked him to pose and he did. I insisted that he had to be paid. When he posed, he was very careful about how I was going to paint him. And he posed his hands a certain way and insisted that I had to get this in, with the finger like this, one finger raised, and that's the way I painted him." Gorky tried to hide his penury with his abundant supply of paints and brushes and books and by wearing well-cut suits and a wide-brim felt hat. Only rarely would he ask for help. De Kooning told a story about Gorky's reaction to an incident in William Saroyan's play *My Heart's in the Highlands* in which an Armenian father sends his son out to beg. Gorky said, "That's not Armenian." De Kooning countered, "Saroyan is Armenian." Gorky explained, "No Armenian would send his son out to the grocery store to beg for credit. He goes out and begs for credit but does not send his son."

Gorky kept the fruit he bought for still lifes until it rotted. One time when Will Barnet visited 36 Union Square in the early 1930s he found Gorky in a rage: "The previous evening he had designed a collage painting of which a part was composed of a piece of cheese. Gorky had gone to bed and in the morning awakened to find that a village mouse, enamored by the choice of materials used in this work, had proceeded to redesign that canvas by eliminating the cheese." Gorky's nephew George Adoian remembers another story about Gorky's financial straits, one that sounds like a Depression-era fairy tale:

Gorky was walking in the Village and he passed by a house out of which came the smell of doughnuts. Gorky loved them and he knocked on the door. A woman opened the door and Gorky said, "What a delicious smell! What a wonderful aroma!" And she asked him what he was, and he said he was an artist. She said, "Come right in." She told him she cooked doughnuts and bread every Friday because her husband, who was a stockbroker, did not like store-bought bread and doughnuts. The next Friday Gorky went to her house accompanied by an artist friend, and the following week he went with three friends and so on until there were about twelve men going there. Finally, the woman's husband got fed up with this. He said, "Let's see if they come back if there are no doughnuts and bread." And the following Friday she made no doughnuts or bread. Gorky and his artist friends arrived and they said, "Where are the doughnuts?" She said, "I'm not making them anymore," and the following Friday and the Fridays after that the artists didn't come back.

Ethel Schwabacher recalled that when she and Mina Metzger went to Gorky's studio three afternoons a week she paid Gorky twenty-five dollars a month while Metzger paid fifty. Two other private students were the future Museum of Modern Art curator Dorothy Miller and her friend Holger Cahill, who would head the Federal Art Project of the WPA and whom she would marry in 1938. At the time Gorky met them, in the autumn of 1931, Miller was between jobs and Cahill was writing and doing some art consulting. The couple had very little money, but Gorky's impoverishment touched them and, wanting to help, they asked him if they could study with him. He took them to Eighth Street to buy art materials and for a brief period they went to 36 Union Square in the afternoons. "Oh he was marvelous," Miller recalled. "He was the most eloquent man I ever met . . . And he was absolutely patient with us although we were not serious students." At twelve dollars apiece, they each bought two copies of Gorky's lithograph of an artist embracing his model. "And Gorky would always make coffee for us. Though desperately poor, he always bought the best coffee, which was Martinson's. We always sat and had coffee after the lessons . . . We paid him some very small sum. In all, we probably went only about six times."

Absorbed in his own struggles, Gorky sometimes lacked empathy for others. Elaine de Kooning remembered Gorky's response to her future husband's litany of his own problems, which included the threat of eviction for nonpayment of rent and a possible operation that would leave one leg shorter than the other. Gorky listened quietly and when de

Kooning stopped talking he responded by saying, "My neck hurts here."
De Kooning always forgave and defended Gorky:

> He had a difficult life. Everything was kind of gloomy and nothing
> really worked so good, paintings and life and the money. And he
> would say, "Ah, that's another cup of coffee, another piece of pie."
> He said it with a certain kind of Armenian accent. He had origi-
> nal mannerisms . . . He would stand there very tall, looking down
> with a drooping moustache, and I knew he was thinking about
> something. "But you see," he said, "you only have to put up with
> me once in a while, but you can imagine how I suffer. I will al-
> ways have to put up with myself." He always had the last word.

Gorky's everyday life in the 1930s consisted of teaching a few afternoons, visiting museums and galleries, and sitting on park benches or in
cheap restaurants talking with fellow artists, mainly about art and artists'
problems. But most of his hours were taken up with work. "He painted
day and night, day and night," said Willem de Kooning. "He lived an ir-
regular life. It had its own rhythm." Elaine de Kooning agreed: "He had
a demon for work. It was literally the center of his life in a way that is uncommon even among artists." When he was not making, looking at, or
talking about art, Gorky took long walks in the Village or in Central
Park. He was proud of his physique, and he liked to invite people to
punch his muscle-hard stomach, enjoying the exclamations of awe that
were forthcoming. "I cannot understand why my stomach is so hard," he
used to say. "Really it can be hit any time and I am not able to feel the
blow." Gorky welcomed challenges to his physical prowess. Stuart Davis
remembered the time Gorky carried Davis's trunk down four flights of
stairs and another time when a contest between Gorky and a wrestling
partner got out of hand and Davis had to intervene. Although he wanted
to be thought of as a sensitive poet, Gorky liked to play the tough guy. He
copied Davis's way of talking out of the corner of his mouth like a mob-
ster. Sometimes he even let his cigarette dangle, Humphrey Bogart–
style. Once at a party he gave during Prohibition, Gorky even came to
blows with Davis after discovering that Davis was about to make off with
a bottle of Gorky's bootleg grappa.

Another time, when Gorky and some friends were returning by train
to Manhattan after an excursion, Gorky took on three or four youths who

were heckling him about his beard. "And we had to restrain him," Davis's wife, Roselle, recalled. "He was very sensitive about being laughed at, and anyone who did so about his beard, did so at their own risk." Mina Metzger's son-in-law Warren McCulloch claimed to have joined Gorky on what he called Gorky's Sunday morning exercise routine: "He would go down south of Houston Street in New York, a solid Italian neighborhood. And he'd go down there and yell, 'Wop, wop,' until two or three would make a run at him. They never made a run singly. And he'd grab them and smack their heads together and throw them aside, wait for the next. As far as he was concerned he was just getting exercise." Another form of exercise was sparring with the painter Peter Busa, whom he met in 1933 and who, though much shorter than Gorky, had trained as an amateur boxer (Fig. 95). Having no talent for boxing, Gorky could not fend off the younger man's punches. Finally he yelled, "God damn it, Busa!" and he picked up his friend and threw him across the room onto the sofa.

Dorothy Miller, too, bore witness to Gorky's potential for aggression. She recalled a fight he had with the painter Joseph Pollet, who "muscled in" on Gorky's table at a downtown Italian restaurant. "And Gorky was terribly angry and they had a fist fight out in the street which Gorky won. O yes, Gorky was strong, physically enormous, you know, very tall, no one to fool with." Gorky's pugnacity could also be verbal, as *Partisan Review* critic (and amateur painter) Clement Greenberg discovered when, on the sidewalk outside Hans Hofmann's Eighth Street school, he held forth on art matters. Gorky, who disliked both Greenberg's paintings and his intellectual arrogance, said, "What right have you got to talk? You're no artist. Do a drawing for me!" There was, of course, a playful side to Gorky's brawn. Raoul Hague recalled that when they left a restaurant and walked out onto the sidewalk, "he'd get you in a neck lock."

For all his love of roughhousing, Gorky was more apt to show off by dancing than by fighting. He was not a drinker—Armenian immigrants tended to be abstemious. Moreover, during the Depression he was too poor to buy liquor. But at parties Gorky drank and, like many other nondrinkers, he didn't know when to stop. If a bottle of wine was on the table, he drank until it was empty. Having little tolerance for alcohol, he quickly became tipsy. This was an occasion for rising to his feet, turning his jacket inside out so that its silk lining looked like a peasant costume, pulling out his handkerchief, and, to the accompaniment of his own voice or to the Armenian records that he sometimes brought to parties, dancing the shepherds' dances of his youth. Mischa Reznikoff recalled: "After a few bottles of Prohibition wine, Gorky would start singing his songs. 'Aaah, aah, aah!' Like these Armenian gypsy songs. He had a way of snapping his fingers onto his knuckles. Davis liked jazz. He would say to Gorky, 'Jazz it up a little, Gorky! Jazz it up a little!' Gorky could sing and snap his fingers and dance, he could do that in the middle of that miserable tea-room. We used to get loaded." Stuart Davis's memory suggests that not everyone was charmed. He felt that Gorky reserved this dancing routine for circles where it would "go over big," and it "took up a lot of room, and the accompanying vocalizations drowned out all competitive conversations. This idiosyncrasy was frowned on by us, who would not tolerate musical deviations of any kind from our profoundly hip devotion to American Jazz. Gorky became aware of this ban very fast, and respected it after being properly indoctrinated in its rationale."

It is easy to understand why Davis found Gorky's singing so trying. Gorky made a wailing, twangy sound. Although his speaking voice was low, when singing he switched to what his friend the Greek-born painter Aristodimos Kaldis called a "high tenor falsetto voice." Like many other tall men, Gorky sometimes stooped over when he was talking to someone smaller, but he generally stood straight and moved with a liquid grace. Holding the handkerchief high over his head, he would turn with smooth, intricate, highly controlled steps. "All his movements and gestures were elegant," Mougouch recalls. Even his long fingers holding a cigarette had an exquisite grace, and when he walked he was "panther-like." The ever appreciative de Kooning remembered: "He sure had terrific style." On one occasion, de Kooning recalled, Gorky danced "with one of those instruments made with just a lot of wires. You held it above your head and you whirled it round, and it made a noise. The faster you whirled it, the louder the noise. That was dramatic enough! He could have taken a man's head off with that thing."

During the Depression most New York artists could not afford a telephone. They sent telegrams and left messages under one another's doors. Meetings tended to be casual. When the painting day was done, an artist might wander out for a chance encounter with a friend on a Washington Square bench or in a certain cafeteria. Gorky drank coffee at all hours of the day and night. Sometimes he went to the greasy spoon in his own building, but mostly he went to a coffee shop around the corner from Union Square at Fourth Avenue and Nineteenth Street or to the favorite haunt of "the cafeteria people," Stewart's on Sixth Avenue, which artists frequented because they could get free rolls. With Reuben Nakian he went to various Automats where you could put twenty cents in a slot and out of a glass-fronted box would come a whole meal. "You have to remember," Nakian said, "that Gorky and I didn't have much money and so sometimes we'd go to a delicatessen and order a piece of bread and a piece of baloney and make a meal of it."

At cafeterias and restaurants Gorky drew on napkins and paper tablecloths. As he drew he talked. He was, friends recall, passionate and serious but also funny. Jacob Kainen said: "I never heard him laugh or saw him smile as though he meant it; his facial expressions ranged from tenderness through earnestness, intentness, vulnerability, contempt, hostility, and sadness." With a few drinks, said Saul Schary, Gorky would "slough off his normal sort of quiet melancholy." He would erupt with high-pitched laughter, and his conversation was often hilarious. He wasn't trying to be witty—what made people laugh was his originality, the odd slant at which he viewed the world. His humor had an innocence overlaid by a somewhat knowing mischief, a need to play the clown. Kainen was with Gorky during one of his more antic moments:

> Gorky had few inhibitions about expressing his feelings, insights, and opinions in public, as I discovered the first time we descended to the coffee shop for coffee and doughnuts. Two girls were seated at a nearby table. They were contrasting types: one thin, animated, and with a light, chirping voice; the other chubby, owl-eyed, with slow movements and a low, soothing speech. Gorky kept looking at them as he drew long horizontal lines with an India-ink fountain pen, lines exquisitely exact, almost as if ruled. Finally he stopped making the wizard lines, arose, and walked over to the girls.
>
> "You," he said to the thin girl, "are like bird—tweet, tweet, tweet." He grimaced coldly in what he might have thought was an ingratiating manner and turned to the chubby one. "You—are like cow—moo, moo, moo-oo." A resounding slap followed and Gorky returned to our table, his eyebrows raised in mock surprise.
>
> "I don't understand. What's wrong with cow?"

Though he did not intend to be cruel, Gorky's peremptory manner and his bursts of unedited aperçus often offended. He was, observed Lee Krasner, "eccentric in terms of saying what he wanted to, which wasn't always the polite or civilized manner to handle things. He might become very abrupt in a discussion if something was said that irritated him." "All of a sudden," recalled de Kooning, "he'd say, 'You know, I'm sick and tired of talking about it.'" And Gorky's tactlessness about people's looks could be brutal: "He'd say, 'You see that woman over there? She's just like an old prune!'" Once Gorky wrote that he liked the "song of a single person." He certainly enjoyed the sound of his own voluble thought. Yet he did not feel at ease with large groups of people, and certain social milieus unnerved him—for example, Albert Gallatin's tweed-suited, pipe-smoking, uptown artist friends or, in the 1940s, Peggy Guggenheim's mercilessly sophisticated Beekman Place salon. On many occasions, especially when there were a lot of people in a room, he was silent. Kainen once noted that Gorky did not have a rapport with many people, and "if he didn't have a rapport with you, he was generally hostile."

Among the downtown restaurants that Gorky favored was Ticino's on Thompson Street. It had sawdust on the floor, a pool table, and you could order a large bowl of spaghetti for twenty-five cents. Another was Romany Marie's, whose owner wore long skirts and ethnic-looking jewelry and was thought to be a Romanian gypsy though she was in fact from Brooklyn. Her restaurant, said Reuben Nakian, "had atmosphere, like homespun gypsy style." There was an accordion player and a bar designed by one of the denizens, Buckminster Fuller. Romany Marie liked artists and she let them run up bills and pay them off with artworks, so her place was, said David Smith, "our hangout. Gorky, Graham, de Kooning, Reznikoff held forth—often Joe Stella presided. He was sort of Papa." Smith remembered designer Frederick Kiesler at Romany Marie's propounding his architectural concepts and Gorky giving "a chalk talk on Cubism." A third place where Village artists could afford to eat was the Jumble Shop, a tearoom on Eighth Street and MacDougal Alley. It had an old bar in the back and tables where you could get a bite to eat. Lee Krasner, who lived in the neighborhood, said: "We'd meet at the Jumble Shop or I'd go to his [Gorky's] studio. The Jumble Shop was a place in the village where you could sit down in the evening and nurse a glass of beer and talk about your art problems . . . We artists could sit there in the evenings and nurse our problems."

Often Gorky and Krasner's conversations about art grew heated. The feisty Krasner said: "I had a great deal of fights with Arshile, o yes, it wasn't a relationship which always flowed in glowing terms. These arguments might, at some point, involve different philosophies of art. At that point, the image of Picasso was dominating the art world very strongly and one might feel, well maybe Matisse is really a better painter," thus provoking Gorky's scorn. For all that, Gorky was, for Krasner, the "big figure," and some of her canvases from the 1930s show the influence of the Picassoid late Cubist mode that Gorky adapted in the early years of the Depression. Indeed, Krasner seems to have understood Picasso through Gorky's eyes.

Gorky sometimes accompanied artist friends to Armenian restaurants along Lexington Avenue in the upper Twenties. His favorite was Arax, where a substantial meal cost fifty cents and where the Armenian waitress, Arpenik Karebian, might give an impoverished artist a free meal. Gorky told her that he was not Armenian, but he always ordered stuffed peppers, pilaf, and *madzoun*. "Arpenik, sweetheart of the artists," he would say. Once he offered her a painting, but she turned it down: "That crazy thing? I don't want it!"

Gorky made frequent forays to the movies, especially to cowboy movies. His favorites starred Bob Steel, Ken Maynard, or Buck Jones, but what he enjoyed was not the drama but the panoply of moving shapes and the beauty of the western mountains, which he said reminded him of Armenia. Having settled into his seat, Gorky would declaim about the way the curve of a hill was the opposite of the curve of a saddle, or how the shadows cast by a galloping horse's legs were like equine ghosts, or how bright sun exaggerated the contrast of light and dark. "Gorky made no attempt to whisper," Jacob Kainen recalled. "He spoke as though we two were the only people in the theater. Soon a succession of outraged calls—'keep quiet!' and 'shut-up!'—came from all sides and continued or subsided as Gorky was moved to speak or remain silent." Occasionally Gorky visited burlesque houses on Fourteenth Street. Raoul Hague told the story of walking with Gorky when suddenly Gorky said, "I'm going home to paint." Hague countered: "I'll go home and read Schopenhauer," but he decided to go to Minsky's burlesque house instead, "and who do I sit next to but Gorky. He was there for the style, not the belly dancers, comedians, and straightmen . . . Gorky saw things differently."

25

Fervent Scrutinizer

✵

When Gorky wasn't standing before his easel, his favorite place to be was in a museum. Although he was interested in the range of art history from Mesopotamian idols to Poussin, usually he would go straight to a painting that he thought might solve some problem he was struggling with in his own work. Sometimes he carried a magnifying glass so that he could examine and learn from the brush strokes of a master like Ingres. The art historian Meyer Schapiro said: "I met him most often in the museums and galleries fixed in rapt contemplation of pictures with that grave, searching look which was one of the beauties of his face. As some poets are great readers, Gorky—exceptional among painters—was a fervent scrutinizer of paintings. No interesting touch or invention of form escaped his eye."

Many of Gorky's artist friends learned by accompanying Gorky to museums. Peter Busa occasionally joined Gorky and de Kooning, and sometimes Elaine as well, on their Saturday pilgrimages to the Metropolitan. It was, Busa said, like going to church. Gorky, of course, was the leader. "He was the best informed art historian of all the artists, merely on the basis of his natural intelligence and his curiosity," Busa recalled. "He could talk for an hour with great depth about a single painting at the Metropolitan." Sometimes Hague joined the group. He remembered Gorky loving Ingres, early Flemish paintings, David's *Death of Socrates*, and Raphael's Madonnas, whose hair, he said, had a lot of electricity. "You couldn't discuss with Gorky," said Hague. "He loved to tell you. He showed the way. He wouldn't give you a chance to talk." In spite of his high seriousness, Gorky liked to play the clown. "He felt a compulsion to be like a fool," said Hague. Busa agreed: "There was an attitude that he was kind of a comedian. And he himself didn't mind that attitude, because it was a way of getting out of his seriousness."

Gorky cut an amazing figure when he visited museums. He acted as though he owned certain paintings, and if he found a stranger in front of one of them he could be annoyed. "He had 'key' works," Elaine de Kooning wrote, "corners of tapestries, pieces of archaic Greek sculpture, to which he returned over and over again. People who didn't meet him until years later remember the tall, black-bearded man coming up to them and launching into unsolicited explanations if they happened to linger before an El Greco, a Raphael or a Bosch that he felt possessive about." Will Barnet recalls standing before a Raphael Madonna at the Metropolitan while Gorky expounded about its abstract qualities: "He looked like a real Messiah." On one occasion Jacob Kainen ran into Gorky at the National Gallery in Washington, DC, standing in front of an Ingres portrait. The two painters wandered into the room showing English paintings and came upon two women admiring Gainsborough's portrait of the duchess of Devonshire. Gorky glanced at Kainen out of the side of his eye, then moved close to the portrait to scrutinize its every part. The women moved aside to watch him. "After a time Gorky stepped back across the room, fixed his baleful eye on the canvas and announced: 'How horrible!' " Not surprisingly, the guards at the Metropolitan Museum disliked Gorky because he would interrupt the tour lecturers, correcting their information and criticizing their ideas.

Most of the art galleries Gorky frequented were on or near Fifty-seventh Street, which was the center of New York's commercial art activity. He would regularly visit Julien Levy's Surrealist-oriented gallery, which opened in 1931. Other galleries he stopped in at were John Becker, Valentine, Pierre Matisse, Knoedler, Montross, Durand-Ruel, and the Daniel Gallery. Once when he was making his gallery rounds with Ethel Schwabacher, Gorky studied an exhibition of Impressionist paintings on Durand-Ruel's velvet-lined walls. Though he had begun his career by working in an Impressionist manner, the style no longer satisfied him. "Gorky's thoughts broke out in snatches," Schwabacher recalled. Frowning at the canvases' shimmering formlessness, he said: "Seductive, yes, they revolted against darkness; there are no lost areas in these paintings as there are in the old masters. . . . The Renaissance discovered chiaroscuro, but the nineteenth century did better, they discovered *light without shadow.*" But suddenly he burst out with: "No, it will not do. Form must be unified again—Why break it up? Why break it up?" and without more ado, Gorky left the gallery.

He was far happier at a Poussin exhibition at the Durlacher Gallery. In March 1940, accompanied by Jacob Kainen and John Graham, he went especially to see Poussin's *Triumph of Bacchus.* "Graham and Gorky took that painting apart in detail," Kainen said. "This sort of analysis was a revelation to me; it included color sequences and shifts, back and forward movements, pulls and pulsations." Gorky observed the way a flaming brazier carried the eye to the end of a long compositional diagonal and the way a leopard skin held the eye at the picture's center. Among Gorky's collection of reproductions are several works by Poussin, including one of the *Triumph of Bacchus* that is covered with lines and circles drawn by Gorky and Graham to indicate the painting's underlying composition.

Sometimes Gorky went to galleries as part of his job as art adviser to Sidney Janis, who in the 1950s was to become a prominent Manhattan art dealer. Gorky met Janis in 1929, four years after Janis moved to New York City from Buffalo and started a shirt company. Janis was collecting mostly School of Paris modernists, and, in his capacity as art adviser, Gorky encouraged him to buy Picasso. Janis and Gorky would drive around in Janis's red convertible. "We used to hit the Fifty-seventh Street galleries and the museums," Janis said, "and used even to travel out of town together. Gorky was terrifically verbal and terrifically informed." Sidney Janis remained a great admirer of Gorky. In 1939, when Picasso's *Guernica* was exhibited at the Valentine Gallery, and Gorky gave a lecture about it in the gallery's foyer, Janis turned to a friend and said: "He is a poet." Both Sidney and his brother Martin Janis bought Gorky's work, and Gorky must have been thrilled to be included along with Picasso, Léger, Matisse, and other of his heroes when the Museum of Modern Art and the Arts Club of Chicago showed the Sidney Janis collection in 1935 and when, in the same year, the Albright-Knox Art Gallery in Buffalo showed the Martin Janis collection.

Gorky was a "fervent scrutinizer" of art in books as well as in museums and galleries. His friends were as amazed by his art book collection as they were by his supply of art materials. When he showed books to friends he did so with great reverence and he refused to lend. The painter David Margolis recalled that during the Depression Gorky bought a rare edition of a book on Brueghel for seventy-five dollars, and he invited Margolis to come and see it. It was late afternoon when Margolis arrived at 36 Union Square. The studio was dark—too dark to see the reproductions in the book. When Margolis asked Gorky to turn on the single bulb that dangled from the ceiling, Gorky said, "Now look, you bastard, to buy a book and pay electricity too?" Margolis was impressed: "His electricity could be shut off but he'd buy a book for $75." Although much of Gorky's library was lost in a studio fire in 1946, what remained is extraordinary for its scope. Books he looked at often are well-worn, and reproductions that he was especially drawn to and that he consulted while he was at work often have oil paint fingerprints in the margins. Certain illustrations prompted Gorky to draw in his book's margins or on the blank pages in the front and back. Sometimes he drew variations on the artworks reproduced.

Erhard Weyhe, who owned an art bookstore on Lexington Avenue, remembered that Gorky would come in the morning and always sit in a certain chair: "He never had any money but he was very welcome here and felt at home . . . O, he loved to see every new book. He'd sit here and use it as a library. They all did that. And my gallery started that way. I'm not an art dealer. So the artists would come in and want a book. So I'd say, 'Why don't you give me one of your drawings or lithographs or etchings, huh?' So what I liked I took and gave them a nice book, a $6 book. And when a customer showed interest, I'd say, 'But I gave him a $50 book for it. You can have it for $50 if you want it.' "

In 1929 Gorky wanted a book he couldn't afford. "That's all right," Weyhe told him. Gorky could give him paintings in exchange. Gorky brought Weyhe two Braque-inspired still lifes. "Can't you sell these paintings?" he asked. "Certainly," said Weyhe. "And hardly had he left," Weyhe recalled, "when a very rich, regular customer, who was a collector, came in." This was John Nicholas Brown, from a prominent Providence family. He had never heard of Gorky, but Weyhe went to work on him. "You better buy that painting. I've bought one too," Wehye said. "So I called Gorky on the phone and said, 'Look here, I just sold your painting. Come on and get your check.' And Gorky was mad. 'How dare you sell that painting?' he said. So I told him, 'I want to tell you something. The customer didn't buy the painting. I sold it to him. You know the difference. So naturally I can call it off . . .' So Gorky finally relented and came in and got the check." This was the inauspicious beginning of Gorky's difficult relationship with dealers. And it was his first recorded sale through a gallery and to someone who was neither a student nor a friend.

Gorky found art outside of museums and books, as well. On his long late-afternoon walks, when Manhattan was alive with shadows, he would exclaim that the patterns of light and dark were what modern painters were trying to achieve. Raoul Hague recalled that Gorky was thrilled by "an old woman, who used to sit on a bench in Washington Square and her clothes were of taffeta and their colors just vibrated in the sun." Cracks on the pavement and peeling walls were, he pronounced, as good as anything in a museum. Rooftops captured Gorky, too. When he saw the hooded tin spouts that projected from the roofs of brownstones he would bend his wrist, splay his fingers, and say, "Look, they're ready to jump." Walking with Jacob Kainen on Second Avenue, he suddenly became transfixed by a marble-fronted Nedick's stand with the remnants of an advertisement picturing oranges and green leaves. As he drew back to the curb and fixed his eye on the stand, the short-order hot dog cook became nervous. "Uneasiness turned to alarm when Gorky rushed to the stand and passed his hands caressingly over the patches of orange and green. 'What chexchures!' he exclaimed. 'What chexchures!'" Sometimes Gorky's outbursts of praise for objects encountered in the street seemed calculated to provoke, as when he proclaimed to Balcomb Greene that a fire hydrant was "more beautiful than any painting ever made." Although Gorky was not specifically looking for motifs or art ideas when he scoured the streets for visual excitement, the experience must have carried over into his increasingly abstract art.

When Holger Cahill introduced Gorky to the Viennese designer and architect Frederick Kiesler as "the greatest artist in America," Kiesler responded, "North or South?" Lillian Olinsey (later Lillian Kiesler), who worked as Hans Hofmann's assistant in the 1930s, met both Gorky and her future husband around 1935. "Gorky and Kiesler were elective affinities," she said. "Kiesler had a passionate relationship to Gorky. He was almost protective of him, and Gorky was so tall and Kiesler was so short. He used to take Gorky to Pappas, a Greek steak house on Fourteenth Street and Eighth Avenue. He was the host. He would pay the bill, and they'd have loud, animated discussions. Both of them were passionate about modern art." Gorky and Kiesler were walking companions as well. Gorky's eyes were "like vacuum cleaners," Lillian Kiesler recalled. They took in "every store sign, every advertisement and display . . . Gorky called it the real American indigenous art, little knowing that later Pop Art would do exactly that." This attitude toward signs was fashionable among the Manhattan avant-garde. Stuart Davis, for example, compared a shoemaker's sign to a Titian, and he frequently incorporated signs into his proto-pop paintings.

On his walks Gorky often stopped in at Hans Hofmann's school in the West Village, and, together with many other artists who would eventually be part of what came to be called the New York School, he attended a series of lectures that Hofmann gave in the winter of 1938–39. From these lectures, through conversations, and probably also through Graham as an intermediary, Gorky picked up many of Hofmann's ideas. Both men spoke about "tensions" between forms in space, about positive and negative space, and about keeping the canvas flat. Although Gorky and Hofmann had great respect for each other—when they met they bowed—both men liked to play the maestro. "Gorky had an attitude of 'Show me,'" Lillian Kiesler observed. "He was resisting Hofmann." Painter Fritz Bultman witnessed one of Gorky and Hans Hofmann's arguments, this one precipitated by differing views of Picasso's *Red Tablecloth with Plaster Cast* (1930). They agreed that nature was the departure point for art, but Gorky, with his symbolic thinking and his impulse to invent metaphors, believed that the motifs in the Picasso and in paintings in general were symbols for something else, whereas Hofmann insisted that the objects in still lifes were simply objects in space with no meaning beyond their transposition into form.

26

Exhibitions

※

Despite the stock market crash in October 1929, the 1930s began on an auspicious note for Gorky's career. Early in 1930 Alfred H. Barr, the young director of the fledgling Museum of Modern Art, came to his studio; shortly thereafter he invited Gorky to participate in *An Exhibition of Works by 46 Painters and Sculptors under 35 Years of Age* to open in April. This was the museum's third show. The previous two had presented French Postimpressionism and modernism. Gorky must have been delighted to be recognized by an institution that championed the Europeans he so revered. The Museum of Modern Art show was his first public exposure and a huge boost to his career.

In fact, Alfred Barr visited Gorky's studio twice. "I was impressed immediately by his seriousness as an artist and his charm as a person," Barr reminisced. "I went back again shortly afterwards to pick out some paintings for our show . . . To be candid I was somewhat put off by his dependence on the painters of the School of Paris such as Matisse, Picasso and Miró . . . In spite of his derivative style one felt grateful for his studies of abstract and semi-abstract painting during a decade given over largely to Social Realism and the American Scene."

The Modern's exhibition catalog listed three Gorky still lifes dated between 1927 and 1929, and it printed the usual falsehoods about his life: "Archele Gorki," it said, was born in 1903 in Nizhni Novgorod. He studied there and at Tiflis, and then for three months in 1920 with Kandinsky. "Gorky's listing was somewhat fanciful," Barr noted. "I recall that about then or shortly afterwards he let it be known that he was a Georgian prince. Anyway the misinformation was his fantasy, not ours."

One of Gorky's three still lifes was listed as being loaned by him. A Braque-inspired *Still Life* with pears, grapes, and a pitcher was loaned by Nathan Bijur and was prominently hung in the center of the entrance hall of the museum's quarters in the Heckscher Building at 730 Fifth Avenue at Fifty-seventh Street. A third entry was identified as courtesy of the J. B. Neumann Gallery. Neumann was a prestigious Manhattan dealer who opened the New Art Circle Gallery in 1924, showing Arp, Calder, Kandinsky, Klee, and Max Weber among others. Very likely the American Expressionist Max Weber introduced Gorky to Neumann, who became the first bona fide dealer to handle Gorky's work. Like future dealers, Neumann found Gorky difficult: according to art historian Robert Reiff, Neumann kept Gorky's paintings for several months in 1930 but was unable to sell them. One day when Neumann was in Philadelphia on a business trip, Gorky stormed into the gallery, told the secretary that Neumann had done nothing for him, and removed his paintings from the premises. He never saw Neumann again. If this story is true, Neumann must have kept a few of Gorky's canvases: three of the four paintings that Gorky exhibited at the Whitney Museum's *Abstract Painting in America* exhibition in 1935 were listed as "Collection J. B. Neumann."

Gorky's representation at the Museum of Modern Art's April 1930 show led to his being invited to participate in a number of group exhibitions. On January 1, 1931, his *Improvisation* was included in a special exhibition organized to inaugurate the new home on Twelfth Street of the New School for Social Research. The show was arranged by the Société Anonyme, an association founded in 1920 by Katherine Dreier and Marcel Duchamp and that functioned somewhere between a modern art museum and a *Kunsthalle*. In March 1931 Gorky took part in *The First Exhibition of the International Group*, at the Art Center at 65 East Fifty-sixth Street, and later in the same year he was included in three group shows at Edith Halpert's Downtown Gallery on West Thirteenth Street. Halpert was one of the few dealers who took an interest in American modernism. She handled Stuart Davis's work, and it was probably Davis who introduced Gorky to her. The Downtown Gallery's papers list seven of Gorky's works, all received in 1931. The four paintings were priced between one hundred and four hundred and fifty dollars. The identity of one is known. *Fruit* (c. 1928–29) was received by the gallery on April 13 and sold for two hundred and fifty dollars to John D. Rockefeller on April 21, 1931. To be included in such a prestigious collection was surely a great satisfaction to Gorky: as usual when his career took an auspicious turn, he wrote to Vartoosh about it.

The third show in which he participated at the Downtown Gallery took place in December and was entitled *American Printmakers: Fifth Annual Exhibition.* It included three recent lithographs by Gorky priced at twelve dollars each: *Painter and Model, Manikin,* and *Self-Portrait.* In April the Downtown Gallery also sent one of Gorky's paintings to the Buffalo Fine Art Academy–Albright Art Gallery—Gorky's first exposure outside New York City. In addition, George McNeil wrote that in 1931 "Davis, Graham, Matulka and Gorky were able to present a strong abstract art exhibition at the Art Student's League to show Léger on his New York visit."

In 1931 Stuart Davis asked Gorky to write a piece about him for *Creative Art.* Knowing that Gorky was not "a glib man with the pen," Davis was anxious, but Gorky kept reassuring him and did not let Davis read the article before it was published. To Davis's embarrassment, Gorky's short appreciation sometimes waxed euphoric to the point of incomprehensibility. But the article gives an idea of Gorky's enthusiasm for Cubism, and it is a passionate defense of abstraction at a time when abstraction needed defending. Gorky wrote:

> Yet the silent consequences of Stuart Davis move us to the cool and intellectual world where all human emotions are disciplined upon rectangular proportions . . . This artist, whether he paints egg-beaters, streets, or pure geometrical organizations, expresses his constructive attitude toward his successive experiences. He gives us symbols of tangible spaces, with gravity and physical law. He, above his contemporaries, rises high—mountain-like! Oh, what clarity! One he is, and one of but few, who realizes his canvas as a rectangular shape with two dimensional surface plane. Therefore he forbids himself to poke bumps and holes upon that potential surface. This man, Stuart Davis, works upon that platform where are working the giant painters of the century,— Picasso, Léger, Kandinsky, Juan Gris,—bringing to us new utility, new aspects, as does the art of Uccello. They take us to the su-

pernatural world behind reality where once the great centuries danced.

Yet there are a large number of critics, artists, and public suspended like vultures, waiting in the air for the death of the distinctive art of this century, the art of Léger, Picasso, Miró, Kandinsky, Stuart Davis. They forget that while the artist never works outside his time, yet his art will go on to be merged gradually into the new art of a new age. There will be no short stop. We shall not, contrary to the expectation of these people, hear of the sudden death of Cubism, abstraction, so-called modern art. These critics, these artists, these spectators who wait for a sudden fall are doomed to disappointment. They have merely not understood the spiritual movement and the law of direct energy of the centuries, and they can never have understood the spiritual meaning of any form of art. If they could but realize that energy is a spiritual movement and that they must conceive of working under a law of universal esthetic progress, as we do in science, in mathematics, in physics.

The twentieth century—what intensity, what activity, what restless energy! Has there in six centuries been better art than Cubism? No. Centuries will go past—artists of gigantic stature will draw positive elements from Cubism.

Clumsy painters take a measurable space, a clear definite shape, a rectangle, a vertical or horizontal direction, and they call it blank canvas, while every time one stretches canvas he is drawing a new space . . . No painter in America has made such [a] definite and developed statement of his thought as Stuart Davis at his exhibition a few months ago. He made his vision clear.

Gorky sounded a Surrealist note when he said that great modernists "take us to the supernatural world behind reality where once the great centuries danced." He also placed great emphasis on precision, logic, and flatness. Similarly, in his work of this period he veered between the Surrealism of the *Nighttime, Enigma, and Nostalgia* drawings and the clarity and rigor of his Synthetic Cubist canvases, in which curvilinear motifs are indeed "disciplined upon rectangular proportions."

Gorky ended his article by quoting three paragraphs from a 1931 letter that Stuart Davis wrote to the Downtown Gallery. These paragraphs could be Gorky's as well as Davis's aesthetic credo: "My concept of form is very simple and is based on the assumption that space is continuous and that matter is discontinuous . . . I conceive of form (matter) as existing in space, in terms of linear direction. It follows then that the forms of the subject are analyzed in terms of angular variation from successive bases of directional radiation. Color must be thought of as texture which automatically allows one to visualize it in terms of space. Aside from this it has no meaning." To conclude, Gorky added one sentence of his own words: "Because Stuart Davis realizes the invisible relations and phenomena of this modern time he is the visible point to the progressive mind in his country." A piece on Gorky that Davis wrote for *Magazine of Art* twenty years later said that Gorky's article "had laid it on thick" and that, although Gorky had probably had a great deal of editorial help, the general tone revealed Gorky's way of thinking. "We kidded about it a lot, but he always stoutly maintained that he wrote it."

By 1932 Gorky had gained a reputation in the tiny New York art world. A sign of his prestige was his being asked to take part, along with Princeton professor Frank Jewett Matther, Jr., in "Two Views of Modern Art," a lecture program presented at Wells College in Aurora, New York, on March 3, 1932. But with the deepening economic crisis and the collapse of the art market, patrons like Nathan Bijur stopped buying. The Grand Central School of Art closed for several years, leaving Gorky jobless. In 1932 and 1933 Gorky had no one-man shows and he participated in only one group show: he sent two paintings to the Wilmington Society of Fine Arts's exhibition of Russian painting and sculpture.

His dream of being a universal artist, of going beyond national boundaries, must have been encouraged by an invitation in 1932 to become a charter member of the Abstraction-Création Art Non-Figuratif group (commonly called "Abstraction-Création"). The association, which began in Paris in 1931 and continued until 1936, included some four hundred abstract artists from Europe, England, and the United States. It sponsored annual exhibitions in which members participated and it published a journal to which it gave its own name. Gorky owned several issues, and one of his *Nighttime, Enigma, and Nostalgia* drawings was reproduced in the 1932 issue.

From February 2 to 15, 1934, Gorky had his first one-man show at the Mellon Galleries at 27 South Eighteenth Street in Philadelphia. The gallery was directed by C. Philip Boyer, of whom Dorothy Miller said:

"That awful man named Boyer stole a great many drawings from him [Gorky]." Apparently what happened was that Boyer kept Gorky's unsold paintings in the hope of selling them over time, and Gorky, having the opposite of a bookkeeper's mentality, did not manage to keep track of what paintings were where. Gorky's Mellon Galleries exhibition included thirty-seven numbered but untitled paintings from 1926 to 1930; the bulk of the show comprised works from 1929 to 1930. There was no catalog, but the checklist (which gives Gorky's date and place of birth as 1904 in the south Caucasus) presented statements by Holger Cahill, Stuart Davis, Frederick Kiesler, and Harriet Janowitz, who was Sidney Janis's wife. Kiesler's observations were the most perceptive. He saw Gorky's art as a coming together of East and West: "Gorky, spirit of Europe in body of the Caucasus, getting the feel of American soil."

Gorky traveled to Philadelphia for his opening and he delivered a lecture about his work. While in Philadelphia, he visited his friend and patron the wealthy textile merchant Bernard Davis, and it may have been at this point that Davis, perhaps realizing Gorky's and Boyer's disappointment with sales, bought a group of Gorky's Cubist still lifes from the late twenties and 1930.

Reviews were disappointing as well. C. H. Bonte in the *Philadelphia Inquirer* (February 11, 1934) gave a sarcastic and double-edged appraisal of Gorky's show. On the one hand, he praised Gorky's "brilliance of pigmentation." On the other hand, he said Gorky's paintings were derivative of European Cubism and looked like modern art as ridiculed in comic papers. Bonte also took a stab at the "ethnological puzzle" of Gorky's "Caucasian" origins: "He is said to be a relative of the novelist Maxim Gorky, in which case he has adopted the pen name of the renowned Alexey Peshkov."

Gorky took advantage of his trip to Philadelphia to visit the Barnes Foundation in nearby Merion. Years later he told his second wife about it. She recalled: "When Gorky went to the Barnes Foundation he was in such a state of excitement over the Cézannes, but Mr. Barnes followed him around and stood just behind him and whistled and made little noises—'sh, sh, sh,' and it drove Gorky mad so he left."

Another major art event for Gorky in 1934 was his inclusion in the First Municipal Art Exhibition in New York, sponsored by Mayor Fiorello H. La Guardia. It took place on February 28 at the Forum Gallery in the still uncompleted Rockefeller Center, and it presented three works each by five hundred New York artists. *New York Times* critic Edward Alden Jewell wrote: "This mile of American Art should be walked by every able-bodied citizen." A year later, in February 1935, Gorky took part in the Whitney Museum of American Art's *Abstract Painting in America.* This was the beginning of a long and happy relationship with the Whitney, which invited Gorky to show in almost all its annual exhibitions. No longer a private club, the Whitney had opened in 1931 as a museum occupying three adjoined brownstones at 10 West Eighth Street. The 1935 abstract show gave special emphasis to the older modernists, people like Marsden Hartley and Max Weber, who had explored Cubism in the second decade of the century but who had returned to more figurative modes in the worldwide retreat to realism in the 1920s. This prompted the younger abstractionists to call it "a kind of old-ladies' affair" and "not truly abstract."

Before the Whitney exhibition opened a group of painter friends that included Gorky, Davis, Graham, de Kooning, Edgar Levy, and Mischa Reznikoff agreed to tell the museum that they would participate only if all of them were invited. All were not invited, and Gorky rather lamely claimed that his works were exhibited without his permission. David Smith told the story this way: "It was in [Romany] Marie's where we once formed a group, Graham, Edgar Levy, Reznikoff, de Kooning, Gorky and myself with Davis being asked to join. This was short-lived. We never exhibited and we lasted in union about thirty days. Our only action was to notify the Whitney Museum that we were a group and would only exhibit in the 1935 abstract show if all were asked. Some of us were, some exhibited, some didn't, and that ended our group."

Gorky had two one-man shows in late 1935. Both were dedicated to drawings—those pen-and-ink drawings such as *Nighttime, Enigma, and Nostalgia* that Gorky had studied and restudied in the early 1930s when they were pinned up on his long studio wall (Fig. 92). The first show opened in September at the Boyer Galleries in the Broad Street Suburban Station Building at 1617 Pennsylvania Boulevard in Philadelphia. Gorky attended the opening and gave a lecture. The *Philadelphia Inquirer* noted that, with his earlier exhibition, Gorky had already "created a profound impression among those who like strong doses of the tenets of modernism."

The second drawing show, Gorky's first one-man exhibition in New York City, took place in December. It was held at the Guild Art Gallery at 37 West Fifty-seventh Street, founded two months earlier by two women artists, Anna Walinska and Margaret Lefranc. Gorky's two still lifes in the Guild's inaugural show had caught the attention of *New York Times* reviewer Edward Alden Jewell: "Archile Gorky's handsome abstract decoration (in soft, indeterminate, romantic treatment, the antithesis of Léger's decorative style) may be said to dominate the show." In November 1935 Gorky signed a three-year contract in which he agreed to make the Guild Art Gallery the sole agent of his work. Anna Walinska had been a friend since the 1920s. She loved Gorky's dash, and he was fond of her Eastern European manner and her flamboyant good looks. In 1937 he painted a Matisse-inspired portrait of her that she acquired in the same year. Gorky would introduce Anna to his friends: "Meet Anna Walinska. The only woman I have never kissed!" Like other of his women friends, she sensed that he was lonely: "It was easy to feel alienated at that time, Americana, flag-waving. He would come up and spend time with my Jewish family. He seemed to be a family man."

The Guild's press releases said that its purpose was to exhibit and interpret contemporary American art "in terms of the conflicts of contemporary life" and to "bring art nearer to the layman." To that end, it set up an educational program that presented a weekly lecture series for which it charged fifty cents. The first lecture was Gorky's. The gallery sent out an announcement saying that on November 24 the "well-known artist" would give an illustrated lecture on "Methods Purposes and Significance of Abstract Art." Despite his imperfect English, Gorky's conviction and knowledge made him a brilliant speaker. Walinska remembered: "He wasn't nervous. He took it very much in his stride."

A few weeks before the December 16 opening of Gorky's first solo show at the Guild, Anna Walinska wrote to Léger asking him to come and see the work. Léger, who had met Gorky in 1931 through either Frederick Kiesler or Stuart Davis, not only came to see Gorky's drawing show but also made a studio visit. Gorky appeared in the gallery and told Walinska that "something unbelievable" was happening—Léger was coming to his studio the next day. A few days later when Walinska asked him how the visit went, Gorky told her that he had panicked and hidden his paintings away before Léger arrived. Having won Léger's approval for Gorky, Walinska and Lefranc went to work writing promotional letters to art-world luminaries. They wrote to Alfred Barr, for example, saying that Léger was "particularly enthusiastic" about Gorky's drawings and had said they were "original and a distinct addition to the field of abstraction." Next they wrote to Albert Gallatin and to Juliana Force, director of the Whitney Museum, again citing Léger's admiration for Gorky.

Gorky's show of eighteen drawings from 1931 to 1932 earned favorable reviews. The *New York Times* called Gorky's draftsmanship "vigorous and personal," and that same Sunday Carlyle Burrows wrote in the *Herald Tribune* that Gorky was "a skillful and ingenious pen draftsman." But Burrows had a caveat, the same criticism that would plague Gorky for years to come: "His is a difficult expression to disentangle from its sources in Picasso, Braque and others." Emily Genauer, who after Gorky's death would take a dim view of his accomplishment, wrote an enthusiastic piece in the New York *World Telegram* (December 21, 1935): "Gorky has an odd manner of almost completely covering his picture surface with thousands of little cross-hatched lines. On this practically black surface float weird, fantastic forms that, having no apparent or obvious meaning, are nevertheless so carefully set in their appointed place they carry the eye deep into the composition, achieve an exquisite balance of shape and tone (amazing how much color the artist has introduced into these black-and-whites), and set the whole arrangement into vibrating, arresting movement."

In *Parnassus* James Lane noted that Gorky's forms were those of "remembered reality," but, like so many later critics, Lane was carried away by the temptation to overinterpret Gorky's forms. In one of the *Nighttime, Enigma, and Nostalgia* drawings, for example, he saw "cronies in Morris chairs blowing smoke-rings," and in other drawings he saw "Durante's Schnozzle," or "the carcass of a man with a horse's head, and what-have-you." Many writers, including this one, have found it difficult not to chase after Gorky's "what-have-you"s. Gorky himself bears part of the responsibility: his shapes are designed to titillate image seekers with hints of what look and feel like objects, figures, or creatures in space.

For all the critical attention, Gorky sold only one drawing from his Guild Art Gallery show. Indeed, it was to be the only sale Gorky made during his contract with the Guild. Perhaps on the recommendation of her good friend John Graham, Katherine Dreier came to see the exhibition, showered Anna Walinska with questions about Gorky's appearance and personality, then bought a pen-and-ink drawing now entitled *Forms* (c. 1931–32). For this wonderfully atmospheric and mysterious version of *Nighttime, Enigma, and Nostalgia* she paid $85. After the one-third commission, the check written out to Gorky on March 18, 1936, came to $56.67. (The expenses of the show were recorded in the gallery's account book: $5.00 for publishing the catalog; $1.50 for cards, $5.50 for cardboards for mounting the drawings, $2.00 for screws and washers, $1.20 for wire, and $10.00 for stamps.) To celebrate the sale, Gorky invited Walinska out to a sumptuous Italian meal. When they finished eating, Gorky said, "That was good. Let's have another!" Walinska declined, but Gorky ate a second meal. On their way home they dropped in on an actress friend of Walinska's to whom Gorky made his usual announcement that Walinska was the only woman he had never kissed. This come-on worked: Gorky escorted Walinska to her bus stop, then returned to the actress's apartment.

Gorky showed in the Guild Gallery's March 1936 group exhibition of drawings, watercolors, and sculptures. His last participation at the Guild was in a group painting show that May. This time he presented three large still lifes. Once again reviewers were appreciative. Emily Genauer in the *World Telegram* (June 6, 1936) said Gorky was one of America's most brilliant practicing abstractionists. She and several other critics singled out *The Antique Cast* (c. 1928–29) for admiration. Anna Walinska recalled that this was one of those paintings that Gorky was especially proud of because he had lavished so much pigment on it. "Lift that!" he commanded. "How much do you think it weighs? You see that spot of cadmium red? That spot cost me thirty dollars. That spot!"

Gorky was not included in the gallery's next group show, in January 1937. Perhaps by then he'd had a falling out with the directors. In a spiral notebook that Walinska and Lefranc used to leave notes for each other about daily matters, Anna Walinska wrote on May 14, 1937: "Gorky was here—wanted to know whether he could have his canvas to show someone & have it photographed. Told him no & said I would talk to you about it. Am taking it home with me, I think I will bring it up to you, before he makes trouble, if any. Don't believe the story because when I asked him to bring the party down—he said it wasn't possible."

In 1936 Gorky participated in several group shows other than the Guild's. He was included in the Pennsylvania Academy of Fine Arts's "131st Exhibition in Oil and Sculpture" and in an exhibition entitled *Modern American Paintings* at the Boyer Gallery at 89 East Eighty-seventh Street in New York. (This gallery was run by the same C. Philip Boyer who ran the Boyer Gallery in Philadelphia.) In mid-September

Gorky was represented in the Museum of Modern Art's *New Horizons in American Art* and in November he took part in the Whitney's third painting biennial. If he did not have many sales, he did have admirers. "In 1934 John Graham, Stuart Davis and Gorky were generally recognized by alert artists as the magus figures in the New York art world," said Jacob Kainen. Among progressive-thinking students at the Art Students League and among Hofmann students, Lillian Kiesler noted, Gorky was a mythic personality: "Gorky was the artist that we all admired." His "bold, luscious" paintings pointed "toward something that we had never known before in America."

Even with this approval, Gorky remained discouraged about the public response to his art. When, back in 1926, he had been interviewed on the occasion of his joining the faculty of the Grand Central Art School and had reflected on the unfortunate situation for the vanguard artist in the United States, he had spoken of American society's lack of interest in its contemporary artists. Some eight years later the artist's situation was even more discouraging. Lee Krasner remembered Gorky calling a meeting at de Kooning's studio and opening it with: "We have to admit we're defeated." Reuben Nakian, who became especially close to Gorky in 1935 when he and Gorky both showed at Boyer's Manhattan gallery, remembered Gorky saying one day, "Come on, there's a friend of mine I want you to meet." Gorky took Nakian to de Kooning's loft and there the conversation turned to the miserable plight of vanguard American artists. "We were all alone," Nakian recalled. "There wasn't anyone who gave a damn for us." Gorky put the matter this way: "The only good artist is a dead one."

Public indifference to the visual arts had elicited complaints from American painters for decades. Puritan pragmatism did not hold painting's sensuousness and imaginative powers in high regard. As a result, American artists felt defensive about their status. Although most of them lived in cities, especially New York, until the 1930s they lacked the camaraderie and the feeling of being embraced by a milieu that Parisian artists enjoyed. This isolation changed during the Depression decade, when the struggle for survival brought artists together in a passionate dialogue about the artist's relationship to society. Yet, even after he joined the Federal Art Project of the WPA, even after hearing the propaganda about artists on relief projects working shoulder to shoulder with other citizens, Gorky never believed that he was part of American society. He

kept on feeling misunderstood and resentful about the way in which social institutions impinged on him. Brought up as an Armenian in Ottoman Turkey, he had no experience at being part of the body politic.
"He felt he was a foreigner in the United States," says Mougouch.
"Gorky was anti-America. He felt that most Americans knew nothing
about life." Gorky, like many other artists and intellectuals, "thought this
was a barn place, that it had no art," de Kooning recalled. "I think it was
logical that artists didn't like it here because, you know, the museums
and galleries were very unfair to us. They felt that unless it came from
Europe, it wasn't any good and what they liked about America or American artists was regional art." To a great extent, Gorky agreed. Although
there were a few Americans, such as Stuart Davis, whom he admired, he
felt that everything of aesthetic excellence came from Europe, especially
Paris. "Gorky didn't like to think of himself as an American painter," said
Balcomb Greene. "Old world, yes. He wanted to belong to the old world
tradition."

Beginning in 1933 the federal government set up various projects for
artists to decorate public buildings. The first of these was the Public
Works of Art Project (PWAP), which Gorky joined on December 20,
1933, at a salary of $37.38 a week. Two days after he was accepted Gorky
filled out an official subject card in which he stated his idea for a semiabstract mural: "My subject matter is directional. American plains are
horizontal. New York City which I live in is vertical. In the middle of my
picture stands a column which symbolizes the determination of the
American nation. Various abstract scenes take place in the back of this
column. My intention is to create objectivity of the articles which I have
detached from their habitual surroundings to be able to give them the
highest realism." Gorky's attempt to combine the Surrealist idea of taking an object out of context with the proposition that his verticals and
horizontals and his column referred to the American scene demonstrates
his awareness of the need to convince the authorities that abstraction was
socially relevant and would mean something to the American public.

The following month Gorky named his mural *1934*, and noted that
it would be suitable for "Port of New York Authority 15 st & 8th Ave
(Fig. 93). Entrance to Museum of peaceful Arts, News building 42 east 3 Ave
in machinery dept." The PWAP required that muralists submit a 30" by
123" sketch of their project. After Gorky brought in a ten-foot-long mural
study, Lloyd Goodrich, who served as assistant to Juliana Force, the

PWAP's regional director for New York, asked him to make a color study of no longer than forty inches. Three days later Gorky wrote that he would proceed with the color study. His mid-March progress report said he was "carefully working constantly" on the color sketch. The color sketch has been lost, but Gorky's pen-and-ink studies show that the proposed mural would have combined themes he had worked on in his early 1930s drawings: *Objects with Ecorché, Column with Objects,* and *Nighttime, Enigma, and Nostalgia.* He laid out these themes as in a medieval predella. Indeed, as Ethel Schwabacher points out, the principal source for *1934* was Uccello's predella panels entitled *The Profanation of the Host,* a reproduction of which hung on Gorky's studio wall (Fig. 94). Gorky copied the design of the balustrades that divide Uccello's four scenes; he made a visual link between his first and last panels by adding a strip of checkered pattern taken from Uccello's floor tiles, and, like Uccello, he used receding walls to create a stagelike space. Gorky never painted *1934*: on April 29, 1934, he was dropped from the PWAP, which was discontinued that June.

27

Marny George

❧

Handsome, articulate, courtly, and funny, Gorky was a magnet for women. His orphan eyes were irresistible; his ultimate aloofness posed a challenge. Clearly this man's wounds called for female succor. Yet he was also powerful. His ethnicity made him seem masculine and exotic: he came from a world where there was no doubt about men's superiority to women and where a good woman was a skilled servant and a faithful wife—almost chattel. In rigidly puritanical Armenian culture women were to be treated with respect and not as objects of sexual desire. Any forwardness on a girl's part was greeted with the word "Shame!" A bride who turned out not to be a virgin was ostracized. Even more punitive was the treatment of adulterous women. They were forced to sit backward on a donkey and to endure insults as they were driven out of their village. By Armenian standards, American women's deportment left much to be desired.

Although in some quarters he had a reputation for being a ladies' man, Gorky was not a flirt. He was awkward and rather formal with women, and he always kept the innocence of the Armenian farm boy. "He shied away from girls, but they didn't shy away from him," said Raphael Soyer. The wife of the sculptor Chaim Gross, who met Gorky around 1930, remembers that Gorky used to sit on the steps of the Forty-second Street Library and tell fabulous stories about his childhood: "Everyone knew Gorky, and everyone loved him, especially women. A group of young people hung around him on the library steps. They sat at his feet, listening." "Gorky related more to women than to men,"

Mariam Davis said. "He had a [new] woman almost every other month. He used to call them Ana, which meant 'dear one' in Armenian." He also called women "skybabies," and he put them more easily on pedestals than in his arms. His method of courtship often fell short of the mark, as when he said to a woman he fancied: "Oh, what charming little wrinkles you have around your eyes." De Kooning remembered one of Gorky's unsuccessful attempts to pick up girls:

> He was sitting at the Jumble Shop and he said to Robert Jonas, who was a lady's man—Jonas had more nerve with the girls—so Gorky said, "Look! Get those girls over here," and Robert Jonas managed to get them over. Gorky was handsome but eccentric. He sure wasn't the American type, right? And Gorky started telling the girls, "My dear, your eyebrows are like caterpillars and your eyes are like butterfly wings." He'd make up those terrific words, you know, and the girls didn't like it. They thought he was nuts. Eyes like caterpillars! He meant it beautiful, but it didn't work so good. The girls kind of left, you know. Jonas, who knew about girls, said, "What are you doing this Paul Eluard business for!?" And Gorky smiled and said, "Oh, you know about Paul Eluard, too?"

Women "were all the time swooning in front of him," Balcomb Greene recalled, but Greene noticed that Gorky often fended off women's advances. "One fell in love with him and she used to practically sit on his doorstep," Greene recalled. "She was quite an attractive girl. And he rebuffed her and finally she wouldn't go away, so he said he really couldn't stand her because her nose was too long. It was a little long actually, but I thought that was a rather nice thing about her, its sort of distinction. Well, anyway, she went to a plastic surgeon and had it shortened. And Gorky had to invent some new reason for not liking her." The Greek-born painter Aristodimos Kaldis had a similar story: a woman who was smitten with Gorky in the late 1930s had a wealthy sister who offered to buy Gorky a house in Woodstock, New York, and to give him a fifty-thousand-dollar dowry if he would marry her sister. But Gorky was unmovable: "Your cheeks are not soft like the Armenian dough my mother used to make," he said. No doubt he was remembering the time when, as a small boy, he asked his mother why she indented her dough with a cross and she told him, "I make this mark of the holy cross so that in the morning, when I make bread, the dough will be very soft. And I hope that when you get married, you'll marry a girl whose cheeks are as soft as Armenian dough." In 1935 Mischa Reznikoff saw Gorky in the company of a striking six-foot-tall woman. She was "the perfect match," Mischa suggested. Gorky disagreed. She had big bunions, he said. "She's a good-looking girl," said Mischa. "Hell! I don't like bunions!" said Gorky.

Not long after his relationship with Sirun Mussikian ended, Gorky met a beautiful young girl named Cerille Miller in a museum. He asked her to model for him. A love affair, which is thought to have been platonic, ensued. Sometime in the 1930s he had a brief liaison with a lovely and well-connected woman called Rene Oakman. It seems that other than his early relationship with Sirun, he was not drawn to Armenian women but was attracted instead to upper-crust Anglo-Saxons. Armenian women, he explained, did not understand his art.

On February 28, 1934, at the opening of the "First Municipal Art Exhibition" at the Forum Gallery in the new RCA Building, Gorky's patron Bernard Davis and his wife, Irmagard, introduced Gorky to a blond Midwestern woman named Marny George. A decade younger than Gorky, she had graduated from college and come to New York City to study fashion art in 1933. Although her first passion was drawing, she needed to make a living. To that end she worked as a model in a department store. Of her first meeting with Gorky she wrote:

> One night I went to a preview of an art exhibit with some advertising people. Pictures of the usual dull sort, when suddenly I saw it! An act of immediate recognition—a powerful abstraction in violent and magnificent color. I don't know how long I stood there before I was conscious of a voice behind me. "You like it?" "Oh yes, this is the first painting I have ever seen!" "Would you care to see more?" I turned to look at the owner of the accented voice and saw a tall, shabbily dressed man with dark, sad eyes—as out of place in that fashionable gathering as his painting was.
>
> He invited the party I was with down to his studio. There were some powerfully beautiful ink drawings tacked on the spacious walls. I remember exclaiming "What magnificent forms!" He

seemed very pleased. "You don't ask 'what are they, what do they mean . . .' "

I saw Arshile nearly every day after that. He sent me poetry. "I am a poet," he would say often. And one day a lovely little gardenia tree accompanied a poem.

Not long after their first meeting, Marny George and Gorky went to Madison Square Garden to see an ice-skating show. Marny was herself an expert figure skater. While watching the skaters, she recalled, "Arshile drew on the program, beautiful rhythmical sketches . . . That night I knew I would marry him. I can almost say, 'whether I wanted to or not.' "

Mischa Reznikoff remembered an evening at Ticino's when Marny borrowed Gorky's pen, picked up a bread stick, and wrote on it: "I would like to be Mrs. Gorky." At a cocktail party at the Janises' apartment Nathan Bijur's wife, Jean, overheard Marny say to Gorky, "Take me and mold me." Jean Bijur disapproved of the relationship—Marny was pretty but her background was too different. Even though Gorky was over her head, as she admitted, she wanted to enter this new bohemian milieu. "We took long walks, mostly through the Village," she recalled. "It was while crossing Washington Square he stopped to point out the beautiful designs formed by the cracks in the cement sidewalk. 'Someday everyone will be his own artist.' It was a moonlight night while crossing the Brooklyn Bridge he asked me to marry him."

Reznikoff ran into the newly betrothed Gorky on Eighth Street coming out of a Russian gift shop with a bundle of little packages wrapped in tissue paper. These, Gorky explained, were gifts for his bride. "Look!" he said as he unwrapped jewelry made of papier-mâché. "Here are my grandmother's jewels!" The night before the wedding Gorky gave a party. Reznikoff and Stuart Davis procured some bootleg liquor and a mass of fruit and vegetables to create an edible still life. "Beautiful colors," Mischa said. "Beautiful carrots, cabbages. He had a round table, we piled the stuff." Alexander and Helen Sandow, the biophysicist and pianist with whom Gorky spent so many evenings in the early 1930s, were among the guests. "That was no wedding," Helen Sandow recalls. "She married him because she saw a good thing. Gorky needed a wife. It was so sad for Arshile. I knew it wouldn't last. Marny George seemed out of place with Gorky. She was not an honest personality. She was duplicitous. All their friends were at the wedding—ten or twelve people. At the wedding I kept saying, 'This can't be true.' " Reznikoff put it this way: "This Marny was a typical happy tappy girl. I thought to myself, Ah ha! This is wrong! What fascinated him about her? She looked exactly like that period of Picasso when he had taken off the walls of Pompeii, women with big rubbery looking fingers and all blown up classical faces. I'm positive that's why he fell in love with her. She had a big handsome figure. Tall and voluptuous." If Gorky made that connection, he also made another, more telling comparison with an opposite physical type: he told Helen Sandow that Marny reminded him of his mother. (Indeed, as Sandow observed, all of Gorky's women looked like his mother.)

At the wedding party Gorky drank too much and talked excitedly. "He was raving," Reznikoff recalled. He made a toast. He kept saying how beautiful his new wife was and how fertile he would be if he ate all those vegetables. Marny, too, "got loaded in no time," said Reznikoff. "No people like parents there. We drank this bloody alcohol. She started playing around with Stuart, not too obvious. 'Come on, say something!' " (Davis could be taciturn.) Always quick to detect flirtation, Gorky intervened: "I cannot permit my wife to be a bathtub gin-drinker." The guests decided it was time to leave. The following morning Gorky and Marny, with Sidney and Harriet Janis as their witnesses, presented themselves at City Hall. Afterward they celebrated with a champagne breakfast at the Janises', and for their honeymoon they visited Bernard Davis in Philadelphia.

From the moment they married, Marny and Gorky were entangled in a battle of wills. She was, as she put it, "encased in bourgeois morals and standards," from which Gorky tried to release her. "From the first," she said, "I was attracted and repelled. I had rushes of passionate feeling. I wanted to be a buffer between this strange, lonely man and the indifferent, materialistic world. At that time I was more a part of that materialistic world than I was of his. I knew what I wanted. I knew from the first moment I saw his painting at the exhibit—but what I didn't realize was how utterly incapable I was of obtaining it." Ethel Schwabacher, who was studying with Gorky at the time, wrote that Gorky's marriage to Marny George had the quality of a brief love affair. "As a foreigner he had no frame of reference by which to assess the character of an American girl. He had fallen in love with beauty, . . . with love itself, perhaps as he imagined it. He had felt he could create a woman, as he had created his art . . . a process of trial and error, infinitely patient renewed efforts toward the full-fledged embodiment of an ideal perfection whose shadow lay cool, abstract and substanceless on the interior wall of his mind." Marny George recalled that Gorky used to say of himself that he was "ferocious as a giant, tender as a little child." The giant's ferociousness soon became intolerable. "First with tenderness, then with force," he tried to "form and mold me into the woman he wanted for his wife." The more violent her husband became, the stronger Marny's resistance grew.

One of their problems was poverty. Marny George remembered that now and then Gorky sold a painting and that his private pupils brought in some income. In addition, she said, "someone else paid the rent." (Mariam Davis said there was a woman who subsidized Gorky's career. Others have intimated the same thing. "Ah, Gorky, he had his mysterious ways," de Kooning observed. "He had all these women who supported him.") "But in spite of usually having to scrape for food (which Arshile often cooked in or over a wood heating stove) he could never pass by an art supply store without emptying his pockets and coming home with new tubes of paint and brushes." Gorky was often in debt to the art stores that he patronized—once for as much as six hundred dollars. His system was to pay them off in rotation so that his credit was always good somewhere. No doubt Marny had a more conservative approach to money and minded Gorky's seemingly irresponsible ways.

Another conflict was over the radio. Gorky liked to listen to soap operas and talk shows while he worked. Marny George wanted to listen to the news but Gorky forbade it. "All the sudden newness of this strange environment was too much for me," she recalled. "I was homesick for the West, for one, for what seemed at the time to be solid, familiar ground. I was miserable, upset, torn. Arshile decided that if perhaps I went home I could free myself of these childish ties and return to him." Marny George went home but her absence resolved nothing. When she came back to 36 Union Square, Gorky said, with bitter resignation: "It will take you ten years before you understand me." Still, he was determined to hold on to his wife and to remake her after his own image of what a wife should be. "For six weeks I did not leave the studio. We fought and fought, then there would be moments of surrender on both sides, moments when it seemed we really would break through to realizing the love that was beneath the conflict of wills. It never lasted. One day he reached the end of his endurance. He hauled out my suitcase and threw my few belongings into it, carried it down the dark, rickety stairs leading from the studio, set it on the sidewalk and went back—to god knows what."

Gorky told one friend that the breakup was precipitated by his finding a letter from Marny's former boyfriend asking her why she had rushed into marriage. Enraged, Gorky woke up his wife and said, "Now get dressed and get out of here!" He told his second wife that the breakup came because one day he returned to the studio and found Marny writing a letter to her former boyfriend. This was bad enough, but the greater affront, from Gorky's point of view, was that she had enclosed a photograph of one of his paintings. Inflamed by paranoid imaginings, he did not listen when she told him that she had simply wanted to give her ex-boyfriend an idea of the man she had married. The painting in the photograph was the very Picassoid *Abstraction with Palette* (c. 1930), given to the Philadelphia Museum by Gorky's friend Bernard Davis in 1942. Marny had written on the back of the photograph, "This is the sort of work my husband does." Gorky did not view her gesture as a demonstration of wifely pride. Instead he flew into a jealous rage and ejected Marny from 36 Union Square. When he filed for a divorce Gorky discovered that Marny was a minor and that the marriage could therefore be annulled. His lawyer, Herman A. Greenberg, filled out the necessary papers and was given a recent still life as part or all of his fee.

After the separation Marny George gave up painting for ten years and earned her living ice-skating. She saw Gorky from time to time, but these meetings were always sad. The bond between them, she said, was stronger on her side than on his. Once when her figure skating show came to New York she met Gorky at their favorite restaurant in the Village. By the time they left the restaurant she had come down with the flu. "He took me back to the studio and nursed me like a sick child." Gorky continued to receive letters from Marny even after he remarried in 1941. In the mid-1940s, Julien Levy recalled, she bought one of Gorky's drawings, but "she made me promise not to tell Gorky." Perhaps she did not want him to know that she still had him on her mind.

Gorky's loneliness—his longing for a family and roots—intensified with Marny's departure, but his life soon filled up again. On December 25, 1934, Vartoosh and Moorad returned from their two-and-a-half-year sojourn in Soviet Armenia. Gorky picked them up when their ship docked in New York, and they stayed with him for a few weeks at

36 Union Square. Vartoosh was pregnant, and Gorky was not earning enough to support them all, so he recommended that until her baby was born Vartoosh and Moorad should go and stay with Akabi in Watertown.

In Watertown, Moorad found a job at the Arsenal. Vartoosh gave birth to a boy on March 25, and she and Moorad named him Karlen after Karl Marx and Lenin. That autumn, when Karlen was six months old, Akabi's son Gurken drove Vartoosh and Karlen from Watertown to New York. Moorad stayed behind for a month because he was earning fifteen dollars a week, which was good money during the Depression. When he joined his family in New York, Bernard Davis gave him an equally well-paying job in the rug business. The Mooradians lived with Gorky for fourteen months. Then in November 1936 they moved to Chicago, where Moorad continued to work for a branch of Davis's La France rug company.

Having his sister and her family with him must have seemed natural to Gorky: in Armenian villages, extended families live under one roof (Fig. 26). But for Gorky the artist it must have been trying. Even though he loved children, living and working in such close quarters with a baby was sometimes a strain. An example of Gorky's remarkable patience was the time when Karlen had just learned to walk and he toddled over to Gorky's easel and painted black lines all over the bottom of the huge canvas entitled *Organization*, which Gorky worked on from 1933 to 1936. Gorky did not get angry, Vartoosh recalled. "O Mougouch," he said to Karlen, using the Van term of endearment, "why did you do that?" He laughed, held his nephew high in the air, then reworked the painting yet again. He was an affectionate uncle. After Vartoosh bathed Karlen she would wrap him in a blanket and place him in Gorky's arms for a long cuddle. A photograph shows Gorky holding Karlen and, pencil in hand, gently touching his nephew's arm. When Karlen was old enough to pay attention, Gorky would carry him down to Union Square to watch the pigeons.

Even with two breadwinners under one roof, Gorky's household had serious economic problems. When a bill collector turned up with an IOU for art supplies that Gorky had purchased on credit, Vartoosh grabbed the paper out of Gorky's hand before he could sign it. She burst into tears and said, "Look, I am here and my brother is supporting me and my little baby. My husband has no work." As a bachelor, Gorky had been in the habit of going downstairs to eat breakfast in the cafeteria on the ground floor of his building. Sometimes he didn't even bother to dress but went down in his pajamas. Feeling that restaurants were an extravagance, Vartoosh would say, "Gorky, don't do that." Another time de Kooning came over for a meal and dropped a bottle of milk intended for the baby. "And at that very moment," Vartoosh recalled, "no one had any money, so Gorky had to go outside to borrow money from a friend to buy more milk. Poor Bill felt so bad."

Doctors' bills were another burden. Gorky's health was not good. He suffered from constipation and had serious skin problems on one hand. Some doctors recommended amputating his fingers, but the condition was finally diagnosed by Mina Metzger's general practitioner, Harry Weiss, as caused by the lead in white paint. Gorky would go off to see a doctor once or twice a week with a painting tucked under his arm. His sister asked what he was doing, and he answered, "Well, I can't pay the doctor, so I give him paintings instead." To pay for a house call by Moses Housepian, an Armenian whom Gorky consulted at Vartoosh's urging, Vartoosh offered one of Gorky's paintings. Dr. Housepian rejected the offer: "The poor boy just scribbles!" he told his wife when he got home. "I asked for a yogurt instead."

Much as Gorky loved his younger sister, Vartoosh irritated him. Her voice was endlessly plaintive. "Too many sighs!" Mougouch recalled. She would stand at the window at 36 Union Square with her arms folded, her head to one side, and with tears rolling down her cheeks. The traumas of her youth in Turkish Armenia had left terrible wounds, and her hopes for a better life in Soviet Armenia had been dashed. Also, she may have been lovesick. Family legend has it that in Yerevan she fell in love. "Vartoosh came to Armenia to get pregnant," Gorky's cousin Azad Adoian affirmed. "Moorad could not give her a child. She met a childhood sweetheart from Van. That's when she became pregnant."

Being lovelorn and politically disillusioned and having a baby but no home of one's own would seem to be sufficient cause for unhappiness, but it is likely, too, that Vartoosh shared with her brother and mother a familial vulnerability to depression. To lift Vartoosh out of her doldrums, Gorky took her to museums and to places near the city like Coney Island. He also gave her art lessons and he drew and painted her, which he knew gave her pleasure. In several letters to Vartoosh after she moved to Chicago, Gorky tried to cajole his sister into feeling less miserable. He agreed with her that in the United States it was hard to find the kind of friends they had had in Van. She should try to paint, he said. She should get out and see people. To comfort her he said that he, too, felt alone, even when he was surrounded by crowds.

After being removed from the rolls of the PWAP in spring 1934, Gorky received no federal support until July 1935, when he applied to the Emergency Relief Bureau for home relief, a prerequisite for eligibility to the Federal Art Project (FAP) of the WPA, which would be established the following month. From the Emergency Relief Bureau he received $24 a week. In August he enrolled as "Master Artist" in the mural division of the FAP with a starting monthly salary of $103.40. (His salary was cut to $91.16 in November 1938 and to $87.60 in July 1939.) The project was headed by Gorky's friend Holger Cahill; another friend, the geometric abstractionist Burgoyne Diller, was in charge of New York's mural division. These connections probably explain why Gorky was able to join so quickly, why he was kept on the project after noncitizens were removed from the rolls, and why he was able to remain in the mural division even after his Newark Airport murals were finished and he was working on easel paintings in the privacy of his studio.

Although a steady income brought Gorky some economic security, project artists were kept on edge by constant cutbacks in annual appropriations to the FAP and the resulting pay cuts and pink slips. Also, in order to qualify for relief, artists had to take an often humiliating "pauper's oath." Once they were on relief, project supervisors made surprise visits to artists' homes to make sure that they had no other means of support. These supervisors opened refrigerators and closets, and they grilled neighbors about possible moonlighting jobs like baby-sitting or delivering newspapers. How Gorky managed to hide the fact that he had private pupils is unknown.

Gorky was a great favorite with the New York office of the FAP. When administrators needed an example of a worthy abstract artist to show off to nay-saying sponsors and conservative congressmen who felt that the Federal Art Project was a boondoggle at the taxpayer's expense and that it was infested with Communists, they could always turn to Gorky: he looked like a radical but he could draw like an academician. "Whenever we had trouble with congressmen and senators against modern art," said Kaldis, "I used to bring them to Gorky's studio on Union Square. And I'd ask Gorky to make drawings of them. 'O, that guy really knows his stuff,' they'd say, 'so we'll let him go.' " One visiting official from Washington noted that Gorky drew as quickly as a draftsman in a vaudeville show. Little did the visitor know that during his student years in Boston Gorky had been just that.

In the later 1930s, when the WPA and FAP were under increasing attack from Congress and the pace of witch hunts, budget cuts, and layoffs picked up, FBI agents came to Gorky's studio at least twice to ask him about the political affiliations of certain friends. They were specifically interested in Moorad Mooradian (who was, in fact, a member of the Communist Party). On one of these occasions Gorky simply pointed out the window and said that, like the unemployed men sitting on benches in Union Square, his friends wanted only bread. Another time when the FBI turned up at his studio, Gorky asked to see the agent's identity card. He looked closely at the photograph and then remarked that it didn't resemble the agent at all. "You are much better looking than the man in the photograph," he said. "The man in the photograph looks like a 'cross cucumber.' "

28

Corinne

In the spring of 1935 Gorky began a romance with a young painter named Corinne West, a blond with a perfect oval face, bedroom eyes, a mouth painted red, and a fetching cleft in her chin. In a photograph from the early 1930s (Fig. 102) she holds a cigarette in such a way as to show off her shapely fingers, and she wears a beret to make it clear she is an artist. Although she adopted the name Mikael and then Michael during this period, and although Gorky thought that the name Corinne sounded like a "debutante daughter," he kept on calling her that.

Born in Chicago in 1908, Corinne moved with her family to Cincinnati when she was seventeen. There she studied piano and art, became involved with the Cincinnati Civic Theater, and eventually married the man with whom she costarred in *The Passing of the Third Floor Back* in 1930. When her marriage failed, she moved to New York, found a place on Bank Street in the Village, and began to study painting with Hans Hofmann and commercial art at the Traphagen School of Fashion. Corinne was introduced to Gorky by Lorenzo Santillo, the monitor of Hofmann's art class and a kindhearted young man who rented a room from Gorky, borrowing money (from Gorky) every month to make the rent. According to Corinne's account, Santillo kept telling her that she must meet this wonderful painter called Gorky. She refused: Hans Hofmann was all she could handle in the way of big egos. On a cold March night she finally succumbed to Santillo's insistence. In notes written decades later in her own peculiar shorthand, full of unfinished sentences and half-developed thoughts, she described the meeting. "Lorenzo and I went to the large studio on Union Square. There were notables there, it seemed private and chi chi to me at the time—Sydney [sic] Janis and his wife, Ethel Schwabacher, the Metzgers, the Muschenheims—etc. [the architect William Muschenheim and his wife, Lisa]. All wealthy people who bought his paintings." Gorky came over and tried to put Corinne, who was unused to being in what she called a "group of intellectuals and intelligentsia," at her ease. Once again it was his art that broke the ice: "As we walked down the long wall of pen and ink I felt that I *knew* him— the best of him—was overjoyed with the style and character of these drawings. His paintings were *tremendous* and were the real influence in my life . . . It was *in Gorky that I found the Great American Painter*."

Corinne described Gorky as an "imposing figure in a greyish brown tweed suit—huge brown eyes—a quiet voice—the intelligentsia loved him—his refinement—humbleness." In Corinne, Gorky had found yet another provincial whom he could mold. Her lack of sophistication both appealed to and irritated him. Her later jottings record a few of the things he said to her: "Corinne, how can you speak this way—you are foolish." But other times she remembered him calling her a "great woman." Like Marny George before her, and like Agnes Magruder (Mougouch) after her, Corinne was a beautiful young art student with the sensitivity and intelligence to be an admirer of his work. "36 Union Square studio was profound, quiet and one tiptoed around in this atmosphere of the maestro and great art."

Although she felt that Gorky did not understand her, there was, she said, a strange identification between them: "I think our *excitement* about art was rather unnatural . . . This tremendous love of art is *where* our identities coincided." Corinne felt connected to Gorky also because he was descended from generations of priests, and, on her mother's side, she came from a long line of Christian ministers. "We were both children of God—ingrained—hereditarily speaking." Both she and Gorky had an inclination toward the spiritual and the poetic. They had, she said, a "sacred feeling for life" that "was in truth—hysterical holiness." As artists, they directed these energies into art, but "behind these gigantic energies—there was a 'time bomb'—or total apathy—opposite yes—here was the battleground on which we were to fight out our lives—I dragged on thru countless grey halls—always ending up contemplating—the beauty of some particular object in a state of 'explosive joy.'"

The couple apparently did not live together. At least part of the time, she lived with her parents at 45 Fifth Avenue. Her life revolved, she said, around the Art Students League and Eighth Street, where Hans Hofmann opened his school in 1936. "[I was] intent on my work and Gorky's criticism. Union Square was not far away." The relationship was serious enough for Corinne to introduce Gorky to her parents: "Father liked him and they discussed athletics—at once—actually Father found him fascinating and looked up to him." In order to impress the Wests, Gorky shifted the facts of his biography, telling them that he had won the broad jump at Brown University. When Corinne's older sister, Faith, visited New York with her friend Colonel James Robinson, Corinne introduced them to Gorky, too:

> Since I was seeing Gorky constantly I took them for a visit to his studio. Gorky liked them and was impressed with army people. He finally succeeded in getting Jim to draw something. We later went to 1 Fifth Avenue for drinks and coffee, the beautiful marble floors large mirrors lining the walls and huge fans overhead plus the bar and marble tables made for a sensational evening. Gorky and Colonel Robinson (millionaire) of many talents 1) discussed military strategy 2) camouflage etc etc . . . My surprise at this side of Gorky was amazing—that he knew so much about the military—He admired Faith my sister and spoke of the bone structure of her face. We took the ferry to Staten Island after this and it turned out to be an exhilarating evening.

Corinne said that she and Gorky "were constantly together in 1936—and for some time before that about 1935—4—after that constantly letters." They made the rounds of galleries, took long walks, talked endlessly about art, and often ate with friends in downtown restaurants. She remembered private pupils coming to Gorky's studio and his occasional lectures at the Grand Central School of Art, "using slides and redrawing Braque and Picasso and Juan Gris on the school blackboard." One of her more stream-of-consciousness notes describes a walk that she and Gorky made after visiting two museums: "Gorky stopping to buy cherries every third block—hot grey asphalt—3 more blocks—6 more blocks—time to stop and eat sandwiches on Broadway and Times Square of all places. Exhaustion! (Not knowing ourselves exhilaration dejection) except [illegible word] had to call someone—always calling—someone.

I thought imagine living this way—He said—it's like a gambler—Could I live it that way—I said I didn't know."

Gorky spent the summer of 1935 preparing for his upcoming drawing show. His pen-and-ink drawings "lined the walls and were hung low so that we could study them," Corinne recalled. He also did a large portrait (now lost) of Corinne. For two weeks she posed in the afternoons and he kept working on the picture in her absence. "When I was there he danced and sang (he was fascinating) then would launch into [a] long discussion of Ingres [or] cubism." In September Corinne borrowed her father's car and she, Gorky, Lorenzo Santillo, and a woman named Geraldine (who, according to Corinne, was in love with Gorky) drove to Philadelphia to see Gorky's drawing show at the Boyer Galleries. En route they stopped outside Philadelphia to see Vartoosh, who must have been there to talk with Bernard Davis about the possibility of Moorad's working for Davis's rug company. "The gallery was beautiful and his pictures looked wonderful standing against the white walls." On their trip home they ran into a storm and fog so thick they had to creep along the side of the road for miles. After reaching Manhattan at about two in the morning, Gorky went on to meet Stuart Davis at Romany Marie's.

He and Corinne often met Davis there late in the evening. They would drink tea and discuss art—Bronzino, Memling, Goya, Tintoretto. "Gorky would start drawing very seriously in pen and ink on napkins— when he finished one he would hand it to me—I would study it carefully for one minute then fold [it] and place [it] in the pocket of my coat. He would do another working twice as hard. Nothing more difficult than paper napkin and pen—nevertheless inspired by what we had seen in the Byzantine Section of the Metropolitan—these choice drawings came about." Returning to Union Square, Gorky would pull his paintings out of his storeroom and give them a critical eye before retiring.

Most evenings Corinne and Gorky dined at home, and often Gorky would talk about his birthplace. "Occasionally he would break into a long chant—and do a Caucasian dance—complete with swirling veil." Gorky was a "natural performer," she said. One night he went into the bedroom and came out wrapped in a blue chiffon robe, which looked "grotesque" in combination with his heavy brown shoes. He began to sing and to whistle and he "flew around in a circle stamping his foot now and then (Lorenzo and I screamed with laughter). He was funny—yet had a serious look on his face." Gorky was, Corinne said, also "a great mimic—he came at people's personalities as he came at his subject matter, from an angle, his own idiosyncratic vision and understanding."

But beneath his animation she could feel despair: "An air of tragedy hung in the air even then—feverish—suppressed—hectic." Armenian friends saw Gorky's melancholy as a specifically Armenian characteristic. Gorky told Peter Busa that in his youth he had received wounds from which he would never recover. One hot July night Corinne, Gorky, and a friend called Louie (who had a job in a jigsaw puzzle factory) were eating spaghetti when the subject of suicide came up. Louie gave a monologue, the gist of which was, if you intended to kill yourself you would never talk about it. Gorky fell into a deep silence that made Corinne anxious: "It was like someone fainting—looking straight ahead. We have all had our rounds with suicide particularly [in] youth . . . But with Gorky it was a different kind of thing—A wealth of talent constantly working in a foreign land—no family except his sister in Philadelphia. Yet his art, deep interest, knowledge, kept him alive for some time— until the fatal time. The subject was always close—somehow—we couldn't talk about it."

In 1935 Corinne's parents moved to Rochester, New York, where her father was president and treasurer of a brick and tile company. She probably moved to Rochester in June 1936. Gorky stayed in New York to work on the designs that would later become his Newark Airport murals. In her notes Corinne said that after she left New York for Rochester "Gorky quickly came there and we discussed marriage but I did not think it would be right—at that time—Gorky said love would come later." In early August 1936 Gorky took the train to Rochester, set himself up in Corinne's studio at the Rochester Arts Club (where sometime that year she had an exhibition), and painted "a huge abstract image . . . Gorky said I inspired him to paint. He finally gave me two paintings which I cherish beyond words." Twice she drove to New York and stayed at the Prince George Hotel, not far from Gorky's studio. "There was an oyster bar there we liked. Mirrors, marble tops and mahogany—we liked this place. It reminded us of the Picasso's and Braque's still lifes with their French mahogany and marble floors." Each time they saw each other, there was a painful separation. She later told Gorky's student and biographer Ethel Schwabacher: "Leaving his presence was agony. We planned to marry but changed our minds at least 6 times, thus there were many letters back and forth, and visits of two days, over weekends."

Several of Gorky's letters and telegrams to Corinne from the summer of 1936 have been preserved. The first telegram, written on July 20 and addressed to her at the Rochester Arts Club, says: "Darling please come to New York for a few days let me know when coming." In three August letters Gorky mixes his own words with snippets from the 1912 love letters of the French sculptor Henri Gaudier-Brzeska, published in *The Savage Messiah* by H. S. Ede in 1931. He also borrows long excerpts from the French Surrealist poets Paul Eluard and André Breton, whose poems he found translated into English in Julien Levy's *Surrealism*, published in 1936. None of these borrowings is attributed.

The opening six lines of his first letter to Corinne, written on August 11, are borrowed from Gaudier-Brzeska:

My precious Love

Now that I have got over the fatigues of the journey, two real impressions remain with me. In the first place, the sweet sensation of perfect and profound love which unites us one to another, and next, the pleasantness of you my Corinne and your work.

I miss you terribly and this place seems to me so big and unhappy because you are not with me.

The fourth and longest paragraph is taken from a section of *The Immaculate Conception*, a prose poem Breton and Eluard collaborated on in 1930. It begins: "My heart my darling [Gorky added the "my darling"] bleeds on thy mouth and closes on thy mouth on all red chestnut-trees of the avenue of thy mouth." After many more sentences in this Surrealist vein, Gorky closes his letter with some slightly altered quotations from Gaudier-Brzeska: "I love you so much my little Corinne dear and I kiss you passionately from the head to the foot of your lovely body and pray the warm sun for your happiness and the success of your work. I love you tenderly, and wait feverishly for the first chance of seeing you again of possessing you fully and fondly. In flames [Breton and Eluard had written, "Thine in flames"] Arshile." In his second letter, this one undated and written from Long Island, Gorky again lifts paragraphs from Breton and Eluard. This time he ends with, "Corinne my love I miss you terribly. I am sending you the picture hope you like it Arshile Will write soon again I am coming nex week."

After returning from his visit to Corinne, he wrote to her on August 24 from New York City. His letter is divided into sections. The first is Eluard's poem "Lady Love," translated by Samuel Beckett and taken from Levy's book. Another section gives Gorky's news: "Beloved, I am very tired; I have done nothing but rush from one place to another, and on top of that have done a lot of work with my murals and started a painting 14 × 9 ft this morning [he refers to one of his Newark mural panels]. have been to Boston with Vartoosh my sister and last weekend to country." Gorky ended his letter with a depressed-sounding passage whose source has not been identified: "So many voices that were calculated even when the speakers smiled had disgusted my ears with hearing. Over the two quotidian cobbles, my feet were dragging—weighted miles lined with a shadow which yet had no thickness, Ill the trees were in gallows wood, and they were innumerable in the forest of repression. With its leaden foliage so thick that from dawn to dusk and from dusk to dawn one did not dare to imagine that some day, beyond the horizon and beyond habit, there would burst a sun all sulphur and Love."

Finally, on September 2, Gorky sent Corinne a telegram: "Dearest why don't I hear from you love—Arshile." The demotion from "Darling" or "My precious love" to "Dearest" may hint at a weakening bond. In the early summer of 1937 Gorky went to see Corinne, probably for the last time. Corinne wrote: "My studio was left with one 50 by 90" *Self Portrait* he painted there—a large grey and green image and wrote to Corinne at the top. He liked the self portrait very much."

Corinne and Gorky's love seems to have been more comradely than romantic. Years later, in a letter to Ethel Schwabacher, she confided that her and Gorky's moments of passion ended in "complete frustration" and that their relation was "a platonic love of two artists driven by love for work, . . . obsessed with painting to a fanatical point." In her notes Corinne reminisced: "—Now for sex—There was no sex between Gorky and I for 3 reasons 1) it was precluded by our feelings for art . . . 2) also I was getting over a divorce from an actor—Randolph Nelson, Gorky from Marny. We felt destroyed by these painful experiences . . . (3rd Reason) I thought he needed a rich sophisticated person who would give him 2 children and *help* manage his career." Corinne's sister Faith said that Gorky, with his "passionate Georgian background," was more than Corinne could handle. He was too "big and fierce, . . . too much a man for her, physically." Moreover, there were great areas of his being that he closed off, even to women he loved. Corinne wrote:

> How could anything please the
> Creator—he lives to create—
> He wants nothing but this—
> No presents (Gorky hated presents)
> (so do I)
> there is *Nothing* you can give
> him but excitement—so he will
> have something to work from.

Corinne, too, held back. She was not prepared to become the woman Gorky wanted. In her notes she said she felt Gorky "needed a strong woman—not an artist . . . I was obsessed with my own work—it stood in the way." Schwabacher recalled the end of Gorky and Corinne's affair: "Infatuation did not steady into love but guttered down, and Gorky was once more alone with his dreams and his phantom companions."

29

Lyrical Man

᠅

Although he thrived in Manhattan's downtown bohemia, Gorky, the farmer's son, longed for the open country. During his summer visits to his sisters in Watertown, he and Yenovk Der Hagopian would take their easels to the Charles River and paint side by side (Fig. 98). Once Gorky left a message for Hagopian at the Hood Rubber Company, then made a trail of arrows on the street so that Hagopian could find the spot where he had set up his easel. Gorky was the mentor figure: after one of his criticisms Hagopian was so upset that he put his canvas aside. Some months later Gorky asked how it was going, and when Hagopian brought his painting out of hiding Gorky announced, "This is beautiful!" Hagopian was puzzled: "Manouk, a few months ago you said it's not good, no more than an Oriental khali design. Now you're admiring. What are you doing to me?" "Don't mind me," said Gorky. "Don't ever take any criticism from anybody, and if you take criticism, put your painting away. Don't let them see it."

If he couldn't afford the time or money to travel to see his family, Gorky contented himself with the seashore or forests accessible from Manhattan by public transportation. Vartoosh said that once when she went with him to Coney Island they could not afford amusement park rides, so they ate frankfurters and walked along the boardwalk. Gorky also liked to take the ferry to Staten Island to visit Reuben Nakian, who had moved to Grasmere in 1936. In those days Staten Island was rural. Gorky would lift Nakian's baby son, Paul, onto his shoulders and set off with Nakian on a two-mile walk to the shore. "And we used to eat, have fun, go to the beach," Nakian recalled. "But being artists, the only thing we were interested in was art. All we spoke about was art."

Gorky was a strong swimmer and loved the seashore. At least once in the late 1930s he visited Provincetown on the tip of Cape Cod, where several of his artist friends rented houses. Around 1936 or 1937 he and David Margolis took the overnight East River boat to Providence and from there took a bus to Provincetown. Unable to afford sleeping berths, they stood on deck and wandered into the gambling lounge, where Gorky stood with his arms crossed and watched people working the slot machines. "Suddenly he looks at me and says, 'Listen, those goddam fools put in so much money. Let's watch those guys. I bet we're going to hit the jackpot.' We put in a nickel and out came four dollars. Gorky jumped up and down like a child. He was so happy. Four dollars was a fortune then."

In Provincetown Gorky and Margolis paid seven dollars a week for two rooms at the Patricks guest house. "We both found ourselves girl-friends," Margolis recalls. "The feeling Gorky gave you as a man was that he had a bravado, a confidence. Gorky liked my girlfriend. I said, 'Al-right, take her.' It wasn't a serious relationship, and I found another girl-friend. Gorky and his girlfriend rented a bike and rode around." The men did not paint in Cape Cod. Instead they went to the beach and drew elaborate pictures in the wet sand. "At the beach we'd come out of the water and we lay naked on the sand. The cold water made our penises small. Gorky, who liked to tease, took a piece of straw and poked my penis and said it was so small it was like a 'little porcupine.' I was em-barrassed in front of the girls. At night we didn't eat in restaurants. We had picnics in the dunes."

When their vacation was over, Gorky and Margolis stopped in Boston, where they went to see Puvis de Chavannes's murals in the Boston Public Library, and then went on to the Boston Museum of Fine Arts to see Gauguin's *Where Have We Come From What Are We? Where Are We Going?*. Standing before this monumental painting, Gorky went into one of his maestro-in-the-museum routines: "Gorky started talking about the Gauguin in a loud voice, and he used his arms to talk. And pretty soon he drew a big crowd and he forgot that I was there, that he had been talking to me."

Rosalind Bengelsdorf and Byron Browne, who would marry in 1940, and who both painted in a late Cubist mode not unlike Gorky's, went to

Provincetown with Gorky in 1938. (It is possible that they went to Provincetown at the same time as David Margolis.) Bengelsdorf remembered that they invited Gorky to join them on their trip because "Gorky was sitting in Washington Square Park by himself and looking very lonely. So I said, 'Come with us to Provincetown.' So we all went on a boat."

Gorky collected driftwood and built enormous bonfires on the beach. "And one windy day," Bengelsdorf remembered, "we had arranged this shashlik party and Gorky made a great fuss about having the meat properly marinated and cut. And when we went out there, to make a long story short, the wind was so strong that everything was full of sand, despite all of Gorky's concern with marination." For a while the vacation was idyllic, but before it was over, Bengelsdorf recalled, "Gorky caused Byron and I to fight and he went home with Byron on the boat and I went home with friends." The problem was that the intelligent and outspoken Bengelsdorf was not the subservient woman that Gorky felt an artist's wife should be. "I had an awfully big mouth and so did Gorky and he once said to me, 'You're a good painter but you make a lousy artist's wife.' And he would walk off with my husband and I'd follow them like a little puppy dog . . . Byron was always going off with Gorky and I was too full of myself at the time . . . to be the kind of woman Gorky thought should be in the background, which is where he pushed me and which I didn't like."

In the late 1920s and through the 1930s Gorky often visited Mina Metzger's daughter Rook and her husband, a doctor, Warren McCulloch, in the house they were building in Sparta, New Jersey. The Mc-Cullochs' middle child, David, remembers Gorky telling him stories about his own childhood: "Gorky told me that when the Turks came in the front door of his house, he ran out the back." Gorky helped install his hosts' windows, and Warren McCulloch was amazed by the speed with which he learned to use American carpentry and stone-carving tools: "He knew how to build a jig to hold a window so that he could plane it right away. And the main bulk of the house is made out of green dike, an extremely difficult stone to work. Gorky went after a couple of bumps on columns in that stone house and chiseled them off. There's still one that he didn't finish. He picked up a piece of that green dike and made a head out of it with the nose recessed into the head. It's an almost impossible stone to work. That's why he found it interesting." The result of this endeavor is Gorky's only surviving stone sculpture, a crudely articulated head tilting from a long neck. In its elongation and stylization it recalls Modigliani. Gorky's admiration for Brancusi comes to mind as well, but Gorky's head is much less refined than the sculptures of either of these Parisians.

In 1941 Gorky made one other stone head, but as he worked he chipped it away to nothing. He also made a few sculptures in wood, works that he probably would have considered handicraft rather than sculpture. Yenovk Der Hagopian remembered that on one of Gorky's visits to Watertown, probably in the 1930s, he and Gorky made miniature plows. Gorky would draw the shapes and Yenovk would cut them with a hacksaw or chisel:

> I remember once we went to work on one and I bought small nails to put it together. "O no," Gorky said, "we didn't use nails like that in Van. We did this instead." And he made his own [wooden] nails. Anyway, we finally made one about a foot long. In the old country, in Van, one pair of water buffalo and three pairs of oxen used to pull one of those original plows. And it would turn up the earth at least two feet deep. So Gorky pulled his miniature plow through some sand but it was so fragile that it broke. We were both heartbroken. But early next morning he was waiting for me in front of my studio in Watertown. "Come on, we have to finish a plow because tonight I'm going to take the train back to New York." We started one but didn't have time to finish it.

There exist three examples of miniature Armenian plows that Gorky carved and assembled in the 1940s. In addition there is a rocking horse from 1942 and a shamanistic-looking *Dead Bird* he made out of a curved piece of wood in 1948.

After Saul Schary and his wife built a house in New Milford, Connecticut, in 1936, they invited Gorky to visit for a week or so each summer. In the mornings, Gorky and Schary would carry their easels into Schary's orchard: "Gorky sat right down among the trees. He looked at this landscape and he was then doing a kind of flat colorful Cubism. He sat there, and he sat there, and he started to paint. He went back about eight years to his Cézannesque way of painting and did a pure, beautiful version, as Cézanne would have painted that spot." Gorky also visited

Balcomb and Gertrude Greene, both of whom were painters. "When he was in the country," Balcomb recalled, "he liked to work from flowers, plants, grass . . . The happiest moments that he had were probably in the country. You know, sitting around after dinner outdoors where he cooked his shish-kebab . . . And he would love to go around without a shirt and with flowers stuck in his hair." At the Greenes' house in Fishkill, in New York's Dutchess County, Gorky was relaxed and in tune with nature. He no longer had to play the role of the "celebrated artist," Greene said. Instead he was "the Lyrical Man, . . . the bronzed swimmer, exuberant with the country air, or sweating in the heat as he swung an axe. In the daytime he fitted in, adjusted to the routines and the work as well as anyone. After dinner he could discuss for hours, omitting all the frills and all the clever knots of ideas. Still later on a clear night, high up on our hill by a fire, he sang the songs which proved he was Georgian, the lonely, haunting laments in a high voice—Georgian, Andalusian, Syrian, perhaps Armenian." The Russian-born abstract painter Ilya Bolotowsky remembered an awkward moment at one of Gorky's shish-kebab feasts at the Greenes' country home. Gorky announced: "The young women will prepare the salad, the old women will cut up the lamb meat." He then assigned his hostess to the older women's task force, whereas her sister was told to join the crew of younger women. "And so," Bolotowsky recalled, "Mrs. Greene was extremely shocked and hurt. And this he could not understand."

A scientist friend of the Greenes' named Lewis Balamuth recalled that at one of these Fishkill gatherings, "Gorky started to talk about his motherland, Georgia. He spoke of the mountains and exhibited a strong feeling of nostalgia towards his early recollections. The conversation became more animated, and Gorky rose to his full height in the twilight to emit a loud cry after the manner of the mountain shepherds of his native land." The party decided to drive to a nearby gorge to watch the sunset. In the car Gorky and Greene talked about various trends in abstract art. "Gorky spoke with a great deal of assurance and without fear of contradiction," said Balamuth. His talk "seemed to reflect a turbulent spirit . . . as though he were torn by some inner conflict which he was ever striving to express." After reaching the gorge Gorky and Balamuth sat on a rock overlooking a waterfall. When Gorky discovered that Balamuth was a mathematical physicist he proposed that Balamuth teach him mathematics and he would teach Balamuth art. Perhaps it was about this time that Gorky, following de Chirico's example, inserted a mathematical equation into one of his paintings and then changed it when the biophysicist Alexander Sandow told him that his numbers were meaningless. It may also have been at this time that Gorky spoke of mathematics in a lecture about abstract art delivered at the New School. Mischa Reznikoff, who was in the audience, recalled Gorky's saying, "Abstract art is a series of numberical quotients." A woman sitting in the front row asked, "Mr. Gorky, what is numberical?" Gorky shouted back, "Lady, I know the word is numerical, but I like numberical!"

❧ PART VII ❧

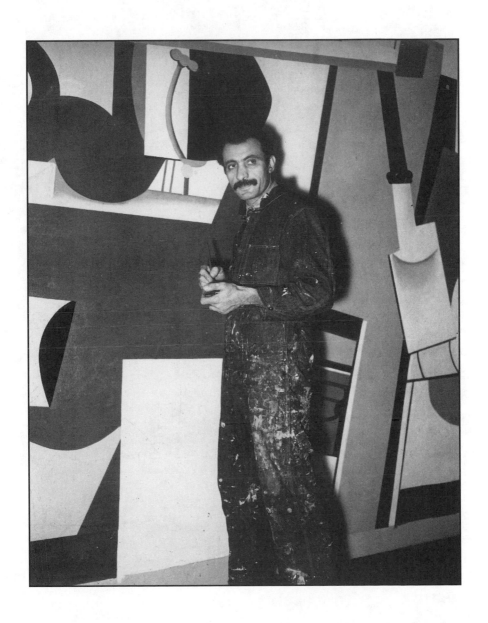

Gorky at work on *Activities on the Field*, left panel, North wall, 1936

30

The Artists' Union and
the American Abstract Artists

※

In the early 1930s the realization that the economic crisis was not about to reverse itself drove artists to establish various groups such as the Artists' Union, formed in 1934. Gorky neither joined the union nor did he take part in many of its demonstrations. He did belong to the union's precursor, the Artists' Committee of Action, and on October 27, 1934, he was one of a group of some three hundred artists who marched on City Hall to demand a place to show their work. For this parade, Gorky designed and, with his friend the painter George McNeil, built an enormous float consisting of a tower made out of painted cardboard over a wooden skeleton and held together with wires. Photographs show the tower to have been closely based on Picasso's Synthetic Cubist *Harlequin* of 1915. Inspiration may also have come from Picasso's costume design for "The Manager from New York," who wore a Cubistic construction made to resemble skyscrapers in the 1917 ballet *Parade*. Stuart Davis remembered that "Gorky had a great big thing made out of pressed wood—what do you call this stuff? Wall board, isn't it? It was a huge thing—you know, like a certain kind of flat sculpture, cubist sculpture, that was in vogue in those days, and when they came to get it out, of course, it was too big . . . They took the window out in the back . . . and they finally had to take it all apart and put it back together again out in the street. It was a big, heavy thing. It took four men to carry it." The protest did not have the desired outcome. Furious to see the artists marching side by side with Communists, Mayor La Guardia went off to officiate at the opening of a new causeway at Jones Beach. The following day, at a stormy Artists' Union meeting, the Artists' Committee of Action resigned—or it may have been expelled—and the group soon dissolved.

Though not a member, Gorky attended many Artists' Union meetings and he clearly shared the leftist political values of the majority of its members. Friends thought of him as left-leaning. Few of them knew he was a Stalinist, for Gorky did not broadcast his Stalinism. He was, Mougouch says, "a Stalinist to the end. He was *not* going to budge, not an inch. He refused to believe that Stalin could do wrong or that he put people in jail. He felt the stories people told him about Stalinist purges were simply anti-Stalin propaganda. Stalin was for him a father figure, inviolable. Gorky's Stalinism was very primitive and childlike. It gave him an identity. He felt that Georgians and Armenians came from the same root and Stalin was Georgian." In addition, for Armenians in the diaspora, Soviet Armenia was a homeland of which they could be proud.

Gorky was not, however, a card-carrying member of the Party. As an immigrant without U.S. citizenship papers, he felt his position in the United States was precarious. He knew that conservative WPA officials were determined to remove Communists from the payroll, and his WPA income meant survival. "Gorky would have been too scared to join the Party," Mougouch says. "He knew about Sacco and Vanzetti. He believed in being subversive, but he was careful because he was an immigrant and he did not want to go back to Armenia."

When he did go to union meetings, his need to be center stage often made him a nuisance. "He was quite an actor," Rosalind Bengelsdorf recalled. "If you were anti-Semitic he was pro-Jewish, if you were pro-Jewish he was anti-Semitic. He loved creating an uproar!" Dorothy Dehner and David Smith attended an Artists' Union meeting in which the topic under debate was what kind of paintings could help the working class. After listening for a while, Gorky rose to his feet and said, "Why don't you just teach them how to shoot?" Bernarda Bryson, a young painter who later married Ben Shahn and who was secretary of the Artists' Union from 1934 to 1935, remembers Gorky's coming to some of the early meetings, but she does not think he was all that politically engaged:

> I found him touching and melancholy. He seemed to be looking for an emotional home and something he could attach himself to.

He never belonged to the union. He'd come up and sit around. He'd draw. He once drew a picture of me. He was a lovely person, very warm—a handsome young man, He had a rather graceful way when talking. He talked slowly and he often hesitated. He would stammer as he looked for the word he wanted. His voice was nice, soft and low. I never heard him laugh. He had a shy smile, but he was not shy. He was reserved. I felt that Gorky in the United States was separated from Russia, which he obviously loved. When he came to the Artists' Union, he was looking for something that would be compatible with his temperament. He came to the union to find a sympathetic milieu, to find interesting conversation with unpretentious people. He and a painter named Phil Bard would sit around a table and chat. Often the talk was about politics. They talked a lot about Russia. There was a lot of arguing. I don't think Gorky found what he was looking for at the union. Gorky was a touching presence because he had a yearning in him.

Gorky gave several lectures at the Artists' Union Hall. Bengelsdorf remembered him explaining "the plastic structure of the picture plane" by cutting an apple in half and drawing it. At union meetings, said Balcomb Greene, Gorky "considered it his mission to instill into the rank and file of the organization a respect for art and a suspicion of the political adventurer. He would gain the floor on the most inauspicious occasions and declaim about the contours in Ingres, which personally I do not think much attracted him. In his broken explosive English, elemental-metaphorical in sound, he seemed to give the impression that Ingres might at any moment lend his support to the cause. I could become furious when he was not on my side. Sometimes he would seem extremely witty. I wanted Gorky with me, intimately."

Some union members were not pleased with Gorky's antics in defense of abstraction. De Kooning, who joined the Artists' Union in 1934, remembered operating the slide machine for a lecture delivered by Gorky at the union. "Every once in a while he would say 'Bill' and then I would [change the slide]." The audience was riveted, de Kooning recalled, "except one particular character . . . who came out with this whole idea about Communist business." But the audience took Gorky's side. "One of them stood up to say that they'd heard enough about what you could have with Communists, but in the meantime they're artists . . . They also wanted to know about painting a bit more. And so it was a very successful evening." The lecture that de Kooning remembered may have been the one Gorky gave in spring 1936, when he pronounced Social Realism to be propagandistic illustration—what he called "poor art for poor people." This now-famous remark earned Gorky many enemies among union members, most of whom were Social Realists. Gorky had drawn the line: he was an elitist. His first loyalty would always be to art.

Mercedes Carles (later Mercedes Matter), who met Gorky on WPA paycheck lines and had an intimate relationship with him in the summer of 1936 (the summer Corinne left New York for Rochester), recalled a time when she and her fellow Hofmann student George McNeil stopped at 36 Union Square to ask Gorky to join them at a protest meeting. Pleased though Gorky was that his young friends wanted him to join them, he refused to stop painting. Since it was Gorky who had introduced her to leftist political thinking by giving her books on Marx and Lenin, Mercedes was amazed and amused by his position.

In attaching himself to Mercedes, daughter of the veteran abstractionist Arthur B. Carles, Gorky once again was attracted to a beautiful young painter whom he thought he could mold. But Mercedes had her own ideas about art, and she was not awed when Gorky played the maestro. "I would preach to Gorky that he should work from looking at nature. I felt it could be ballast against art." Together they went to the Frick and he "fell into a trance" in front of Ingres's portrait of the Countess d'Haussonville. When they walked the streets of Manhattan Gorky exclaimed over the images he saw in the cracked pavement. They spent a day taking photographs of things like shop signs that they thought might amuse Léger, with whom in 1936 Mercedes worked briefly on an abortive mural project for the French Line pier.

Gorky told Mercedes that he was Georgian:

When he told stories about his childhood, he'd go into a kind of chant. I was fascinated and intrigued. I wasn't in love with him. Gorky had a crush on me for a while. There was a time when he couldn't stay away from me and he came to my studio every day. He would quote the punch line from a popular song that played frequently on the radio: "Life is just a bowl of cherries." I had a little studio on a high floor with a terrace, on Twenty-eighth Street, just west of Fifth Avenue. After coming to my studio for a while, Gorky said he was spending too much time there and why didn't I come to work in his studio? I did, and I began painting in a way that was alien to my usual way of working.

Gorky was not flirtatious or romantic. He was very attentive, and he focused on one. He was very sensuous, but he had a problem. He was definitely interested in sex and very sophisticated about it and about everything else. Any sexual connection we might have had wasn't romantic. I don't think Gorky was really in love.

It all came to an end when Mercedes' regular boyfriend, the sculptor Wilfred Zogbaum, returned from Cape Cod. He "arrived at Gorky's studio and took me out."

Sometime in the mid-1930s the friendship between Gorky and Stuart Davis broke up over the issue of political engagement versus commitment to art. Davis gave endless hours to the Artists' Union and the Artists' Congress, which was called in New York in 1936 to discuss issues of culture in a world in crisis and for which Davis served as secretary. As a result, he had little time for painting. In his memoir of Gorky, Davis wrote: "I was in these things from the beginning and so was Gorky. I took the business as seriously as the serious situation demanded and devoted much time to organizational work. Gorky was less intense about it and still wanted to play. In the nature of the situation, our interests began to diverge and finally ceased to coincide altogether. Our friendship terminated and was never resumed." About this falling out, Mariam Davis recalled: "He and Stuart would not speak to each other for a while. There was a magazine *Art Front* that Stuart was editing, and he asked Gorky to write a little paper and Gorky wouldn't do it. Gorky didn't want to get political. He wasn't political at all. He wasn't a joiner."

Besides the WPA and the Artists' Union, various groups and organizations helped bring artists together during the Depression. One of these, formed in 1935 and called The Ten, was a group of nine independent artists, most of whom worked in representational modes. Their purpose, as one critic described it, was to "attempt to combine a social consciousness with [an] abstract, expressionistic heritage, thus saving art from being mere propaganda on the one hand, or mere formalism on the other." Among the members, whose roster changed slightly over time, were Mark Rothko, Adolph Gottlieb, Joseph Solman, and Ilya Bolotowsky. Gorky was invited to join but declined. In December 1935, armed with his book on Ingres, he attended the opening of the group's first exhibition at the Montross Gallery and carried on about Ingres being more abstract than modern artists.

More important than The Ten in terms of the formation of an artistic community in Manhattan was the American Abstract Artists. Founded in 1936, its purpose was to counteract the neglect and misunderstanding of abstraction during a period when regionalism and Social Realism held sway and when museums ignored contemporary American abstraction in favor of European modernism. The idea of forming a group modeled on the French Abstraction-Création and the British association called Circle began to be discussed, and late in 1935 Rosalind Bengelsdorf, Byron Browne, geometric abstractionist Albert Swinden, and sculptor Ibram Lassaw met in Bengelsdorf's studio to talk about the possibility of a group exhibition. The group expanded with each subsequent meeting and it attracted artists of radically different political and aesthetic viewpoints. There were Stalinists, Trotskyists, and simply left-leaning liberals. There were hard-edge geometric abstractionists as well as semiabstract painters working in painterly, biomorphic, and sometimes Expressionist modes. Naturally, when they came together there were scuffles. As George McNeil recalled: "The group manifested contradictory and irreconcilable views about art quality and significance, and there was some fear that the group would be dominated by personalities." Gorky was one such personality. At a November 1936 meeting at painter Harry Holtzman's studio, Gorky was a troublemaker. With the idea of setting up a workshop/school or an intellectual community of abstract artists, Holtzman had equipped the studio with white easels in homage to Mondrian's Paris studio. It soon became apparent that the assembled artists were divided between those who, like Holtzman, wanted the group to be a discussion center and those who wanted it to focus on organizing exhibitions of members' work. Gorky supported Holtzman. Ever the teacher, he proposed that everyone complete an assignment before the next meeting. Ilya Bolotowsky, whose memories tend to exaggerate Gorky's high-handedness, spoke of the occasion this way:

> In any crowd, he had to be the center of attention . . . and of course Arshile could lecture us like a master, and he said, "Before you go into all this abstraction, see what you can do with a simple thing, then make it abstract. Now take for example, a piece of string, an electric bulb and that's all. And see how you can compose it so that it's still abstract." And most of the bunch very obediently, for they were all school trained, immediately went home and did their homework. He was the one who didn't. And he criticized it severely. After a while, the bunch got wise that it was a delaying tactic and so they decided to start an exhibiting group.

The German-born painter Werner Drewes, who was a few years older than Gorky and who had studied at the Bauhaus in the 1920s, objected to Gorky's setting himself up as the authority who would critique the other artists' projects. Drewes put forward once again the idea of organizing a group exhibition. Gorky countered by saying that the group was not ready to exhibit: "Right now, there is no room for abstraction in this country except for one strong personality, and if he is propped up by his friends who have understanding . . . then eventually more can go up there. But first you have to push through." Who, Werner Drewes asked, would be the first to be pushed through? "Of course, somebody who is deserving," Gorky answered. "Is that you?" Drewes now asked. "Of course," Gorky said, and Drewes said, "The heck with you." "What do you mean 'the heck with me'? Of all the bunch here, I exhibit at the Whitney Museum any time I want and you people still hardly can make it. And so I'm the natural one to open the field." Drewes said, "Just for your own career." Gorky retorted, "I see you're not serious. I'm leaving." As Gorky walked toward the door, Drewes said, "Good-bye, Gorky," but everyone else was silent. Bolotowsky recalled: "He goes out, bangs the door, puts his face in and says, 'You are making a big mistake. I am leaving.' And afterwards, we went after him, all over the place, but he would not join the group. He would come to our openings though, but it didn't quite suit his means. Underneath, it was really humorous, although the prima donna attitude was genuine, of course." The loyal de Kooning, a kind of younger-brother figure to Gorky in these years, followed Gorky out the door a few minutes later.

Two months after that meeting, the group formed an exhibiting society and named itself the American Abstract Artists. Gorky and de Kooning were invited to join but refused. The AAA held its first exhibition on a high floor of the Squibb Building at 745 Fifth Avenue in April 1937. The opening night was a crowded and lively affair at which, according to McNeil's memory, "Gorky was in his usual jocose mood as he went about with an Ingres reproduction insisting that Ingres was more abstract than any of the pictures on the walls." Another time Gorky attended an AAA opening carrying a book on Uccello under his arm. Mercedes Matter recalled: "He would be disdainful and spoke of the arrogance of the American Abstract Artists, who thought they had discovered geometry, whereas geometry was in the old masters." Gorky was invited to lecture at one of the AAA meetings, and the gist of his talk, according to Bolotowsky's hearing of it, was: "We are all apprentices, we all steal from the [past]. The only difference is that I admit it."

Gorky did not approve of the AAA's dogmatism in rejecting artists like John Graham, who the members felt were modern but not abstract. After all, Gorky himself painted portraits and even the occasional landscape. Also, though he loved Mondrian, he disliked most geometric abstraction, and he perceived the group to be dominated by artists working in purely geometric abstract modes. Vaclav Vytlacil, an AAA member who alternated between geometric abstraction and figuration in the 1930s, observed that Gorky felt geometric, nonobjective art was too austere: "He wanted to enrich it. He felt that pressure was narrowing the art of painting down towards geometric form . . . He liked the painterly. He loved sensuality . . . Flat things irritated him."

In fact, the AAA's membership included many artists who mixed geometry with a clean-cut version of biomorphism and many others who worked in a painterly manner, often abstracting their free forms from nature. Pure plastic values were the order of the day, and, even when members used biomorphic shapes, they scrubbed them clean of their murky Surrealist aura. Harry Holtzman expressed the group's anti-Expressionist and anti-Surrealist bias when, in the catalog of one of the group's 1938 exhibitions, he attacked "the solipsist [who] would have the means become a merely egoistic function," so that a painting, instead of having "universal meaning," becomes an "individualistic symbol." Gorky, of course, believed that a painting could be personal and universal at the same time.

Gorky's attitude toward the AAA was colored also by his sense of not being a mainstream American. He was uncomfortable in the company of the so-called Park Avenue Cubists, the uptown contingent of the group's membership, which included painters like Suzy Frelinghuysen, A. E. Gallatin, Charles Shaw, and George L. K. Morris. "Gorky couldn't stand the AAA," Mougouch recalls. "He felt that its members were Anglo-Saxon snobs." The group of artists connected with Gallatin "all wore tweeds and smoked pipes and Gorky didn't feel any kinship with them. Instead he used to sit in the cafeterias on West Twenty-third Street with whoever turned up." Indeed, Gorky's foreign and bohemian appearance might have made some of those blue-blooded establishment New Yorkers uneasy. Mercedes Matter says: "Gorky was not acknowledged by uptowners. Once I was uptown at the [James Johnson] Sweenys' for drinks with my husband, and Sweeny said, 'Oh, I saw you walking along the street with Gorky,' as if that were almost reprehensible. The uptown people were very snobbish."

31

The Newark Airport Murals

꽃

Soon after Gorky joined the WPA mural project he was assigned to make sketches for a mural on the subject of aviation for the Administration Building of Floyd Bennett Field in Brooklyn. Burgoyne Diller recalled that one of his rationales for picking Gorky for the job was that "an airport was a very contemporary activity and a place that could stand a good contemporary painter's work." To ensure that Gorky's mural would be understandable to the public, Diller decided that it should incorporate enlarged photographs of airplanes and airports by Wyatt Davis. Accompanied by Davis, Gorky visited an airplane factory in Farmingdale, Long Island, where he studied engineers' drawings of airplane parts. In late November or on the first of December 1935, he submitted a collage study for a mural called *Mechanical Aspects of Airplane Construction* to the WPA/FAP office.

Although Gorky had the support of project officials, there was another contender for the job, a conservative muralist named Eugene Chodorow. In a letter dated December 2, 1935, Audrey McMahon, regional director for the WPA/FAP, asked Alfred Barr for his opinion as to the relative merit of Gorky's and Chodorow's proposals for the Floyd Bennett Field mural. Barr responded the following day saying that he preferred Gorky's proposal and that "pilots and mechanicians [sic] would find Mr. Gorky's composition with its photo-montage far livelier and more interesting." Three weeks later McMahon wrote to Barr to inform him that the City Art Commission had not yet taken any action on Gorky's proposal. The WPA/FAP planned, she said, to include Gorky's sketch as well as a small print of his photo mural project in the soon to open *Murals for Public Buildings* exhibition.

Much fanfare attended the December 27, 1935, opening of the exhibition, which comprised works by twenty-seven project artists and which inaugurated the Federal Art Project Gallery at 7 East Thirty-eighth Street. Reviewing the show for the *World Telegram*, Emily Genauer said that Gorky's mural study incorporating "bits of aeronautical photographs by Wyatt Davis" was "an aesthetically thrilling work in which shapes, colors and textures have been organized with sensitive regard for spatial relationships, equilibrium of forms, distribution of weight tensions, and movement rhythms."

Mayor La Guardia was less impressed. He came to the opening accompanied by Thomas E. Dewey, the city's special rackets prosecutor, and Adolf A. Berle, Jr., city chamberlain, and gave a speech about art and society. "After the applause," the critic and poet Edwin Denby remembered, "Gorky who was on the reception committee stepped forward unexpectedly and began, 'Your honor, you know about government, and I know about art.' " Gorky addressed a few more sentences to the mayor, but their exchange was not recorded. The most reliable source for what occurred when the mayor was shown the various mural projects is the *Herald Tribune*'s December 28, 1935, article headlined, "W.P.A. Murals Are Too Much for La Guardia." The mayor, according to the *Herald*'s reporter, found that several of the murals planned for New York City's public buildings were "beyond his comprehension." First he studied a mural design by Albert Swinden. "What is that?" he asked Audrey McMahon. When she told him it was a mural, he said, "I'll admit I don't know what it is." "It's a map of Manhattan," quipped a facetious bystander. "Well, if that's art," said the mayor, "I belong to Tammany Hall!"

McMahon and several of her assistants now steered the mayor to a dreary realistic painting entitled *Preventative Medicine*. Here La Guardia felt more at home, but, "reinforced by a few sips of kickless fruit punch," he moved on to a wall where Gorky's *Aviation* hung. Anticipating trouble, McMahon's assistants had "rounded up some experts on abstraction, including Arshile Gorky . . . Mr. Gorky told the mayor that the abstractionist did not use 'old-fashioned colors,' tried to show all sides of an object at the same time, and viewed a round ball as flat." Gorky explained that he'd been inspired by aviation lofting plans and that he had taken a section of the fusilage and turned it into an abstraction. The mayor wrinkled his brow. "I'm a conservative in my art, as I am a progressive in my politics," he said. "That's why I perhaps cannot understand it."

FAP press agents decided that La Guardia standing in front of Gorky's design for *Aviation* was an excellent photo opportunity (Figs. 105 and 106). Even that turned into a fiasco when an aggressive salesman for *Art Front* jumped into the picture holding up the magazine. Although La Guardia laughed, Audrey McMahon was upset. The photographer took another picture without the salesman. The resulting photographs show Gorky's talents as a teacher brought to bear upon the short, rotund mayor, who in one shot leans forward for a closer view but whose expression remains incredulous. As he was leaving the party, the mayor was asked whether he thought the works in the exhibition were a good return on WPA money. "Well, it has employed lots of artists, hasn't it?" he responded. "They have to eat, don't they?"

Soon after this encounter between Gorky and La Guardia, Gorky's mural project was reassigned to Newark Airport's recently completed and highly modern Administration Building. Years later, Burgoyne Diller said that the reason for the reassignment was Mayor La Guardia's negative response. By the end of January 1936, Gorky, much to the annoyance of some of his fellow artists, was making preliminary sketches for Newark at an accelerated pace. Three days after being asked to produce studies, he turned up in the FAP offices with about fifty color sketches. "And when Gorky brought in all these sketches that he'd done so quickly, by god, they hauled him up in front of the Artist Union and raised hell with him, because they said he was ruining the project," Saul Schary recalled. "He was doing too much work and showing the others up."

At first Gorky was to incorporate Wyatt Davis's photo enlargements. Sometime in late spring or early summer 1936 he persuaded the authorities that he and Wyatt Davis should work on separate murals. By August 1936 his designs were done and project officials were able to present the Newark Art Commission with a scale model of the Administration Building's second-floor foyer with tiny versions of Gorky's ten proposed murals placed on its miniature walls (Fig. 103). "The Commission was made up of rather elderly gentlemen," Burgoyne Diller remembered. "When we presented the mural I deliberately presented it as decoration so they wouldn't quibble about art. But one of them, probably brighter than the rest, said 'Well, that's abstract art, isn't it?' That unleashed the devil . . . Beatrice Winser [director of the Newark Museum], who is socially and economically their equal, shamed them into accepting it."

By mid-September, when the Museum of Modern Art opened *New Horizons in American Art*, featuring work made by artists on the WPA/FAP, Gorky's mural panel *Activities on the Field* was ready for the show. When, in November, certain conservative Newark Airport officials saw Gorky's mural project in the Newark Museum's *Old and New Paths in American Design: 1720–1936*, they were horrified. Gorky's works in these two exhibitions prompted a brouhaha in the Newark press. Some pronounced the murals to be incomprehensible or outmoded. Others said they represented the most up-to-date abstraction. The *Newark Evening News* reported that "everyone has tried to be polite about the Federal Art Project Murals for the new administration building, but aviators and aeronautical engineers, no word-mincers, have found it tough going . . . Everyone is happy that the murals are not frescoes—i.e. painted on the walls so they are permanent."

Concerned that the negative publicity might jeopardize future mural projects, Olive Lyford, special representative to the Federal Art Project in New Jersey, asked Alfred Barr for a letter in support of Gorky's murals. Barr responded that Gorky's murals were appropriate for a modern airport: "It is dangerous to ride in an old-fashioned airplane. It is inappropriate to wait and buy one's ticket surrounded by old-fashioned murals." Perhaps to create a better understanding of what Gorky was trying to do at Newark, a fact sheet about Gorky and his proposed mural was prepared. The writer clearly spent hours talking to Gorky, for the piece captures Gorky's turn of mind. The most illuminating section comes under the heading "Philosophy of Painting." The central problem for the contemporary artist, Gorky told the writer, was the way an object occupies space. At Newark, Gorky said, he "distilled" aviation and airplane forms to their essentials, organized shapes in such a way that they did not "break through the wall," and tried to convey the "mood of aviation, . . . suspension in space, the sense of objects floating in space."

By June 1937 Gorky had squared up all ten of his mural sketches and transferred their compositions to canvas panels. Because his Union Square studio could not accommodate such large murals, he had been given a studio space at the WPA/FAP's midtown headquarters. He was also assigned three assistants. One of them, the painter Giorgio Cavallon, remembered that Gorky refused to delegate any part of the Newark job. Occasionally he would tear downstairs to the administrator's office and complain about being bothered by amateurs who wanted to help. It was only after much pleading that Gorky, after looking Cavallon up and down with an air of sad resignation, took him on. Cavallon's principal contribution was constructing scaffolding and performing odd jobs. Mostly he watched Gorky work. There was almost no privacy in the WPA studio, Cavallon recalled: "I remember one morning it turned out that somebody had stolen Gorky's brushes, and there was hell to pay." Another day when several restless assistants were milling about in the back of Gorky's WPA studio, one of them piped up: "I've got work of my own I could be getting on with. I think I'll complain to the Artists' Union. He won't even let us touch his mural." Another assistant laughed. Gorky kept on painting as though he'd heard nothing.

Cavallon became Gorky's WPA assistant again in 1939, and once a week he clocked in at Gorky's Union Square studio. But Gorky still would not let him touch a brush. Instead Cavallon read art books out loud while Gorky painted. "You're wearing out the couch," Gorky would say. But the two became friends: "We went to an Armenian restaurant on 30th Street, for about 30 or 50 cents, shish kebab or lamb stew and those vine leaves. Every time he had a Turkish coffee, he turned his cup to see the fortune. Every time, he found it was no good."

Painter Arnold Blanch saw Gorky begin his Newark panels: "And when I came up about three weeks later he had completed them. I said to him, 'You fellows that are abstract painters surely can paint with a lot of speed.' And he said, 'Well, that's because we are of our time.' " When an artist is in tune with his time, Gorky explained, he can paint with greater ease. As an example, Gorky went on to tell the story of how Tintoretto won the competition for the Scuola di San Rocco's frescoes. Instead of presenting a sketch, Tintoretto produced a finished fresco in the very space that had been designated for the winner's picture. Naturally, he beat out the competition.

Gorky's mural panels were installed in June 1937. Indeed, they were affixed to the wall twice: the first time they were attached with a new kind of glue, and they sagged and had to be rehung, this time using white lead-resin adhesive. In August 1937 Gorky exaggerated his problems in a letter to the Mooradians: "Some of my pictures fell apart while being hung—which was not my fault at all, as others had applied the glue—I have to do those all over." Gorky's August letter gave other news: his studio was being painted and the landlord was hounding him for $165 to cover the work. His finances were, as usual, shaky. He felt especially insecure because noncitizens were being dropped from the WPA/FAP. "That applies to me as well, since I have not got my second papers yet." He had some good news, though:

> I sold two very excellent paintings, and very cheap too. But it does not matter. If everything turns out all right, I have done about $500.00 worth of painting.
>
> Darling, light a few candles at the altar, and pray that all goes well. I am expecting some new students in a couple of days. Everything is fine with me these days; don't worry about me. I am expecting to paint a portrait and then a large mural if the deal goes through, just fine. I am thinking so much of you. You are before my eyes every minute. I seem to speak to you so often that I don't feel it necessary to write any more.
>
> [On the reverse side of his paper he wrote:] Dear Vartoosh. I miss you all very much. I am speaking with you every moment. My little cat is in Karlen's condition; I call her Boujik. The poor thing fell out of the window, and one leg is badly hurt, though not broken. She'll soon be O.K., says the doctor.

Controversy about Gorky's Newark murals broke out in the press again in the summer of 1937. Texaco's red star logo on the gasoline truck in *Activities on the Field* was mistaken by government officials for the Communist star. Another objection came from the airport manager who feared that the red star might be construed as a free advertisement for Texaco. Gorky was asked to repaint the star in blue. On June 10, the day after the murals were unveiled, the *Newark Ledger* fanned the flames. The level of philistine ignorance makes understandable the bitterness that American abstract artists felt at the public's indifference to their art. The *Ledger* reported on the problems the FAP's technical crew had in hanging Gorky's murals:

> Visitors to the new Administration Building at Newark Airport were walking around in a daze yesterday trying to decipher a series of startling murals. Equally puzzled were two Russian artists

assigned by the WPA to paint the Cubistic brain children of Arshile Gorky the WPA maestro who conceived the murals. They had a sketch on the floor and were gazing at it in awe. It was a frightening assortment of multi-colored angles and planes with something that looked like a silhouette of Popeye the sailor on his back eating two telephone poles.

"This is the top," hazarded the first artist, pointing a tentative finger toward a Japanese sunset.

"No," said the second artist, turning the sketch around and cautiously touching a character study of Old Faithful. "This is the top."

Came ponderous steps along the floor—a man with a handlebar moustache and long hair tied in a knot at the nape of his neck.

"What makes the trouble?" he demanded.

"I'm sorry, Mr. Gorky," said his first assistant, Mr. Bodna, "but we can't tell which is the top."

"No difference it makes," roared Mr. Gorky. "Top is bottom, bottom is top, it is all comprehensible to the artistic eye of the cultured!"

And "no difference it makes," is right, according to the remarks of visitors!

When Gorky explained that one of the murals, *Mechanics of Flying,* was "an artistic conception of the construction of a plane," one onlooker declared, "If that's art then I'm a shoemaker," and others chimed in with equally inane comments. Gorky gave them all a pitying look and tried again to illuminate his mural's meaning: "The blue there is wacuum," he said, pronouncing, as was his habit, *v* as *w.* "When a plane through the air goes the air it pushes aside and a wacuum created is behind, so? Planes are made not by pouring iron in a mold. They are made in pieces. Here I have taken apart the pieces." The *Newark Ledger* had the last word: "Granting that vacuum is a blue spot behind a purple egg in a forest of orange pencils, Mr. Gorky, who is going to put together again the pieces?" So much for the heralded new understanding between the artist and the public brought about by the government art projects! The negative criticism led to difficulties with local officials, but it did not obstruct the murals' formal acceptance by the Newark Art Commission (with Gorky in attendance) on June 24, 1937. In the end, however, the philistines triumphed. During World War II, when the Administration Building was turned over to the War Department, some of Gorky's murals were removed and probably destroyed; two (*Mechanics of Flying* and *Aerial Map*) were painted over and in the 1970s discovered and restored.

In November 1936 Gorky was asked to write a five-hundred-word essay about the meaning and design of his Newark murals for *Art for the Millions,* a report on the WPA/FAP's achievements. What he wrote gives an idea of how his thoughts flowed, and it shows how his ideas about the creative process combined Cubist and Surrealist theories. From Cubism came his notion of dissecting an airplane into its constituent parts and his concept of art as an operation in the "given space of the canvas." Taking the object out of its context in order to make "from the common— the uncommon" is a Surrealist concept.

MY MURALS FOR THE NEWARK AIRPORT: AN INTERPRETATION

The walls of the house were made of clay blocks, deprived of all detail, with a roof of rude timber.

It was here, in my childhood, that I witnessed, for the first time, that most poetic image for a calendar.

In this culture, the seasons manifested themselves, therefore there was no need, with the exception of the Lental period, for a formal calendar. The people, with the imagery of their extravagantly tender, almost innocently direct concept of Space and Time conceived of the following:

In the ceiling was a round aperture to permit the emission of smoke. Over it was placed a wooden cross from which was suspended by a string an onion into which seven feathers had been plunged. As each Sunday elapsed, a feather was removed, thus denoting passage of Time.

As I have mentioned above, through these elevated objects, floating feather and onion, was revealed to me, for the first time, the marvel of making from the common the uncommon!

This accidental disorder became the modern miracle. Through the denial of reality, by the removal of the object from its habitual surrounding, a new reality was pronounced.

The same sense of poetic operations manifested itself in the handiwork of the ancient Egyptian undertaker. Knowing that the living could not live forever, with the spiritual support of the priest, he operated upon the dead, so that the dead might live forever—never to die! To ensure the perpetuation of Life, portraits of the beings, glassy-eyed, enigmatic, were painted upon the mummies.

This operation has transferred itself to the clinical image of our Time. To operate upon the object! To oppose the photographic image, which was the weakness of the Old Masters. Their painting was complete when the outline of the object was correct. The realism of Modern Painting is diametrically opposed to this concept, since the painter of today operates on the given space of the canvas, breaking up the surface until he arrives at the realization of the entirety.

I am definitely opposed to the interior decorator's taste in mural painting, which seems to be that everything must "match." Mural painting should not become part of the wall, as the moment this occurs the wall is lost and the painting loses its identity.

In these times, it is of sociological importance that everything should stand on its own merit, always keeping its individuality. I much prefer that the mural fall out of the wall than harmonize with it.

Mural painting should not become architecture. Naturally, it has its own architecture and limits of space, but it should never be confused with walls, windows, doors, or any other anatomical blueprints.

A plastic operation is imperative, and that is why, in the first panel of "Activities on the Field" I dissected an airplane into its constituent parts. An airplane is composed of a variety of shapes and forms and I have used such elemental forms as a rudder, a wing, a wheel and a searchlight to create not only numerical interest but also to invent within a given wall space plastic symbols of aviation.

These symbols are the permanent elements of airplanes that will not change with the change of design. These symbols, these forms, I have used in paralyzing disproportions in order to impress upon the spectator the miraculous new vision of our time. To add to the aggressiveness of these shapes, I have used such local colors as are to be seen on the aviation field—red, blue, yellow, black, gray, brown—because these colors were used originally to sharpen the objects so that they could be seen clearly and quickly.

The second panel of the same wall contains objects commonly used around a hangar, such as a ladder, a fire extinguisher, a gasoline truck, and scales. These objects I have dissected and reorganized in a homogeneous organization comparable to the previous panel.

In the panel "Early Aviation" I sought to bring into elemental terms the sensation of the passengers in the first balloon to the wonder of the sky around them and the earth beneath.

This sense of wonder I also attempted to create in the second panel. From the first balloon of Montgolfier, aviation developed until the wings of the modern airplane, figuratively speaking, stretch across the United States. The sky is still green, and the map of the United States takes on a new geographical outline because of the illusion of change brought about by the change in speed.

The first three panels of "Modern Aviation" contain the anatomical parts of autogyros in the process of soaring into space, and yet with the immobility of suspension. The fourth panel is a modern airplane simplified to its essential shape and so spaced as to give a sense of flight.

In the other three panels I have used arbitrary colors and shapes; the wing is black, the rudder yellow, so as to convey the sense that these modern gigantic implements of man are decorated with the same fanciful yet utilitarian sense of play that children use in coloring their kites. In the same spirit the engine becomes in one place like the wings of a dragon, and in another, the wheels, propeller, and motor take on the demonic speed of a meteor cleaving the atmosphere.

In "Mechanics of Flying" I have used morphic shapes. The objects portrayed, a thermometer, hygrometer, anemometer, an airline map of the United States, all have definitely important usage in aviation, and to emphasize this I have given them importance by detaching them from their environment.

Mural painting does not serve only in a decorative capacity, but an educational one as well. By education I do not mean in a descriptive sense, portraying cinema-like the suffering or progress of humanity, but as to the plastic forms and treatments in the art of painting. Since many workers, school children, or patients in hospitals (as the case may be, depending on the type of institution) have little or no opportunity to visit museums, mural painting could and would open up new vistas to their neglected knowledge of a far too-little popularized Art.

Rimbaud has epitomized for me the true function of the Artist when he wrote: "The poet should define the quantity of the unknown which awakes in his time, in the universal soul. He should give more than the formula of his thought, than the annotation of his march toward progress. The enormous becoming normal, when absorbed by everyone, he would really be a multiplication [Rimbaud wrote "multiplicator"] of progress."

For his murals' subject matter Gorky stuck close to the iconographic program set forth in January 1936 by FAP supervisor Olive Lyford, who said the Newark murals should depict "forms which have evolved from aerodynamic limitations." Given Gorky's predilection for protean organic shapes, the Newark murals, based on the mechanical shapes of airplanes and other objects associated with aviation, can hardly have been an easy subject. Gorky turned to Picasso, Miró, and Léger for help. Like several other abstract muralists on the WPA—Ilya Bolotowsky, for example—he combined geometric shapes with free forms inspired by Miró and Picasso. In his *Early Aviation* panel on the west wall (lost but recorded in a photograph of the model), Gorky based his barbell-shaped cloud on the shape Picasso used to designate a compote or a cake dish in several Cubist still lifes. *Mechanics of Flying* appears to be based on Picasso's *Three Musicians*, which we know Gorky admired in the Gallatin Collection (Figs. 29 and 30). Turn *Mechanics of Flying* upside down and you will find something resembling three figures in descending order of size from left to right, just as in Picasso's *Three Musicians*. The figure to the left in Gorky's mural might even hold an instrument!

In the two extant Newark panels, *Mechanics of Flying* and *Aerial Map,* colors are dissonant and personal. The yellow of the background is not Crayola crayon yellow; it is slightly off and it predicts the yellow grounds that Gorky used in several Miróesque paintings of the early 1940s. *Activities on the Field*, on the other hand, was, as one study for it shows, primarily red, yellow, blue, black, white, and gray, bearing out Gorky's statement that he used the colors he saw on the airfield. Gorky's departure point for abstraction in *Activities on the Field* was photographs of airplanes provided by the FAP and by Wyatt Davis. No doubt the photographic source accounts for the more geometric and mechanical look of this panel compared with the two extant panels. Another source for the hard-edged, mechanical feel of *Activities on the Field* was Léger's *The City* (1919) (Fig. 104). Gorky had a full-page color reproduction of this Léger, but he did not see the canvas itself until it arrived in the United States and was installed in the Gallatin Collection at New York University in 1937. In addition, Gorky surely saw Léger's retrospective at the Museum of Modern Art in fall 1935, which is about the time he began making studies for *Activities on the Field*. Like Léger's *The City*, *Activities on the Field* has a musical phrasing of clusters of semiabstract shapes across the canvas. Also similar is the proportion of shapes in relation to the whole. In addition, several details seem to be quotations from the Léger. For example, the two black lines with a black circle on the left margin of Gorky's panel are taken from a similar configuration in the upper left corner of the Léger. The lamppost that bisects the Léger is reiterated in the similarly modeled "leg" of a landing gear mechanism on the right in the Gorky.

Another source for Gorky's murals could be the machine-age forms used by the Parisian Purist painters of the 1920s Charles-Edouard Jeanneret (Le Corbusier's painting name) and Amédée Ozenfant. From the Purists Gorky appears to have taken the simple, clean-contoured shapes covered with uniform flat, strong color—a style suitable to the large scale and public function of murals. The bracing example of Ozenfant's precise and smoothly painted forms with their matte finish and chalky colors was close at hand: Ozenfant lived in New York City in the mid-1930s and Gorky knew him. Elaine de Kooning recalled a story told to her by one of Gorky's FAP assistants: "Gorky, after visiting Ozenfant in his studio, rushed back to his own easel, and, picking up some brushes similar to Ozenfant's, immediately began to experiment with that artist's method of applying paint." In his *Art Front* piece on Gorky's Newark murals, Frederick Kiesler described Gorky's Ozenfant-inspired method: "Gorky tried to invent a new oil paint technique for this departure from common mural treatment [i.e., fresco]. He used oil paint in an outflattened equalizing cover."

The Newark murals are at the furthest remove from Gorky's pen-and-ink mural studies of 1934. In adopting a mechanistic and geometric style that could celebrate modern technology, he went against his grain. He went against his grain also because painting public murals did not allow him to follow his usual procedure of reworking his canvas again and again. Nor could he heap up pigment to make it luscious and tactile. His shapes had to be clearly defined—they couldn't look as if they were about to metamorphose into some creature or personage, and he had to give up the intimation of sexuality that the biomorphic shapes in his easel paintings often projected. His designs were to be taken in at a glance by passengers rushing to purchase airline tickets. Thus he tried to give them the bold impact that he and Stuart Davis had so admired in street signs during their Manhattan strolls. This meant curtailing the personal feeling and fantasy that are the wellspring of Gorky's art.

While working on the Newark murals in the mid-1930s, Gorky also did easel paintings such as the very large *Organization* (1933–36), whose severe style reflects his current focus on public murals (Fig. 16). "If Picasso drips, I drip," Gorky had pronounced, and, unabashed by detractors who called him an imitator, he cleaned up his edges when Picasso did. *Organization* is based on Picasso's two semiabstract and rigorously rectilinear studio interiors, *The Studio* (1927–28), which Gorky would have seen at the Valentine Gallery, and *Painter and Model* (1928) (Fig. 17), which he admired when he baby-sat for Sidney and Harriet Janis's two sons. From Picasso's studio interiors (and possibly inspired also by Mondrian), Gorky took the armature of straight black lines that holds *Organization*'s flat color planes in place like the leads in stained glass. Turning his back on the interpenetrating curves and the suggestion of a shallow interior space seen in works such as *Nighttime, Enigma, and Nostalgia,* he flattened rectilinear planes of uninflected color against a white background. Only one biomorphic shape survived Gorky's paring-down process. This is the large black three-lobed form with a yellow eye and a red pupil at *Organization*'s center. It must be a palette: there is a similarly unconventional palette shape in the same position in Picasso's *Painter and Model.* But, given Gorky's habit of transforming palettes into bodies, the shape is likely to stand for the figure of the artist or his model. For all *Organization*'s clean-lined geometric rigor, Gorky's sensibility comes out in the painting's thick impasto and in the idiosyncratic color choices: pale pink, turquoise, green, red, brown, several yellows, blues, grays, plus black and lots of white.

In *Organization* lines interconnect at dots in three places, and a series of drawings for the painting is full of black dots at the ends of straight lines. These lines and dots suggest that Gorky was looking at Picasso's 1926 dot-and-line drawings in which black dots are linked by black lines and dots punctuate the lines' intersections. Or Gorky could have taken the idea from Picasso's *The Studio,* in which there are dots at the base of the lines that form the table legs. A photograph of Gorky standing with de Kooning beside *Organization* (Fig. 96) shows that at an earlier state, probably around 1935, the canvas had many more black lines ending in black circles. A slightly later photograph of Gorky at work on *Organization* (Fig. 18) shows that he slowly painted out unnecessary forms. Sometimes he reconsidered and brought banished forms back, as with the white rectangle just below the palette.

Gorky reworked *Organization* so many times that its paint surface is several inches thick. "That's worth a lot of money in paint," he would say those times when he asked visitors to pick up his many-layered canvases and stood by as they struggled with the weight. To his old friend and neighbor the painter Max Schnitzler he explained that form must be made tactile: "He liked to touch it, so he put so much white paint on that the form was actually like bas relief." When his assistant, the young painter Herman Rose, first turned up for duty at 36 Union Square, Gorky met him at the door wearing a dark red bathrobe and a towel wrapped around his head like a turban. On the easel was a large painting with a red free form in the middle—probably *Organization*. To Rose's astonishment, Gorky picked up a palette knife, pried up the red pigment, and peeled it off. Finally Gorky made up his mind that *Organization* was finished. He signed and dated it on the back, "A Gorky/33–36," and he sent it to the Whitney Museum's third painting annual.

Some artists were annoyed by Gorky's profligacy with pigment. The way he brushed great gobs of expensive cadmium blue onto his canvas and then scraped it away seemed a form of showing off. Other artists were admiring: Aristodimos Kaldis remembered that Gorky kept huge quantities of paint in his small storage room and would carry it out to his studio "like precious icons." Gorky squeezed out paint into luscious heaps on several palettes and left them until they had become viscous. When he applied paint to his canvas with a brush or a palette knife, he was as lavish—it was as if the pigment were an offering. Fortunately for Gorky, some of his art materials were supplied by the Federal Art Project. Occasionally his sisters would send him paints as well. On one occasion de Kooning told Gorky about an art store that was going out of business and was selling paint for next to nothing. Without more ado, and with de Kooning following in his wake, Gorky went straight to the shop, swooped down on all the expensive colors—blues and reds—and left the inexpensive earth colors behind. De Kooning expected that Gorky would share his haul, but it never happened.

Gorky's artist friends have described Gorky's painting process as a mixture of discipline and frenzy. "See the excitement of the brush!" he would exclaim, and he would pace back and forth, then stand and contemplate his canvas. David Smith remembered watching Gorky "working over an area edge probably a hundred times to reach an infinite without changing the rest of the picture, based on Graham's account of the import in Paris of the 'edge of paint.' " David Margolis found Gorky's manner of painting violent: "By violent, I mean emotional. His easel was quite big, a crank easel. And he would crank it up. So he mostly stood up to paint because with an easel like that you can't sit. He used to wear sandals and a kind of blue-green smock. And he also wore overalls like a mechanic. He used to walk away from a painting, come back to it, grab the paint." Max Schnitzler watched Gorky standing poker-faced before his easel. Then he went at it with brushes and a palette knife. "You've got to attack, you've got to attack," he told Schnitzler. "He didn't want to instill doubt into anybody. He fought it, he burned up his doubts on his canvas in two or three minutes."

Balcomb Greene recalled another aspect of Gorky's creative process—his combination of confidence and anxiety:

> In this earlier period when we were all suffering so collectively, so economically, and often so theoretically, Gorky increasingly suffered in a way of his own. He seemed to become entangled completely within his art, a Dostoevski character with a specialized conscience. I have never known an artist to whom a sense of fail-

ure, or a feeling of not quite making it, could be so painful. It was a technician's pain, but it was also intangible. When friends protested to him that his half-inch masses of pigment would some day crack, he denied this. He insisted, against all authorities, that pure zinc white was more permanent than any titanium or lithopone product. When the evidence seemed against him, he undertook to grind and prepare his own paints, with the aid of a machine built for him by Giorgio Cavallon. It was necessary that his paintings be laboriously made. The issue about physical permanence, which he kept undecided, surely was related to the pain which he nursed and of which he spoke so often to those who knew him.

De Kooning, too, observed Gorky's doubt. To him, Gorky's piling on of paint was a compulsion. "He'd be stuck with the drawing. It was agonizing. He'd have this Greek profile in black. The background was white. And day after day, he put more paint on, day after day. The paintings, they looked gorgeous. He had a peculiar way—it's almost like torturing yourself. Coat after coat of paint."

After his excursion into the chastened geometry of *Organization*, Gorky returned, by stages, to the biomorphism of the *Nighttime, Enigma, and Nostalgia* series. As his art developed, his conflations became more subtle and complex. In a few paintings such as the large *Composition with Head* and *Still Life on Table* (Fig. 19), both from around 1936–37, Gorky picked up on Picasso's Expressionist/Surrealist or "cloisonné" Cubism of the late 1920s and 1930s, a mode in which the heavy black outlines that define Cubist planes are like the metal bands, or cloisons, that separate the colors in medieval enamels. Cubist facets are no longer parallel to the picture plane as they were in *Organization*. Instead they poke back and forth, creating a limited depth. Gone is the classical equilibrium supplied by *Organization*'s horizontals and verticals: colored planes look as if they are about to burst out of their grid lines and make a dash in the direction of Expressionism.

In three very similar paintings from 1936–37—*Painting, Composition*, and *Organization No. II*—Gorky combined the strict horizontal-vertical structuring of *Organization* with biomorphic shapes that move to and fro in a shallow space (Figs. 20, 21, and 22). Space is made stagelike by a shape on the left that resembles a drawn curtain. In all three of these canvases there is a central biomorph with a kite-shaped head flanked by what appear to be birds—one with a hanging head on the left and a standing, turkeylike creature on the right. The central protozoan creature with a single round eye and an oval mouth (in *Painting* Gorky gave it two mouths—or possibly one mouth separated into two oval lips) is modeled on Miró's kite-headed biomorph seen in his *Painting* and *The Siesta*, both of 1925. In discussing *The Siesta*, Miró identified this creature as a figure asleep on the beach. We do not know what kind of a being Gorky's kite-headed biomorph stands for, but several pen-and-ink studies for this series are based on Picasso's 1932 ink drawing entitled *Women Playing at the Edge of the Sea*. In one study (Fig. 38) Gorky transformed the heart-shaped torsos of Picasso's women into oblong shapes that, in the three paintings, become avian. Given the fact that the theme of both the Mirós and the Picasso was women on the beach, perhaps Gorky had a similar subject in mind.

32

"Deeper and Purer Work"

In spite of his being criticized as a Picasso imitator, Gorky's reputation grew in the second half of the 1930s. He sold a few paintings and drawings, mostly to friends; he was included in important group shows in New York and in various parts of the United States; and, being a good speaker, he was occasionally invited to lecture. Gorky was pleased with any attention, and in his letters to his sister he reported not only on his economic straits but also on his achievements, usually sifting the facts to make a success seem a triumph. On January 11, 1937, he wrote the first letter to Vartoosh, who with her family had left for Chicago the previous November:

> My dear ones,
>
> I wish I could be with you now so that I could embrace you all.
>
> Sweet Vartush, I always mean to write but you know my laziness. Today I finished a big photograph [he means a portrait done from a photograph]. I wish you could see it. It is very beautiful.
>
> The way forward in my work is clean [clean probably means painting with precise contours] and much closer to me. Just 10 minutes ago Mr Kisler [Kiesler] went to my studio and took away with him my drawing of an aeroplane to publish it in an important magazine. I'll send it to you when it's published. I haven't sold a painting yet, but I have hopes.
>
> My dear ones I received a parcel in which was a bottle on

which was written take 2 teaspoonfuls mixed with water. But I haven't received the other ointment. Maybe you could send it.

Dear Vartush Misis Mitzkirt [Mrs. Metzger] wants to study with me again. I'll write to you about it. My dear how are you. I miss Karlen a lot. I see his smile before me constantly. And up to now I've heard his words in my ears.

Dear Vartush how is Murad's work. Please write to me. I haven't yet seen Davis and Imgard

I miss you greatly. Kiss Karlen ten times and hug him hard and kiss Murad from me.

I'll send you a beautiful photograph. It's of me.

I'm working hard hard

> With kisses
> Ever your affectionate
> Brother Gorghi

On March 23, 1937, Gorky again complained to Vartoosh about insufficient sales:

Dear Vartoosh:

I have received all your letters long ago and have always intended to answer them, but I have been waiting, hoping to give you some good news.

Dearest, for the third time prospective purchasers have come to my studio, seen my painting, and admitted in so many words that they are good, but [they] always put off buying them. For instance, last Wednesday night, Mr. Janovitch's brother and his wife came over and selected three of my paintings. However, we did not agree on the price. They were to call again last night to close the deal, but failed to come. Today over the telephone I was told that the wife had a bad cold and therefore the visit was postponed until next Tuesday. And so it is with others.

As I had written to you, my mural was published in the Architectural Forum [Architectural Record], a copy of which you will soon receive.

Yes, I did sell two pictures, for one hundred dollars apiece: one to Mrs. Metzger's daughter, the other to Ethel [Schwabacher].

Now a news of interest: I have been invited to Washington,

D.C. to speak (May 13) before the American Federation [of Art]. I shall write you about it later.

Dear Vartoosh, I am fine and working very hard. Been doing some very successful paintings with a view to an excellent exhibit next year.

You are always in my thoughts. Never forget little Karlen.

I liked Ado's poem very much, and yours also.

I expect to visit you this summer, as I really miss all of you.

Will write you a very long letter soon—next Wednesday.

With love and kisses

GORKY

The Mrs. Janovitch to whom Gorky referred was Harriet Janis, wife of Sidney Janis (whose original name was Janowitz) and one of three contributors to the brochure for Gorky's first show. Concerned about Gorky's financial straits, Harriet called her brother, I. Donald Grossman, and his wife, Isobel, and told them that Gorky was too poor to buy paints or to pay his rent. Would they help by purchasing pictures? Since their apartment was in the midst of renovation, Isobel Grossman had no interest in buying art, but her husband did, and he proceeded to make an appointment to visit Gorky the following day. Isobel Grossman recalled that Gorky's greeting was "friendly although tinged with a degree of cautious restraint. His pride and dignity were carefully guarded. I observed his long sensitive fingers, the rather tired droop of his shoulders . . . There was an unresolved drama in his person yet the atmosphere in which he worked remained untouched by confusion or social considerations."

Gorky asked the Grossmans to sit on two folding chairs that he had placed at the proper viewing distance, and he began to bring his paintings out from the storage room. As they responded with enthusiasm, he relaxed and explained his method of working out paintings with numerous studies. He spoke of the anxieties and frustrations of his search for perfection. "Was it worth the struggle?" he asked. The Grossmans responded, "Perhaps, an artist such as you has no choice." Gorky ended the conversation with a line from a Duke Ellington song: "It don't mean a thing, if it ain't got that swing."

The Grossmans chose three paintings, one of which was *Composition* (1936–37). As they were leaving, Isobel noticed Gorky's *The Artist and His Mother,* the only picture that hung on Gorky's studio walls. When she commented on it, Gorky cut her short. The painting was not for sale, he said, in a voice that made her feel she had "intruded into his private world." A few days later Gorky brought the three paintings that the Grossmans had purchased to their Gramercy Park apartment and with them drank champagne to celebrate the sale.

On the morning of May 12, 1937, Gorky sat in his room at the Wardman Park Hotel in Washington, DC, and wrote a note to Vartoosh: "This morning I have to speak to the American Federation [of Arts]." He told his sister that he was drawing a lot and that if things went well he would visit her the following summer. Later that month Ethel's husband, Wolfgang Schwabacher, bought a painting in progress for $650, to be paid in monthly installments of $50. Schwabacher wrote to Gorky on May 28: "You are, we feel, a great painter and some day you will come into your own. In the interim, we know you will carry on with your usual courage and high hope." The following August, Gorky wrote Vartoosh that he had sold "two very good paintings at a low price, but it cannot be avoided." He expected to earn $500 from them, and he was hoping as well for some new students.

During this period Gorky needed money not only for himself. He also felt he should help support his father, perhaps buy him a farm. After the death of Sedrak Adoian's second wife early in the 1930s, Sedrak returned to live with Hagop, who, having lost his job at the Iron Winding Company during the Depression, had been moving his family from house to house and now did piecework at the New England Butt Company. Conflicts between father and son soon forced Sedrak to move out and into the home of a shoe salesman to whom he gave his Social Security check and some baby-sitting hours in exchange for room and board. Gorky's October 18 letter to Vartoosh said:

Next Monday evening I am to teach several students. If I receive any money from them, I shall be able to mail $15.00 to Akaby for father.

This very minute I sighed very bitterly.

My cat is on my desk bothering me. She leaped on the first sheet and dirtied it up. But she is very pretty, and just as Karlen used to do, she keeps running after me, watching me paint.

Vartoosh dear, I don't know whether you remember that on your last visit here I did a pencil drawing of you. I have done four lovely paintings from it and if I can come for Christmas, I shall bring them along.

Well, I miss Karlen very much. Kiss his eyes for me. I am gathering some pictures for him; will send them soon.

Don't worry about me! I am fine.

So much for the present. Will soon write again.

With yearning kisses, ever yours,

GORKY

P.S. The Cat says "hello" to Karlen. Sis, she looks just like a tiger—rears on her hind legs and fights. She ran away; I could not finish her picture.

His letter said that he hoped to be able to help pay his father's traveling expenses so that Sedrak could be with his daughters for Christmas.

The most auspicious event of 1937 was an invitation to participate in the Whitney Museum's fall painting annual. This led to the Whitney's purchase of *Painting* (1936–37) (Fig. 20), which was included in the show. Gorky's first sale to a museum was a real boost to his confidence. He had written to Vartoosh on October 18: "I have a painting in the current exhibit at the Whitney Museum, which is to purchase paintings worth some $20,000.00. Mine is priced very reasonably. If only they would buy it, I should be able to help father, and what is more I could pay you a visit on Christmas. Oh, I miss you all so!" On December 13 Gorky sent his family a telegram: "My Dears, Whitney Museum purchased one of my paintings for $650. Will write soon. Love Gorky." In a January 1, 1938, letter, he said: "My dear ones, they bought one of my paintings for $650 but I haven't yet received the money but on the 4th of the month I will."

Gorky's New Year's Day letter continued:

My sweet one, I received your gift. It was most beautiful. I have not forgotten you all, but these days I have no money, but when I receive my money either this week or next week I will have an appropriate gift for you. And I am sorry that I have been unable to help Father. I will do that also when they send me my check . . .

Vartoosh dear, I will send you three or four paintings so that you will be able to ornament your rooms and I will send Karlen paintings. Write me as to when Akabi will be there . . .

My sweet ones, write more frequently. Yes I am the King of the Lazy (again the champion!), but Vartoosh dear, being a champion is a very difficult thing. Moorad dear, what is your work like? Write me about it. Missing you and with very soulful kisses.

Your loving

Gorky

Kisses to Karlen. I am keeping a cat in the house illegally and when I take him out and he sights another cat he is not brave. I tell him, "very well, cat," and call him Mougouch.

The unfinished painting (Fig. 33) that Wolfgang Schwabacher bought from Gorky in May was one of three versions of *Khorkom*, a series that, because it was named after Gorky's birthplace, must certainly explore memories of Armenia. The series is based on a group of at least eight drawings from 1933 to 1936 that evolved out of the *Nighttime, Enigma, and Nostalgia* theme and in which a whole new cluster of shapes—heart, bird, egg, phallus, belly, and embryo—is generated out of line's sweep (Fig. 90). Either on paper or on canvas, the *Khorkom* theme suggests some crepuscular drama, perhaps, as in *Nighttime, Enigma, and Nostalgia*, a battle between the sexes. I see the principal protagonist as a round-bellied female (slightly to the right in the drawings and centralized in the paintings). She holds up a small, lobed creature; my guess is that this is her child, and she appears to be protecting the child from a phallic shape that swoops toward her from the left.

In *Image in Khorkom* (c. 1936–37) (Fig. 31), the first of the series, the threatening phallus, amalgamated with a shape that looks like a boomerang and is painted various shades of red, appears to penetrate the flesh-colored belly of the female. Gorky emphasized this penetration by curving a brush stroke around the place where the boomerang enters the woman's belly. Adding to the visceral—even pubic—quality of this image, he slathered black pigment in this area. In another reading, the phallus can also be seen as a projection from the belly, turning the female into a male (and predicting the phallic shapes seen on the right in the *Betrothal, Pastoral,* and *Agony* themes of 1947). Either way, it looks aggressive. The drama of the phallus penetrating or emerging from the belly is underscored by the background color, which bursts into flaming red-orange; it is as if everything close to the phallus were on fire.

In general the colors in *Image in Khorkom* are earthy and warm. Gorky's combinations of lavender, jade green, yellow, red, pink, apricot, brown, plus black and white seem un-European. Surely they are colors he remembered when he closed his eyes and thought about his Khorkom boyhood. Their richness is enhanced by layering—layering of pigment, layering of memory. The lumps and grains embedded in his pigment are the result of Gorky's habit of squeezing out large quantities of oil paint and, after it formed a skin, incorporating pieces of that skin into his painting. To call attention to the gritty materiality of his surface, Gorky sometimes laid on paint with a brush that did not hold enough to cover the rough-textured color underneath. In other places he loaded his brush and allowed paint to dribble and drip. But these drips are unusual in Gorky's paintings of the 1930s: it was not until the early 1940s that he thinned his paint and let it run.

Given the title of the series, one wonders whether the imagery has anything to do with the fate of the village during the 1915 massacres. Many of Gorky's relatives in Khorkom were slaughtered. After the villages were pillaged and burned, Gorky witnessed the hordes of bloodied, ravished, and starving refugees—mostly women—that poured into besieged Aikesdan. He would have heard tales of rapes and babies murdered in front of their mothers. It is difficult not to associate the posture of the woman who seems to be protecting her child with Gorky's early experience.

Alternatively, the *Khorkom* series can, of course, be viewed as the image of a proud mother holding up her child. The filled-in lobed shapes formed by the swing of Gorky's pencil in the early *Khorkom* pencil drawing evolve in later drawings and in the first two *Khorkom* paintings into a seemingly jolly image of a crested bird perching on a boomerang. Indeed, the second and third versions of *Khorkom* have none of the first version's feeling of anguish (Figs. 32 and 33). They are lighter in color: both were to have had white backgrounds, but Gorky overpainted part of the background of the version Wolfgang Schwabacher bought (now in the Albright-Knox Art Gallery) with a greenish brown. In the Albright-Knox version, the phallus/boomerang no longer penetrates the belly. Instead it is a separate red shape connected to the female's head by two straight black lines that read as trajectories of vision and that possibly derive from the diverging black lines with dots on their ends that descend from the eyes in Picasso's series of weeping women from 1937. If indeed Gorky meant the black lines to refer to falling tears, my idea that the female creature in the *Khorkom* series is under extreme stress is borne out.

In the 1937–38 version of *Khorkom*, the baby and the bird have become almost abstract and the mother's platypuslike feet have been transformed into a trapezoid. All three *Khorkom* canvases were reworked many times over the years. As a result, some sections of the black contour lines are like recessed channels between more heavily built-up color areas: when Gorky repainted a canvas he changed the colors more often than he changed the arrangement of line and shape. Other times he heaped paint onto the contour lines so that they are raised above the general level of the paint surface. In his January 1, 1938, letter to Vartoosh and her family, Gorky wrote about *Khorkom*: "You know how fussy and particular I am in painting. I am ever removing the paint and repainting the spot until I am completely exhausted. I can't eat, I can't drink, I can't sleep! For example Ethel and her husband came to my studio some time ago and picked a picture for $175. However, since it was not quite completed, I proposed to work on it some more, and have been laboring on it ever since. My soul is in agony, I don't know what to do! It is such things that overcome me, get me down. But I have to finish it in a few more days."

In *After Khorkom* (c. 1937) (Fig. 34), the boomerang is gone and the "child" has been transformed into a Cubistic head with two frontal eyes and an open mouth seen in profile. The embryonic creature inside the female's belly has become birdlike and the belly itself has turned into an oblong with a point at one end: it begins to take the shape of the famous boot/butter churn motif that first appeared in two 1929 still lifes and that would soon emerge full-blown in the *Garden in Sochi* series. With its multiplicity of shapes thrusting back and forth against the picture plane, *Enigmatic Combat* (c. 1937) (Fig. 35) takes off from *After Khorkom*. The subject must be some avian skirmish: the circle, palette, and wishbone-shape in the upper right form a bird with its open beak facing right while various bird heads seem to hang downward like slaughtered poultry. Seeing birds in this thicket of shapes may be the result of the human tendency to read abstract shapes as images (just as Gorky was constantly seeing figures in trees and clouds). Gorky, I think, played on this human proclivity: knowing his viewers would read his shape clusters as bodies, he made sure no clearly identifiable image emerged.

Art historian William Rubin says that the cloisonné Cubist mode of *Enigmatic Combat* derived from Picasso's *Girl before a Mirror* (1932), and I see Picasso's 1928 *Painter and Model* as the source for Gorky's placement of the circular bird head above the palette and his use of a black rectangular plane to hinge his composition to the canvas's top edge. Sources in Picasso's 1934 *Bullfights* and in Masson's *Combats* have also been suggested. But Gorky went further: in *Enigmatic Combat* he burst open Picasso's cloisonné Cubism and set feathers flying. The fracas stirred up by triangular shapes poking this way and that was really a battle that Gorky was waging within his own art as he freed himself from the rigidities of Synthetic Cubist structure and tried to invent an art that could express feelings about memories long suppressed. In a February 28, 1938, letter to Vartoosh and her family, he spoke of his struggle to change his art: "Nowadays an extremely melancholy mood has seized me—and I can concentrate on nothing except my work. Dearest ones, lately I have been well and am working excessively and am changing my painting style. Therefore, this constantly gives me extreme mental anguish. I am not satisfied and from now on I will never be satisfied a single day about my works. I desire to create deeper and purer work." He wrote again a month and a half later saying that he was working himself to the point of exhaustion: "Dear Vartoosh, today I painted so intensely that my knees are trembling from standing so long. Painting is an excruciatingly tedious career. Had I only known that, I would not have entered it. Yet the agonies and torments in my mind impel me to recognize that I must have been born to suffer for art . . . I have drawn a most priceless picture of Mother in charcoal. It required considerable time and is extremely successful" (Fig. 49).

As Gorky's paintings from the second half of the 1930s evolve from the *Khorkom* to the *Sochi* themes, colors change, shapes metamorphose, and new forms are born as Gorky brushes the ground color over earlier paint layers, thus leaving shapes in reserve. In *Summer in Sochi, Black Sea* (c. 1936–37) (Fig. 36), the boot/butter churn is no longer attached to a figure as if it were a belly. Instead it floats free and has developed the two-lobed lower profile that will become a constant feature in the *Sochi* series. The lobes suggest pendulous breasts, but they probably conflate several ideas—buttocks, heart, palette, and pelvis.

Apricots, also called *Painting* (c. 1938) (Fig. 37), was the next step in Gorky's move toward *Sochi*. Here, as in *Summer in Sochi, Black Sea*, the lobed boot/butter churn is situated above a tripod shape, and, as in several versions of *Sochi*, there is a ball with a dot in the middle balanced over the boot's left tip. *Apricots* also has vestiges of the heart and kite shapes seen on the left in *Summer in Sochi*, but the background color swarms in, around, and sometimes over shapes, leaving disconnected vestiges floating in an impastoed sea. Mougouch said of *Apricots* and of several other *Sochi* precursors: "They have to do with memories of the orchards of his childhood, apricots, apple trees." During the late 1930s loneliness made Gorky long for the lost agrarian world of his childhood, for treasured memories like gathering apricots for his grandfather. Gently lobed apricot shapes had already turned up in his Cubist still lifes; they would continue to haunt his paintings of the 1940s.

Argula (1938) (Fig. 39) is the first painting that clearly belongs to the *Garden in Sochi* series. For the first time the the bi-lobed boot shape—which I believe is a butter churn, although it surely has other meanings as well—hangs from a vertical black line. In Khorkom, butter churns made of a goatskin were suspended from the rafters or from a wooden structure with three or four legs. Milk was poured in through an opening at the churn's neck and women stood on either side and rocked. The black line descending from *Argula*'s upper edge could be the rope from which the butter churn was suspended. This black line may also be a vestige of the black lines that anchored shapes to the framing edge in such paintings as *Organization* and the Whitney's *Painting*. Gorky loved suspended forms that jostle and tilt like shapes in a Calder mobile. Many of his paintings from the 1940s have shapes that orient themselves in relation to a vertical that enters the composition from the canvas's top edge. Perhaps the floating shapes reminded him of his family's butter churn or of the traditional Lenten calendar.

Flanking the boot/butter churn in *Argula* are ideographic female figures (presumably churners) with raised arms, their bodies made out of the hanging-bird-head motif seen in the *Khorkom* series. They recall the women with upraised arms in Gorky's drawing based on Picasso's *Women Playing at the Edge of the Sea* (Fig. 38), and they also bring to mind the sprightly female celebrants flanking a central motif in a group of *Garden in Sochi* precursors from the late 1930s and early 1940s including *Tracking Down Guiltless Doves* and *Composition*. The ball inscribed with a pinwheel pattern, balanced above one tip of the boot/butter churn, may be derived from the Armenian symbol of eternity carved into the facades of many eleventh-century Armenian churches, or it could be a reminiscence of the apples stuck with little wooden flanges that Gorky suspended over Khorkom's irrigation canals to kick up a spray. Certainly the ball is a playful motif: it brings to mind Miró's circles inscribed with rosettes and Picasso's women playing ball on the beach.

Argula has the feeling of a folk ritual—it seems a celebration of fertility and abundance. Gorky avowed that it was connected with childhood memories: when Bernard Davis gave it to the Museum of Modern Art in 1941 and it was exhibited in "New American Acquisitions," the museum asked Gorky to fill out a questionnaire. *Argula*, Gorky wrote, was a memory: "No specific scene but many incidents—The first word I spoke was Argula—it has no meaning. I was then five years old. Thus I called this painting Argula as I was entering a new period closer to my instincts." To describe the technique he used in *Argula*, he said: "Hundreds and hundreds of layers of paint to obtain the weight of reality—At this period I measured by weight." And about the significance of the work he said: "If the painting doesn't tell what can I say?"

Argula's bright yellow ground color moves in and around forms like floodwater covering up and cutting out terrain. Yellow submerges whatever might have been left of the Cubist grid, and it eliminates any suggestion of a horizon. As a result, images seem to float in a golden firmament like the holy figures in Byzantine mosaics and Russian icons, both of which Gorky loved. The most immediate source for Gorky's way of floating shapes on a yellow ground is Miró, whose influence had begun to replace that of Picasso. Miró, like Gorky, often took his inspiration from his native roots. Thus, Catalan Romanesque murals and manuscripts informed the Spaniard's work just the way Armenian carpets, frescoes, manuscripts, and relief carvings were deeply ingrained in Gorky's vision. Miró's early farm themes, painted in Paris, were a paean to Catalonia, just as Gorky's work from *Khorkom* to *Sochi* was a visual memoir of Van.

33

Armenian Portraits

✳

Gorky's friends—especially his Armenian friends, with whom he did not pretend to be Russian—recalled his attachment to his Armenian heritage. "It was understood that he was Armenian," said Reuben Nakian. "You could tell as soon as you met him on the street . . . He used to speak about it nostalgically." To Yenovk Der Hagopian, Gorky loved to talk about Khorkom: "He did not care what you thought about him as long as he knew what he was. And he knew he was Armenian." Greek-born Aristodimos Kaldis understood this well: "Anybody who goes away from those countries and comes to New York City has nostalgia for the landscape, the form of life," Kaldis said. "He was uprooted by the brutality of the Turks, and that gives some kind of trauma, a wound . . . He'd go into a chant—'Alolialooi!' and he'll go on for hours." Gorky felt a special kinship also with the sculptor Isamu Noguchi, who, being half Japanese, experienced a similar separateness from American culture. "He talked about his childhood, about Tiflis. He'd tell tales about his mother often," Noguchi recalled. "He romanticized his childhood. His images were always tinged with a Middle Eastern viewpoint . . . He felt that he wasn't totally American . . . We had a certain loneliness here, which we shared, and art was something that kept us going." The artist Robert Jonas put it this way: "Gorky's Armenian past saturated his consciousness. You felt it all the time, as if he was never really here, as if his umbilical cord to his past was never broken . . . He had to break through and translate what he knew as an Armenian before he became Gorky and the germinating force behind the abstract expressionist movement."

To his second wife, Gorky often spoke about his childhood, but only in legendary terms. She remembers Gorky coming home in a furious mood after visiting his sisters in Watertown. They had tarnished his memories by giving him facts. He would never visit them again, he said. "Gorky couldn't stand being contradicted. Because his sisters were older, they were more knowledgeable about their mother and father and about their life in Armenia." To Gorky, his father was "a great guy sitting on a horse, commanding men and telling all the men what to do," said de Kooning. When he talked about his childhood, Gorky spoke "about a certain kind of happiness," but from de Kooning's point of view, Gorky's tales about his family were "like folklore." "I like my family too, but I can do without them. He's a terrific artist. Why should he worry about his sister? . . . I always thought he gave me the business about it, but maybe he really meant it."

What continued to bother other friends was the way this "business" shaded into performance. "In a way," painter Milton Resnick observed, "he always made himself a little ethnic. Somehow, you felt that he wasn't going to be mistaken for an American." As Stuart Davis noted, Gorky would exaggerate his curious syntax in social milieus where he knew it would charm. Many friends remember Gorky's dancing and cooking shish kebab as a one-man show. What they didn't realize was that shish kebab picnics at which men sang and danced were popular with Armenian immigrants in the United States. Jacob Kainen saw another side of Gorky's holding on to his past when Gorky spent a whole Sunday going from butcher shop to butcher shop all over Manhattan, looking for a calf's heart so that he could strip off the heart's surface layer, cure the membrane, and then stretch it over the face of an Armenian stringed instrument that he sometimes strummed to accompany his song.

In Harold Rosenberg's view, the play actor in Gorky, like his need to act out other artists' styles, was impelled by the uprooted immigrant's will to remake himself: "All his life Gorky took pleasure in trotting out as an exotic souvenir the Armenian peasant he might have been . . . His Armenian childhood became, in sum, a decorative motif on the identity he chose for himself in deadly earnest; that of vanguard artist." The truth is perhaps not so simple. Far from being a mere "decorative motif," Gorky's past was a huge part of his present—especially the present out of which he painted. If he played the exotic foreigner to the hilt, he did so partly out of a powerful need to cling to the past even as he re-created it. Before he could become an independent artist he had to explore his past and reweave it into his life and art.

Gorky's first clear expression in painting of his longing for Armenia was the group of drawings and paintings on the Khorkom theme. Another group of works in which he revisited his homeland through the act of painting was his so-called "Armenian portraits," most of which are probably from the mid-1930s. Gorky's absorption in these portraits of family members, of himself, and of the occasional friend might have been prompted by his sharing his studio with Vartoosh and Moorad after they returned from Armenia. Vartoosh, who sat for him often, said: "He wanted to interpret Armenian eyes and sensibility in portraits . . . Our tragic history produced sadness amid beauty, a combination for which he had much affinity."

Gorky's portraits are indeed melancholy. Except in self-portraits, for which he had to look in the mirror, his models never look at the viewer. Most have a far-away look, as if they were in meditation. Color is usually quiet, subtle, autumnal, with few primary hues. *Portrait of Vartoosh* in the Hirshhorn Museum (Fig. 25), begun before Vartoosh left for Armenia and finished after her return, is a cool mixture of slate gray, olive, ivory, and brown. Several circa 1937 portraits are pinky apricot and terracotta in tone, recalling Gorky's love for the Pompeiian frescoes in the Metropolitan Museum. "I was often with Gorky when I saw those murals," de Kooning said, "and he couldn't get over the idea of painting on a terra-cotta wall like the Pompeiians were doing."

In one of the pinkish portraits, *Portrait of Ahko* (Fig. 24), his older sister holds her right hand under her chin in a classical gesture of contemplation that is very like that of the seated women in the Pompeiian frescoes in the House of Vettii or in the Roman frescoes in the Basilica at Herculaneum. This gesture also recalls that of Mme d'Haussonville in the Ingres portrait that Gorky so admired. On a more personal level, the symbolic portrait of Armenia, a woman resting her head on the back of her hand as she mourns the destruction of her homeland, could have been in the back of Gorky's mind. (This ubiquitous image, engraved on cigarette cases, woven into rugs, and pictured on post cards, was one Gorky surely knew.) In a letter to Vartoosh on May 29, 1939, Gorky said: "This morning Agapi [Akabi] came with Azat [Azad Adoian, Gorky's cousin]. I was very happy. They're staying here today and tomorrow evening they have to go . . . I am making a portrait of Agapi and she is posing for me." Perhaps he was retouching *Portrait of Ahko* or perhaps he was referring to another of his Armenian portraits, many of which he worked on from about 1936 to 1942.

In 1942 Gorky chose *Portrait of Ahko* to send to the Museum of Modern Art's *Twentieth-Century Portraits*. Because he backdated it to 1917, it was hung in a room with portraits by an older generation of European masters. Gorky was delighted to see his painting placed beside one of the three Matisses included in the show, probably *Laurette in a White Blouse* (1917). Actually, Gorky's and Matisse's portraits have many points in common: though Gorky's chief source for portraits was Picasso, he looked hard at Matisse as well. Laurette, like Akabi, holds her right hand to her chin, and her dark hair is similarly stylized and abstracted.

Eyes are enormous in Gorky's portraits, and large, dark irises with tiny highlights give them a peculiar intensity. The rapt, reverential expression of Gorky's sitters brings to mind faces in medieval Armenian art, Romanesque Catalonian frescoes, and especially Fayum mummy portraits, which have a similar highlight on the black iris and which Gorky called "glassy-eyed, enigmatic." He often added to the enigma and the intensity by giving his sister's eyes a slight cast (seen also in Ingres) that predicts John Graham's and de Kooning's portraits of cross-eyed women. Although the gloomy mood and subdued coloring of *Portrait of Vartoosh* in the Hirshhorn Collection has been compared to Blue Period Picasso, the bold schematization of features, especially the eyes, is much closer to Picasso's paintings of 1906 and 1907, which show the influence of Iberian sculpture of 400 to 200 B.C.

Gorky painted himself, his mother, and his sisters in part to allay his loneliness during the Depression years. Early in 1938 he wrote to Vartoosh that when he painted portraits of family members he felt he was talking to them: "Yes every day you are in the pupils of my eyes. . . . I thought that you Moorad and Karlen were here and together we were singing sad songs." By painting his family he could gather them around him again. But in order to give the image lasting formal interest, he departed from the facts of appearance. As in his Cubist still lifes, he separated out parts of the figure so that, in his *Portrait of Vartoosh*, for example, hair, shoulders, neck, ear, and clothing become abstract shapes. The broad handling of paint and the rich impasto seen in Gorky's portraits likewise parallel the sensuous surfaces of his abstractions of around 1937. And, as in many of those abstractions, in all three portraits of his younger sister the ground color flows over and covers up parts of her body, thus welding the figure to the background and flattening space.

Gorky often went to the home of Raphael and Rebecca Soyer at 1 Union Square to talk and to draw. At the Soyers' he found other artists, especially Russians, who came to work from a model. David Burliuk's painting *In Moses Soyer Studio* (1943) gives an idea of the atmosphere. It shows Moses Soyer (Raphael's brother) painting Burliuk. Raphael Soyer and painter Nick Cickovsky are seated nearby, and a bust of Gorky looking more Russian than the Russians sits atop a classical pedestal. This may be a spoof about the way some of Gorky's artist friends put him on a pedestal, but it is more likely a joke about the way Gorky put himself on one. Raphael Soyer did not, however, perceive Gorky as a "big ego." "Gorky was a sad fellow," Soyer said. "Very melancholy, thin voice, melancholy intonations and very melancholy laughter. A gentle fellow, actually."

Gorky would turn up at Soyer's studio several times a week to sketch from the model. "When the Burliuks posed for me," Soyer recalled,

> Gorky sat quietly to one side and diligently drew them. His Seurat-like profile of Burliuk hangs on my wall today. He made many drawings of me too, and I painted and drew him whenever I had a chance. He was a fascinating subject—tall, thin, with deer-like eyes, a naïve and haunted expression and blue-black hair.
>
> He had beautiful hands. His clothes were like his paintings in color and texture, harmonious and esthetic: a brown corduroy jacket, a red scarf loose around his neck, its folds arranged with deliberate intent. How he kept it in place, even when he moved about, was a mystery.

Soyer's drawings of Gorky have that same desolate, hollow-eyed expression seen in the jobless and homeless people he portrayed with his characteristic soft-edged realism, but Gorky's morosity may simply reflect the meditative mood that comes when posing.

On one of his visits to Soyer's studio, Gorky looked around and said, in his usual melancholy voice, "Gee, you still have a romantic life with pictures!" Though touched, Soyer wasn't sure what Gorky meant. Another afternoon, when Soyer visited 36 Union Square, Gorky suddenly took two small paintings from his storage room, a self-portrait and a head of Vartoosh, and gave them to Soyer. Remembering this generosity, some time later Soyer offered Gorky a portrait he had made of Gorky's pregnant second wife. Gorky became sullen and turned down the offer, even though Mougouch wanted to accept. "Don't give it to me," he muttered. "I don't collect. You have a romantic life with pictures. I may someday suddenly paint over it." In the 8-by-10-inch *Self-Portrait*, from 1933–34 that he gave to Soyer (Fig. 75), Gorky presents himself no longer as Cézanne, Picasso, or Matisse but as a soulful Armenian with huge, dark, almond-shaped eyes, high arched eyebrows, and a long nose that curves downward over his moustache. (This is the first painting in which he made his nose so emphatically large: Mougouch recalls that Gorky took great pleasure in the resemblance of his nose to Cézanne's—both of their noses, he said, looked like half a pear.) Gorky's face is still shaped like a palette and his ear is a calligraphic swirl. In front of him is the corner of a stretched canvas, and his gaze appears to be directed beyond the canvas to an invisible mirror.

De Kooning once observed about Gorky's portrait method that "sometimes he would look at you for a long time and then walk away and paint without looking at you." In a sense, Gorky looked away even when he was looking at you, for he was looking not just at your features but at the shapes into which he could transform them. He developed certain habitual ways of rendering human features. Thus, the eyes in his *Portrait of Jacob Kainen* (Fig. 97), a canvas that Gorky began in 1934 and had mostly completed by 1937, are very like his own eyes in *The Artist and His Mother*, and Kainen's vulnerable mouth, with its upper lip made of two curved strokes like bird wings, is similar to the mouth in the *Self-Portrait* that he gave to Raphael Soyer.

Soon after they met, Gorky asked the twenty-five-year-old Jacob Kainen to pose for him. Since Gorky was, in Kainen's view, one of the "magus" figures in the art world, Kainen accepted with alacrity. He recalls that he posed in conventional clothes—a nondescript jacket and tie—and that he sat for Gorky only once a week in order to give each new layer of oil paint time to dry. After about four sessions Gorky sanded down his 22-by-18-inch canvas and applied colors that were almost the same as those he had placed there before. After this, Gorky sanded or scraped his canvas with a razor and repainted it each week. "I want surface smooth, like 'glahss'," he explained. He told Kainen how a dark blue in a Cézanne painting "appeared as solid as a rock" because of the layers of other colors underneath. "Keep things flat," he said, "don't over-model or you will lose the clear, flat shape. You don't want it round like a sausage. You just need a touch of shadow at the edge." While Gorky was painting Kainen's portrait his concentration was fierce. "Not only didn't he talk, but he didn't tell me when to rest. You know I was leaning on my hand. After a half hour, it got very tiring. So I'd put my hand down and he'd look kind of impatient." Since Kainen's portrait was small, Gorky was able to work on it while seated. He held his big palette in his left hand and he sometimes rested his right hand on a mahlstick, a stick with a padded ball on its end used by painters to steady the brush.

In Kainen's portrait Gorky defined the shapes of the left hand and the contour of the face and neck with a heavy dark outline reminiscent of the black contour lines in Catalan frescoes. Following his own advice to simplify, he eliminated details of texture and light so that hair becomes an expressive but flat biomorphic shape. As with the folds of Vartoosh's sweater in the Hirshhorn portrait, he abstracted the shapes of Kainen's jacket and gave the jacket several different shades of green, gray, and tan. As a result, the sitter's clothes camouflage the body rather than reveal it.

As always, the place where one color plane meets another is full of tension: obsessed with the need to make his contours exact yet free, Gorky sanded and repainted them over and over again. Then, to keep his surface alive and fresh, he scumbled. He scumbled over both the flat shapes of Kainen's jacket and the gray-green and terra-cotta expanses in the background. These loose, brushy strokes may have been added several years later: Mougouch said that she remembered Gorky painting on many of his portraits from the 1930s, including the one of Kainen, in 1941 or 1942. After 1936 Kainen saw Gorky less frequently. He recalled that the last time he went to 36 Union Square to model, Gorky said he no longer needed him to sit. "I caught a last glimpse of the portrait, which he didn't seem particularly pleased with. . . . I was saying good-bye as he gave me two ink drawings, diffidently, as though he didn't want to press on me anything I didn't want."

In his *Self-Portrait* from circa 1937 (Fig. 27), Gorky stands in three-quarters view looking out at us with something of the cool hauteur of Ingres's Mme d'Haussonville. The sanded-down forms recall also Gorky's love of Bronzino's cool perfectionism. After he finished this *Self-Portrait* he wrote his sister on April 18, 1938: "And I have painted my portrait. I have given my eyes the shape of leaves. These two leaves told me constantly YES, yes. It's very sad, a month ago I cut my hair and I really look like a peasant. From this you can guess, dear Vartush, that I don't like my hair at all. When I come there, my dear, I'll paint you and mother. I've made a wonderful painting . . . It came out very well and when I come I'll bring it to you." Though clearly sad, Gorky's expression is hard to read. As he looked in the mirror his face took on that peculiar intensity that is often seen in self-portraits. Beneath his unbuttoned jacket he wears an undershirt cut low. The shirt, the awkwardly placed rectangular palette, the palette-shaped face, and the stiff position of the arms all recall Picasso's *Self-Portrait* from 1906 (Fig. 6). But the feeling in Gorky's and Picasso's self-portraits could not be more different: Picasso has all the pugnacious determination of a small but fiercely confident young man. Gorky looks like a man in his mid- to late thirties who has suffered. His posture seems diffident—sensitivity was what Gorky valued in himself, not aggression. He stands slightly stooped, and his shoulders slope downward. His arms, defined by disconnected, substanceless, semiabstract forms, seem inert, demuscled, passive.

As in *Portrait of Master Bill*, which depicts a Swedish housepainter to whom he gave lessons in exchange for having his studio painted, Gorky's arm appears detached: this was a visual idea that de Kooning and John Graham would take up a few years later in portraits that dislocated anatomy even further. His right hand and left forearm are encased in unarticulated masses of paint, as if the hands whose job it is to hold his palette and brush were entrapped in plaster casts. This oddity, seen also in *Portrait of Master Bill* and *The Artist and His Mother*, may reflect Gorky's insistence on the elimination of distracting details. Or it may be that Gorky left his *Self-Portrait* unfinished—the palette is only tentatively blocked in; perhaps he planned to continue working on the hands. Or the unarticulated hand and arm may be explained by his difficulty in drawing hands—unlike an arm draped with folds of cloth, the hand and bare forearm could not easily or convincingly be transformed into abstract shapes.

Gorky turned this awkwardness into an asset: the bulbous hand and forearm in his *Self-Portrait* have a strong psychological resonance. Ethel Schwabacher got it right when she saw in this *Self-Portrait* a "mixture of potency and impotency—the potency of the inquiring eye and the impotence of the hand which, though it suggests endurance and contained energy, is heavily frozen, immobilized." A mood of quiescent despair and spiritual exhaustion pervades this portrait—a similar mood emanates from the portraits that de Kooning painted of men toward the end of the Depression. Only Gorky's alert, gaunt eyes, boring into space, hold the abstracted parts of his figure in place as he lets his body meld into a background painted in the same flesh tones and grayish greens that form the figure itself.

34

The End of the Decade

✼

The years 1938 and 1939 were ones of continued hard work, poverty, and neglect. A still life of Gorky's was included in a traveling exhibition presented at two Midwestern universities, but his feeling of rancor at having no gallery representation persisted. Just as in the early part of the decade Gorky went back and forth between Cubist abstractions and the two versions of *The Artist and His Mother*, so in the second half of the 1930s he worked in both abstract and representational modes. He not only drew from the model at Raphael Soyer's studio but also joined his friend Conrad Marcarelli's class at the Leonardo da Vinci School on Thirty-fourth Street between Lexington and Third Avenue. "It was," Marcarelli recalled, "one of those schools where you just pay a few dollars a month and you could study there. And we had a model and so he used to come in two or three times a week . . . He never took lessons. He was just taking advantage of the model . . . We all knew that he was already an artist, that he didn't pay tuition for any kind of instruction . . . He'd just bring a pad and make these drawings, which were complete abstractions out of the figure. But to spectators it was just like doodling. The students looked at him as some kind of freak."

In his April 18, 1938, letter Gorky told Vartoosh about the favorable response to his work exhibited in *Trois Siècles d'Art Américain*, a huge survey of three centuries of American art sent by the Museum of Modern Art to the Jeu de Paume in Paris: "The Paris newspapers liked all my paintings a lot and had written that Arshile Gorghi is the most original-original painter in America." In fact, the show included only one Gorky,

Painting (1936–37), lent by the Whitney Museum, and the French response was lukewarm. Although Parisians were enthusiastic about Buster Keaton and Edward G. Robinson, recent American art was labeled "L'Ecole Frigidaire." But James Johnson Sweeny, a critic closely associated with the Museum of Modern Art, used Gorky's *Painting* to illustrate a piece on contemporary American art published in *Cahiers d'Art*, and he mentioned Gorky (together with Stuart Davis, Saul Schary, and Charles Biederman) as one of a group of painters "who give considerable promise of development once they have found sufficient confidence to find new ways of their own." Full of pride, Gorky wrote to Vartoosh: "Then the painting was published in the best review on art in Paris and in the world, called *Cahiers d'Art*. You know, the one I always used to get in order to see the works of Picasso."

Perhaps as a relaxation from his struggle to free himself from Picasso, Gorky painted a number of flower still lifes in the late 1930s. Giorgio Cavallon, who was still on hand at 36 Union Square as one of Gorky's WPA assistants, recalled a day when two ladies from Philadelphia brought Gorky fresh flowers and he set to work producing one flower painting after another until the blossoms had drooped and died. He sold one of these for fifty dollars. Another he gave to Gaston de Havenon as a wedding present; Mina Metzger acquired two others. Gorky clearly loved painting these modest bouquets: they brought him into direct contact with nature, and (unlike hands) blossoms, leaves, and stems were perfect subjects for him to metamorphose into shapes that could be redeployed in his more ambitious abstract work.

One of Gorky's 1939 flower paintings is inscribed: "To My Lovely Leonora With Love Arshile 1939." It was a gift to Leonore Gallet, a tall, slender, blue-eyed redhead who played the violin in a symphony orchestra and whose father was a Michigan steel manufacturer. Their love affair began early in 1938 when he made her a valentine painting with doves and a heart contained inside what looks like an apple. Leonore appears in at least two of Gorky's drawings, once with her violin (Fig. 107) and once lying in bed with the covers pulled up—likely a sickbed picture.

When Gorky's sixteen-year-old niece, Liberty, visited his studio, Gorky, having informed her that everyone who comes to New York must see the Cloisters, called Leonore to ask her to be Liberty's escort. Liberty was shocked when she first met Leonore, who wore heavy makeup: Gorky had only just given Liberty a lecture about the vulgarity of using cosmetics.

In the spring of 1938 Leonore wrote Gorky from Europe that she had seen his painting at the Jeu de Paume. Missing her, Gorky often sought comfort in the Sandows' company. Helen Sandow recalled: "He was always in love and he used to come and just let it all out to me—how much he loved this person, this girl he went with. She was beautiful. I remember saying to Gorky that all his girlfriends looked like his mother. They were all tall and dark. He was ready to love and to marry Leonore. She was in love with him but her father broke it up. Her father didn't think Gorky was a good catch, and he made it very difficult for her to see Gorky." When he couldn't see her, Gorky wrote Leonore passionate letters. He also gave her numerous drawings. But something was askew. In March 1939 he wrote to Vartoosh, "Life here is the same, I don't see Linora very often. And now I understand a bit better." In October he wrote: "Don't worry about me I am well and working hard. If ever I get this money I will be with you in April, or else this summer Linora and I will come to you."

That was the last mention of Leonore. What went wrong between her and Gorky might be hinted at in several friends' comments: "He wasn't a womanizer," Gaston de Havenon observed. "He wanted affection. He wanted a love affair. That's really what he wanted. A romance." The implication here may be that Gorky was more romantic than sexual or that the emotional aspects of sexuality engaged him more than the physical act. De Kooning, always ambiguous but perceptive, described the relationship this way: "He was very jealous of her, you know. I mean like a man and woman. I mean I think he really made it out good with her. . . . She really likes him and I think he really likes to make love to this woman. It clicked. Because Gorky was a peculiar guy in front of American girls, you know. She knew how to handle, or he knew how to handle—they clicked. They had a real passion. Their love life truly was really Hallelujah! I mean it was right in the right time and she was a violinist in an orchestra." Whatever the problems were—Gorky's morbid jealousy or his sexual inhibitions—Leonore, no doubt to her father's gratification, gradually put distance between herself and Gorky. According to Raoul Hague, she began to see another man: "He had difficulty with girls," Hague said. "On the weekend he'd come see me." Gorky confided his troubles and he explained away Leonore's absence by saying she had a sick mother. But Hague knew better: "She went to New Jersey with another boyfriend," he said, and before long Gorky found out.

In Giorgio Cavallon's view, it was unrequited love for Leonore that prevented Gorky from finishing a WPA project to design a stained glass window for the Catholic chapel in the prison on Rikers Island. Instead of completing his window, the normally abstemious Gorky drowned his sorrows in alcohol. "Gorky had a beautiful girl who was playing the violin and he had problems," said Cavallon. "He was secretive about women but I sensed that I was in the way. He had problems. Here was this good-looking guy, this girl left him. He was trying to call her, and couldn't get her. He was so depressed, he bought a bottle of whiskey and got drunk. He had quite a good voice and sang. Then he got depressed again. He repeated it the next week. He suffered a lot."

Although Gorky remained on the mural project until July 1941, after he finished work at Newark Airport he produced no more murals for the WPA. He did, however, execute two murals that were not sponsored by the WPA—one (*Man's Conquest of the Air*, Fig. 108) at the Aviation Building at the New York World's Fair, which he worked on during the winter and spring of 1939, and one at the Riviera Club in New Jersey, painted in the winter of 1940 to 1941. (There were several uncompleted murals as well. Gorky's architect friend William Muschenheim suggested, for example, that Gorky receive a commission for a mural at the World's Fair's Marine Building, but Gorky's proposal was rejected in favor of a design by Lyonel Feininger.)

Gorky's earliest mention of the Aviation Building project is in an August 1937 letter to Vartoosh: "I am expecting to paint a portrait and then a large mural; if the deal goes through, just fine." On October 18, he wrote again: "The last two months I have been working on sample drawings for the New York World's Fair (of 1939). God helping, they'll be accepted . . . But, honey, I finished them a month ago and here I am still waiting and hoping—to hear from them any day now, and as a consequence I postponed my letter with hopes of giving you some good news. I am always thinking, it would be so nice for all of us if they would accept my pictures." Early the following year Gorky wrote Vartoosh: "I have been painting samples for the World's Fair, and if they are acceptable they will mean an income upwards of $2000 to me. However, as you know, politics is in everything and everywhere. So, I've been working until three and four o'clock every morning the last four months." In late February 1938 he told his sister, "A melancholic mood has taken hold of me . . . My dear ones this work of the World's Fair is still in the same situation and surely you know that these things take a lot of time but I hope that something will come of it."

In May Gorky's mural proposal was finally accepted. When he wrote Vartoosh again on October 12, 1938, the job was in full swing:

> You recall my writing you about some murals for the World's Fair. I was invited there yesterday after dinner and was given the blue prints of the wall plans. I am beginning on the sketches as soon as my studio is done. I believe they will be acceptable and worth about $3000.
>
> These are the murals in the Aviation Building. The architect in charge is Mr. William Lescaze, the best architect in America today. He is not a native, but a Swiss, and likes my paintings very much. He had written to the World's Fair Administration, insisting that I should be given the assignment. Well, that will be just fine, and I'll do my best, I'll work very hard.
>
> So much for the present. Friday, I'll be at the Fair site again for other arrangements.
>
> > Many kisses to Karlen,
> > Your loving brother,
> > Gorky

On January 11, 1939, Gorky resigned temporarily from the WPA because he now had another source of income.

On March 17, he wrote to Vartoosh that his mural was finished:

> I received your sweet letter two weeks ago. I'm so glad you are all better. I instead these six weeks had a bad cold. Because with a tiny stove in the winter's cold I painted my painting (World's Fair) and finished it a week ago. It's beautiful and everyone's pleased with it. The proposal pleased them so much I was obliged to paint it on canvas with oil paints. You know that oils need a lot of time to [dry] . . . I had a lot of trouble, thank goodness it's finished.

When the World's Fair finishes in 2 or 3 years they'll take my painting off the wall and hang it in a new airport.

I had many expenses. There were few colors and then I needed more and so when I finished (in the end) I had $1,500 left. But it's been four months since I've been off the WPA, since they gave me the job at the World's Fair, they sent me away, so Monday I must go quickly to see if they'll take me back.

My dear that money I've put safely in the bank. . . . I'll take out 10–15 $ but I have to keep 1000 under my real name. The bank already knew that.

Sometime that spring Gorky wrote to Moorad Mooradian: "Soon I'll get my naturalization papers and then as you can understand it will be much easier for me to take some time off and move about. I'm writing about the Project obviously, as I am not a citizen and I don't want them to have to make an exception in my case Dear Murad as you know in all the Project I am the only one who isn't a citizen and those who aren't citizens are immediately kicked out." On May 20, 1939, Gorky became a U.S. citizen. Armed with his citizenship papers, he applied to be taken back on the WPA/FAP, and on June 16, 1939, he was accepted. He wrote to his family on July 1: "I am well and I've received the last paper for my American citizenship. Now I'm back working for the WPA. But this Thursday they [FAP supervisors] are coming to my house and to make sure if I have the money or not. And to see how much I pay in rent . . . and if I've got any furniture . . . There's sure to be something. Dear Vartush, I'm working to find a good job teaching in a school. That will be much better."

The following autumn Gorky wrote Vartoosh that he feared the WPA was "going to close down forever." Starting in 1939, project artists were automatically laid off after eighteen months and had to apply for home relief before they could be readmitted; sure enough, on December 9, 1940, Gorky was forced to resign. He reapplied and was back on the project by December 17. He stayed on for another six months, before resigning on July 2, 1941. At this point, with the United States preparing for war, the WPA/FAP was being phased out. Hoping for a year of financial security, late in 1939 Gorky applied for a John Simon Guggenheim Foundation Fellowship. He asked Holger Cahill and Max Weber to write letters of recommendation, but he was rejected in spring 1940. Gorky

Fig. 44. Church of the Holy Cross, tenth century, Akhtamar Island, Lake Van

Fig. 45. Armenian plough

Fig. 46. Virgin enthroned, south facade, Church of the Holy Cross, Akhtamar Island

Fig. 47. Gorky and his mother in Van City, Turkey, 1912

Fig. 48. Gorky's father, Sedrak Adoian, at age forty-seven, in Providence, Rhode Island, 1910

Fig. 49. *The Artist's Mother*, 1938

Fig. 50. Armenian family, early twentieth century

Fig. 51. Street in Aikesdan, early twentieth century

Fig. 52. Armenian manuscript: Toros Roslin, page from a canon Table, 1256

Fig. 53. Elizabeth Barrows Ussher and Dr. Clarence D. Ussher, c. 1910

Fig. 54. Refugees waiting for bread at a public oven during the siege of Van, 1915

Fig. 55. Armenian soldiers during the siege of Van, 1915

Fig. 56. Gorky in Watertown, 1922

Fig. 57. Akabi Amerian (Gorky's half sister), Boston, 1918

Fig. 58. Vartoosh (Gorky's younger sister) and her husband, Moorad Mooradian, Boston, 1929

Fig. 59. Gorky with violin on the banks of the Charles River, Watertown, 1922

Fig. 60. Gorky with palette, Watertown, c. 1923

Fig. 61. Gorky (seated) with Miss Lisle and Ethel M. Cooke, friends from the New School of Design, and Felix Chooligian, a friend from Van, 1924

Fig. 62. *Park Street Church*, 1924

Fig. 63. Gorky painting in Central Park, c. 1926

Fig. 64. Gorky drawing, New York City, c. 1926

Fig. 65. Gorky with a chain, c. 1926

Fig. 66. *Nude (After Rodin)*, c. 1925–26

Fig. 67. *Self-Portrait*, 1923–24

Fig. 68. *Self-Portrait*, 1926–27

Fig. 69. *Self-Portrait at the Age of Nine,*
1913, 1927

Fig. 70. *Self-Portrait*, c. 1928

Fig. 71. *Self-Portrait*, 1928

Fig. 72. Henri Matisse, *Self-Portrait*, 1906

(*left*) Fig. 73. *Self-Portrait*, 1928

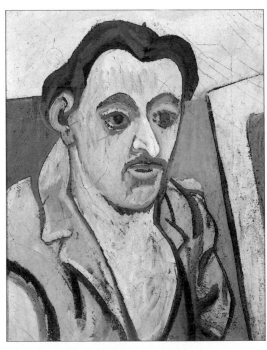

(*left*) Fig. 74. *Self-Portrait*, c. 1928
(*above*) Fig. 75. *Self-Portrait*, 1933–34

Fig. 76. *Still Life with Skull*, c. 1927–28   Fig. 77. *Still Life with Horse*, 1928

Fig. 78. *Still Life with Pears*, 1928

Fig. 79. Georges Braque, *Basket of Fruit*, 1922

Fig. 80. Gorky with Vartoosh and Sirun Mussikian in the Mooradians' backyard, Watertown, 1930

Fig. 81. *Reclining Nude,* c. 1929

Fig. 82. 36 Union Square studio with dining table

Fig. 83. View of Sixteenth Street and Union Square from Gorky's bedroom

Fig. 84. *Cubist Standing Figure,*
c. 1931–32

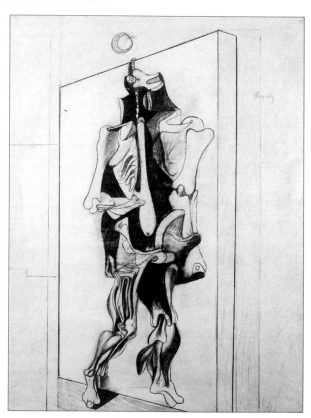

Fig. 85. *Ecorché,* c. 1931

Fig. 86. *Nighttime,
Enigma, and
Nostalgia* c. 1931–33

Fig. 87.
*Nighttime,
Enigma, and
Nostalgia*
c. 1931–33

Fig. 88. Giorgio de Chirico,
The Fatal Temple, 1913

Fig. 89.
Untitled (related to
Nighttime, Enigma,
and Nostalgia),
c. 1933–36

Fig. 90. *Khorkom,*
c. 1933–36

Fig. 91. André Masson, *Cock*
Fight, 1930

Fig. 92. Gorky at 36 Union Square, 1933

Fig. 93. Study for *Mural*, c. 1933–34

Fig. 94. Paolo Uccello, *The Miracle of the Host*, c. 1467–68

Fig. 95. Gorky (carrying a book on Ingres) with Peter Busa, New York, 1933

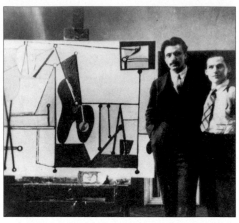

Fig. 96. Gorky and Willem de Kooning standing next to *Organization* at 36 Union Square, c. 1935

Fig. 97. Portrait of Jacob Kainen, c. 1934–37

Fig. 98. Gorky and Yenovk Der Hagopian, Watertown, 1935

Fig. 99. Gorky and John Graham, c. 1938

ended an April 21, 1940, letter to Vartoosh with "the art business has not been so good this year—not a picture sold yet."

When the World's Fair opened at the end of April 1939, a catalog of the art works on display printed Gorky's curriculum vitae with the usual lies: "Arshele Gorky" had studied at the Académie Julian in Paris and had pursued study and research in Italy, France, and Switzerland. Contrary to the assurances Gorky had been given that *Man's Conquest of the Air*, above the main stairway of the Aviation Building, would be moved to an airport when the fair closed, the mural was destroyed along with the Aviation Building itself, but it is recorded in a souvenir postcard that shows a mixture of organic and geometric shapes based on autogyros, flying balloons, early flying machines, and airplanes. One Miró-esque shape on the panel's left side looks like the boot/butter churn in the *Garden in Sochi* series, whose main elements were conceived during the period of the mural.

The mural's overall look is more severely geometric, more decorative and less personal than the Newark murals. Again Gorky went against his own artistic temperament. A 1949 letter to Wolfgang Schwabacher from architect William Lescaze about *Man's Conquest of Air* says, "I don't think Gorky was too happy about that particular mural." Gorky was clearly in a bad mood when journalist Ruth Carson interrupted his work with inane questions for an article on the World's Fair that she was preparing for *Colliers* magazine. "Abstraction?" he growled. "Always people talk about abstract art. What is it? I don't know. A machine maybe. An airplane—better a sphere with wings." Though Gorky surely gave her one of his withering looks, Carson was not to be put off. She concluded: "Maybe he can't describe it but he paints it."

The winter he worked on the World's Fair murals appears to have been an unhappy one for Gorky. When the young Agnes Magruder (Mougouch) met him early in 1941, she saw that the strains of the Depression "had proved almost fatally exhausting to him." The months when he was off the WPA made him feel financially insecure. His career was not moving ahead, and he knew that many people in the art world had dismissed him as a pasticheur. In one of his letters to Vartoosh, he grumbled: "Recently every week something [bad] has happened to me that is last month I had a nail in my foot, three weeks after that a bench fell on my foot and after that I had an ingrown fingernail so that I've been to the doctor every day for two weeks and now I have a sty in my left eye and so when one thing finishes another starts up." The final blow was the termination of his relationship with Leonore. "Towards the end of the 30's," Mougouch recalled, "he felt a terrible isolation which no amount of subsequent friendliness on the part of the surrealists or anyone else could eradicate."

In May 1939 Gorky was invited to take part in a panel discussion organized in conjunction with the Valentine Gallery's exhibition of Picasso's *Guernica*. The other panelists were Leo Katz and Walter Pach, the author of Gorky's favorite book on Ingres. The American Surrealist painter Dorothea Tanning was in the audience:

> We listened as a gaunt, intense young man with an enormous Nietzschean moustache, sitting opposite us talked about a picture. It was not his accent, which I couldn't place, that held me, but the controlled passion in his voice, at once gentle and ignited, that illumined the painting with a sustained flash of new light. I believe he talked about intentions and fury and tenderness and the suffering of the Spanish people. He would point out a strategic line, and follow it into battle as it clashed on the far side of the picture with spiky chaos. He did not, during the entire evening, smile. It was as if he could not.
>
> Only afterward I was told that the man's name was Arshile Gorky.

When Vartoosh's letters complained about loneliness, Gorky wrote back promising to visit her in Chicago and saying that he had problems similar to hers. "This morning I received your sad letter which made me very sad," he wrote in spring 1939. "My dearest, you must take care of yourself and your eyes. You surely need glasses . . . I don't know whether I wrote about it or not, but my eyes are much weaker so that I had to pay 30 dollars to buy glasses and now I cannot use them because I cannot get used to wearing glasses." He went on to recommend that she try to cheer herself up by seeking friendship and "good surroundings." He too suffered for lack of these things:

> My dearest, I want to tell you from my heart that . . . I always feel alone when I talk to others, but my heart is always looking for something and does not know what it is. And I know that here or

there you cannot find those kind of armenians that one does not find them even in Armenia, but you see the armenians of that place are not those you think because I know that you loved Ato a lot and you see how they treated him and they sent him away from the things for which he worked so hard and loved so much. [Ado Adoian was sent to Siberia.]

So you see that deep down all men are the same, above all our armenians if only you did not suffer for the armenians on account of whether they are good or kind. In life, dear Vartush man has to, since the moment he is born, look for a peaceful cradle or else a really good surroundings and when he finds a loving and gentle or else just his own loved surroundings, then he is no longer sad and he can remain alone even without friends. So man is forced to learn this truth of life and the importance of his surroundings. My dearest, I do not mean to upset you in writing this, but I want to tell you that within us, as within all men there is a desert and we constantly seek the one thing that enables us to escape from being alone.

This has always happened and always the weight of loneliness is with us, and for this reason we think of this thing or that so as not to feel alone. Believe me, dear Vartush, that I understand you and I too have those terrible days and I too lack those kind of friends that is true friends . . .

> With hugging kisses
> Your loved brother   Gorghi

In a letter from May 1939 he spoke of the negative influence of their ancestry, perhaps referring to the curse put on their family by their grandmother's burning Charahan Surp Nishan. "My dear I have to tell you something . . . Our ancestry I know is not so good, but we must make the effort to make friends." An undated letter, probably from fall 1939, again urged Vartoosh to be more social: "I think of you constantly. When you write that you are always lonely, truly my heart fills with great bitterness. Surely that was our destiny. I too feel lonely always, even if I see lots of friends, even if I am among thousands of people I always feel lonely."

Gorky fought loneliness with hard work, but his struggle for perfection often left him dissatisfied. Ilya Bolotowsky was at Balcomb Greene's studio one day when Gorky turned up with red paint in his hair and a despondent look on his face. Without saying hello he announced, "I worked on a painting for years and today I ruined it." Then he greeted Bolotowsky and said, "I feel so terrible. I feel like getting a row boat, rowing to the middle of the ocean and drowning myself." Bolotowsky joshed, "Look Arshile, I mean it's a rather difficult job. If you are a poor swimmer, you may as well swim and drown yourself without getting a boat." "That's not funny," said Gorky. Later Bolotowsky regretted teasing Gorky. "He was being a bit funny, but actually he was tragic."

There are many such stories that reveal Gorky's sometimes tender, sometimes humorous gloom. One of them tells of a toast he gave at a testimonial dinner for A. Conger Goodyear, probably in 1939 on the occasion of Goodyear's retirement as president of the Museum of Modern Art. After museum officialdom had said its words of praise, Gorky rose to his feet. "May I say a word? Everybody says what a strong man Conger Goodyear is, that he can throw a bull, that he can jump, but nobody says that one day he walked down Broadway and found a wounded bird, picked it up, caressed it and put it in his handkerchief and took it away. Thank you. That's all I want to say."

The story that best captures Gorky's flair for melancholy was told by the dance critic and poet Edwin Denby. A party at de Kooning's Chelsea studio had begun cheerfully enough with artists performing various stunts. Elaine Fried (later Elaine de Kooning) put a handkerchief next to her foot and, keeping her hands behind her back, tried to pick it up with her teeth; de Kooning did a Russian dance, and Gorky did his Armenian shepherd dance. "Suddenly Bill was on the floor," Elaine de Kooning recalled, "and his leg began to swell up." The guests' spirits plummeted. Gorky fell into one of his silent moods. Indeed, he was so quiet that people forgot he was there. The conversation "turned to the condition of the painter in America," Denby recalled, "the bitterness and unfairness of his poverty and disregard. People had a great deal to say on the subject, and they said it, but the talk ended in gloomy silence. In the pause, Gorky's deep voice came from under a table, 'Nineteen miserable years have I lived in America.' Everybody burst out laughing. There was no whine left. Gorky had not spoken of justice, but of fate, and everybody laughed open hearted."

Adding to the feeling of despair that pervaded the art world in the late 1930s was the rise of Fascism, the Hitler-Stalin pact, and the threat of war. When war broke out in Europe, Gorky felt the United States should remain neutral. From the Communist point of view, the Allies were driven by capitalist greed for money and power and did not deserve to be supported in their fight against Hitler. When Stalin called World War II the "second imperialist war," Gorky, along with American Communists and Communist sympathizers, echoed him.

Stalin's pact with Hitler on August 23, 1939, prompted many artists and intellectuals to drop out of the Party, but many others, including Gorky, remained loyal Stalinists. In spite of the fact that about half the members of the American Communist Party were Jewish, American Communists were not supposed to speak out against Hitler or the Soviet-German nonaggression pact. During this agonizing period, Stalinist stalwarts went into contortions of denial as they invented excuses for Stalin's act. David Margolis recalls going with Gorky to a rally at Irving Place in support of the Soviet-German pact, probably one of the many mass meetings to rally the Communist membership that took place in the first weeks of September 1939. But after Hitler invaded Russia on June 22, 1941, the American Communists (and Gorky) naturally relinquished their antiwar and pro-Hitler stance and supported the Allies and the Soviet Union in the fight against Nazi Germany.

During the dark days of late summer 1939, Americans stayed close to their radios. Eleven days after making his pact with Stalin, Hitler marched into Poland, and two days later, on September 3, radio listeners heard the quiet, sad voice of Neville Chamberlain in London: "This country is at war with Germany," he said. After hesitating for fifty-six hours, the French declared war, too. Although the United States stayed out of the hostilities until the Japanese bombed Pearl Harbor on December 7, 1941, it was clear to Americans that a new era had begun. Isamu Noguchi remembered that on September 1, 1939, he and Gorky were together at his Greenwich Village studio when the news came over the radio of Hitler's invasion of Poland. Gaston de Havenon and an artist named De Hirsh Margules were there as well. As he often did when he felt anxious, Gorky began to draw. He suggested that he, Noguchi, and Margules make a communal drawing to express their feelings about the now-inevitable outbreak of war. Noguchi, who saw Gorky as "not a political animal," recalled that "when Hitler came along, for a while he [Gorky] was rather fascinated by the man. He thought he might be an artist, which perhaps he was in a rather gruesome sense. We spent the night together when Hitler invaded Poland, and we did drawings together at the time. I have one of them left." De Havenon remembered the drawing: "Each one of the painters drew on what Gorky was doing, their own feeling. Pencil, black and white and colour drawing. It was completely abstract. Then they decided to make an anti-war drawing with colour pastels. They expressed their heart out by drawing, each one over the other one. We didn't have a feeling for money then. I don't know if he [Gorky] took it [the drawing] or Noguchi." When they finished drawing they talked about art and, for a moment, forgot about war.

Gorky followed the war's progress, and he was, said Raphael Soyer, "very much imbued with the spirit of the Red Army." Around the time of the battle of Stalingrad, Gorky wanted to make a "symbolic painting of the Red Army." It was, Soyer recalled, to be a single figure with an enormous open mouth yelling "hurrah!" But, Soyer went on to affirm, for Gorky art came before politics. When Gorky lectured at the Communist John Reed Club, he used chalk and a blackboard to make points about art, not about revolution: "Gorky made a dot here and a line there. 'This is not a composition,' he said. But then he changed the dot to say, here, and the line to somewhere there, and said, 'That is a composition.'"

35

A Language for All to Understand

Poverty remained a central theme in Gorky's letters to his sister in 1940. In April he wrote: "I don't know how to start writing, but I want to thank you for the ten dollars, and if things turn out well I'll send them back to you very soon." He had been to Buffalo to meet a potential client for a mural: the job would mean two thousand dollars. "At the moment, nobody is buying any paintings and everything is very difficult. I want to change my studio for another place, but at the moment it's difficult because everything is very expensive and I'd like to find something for 25 dollars, but I think this is impossible. This Friday I'll see mister Davis and I'll ask him if he can buy a painting of mine." He did see Bernard Davis, but because of something his old patron said, he realized that he could not ask him to buy a painting. A more awkward failure to make a sale came when Mina Metzger's husband made a studio visit and said that he would like to buy a painting for his daughter, but at the moment he did not have enough money. Metzger then suggested that there were "plenty of jobs" to be had and that Gorky should find some other way to make a living. "So I don't think I'll see him again," said Gorky.

The Buffalo commission did not materialize. Gorky's finances continued to be precarious. An August 11 letter said that he had sold all his books. On a more positive note, he told his sister that he had sold a painting to Wolfgang Schwabacher for fifty dollars, and he had had a two-week visit with a friend who lived seventy miles from New York and a weeklong visit with the Muschenheims. "My dearests don't worry about me. Somehow I'll get through. Something will turn up . . . Surely one day things will go better for me and I will be able to visit you . . . Thank you my sweet, I have just received the two letters from you and Murad, in which there were also 2 dollars. I feel deep shame when you send me money. Perhaps I will one day be able to help you."

When Gorky visited William and Lisa Muschenheim at their beach house on Long Island, he was always a favorite with their children. "He would make things for us," said the Muschenheims' son Art. "He whittled a bow and arrow out of a piece of wood. He used to carve things and played with us." He was usually a hit with the Muschenheims' cosmopolitan friends as well, but once he organized a shashlik picnic and made the same mistake he had made at the party at Balcomb and Gertrude Greene's. The "older" ladies should cut the meat, he said, and the "young" ladies should prepare the salad. The picnic turned into a fiasco when Boy Scouts informed the assembled company that they were sitting in poison ivy. Mrs. Muschenheim was hospitalized for a week.

On September 3 Gorky wrote to Vartoosh that he planned to advertise in a newspaper saying that he was opening an art school: he had applied to Edmund Greacen, director of the reopened Grand Central School of Art, for the use of a classroom in which to teach camouflage. He thanked his sister for sending him five dollars and said, "Do not worry about me, I'll get by somehow. Such is life, and it is nothing new to me or to any artist." Greacen asked him to wait a few months to see if there would be sufficient enrollment—many young men were being drafted. The job teaching camouflage did not come through until the following autumn.

Through Noguchi and Willie Muschenheim, Gorky was commissioned in fall 1940 to paint murals for nightclub impresario Ben Marden's Riviera Club, which was nestled into a Palisade cliff at Fort Lee, New Jersey, just on the other side of the newly completed George Washington Bridge. Again he was put off because of what he called the "war-created situation." "I really worked hard on these pictures," he told Vartoosh, ". . . slaving on them—then a few words are spoken and all my plans are upset." A month or so later the Riviera Club's architect Louis Allen Abramson told Gorky that he could proceed with the murals on curved walls that flanked the Club's stage.

The club was a sleek, glamorous building with a curved facade and a huge dining rotunda that featured a revolving dance floor and an oculus in the roof that retracted so that couples could dance and dine beneath the stars. Besides dancing and gambling, it offered floor shows. Planned for the 1939 season, for example, were lavish productions with "seventy-five of the most beautiful girls in the world . . . arranged into production numbers by a well known producer." The daily bus commute across the George Washington Bridge was spectacular and the certainty of a good income helped lift Gorky out of his doldrums. On January 10, 1941, he wrote to Vartoosh and Moorad: "I am writing you so briefly because I am on my way to the place where I am working." He would be able to repay the five dollars they had sent on the fifteenth. "Thus I will keep my word and I thank you very much."

Gorky's daily stints at the Riviera Club were enlivened by the comments of the various employees. An Italian contractor, for example, proffered advice on how to make the mural beautiful. A black janitor watched the progress of Gorky's mural and said: "If I was a bird, that's what the world would look like to me." Saul Schary was painting a mural for Ben Marden, too, and de Kooning served as Gorky's occasional helper. Because this was the first time Gorky had worked directly on wet plaster, de Kooning gave him advice on pigments. He also helped Gorky with problems of scale for, to de Kooning's surprise, Gorky was "a little bit out to lunch" when it came to transferring his squared-up mural studies to a large wall: "So I said, 'Then I'll do it and you follow me . . . and you do your drawing over it.'"

Another thing that surprised de Kooning was Gorky's submissiveness in the face of authority figures. One day he and Gorky were hard at work at the club when a "gangster character" in a wide-shouldered polo coat sauntered into the room accompanied by his sidekicks. Gesturing to the two painters to come down from their scaffold, the gangster said to Gorky in a gravelly voice: "I understand you're tops in your field. . . You can do anything you want, paint any way you want; only remember, *no green.*" When the man and his cronies had gone, Gorky and de Kooning looked at each other, amazed. The gangster turned out to be Ben Marden and he disliked green because it was the color of billiard tables. According to de Kooning, Gorky immediately agreed: " 'Well, I never did like green,' he said." "That," said de Kooning, "was something about him which you couldn't figure out . . . I guess he was influenced if somebody made up their mind that they wanted it a certain way. He right away went on the side of that character, you see."

Gorky's Ben Marden murals are recorded in two gouache studies

(Fig. 109), in both of which sprightly biomorphic shapes painted in blues and grays, plus beige, brown, terra-cotta, and tiny touches of yellow and pink, disport themselves against the background color. The background in the study for the mural to the left of the stage was pale blue edging toward gray and lavender. The mural to the right of the stage had a warm beige ground. As in the contemporaneous *Garden in Sochi* series, Gorky, inspired by Miró, abandoned the Cubist grid and opened up space. Because the fresco medium forced him to give up his habitual method of adding layer upon layer of pigment, the mural was a step in the direction of the more open and more thinly pigmented canvases that he began to paint in 1942. Years later, Gorky pointed out the Palisades to his friend Jeanne Reynal and said (as if he had foreseen the changes in form and scale that came about with Abstract Expressionism) that "painting in the future would be like that long, bright cliff—the subject matter 'plein air' and the scale limitless."

Although the Ben Marden murals were abstract, Gorky had specific subjects in mind. His shape clusters form almost recognizable creatures, three of which, in the blue-ground mural, appear to be vaguely human: to the left is a man with a bird head that recalls Gorky's early écorché drawings. Above the door are what appear to be two or three recumbent figures shaped like Henry Moore sculptures but also recalling the looping shapes of Gorky's embracing figures in *Nighttime, Enigma, and Nostalgia*. There are also several other biomorphs to the left and right, and what looks like a blue quarter moon in front of a burnt sienna sun with a lavender halo. The gouache with the beige background (Fig. 109) has animallike creatures—the one in the lower right corner resembles Gorky's boot/butter churn motif, but, with its sprout shapes, it also makes one think of a bull. Gorky said that his mural's theme was sky and river— no doubt to honor the grand view from the club's huge windows facing east over the Hudson River. Perhaps the mural with the blue background and a sun and moon signifies the idea of sky and the mural with the earthy beige background and mostly blue shapes interlinked to form one long, rippling flow stands for the idea of a river. In keeping with the mood of the opulent floor shows that took place on the circular stage that separated his two murals, Gorky gave his compositions a freewheeling carnival spirit. Indeed, they have none of the melancholy that usually flavors his art.

On August 22, 1941, the *New York Sun* ran an article about Gorky's

Ben Marden murals called "Café Life in New York." The author, Malcolm Johnson, wrote that the Russian-born Gorky had done murals at Newark, the World's Fair, and the American Music Hall. (Gorky mentioned the music hall commission as one of his accomplishments in his curriculum vitae submitted in 1934 to the PWAP. No other information about it exists.) Johnson quoted Gorky on the Ben Marden project:

> I call these murals non-objective art, but if labels are needed this art may be termed surrealistic, although it functions as design and decoration. The murals have continuity of theme. The theme— visions of the sky and river. The coloring likewise is derived from this and the whole design is contrived to relate to the very architecture of the building.
>
> I might add that though the various forms all had specific meanings to me, it is the spectator's privilege to find his own meaning here. I feel that they will relate to or parallel mine.
>
> Of course the outward aspect of my murals seemingly does not relate to the average man's experience. But this is an illusion! What man has not stopped at twilight and on observing the distorted shape of his elongated shadow conjured up strange and moving and often fantastic fancies from it? Certainly we all dream and in this common denominator of everyone's experience I have been able to find a language for all to understand.

Although Gorky aimed to "find a language for all to understand," not many people did understand his work. Their lack of comprehension did not help the fate of his murals. Already in the 1940s, Gorky's Riviera Club murals had been very much altered by repainting. Warren McCulloch remembered "Gorky's bitter laughter when they painted them out later . . . This was as though you gave a man something very valuable and he threw it away." When the club was torn down in the 1950s, Gorky's murals were lost for good.

PART VIII

Gorky and Mougouch on the beach in New Jersey, 1942

36

Mougouch

In February 1941 de Kooning introduced Gorky to Agnes Magruder, a beautiful, vibrant, and highly intelligent nineteen-year-old whom he soon nicknamed "Mougouch (or Mouguch)," the Armenian term of endearment that he had sometimes used for his nephew Karlen—and even for his cat (Figs. 110, 111, and 112). He told Agnes that Mougouch meant "little mighty one." "I'd met Bill de Kooning through a girl named Elsa Combe-Martin in whose flat I'd rented a room," she recalls. "I worked for the Chinese Communists on Twenty-third Street and Second Avenue and Bill lived on West Twenty-second Street, and he was painting those rather lopsided women with long necks and no shoulders. Bill and Elaine were talking about Gorky and they said I must meet him." Elaine Fried, an enthusiastic matchmaker, described Gorky to Mougouch as a "terrible showoff who sings and dances and makes everyone dance in a circle with a handkerchief." Fond though Elaine was of Gorky, she was glad that de Kooning was seeing less of him, and that he was, as she told Mougouch, freeing himself from Gorky's overpowering influence.

A day or so after Elaine Fried and de Kooning described the pros and cons of Gorky to Mougouch, Gorky dropped into their loft and, Elaine recalled, he kept talking about how much he wanted to have a young girlfriend like de Kooning's. "They're so strong, these American girls," he said in a mournful tone. "Well, there will be a girl at a party we are going to whom you would like very much," Elaine said, "so why don't you come with us?" At first Gorky didn't want to join them, but with Elaine's coaxing he finally agreed.

The meeting took place at a Sunday afternoon party at the Twenty-third Street studio of Fred Schrady, a rich artist friend of de Kooning's. During the course of the evening, Elaine noticed that Gorky kept hovering around the host's girlfriend, so she went over, tugged at his coat sleeve, and whispered, "No, not this one, *that* one!" She then brought Gorky over and introduced him to Mougouch. After the party, Elaine recalled, Gorky and Mougouch were "inseparable."

Mougouch remembers her first encounter with Gorky slightly differently. She says that Elaine and Bill had described her to Gorky as a blond, whereas her hair was dark brown. Since she was expecting Gorky to be a showoff and he was expecting her to be a blond, they did not recognize each other:

> I went with Bill and Elaine to this party and sat next to Bill on a bench. On the other side of me was a man with a moustache who was very quiet and rather pokey. Meanwhile I was waiting for this fascinating horror to arrive, so I was at the party practically to the last. Everybody else had gone home, including Elaine and Bill, and I was left with the man with the moustache. We did not say a word to each other. And the man with the moustache put on a porkpie hat, which reminded me of my father, and a nice sort of tweed coat with raglan sleeves. He looked different from everyone else—his way of being, his physical ease and grace of movement. I went out the door and he looked at me and said, "Miss Maguiger?" And I said, "Oh, Gorky!" "Would you like a cup of coffee?" he asked. And we went downstairs and sat and chatted and drank coffee.

When they had drunk their coffee, Gorky read their fortunes in the coffee grounds. He asked Mougouch so many questions about her life that she finally dumped the meager contents of her handbag onto the table to present a picture of her identity. Her boldness delighted Gorky. Also in her favor was the fact that, like several of the women with whom Gorky had been involved, Mougouch had thoughts of becoming an artist. When they were ready to go home, he invited her to have dinner with him the following evening:

> The next evening he appeared at my apartment to take me to dinner. It was snowing. He took me down to a tiny Armenian restau-

rant on Twenty-fifth Street between Lexington and Third Avenues. It had about six tables and you went down some steps to a basement. I think it was called Vartan's. I was so hungry, I just couldn't think of anything to say. I just ate and made a few polite remarks about "Where do you come from?" He said he came from Lake Van. It meant nothing to me. I didn't know where Armenia was on the map. Because Gorky's Armenia had become Turkey, and eastern Armenia was part of Russia. It was not clear if he was Russian, but I did not want to be very precise about this. I was extremely young and was just taken up in the life of the moment.

Born in Boston on June 1, 1921, Agnes Magruder was the daughter of a naval officer who was often posted abroad, which meant that she had traveled a great deal. Five foot seven, slim, and graceful, she had full, sensuous lips, a firm jawline, and slightly bulging hazel eyes that often twinkled with a kind of impudent amusement. Her sense of fun was contagious. Here was one of those strong American women that Gorky had told de Kooning he hoped to find. "There was a straightness about her," Ethel Schwabacher wrote, "a something mysteriously alerted, springy, very beautiful. More important for his life, Gorky felt that she was fearless, while he, though strong, was full of fear, disaster-haunted." For a girl of her upper-class background to choose a man like Gorky was indeed courageous. But then, Gorky was tall and commanding and he wore a hat that reminded her of her tall, commanding father. Moreover, he suited her rebellious nature—he was exactly the kind of man her parents did not want her to marry.

Mougouch's mother, Esther Hosmer Magruder, came from a distinguished New England family whose roots were in Watertown, Massachusetts, and Rhode Island. One of her ancestors was Harriet Hosmer, a renowned neoclassical sculptor who dismayed Watertown society by setting up her own studio in Rome—an unheard-of act of daring in the 1850s. Esther Magruder was a pretty woman, endowed with well-bred charm and a feisty spirit buttressed by that sense of superiority that comes with privilege. Agnes's father, John Holmes Magruder, was from an established Washington, DC, and Maryland family. Immensely tall, he had a deep and powerful voice and an aura of authority that belied his affectionate and playful nature. Around 1943, when Magruder was on a brief leave from his naval duties, Gorky made a detailed pencil drawing of him sitting with his head against a pillow, smoking a pipe and apparently listening, one assumes to Gorky. The touch of skepticism in the captain's eyes suggests that Gorky felt tolerated rather than embraced by his father-in-law.

When Gorky met Mougouch in 1941, she had been in New York City for only a few months. The previous year she had lived in Shanghai, where her father was in command of the flagship *Augusta* of the Pacific fleet. There she had fallen in love with a handsome young diplomat from New York. After spending the night with him at his hotel, she ran into a diplomatic friend of her parents in the lobby. Asked what she was doing there, she said, "Fucking!" According to her, she had only just learned the word and had little idea of how it sounded on a young woman's lips.

Mougouch's love affair and her new fascination with Mao Zedong and Chinese Communism were enough to persuade her parents that she needed to leave Shanghai. They said she could go either to Japan, where they had a friend who could keep an eye on her, or to America to study art. Having seen a *Life* magazine article about the flowering of American regionalist painting, she decided to go to Iowa City to study with Grant Wood. "I didn't want to go into any more embassy life. I wanted to get cracking on the revolution. So I chose to go to America."

At the University of Iowa she joined the class of the modernist painter Karl Knaths, who advised her to study with Hans Hofmann in New York, so she boarded a bus headed east. Upon her arrival at Manhattan's Port Authority bus terminal, a scruffy-looking man who had made a nuisance of himself by talking nonstop to all the passengers overheard her asking at the ticket window where she could stow her trunk. The man approached her. "Where are you living?" he asked. "I have no idea," she answered. "You'd better come with me," he said. "You can't just go out at four o'clock in the morning and find someplace to sleep." Mougouch stayed with him for about a month, fending off his advances and spending her allowance on food for him and his friends. "Then I got a room just south of Washington Square. The ceiling fell in and the landlord wouldn't give me back my money. I learned a lot about New York life. I was taken up to Harlem, to the Apollo Theatre. I had forgotten about studying with Hans Hofmann."

She moved to an apartment at 19 East Seventy-first Street that belonged to Else Oak Snapper, a young hat designer who had befriended her on the boat from China. In September 1940 Mougouch enrolled in the Art Students League, where she met the German-born painter Peter Ruta, who shared her interest in left-wing politics. "In Robert Laurent's sculpture class," he recalls, "I met Agnes. She was very attractive in a New England way. You had the feeling she knew what she wanted." With Ruta's help, Mougouch moved out of Else Snapper's apartment and into the apartment of Michael and Elsa Combe Martin at 121 East Fifty-seventh Street. Elsa was an ex-Communist from Brooklyn; he was a Cambridge-educated poet. In the spring of 1941 Peter Ruta began to realize that he was losing Agnes. "I felt a coldness between Agnes and me," he says. "One day I came to see her and she said she was going to San Francisco with Gorky."

Before she met Gorky, Mougouch gave up studying art and took a job as a typist for a monthly magazine called *China Today*. Every day as she walked from the subway to her office she stopped at the same newsstand, hoping that the vendor would smile and say hello. "I longed for contact. That was the state I was in when I met Gorky. He was very keen on my involvement with the Chinese Communists. He liked my being a revolutionary—a wild force, and all that. I adored being with someone who loved to walk and talk. I suppose I was enormously lonely. Lost and lonely. I threw myself from one deep water to another." Although she was strong, Mougouch was drawn to men who had authority and conviction. As she recalls: "The feeling Gorky gave me was of an enormous security. I felt I'd attached myself to the Rock of Gibraltar—absolutely. I felt I'd finally found a rock. I totally believed in him. He totally believed in himself. Everything that had anything to do with him was the best of everywhere."

On the evening of their first "date," when Gorky took Mougouch to the Armenian restaurant, they ate yogurt soup, shashlik, and baklava. "I had two or three dishes of yogurt soup. It was cheap. Gorky could afford it, because he had the job at Ben Marden's Riviera Club and he'd finished the murals at the World's Fair. After dinner we walked in the snow from Twenty-third Street to the top of Central Park and back downtown again. There was deep snow. It was beautiful. He told me all about himself— about Van, which he placed somewhere in Georgia or the Caucasus."

Gorky had a very nice easy loping walk, not jerky, not self-conscious. He used to say he was like a lion. He was physically at ease. His gestures were part of him; everything he did came from the center of his being and unfolded from inside out. He sat very well, but not ramrod straight. He was a big man, six feet two inches. He was rather elegant. He always wore very well-pressed suits and trousers and he had a tailor on Eighth Street where he used to buy his clothes. He had a three-piece suit. For painting he wore overalls. He had narrow shoulders and wide hips, a slim chest. His chest was very furry, and when I first saw it I was deeply shocked. He had a black line of fur going down the middle of his chest.

When Gorky talked, he had a habit of pushing back the hair that hung down on either side of his high brow. His enormous but sensitive hands amazed Mougouch. The palms were not rounded, she recalls: "They were large flat hands and his fingers were all the same length." She not only found Gorky physically appealing but also loved the way he observed and spoke about the world: "Like many foreigners, he sometimes hit the nail on the head. He was inventive with language. He'd make mistakes but it would come out right. He was not grammatical and he had a thick accent. For example, he said the letter *t* for *th*. He said 'tink' instead of 'think,' 'ting' instead of 'thing.' When he wanted to be tough or to impress me he would talk out of the side of his mouth."

Having walked with Gorky through the snow to the top of the park and then back down to Fifty-ninth Street, Mougouch was hungry again. "He took me into a delicatessen—a fancy Madison Avenue delicatessen—where we had hot pastrami sandwiches and hot buttered rum. Then he took me home to my apartment. We arranged to meet the following day. He was going to take me to the Metropolitan Museum. We said good night. I think he kissed me on the cheek."

Soon after they met, Gorky took Mougouch to 36 Union Square to show her his work. He carried painting after painting out from the storeroom off the entrance hall and set each down in his studio for her to see. Although she knew very little about modern painting, she loved what she saw, especially the portrait of Gorky with his mother. Gorky was pleased by her response and by her innocence in matters of art. Once again he had found somebody he could mold and teach. The next time she visited him she couldn't find his studio. Frantic, she walked up and down Sixteenth Street. Finally Gorky spotted her from his window and came to her rescue. He told her that from now on she could find his apartment by looking for his shoes in the window. "Gorky always put his shoes on the windowsill to air. He told me to look for them so that I would recognize his apartment, because from the outside you could not see that it had a large studio window facing north."

As with many a Manhattan courtship, real estate played a role. The apartment Mougouch had inherited from Michael and Elsa Combe Martin, who had left town, turned out to have bedbugs. She showed her bites to Gorky, who said, "You'll have to find someplace else." He found her a one-room apartment on Seventeenth Street and Fifth Avenue. "And he set about cleaning it and painting it. He was so sweet. I moved in on St. Patrick's Day. I remember, I stood on the sidewalk on Fifty-seventh Street with an ironing board and an iron and Gorky went to find a taxi." Now that they were near neighbors they saw each other constantly:

> Gorky used to go downstairs to this little quick and dirty diner on the ground floor of his building. The diner would be packed. Everyone was having breakfast at the same time, and Gorky always started off by saying, "Please, Miss, may I have . . ." And by this time the waitress would turn her back on him. So he never got what he wanted. He had to learn how to just say, "Two fried eggs." But he told me the eggs were greasy and they weren't any good.
>
> I was moved by the terrible plight of this man who had no one to make breakfast for him. So I used to cross Union Square from my little studio and make him poached eggs and bacon. I even tried to make waffles. He had a waffle iron left over from life with Vartoosh, and I can remember endlessly trying to make waffles. They all stuck to the iron and went up in smoke and finally he and I in a rage threw the waffle iron out the window and onto the roof that was just outside of our bedroom window. It was so hot that it stuck in the tar and it was there for a long time sitting sort of on one ear. And that was the beginning of my domestic life.

The pace of Mougouch and Gorky's courtship picked up again when it turned out that Gorky's washing of Mougouch's skylights had been so scrupulous that he'd removed the putty and rain poured in. "Well," says Mougouch, "the upshot of it was that I left my apartment on Seventeenth Street after about a month and moved in with Gorky."

37

Cohabitation

꒰꒱

Soon after Mougouch moved in with Gorky, she began to take over certain household chores. One evening when she had deployed her new-found culinary skills and cooked an especially good dinner, he informed her that he had to go out. She asked why, and he said that a woman had invited him to dinner and to an ice skating show. Mougouch was furious. "Well, you can't go," she said. "I'll throw the food out on the street!" Gorky went down to the tobacco shop on the corner (Fig. 83) and telephoned to cancel his date. Mougouch watched him from a window. "When he came out of the tobacco store he waved at me and then came back upstairs. He was very pleased that I minded."

During the winter of Gorky and Mougouch's courtship, Captain Magruder and his wife returned from China. After a stint at a navy yard in California, Magruder took his ship to Newport, Rhode Island. Early in May Mougouch went to visit her parents. "I spouted Communism to them. I was full of phrases like 'dialectical materialism,' which made my father think I had lost my mind. Daddy was terribly pleased when I came down with measles, because he thought my Communism was all part of having the measles." Mougouch did not tell her parents about Gorky. Although she was living with him, she kept her Seventeenth Street apartment as a front.

Gorky and Mougouch's exchange of letters during her two-week absence reveals the tone of their relationship—affectionate, tender, and comradely. She used several nicknames for Gorky, most often "Pook," and "galupchig," a familiar Russian term of endearment meaning "my little dove." From Newport, she wrote:

> Gorky galupchig have you been working hard eating drinking have you finished your mural have you written your explanation. . . . did you get my telegram . . .
>
> what did you do?
>
> what are you doing now?
>
> I look very funny I am covered with the nastiest red spots . . . My family was terribly relieved to find that it was the measles and not socialism . . . Of course it is most inconvenient for me to be sick this week as regards the magazine [*China Today*]. I am going to call Manny [Manny Gold, the editor] because the lettering on the cover is not perfect someone must do that.
>
> Gorky dear I have just talked to Dorothea [a colleague at *China Today*]. She is going to come around to see you about the cover. You will be a great help if you could do that lettering or if you don't want to or don't have the time take it to your friend I can pay her. Please darling don't scare Dorothea she is neurotic and a serious scare might be her finish!
>
> Please try and get them to do that cover right. I shall be so dis-appointed if they do it wrong and it looks gavnoy.
>
> Bolchoy soudkinsin I am to have the measles.
>
> I miss my bolchoy galupchig
>
> > Xxxxx
> > Moguch
>
> Please write to me

On May 7, after Mougouch cabled him that she couldn't return to New York as soon as planned, Gorky wrote her the first of two long let-ters:

> My dearest love,
>
> I miss you terribly—this place seems so big with out my Mouguch—and the telegram with it come the sad news that you are ill. But why why my Galupcheg you. Having the measles— and your sweet letter—I have been praying to God—that it will be soon over—so that I might be with my Mouguch.

Dorothea came to see me this morning. Please Dear don't you worry about the magazine. I will work over it and everything will be all right—

Cheer up Mouguch, Dear. I am feeling well and looking after myself. I have provided myself with lots of vegetables and fruit. Most every morning I am back to the house at 7, and work hard until seven 7 in the evening. And at night I draw or look at the art book and dream about you—then I curse that measles. Mouguch xxx. The explanation is written and they are happy about and the mural is about finished—

Yesterday I had lunch with Mrs Metzger. Then I went to the zoo.

At this point Gorky's letter turns into a meditation on war, love, man's bestial nature, and the fragility of art and civilization, all lifted, with a few minor changes, from the 1912 love letters of Henri Gaudier-Brzeska, a source from which he had borrowed for his love letters to Corinne. He ended his letter with more words from Gaudier-Brzeska: "Dear, dear love, I press you to me with all my force, and only your help enables me to work. I thank you, dear Sun lovely Star, for having created women and men that we may be united, mingle our personalities, melt together our hearts and, by the union of our passionate bodies, better liberate our souls, making of us a single creature . . . Good-night, dear heart, sweet sister, Mother. Think that we are together in the same bed, and by our perfect union, making prayer to God."

Some critics, such as Hilton Kramer, have seen Gorky's plagiarism as a reflection of his feelings of inadequacy. Since his English was not fluent enough to express his feelings, he borrowed someone else's words. The parts of Gorky's letters that he actually wrote are indeed awkward and full of mistakes. Even his letters in Armenian are not eloquent; Gorky's education in Armenia was rudimentary. Curiously, Mougouch recalls, Gorky no longer liked Gaudier-Brzeska's work. When a Gaudier-Brezska exhibition was mounted at the Museum of Modern Art he told her not to see it, but she went anyway. Fearful that she would discover his plagiarism, he got rid of all his books on Gaudier-Brzeska. His explanation was that he did not like artists of whom people said, "Had they lived longer they would have done this or that."

From Newport, Agnes wrote Gorky a second letter. Postmarked

May 8, 1941, it reveals her skill at making Gorky feel that he was important to her:

> Gorky galupchig. I was so happy with your letter . . . Please fin-
> ish your mural and give it to teacher I wish I could see it before
> you turn it in but they must be sore by now. What did you write
> to explain the other mural. Please remember and tell me about
> it . . .
> You are the dearest most reliable Gorky to have helped with
> the Magazine. I can now be sure that it will be done as well if not
> better than had I been there . . .
> Please drink a lot of water. I do not want you to have the
> measles. A cold is the first sign so watch out . . .
> Goodnight darling. Sleep well Boo from
>
> Mouguch

By mid-May Mougouch was back in New York. It was probably at this
time that Gorky helped out again with *China Today*. Mougouch's Communist colleagues asked her to see if Gorky would make a poster to show
that the war in Europe was an imperialist war and that capitalist countries were fighting for the sake of oil. "So Gorky drew a man with very
black hair and a big huge nose (the capitalist!) holding an oil can that
really looked like a watering can! Nothing came out of that venture." Although he loved Mougouch's fervor, he himself did not become engaged
in her political activities. On May Day 1941, when she and her friends
from *China Today* joined a workers' parade, Gorky merely waved to her
from the sidewalk at Union Square.

Asked if Gorky talked much about politics, de Kooning observed that
Gorky's approach was "kind of funny," and "kind of left, you know." De
Kooning remembered going with Gorky to a loft in the lower twenties
that was the headquarters of a Chinese organization (probably the office
of *China Today*) where "a lot of young people were working for China
against Japan." Gorky, with his genius for inappropriate remarks, burst
forth with: "Japanese art is much better than Chinese art." De Kooning
was aghast: "I mean he put his foot in it, so naturally they wanted to cut
his throat almost. He did that all the time. He stayed faithful to all his
ideas but with gyrations. He was like shaking up everything. He was a
pain in the ass!"

When Mougouch returned to Union Square she introduced Gorky to her mother, who was in New York for a week. Pleased that their relationship was no longer a secret, on May 20 Gorky wrote to Vartoosh:

Dear Vartoosh, recently about three months ago, you remember Bill [de Kooning] who was the friend of Mrs. Metzegri [Metzger] introduced me to a young woman very honest and modest who is called Agnes, whose father is the admiral [captain] of an american ship. I am seeing her and I talk to her about you. Recently she introduced me to her mother who came here from Washington for a week. If you saw her you would like her a lot. In a few days I'll send you her photograph. Last night her mother invited me out to supper and the whole evening Agnes said that I should write to you. We speak constantly of you, she has learned a few words of armenian and can sing "the shepherd grew sad on the mountain" and I call her Mogik. Write, she is longing to meet you. Here in New York she works on a journal and as you know in these terrible days nobody is thinking about painting.

Last night I went to the house of Miss Metzgri for dinner, and they were so worried, so my dear, I'll write to you again, very soon every week and we'll see what happens. Agnes said that she wants to send you a card and longs to meet you and get to know you.

Write, with affectionate embraces from
your affectionate
Gorghi.

At eleven o'clock exactly when Agnes came to see me she is pleased I have written to you and now tells me I have to write to Agop [Akabi] and Satenik.

Mougouch visited her parents a second time at the end of May. The day before her twentieth birthday on June 1, Gorky wrote her a second long letter:

My Precious Love
Good morning my pet; Good morning my goulupikeg, my adorable Mougush.
It is four O'clock in the afternoon and the bells are pealing as

[I] am writing to tell you happy Birthday to you. I promised to write to you, you scc I am keeping my word. —

Most of the rest of Gorky's letter—a discussion of the relative merits of primitive versus modern European sculpture—is borrowed from Gaudier-Brezska. Gorky's quotation ends with Gaudier-Brezska's statement that artists should transform nature rather than inventing pure forms, as the so-called nonobjective abstractionists were doing:

> To conclude, in order not to inflict on Mouguch's ears too much, I am in entire sympathy with the modern European movement to the exclusion always of those moderns who belong to the other class, those who invent things in stead of translating them.
>
> I hope that you are no longer feeling so poorly and that you aren't tired.—after your long journey. Don't miss your train on Monday and don't tire yourself out by worrying My dear heart of Goulupcheg I kiss you with such passion I lavish upon your lovely body all the deepest expressions of my love and my soul is inseparably held in yours . . . xxx
>
> your Goulupcheg
Gorky—

At 36 Union Square, Gorky and Mougouch spent most of their evenings alone. "We didn't have much social life," she recalls. "I was out a lot because I was working all day. Gorky's attitude was, once he had me he didn't have to go out looking for company. He stopped seeing many friends and they blamed me." Although she thought Gorky was a wonderful artist, she realized that his reputation was at a low ebb:

> He wasn't the lion of the moment at all. When I met him, the Surrealists were center stage. People would say to me, "Oh, he's just an old ham. He's been doing the same painting over and over for years." It wasn't as though he was a new boy like Matta, who had just come from abroad, or Max Ernst, who Peggy Guggenheim brought out of France. Gorky exhibited in the Whitney Annuals, but he hadn't had a show in years. He felt that all the people he knew saw him in a certain way, and he felt he didn't have to be this person anymore. So he decided to dismiss them;

therefore he was lonely. Gorky could be very dismissive of his artist friends on Eighth Street. He'd say, "If you don't take what I say as gospel truth, I'll go my own way."

Gorky did keep up with some old friends and patrons. "Maybe once a month we'd go to Ethel Schwabacher's and once a month to Mina Metzger, and once a month to Willie Muschenheim. And we saw Gorky's patron Bernard Davis. We would go to the Schwabachers' Park Avenue apartment for dinner and servants would serve the food, and Ethel and Wolfgang would be in their pajamas." Mougouch remembers visiting Hans Hofmann and that Gorky went to his studio. They also saw the Burliuks, the Nakians, and the Soyers (Gorky continued to go to Soyer's studio to draw and Mougouch sometimes served as model). "Peter Busa used to hang around us all the time in the early days," Mougouch recalls. But when Busa told Gorky that Mougouch had a figure exactly like a woman in a Salvador Dalí painting, he aroused Gorky's jealousy. "After that we saw less and less of Peter Busa."

De Kooning and Gorky were still close, although Mougouch suspected that Elaine was trying to discourage their friendship. And there was another difficulty, ominous in retrospect: "I would have loved to see de Kooning, but Gorky said he wasn't going to see any of these people, because they stole his ideas. This was part of his paranoia. I saw this early in our marriage." Aristodimos Kaldis likewise observed Gorky's fear that other artists would steal his ideas: "De Kooning always followed Gorky, to the point where in one period Gorky wouldn't even talk to him, because he gets his ideas . . . Not only de Kooning. They all took his ideas."

Gorky and Mougouch saw a fair amount of the architect and engineer Buckminster Fuller, whom they met in 1941, probably through Noguchi. When Fuller came to see them at the studio he would climb up on the model stand, which served as a coffee table, and talk endlessly about gestalt. "Gorky and I simply went off to sleep. The light in Gorky's studio was terrible at night—there was just one bulb hanging from the high ceiling, no lamps at all."

Late in the spring of 1941, Gorky and Mougouch attended a dinner party at the home of his friend and patron Margaret (Peggy) Osborn, the daughter of the painter John La Farge. Margaret Osborn wrote fiction, collected modern art, and had a house in the East Sixties to which she invited her artist friends. She was intelligent, well-informed, high-powered, and high-strung. "Peggy Osborn was very splendid and impossible," says Mougouch. "She was dotty on left-wing issues and Gorky liked her because he said she was like a 'wild horse.' He thought I had a lot of her in me." Isamu Noguchi, who had introduced Gorky to Osborn, was at the party, too, and so was a good friend of both Noguchi's and Margaret Osborn's, the mosaicist Jeanne Reynal. Reynal had been living in California since her return from Paris, where she had served as apprentice to Boris von Anrep, who had become her lover. A few years older than Mougouch, Jeanne Reynal was a good-looking, generous-spirited woman who did not step aside when Gorky tried to dominate.

At Margaret Osborn's dinner party Jeanne and Gorky were at loggerheads. She had negative things to say about three of Gorky's gods: Ingres, Poussin, and Léger. Gorky was about to launch into his counterarguments with his favorite conversation opener, "Permit me, Madam"—pronounced "Modom"—when Jeanne started talking with enthusiasm about the fourth dimension; she, too, had had an earful of such talk from Buckminster Fuller. Gorky's retort was, "Why not the fifth or the sixth dimension? Where are you going to stop?" This contretemps only made Gorky and Jeanne like each other more.

"Our friendship took off," Mougouch recalls, "and that made Peggy Osborn jealous. She had a terrific rivalry with Jeanne, who was an old friend of hers. Peggy thought she owned Gorky—she had bought an early painting and later bought a newer one and a drawing or two." Jeanne Reynal soon became Mougouch's best friend. "She was in and out of our house, our lives, our pocket book, our babies, our quarrels." The day after she met Gorky and Mougouch, Jeanne went to 36 Union Square and immediately bought a painting for the then huge sum of five hundred dollars, much more than most of his other patrons were paying. Not long after that she bought another painting. Her love for and understanding of his art were enormously important to Gorky. He was careful to show an interest in her work as well, and her mosaics of the 1940s are full of organic shapes and fluid movement that reveal how much Reynal learned from her new friend.

38

San Francisco

In the weeks after Margaret Osborn's party, Gorky, Mougouch, Jeanne Reynal, and Noguchi had several country outings, during one of which they escaped the tedium of a formal luncheon at a Connecticut estate by swimming in the pond and wandering among the flowering fruit trees. Noguchi picked a sprig of plumbago and wore it as a moustache. Gorky taught Mougouch (who had no singing voice) Armenian songs and whittled flutes for his companions, all the while keeping up a steady narrative of childhood lore interspersed with his own rather innocent brand of dirty jokes whose funniness lay in the telling. With Mougouch in his life, Gorky's melancholy lifted: his mirth made everybody laugh.

It was on this trip to Connecticut that Jeanne, full of her habitual generosity and enthusiasm, came up with the idea of asking the San Francisco Museum of Modern Art to put on a Gorky exhibition. She would talk to her friends in San Francisco, the show would be arranged, and Gorky and Mougouch must come. A change of scene would be good for Gorky's painting, she insisted, and he could use a studio on a farm near San Francisco that belonged to her companion, Fred Thompson. It may have been on this occasion, too, that Noguchi warned Mougouch that it would be a mistake for her to marry Gorky. "He told me that Gorky was a wonderful person and painter, but he was 'stuck in a rut' and kept scraping and repainting his canvases and couldn't finish anything."

It was decided that Gorky and Mougouch would join Noguchi, who planned to drive to Los Angeles to see potential clients. To allay concerns about propriety, she told her parents that she would be traveling with friends whose parents were friends of her family. Equally circumspect, Gorky wrote Vartoosh on June 23, 1941, and told her a string of white lies about his traveling companions and that Mougouch's father would be in San Francisco:

My most cherished ones,

. . . Vartoosh dear, sometime during the next three weeks I am going to San Francisco by auto with several friends. A very dear and pleasant friend, who is an artist, visited here a few days ago and liked my paintings so much that she purchased one for which she immediately paid $500. And she invited all of us to go and paint out there this summer. Frankly it would be quite pleasant as it has been 16 years since I have been out of New York.

And as you know, my acquaintances here will pay no more than $25 or $50 for my paintings so that when I sell a painting I am unable to paint another one with this money because supplies are so expensive. Two weeks ago I approached Mrs. Metzger, who for 14 years had been wanting to buy a painting, and when I explained to her my pronounced need for money, she replied, "We are all in a similar situation."

My friends believe that a change of scene is most necessary for all artists. Therefore, I want to hear from you concerning this matter so write me immediately. Agnes will also come since her father will be there on naval matters.

I am taking with me a letter of introduction from the Modern Museum. I would like to see you on the way but Noguchi, who is driving us in his auto, will take a different route for his sister and two other riders. As a result, Agnes and myself are most anxious to visit there this summer.

But as I said, when one of my friends here buys one painting for $50 they won't pay for weeks or months. But notice, someone from a new city arrives, speaks with me, and twice purchases a $500 painting. I desire to rent my studio to someone else for four or five months. Enclosed in this letter is a picture of Agnes which we took on 14th Street. Agnes and I speak about you all constantly every day, miss you, and send you warm kisses. Kiss Karlen and

Moorad for me. . . . On our return we will visit there for two weeks. With kisses,

Always loving you all,
Gorky

On July 2 Gorky resigned from the WPA, which meant that his monthly income of $87.60 came to an end. Needing money for the cross-country trip, he tried and failed to rent his studio. He went to see Dorothy Miller at the Museum of Modern Art and asked her if she could think of any purchasers for his paintings. She herself bought a painting related to the *Garden in Sochi* series, paying for it in two seventy-five-dollar installments. Besides this sale and the two sales to Jeanne there were a few others.

Early in July Gorky, Mougouch, and Noguchi climbed into the front seat of Noguchi's new Ford station wagon. The back was full of Noguchi's sculpture tools, for he planned to work on commissions in California. They took the southern route via Pennsylvania, Ohio, Indiana, and Oklahoma. Noguchi drove the whole way: Gorky couldn't drive and, although Mougouch could, she did not have a license. In the beginning there was a lot of teasing and banter. Gorky and Noguchi talked about gestalt theory, which Noguchi, like Jeanne Reynal, had learned about from Buckminster Fuller and which he spoke about with the enthusiasm of a recent convert. Finally Gorky said, "To hell with gestalt!" They had political discussions, as well. Mougouch wrote to her mother on July 14 that Oklahoma had been "the scene of violent arguments on the future of mass production many being of those believing that mass production and the perfecting of the machine frees man and is most certainly the ultimate [goal] of nations today. Others believing that the machine perfection is useless and aggravates the contradictions of time and that until man has invented the mechanical heart which will thump at a universal measure etc etc you know the arguments."

A bigger bone of contention was clouds. "Gorky kept seeing warriors and Saint George and the dragon and all sorts of fascinating battles in the sky. Everything was always vicious or aggressive. He saw these things in the trees, as well. Noguchi said, 'Gorky, you turn everything into something else.' " Years later Noguchi had not forgotten his arguments with Gorky: "On this trip he'd be always seeing some peasant woman up in the clouds," Noguchi said. "And we had terrible arguments about it because I said, 'That's just a cloud.' And he'd say, 'O no, don't you see that old peasant woman up there?' Nature didn't look the same to him as it did to somebody else. He was always elaborating a lacework of imagery into what he saw."

As they crossed the country, Gorky made unfavorable comparisons between the American landscape and the splendor of Armenia (which he identified only as the Caucasus). He would say, "Oh, but we have bigger trees in Van and the hills are far more beautiful, and the grass is higher, and the fruit is redder and everything is better." "He drove me and Isamu crazy," Mougouch recalls, "and he managed to spoil a lot for himself, because he was always saying that anything marvelous that we saw out the car window was better in the Caucasus."

One of the things that Gorky felt was lacking in the United States was peasants. The roadside diner waitresses horrified him. So did the food. "They fry everything but ice cream!" he grumbled. No doubt two such foreign-looking men as Gorky and Noguchi horrified the waitresses as well. Mougouch recalls: "The waitresses in the places where we stopped to eat would simply move a tin can from one shelf to the hot shelf and dig a hole in it and then turn it out on a plate. So Gorky was always attacking the girls and saying, 'How is it that you spend so much time putting *foutra* [makeup] on your faces and you can't even try to make a plate look like something anybody would want to eat!?' "

The three travelers had some lighthearted moments, for in spite of irritations, they had a deep fondness for one another. Noguchi loved the "streak of gaiety" that burst through Gorky's melancholy, and he loved talking to Gorky about art. In their friendship Noguchi wisely let Gorky play the dominant role: "He was a very sweet person. Gorky was always educating me, I felt."

Although Gorky had looked forward to escaping the hot, sooty Manhattan summer, leaving the city and his studio made him miserable. "New York was what he was tied to," Mougouch says. "It was his home. As we got further and further away from New York, he got more and more frantic. He had not been very far from New York for many years. He panicked. By the time we got to Mississippi, he thought the whole trip was a terrible mistake." Exacerbating Gorky's anxiety was Mougouch's occasional siding with Noguchi about clouds being just clouds.

During the men's arguments she went back and forth, from one side to the other, trying to keep everybody happy. Gorky became annoyed:

> I was not supposed to ever agree with anything Isamu said. If I said to Noguchi, "Well, that's interesting," Gorky would say I was being terribly disloyal. He said my siding with Noguchi was typical of how people in the West betray people in the East. He got so angry when we were crossing the long bridge over the Mississippi. There must have been some argument about clouds or gestalt going on, and I must have held up some poor little flag for Noguchi, and as a result of that, Gorky said, "Stop the car! I want to get out. I'm going to walk home!" He got out of the car in the middle of the bridge, and of course I got out and went after him. He almost threw me into the Mississippi River! I was pinned against the edge of the bridge. Fortunately someone had thought to put some barbed wire or something on the wall and I did not go over. I think Noguchi got out of the car and tried to help.

With some cajoling, Mougouch and Noguchi got Gorky back in the car, and they headed toward Santa Fe, where they spent several days with Noguchi's friend (and Margaret Osborn's brother) Oliver La Farge, who lived on an Indian reservation outside the city and was an authority on Indian culture. Santa Fe itself they found overly precious: Mougouch wrote to her mother that the atmosphere reminded her of Bali in that it was an "indigenous culture preserved by discriminating white men." To her and Noguchi's relief, Gorky actually liked New Mexico. He admired the Indian artifacts, the adobe houses, and the domed adobe ovens, which he said reminded him of the ovens outside the houses in his country and were soft to the touch like breasts. (Actually he was probably remembering the piles of dung and straw bricks that stood outside each Lake Van home and that were used for fuel.) In her letter to her mother, Mougouch reported:

> Lafarge did us a very good turn in sending [us] off to Tuba City, a real oasis in the Painted Desert behind the Canyon. We reached the desert after dark large dark clouds all around us and the obvious beginnings of a storm which soon worked up to lightening

and thunder a terrifying wind which lifted the desert into our faces. By the time the storm was over we had lost the road but had somehow reached the back door of westernmost fringe of a tribe of indians called Hopi and there we slept the night in a very fine hut. The rocks around there and various earth formations sent the sculptors and painters into fits . . . the works were labelled Modern Art and canyon beds were set aside as studios.

Since part of the purpose of their trip was to see the United States, they stopped at the Grand Canyon, where Gorky and Noguchi sat with their backs to the view and refused to display any touristic awe. "At the Grand Canyon," Mougouch recalls, "Gorky and Isamu behaved like two clowns. They felt it was too big, that it looked like a picture postcard." A blue haze softened the canyon's bold forms, diminishing their majesty. Mougouch was longing to walk down into the canyon, but her blasé traveling companions were only interested in smaller canyons. Brooding over their disappointment, they ate lunch in a restaurant with a view of the canyon, which, Gorky grumbled, had "no signature, no identification!" They discussed what kind of incident—a clown on a bicycle crossing the chasm on a tight rope, perhaps—might "create interest." They decided that, as Mougouch put it, "the beautiful when it is so beautiful that it no longer excites a remark is no longer beautiful."

Finally the threesome arrived in Los Angeles and settled into a hotel, and went out to dinner. Unused to sleeping in hotels or eating out, Gorky was upset. He wanted to find cheaper lodging. Mougouch refused to move:

I had terrible crabs. I'd gone to the drug store and the pharmacist gave me a bottle of kerosene, and he told me to bath my parts with it. Well of course I went up in flames! I said to Gorky, "I can't move to another hotel. I'm just going to sit here with cold wet towels around me. I can't bear it!" Gorky and Noguchi went out. I guess Gorky had had too much to drink. Anyhow, he and Isamu must have disagreed about something, and Isamu came back, knocked on my door, and came in and stood by the bed to say good night to me, and Gorky suddenly burst into the room and dumped a whole bagful of lawn clippings on top of me. He must have gathered them from the hotel garden. He thought that I was flirting with Isamu. But there was not a murmur of electricity between me and Isamu. Isamu would not have done that to Gorky. Isamu was just saying good night to me and asking whether I was feeling better. When Gorky dumped the grass cuttings on me, I said, "Well, it's lucky it's not horse shit." Isamu vanished promptly, and Gorky stormed out of the room. He was an awful old tyrant, really.

At one point during their stay in Los Angeles, Gorky became so disgruntled that he announced he was going to take a bus back to New York. His obsessive jealousy cannot have been helped by Mougouch's youth and beauty. She was irrepressibly amusing and willing to be amused. Even if she was not attracted to Noguchi, she probably flirted with him. As Jeanne Reynal recalled, Mougouch was "a very tempestuous and attractive young woman with half the world in love with her. Wild and witty, . . . she was not a tamed colt." Mougouch had been brought up in a family where social poise meant, for women at least, a kind of flirtatiousness. This seductive behavior was not directed only toward men. It was supposed to make people of both sexes feel that they were delightful—what it amounted to was good manners and charm. Gorky, brought up in a culture in which men and women treated each other with great reserve, and accustomed to his somber mother and younger sister, did not understand that flirting was a social skill.

While in Los Angeles, Gorky and Mougouch were roped into seeing Noguchi's clients. "Yesterday," Mougouch wrote her mother, "we lunched with Anatole Litvak and swam in the Pacific . . . and I have met walt disney and Miriam hopkins and tweedle dee and dum etc which is all nice but exhausting and possibilities for a job in disney studios which are on strike in a very complicated way so I cannot visit not wanting to be a scab. Pop Disney had desires a cross between lady Bountiful and Robert Owen and suddenly must wake up to the facts of the harsh brutal world and the AFL." Their visit with the actress Miriam Hopkins (then living in Hollywood with the ex-husband of Dorothy Parker) did not go well. Gorky was horrified by their hosts' drinking and by huge photographs of their hostess displayed in the master bedroom. He was also scornful of the lavish sculpture portfolios Noguchi brought out to make a sale. "Gorky was very scathing about publicity, because he wasn't good at it," Mougouch observed.

By the time they arrived in San Francisco on July 16, Gorky was feeling more than sour. Although he liked the rocks and mountains in California, it was hard for him to be cooped up in the car. His spirits were not improved when he learned that, because Jeanne's relationship with Fred Thompson had ended, the country studio he'd been promised was no longer available. Jeanne now had a new companion, named Urban Neininger, a genial, handsome, and unsophisticated man with a terrible stutter and no money.

Fortunately Jeanne had already secured, through Thompson's contacts, an exhibition for Gorky at the San Francisco Museum. Thompson's brother, an editor at the *San Francisco Chronicle*, would make sure that the press would take notice as well. And Jeanne had connections of her own. Indeed, says Mougouch, "Jeanne was the muse of the art world. She'd come back from Paris and had some money, and she took us to everybody's studio and Gorky was simply dreadful. He did not put himself out to make Jeanne feel that the people she was introducing him to were worth five minutes' conversation." What Gorky especially disparaged was the way the whole town of San Francisco emptied out on weekends, when people went to their country houses. "Gorky couldn't understand how artists could live like that. How did they turn it on and off like hot and cold water?"

Through Jeanne, they met the Surrealist painter Charles Howard, whose art Gorky scorned. "I think it was at Charles Howard's studio where all Gorky would say was, 'The frames are very nice,' and then he spied a trapeze and he decided the best thing he could possibly do would be to hang from it." On another occasion Gorky was introduced to the Greek painter Jean Varda, who was teaching at the California School of Fine Arts, and to Douglas MacAgy, who had just taken a job at the San Francisco Museum and was helping to organize Gorky's show. Both men were sympathetic to vanguard art. It behooved Gorky to be agreeable, but he wasn't. When he overheard Varda denigrating Dalí—many people in the art world thought of Dalí as commercial and exhibitionistic—Gorky told Varda that Varda himself would have sold his soul to the devil but the devil wasn't interested in such a trivial purchase. In spite of Gorky's rudeness, Jeanne was proud of him. "She liked the whole setup. She liked me, she liked Gorky, and she thought it was worth putting up with his difficult behavior. She was like a fairy godmother."

In San Francisco, as in Los Angeles, Gorky was upset because he felt his money melting away. Though Jeanne had given him her own studio at 712 Montgomery Street, while she stayed with Neininger in his tiny room with a kitchenette on Telegraph Hill, Gorky remained disappointed that he was not able to work in the country. "What Jeanne called her studio," Mougouch recalls, "was a little apartment that Jeanne had fixed up in chintz, and Gorky couldn't paint there at all. There was a sofa and chairs around a fireplace and a bed in an alcove." On July 20, 1941, Gorky wrote to Vartoosh and Moorad from San Francisco:

My dear Vartoosh and Moorad:

I have been in San Francisco four days now. Maybe I am crazy. My friends promised that upon my arrival here they would take me to their farm where I was to be free for three months to do my paintings, etc., etc., That was to be followed by an exhibit— which I still believe that will take place. Now, it appears, I am to foot the whole expense, a sum of $250.00, for the price of my moving from New York to San Francisco.

This was a mistake, the worst mistake I have made in my life. My friends, it seems, were coming here anyway, so asked me along just to share their expense!

I am at loss—don't know what to do. I shall wait a few weeks and then probably return to New York, though it's doubtful whether there is anything for me to do there either. Luckily, I did not rent my studio.

Too bad, I cannot write you better news from here right now. But perhaps that's my nature. Ever since I left New York, I have not had a good night's sleep. I hate all this! Oh, yes, the hills and the mountains are beautiful!

If by good fortune, I should be able to sell a few pictures, I will visit you on my way back to New York.

It's six in the morning, and it's raining. As if it must rain here every morning; but the sun shines through in the afternoon.

I am trying to find me a place to live in. And the prices are so high!

Next week I hope to write a better letter.

Kiss Karlen for me. He must be well by now.

With many kisses to all of you,
Gorky

According to Mougouch, Gorky's complaint that he had been invited to drive to California with Noguchi only so he could share expenses was unfounded. It was true, however, that Gorky had to spend more money on restaurants than he was used to. "In the evening," she recalls, "we'd go off with Jeanne and Isamu to these various dives on Montgomery Street." One night when Gorky, Mougouch, Jeanne, and Noguchi were at a nightclub, Mougouch asked Gorky to dance. Knowing nothing about social dancing, Gorky reluctantly followed Mougouch out onto the dance floor, but after a few minutes, without saying anything, he absentmindedly walked away. "Then Isamu came and danced with me, and Gorky spent the whole time eyeing me with horror." When Mougouch returned to the table she overheard Gorky saying to Jeanne, "Look at her! She's just a frivolous person who likes to dance! All she cares about is clothes!" Four years later Mougouch laughingly reminisced about that evening in a letter to Jeanne. In her unpunctuated e.e. cummings style, she wrote that Gorky had once again had that "wild dishevelled look that I associate with our san francisco bouts remember that night in the spanish night club with isamu and others when he told you I cared for nothing except clothes a sort of frantic undone but I'll-have-the-last-bitter-drop look."

To Gorky, vampishness was repugnant and social dancing was immoral and vulgar. "I wasn't supposed to have any dealings with any man. But it was all right if it was a man who adored Gorky," Mougouch explains. Too high-spirited to conform to Gorky's idealized image of his mother, she put up with Gorky's jealousy by making light of it. "If a man looked at me in a restaurant, Gorky would turn around giving them the evil eye by pointing at them with two fingers." This familiar Armenian gesture, a thrusting forward of the hand with index and pinkie fingers extended, is also called a "horn's hex" sign.

Gorky wanted full possession of Mougouch. He began to talk about marriage but she successfully sidestepped the question. Having only just turned twenty, she was not quite ready to settle down. Indeed, she seems to have thought seriously of leaving Gorky, for she had taken it into her head to go to China after San Francisco. Knowing that during wartime she would not be given papers to travel to China, she thought she might get there as a war correspondent, but her application for a job at the *San Francisco Chronicle* was turned down.

One day when the subject of marriage came up, Mougouch told Gorky that she had to see what he looked like without a moustache. "I couldn't marry a man whose lip I had never seen," she explains. Gorky obliged. "His upper lip was tremendously vulnerable," Mougouch recalls. With his clean-shaven face he made the rounds of Fifty-seventh Street galleries that fall, and he came home bemused because all the art dealers had been so cordial. Had his moustache scared them? he wondered. "I've got to grow my moustache back on because the dealers are all too friendly," he said.

While they were staying at Jeanne Reynal's Montgomery Street apartment, Jeanne introduced Gorky and Mougouch to their neighbor, the sculptor Ralph Stackpole, a kind and generous man who had befriended Diego Rivera and Frida Kahlo when they lived in San Francisco in 1931. Stackpole had a large garden where he sometimes worked. When Gorky suggested that he would like to try his hand at sculpture, Stackpole invited him to use the garden, gave him a piece of stone, and loaned him sculptor's tools. Mougouch posed for a portrait bust: "I sat while the chips flew around my head." Gorky was so engrossed in the process of hammering and chiseling that he lost sight of the image he had in his mind. Suddenly he saw that the block of stone had become too thin. "There's no room left for you in it," he said.

Gorky and Mougouch finally rented a small house that Stackpole found for them in a garden compound on top of Telegraph Hill. Many of their new artist friends lived nearby. On August 4, Gorky wrote again to his sister, this time in a more sanguine mood:

My dear ones:
    Despairing though my last letter was, I believe everything is going to be all right. I have met many friends who in turn have introduced me to many others here, all helping me to succeed.
    Agnes too is here, And with the aid of her parents' many acquaintances, all will turn out well. She is really working very hard to make my exhibit (Aug. 9) a success.
    After lunch Agnes and I are going to the Museum, where my works are shown. We have had no rest or sleep the last ten days, what with running here and there to contact necessary people.
    This city has beautiful scenes and a pleasant climate, just

like our homeland. The temperature reminds me of April and May.

I shall write to you next Wednesday about our visit to the Museum.

Do not worry about us. Agnes is a very capable woman. Gradually after knowing this city a little better, we shall be able to do better.

The situation was different and bad the first few days I was here. Our friend Miss Reynal, who purchased one of my paintings in New York, is here now and doing her best to help me.

Agnes is really fine and always asks about you. She sends you her love and regards. She wants us to stop in Chicago for two weeks on our way back. And also suggests holding exhibits in Los Angeles and Chicago.

So, you see, you should not worry at all about me. Everything will be fine.

I embrace and kiss you all,
Your Gorky

P.S. what do you think of this war? How do things look with the Soviet Union? Would like to hear from you.

I forgot to write that we have rented a pretty house, surrounded by trees on three sides, while the ocean is on the fourth.

Among the many people whom Gorky and Mougouch met that summer were the Russian-born architect Serge Chermayeff and his English wife, Barbara. Although the Chermayeffs' stay in San Francisco did not overlap with Gorky and Mougouch's for long, the two couples hit it off, and they continued to see each other in New York, where the Chermayeffs found an apartment on East Twenty-second Street. "Gorky would get these fixed ideas about things," Barbara Chermayeff recalled, "but he and Serge never quarreled, because they came from similar backgrounds. Serge was born in Grozny [Chechnya, in 1900], not far from where Gorky [said he] was born." Gorky, of course, had a special liking for Russians. As tall or taller than Gorky, Serge was handsome but rather fierce in both looks and manner. By contrast, Barbara was small, dark, and pretty, and, of necessity, soft-spoken. "We all became friends immediately," Mougouch says. "Serge knew how to treat someone like Gorky."

In San Francisco Gorky and Mougouch had dinner several times with Fernand Léger, who was preparing for a show at the San Francisco Museum that would run concurrently with Gorky's. "Léger was very sweet," says Mougouch, "and he said he wanted to come and cook a pot au feu. So I bought a pot au feu and the ingredients for it. Ralph Stackpole's wife was French and she told me what to get and where. What I didn't know was that it took seven hours to cook; so when Léger arrived at our house with Marshal Pétain's niece he looked in dismay at this material I had assembled and said, 'What shall I do? Shall I go to the butcher? My dear girl, we won't eat until midnight or way past!' " They laughed and had scrambled eggs instead.

Another person who turned up in San Francisco was Gorky's first wife, Marny George. For years she had been writing to Gorky from California, but Gorky never opened the letters. "Gorky would throw away her letters," Mougouch recalls, "but I'd open them. Marny George wanted him to take her back. She said he meant everything to her. She found us in San Francisco. She probably read about Gorky's show in the newspaper. Gorky went to meet her and brought her back to our cottage on Telegraph Hill. She was very pretty. He asked her to stay to dinner. The meat was very tough. I was pleased."

39

Marriage

❧

During their two months in San Francisco, Mougouch discovered that she was pregnant. Gorky wanted her to have the baby, but she did not want a shotgun wedding and was not ready to be a mother. Gorky insisted that everything would be better once they were married. They had terrible arguments. A neighbor, the Armenian artist Manuel Tolegian, who had known Gorky from the days when Gorky hung around the Art Students League cafeteria, recalled: "I heard all this commotion. Things tumbled. I thought there was a party going on. I ignored it, then, again at 3:30 in the morning. Well, they were having a big fight. I settled the whole thing and I asked him to come up to my room with my wife, which he did with this girlfriend . . . We sat together until eight that morning. Then we both went out somewhere and had some nice food. We got reacquainted. He was happy to see me again and we remembered old days."

Finally Jeanne convinced Gorky that they should not have a baby because they were not married and were too poor. She arranged for an abortion. "I had an abortion down on the San Francisco waterfront where tarts go," Mougouch recalls. "It was a very scary place. They slapped me and told me I mustn't shout. 'Stop that or we'll have the police in here,' they said." When it was over she went downstairs, where Gorky and Jeanne were waiting. They took her home and put her to bed. During her convalescence Gorky made a pencil drawing of Mougouch lying in bed wearing a little hat that Jeanne had bought to cheer her up. He drew her eyes so large that she resembles one of his so-called Armenian portraits. Like Akabi in Gorky's portrait, Mougouch rests her head on her rather atrophied-looking hand. She looks miserable. After the abortion she was stricken with guilt. "I knew I wasn't going to leave Gorky, because I'd had the abortion and I suddenly felt terrible about it. I felt that I'd hurt Gorky so much that I had to make it up to him by marrying him." When Dorothy Miller and Holger Cahill visited San Francisco that summer they noted Gorky's happiness: "She had written a magnificent letter to her parents, who opposed the marriage, telling why she was going to marry Gorky, and Gorky was so proud of her, and in love with her."

Loan Exhibition of Arshile Gorky at the San Francisco Museum of Art, which opened on August 9, was Gorky's first museum show, and it came after a period in which he had felt ignored. Among the twenty-one works exhibited was a portrait of Vartoosh, several canvases from the *Khorkom* series, including his favorite, the one Jeanne had bought, and *Enigmatic Combat*, also loaned by Jeanne but soon to be donated by her to the museum. Mougouch was struck by one of the guests' strong reaction to the work:

> This nice old gentleman was a big wheel in the San Francisco art world and he got hold of me and asked me to come outside with him and he sat me down outside and said, "I can't stay in that room. Those walls are too full of misery and agony for me to be able to stand it. I just can't stand it." And I felt sorry for him and said, "Well, life has been very difficult for Gorky and I hope it's going to get a little better now." When I told Gorky about this he was quite quiet about it. He said, "He must be a very sensitive man." Perhaps Gorky was disappointed because he would have liked this man to buy something. I think he was upset by this man's reaction, because even though his art came out of his life, he wanted it to be seen as independent of his personal life.

The press response to Gorky's exhibition was generally favorable. The *San Francisco News* described Gorky's work as "opulent and turbulent," "exotic," and "partly abstractionist, partly expressionist." It quoted Gorky's aim: "To paint the common, uncommonly." The *San Francisco Examiner* called Gorky a Surrealist whose "ominous ogre-like abstract fantasies may make you want to take them or leave them." Alfred Frankenstein in the *San Francisco Chronicle* noted Gorky's debt to Picasso, Braque, Miró, and Mondrian but said "the synthesis is ultimately Gorky's own," and the paintings "buzz and sizzle with power and excitement."

After the show closed on August 24, Gorky, Mougouch, Jeanne, and Urban Neininger decided to go camping in the Sierra Nevada mountains. Saying that she did not want to get in trouble with the Mann Act laws by taking a minor over the state border for "immoral purposes," Jeanne encouraged Gorky and Mougouch to marry. Mougouch, who loved to act on impulse, agreed. On September 12, 1941, Gorky wrote from San Francisco to Vartoosh and her family:

> My beloveds,
>
> This morning Agnes and I are driving by auto with our two friends to Dodge City to be married tomorrow morning. [Gorky was confused: Dodge City is in Kansas] We are very happy and know that you will be happy. In one week we shall return and when we arrive in New York will live in the studio. Vartoosh dear, you are going to like her very much. On the way back, we shall stay in Dodge City several days. I'll write you all when we can come and will make preparations to stay with you several days. Also I'll write you about my exhibition. Did you enjoy your vacation?
>
> I am most anxious to see you both and Karlen, whom I haven't seen in such a long while. My friends came just now and my beloveds we are about to leave. The two of us send our greetings and embraceful kisses to all of you.
>
> Agnes and Gorky

The four friends packed their camping gear into Jeanne and Urban's car and drove to Virginia City, Nevada, a nearly deserted gold-rush town with several opulent old buildings, including an opera house. They stopped at a five-and-ten and bought a curtain ring. Then, dressed in their camping clothes, the wedding party asked at the local bar for directions to the office of the justice of the peace. "Knock on his door," they were told. "He's either in or out." When they drove up to the Storey County courthouse, they saw the justice standing in the window "like an old spider waiting to catch a fly." Thrilled to have something to do and overflowing with sentiment, the justice looked over his half-moon spectacles at the loving couple and said the necessary words. Jeanne and Urban served as witnesses. It was September 13, 1941. Gorky was probably forty-one. Mougouch was twenty.

Marriage certificate in hand, they went back to the bar to celebrate. "We had a drink of something warm and fizzy at a very long bar with lots of photographs of gold diggers with pickaxes and with their names signed underneath." They stopped at the booth of one of those street-fair photographers who have humorous screens through which customers can poke their heads and have their picture taken. The screen Gorky and Mougouch chose had a cartoon-style image of a man giving his betrothed a ring while a bald justice of the peace reads the wedding vows from an open book (Fig. 113).

The newlyweds and their witnesses drove up into the Sierra Nevada woods, found a campsite on the banks of the Yuba River, built a fire, and cooked baked beans for dinner. They spent their wedding night in a new double sleeping bag, a gift from Jeanne. In the middle of the night Mougouch woke up and said there must be a skunk at the bottom of their nuptial bag. They struggled out of it and Gorky held it up and shook it. Since no animal dropped out, they climbed back in. "And there it was again!" Mougouch recalled. "Pouff! The beans!" Another time during the night, the river's warble was drowned out by the roar and whistle of a passing train. Terrified, they jumped up and back and tripped over their sleeping bag.

On September 17, 1941, the day after they returned to San Francisco, Gorky wrote to Vartoosh and Moorad:

My Dearest ones,

Agnes and I got back yesterday afternoon at eleven o'clock from Virginia city, as last Saturday we got married at about eleven forty-five, with no problems. Our friends there took us by car and we came back together. About 6 hours away there are huge forests surrounded by a tall and beautiful chain of mountains. And in the forests there are big lakes and torrents with clear running water, rushing through the stones and rocks. And beside the torrents are enormous cypress trees as still as sentinels with their heads in the cloud. They seem to press upwards against the blue of the sky to stop the bright blue sky from one day falling down.

We are very happy and Agnes is a very beautiful and well-educated girl and has studied in Switzerland, France, England, Holland and has visited every country in the world. now she is studying a lot and every day she reads Marx, Engels, Lenin, Stalin. She's also studying armenian and russian. For example she told me in armenian: "Ah, you man without God"!

My dearest ones Vartush and Murad, next Monday at 7:30 in the morning we'll take the bus and Friday next at 5–6 in the morning we'll arrive in Chicago and we long to see you as every day Agnes and I speak of you, and like me Agnes wants to meet you as soon as possible. Yesterday evening when we got back we found your telegram and your letter, dearests, arrived this morning.

I am so glad you are all well and I miss Karlen a lot, surely he has grown a great deal now . . . And so with this letter I send you on behalf of both of us all our love and soon we will see each other . . .

With affectionate greetings and kisses
Your Gorghi and Agnes

In their last days in San Francisco, they said good-bye to friends, packed their belongings, and organized their trip home. "We found a bus that would take us from San Francisco to New York in thirteen days for thirty dollars, and that would let us get off in Chicago to visit Gorky's sister. We slept on the bus sitting up. I was terrified because the driver went around corners very fast and it was a jalopy of a bus." In Texas, near the Mexican border, they were stopped by military police, who asked to see Gorky's passport and identification papers. Because of Gorky's dark complexion and because he had not brought his citizenship papers with him, he was afraid he would be deported to Mexico as an illegal alien. Finally they were free to go after Mougouch showed the officer their marriage license and a document identifying her as her father's daughter.

The newlyweds arrived in Chicago on September 26 and stayed for two or three days at Vartoosh and Moorad's apartment on Ardmore Avenue on Chicago's North Side, near Lake Michigan. Vartoosh recalled:

He was happy to be married, but because of traveling by bus they were so dusty, so tired, that the first thing they did was to take baths. Agnes slept for nearly two days, one night and one day.

Gorky awakened early in the morning and while I was preparing breakfast he sat at the kitchen table and began to draw me. We spoke of life, of its difficulties. Later, Gorky and Agnes walked all the way from our north side apartment (5800 north) downtown to the Art Institute on the park paths along the shore of the lake.

Although Gorky did not like Chicago, he loved its art museum, and he enjoyed walking along the lake's shore. Mostly he was glad to see Vartoosh and his six-year-old nephew, Karlen. "Vy, Mougouch, vy," he laughed as he lifted the boy into the air. Vartoosh organized a party in honor of her brother and new sister-in-law. There were toasts and songs and all kinds of Armenian dishes that Vartoosh had spent hours preparing. Vartoosh obliged her brother by singing "D'ele Yaman" and he returned the favor with a song of his own. When Vartoosh's great friend Alice Kelekian was asked to sing and said, "I don't sing in small rooms, only in a concert hall," Gorky told a story about the great opera singer Boris Chaliapin's refusing to sing at a friend's banquet on the grounds that his performance was worth two thousand dollars. The host called the butler over and said, "Give Mr. Chaliapin two thousand dollars. Now give Mr. Chaliapin his hat!" Vartoosh remembered the evening with some regret: "In retrospect I wish that I had instead given the money spent on that dinner to my brother because he needed it more. But I gave him $15 which he gave to Agnes to keep."

Since Vartoosh spoke very little English, she and Mougouch could not converse. In any case, Gorky was so afraid that Vartoosh or Moorad would reveal the truth about his origins or mention that Gorky had a father living in Rhode Island that he never left his wife alone with her new in-laws. When he wrote to his sister that Mougouch was learning Armenian and Russian, he probably was trying to please: in fact, Gorky never told Mougouch that he was Armenian, or about the genocide, or that his father was alive and, at seventy-eight, a laborer on someone else's farm. Instead he told her that his father was dead and that he had last seen him riding off into the mist along the shores of Lake Van—a paradisical place in Russia or Georgia. His stories gave her a mental picture of Gorky as a boy riding in the Caucasian mountains, where snakes reared up under his horse's hoofs. In a November 1942 letter to her mother, Agnes said that she and Gorky were reading a life of Tamerlane and that "Gorky knows the land and language and gestures of the Tatars so well that it seems incredible that this is today, so far distant from those wonderful acts. Gorky's memories have the same quality, the same speech, with peat roofs and apricot trees in the sun etc—that world must have changed very slowly . . . Gorky's mother came from Kurdistan which had been conquered by the Tatars and I guess that's how she came to be such a wild horsewoman." Mougouch was happy to believe what Gorky told her, but one day, back in New York, she came close to finding out the truth. In conversation with an Armenian grocer on Third Avenue, she learned that Van was the heart of Armenia, that the people of Van were very pure Armenians, and that Gorky's family was particularly distinguished. When she returned to the studio and told Gorky what the grocer had said, he was furious. He forbade her to go to that grocer again. Mougouch did not learn that her husband's real name was Vosdanig Adoian and that he was not Russian but Armenian until the publication, almost a decade after Gorky's death, of Ethel Schwabacher's monograph on him:

> I had a very vague sense of geography and he spoke a little Russian. We did not have an atlas! I did not know how far Van was from the Caucasus. But it was high in some mountains . . . The Caucasus were mountains that everyone knew about. In America he needed to come from a known place, so he sort of took over the Caucasus. He didn't *not* say he was Armenian, he just seemed to belong to Van . . . He hated the shame of losing his country, the terrible suffering the Armenians went through. It was really a case of protective fudging. So I did and did not know he was Armenian. After my excursion to the Armenian grocer, I left the whole subject to Gorky . . . I did know he was Armenian, but this did not matter to me since Gorky did not make it matter. . . . I had to protect Gorky somehow.

Given Vartoosh's passionate attachment to her older brother, there must have been some ambivalence in her attitude toward her new sister-in-law. She was glad that Gorky was no longer alone, but she wondered how a well-brought-up girl could marry a man without her parents' being involved. Vartoosh would surely have preferred to see Gorky bring home an Armenian wife.

From her point of view, Gorky and Mougouch's visit was much too brief. She tried to persuade them to move to Chicago. At the bus station she hugged them, gave him a bundle of food for the trip, and wept. "They needed to return to New York quickly," Vartoosh recalled, "so that no one else would take the 36 Union Square studio, because he had not been able to pay the rent on time." Vartoosh kept up her tie with Gorky through frequent letters. She sometimes sent money and packages as well: "During the war, when many foods were rationed, I always sent them coffee, flour, rice, sugar, whatever amounts came into my hands." The parting at the Chicago bus station was to be the last time Vartoosh saw her brother. "He always wrote that he would come this year, next year, the summer, but he had no money." Gorky's letters over the next seven years are full of excuses (mostly to do with work and lack of funds) for not fulfilling his promises to come see his sister in Chicago. As time passed, Gorky became part of a world different from that of his sister, and his desire to see her seems to have waned. Possibly he avoided visiting his sister because he felt guilty that he had not told her about lying to Mougouch about his background. Surely also that lie created a wedge between him and his wife. But his letters to Vartoosh show that his need to maintain a family bond and to keep hold of the Armenian side of his identity never died.

40

Garden in Sochi

꙱

Upon their return to New York in early October 1941, Gorky found waiting for him a letter from Lloyd Goodrich, now curator at the Whitney Museum. Goodrich wanted to come to the studio to choose a painting for the Whitney Annual, which that year was to be devoted to work by painters under forty. (If Gorky was in fact born in 1900, he would have been forty-one.) Since the Annual was to open on November 12, Goodrich needed the painting soon. "Gorky stayed up all night the night we came home," Mougouch recalls, "and he made *Garden in Sochi*—the one with the olive green background—in one night (Fig. 149). He painted it on top of an earlier painting [a version of *Khorkom*]; that's why the paint is thick. The green background is the last layer. And Lloyd Goodrich put it in the best place. You saw it facing you on the wall of the entrance hall as you came into the museum, which was then located on West Eighth Street. It looked very grand. But it wasn't mentioned in any of the newspaper reviews. Gorky was very disappointed."

The *Garden in Sochi* series has always been seen as a bridge between Gorky's early work and his so-called mature style, that extraordinary flowering of his art that began in 1942 and lasted through the summer of 1947. Having evolved out of the *Khorkom* theme, the *Sochi* paintings share with that earlier group a preoccupation with Armenian memories. The first versions of the *Sochi* theme—*Argula* (Fig. 39), for example— showed what appear to be two women on either side of what is probably a butter churn. As the series went along, the butter churn developed into a shape that looks like a boot with a pointed toe. Some viewers have gone so far as to identify this shape as one of the Armenian slippers that Gorky's father gave him when he said good-bye. The more Gorky delved into his childhood as a source for imagery, the more he freed himself from European precedents. The movement and texture of the paint took on an ever more expressive role, and Gorky's metamorphic shapes were charged with deeper levels of personal feeling.

The sequence of the three principal versions of the *Garden in Sochi* series has been debated by various writers. Jim Jordan seems to have settled the matter, placing the yellow-ground version first because of its closeness to a yellow-ground gouache *Sochi* (Fig. 42) that Gorky painted for the WPA. Since Gorky withdrew from the project in the summer of 1941, the gouache and the yellow-ground oil would, Jordan surmised, have to have been painted in 1940–41. Thus the blatantly Miróesque yellow-ground *Garden in Sochi* belongs to the same moment as the similarly Miró-inspired Ben Marden murals.

Mougouch corroborates Jordan's judgments: she says that Gorky did not work on the yellow-ground *Sochi* after she met him in February 1941. She also says that by the time of the 1941 Miró retrospective, Gorky was no longer so dependent on Miró. He saw the Miró show a number of times and came home full of praise for Miró's early *The Farm*, which, like his own *Garden in Sochi* series, looks back to an agrarian childhood in a distant land. But Gorky felt that such huge exhibitions "killed" artists. Miró had nothing more for him, he said. Gorky protested too much: Miró's influence, albeit very much assimilated, remained with him to the end.

If Mougouch and Jordan are correct that the yellow-ground *Sochi* is first, then Gorky must have gone back to *Argula* or *Composition* (Fig. 41) in October 1941 when he needed a starting point for the green-ground *Sochi*. Later, possibly as late as 1947, when he painted the looser and more painterly white-ground *Sochi* (Fig. 150), he based it not on the green *Sochi* but on the earlier yellow-ground version. In the white-ground *Sochi* Gorky simplified and abstracted the yellow-ground version's grouping of forms. Freed from its job of defining shapes, Gorky's tensile line skirts around color areas and dazzles on its own. The separation of line and colored shape aerates the composition so that every part of the painting expands and breathes. Because foreground and background are united, the image merges with the field instead of floating in or before the background. Imagery has become less important as a carrier of content. Now, to a great extent, meaning and feeling are communicated directly through the sensuous properties of the medium itself.

While the green-ground *Garden in Sochi* was hanging in the entrance to the Whitney Museum, Lloyd Goodrich told Alfred Barr that it was the best thing Gorky had ever painted. On that recommendation, in the spring of 1942 Barr made an appointment to see the painting. "Goodrich tells me you have painted your best painting," he said on entering Gorky's studio. When Gorky fetched *Garden in Sochi* from the storeroom and placed it on an easel, all Barr said was, "Yes." He arranged for the Museum of Modern Art to take *Garden in Sochi* in exchange for *Image in Khorkom*, which the Schwabachers had donated the previous year. The museum would pay Gorky an additional three hundred dollars to cover the difference in the two paintings' value. Gorky was disappointed that the museum did not buy his *Sochi* painting outright, but he was pleased to have an example of his recent work in the bastion of modernism.

When the green-ground *Sochi* entered the Museum of Modern Art's collection, Dorothy Miller wrote to Gorky to ask him to write something about it for the museum files. In response, on June 26, 1942, Gorky sent Miller his well-known prose poem on the Garden of Wish Fulfillment, along with a cover letter that is full of the usual fabrications:

Dear Dorothy

My biography is short and in fact I would prefer to omit the references to Paris and Mr. Kandinsky as such brief periods that mention of them is out of proportion to the actuality.

I was born in Tiflis, Caucasus, South Russia, October 25, 1904 and after the usual studies I came to America in 1920. I had been painting steadily since I was seven and continued to do so during my 3½ yrs. at Brown University where I studied engineering. In 1925 I came to New York and taught at the Grand Central Art School for seven years. I have been living and working ever since in New York.

For anything more personal perhaps there is something in the little writing I am sending you which would make the "label" more interesting. It is very difficult for me to know what to say . . .

Affectionately Arshile

Mougouch recalls that because Gorky did not write easily, she persuaded him to dictate to her his thoughts about *Garden in Sochi*. She wrote down the parts that seemed evocative. The result is a poetic reverie that illuminates the painting and that, according to her, captures "the cadence that Gorky used when he spoke," as he often did, about the garden. But it defines and explains nothing:

Garden in Sochi   June 26, 1942
    I like the heat the tenderness the edible the lusciousness the song of a single person the bathtub full of water to bathe myself beneath the water. I like Uccello Grunewald Ingres the drawings and sketches for paintings of Seurat and that man Pablo Picasso.
    I measure all things by weight.
    I love my Mougouch. What about papa Cézanne.
    I hate things that are not like me and all the things I haven't got are God to me.
    Permit me—
    I like the wheatfields, the plough, the apricots, the shape of apricots those flirts of the sun. And bread above all.
    My liver is sick with the purple.
    About 194 feet away from our house on the road to the spring my father had a little garden with a few apple trees which had retired from giving fruit. There was a ground constantly in shade where grew incalculable amounts of wild carrots and porcupines had made their nests. There was a blue rock half buried in the black earth with a few patches of moss placed here and there like fallen clouds. But from where came all the shadows in constant battle like the lancers of Paolo Uccello's painting? This garden was identified as the Garden of Wish Fulfillment and often I had seen my mother and other village women opening their bosoms and taking their soft and dependable breasts in their hands to rub them on the rock. Above all this stood an enormous tree all bleached under the sun the rain the cold and deprived of leaves. This was the Holy Tree. I myself don't know why this tree was holy but I had witnessed many people whoever did pass by that would tear voluntarily a strip of their clothes and attach it to this tree. Thus through many years of the same act like a veritable pa-

rade of banners under the pressure of wind all these personal inscriptions of signatures, very softly to my innocent ear used to give
echo to the sh-h-h of silver leaves of the poplars.

Many critics have discerned one-to-one relationships between the details of the garden described by Gorky and the imagery in his *Garden in
Sochi* paintings. The black vertical, for example, is seen as the Holy
Tree. The many sprout shapes could be carrots or strips of clothing
waving in the wind, or poplar leaves, or "shadows in constant battle."
The voluptuous lobed shapes could be the village women's pendulous
breasts. What I see in the *Sochi* paintings is not any specific object mentioned in Gorky's text but rather Gorky's childlike awe at the marvelous-
ness of nature and recollection. As Gorky mulled over his memories,
images came and went and some of them entered his paintings, but not
usually in recognizable form.

The myths that Gorky made up about his youth (and that resonate
in his paintings) are embedded in the cultural tradition of Armenian
villagers, who revered earth, water, and fire. Birds of spring, storks, and
cranes were considered to have magical properties and it was forbidden
to kill them. The villagers also saw special powers in mountain peaks,
and believed certain stones could heal illness, bring rain, or make barren
women fertile and dry women give milk. Springs and flowing water were
considered holy, and some trees, especially large trees that were rare in
the deforested Armenian tableland, were said to be sacred. "Let my illness stay behind," believers might say as they tied a strip of their clothing
to such a tree.

Although the shapes and colors change from one *Sochi* to another, all
three paintings have more or less the same imagery. Each conglomera-
tion of shapes has a particular identity and seems to refer to an animate
being. Though Gorky's shapes remain just below the threshold of deci-
pherability, as in his Ben Marden murals, they had specific meanings to
him. By never putting "a face on an image," Gorky kept the viewer prob-
ing his canvas in search of meanings. I, for instance, see two women
pushing a suspended goatskin butter churn to and fro. But the butter
churn, the womblike central shape suspended from the black vertical,
could also be a boot (it has been compared to the shoe in Miró's *Still
Life with Old Shoe* of 1937, which Gorky admired), or it could be meant
to suggest buttocks, belly, or breasts—perhaps the breasts that the child

Gorky saw or imagined seeing rubbed on the magical rock in his father's garden.

One thing is clear: the consistency of certain images from one painting to the next in the *Garden in Sochi* series suggests some hidden narrative. That the two biomorphs flanking the boot/butter churn motif are meant to be female figures is all but proven by two gouache versions of the yellow-ground *Garden in Sochi*. In one (a gouache in the High Museum of Art in Atlanta) the figure on the left even has a face with three black dots for features, very like the faces in Miró's 1936 gouaches. She also has an exposed breast with a nipple. The voluptuous creature on the right is bare-breasted as well. The other gouache (in the collection of Mr. and Mrs. Michel J. Berberian) has a female on the left with easily decipherable features; the figure on the right is less clearly human, more like one of Miró's fantastical quadrupeds in his 1936 gouaches. Perched above the "females" in the *Sochi* series are what look like birds—a favorite Gorky motif and a motif that appears constantly in Armenian poetry and manuscript illumination (Fig. 52). Perhaps Gorky followed Max Ernst in taking a bird for a kind of pictorial alter ego. Galupchig, the term of affection he used in letters to Mougouch, means little dove, and the name of Gorky's beloved Uccello means little bird, too. Whatever he intended them to be or mean, Gorky's birds are well camouflaged: when he described the *Garden in Sochi* series to Mougouch he spoke of painting "the bird singing without the bird being there."

All the *Sochi* paintings are sprightly and festive in feeling. The olive green ground in the 1941 version is a bit lugubrious, but the vivacity of color and stroke both on the surface and in the painting's partially revealed underlayers brings the green to life. The yellow-ground version opens the painting's space and creates a feeling of abundance and release. Its burst of radiant yellow brings to mind those curious lines that Gorky copied into one of his love letters to Corinne: "Some day, beyond the horizon and beyond habit, there would burst a sun all sulphur and Love."

The yellow- and green-ground versions of *Garden in Sochi*, plus several other versions painted between 1940 and 1942, are transitional paintings and, appropriately, they came at a moment of transition in Gorky's life. When he began living with Mougouch he may have thought back to moments of happiness as a boy embedded in an extended family and living on a farm. In terms of his stylistic development, the *Sochi* series, like the World's Fair and Ben Marden murals, shows Gorky freeing himself from the Cubist grid and from Picasso by assimilating ideas from Miró. In particular, he took from Miró the idea of floating shapes against a single colored ground that can be read as infinite extension or as a flat color on the canvas surface. Gorky loved the feeling of suspension in Miró's paintings, Mougouch recalls. He loved the way forms oscillate in space and the way Miró eliminated the horizon line so that space becomes ambiguous and limitless. As with Miró, Gorky's paintings look spontaneous, but their basic compositions are, for the most part, carefully worked out beforehand. The final white-ground *Sochi*, with its separation of line and color, its expression of feeling through painterly gesture, leads to the extraordinary freedom and expressive intensity of Gorky's late work.

41

Camouflage

✵

Soon after Gorky and Mougouch returned from Chicago he wrote to his family:

Dear Vartush, Murad and little Karlen.

We got here without any trouble and for a week we cleaned the studio. Just now I received a letter from an architect [William Muschenheim] who wants to see me. To make a mural and after I've written this letter I'll go and see him. Agnes and I are happy, and after this week we will go to Filadelfia to see her father and mother.

Dear Vartush, truly you cooked a wonderful meal and Agnes always talks about it. She loves you a lot and not a day goes past that she doesn't say "I wish we were there so that Vartush could teach me how to cook." Today was a beautiful day. Don't worry about us. We are well and we have started working. Agnes today is going to the Modern Museum to see someone and to get some kind of a job. Today I am going back to see the architect when we I get back from filadelfia I'll write more. With nostalgic kisses. Your loving

Gorghi

Kiss Karlen for me XXXX

When Mougouch wrote to her parents to tell them that she had married Gorky, they were distressed. "They felt I'd thrown everything down the drain," she recalls. "I was meant to marry someone from the State Department." Nevertheless, they invited Mougouch and Gorky to come and visit them in their temporary home outside Philadelphia. It was Gorky's first meeting with Captain Magruder. He also met Mougouch's favorite uncle, Henry Hosmer.

> Gorky offered to make shashlik and he made a bonfire in the garden which nearly burned the house down. Then he performed. As he made the shashlik, he sang and danced and I remember my uncle slapping his thigh and saying to my mother in his very Bostonian way, "Esther dear, this is the kind of thing people pay money to see!" At the end of the evening, after my mother had gone to bed because she couldn't bear it anymore, my father and uncle listened to Gorky telling about how he had robbed birds' nests as a boy. As we went up to bed, my father said to me, "Well, darling, don't forget the latch key is always in the door." He obviously thought I'd be on the next train home.

While staying with the Magruders, Gorky and Mougouch walked to the Barnes Foundation in Merion. "We got nice and dusty but we weren't allowed into the museum. Because in order to get in we were told you had to be poor or black or an artist. We did look poor, but Gorky was shy and he didn't insist on getting in. He didn't say: 'I've already been here.' He did say he was an artist, but we withdrew, terrified."

How Captain Magruder felt about his eldest daughter marrying a swarthy foreigner can be inferred from his derogatory comments about his youngest daughter Esther's future husband, Paul Makanowitzky, a Russian Jew and a concert violinist. To his own son and namesake, John Magruder III, he wrote: "You now are my only hope son—for keeping the true Magruder strain." But after young Esther's marriage, he did give Paul credit for having joined the army: "I'll say this for him—which I can't say for the big shaggy Archile—he had enough guts to get into the fight and is a bow gunner on a flying fortress due to go overseas very soon."

Gorky and Mougouch's chief worries in the autumn and winter of 1941–42 were finding enough money to pay the rent and figuring out how to avoid his being drafted. Mougouch took a secretarial job paying twenty-one dollars a week at the United China Relief Agency. Thanks to Willie Muschenheim's connections, Gorky was invited to make studies for a mural commission—the one mentioned in his letter to Vartoosh. His second letter to Vartoosh that fall said: "I have already started my preparatory drawings. I hope they get accepted and then I will rent a house and you can come here whenever you like." Again he encouraged his sister to escape loneliness by painting: "It is company," he said. His next letter, undated, said, "I am still painting the preparatory sketches and I have shown them. And the director liked them a lot. So that before next Friday I have to take them and get the OK of the Board of design so then I will get a contract and do the job. I hope it works out. That would be great." His hopes of winning the mural commission were disappointed.

After the Japanese bombed Pearl Harbor on December 7, 1941, and the United States entered the war, Gorky and many of his artist friends felt threatened by the draft. Mougouch recalls: "Peter Busa, de Kooning, Saul Schary, and Gorky all sat around thinking up answers to the draft board. They talked about camouflage, because it was a way not to be drafted." Gorky wrote to Vartoosh on December 28: "We artists are getting organized so that if called we shall serve as painters and not as soldiers." Mougouch recalls another fear shared by Gorky and his friends: deportation. In the furor over the Red menace, aliens and radicals became scapegoats. In June 1940 the House and the Senate passed the Smith Act, which required the registration and fingerprinting of all resident noncitizens. They also passed a federal sedition law and authorized the deportation of aliens who were members of revolutionary groups. Even though he was now a citizen, Gorky, having lived through the deportation and massacre of Armenians in Turkey, was wary. Busa remembered Gorky's attempt to get into a camouflage unit:

I recall meeting Gen. Drum, who had some command post with the New York Militia. Gen. Drum suggested we write to the army's camouflage department to see if we could qualify as camoufleurs by taking some test to see if we could camouflage a building located at West Point. Gorky was pretty good at it. I remember his solution, a monstrous addition to the roof which eliminated the visual shadow of the building by dropping the roof lines to the ground, but then there was a problem with egress and access. Gorky suggested chopping holes in the extended eaves as well as planting trees on the roof.

Gorky finally presented himself to the draft board. He wrote to Vartoosh on August 2, 1942: "Yesterday I received my papers from the draft to fill in, but I don't know what class they'll put me in 1A 2B 3A I don't know yet." At the draft office he was examined by a cross-eyed doctor whose drooping face reminded him of a portrait by Chaim Soutine. After examining Gorky the doctor asked him what he thought of the pictures hanging on the wall. Gorky said, "I don't like them!" "What's your problem?" the doctor asked. "I don't have a problem," said Gorky.

Rejected by the draft because he was overage, Gorky went straight to Busa's house at 10 East Fifteenth Street. "He came to my studio about 8:30 one morning . . . He said, 'The doctor said I'm 4F.' I said, 'Gee that's good, Gorky. That means you don't have to go in the army.' He said, 'Is it really so good? Maybe there's something wrong with me.' I said, 'Don't worry, you can paint now.' He said, 'I don't know, the doctors know something.' He spent the whole morning till 11:30 till I was exhausted. Then he said, 'Well, I've got to go home and paint.' Ruined the whole morning."

For a year Gorky had been hoping to organize a camouflage class at the Grand Central School of Art. Edmund Greacen agreed late in 1941. In an undated letter to Vartoosh, Gorky wrote:

Just now I received your letter and I shall reply immediately. Sweet one, today I received the two letters you had sent in which you had asked what age I have put down in my American citizenship papers. I have written that I was born on april 15, 1904 . . .

So, Vartoosh dear, this Friday I shall once again have a class at the Grand Central School and I shall send you one of the teacher's catalogues of camouflage in this letter. I shall give two classes, that is an afternoon class and an evening class, and each student will pay me $5. If within my two classes I have 20–30 students, it will be relatively good . . .

Always loving you,
Gorky

Gorky worked hard to prepare his camouflage course. He read every book he could lay his hands on and he picked the brains of his scientist friends Alexander Sandow and Warren McCulloch, who remembered Gorky's concern that camouflage might be perceived by the color-blind. To an Armenian friend, Oksen Sarian, Gorky spoke with enthusiasm about his plan to camouflage the whole of New York City. He said he wanted the *New York Times* and other newspapers to publish his idea.

Only a little less ambitious was his statement in the prospectus for his camouflage class (written with the help of his friend Robert Jonas). It began: "An epidemic of destruction sweeps the world today. The mind of civilized man is set to stop it. What the enemy would destroy, however, he must first see. To confuse and paralyze this vision is the role of camouflage. Here the artist and more particularly the modern artist can fulfill a vital function for, opposed to this vision of destruction is the vision of creation." Gorky then launched into a discussion of the modern artist's superior visual intelligence and the "new magic of space and color" created by Cubism—a magic that could make an object visible or invisible. "Mr. Gorky plans a studio workshop in which every student becomes a discoverer," the prospectus said. Students would make scale models, build "abstract constructions," and study the "history and aesthetics of modern art." With the knowledge gained, they would contribute to "civilian and military defense." There were day and evening classes. Registration was five dollars; tuition was fifteen dollars a month.

The future art dealer Betty Parsons was among Gorky's students. "He was witty and brilliant as a camouflage teacher, she said. "His camouflage class met twice a week. There were about 20 to 30 students in the class and they admired him. I was in the class about three, maybe six months. And then after that we organized a drawing class together in my studio on 40th Street . . . I think Gorky probably knew more about aesthetics than anybody I ever met in my life, then and now." Parsons remembered that Gorky's teaching was "full of imagination . . . He could yodel marvelously. Oh, that fantastic Russian yodelling! And [he] told marvelous stories. The most beautiful stories of his childhood. And very poetic. A fantastic kind of Paradise scene." Aristodimos Kaldis had a different sort of recollection. He said that when Gorky began to teach camouflage, the FBI came after him because they could not figure out how Gorky had obtained the kind of technical information he was imparting to his students. "Well, Gorky became so angry that he didn't want to teach. Then we had a big session the first night and several people came and that calmed Gorky down."

For the drawing class that was held in Betty Parsons's studio after his stint at Grand Central ended, Gorky and Parsons hired models, and, when none was available, students drew from casts. Gorky would say, "Bring it alive! Bring that cast alive!" He was, Parsons said, "a tough, tough teacher because as soon as you started to show a little skill he'd say, 'Use your left hand.' Or 'Stop doing that. Start something else.' Because he was trying to keep you always seeking and searching . . . In other words, not to rely on technique." Another method Gorky had for preventing bland facility was to dip a piece of string in a bottle of ink and tell the student to use it to draw. "It could be discouraging," Parsons said, "because just when you felt you'd mastered something, he'd say, 'Now, Miss. You've got that. Start on something else.' . . . He didn't like anything overly confident."

During the first winter of their marriage, Gorky and Mougouch's life settled into a routine. She worked during the day and learned to be a housewife in her spare moments. Because she was so young, daily chores had the novelty of a new game. "I could hardly boil an egg when I met Gorky. I used to dust by blowing the tops of the tables. One day Gorky found me pushing the dust out of the window with the vacuum cleaner. I had the hose attached at the wrong end. We laughed a lot over the hoover."

Gorky put in long days before his easel, repainting his old canvases. He started early in the morning, placing the canvas he wanted to work on on the easel, then lighting a cigarette and looking for a while before dipping his brush into one of the many colors that had formed a skin that Gorky said smelled like melon. "When I first knew Gorky," Mougouch recalls, "there was a rotation. He'd pick a dry canvas and paint on top of it. The painting would be completely changed. While he was painting, he listened to the radio all morning long, at full volume—the silliest women's programs, soap operas, people talking about baking cakes, and people telling their troubles and getting advice." Gorky talked back to the radio—"Silly cow!" or "Poor t'ing!" One of his favorite programs was Major Bowes's hour in which people telephoned in and spoke about their problems. "We used to die laughing, because as soon as these people got to the nitty-gritty of their problems, Major Bowes said, 'No details, Madam! No details!' But what they'd said wasn't a detail at all. It was the crux of the problem!"

At the end of the day, when Gorky finished working on a painting that he planned to rework soon again, he turned it so that it faced the wall. Or, if he'd done with it for the moment, he put the canvas in the storeroom to dry. The storeroom was fuller than ever. "Just before the United States entered the war, Mougouch recalls, "Gorky laid in a tremendous stock of Winsor & Newton paints and brushes, because you could still get them from England and he was afraid he would be cut off. So he had a little shop full of supplies in one of the bureaus in the storage room off the entrance hall. He had masses of paper and lots of lovely canvas. He would use inferior canvas and keep the good canvas for when he knew how to paint better."

Gorky continued to keep 36 Union Square uncluttered and spotless except for his collection of twenty or thirty glass vases. These were allowed to go undusted because he thought dust gave them beautiful colors. He or Mougouch scrubbed the floor once a week. In her effort to become the next best thing to an Armenian wife, she learned to cook soups that would "feel like a meal," rarely meat, which was too expensive. Gorky washed the dishes with the kind of care associated with obsessive-compulsive behavior:

> He scraped, rinsed, washed, and then washed them over and over. At least three times, and then he dried them. He sang as he washed the dishes. He would tell me what dishes from his childhood tasted like, and then he'd write to Vartoosh to ask her for recipes for me. She sent a recipe for bread. We bought a huge quantity of flour and yeast, which was difficult in wartime. We kept the dough warm under an eiderdown and the next morning the dough was the size of a pillow. Everything Gorky did he did to excess. If he built a fire, he would nearly burn the house down. If he cooked rice it overflowed and we'd have to put it in the bathtub. He always made too much. Once in Virginia, he made peach ice cream and he churned it with such vim and vigor that it was not ready to eat until very late at night. And by then it had turned into butter.

In the early years of their marriage, Gorky and Mougouch visited museums two or three times a week. He taught her how to look at paintings, so much so that she learned to see them through his eyes. "In museums, he was quick and selective," she recalls. "He went to look at a specific thing. At the Metropolitan he loved the Persian rugs. He liked Cycladic sculpture, early Greek and Sumerian art, Byzantine and Islamic. He loved Coptic textiles—he was mad about the Copts, and he had a fat book on Coptic art." As the years passed and Gorky found his own pictorial language, he stopped haunting museums and art galleries. He no longer needed to get ideas from other art.

Most of Gorky and Mougouch's evenings were spent at home. Often he would paint or draw. The light of the single dangling light bulb in the studio was insufficient, so he would turn on the photographer's flood lamp attached to his easel. Sometimes she would sit on the narrow daybed with its scratchy horsehair mattress and read to him. Other times he looked at his art books himself. Though he especially liked books on the methods of the old masters, which he called "cookbooks," he always grumbled that these were a waste of time. Before retiring, Gorky would take a walk around Union Square and buy the evening newspaper. He followed the progress of the war closely, and after Hitler invaded Russia in the summer of 1941, he would be pleased when the Red Army beat out the Germans. But his favorite reading was the gutter press—the *Daily News*, the *Mirror*, and the *New York Post*. "He did not want to read measured, objective news. He loved all those human-interest stories. He'd have a cup of coffee at Horn and Hardart. Then we'd go to bed."

From time to time Gorky and Mougouch would eat at Horn and Hardart Automat, and it was here that she discovered a side of Gorky that she found reprehensible. He was an anti-Semite. What was happening to the Jews horrified him, particularly as it brought back memories of the Armenian deportations and massacres. Yet, according to what Mougouch surmised after learning in the mid-1950s that Gorky was Armenian, "Gorky did not have much sympathy for the Jews. He felt that the Jews had the best publicity in the world and that the Armenians had none. He felt that because the Western democracies had not stopped the Turks from massacring the Armenians during World War I, this had given the green flag to Germany to get rid of German Jews." (There was some truth in this: when on August 22, 1939, Hitler informed his military commanders of his plans to invade Poland, he said, "Who, after all, speaks today of the annihilation of the Armenians?")

Gorky's anti-Semitism was fueled by his perception of the way established New York Jews treated the recent influx of Jewish refugees. At the Automat, he observed the bafflement of the newly arrived refugees when faced with the problem of putting coins in a slot in order to extract plates of food from little glass-fronted compartments. Gorky was upset to see that the Jews who had been eating in the Automat for years did not get up to help the newcomers. For Armenian Americans it was a moral imperative to help recent immigrants adjust to their new environment. When Mougouch discovered that her new husband was an anti-Semite, she was aghast: "I went into the bathroom to find iodine. 'I'm going to kill myself,' I said. 'I'm jailed with a bigot!' I was crying, and Gorky rushed into the bathroom and took the iodine out of my hand." In retrospect she came to terms with his anti-Semitism: "Gorky's feeling was that no one cared about the Armenian holocaust. I don't think Gorky felt that the same thing was happening to the Jews. He felt it only happened to the Armenians. It was racial jealousy—who had suffered the most."

Some evenings Gorky and Mougouch went to cowboy movies in the downtown movie theaters. "He thought they were the best thing about America, the more grade B the better, and Third Avenue provided a fresh one daily in those days and they were very often his evening meal." They also saw films about Soviet Russia and once or twice they traveled uptown to see a film at a Broadway movie palace. "He liked Bette Davis. He told me that in the 1930s he used to go to Broadway and go from one movie to another."

The early years of their marriage were full of laughter as he told her childhood stories and observed with his extraordinary acuity the hilarity of everyday life. Because they were happy, there was much to laugh about, from the infuriating waffle iron to the nightly symphony performed by the elderly black janitor who lived upstairs and had a squeaky bed. To Mougouch's delight, Gorky called sex "push-push." He had a boyish, playful side, and he loved to roughhouse and wrestle.

But money problems plagued them, and it was always difficult to come up with the monthly rent of fifty-five dollars. Gorky earned a little by teaching, and Vartoosh occasionally sent him five dollars or a food package. Once Mougouch was married, her father cut off her allowance of a hundred dollars a month. "He thought I was giving all my money to the Communists," she says. (A year and a half later, when she gave birth to her first child, he restored her allowance at the reduced amount of fifty dollars.) In addition, Mougouch occasionally had a small influx of cash: in May 1942, for example, $659.33 was transferred from a Washington savings bank to her Manhattan account, and she had a $1,000 U.S. Treasury bond that paid 3¼% interest. In spite of penury, she and Gorky entertained. Mougouch wrote her mother on June 4, 1942, that "30 artists are coming here tonight for a rebellion against a dirty deal a publishing house gave a man writing a book on modern art. They ditched him & stole his list of top artists to reproduce & we are supposedly to refuse to cooperate in letting them use plates of 'our' pictures."

For a while Mougouch kept her job at United China Relief. In July 1942 she took a secretarial course. For a month or so during the summer of 1942 she sold the *Daily Worker*. Once, when she was distributing this Communist newspaper to residents of tenements near the docks, she found herself in the middle of a brawl between Communists and anti-Communist stevedores. When she finally came home, Gorky was terribly worried. He told her she must stop peddling the *Daily Worker*. "Also I'd go to night classes in Communist doctrine," she recalls, but Gorky did not like to have his wife staying out late, so she dropped the class. Fortunately for Gorky, Mougouch was not a woman with conventional notions about financial security. Yet, early in her marriage, she discovered that some aspects of the change from being a footloose girl to a married woman grated: "I realized the confinement of marriage—that you have to sleep in one bed. Gorky was upset when I got out of bed and wandered around. 'What's the matter?' he would ask. I felt I couldn't move."

Gorky's jealousy made his young wife feel hemmed in as well. The first party he took her to was given by Jane and John Vandercook in their house on Park Avenue and Thirty-eighth Street. Gorky had met them through Mina Metzger, one of whose daughters had been married to John but had died. "Gorky and Jack argued about politics and Jane often took our side. We both loved her. She was very beautiful—so thin as to be almost transparent. I wore a slinky taupe-brown dress and I made friends with a young man who was in publishing. He wanted to see more of us. Gorky thought he was flirting with me. The man came to the studio to see us twice, and the second time, Gorky said: 'Why don't you come out with it? We know perfectly well you're working for the FBI.'" Although Mougouch sounds amused when she looks back on her early experiences with Gorky's possessiveness, it was never easy to live with.

Since Gorky was twice Mougouch's age when they married and since, as an Armenian, he expected a wife to be submissive, he was the dominant spouse. Mougouch, for her part, may have had the temperament of a "wild horse," but she wanted her husband to be her "Rock of Gibraltar." She deferred to him. He was thrilled to have a woman to look after him. He loved her eagerness for him to succeed as an artist and the way she did everything in her power to give him the strength and freedom that that required. Early on, Serge Chermayeff, an emphatically dominant man himself, commented to Mougouch: "You're bad for Gorky. He's becoming a pasha." Raphael Soyer, for whom she posed when she was pregnant in 1942, recalled that Mougouch was "very bohemian-looking at that time with a cape. She actually became so much like Gorky himself, for a while, in behavior, in appearance." Peter Busa likewise watched Mougouch conforming to Gorky's ideal: "When he first married her she was the right type. He imposed an attitude on her, which was his own. He wanted a mother. His whole psyche, he was transferring his whole affection for his mother onto his wife. He used to have Agnes scrub the floor. She was a socialite!"

Mougouch herself recalls adapting to Gorky's demands: "Gorky was a man of enormous experience. I always agreed with Gorky. I didn't know enough to differ with him. I was virgin soil, which he liked. I wasn't brought up to think that I had anything to say for myself. He could tell me anything and I'd believe it." The flow of ideas was mostly one-way: "I was very nervous about talking with him about his art. He didn't like people to say they understood what he was doing. He never explained his painting. If you said, 'I understand,' as if you thought you had got Gorky's point, he would say, 'You don't. It's not at all like that.' As soon as someone said anything similar to what he had said, he changed his position."

For all that, Gorky was, she says, enormously loving. "He was everything—mother, sister, aunt. He showed me love in every way." Coming from an undemonstrative family and having been brought up by a series of nannies, Mougouch reveled in her husband's adoration. "It was incredible the way he was with me, making any little thing for me, carving combs out of wood. Any little pebble I picked up he loved, anything I did was wonderful."

PART IX

Gorky, c. 1938

42

Surrealists in Exile

꙰

With the outbreak of World War II in September 1939 and the capitulation of France in June 1940, many European artists, especially those of the Surrealist group, took refuge in America. Although Gorky had been aware of Surrealism for a decade, the presence in the New York area of artists like Roberto Matta Echaurren, André Masson, and Max Ernst had a profound effect on his painting. In his drawings from the early 1930s he had experimented with the improvisational look, but not the method, of Surrealist automatism, a technique that gave free play to the movement of line and was somewhat like stream-of-consciousness writing or free association in Freudian analysis. Line, according to automatist method, was supposed to look as if it were propelled by energies coming from the unconscious, and these energies were supposed to be unchecked by the conscious mind's desire to create logically coherent or beautiful forms. In his Surrealist Manifesto of 1924, the poet and essayist André Breton described automatism in his definition of the movement: "SURREALISM. Noun, masculine. Pure psychic automatism, by which one intends to express verbally, in writing or by any other method, the real functioning of the mind. Dictation by thought, in the absence of any control exercised by reason, and beyond any aesthetic or moral preoccupation."

Now that he had broken free of the rigidities of Cubist structure, Gorky could more fully engage in Surrealist ideas and techniques. But he was never, properly speaking, a Surrealist, for he was too much in love with beauty, control, and perfection. In his drawings from the early

1930s, line loops and meanders as if moved by labyrinthine urgencies, yet it is always strictly controlled by rigorous aesthetic choices. Indeed, since Gorky's habit was to trace the outlines of a completed drawing to use as the basis for the next, nearly identical loops and meanders reappear from one drawing to another in a series. The same kinds of controls continued to be part of Gorky's creative process in the years to come.

Among the Surrealists, Kurt Seligman, Yves Tanguy, Kay Sage, Roberto Matta Echaurren, and Salvador Dalí were the first to arrive in America. In June 1940 came Gordon Onslow Ford, an English painter who had worked closely with Matta and who joined the Surrealists in Paris. The next year brought Max Ernst, André Masson, and the man who came to be called the "pope" of Surrealism, André Breton. Gorky would presently meet them all. The Julien Levy and Pierre Matisse galleries (Pierre Matisse was Henri Matisse's younger son) became meeting places and showcases for the so-called Surrealists in exile. Another venue was Peggy Guggenheim's Art of This Century gallery, which opened in October 1942.

Three years before the arrival of the first Surrealist émigrés, the Museum of Modern Art had thrown its weight behind the European Surrealists by mounting *Fantastic Art, Dada, Surrealism* and publishing a fine catalog (1936). One year earlier, James Thrall Soby's *After Picasso* was the first American book to focus on Surrealism. More important to Gorky, though, was Julien Levy's *Surrealism*. With its imaginative layout, this anthology of writings and pictures is almost a Surrealist work in itself. Levy recalled, "When my book *Surrealism* was published in 1936, [Gorky] straightaway read it in the back room of my gallery and soon borrowed it to take home." Gorky actually owned a copy of Levy's book, sections of which he lifted in 1936 and 1941 for use in his love letters. Levy's definition of Surrealism must have appealed greatly to the antirationalist Gorky: "SURREALISM is not a rational, dogmatic, and consequently static theory of art . . . SURREALISM attempts to discover and explore the 'more real than real world behind the real,' meaning which is expansive behind contractile fact." Levy said that, although artists cannot explain the symbols prompted by the subconscious, those symbols will arouse "a corresponding intuition in others." Citing Engels, Levy proposed that the world is "a complex of processes" in which objects are in a state of flux. Gorky would have found all these ideas congenial, as would the future Abstract Expressionists.

Levy's book quoted from a lecture Dalí had given at the Museum of Modern Art in 1934, and Dalí's words, too, must have fallen on Gorky's receptive ears. "The subconscious," Dalí wrote, "has a symbolic language that is truly a universal language, for it does not depend on a special habitude or state of culture or intelligence." Gorky must also have been intrigued by Dalí's concept of the "great vital constants," meaning sex, death, and "the physical melancholy caused by time-space." What Dalí called his "paranoic critical method" had a parallel in Gorky's ideas about the creative process. Dalí's method involved the deploying of Surrealist techniques of free association to unearth the contents of the subconscious. Thus, an artist might look at an object, but, using his imaginative or hallucinatory powers, he would see something else. For Gorky, this was a way of life. On those frequent occasions when he had to stick up for Dalí, Gorky would say: "If a man can give you one image becoming another, that takes a lot of plastic ability."

Peter Busa remembered that Gorky once asked Dalí how to become famous. "Dalí told him to pick on the St. Marks church by peeing against the wall, exposing himself to full public view, and be arrested, and in that way he would become well known for indecent exposure." Dalí's recipe for instant fame stayed with Gorky, for he recycled the joke a few years later when he ran into William Freed and Lillian Orlowsky in the Union Square subway station. The two former Hofmann students had just returned from Provincetown, and William Freed was feeling neglected by the art world. "Bill was a complainer," Orlowsky remembers:

> He and Gorky were comrades in moans and groans. In those days Bill complained about the situation of the artist—you can't exhibit, you can't sell. He complained to Gorky when we met him in the subway, and he asked Gorky how he could get his work shown. Gorky's advice was to get a sandwich board, put your name on it and write that you are an artist. Then have a little cart and put your paintings in it and take it up to the Public Library on Forty-second Street and Fifth Avenue. Stand at the bottom of the library steps in front of the sculptured lions. Make sure you have arranged for the press and photographers to be there. Then pee on the lions.

William Freed considered the advice and said, "I can't pee in public." Gorky answered, "Then you do have a problem!"

Two Surrealist magazines, *View*, founded in 1940, and *VVV*, founded in spring 1943, added to Gorky's understanding of Surrealism. Early in 1941 he went to the New School for Social Research to hear Gordon Onslow Ford's series of four slide lectures advocating an abstract and symbolic Surrealist art as "an adventure into Human Consciousness." To coincide with Onslow Ford's lectures, Howard Putzel, Peggy Guggenheim's art adviser, organized several exhibitions of Surrealist paintings at the New School. Onslow Ford's lecture notes show that what he had to say about Surrealism was just what the New York painters, especially those who would later become Abstract Expressionists, were hungry to hear. In his introduction he encouraged his listeners to explore their own "psychic landscape," the "marvelous world that is perhaps buried in each one of us." He stressed the importance of dreams and of the collective unconscious. If an artwork delved into the "unknown self," he insisted, it would "speak to the unconscious of every sensitive person." Surely Gorky was one of Onslow Ford's more alert and absorbtive listeners. Indeed, Onslow Ford recalled that Gorky came to his Eighth Street apartment several times to find out more about Surrealism.

The intellectual ferment that the arrival of the Surrealists in New York precipitated gave support for Gorky's move away from strict Cubist structuring and toward a freer, more fluid way of painting. In Julien Levy's opinion, the Surrealist technique of automatism was for Gorky a "redemption": it helped him to "realize that his most secret doodling could be very central." In a memoir published in 1977, Levy suggested that Gorky had listened when he told him what Eluard had said about poetic inspiration: "I hum a melody, some popular song, the most ordinary. Sometimes I sing quite loudly. But I echo very softly in my interior, filling the melody with my own errant words." The Surrealists encouraged Gorky to go back to his childhood memories, to explore his fantasies, and to let his subconscious play a stronger role in the invention of form. Later, in connection with his 1944 painting *How My Mother's Embroidered Apron Unfolds in My Life* (Fig. 157), Gorky would tell Levy how he told himself stories while he painted. Often they were stories his mother had told him, and they often had little to do with the canvas at hand: "Her stories and the embroidery on her apron got confused in my mind with my eyes closed. All my life her stories and her embroidery keep unraveling pictures in my memory."

Around 1942, when he became involved with the Surrealists in exile, Gorky's paintings became much more improvisational, but even though the Surrealists confirmed Gorky's belief in the importance of fantasy and memory, it must be remembered that when they arrived Gorky was ready for them. His fantasy had been nurtured early on by the hybrid creatures he saw in Armenian manuscripts, carpets, and stone carvings. As de Kooning put it: "He had all those things before the Surrealists and the Surrealists told him he had it already. I mean he had a fantastic instinct, a gift of seeing it the right way . . . and he would say, 'Look at these feathery trees and that's why they're so wonderful. You know, I really feel like painting feathers.' "

Gorky met Roberto Matta Echaurren soon after the twenty-seven-year-old painter arrived in the United States in 1939. Reared in an upper-class family in Santiago, Chile, Matta had gone to Paris to study architecture with Le Corbusier but turned to art, making his first drawings in 1937, the year he joined the Surrealists. He began painting in 1938 and before long was creating what he called "inscapes," in which thin layers of rubbed pigment coalesce into biomorphic forms that suggest psychological states (Fig. 117). Gorky and Matta could have met through Onslow Ford or at Matta's first exhibition in the United States, which took place at the Julien Levy Gallery in spring 1940. Peter Busa said that he introduced Gorky to Matta at a small gathering at Matta's house:

> Gorky was saying, "You know, I think that you paint too thin." And Matta graciously replied, "Oh, I don't think I paint so thin." It was an infantile conversation that went on in that way for a while. Gorky, if you remember, was painting very heavy in those days . . . Exasperated, finally, Gorky pulled himself up to his full height (I thought he was going to fight), and he said, "Well, let's put it this way—you don't paint so thin, I don't paint so thick." With that we all relaxed. His sense of humor, which ranged from the ridiculous to the sublime, endeared him to all of us. We all laughed, but Gorky laughed the most.

Matta described his relationship with Gorky as one of "unreserved exchange but basic misunderstanding." The two artists certainly learned a great deal from each other: they are said to have borrowed each other's drawings specifically to get ideas from them. But Matta's improvisational approach was at odds with Gorky's aesthetic perfectionism. In appearance and personality, the two men made a striking contrast. More than a decade younger than Gorky and much smaller, Matta had a crown of straight black hair and deep brown eyes that brimmed with mischief and a mind that moved like quicksilver. Among the Surrealists in exile, he made friends the fastest—he had an irrepressible charm.

Gorky and Mougouch began to see a lot of Matta and his wife, Anne Alpert, whom he called "Pajarito," or "little bird." The hyperactive "*enfant perpetuel*," as Julien Levy called Matta, brought out the outrageous funniness in his often saturnine Armenian friend. Matta laughed readily—his giggle was catching. "It trilled and trilled, going up, up, upward, on soprano wings," wrote his and Gorky's friend the writer Lionel Abel, who was part of the Surrealist circle in New York and who in 1942 helped to edit the Surrealist review *VVV*. "Having heard Matta laugh, you wanted to say something to make him laugh again, but as it turned out, it was Matta who said the things which made *you* laugh, and him too." Gorky's laughter was equally surprising: people expected a deep laugh from such a giant of a man, but his laugh was a high-pitched "Hee, hee, hee." He didn't open his mouth much—he felt opening the mouth wide while laughing was very American, meaning vulgar. He told Mougouch that in his country it was considered to be unseemly, "without shame." He smiled with his mouth closed, too, for he was self-conscious about his teeth.

Gorky and Matta became best friends, but, as Max Ernst's son, the painter Jimmy Ernst, used to tell it, they kept certain reservations about each other:

> One evening at the Jumble Shop after one of Gordon Onslow Ford's lectures we were all sitting around. Matta and Gorky were there. Gorky didn't have much use for Matta personally and they were always at each other's throat, particularly since Gorky then was seemingly heavily influenced by Matta in his approach. Matta, referring to a prior visit to Gorky's studio, said, "There's something in the upper right-hand corner of the last painting— how did you do that?" . . . Gorky said, "Well, first you take a glass or a palette and you squeeze paint on that, then you have brushes,

then you have a little cup with turpentine and some oil. You dip the brush in the cup and in the paint and you transfer it to the canvas." Matta said, "Yes, but how did you do it?" "That's how I did it," said Gorky.

The undertone of brotherly competition showed up again in the early 1940s when Mougouch heard Gorky saying to Matta, "You've gotten a lot of attention and you are just a kid. What would you do if no one paid attention to you?" Matta came back with, "Then I'd have done something else." Gorky said, "You have to work forty years, forty years of hard work. Then you might become a good painter." Matta held his ground: "If I can't stun the world with my painting, I'd do something else." Even as his friendship with Matta deepened, Gorky remained envious. "Give Matta another twenty or thirty years," he said, "and see how he paints."

The paintings that Matta produced during his first years in New York were called "psychological morphologies." Amorphous, ever-changing shapes in bright glowing colors were signals of feelings, thoughts, and impulses. Somehow he managed to combine ideas about biology and psychology with notions about the earth and the vastness of space and time. Matta, like many other artists at that time, talked a lot about cosmic, non-Euclidian space and the fourth dimension. His method — and he was enormously facile — was to spill thin washes of paint onto the canvas and then rub and spread the liquid with rags. Details and thicker areas were brushed on later, but drips and runs were allowed to remain. Once he tried to explain his work to Breton: "I call psychological morphology the graphic mark of the transformations resulting from the emission of energies and their absorption in the object from its first appearance to its final form, in the geodesical psychological milieu . . ." and so on. If Gorky had a hard time decoding Buckminster Fuller, he must have been equally at a loss when confronted by such statements by the voluble Matta. Very likely he caught Matta's drift by watching him paint.

Matta admired Gorky's talent, but, like Noguchi, he saw that Gorky needed to change. Assuming that Arshile meant Achilles, Matta warned Gorky about putting too much faith in the School of Paris. "You must not think of Paris, for Paris will shoot an arrow into your heel." Often Matta teased Gorky about the way he worked so long on one painting. He couldn't understand why for Gorky painting was such a struggle, why the endless revisions, the layers and layers of paint. "You must just let it go. Let it rip," he said. But, Mougouch recalls, "Gorky had a workman-like attitude toward painting. 'I'm a worker,' he would say. He had arguments with Matta. Gorky said, 'Art is not all inspiration. A lot of it is just plain hard work.' " Nevertheless, Gorky decided to try to be freer. "The endless repainting of the same canvas had had something to do with economy. Now he had more money. Things were looking up. I was earning money. Even Mrs. Metzger and Ethel Schwabacher upped the ante. Matta said, 'You must move to another canvas. Stretch a lot of canvases and just fill them up.' Gorky decided not to scrape the canvas down. Instead he now worked on three or four canvases at once, and he'd work on another one while the first one dried." Thus, in the winter of 1942–43 Gorky was urged by Matta to thin his paint with turpentine and let it drip and run. He learned to accept the idea of accident and to make chance marks the starting point for the invention of new forms. Now the movement of paint could carry its own narrative.

But, for all of Matta's liberating influence, Gorky was much too controlled to follow Matta's improvisational methods completely. As the critic and art historian Meyer Schapiro astutely observed, Gorky had chosen successively younger artists as his models and Matta, instead of being a father figure, was a younger brother: "From Matta came the idea of the canvas as a field of prodigious excitement, unloosed energies . . . The encounter with Matta was, it seems to me, a decisive point in Gorky's liberation from copying."

Since many of the Surrealists did not speak English, their contacts with New York artists were not casual or easy. The sculptor Philip Pavia recalled that New Yorkers' awe of the Europeans put a distance between the two groups. The Americans, Pavia said, would see the Europeans and not say hello because "we were too humble." Very likely the émigrés appeared arrogant or aloof. Displaced by the war, most of them had to struggle to make ends meet, and they had a hard time even keeping in touch with one another. Naturally there were moments of resentment toward the country in which they had found refuge. In December 1939, for example, Tanguy wrote to the Seligmans to ask them to buy a picture from Matta: "The Mattas are in a bad situation, no money and little hope of selling in this terrible country. We have tried to help, but our means in this accursed country are too limited." Some of the Europeans felt that America was an uncultured place. Max Ernst complained that in New York it was difficult to maintain the intense level of artistic exchange that he and other painters had enjoyed in Paris: "The café life was lacking. As a result we had artists in New York but no art. Art is not produced by one artist but by several. It is to a great degree a product of their exchange of ideas with one another."

For all that, the presence of the Europeans in Manhattan made a difference. Artists whom the Americans had worshiped from afar were now flesh-and-blood people walking the sidewalks of Manhattan. As Jackson Pollock said: "American painters have generally missed the point of modern painting from beginning to end . . . Thus the fact that good European moderns are now here is very important, for they bring with them an understanding of the problems of modern painting. I am particularly impressed with their concept of the source of art being the unconscious." For Gorky, the arrival of the Europeans, and their gradual desanctification, was an enormous boost, especially because, with time, they accepted him as one of their own.

It was not long before young American painters became competitive with their European colleagues. The dominance of the School of Paris irked them, and they especially resented the fact that museums and art galleries paid far more attention to (and higher prices for) contemporary Europeans. Thus, while Gorky was ignored, a newcomer like Matta was included in a two-person show at the Julien Levy Gallery within months of his arrival, and in 1942 Pierre Matisse mounted Matta's first one-person exhibition. By the mid 1940s there was a growing feeling among Manhattan artists that it was time to break free from European influence and to create an art that expressed the energies of contemporary America.

Gorky was, Mougouch says, thrilled by "the awesome presence of these mythical giants from the culture he loved." But he did not immediately become part of the Surrealist group. It seems that Matta and other friends, among them Noguchi and Kiesler, were reluctant to introduce Gorky to the Europeans. Gorky was out of fashion—most people were unaware of the change in his work exemplified by the *Garden in Sochi* series, and they continued to think of him as a Picasso imitator. When, in October 1942, the Surrealists in exile and a handful of their American colleagues were presented to the Manhattan public in a large exhibition titled *First Papers of Surrealism* at the Whitelaw Reid mansion on Madison Avenue, Gorky was not included. Nor was he invited to the opening. Mougouch remembers that in the early days of their marriage, on those few occasions when they were invited to openings, no one paid any attention to them.

On the twentieth of October Gorky and Mougouch went to the gala inauguration of Peggy Guggenheim's Art of This Century gallery at 30 West Fifty-seventh Street. According to Mougouch, Gorky never felt at home in the highly sophisticated and rather racy Guggenheim milieu. Judging from Guggenheim's memoir, *Out of This Century*, her every moment had to be a madcap adventure. Life was a spree. At the crowded opening for her gallery, Guggenheim wore one earring made for her by Alexander Calder and another by her one-time lover Tanguy, in order, she said, "to show my impartiality between Surrealist and abstract art." The gallery's designer, Frederick Kiesler, had created an unusual exhibition space. The Surrealist gallery had curved gumwood walls from which projected baseball bats on which unframed paintings were mounted. The abstract and Cubist gallery had blue canvas-covered walls, and paintings were hung from strings so that they seemed to float in space.

Gorky, whose notions about exhibition space were conventional, must have been both amused by and contemptuous of the avant-garde atmosphere. It was, he said, "like a circus," and he complained that one couldn't really see the paintings. Nevertheless, he might well have wished to have been taken up by Peggy Guggenheim. Although she did buy a painting from him in 1944, she never offered him a show or included him in any of her group exhibitions. Gorky's high seriousness would have seemed heavy to someone as giddy as Peggy Guggenheim, and she, no doubt, appeared to him to be one of those spoiled, headstrong, promiscuous American women of whom he disapproved. But he surely recognized her astuteness with regard to contemporary art, and he was probably envious of the attention she lavished on other Americans, such as Pollock, Robert Motherwell, William Baziotes, Clyfford Still, Mark Rothko, and David Hare, all of whom were given shows at Art of This Century.

Guggenheim's enthusiasm for Pollock would have been particularly galling. Gorky and Pollock disliked each other and bristled whenever they met. In 1942 or 1943 Pollock asked Busa to take him to see Gorky's work. Busa remembered Gorky offering some kind of liquor that turned milky with the addition of water. Most likely it was Pernod or ouzo. Pollock drank the liquid and began to give Mougouch lascivious looks. When Gorky brought his paintings out of the storeroom to show to Pollock, Pollock turned nasty: "Why don't you get a little shit in your work?" he said. What Pollock meant, Busa explained, was that Gorky's paintings looked "a little clean." Gorky's response was to be irritated but not flustered. Busa was angry, because he felt that Pollock had asked to be taken to 36 Union Square only in order to insult the older artist—an artist for whom he had, in fact, a grudging respect. When Busa told Pollock to keep his mouth shut, Pollock had a tantrum. "He was very envious of Gorky," Busa recalled. "Krasner's early paintings were copies of Gorky. He knew that Gorky was highly respected, but Jackson always had to be a star." Pollock may also have known that Gorky went around pronouncing Lee Krasner, Pollock's companion (and after 1945 his wife), the stronger painter. When things calmed down, Pollock and Busa "left with a cool good-bye." "Pollock was a very belligerent man," de Kooning said.

> I was at a party once and he started insulting Gorky and Pollock was drunk. He was going to do this, he was going to do that, and he said to Gorky, "You're a lousy painter." Gorky didn't bat an eyelash. He took a long knife which he always kept in his pocket. He used it as a pencil sharpener, used to make piles of pencils with long lead because of the way he drew. Like he used to say he used pencils in drawing "like a surgeon's tool." . . . So it became a habit for him to take that big knife out and sharpen a pencil whenever somebody wanted to make trouble. People knew they shouldn't fool around with him, you know what I mean. And Pollock didn't either. Gorky just answered him, "Well, we're different artists."

In 1942 Gorky was included in several group exhibitions. His career was picking up. Mougouch wrote to her great-aunt Nathalie Campbell in February 1943: "1942 was a pretty successful year. Gorky has sold about six paintings since last spring and plans exib. in fall *if not drafted* in war plant." One of the shows in which Gorky took part was *Contemporary American Painting*, organized by Samuel M. Kootz and presented in January on the eighth floor of Macy's department store. Among the other participants were John Graham, Adolph Gottlieb, and Rothko. The show's aim was to sell modern art to the middle class. Kootz's announcement in the *New York Times* said that 179 framed paintings by seventy-two contemporary American artists would be sold for prices ranging from $24.97 to $249. "Choose the picture that speaks to you; be assured that any one you choose will possess real merit. All are priced with great modesty." What, one wonders, did Gorky—who, although he always maintained that he painted to "earn his bread," was also convinced that artists live on a higher spiritual plane—feel about Kootz's commercial fanfare? He must have been displeased when he read the paragraph Kootz wrote about him in his 1943 book *New Frontiers in American Art*: "Arshile Gorky is pursuing abstraction in a manner that should make the sensitive spectator howl in dismay. Gorky has genuine talent; he is definitely intelligent about his art, his painting is superb, and he has great sensibility. But somehow he has never jelled these talents, at one moment pursuing Cézanne, at another hot footing after Picasso or Miró or Léger. He has been too busy to become Gorky."

That fall Gorky donated two oil paintings to an "Art Exhibition for the Benefit of Armenian War Relief" presented at the Art Students League. The show featured the collection of Armenian art belonging to Haroutune Hazarian, whom Gorky had known since the 1920s. When Hazarian came to 36 Union Square to pick up Gorky's contribution, Gorky handed him *The Head* (c. 1930–31) and *Summer in Sochi, Black Sea* (1936) (Fig. 36). At the October opening Gorky admired a group of drawings by an early-twentieth-century Armenian artist named Vanno Khojabedian, who had been a porter in Tiflis. "I kneel down before this artist," Gorky said. When the Armenian guests at the opening expressed bewilderment about his *Summer in Sochi, Black Sea*, Gorky helped them out by inventing a possible meaning: "This picture shows the sea coast of Sochi, and there, standing, are my mother and I." He told them they could find their own meanings in his work. After the show closed, Gorky was furious to learn that Hazarian had bought both of his paintings for five dollars each. Gorky offered to buy them back for the same amount, but Hazarian refused to part with them. Indignant not only with Hazarian but also with the Armenians involved in organizing the show, Gorky snorted, "Never again!"

Probably thanks to Dorothy Miller's having become a curator at the Museum of Modern Art, Gorky's work was included in two 1942 exhibitions there. The first, which opened in June, was entitled *New Rugs by American Artists*. (Actually the show was a competition organized by the museum in cooperation with rug manufacturers looking for new designs.) Gorky was represented by *Bull in the Sun* (1942), a wool rug woven by V'soske, plus two related preliminary studies and a gouache design of the "bull" (Fig. 114). Closely resembling Gorky's creatures in his Ben Marden murals, the bull, or what Gorky said was the "skin of the bull drying in the sun," is a black biomorph with a human-looking profile and long flanges that might be horns. The bold graphic quality and the clean-cut contours suggest that Gorky turned not only to Miró but to Matisse's cutouts for *Jazz*. In a letter to Miller, Gorky said of *Bull in the Sun*, "The design on the rug is the skin of a water buffalo stretched in the sunny wheatfield. If it looks like something else then it is even better!" Gorky's design did not win, and when the rug made after his design was offered to him for sixty dollars, he was too poor to buy it. On July 15, 1942, he wrote to Vartoosh:

> Dear Vartush, the Modern Museum has bought a big painting [*Garden in Sochi*] of mine two weeks ago and they are going to spend $350 in order to make a colored print so that it will be published in a book. Four or five months ago they asked me to make a design for the Modern Hall [?] and so I did it. They have sent it to the factory which makes modern carpets and two weeks ago they put it on show in the Modern Museum and many people were invited to see it in the exhibition and it looks great. And it will be shown in the major american cities and will be sold. Then they will pay me.
>
> Many journalists from the magazines came to the exhibition and they took a photo of me and Agnes and the head of the museum in front of the carpet. It will be published in town and country and I'll send it to you. We are well and I am very lucky to have a woman like Agnes. . . . For the last three weeks I've been working fifteen hours a day to finish a painting. It looks good and is a commission.

The other Museum of Modern Art show in which Gorky took part was *Twentieth-Century Portraits*, organized by Monroe Wheeler. This was the show in which *Portrait of Ahko* hung next to a portrait by Matisse. "Gorky went to the Museum of Modern Art practically every day to enjoy this beautiful cousinship," Mougouch recalls. "Look how beautiful it is!" he would say.

One 1942 exhibition in which Gorky should have been included was arranged by John Graham for the McMillen Gallery. It presented paintings by Americans such as Stuart Davis, de Kooning, Krasner, Pollock, and Graham himself alongside works by Europeans like Picasso, Braque, and Matisse. The event was considered a breakthrough for the Americans. Gorky must have been disappointed to be left out, but by this time he was no longer a close friend of Graham's. Their friendship had ended when Graham turned from Marxism, modernism, and psychoanalytic theory to autocracy, classicism, and the occult. He rejected abstract art and rescinded his admiration for the artists he had discovered and supported in the 1930s. Even Picasso fell from grace. "Picasso," Graham wrote to David Smith and Dorothy Dehner, is the "best of the international art crooks." After Graham's conversion from modernist to magus, Gorky rarely saw him: Graham had become "too obscurantist," Gorky said.

43

Waterfall

"Agnes and I are leaving town tomorrow morning for a week in Connecticut to the house of a friend of mine who is an artist," Gorky wrote to Vartoosh on August 2, 1942. The friend was Saul Schary, whose country house in New Milford Gorky had visited almost every summer for the past six years. Of Gorky's visit Schary recalled:

> We'd take our painting stuff and go out to do a landscape. He made a beautiful drawing of my apple orchard, where he sat right among the trees. He sat there and he sat there and he looked at this landscape and then he started to paint . . . And I took him down to a ruined mill on the Housatonic River. It was an old silica mill and there were these huge grindstones lying about . . . And just below it, where they took the power from, was a waterfall. And Gorky's drawings of it evolved out of the water falling over the rocks, and splashing up from the rocks and making these kind of strange forms.

Near water Gorky was happy. The Housatonic spilling over boulders brought back memories of the Khoshab River rushing down out of the mountains to his village in Van. "He stood on a rock and he wouldn't come out of that water," said Schary. "He loved it so. It reminded him of a spot back home. He just stood on the rock and let the water flow past him." Schary and his wife kept Gorky's first drawing of the waterfall. Now in the Hirshhorn Museum, it shows how the shapes suggestive of human anatomy in Gorky's two subsequent and more abstract paintings of *Waterfall* (Fig. 151) were conjured as Gorky stood and watched the tumble and curl of falling water.

It was during this sojourn that Gorky began to explore and extend the new freedoms encouraged by Matta. Painting directly from nature helped him loosen his brushwork and trust the movement of turpentine-thinned pigment. The result was the new ease and luxuriance first seen in paintings like *The Pirate I* and *Waterfall*, both begun in 1942. Eight months after his visit, Gorky wrote to Vartoosh: "Last summer Agnes and I spent two weeks outdoors, in the sun, and it worked wonders for us." In her February 1943 letter to Nathalie Campbell, Mougouch said: "Last summer we spent 2 weeks in the country away from N.Y. and during those two weeks Gorky did some very inspiring drawings from nature which have given him great impetus in his work and something quite new and miraculous is resulting, which has meant great exhilaration and of course much tearing of the hair and despair for what he is doing is entirely new for him and at times he feels like a drowning man."

In September Gorky and Mougouch visited her parents in Cape May, New Jersey. They spent many happy hours lying on the beach (Fig. 119 and p. 319) and bicycling over the flat, warm roads. During the visit Gorky met Mougouch's older brother, John Magruder. Like his father, John disapproved of his sister's choice of husband. To both father and son, any man who wasn't involved in the war effort was a shirker. Their views were conservative, and if they were perplexed when Mougouch spouted Communist propaganda, when Gorky made pro-Stalin pronouncements they were furious, even though they saw Gorky's political opinions as something of a joke. One night at dinner everyone began to shout. Gorky pitched in by reciting Mayakovsky's poem "Tovarich Soldat" as loud as he could in Russian. Mougouch recalls with amusement the platoon of naval guards who, on hearing shrieks and raised voices, rushed into the dining room to rescue her father.

Shortly after their Cape May visit, Mougouch discovered that she was pregnant. Gorky's happiness was profound. Now he would establish an American family to replace the Armenian family he had lost when he fled Khorkom and the one he left behind when he changed his name and moved from Boston to New York. Without telling Schary his news, Gorky asked, "What you t'ink, Schary, I have a baby?" Schary warned him that he couldn't afford a child and it would distract him from painting. Gorky was offended. They argued. Schary had always felt that Gorky should have married an Armenian girl who would have taken care of him and made no demands. He didn't really like Mougouch, because he felt she had behaved in a snobbish manner toward his wife, who was in the clothing business. It is easy to imagine Mougouch's aloof response to his suggestion that she join her in the garment industry. She recalls, "We broke off our friendship when Saul came to see us that fall and I was pregnant and he turned on me and said I was going to reduce Gorky to slavery for my own biological fulfillment. Gorky threw Schary out of the studio."

It was not just the sojourn in the country and the nudging of Matta in 1942 that moved Gorky to apply paint to canvas with a greater confidence and expressive power. The change in Gorky's work came also from his feeling of contentment and security in his marriage. His love for Mougouch, his anticipation of fatherhood, and his delight in her appreciation of his work freed his hand and heart. He now gave up his cautious habit of repainting the same canvas over and over again. Fiercely positive in her approach to life, Mougouch made her strength a gift to Gorky. All that mattered was that Gorky should be surrounded by an atmosphere in which his art could flourish.

Although Gorky had none of Vartoosh's snobbery about their mother's priestly heritage and although he had leftist sympathies, in the early years of their relationship he was delighted with Mougouch's blue-blooded Anglo-Saxon background. "He thought my parents were hopeless, but he liked my being upper-crust. I was a catch, Gorky said." He often boasted to friends that his wife's father was an admiral. (In fact he was a captain and, after retirement, a commodore.) "Gorky hated being an immigrant," Mougouch says. He did not seek out other Armenians in New York. "He called Armenians 'these claiming people.' He felt that all minorities are 'claiming people.' " Years later, in a letter to Ethel Schwabacher, Mougouch put it this way: "g. [Gorky] was east, he wanted west, he steeped himself in western painting but he couldn't help his east . . . if only he had not felt the stigma of refugee if he could have been free and proud of his difference but then ifs are not interesting. I know this was one reason I was so important to him because he saw me as the Brooklyn Bridge, I was west. He was very naïve and very dissapointed fundamentally when he found my family for instance just as full of the same human weaknesses as his."

On October 15, 1942, after a visit from Moorad Mooradian (who had taken a film of Gorky and Mougouch dancing on the roof outside their bedroom window), Mougouch wrote Vartoosh with the news that she and Gorky were going to have a baby in March or April. Although she had very little experience with babies, New York Hospital was offering a course in baby care. Moreover, she said, "Gorky is especially wonderful with babies and he had some practice with little Karlen." She and Gorky were "both very well and happy. You would not recognize Gorky if you saw him he had grown so fat . . . not really fat, you know, just solid. Everyone says he looks better than ever before, which of course makes me very happy." Her letter's housewifely tone suggests that she wished to impress her sister-in-law with her domestic virtues: "Gorky has been asking me for a long time to write and ask you how to cook some dish he is very fond of and which he will describe to you at the end of my letter. You would be sweet if you could tell me this because I would love to learn how to cook some more of your country's dishes. I still do not know how to cook lentil soup, and also I want to learn to cook anything else that you might know of as one of Gorky's favorite dishes." At the end of the letter, Gorky added half a page of writing in Armenian: "Dear Vartoosh: Will you write out in very plain letters the recipes for making Chelbour and also lentil soup as they used to make them back at home? With love and kisses—Gorky."

Gorky's work from the early period of his marriage is various. There are a few paintings and studies connected with the *Garden in Sochi* theme. He also worked on portraits and still lifes of flowers, a motif that he took up at different moments in his life, perhaps as a way of staying in touch with nature (Fig. 115). "Gorky spent one winter, 1942, doing many little bouquets," Mougouch recalls. "He sold one painting to an old friend Gaston de Havenon, and he gave a different color scheme to this painting every night for weeks. He was inspired by the flowers of Manet, Zurbarán, and Chardin's painting in Edinburgh." The flower paintings were modeled also on Cézanne and Matisse. Some are nearly abstract. He gave one of the more realistic bouquet paintings to Mougouch's mother on her birthday, May 26, 1942.

After his weeks of working outdoors in Connecticut in the summer of 1942, Gorky's style changed radically. The transformation can be seen in the first version of *Waterfall*, a nearly monochromatic oil on board that was probably done at Saul Schary's and was based on the waterfall at the abandoned mill. The nearly abstract painting appears to show what Schary remembered Gorky to have drawn at the site—water falling over rocks, splashing upward and creating "strange forms." In the painting's top register, the shapes created by splashes look rather like the flowers in some of Gorky's more abstract still lifes. One shape to the right of center has two pointed "ears" and suggests a biomorph, possibly a forebear of the voluptuous creature in the upper right corner of his slightly later *Waterfall* (1942–43) (Fig. 151), now in London's Tate Gallery. In both waterfall paintings, the biomorph seems to dance on top of the water that cascades over rocks and forms a pool below.

Gorky's real breakthrough came in the Tate's *Waterfall*. Here, encouraged by Matta, he added turpentine to his pigment and, to some extent, let the movement of paint discover forms. Another liberating influence at this moment in Gorky's career was Kandinsky, with whom he falsely claimed to have studied. Kandinsky was highly visible both in New York art galleries and on the velvet-clad walls of the Museum of Non-Objective Painting, which opened in June of 1939. (In 1950 it was renamed the Solomon R. Guggenheim Museum.) Gorky had been familiar with Kandinsky's writings since the 1930s, and his library contained various works on Kandinsky. But when Mougouch read the Russian-born Expressionist's *Concerning the Spiritual in Art* out loud to Gorky, Kandinsky's idea that beauty comes from "internal necessity, which springs from the soul" must have appealed to him. From the evidence of Gorky's paintings, what he admired in Kandinsky's work from around 1913 were the plumes of raw color and the way nature-based abstract imagery hovers on the threshold of recognizability. He must also have loved the feeling of flux in Kandinsky's shapes and the way color often separates from line. Starting around 1943, Gorky's color takes on a Kandinsky-like intensity: at first glance the colors in some of his crayon drawings and paintings seem raw, as if they belonged to some primitive Caucasian tradition rather than to the School of Paris. (On second glance, of course, Gorky's color is as subtle and nuanced as in any French painting.)

In the Tate's *Waterfall*, Gorky let turpentine-thinned green paint run, suggesting not only water's fluidity but also a joyous melding of earth, foliage, sky, water, and the human body. Although the painting is abstract, certain shapes are almost recognizable. Various anatomical parts have become detached in a process that Gorky once called the "elevation of the object," that is, the separating of a part from a whole or an object from its context. On the right, what might be an ankle and part of a foot could also be a fallen branch or a boulder. To the left of the "foot," drawn in a black outline over an area of pink and yellow, is what appears to be an erect penis. In a drawing for *Waterfall* (now in the Hirshhorn Museum) the penis is more clearly defined, and just to its left are curving and lobed shapes suggestive of human buttocks and breasts.

Above and to the right of the phallus, an abstract configuration with a black arrow penetrating a red heart surely must allude to the female sexual anatomy. With a child in his wife's belly, Gorky might well have been rejoicing in his own fecundity. Indeed, the idea of fertility, central to Gorky's art, is everywhere in the Tate's *Waterfall*. It resides not only in the painting's more obviously sexual shapes and symbols but also in the merging and metamorphosis of forms, the lushness of greens, the surrendering vulnerability of reds, the urgency of pinks, the melting yellows. Gorky does not just symbolize fertility, he makes colors and shapes correspond to sensations so that the viewer feels it. For example, in the center of *Waterfall*, excitation is conveyed by a small black dart that embeds itself in the surrounding fleshy pink. Just to the left, a curve of pigment begins to drip. Every part of *Waterfall* carries a heightening of the senses. One is reminded of Matisse's insistence that it was not the bodies of his odalisques that were sexual but rather the entire surface of his painting. Likewise in Gorky, the canvas itself becomes an erogenous zone.

The Pirate I (1942) and its sequel, *The Pirate II* (1942–43) (Fig. 116), convey a similar mood of lightness and well-being. Although the imagery is ambiguous, both paintings have a barnyard feel. They seem to be full of rumps and feathers, beaks, bones, and tails. What might be a cat or a dog sits before a descendant of the roosterlike birds in the *Khorkom* series. The lobed shape on the lower right could be a phallus or a bone—what may be another bone with a two-lobed end sits in front of the cat/dog.

Julien Levy knew that it was a mistake to try to pinpoint images in Gorky's work, but often he couldn't resist. In Levy's view, Gorky's abstractions were derived from nature and "basically representational." But they were nature camouflaged. In the upper left corner of *The Pirate I*, for example, he saw the foreshortened rumps of a pair of horses, and he said that Gorky had told him that the painting's subject was based on the "Old Pirate"—a mongrel that occasionally appeared in Gorky's yard. The problem with this theory is that in 1942 Gorky lived in the city and did not have a yard. Perhaps Levy meant Schary's yard or some yard that Gorky remembered from childhood. In any case, Levy had a point—it is hard not to see a seated animal, be it a cat or a dog, in both versions of *The Pirate*. The animal has sproutlike ears and a piratical black patch over one eye. Once you see such an image in one of Gorky's paintings, it is difficult to get rid of it. Had he wished, Gorky could easily have blurred the contours of the cat/dog to make it read as pure abstraction. When he left shapes teetering on the edge of recognizability, he did so for a reason.

Although his financial condition was less precarious than it had been during the Depression years, Gorky continued to worry about money, even more so now that he would be feeding a family of three. Mougouch's mother, Esther, sent them sugar and Vartoosh occasionally sent sugar, rice, and coffee, which Mougouch described to Esther as "pure gold in this town." One of Vartoosh's packages included "all sorts of precious herbs in the cutest white cotton bags she has carefully sewn and marked with the Georgian names which looks ever so attractive but I must confess hasn't helped as Gorky is unaware of their existence in the English language."

Friends tried to help as well. In the summer of 1942, for example, Buckminster Fuller attempted to get Mougouch a job as a magazine researcher and to secure Gorky an assignment to design a *Fortune* magazine cover. The subject of the cover was paper manufacture and "energy per pound foot." Since Gorky had no idea how to illustrate energy per pound foot, Mougouch went down to the corner cigar store and telephoned Fuller. "And clear as a bell, he explained energy per pound foot to me, and I said, 'OK, OK, I'll rush back and tell Gorky.' I rushed back upstairs, and I went blank, absolutely blank. I must have called poor Bucky about six times. Finally, I couldn't anymore, and Gorky and I weren't any closer to understanding it. Nothing came out. All Gorky made were spirals."

It was decided that Mougouch should be the emissary in Gorky's quest for the *Fortune* commission, so, with Gorky's drawing portfolio and Buckminster Fuller's letter of introduction in hand, she went to see Peter

Piening, the magazine's art director. Piening looked through the drawings and stopped at Gorky's poster-paint copy of Picasso's *Lysistrata*.
"Can't this man make up his mind what he wants to be, Léger or Picasso?" he asked. Mougouch, who had no idea that Gorky's Lysistrata
drawings were copied from Picasso's, drew herself up and said, "What do
you mean?" Piening told her, "This is just straight Picasso." Mougouch
said, "I don't believe you." Piening said, "Well, come back tomorrow and
I'll bring you the Picasso. Just leave this portfolio with me. I'll think
about it."

Mougouch returned home and said nothing to Gorky about Piening's reaction. When she returned to *Fortune* the next day and Piening
showed her a reproduction of Picasso's *Lysistrata*, she was mortified. "I
couldn't see how Gorky could let me get into such a mad trap, and I
never ever told him. I did tell him about Piening's remark that his work
looked like Picasso and Léger, because he was quite used to that kind of
reaction." The upshot was that Piening asked Mougouch to bring in
some of her own drawings. Perhaps he might be able to give her a job in
the layout department. But when she tried to draw she realized that her
drawings were not good enough, so Gorky made some pen-and-ink drawings for her. "I drew a little bit, and he did most of it. I drew, for example,
a part of a pair of gloves, which Gorky finished. And Peter Piening said,
'You are just bursting with talent! I'll take you on right away. You're
hired.' You see, Gorky was very relaxed when he was drawing something
that was supposed to be by me. He didn't worry about making something
perfect." Gorky was pleased that his wife had landed a well-paid job,
but when he learned that each month when the magazine was "put to
bed" she would have to work overtime, he was suspicious. Overtime, he
thought, was just an excuse for Piening to be alone with Mougouch.
"Anyhow, I then discovered that I was pregnant, so I called and said I was
pregnant and couldn't take the job."

Pregnancy notwithstanding, Mougouch took another job, with the
British Purchasing Commission (working on lend-lease) secured for her
by Barbara Chermayeff, who was employed there as well. For four or five
months she earned thirty dollars a week. She wrote to her mother in November not to worry about her getting tired, for "Gorky cooks & cleans."
A December 8, 1942, letter from Esther Magruder to Mougouch's
brother, John, said, "Aggie still has her job with the British Purchase
Company and hopes to keep it till after Xmas. I bought her some nice

dresses for her form when I was last up [in New York] and she is so lucky to feel well." A month or so later, having become visibly pregnant, Agnes was fired.

In November 1942 Dorothy Miller wrote to Gorky inviting him to participate in a show juxtaposing abstraction with various kinds of realism that she was organizing for the Museum of Modern Art. Scheduled to open in 1943, it would be one of a series of American shows Miller would curate over the years. Gorky wrote to the Mooradians:

Dearest Murad and Vartush.

I received your telegram and the 100 dollars you sent me. Many thanks from my heart. Next Monday I'll send you 40–50 dollars and after a week or two, my dear ones, the remainder. I wanted to come to visit you but only after I have finished this work and a few days ago the head of the Modern Museum came to the studio and wants to take seven paintings to the Modern Museum and he said they would buy two of them. And so after that I will come and stay with you for a short while. I wish you a happy New Year. Health and success and I know that Karlen is better

With kisses and lots of love

Your Gorghi

Gorky was soon to be disappointed. Dorothy Miller's superiors at the Museum decided that it would be better to show only the figurative artists on her list. In December she wrote to the abstract contingent telling the artists that their part of the show was postponed. Gorky had to wait until 1946, when Miller put together *Fourteen Americans.* For the forty-two-year-old Gorky, who longed for recognition and who hadn't had a New York exhibition in seven years, that was a long wait.

On February 17, 1943, Gorky wrote to Vartoosh: "Two weeks ago we sold two more paintings. That will tide us over the next few months. Mrs. Metzger also is contemplating buying a picture. I am doing very lovely personal pictures these days." Sorry to hear that Vartoosh had been sick, he offered his usual remedy: "When summer comes, you must get a lot of sunshine; you must give the sun's rays a chance to work into your body." He went on to give his sister important news. After their baby was born, he and Mougouch were planning to go to the farm her mother had just bought in Lincoln, Virginia:

Agnes's parents have acquired a large farm, some 110 acres, this year. We are going there this summer, where I shall do some work on landscape, provided, of course, that the place is sufficiently furnished for habitation; it's bare right now. If this succeeds, even you and Karlen should come to spend a month or so there. I think it will be fine.

I'm writing to Satenik and Akaby tonight. Have received no letters from Akaby. Wonder if she is peeved. Why, I would not know . . .

We just had a telephone installed in our apartment, and Agnes is busy on it . . .

Darling, I am very happy. Agnes takes good care of me, she's just wonderful. If you were closer it would be so much better . . .

Always your loving brother, Gorky

On a snowy February evening, Gorky and Mougouch, now seven months pregnant, prepared a dinner party for Fernand Léger. At nine o'clock, together with David and Mary Burliuk, they were still awaiting Léger's arrival. Mougouch passed the time by knitting, Burliuk by drawing Gorky, who was nervous with anticipation. Mary Burliuk's gaze traveled around the studio and lit on a huge red sofa with white pillows. "It does not belong to us," said Mougouch, knowing that the sofa looked out of character in this spartan environment. "A friend of my mother moved to California and gave it to me to make my home more comfortable, more—as she put it—rich looking." Next Mary's gaze shifted to six pen sketches thumbtacked to the studio wall, and then to Gorky's work table beneath the dust-layered north window. There lay Gorky's palette, "cleanly scrubbed and bare," and a tumbler with dried-out flowers stood beside the faded photograph of Gorky and his mother.

Finally, when the four friends had begun to feel tired and hungry, the buzzer rang. Mougouch opened the door to the hall and called out in French, "Come up one floor and you will find us." "Oh, what a dreadful storm!" bellowed Léger from below. "New York is a cold city!" he exclaimed as he entered. "Look at the muffler, gloves, overshoes, but still I feel among your tall New York buildings as if I were in Switzerland!" Gorky was, Mary Burliuk recalled, "overwhelmed with emotion. Fernand Léger was in his studio. Fernand Léger was his guest." Perhaps remembering the uncooked pot au feu disaster when Léger dined with them in San Francisco, this time Gorky and Mougouch had prepared most of the meal in advance. Léger, who had the reputation of being a great cook, took over the tiny kitchen and began to prepare steaks in the French way.

It was, according to Mougouch, a lighthearted evening. Gorky adored Léger's peasantlike warmth and energy, his robust humor. He listened with delight when Léger told him that he wanted to paint a huge mural in Times Square using a broom as a brush or when Léger said, "In France we put the Surrealists in our pocket. They served us. We didn't serve them." Gorky was even more gratified when the childless Léger told him that he envied Gorky's imminent paternity. In a 1949 issue of *Color and Rhyme*, Mary Burliuk described the evening at 36 Union Square:

> The food served and eaten. It is late now. Léger is on the giant sofa. He speaks. He speaks French only. In five years in the States he did not learn one English sentence.
>
> "I always have an interpreter," he explains. "A study of a new language would take me away from my art. I am a Frenchman, and that is good enough for me. Now if you are not in the mood to show me your paintings—don't do it. One's heart belongs to his art and not always one can open his heart. But I would like for Agness [*sic*] to tell me everything about Arshile's childhood. I want to know what made him feel that he must paint."
>
> I felt sorry for poor Arshile. I felt sorry to see him so confused, shaken, almost crushed by the presence of Fernand Léger in his studio. Agness began to translate her husband's quiet, deep, moving words.

Gorky retold a favorite story from his childhood—a story that clearly had archetypal significance to him:

> I remember myself when I was five years old. The year I first began to speak. Mother and I are going to church. We are there. For a while she left me standing before a painting. It was a painting of infernal regions. There were angels on the painting. White angels. And black angels. All the black angels were going to Hades. I looked at myself. I am black, too. It means there is no Heaven for

me. A child's heart could not accept it. And I decided there and then to prove to the world that a black angel can be good, too, must be good and wants to give his inner goodness to the whole world, black and white world . . .

After that I remember faces. They are all green. And in my country in the mountains of the Caucasus is a famine. I see gigantic stones and snow on the mountain peaks. And there is a murmur of a brook below, and a voice sings. And this is the song.

Gorky now began to sing.

David Burliuk was one of a number of Gorky admirers who tried to find buyers for his work. When he succeeded, he took a commission— sometimes money, sometimes art. Mougouch recalls that when the Burliuks came to dinner, Gorky would always give them one of his paintings—usually a gouache—done on the cardboards that came inside his laundered shirts. The Burliuks would be halfway down the stairs when the voluminous David would rush back upstairs saying, "You haven't signed it!" Gorky was always amused by this performance. When he signed such pictures, he often put the date when the gift was made rather than the date when the painting was made. Sometimes he inscribed a gift. A 1942 ink drawing of a Picassoid head says: "To dear Mrs. Burliuk and dear Mr. David Burliuk—thinking of the joy you give people—gave to the Gorkys Arshile & Mougouch."

Not long after the dinner for Léger, Burliuk told Gorky that he had a patron who wanted to get to know painters, and on March 20 Burliuk brought the collector Joseph H. Hirshhorn to the studio. Mougouch remembers Hirshhorn as "a small dark man, full of enthusiasm. He made nouveau-riche remarks, and he chose very nice things. He liked the little paintings with people in them, not the abstract ones. For about six hundred dollars he got a large pile of Gorky's little paintings on shirt cardboards—the ones Gorky called "valentines"—and gave away when people came to dinner. Gorky did not show Hirshhorn his larger paintings." Hirshhorn's reaction to Gorky is recorded: "He looked like a great big Turk. I loved him." On that first buying spree Hirshhorn bought sixteen of the Gorkys that are in the Hirshhorn Museum. Eventually he added thirteen more to the collection. After Hirshhorn left that March evening, Gorky, Mougouch, and Burliuk celebrated with a whiskey cocktail and Gorky gave Burliuk a painting in gratitude.

Shortly before or after Hirshhorn's visit, Gorky signed, dated, and titled some of the paintings that he sold to Hirshhorn. He did not think dates or titles were important, and he tended to name his paintings only when a buyer or a dealer asked him to. "I'd been reading Mallarmé to Gorky and that's why he titled one of the paintings *Child of an Indumean Night,*" Mougouch recalls. The dates he put on the Hirshhorn paintings were mostly wrong. Paintings from the 1930s were dated in the 1920s. Gorky is said to have checked on the age at which an artist idol painted a certain work and then adjusted the date of his own painting so that it would appear to have been made at the same age.

On April 5, two days after her doctor told her that her baby would not come for another two or three weeks, Mougouch gave birth to a daughter whom she and Gorky named Maro. The previous evening Esther had come to dinner, after which she and Mougouch and Gorky had gone to a movie. "I suddenly realized I was sitting in a puddle of water and my mother said, 'Oh, your water's dripping, darling!' and we rushed around the corner to the studio to pick up my little suitcase, and Gorky and my mother took me in a taxi up to New York Hospital. It must have been about ten o'clock at night." Esther wrote to her son, John: "They sent Gorky and me away at about 1:30 and I went home with him and we sat up most of the night keeping each other's spirits up and throwing Bubbles's ball!" (Bubbles was the Magruders' dog.) Maro was born at about 8:30 the following morning. According to Mougouch, when her mother telephoned, she asked, "What color is it?" After seeing the eight-pound baby, Esther wrote to John: "Aggie is very well and the baby looks like all babies tho I think she has a lot of personality in her small face. A nice shaped head with flat little ears and a cute deep cut chin. So far the much talked of nose is only a small button. She has the usual amount of dark hair which will all come off anyway. She seems very healthy and everything is fine all around. Gorky behaved very well thru it all." Captain Magruder's response to becoming a grandfather is recorded in his May 24 letter to John: "The little Gorky MARU—seems to be shaking down in fine order from reports from 36 Union Square . . . Wait till the button of a *nose* develops, say I!!"

Mougouch's hospital table was full of flowers. Serge Chermayeff sent a bouquet addressed "To Princess Mougouch," which intrigued the ward nurses, who decided that she must be some kind of royalty. The hospital kept strict visiting days and hours and Gorky had to wait two days before he could see his wife and child. When he finally came into the maternity ward he had just seen Maro in the nursery. "He'd done a dance in front of the window." Having been terrified of having male offspring, Gorky was delighted with his small daughter. Maro looked just like a Leonardo da Vinci, he said, and indeed, as she grew older, she did resemble a Leonardo angel. "She arrived all smooth," Mougouch recalls. "Her features were exactly as they were later, and her eyes were a wonderful spinach green." Gorky wrote a kind of poem to Mougouch and sent it to the hospital:

> My Darling Mougouch
> My sweet Heart
> My Wife
> [Here he drew a small sketch of a family of three.]
> I love you and love you
> And love Our little
> Maro
> I miss you my
> Dearest
> The House is—all right the painters are working at
> Forgive me my Darling, I can't write clearly— . . . I love you
> Our Maro.—[Here he drew two hearts.] yours
>   All yours my
>   Darling
>   Arshile

On May 3 Gorky wrote to Vartoosh and Moorad: "Sweet ones, we are most happy and our little Maro is so beautiful. She is a quiet baby and cries only when hungry. And we all express out heartfelt thanks for your present which we have put in the bank. We wish to buy a war bond for Maro with it. And so we are happy."

Gorky and Mougouch chose the name Maro because they wanted a name from his part of the world, and Maro was the pseudonym of the revolutionary heroine Miriam Vardanian, who, with her husband, Avetis Nazarbekian, was a founder of the Hunchak Party. (Nazarbekian visited Gorky in New York in 1934.) "Gorky said Maro was a fearless horse-woman who led a troop of revolutionary men in the mountains. (He said Caucasus, but it was Armenia.)"

In preparation for Maro's return from the hospital, Gorky went into a frenzy of fixing up 36 Union Square: "He washed the studio from head to foot and he scraped all the black paint off the round oak pedestal table. He bought flowers and put up a welcome home sign. He tried to build a cradle but it fell apart. He built a sort of screen around the studio sink where he washed his brushes so that I would have a place to put dishes and food. Before that, I'd washed the dishes in the bathtub be-cause I didn't want to disturb Gorky."

After ten days, Gorky brought Mougouch and Maro home. A Miss Wilkes, a tall, gray-haired Yorkshire woman hired by Esther, was waiting for them:

> She was used to taking care of much grander people where her meals were brought up to her on trays. I put the baby in a basinette that was a laundry basket. This was already pretty hard on Miss Wilkes, who tried to make pads so that the baby's head wouldn't get bumped by the basket. She slept with the baby in the spare room, which Gorky had cleaned and painted and put a bed in. The first evening we were home Miss Wilkes and Gorky got drunk. Gorky was exhausted. To relieve Miss Wilkes's despair, Gorky plied her with whiskey and he and she collapsed on the couch in a state of euphoria.

For about ten days, Mougouch tried to breastfeed Maro, but her milk dried up and Maro was put on formula. When the time came for the first home visit from a pediatrician, Miss Wilkes recommended a Dr. Bartlett. Mougouch made an appointment, but when she learned from her great-aunt Marion Hosmer that Dr. Bartlett was the most expensive doctor in New York, she canceled the appointment, saying that she couldn't pay his fees. He came the next day anyway and never charged for his services:

> He came in and took off his fedora with a great swoop, and he said "Maestro" to Gorky. Then he offered Gorky a cigar and Gorky was

appalled and went green after the first puff. And Dr. Bartlett went on smoking his cigar and he blew a large cloud of smoke at Maro. "She's perfect," he said, and he told me nothing would go wrong. However, on Mrs. Wilkes's first day off it was terrible. Maro had hiccups and we watched the hiccups and Gorky said, "Oh, Mougouch, she's going to die!" I shrieked out of the window for Miss Wilkes: "Miss Wilkes! Come back! She's dying!" Miss Wilkes came rushing back and told us what to do.

Ethel Schwabacher gave them a huge English pram that her own two children had used, and Miss Wilkes taught Gorky how to maneuver it down the stairs. Greatly enjoying the splendid carriage and proud to show off his child, Gorky took Maro for frequent walks. "The first time Gorky took the baby out," Mougouch recalls, "he practically dumped her on the sidewalk, because he ran right into the curbstone." An extraordinarily tender father, Gorky gazed at his baby with a rapt expression on his face. He sang and danced holding Maro in the palm of his huge hand. A photograph taken when Maro was about four months old shows him squatting on the grass and bathing Maro in what looks like a baking pan (Fig. 121). "Gorky's life was transformed by having children," says Mougouch. "He was a family man. It made him feel alive."

Being a father also made Gorky's life as a painter more difficult, by both straining his finances and disrupting his work. "The studio, me, and the baby, and the formula, and the clutter, and the bang," Mougouch recalls. In spite of the tumult, they were happy. "Gorky painted and sang and played his radio, and that part was all right, but it wasn't going to be all right for very long. I would put the baby in the carriage beside the window. I wasn't keen on promenading this ridiculous carriage. I took Maro out and the soot in New York was terrible. I would put her near the window to get the sun and she'd get covered with black soot—she'd have black spots on her eyelids."

When the possibility of spending some months at the Magruders' farm in Virginia was offered to them, Gorky and Mougouch were delighted. They didn't care if the house was not yet furnished—they would fix it up. Their idea had been that they would be alone at Crooked Run Farm until her father came back from the war, but when Esther heard that they wanted to go to Virginia, she said, "Oh, what a lovely idea! We'll all go out." Captain Magruder's May 24, 1943, letter to his son said: "They will soon be moving down to the farm. They haven't much to furnish it with except packing cases & the Filipino furniture I had down at Cape May—& oh yes the ubiquitous 'screens' & 'scrolls.' But I wish I could be with them. Your ma will probably get gyped on every turn as a 'city slicker' and I bet Gorky will be a scream."

❈ PART X ❈

Gorky drawing at Crooked Run Farm, 1943 or 1944

44

Virginia

※

In early June 1943, Jeanne Reynal and Urban Neininger drove the Gorky family from New York to Crooked Run Farm in Lincoln, an old Quaker town in northern Virginia. Since "Ma's folly," as Mougouch's father called his wife's new property, was not yet habitable, the foursome spent several nights at a house that Esther had rented from neighbors named Maclean. The morning after their arrival, they went to look at the farm. Situated on a hilltop, the farmhouse (Fig. 123) had (and still has) a view of sloping fields rimmed by rolling hills. At the bottom of the hill, hidden by trees, was Crooked Run, a shallow, stone-filled creek beside which grasses and weeds grew six feet tall. Being on a farm reminded Gorky of his childhood in Khorkom, although the Virginia landscape, with its low, gently curving horizon softened by treetops profiled against the sky, could not have been more different from the often snow-covered rock mountains, the volcanos, and the vast expanses of parched straw-colored earth around Lake Van. The fields that spread downward in all directions from the farmhouse were delimited by trees, gates, fences, and hedge-rows. These boundaries and signs of ownership were comforting. Open yet encompassing, Crooked Run Farm felt to him like a haven that could not be taken away. Here Gorky's bitter feeling of dispossession clawed less fiercely at his refugee soul. But fear of loss was never far from his heart: a year later he would name a painting *They Will Take My Island.*

Gorky described this new landscape to his wife as having "no out of bounds." In spite of the fences and hedgerows, one stretch of green flowed into another. As with the abstract landscape drawings that he would produce that summer, there were boundaries but no barriers for the eye. And, solace to a man who had witnessed starvation, the earth was so fertile that the idea of hunger seemed remote. In the moist summer heat, the land seemed to crackle and hum. Such heat dissolves separateness and Gorky rejoiced in being part of Virginia's burgeoning growth. "Gorky adored Virginia," Mougouch recalls:

> He'd never seen fireflies before. He'd never seen milkweed before. We were there until late November. We had a change of seasons—the ripening in the fields. Gorky loved to watch the seasons change. He loved spring. He did not like the cold. He loved dawn and nightfall. He loved the hills and he loved to explore the countryside. We used to take long walks over the hills and we discovered houses that we were going to live in forever. He found Virginia's soft light was very different from the light in New York. The landscape in Virginia was very *accidenté*. It was full of variety. He loved the weeds. He liked things that happen, things that stood out. He liked features. He didn't like a landscape to be just a monotonous woods. Louden County had a large variety of shapes, hills, rills, trees bending over brooks. All this he observed rather like going to the theater and looking at the stage set. If he was interested in the play he would look also at how someone had set the stage up to accentuate the thought in the play.

Mougouch's theater image is apt: many of Gorky's Virginia-inspired works have a stagelike space that does not take away from the idea of boundlessness.

A few old maples shaded Crooked Run's modest two-story white clapboard house, built between 1760 and 1790. (The kitchen wing, shown to the right in a painting Gorky made of the house that first summer, was a later addition.) Downstairs in the oldest part of the house was a low-ceilinged living room with walls so thick they made the windows look like niches. Off the living room was a small room where Gorky and Mougouch put Maro's crib. Upstairs were two bedrooms separated by a bathroom. Esther slept in one, Gorky and Mougouch in the other.

In the summer months they spent most of their time out of doors. Gorky was, as Mougouch put it, "fearfully attached to the sun." To him the sun was not only a source of health but a determiner of mood. On bright days they put Maro's cot outside. "We cooked her several times," says Mougouch. Esther bought garden furniture—a chaise and white Adirondack chairs and a small rolling table for endless pitchers of lemonade or for cocktails. A photograph taken in July or August of 1943 shows Gorky and his mother-in-law sitting in the Adirondack chairs (Fig. 122). Esther, a dainty and elegant woman in her midforties, smiles as she listens to a barefoot Gorky, who holds Maro and, as was his habit, talks with his hands and with his amused and engaging eyes. Beside his patrician companion he looks like an exotic creature, but he was unabashed by Esther's upper-class airs. "He got on very well with WASPs, especially WASP women," Mougouch recalls. "They liked him and he liked them. He was a big hit with a wealthy Washington dowager who was the hostess at a wedding we went to that summer. Gorky had great self-confidence. He poured himself out to Mrs. Wilson, the bride's godmother, and she fell in love with him. She made Gorky dance about the dining room and she danced with him."

Esther and her husband developed a guarded affection for Gorky. They loved to tease him, and, although he was more formal with his father-in-law, of whose underlying disapproval he surely was aware, Gorky teased Esther, who was only a few years older than he. "Mother knew Gorky very well in a purely human way," Mougouch observed to Ethel Schwabacher. His understanding of Esther was "without any psychological involvements and though g. complained a lot about her (he was vicious about everyone at times) he was very fond of her and she of him." For all this geniality, Gorky continued to scorn the conventionality that he thought came with his mother-in-law's WASP upbringing. "He disapproved of American women's estrangement from tears and tenderness. He thought they had a princess complex, all of them—except me!" Once when Esther and her husband were arguing, Gorky advised: "Why don't you just put her over your knee and spank her?" The Magruders thought this was funny. They did not understand that Gorky meant it, or something like it, and that such an attitude toward women was part of his culture. Another time, when Gorky and Mougouch were asked to dinner by a Quaker gentleman farmer who advised the Magruders on agricultural matters, Gorky shocked his host by calling his mother-in-law spoiled. His host's response was, "Gorky, that would sound much better if you weren't living in her house."

Esther's frequent returns to her Washington home eased family tensions. One of those tensions came from conflicts in taste. Esther wanted her home to be proper and her lawn neatly mown, whereas Gorky wanted to strip the furniture and let the lawn grow into a field of tall grasses. When he and Mougouch went on strike and refused to mow, Esther, knowing that her daughter would rush to her aid, began to wield the mower herself. Another bone of contention between Gorky and his mother-in-law was her hair. "Gorky attacked my mother because she curled her hair." Curling hair, like mowing grass, was against nature. Worse still, it was vampish—not modest and pure like his mother.

Mougouch remembers the daily routine in Virginia as follows: "I got up at six to feed the baby. Gorky woke at about this time. I would take a breakfast tray upstairs to my mother to keep her out of the kitchen." Some days they would wake to find the neighbor's cows outside the house, and they would all race out to chase them away. Mougouch's sister remembers waking early one morning to find Mougouch and Gorky nearly naked trying to eject the cows from the vegetable garden. After breakfast Mougouch would clean up, put Maro in the sun, and work in the vegetable garden, while Gorky went to his improvised studio to prepare paper on a drawing board. The first summer in Virginia he produced one or two drawings each day and did almost no painting. Getting ready for work was, for Gorky, always an elaborate ritual. He would take his drawing materials, his drawing board, and a small folding stool and go out into the fields for three or four hours in the morning, come back for lunch, and go out again in the afternoon (p. 411). Each day he carefully considered his choice of motif. He had a number of favorite drawing spots—for example, by the brook or near the house looking down the field to the line of trees at the bottom. He would return to these places again and again. "It took Gorky a long time to settle down to draw," Mougouch recalls. "First he had to beat the bushes with his stick and he had to flatten the grass because he was terrified of snakes. Then he'd talk to the cows." When his site was cleared of dangers he would place his stool on the grass and his drawing board on his knees and go to work. Once he began working, his concentration was total. If cows gathered around him he didn't notice. Even his wife and mother-in-law chasing and hooting at the neighbor's trespassing cows escaped his attention.

"Gorky hasn't been doing anything," Esther would tease when Gorky came home for lunch. "We've been hoeing the garden, so we get two kidneys and Gorky only gets one." This kind of remark infuriated Mougouch. Sometimes after lunch he joined her in the vegetable garden. He loved working the soil and watching things grow. In the evenings she cooked and they ate in the living room. When the nights grew chilly, Gorky built a fire and after dinner Mougouch read to him as he drew. "He used to make those little drawings after tea or dinner when we were all sitting around talking or playing Chinese checkers . . . all being mother and myself." Occasionally Gorky and Mougouch went for an evening stroll. Once, on their way home, the moon came up over a hill and Gorky spoke of being a small boy in the mountains and seeing for the first time the full moon rise. He was so terrified, he said, that he ran the whole way home.

During his first days at Crooked Run, Gorky was preoccupied with sweeping and fixing up the cow barn as a studio. He loved the rough-hewn barn with its view of distant hills and of the pump house, the milking shed, and the house's kitchen wing. He found ancient farm implements rusting in the fields and hung them from the barn beams. He collected weatherworn cow bones and the pelvic bone of a horse, which he compared to the Winged Victory. "When the studio was all fixed and laid out just so and his tables and easel were set up, Gorky went out into the fields. The first drawings he made that summer were very hesitant. They were Cézannesque watercolors. Then he abandoned watercolor and took to pencil and crayon." Very likely the idea of using pencil and crayon came from Matta's early drawings. Indeed, it is in Gorky's drawings from the summer of 1943 that he comes closest to Matta.

After several days of struggling with the landscape and not feeling able to make a drawing that satisfied him, Gorky produced one that looked different from anything he had done before. "Gorky came back one day with this rather complicated drawing," Mougouch recalls, "and he said, 'Will anybody understand this? What do you think it is? Do you think I'm mad? Does it look like a drawing to you?' I said I thought it was marvelous and told him to go and make more of them."

The extraordinary transformation in Gorky's vision in the summer of 1943 came from having months in which to embed himself in the landscape through drawing it. After his endless training, his effort to equal Ingres, Cézanne, and Picasso, he was confident that his fingers had the skill to create the forms that he saw, felt, and imagined. Now that intimacy with nature brought him closer to himself, parts of Gorky's form-making genius that had lain dormant came to the surface. In a letter to her great-aunt Nathalie Campbell written the following December, Mougouch spoke of what Gorky's first full exposure to the country meant:

> The country was a great inspiration to Gorky. He was again a small child, not having been to the country for any length of time since he was 6 yrs old and his vision was clear and untramelled by habit. He made only drawings, as he found that paintings took too long and he had too much to put down, and paintings anyway are better when not done from nature. Nature (he says) is so complex and confusing and one is too apt to get tired and take the easiest way out. A drawing is more direct and automatic, or should be, to have the lyrical freshness that a drawing should have, like a poem. He made well over 100 drawings. This summer was the real release of Gorky. He was able to discover himself and what he has done is to create a world of his own but a world equal to nature, with the infinite complexities of nature and yet sweet, secretive and playful as nature is. They are not easily understood but then neither is nature, and to those free enough to follow him they are v. wonderful. There is talk of his having a show of these drawings and if it does come off and has any success we can go back next year.

Mougouch's admiration for Gorky's new work was a necessary support. She was the only person around who understood. The taste of the local Virginians was too conservative for them to have any inkling of what Gorky was doing. To this day there are people in the nearby town of Lincoln who smile at the memory of the crazy Gorky who sat out in the hot fields wearing overalls, a Navajo vest embroidered with a bold red, white, and black zigzag pattern (a gift from Jeanne Reynal), and a wool cap or a bandana tied around the crown of his head. Asa Moore Janney, who owned A. M. Janney & Co., the local store in Lincoln, recalls: "We all thought he was nuts. Someone told me that Gorky just dips his brush and throws paint at the canvas. Then he charges money for it. All the stick-in-the-muds around here thought Gorky was crazy as hell. He went around in overalls with a bib and that's all. I don't believe he had shorts on underneath the overalls. To a staid old Quaker like me that was something. No one except Gorky walked on these roads in bare feet. He had a very tall stick like a shepherd's crook and he'd walk up the road with it."

The postman, Louis Magvich, was "flabbergasted" at Gorky's appearance. He would tell stories about his encounters with this "barefoot wild man wearing odd clothes out on the road." Once when he went to Crooked Run Farm to deliver a special delivery letter, he passed Gorky seated on his drawing stool near the gate. The postman asked Gorky, "Will you sign for this special delivery letter for Captain Magruder?" Gorky said, "Can't you leave me alone? Can't you see what I'm doing? I'm inventing, just like you invented corn liquor!" On one of her rambles through the fields Mougouch met up with a farmer. "Have you seen Gorky?" she asked. When the farmer replied in the affirmative, she asked, "Was he working?" The farmer answered: "He was looking up and then down, if you call that work." For all their bafflement, the local people liked Gorky, because, as Asa Janney put it, he was full of fun: "He'd make you laugh. But there was a seething somewhere down underneath there. Gorky came to Lincoln two or three times a week to pick up the mail. He'd come to my store to chat. He and I would talk for an hour or so. Gorky said he came from Odessa and that he had been glad to get out of Russia. He said that he came out under cover, that he had sneaked out."

A local farmer who liked to stand behind Gorky and watch him draw once patted him on the back and said, "Well, if you keep going perhaps you'll get somewhere eventually." Gorky loved to tell about the time he organized a private showing of his drawings in his barn/studio, and Jim Cole, a farmer and neighbor, looked around and, feeling he must say something, said, "Flashy, ain't it?" At a shish kebab party that Gorky and Mougouch organized for local friends, Gorky grew mischieveous after a few drinks and shocked his Quaker neighbors by telling one of his favorite outrageous stories. He said that he could prove that Christ had returned to the world because a pubic hair identifiable as belonging to the Savior had been found on a prostitute's belly. (Actually, Gorky stole this story from that Surrealist bible Lautréamont's *Les chants de Maldoror*.) Fortunately, none of his Virginian guests took offense. They had already decided that Gorky was a lunatic.

Even as they purchased, fixed up, and inhabited in their imaginations every old farmhouse they passed on their walks, Gorky and Mougouch realized that they could not live permanently in Virginia. They found it lacking in cultural nourishment. But they did make a few good friends. Among the closest were their neighbors Thomas and Mary Taylor, who, like everybody else, were astonished at Gorky's attire and at the way he walked barefoot on the rock-strewn roads. The Taylors and the Gorkys occasionally shared picnic dinners at which Gorky made shashlik and helped with the dishes. "He had to have the dishes clean before he started washing them," Thomas Taylor recalls. After supper they sat around talking of the land, the crops, their children—the Taylors had a one-year-old son and a daughter Maro's age. "My favorite Gorky story," says Thomas Taylor, "happened soon after we'd remodeled our house. Our son was born in 1942 and our daughter in 1943, and we had a room off our bedroom called the children's room. The children were allowed to do what they pleased with crayons. They crayoned the walls and even the ceiling. We suggested that Gorky come up to see this. He walked in and said: 'But, this is wonderful! This is what I am trying to do!' " On one of these evenings, Taylor recalls, they were sitting on the back steps of the Taylors' house after dinner when Gorky complained that in the United States nobody sang. He insisted that the Taylors and Mougouch sing. "In my country everybody sings," he said. "In my country peasants sing at their labor." Mr. Taylor remembers Gorky as being "awfully good company. He told jokes, laughed. He had a light laugh. Sometimes you'd think this guy wasn't entirely reliable about what he said. He said he spent years in museums copying painting. If he'd spent that much time, he'd be twice as old as he was."

Mary Taylor, a kind and gentle woman, was, she says, much too timid to talk with Gorky about art. But one evening at Crooked Run Farm she noticed a representational painting, perhaps the flower painting that Gorky had given to Esther, hanging over the fireplace. "It's lovely!" she exclaimed. "It's like a dream!" Gorky said. "That's right! It is a dream!" But Gorky knew that his abstract drawings and paintings baffled the Taylors, and one day he attempted to clarify what a drawing that he had given them was about. "Gorky took us down by the hill, thirty or forty yards southeast of the Magruder house," Thomas Taylor recalls. "We had our backs to the driveway and the house behind us and to the right and the barn behind to the left. He was facing the creek at the bottom of the hill, almost straight south. The peach tree that you see in the drawing was near him and the fence line. He said, 'Here is this and this and this and this.' You could see it in the drawing, but you couldn't see it before he pointed it out." Gorky's in-laws, too, were dismayed by his work. One day when Gorky was sitting to the side of the house drawing a view that included two sycamore trees, Esther came out, looked back and forth from drawing to landscape, and said, "How on earth could you make a drawing like that out of two such beautiful trees as these?" Gorky answered, "I'm not drawing the trees. I'm drawing the space between the trees."

To understand the blossoming of Gorky's draftsmanly imagination in 1943 and in two subsequent summers at Crooked Run, it helps to picture him spending hours and hours in the sun-drenched fields, sitting on his low stool, his drawing board propped on his thighs and steadied by his left hand. What happened as he held the sharp lead of his pencil to the paper pinned to his board was a strange kind of mental combustion that freed him to look in and out at the same time. He looked at the landscape and, almost without thinking, made his mark on the paper. When he looked at the landscape again, the lines he had drawn altered what he saw and prompted what his next mark would be. Neither doubts, nor self-consciousness, nor the burden of art history blocked the flow of invention. As time passed and Gorky became more and more a part of the landscape, everything that surrounded him seemed alive. And it was: in the heat of a Virginia summer, the peep, rustle, and buzz of creatures and grasses was all-encompassing.

Later Gorky explained one of his drawings to his friend Robert Jonas: "You see, these are the leaves, this is the grass. I got down close to see it. I got them from getting down close to the earth. I could hear it and smell it. Like a little world down there." When James Johnson Sweeny wrote about Gorky's drawings from the summer of 1943 in a 1944 issue of *Harper's Bazaar*, he said that Gorky had told him he had decided to "look into the grass." When he looked into the grass, he looked with such fierce concentration that his vision turned inward and scooped up memory.

"Gorky worked *in* the landscape," Mougouch says. "He thought the landscape was a part of the drawing. The landscape was *in* the drawing, as opposed to looking at it and then drawing it." Gorky's immersion in the fertile Virginia earth resulted in a series of drawings in which space seems to surround the viewer. In *Composition II* and *Drawing* (Figs. 125 and 154), for example, there is no horizon line and biomorphs drawn in pencil and frolicking in the midst of crayoned plumes of color give us no sense of here or there. We are not outside looking at the scenery but rather in the midst of stems, petals, leaves, branches, and twigs.

Gorky's swift, firm pencil lines moving around and between bursts of colored crayon responded as much to his emotion as to what his eyes saw. As they curve and loop they seem to trace some dream anatomy located deep within his psyche. The mixture of sensuousness with intricacy and precision in his drawings justifies Ethel Schwabacher's naming Gorky the "Ingres of the unconscious." When he drew, the circuits between his eye, his hand, the shapes and lines appearing on the paper, and the complex interplay between feeling, memory, and knowledge, seem to have functioned perfectly. The connections happened so quickly that Gorky himself was surprised at what emerged on his drawing board. In her 1949 letter to Ethel Schwabacher, Mougouch wrote: "The aesthetic intention as seen from Gorky's point of view is practically impossible to define . . . In the first place G himself did not always know what he intended and was as surprised as a stranger at what the drawing became after an hour of work . . . It seemed to suggest itself to him constantly, the way it does to children except of course he had all the techniques and mastery of his art and other idioms at his fingertips."

From the beginning Mougouch had an intuitive understanding of Gorky's creative process. "Nature to Gorky was a jumping-off point," she says:

> He felt the earth as a swell, a bosom, an expansion like a sigh. Nature was part of him. There were things that he did as he drew from nature—there were shapes that were transformations or incantations or representations of images he had inside him already. He saw fantastic animals and menacing heads in the shapes of trees. And he saw it all in terms that were activated.
>
> The interaction of shapes was terribly important to Gorky—the space between the trees, the tensions he felt between the branches were just as important to him as anything on the tree. Space for Gorky was very active. It came forward or went back. The shape of a space wasn't just a static shape. He used words like *aggressive* to describe these shapes.
>
> Gorky's idea of line was like a song. That's why he used to say he liked the sound of a single voice. We did listen to Gregorian

chants, but on the whole he liked the single solitary line of the voice.

Although Gorky had, by 1943, freed himself from his dependence on other artists, he continued to use what he had learned from the past. During his years of apprenticeship, his knowledge of art had penetrated his very muscles. Miró's and Picasso's line ran, as he said, through his fingertips. Many of Gorky's 1943 drawings are close to Miró's metamorphic landscapes of 1935 and 1936 in which biomorphic creatures confront each other in strange lunar terrains (Fig. 43). From Miró (or from Miró via Matta) he borrowed the motif of a circle or oval made up of small dashes or dots. The dotted circles and ovals may allude to conception. Certainly they suggest some idea of connection or fusion. They often contain embryonic shapes that look like fledglings getting ready to hatch. Although Gorky's predilection for sprout forms could derive from the decorative flowers and birds in Armenian manuscript illumination, forms remembered from childhood were mediated through his knowledge of Western art. His sharp sprout shapes with their points filled in with dark pencil, for example, came straight from Miró. These sprouts are sometimes arranged to look like petals. Sometimes they suggest ears, beaks, claws, or tails. In any case, they make the rounded organic forms in the 1943 drawings look sprightly and alert. Mougouch wrote to Ethel Schwabacher of Gorky's not being able to escape Miró's influence:

> Sometimes it worried him enormously that he recognized too readily and easily another artist's vision in the nature he was working from. This would bring him to me with the question that worried him so much "whose influence do you see here" and sometimes it was just the introduction of those little black pointed Miró shapes that would appear like a mannerism he couldn't help falling into, which he didn't need or want at all. Such seeming details sometimes dictated a complete change in the painting that would follow. Certainly Gorky never had a program never while I knew him and I am pretty sure never before though he may have adopted [intellectual] programs once he began talking [about art]. He wanted always an excuse to paint and I think this is one reason he could be such a student of Picasso or Miró or Léger or who-

ever he chose to work through. And when they failed him, that is when he finally realized that people expected something from HIM it was despair and a stroke of luck, ie our going to the country, that brought him a sudden wealth, nature, on which he could draw without the stigma of derivation . . . but actually the two periods were alike in intent and motive.

Gorky's 1943 drawings often have a strong sexual atmosphere, and they are full of shapes that suggest genitalia. In drawings like *Anatomical Blackboard*, orifices seem to be everywhere. They could, of course, be parts of flowers. In his passion for fertility of all kinds, Gorky dissected and transformed flowers, whose pistils and stamens, cavities and petals are, in themselves, erotic. Gorky's visceral shapes bring to mind the wonder and seductiveness of Odilon Redon's flower pastels, but a more immediate source for his erotic imagery was Matta's explicit sexual narratives in the drawings he showed at Julien Levy in April 1943. Compared with Gorky's, Matta's imagery was more deliberately scatological and *méchant*. Matta liked to draw recognizable figures in all sorts of naughty positions. Often those positions are painful: the sadistic sexuality of Matta's work was something that Surrealism encouraged. By contrast, Gorky's 1943 drawings are more abstract, lyric, and tender. His sexual cryptograms were a paean to nature's fertility, and as he celebrated the Virginia fields he also rejoiced in his paternity. A few years later the sexual imagery in Gorky's work would become more painful, less loving and sensuous. It would suggest feelings of frustration and menace, yearnings that could never be satisfied. Where Matta was mischievous and playful about sex, Gorky would become agonized.

But this was later. In the first group of Virginia drawings Gorky's creaturelike forms are light and exuberant. Their antics sometimes recall cartoon characters. Perhaps Gorky shared the Surrealists' admiration for comic strips. In 1938 he would surely have seen Julien Levy's exhibition of the sketches for Milt Caniff's cartoon strip *Terry and the Pirates* and the Walt Disney studio watercolors for *Snow White*. Matta's figures are distinctly cartoonish, and in 1942 Matta, following the comic strip format in Picasso's *The Dreams and Lies of General Franco* (1937), began to present a sequence of drawings on a single sheet of paper.

Gorky's 1943 drawings relate to Matta's drawings in other ways as well. As in Matta's drawings of the early 1940s, Gorky separates line and color. But Matta's drawings are deft and clever: they lead the viewer to believe that they erupt from the subconscious in accordance with the method of Surrealist automatism. In fact, Matta's lines have a chilling deliberateness. Gorky's drawings, while acknowledging certain formal aspects of Matta's draftsmanship, seem propelled by strong and immediate feeling. And while his pencil might meander in an improvisatory fashion, he always kept a watchful eye on aesthetic quality.

As the days grew shorter and colder, Gorky, Mougouch, and Esther spent long evenings by the fire with Gorky drawing incessantly. Esther's letters from the autumn of 1943 offer glimpses into family relations. One of them suggests both her affection for Gorky, her husband's disapproval of him, and her eagerness to smooth relations between the men her daughters had chosen. Esther wrote to her son, John, that his sister Esther was reluctant to tell her father about her attachment to Paul Makanowitzky because

Paul is also Russian . . . and she feels that may prejudice Dad against him and that he wants her to marry "a nice clean-cut American boy." So I have to do the diplomatic stuff again and give him a build-up. I shall have my hands full while they [Esther and Paul] are here keeping the family off the subject of Communism etc which . . . [Paul] is violently opposed to along with a lot of other things. And the fact that he is taking part [in the war] and not just talking rather tips the scales on his side. I'm wondering how Gorky is going to behave . . . I bought tulip, jonquil and narcissus bulbs to plant now for next spring also a lot of crocuses for the lawn.

Eight days later Mougouch's mother wrote that, thanks to Paul's tact, during the three days that he and young Esther had been at Crooked Run there had been no "acrimonious conversations" between Gorky and Paul about politics. "There was only one embarrassing moment when he spoke Russian to Gorky. Evidently Gorky never learned real Russian. I suppose they have a dialect in his part of the country and he did not have the kind of education which included languages . . . Maro has six teeth and Gorky shaved the other day. That's about all the news."

As the mild Virginia fall came on, the fields went golden and the milkweed pods turned brown, shriveled, and burst. In drawing after drawing, Gorky kept on finding an ecstatic union with the land. The drawings are spontaneous and controlled, lucid and ambiguous, tender and sensuous, but with an edge of abrasive intelligence. Always they are tinged with melancholy. Finally, in the first week of November, Gorky, Mougouch, and Maro took the train from Washington to New York City. With him, tucked in a portfolio, was his first great harvest of Virginia drawings. He knew that it would provide excellent fodder for his winter's work.

45

The Leaf of the Artichoke Is an Owl

Their happiness at Crooked Run made Gorky and Mougouch's return to the city in the fall of 1943 difficult. "When we left Virginia after that summer we had thirty dollars to our name," Mougouch recalls. "It didn't look as though we could ever come out of the tunnel of poverty. If I got the flu and Gorky had flu and we were immobilized inside the house, then my aunt Marion would take a Lexington Avenue bus downtown to bring us a little chicken in a basket. I didn't have anger, but I did have to fight a bit of my own depression." About this time Mougouch ran into her former boyfriend Peter Ruta. At first he didn't recognize her because it was dusk and she was standing in the shadowy doorway of a tenement building. "She seemed harassed. She complained about lack of money. She said she had not enough money to give a party and she couldn't even afford a bottle of whiskey."

Nevertheless, she and Gorky managed to entertain the occasional art dealer and museum person in the hopes that Gorky would find a gallery. Dorothy Miller recalled: "I remember several of those dinners that he made, even though he was so poor. Sidney Janis and his wife were at the first one. . . . He made a dinner for the dealer, Kurt Valentine, a German refugee who started his gallery in 1937 . . . Kurt Valentine liked Gorky so much personally that he wanted very much to take him . . . but he really didn't understand abstract art or like it or respond to it."

Besides money and lack of gallery representation, there was also the problem of space. Mougouch tried to protect Gorky from the onerous aspects of domesticity, but now that they had a baby, he had trouble working at 36 Union Square, and not being able to paint ruined his peace of mind. "I can't work anymore with a wife and baby in my studio," he told Dorothy Miller. "I simply can't work." He soon solved the problem by renting a separate space on the other side of Union Square for twenty dollars a month. "He hated this new studio," says Mougouch. "It was too small and his things weren't there. But he didn't complain."

One consolation was Dorothy Miller's and other friends' positive response to his summer's haul. Miller said:

> After he spent the summer in Virginia, he came back with this huge portfolio full of those wonderful crayon-and-pencil drawings. And he brought them right to my office and showed them to me. And I was crazy about them. "Now you must have one," he offered. And I said, "Oh no, Gorky. I'm sorry. I buy what I can but never accept a gift from an artist." And it was a principle that we had here at the museum, unfortunately. So I said, "No, I won't take one but I'll take three of them for an exhibition that we are going to send out on the road." So that we did. And then he began selling those drawings. I mean a great many of his friends bought them.

The Museum of Modern Art's circulating show *Twelve Contemporary Painters* included Gorky's *Composition II*, a pencil-and-crayon drawing from the summer in Virginia. Soon after he returned to New York, Gorky showed another Virginia drawing, *Shenandoah Landscape*, at the 1943 Whitney Annual.

Esther wrote to her son on November 15 that she and her daughters would probably spend a quiet Christmas in New York with "poor old Gorky to whom Xmas doesn't mean anything anyway." Four weeks later she wrote again, this time complaining that thanks to Mougouch and Gorky's carelessness, Bubbles had been "ravished" by a "farm wonk." Gorky and Mougouch's solution to this problem was to have the pregnant dog sent on a naval transport plane to Captain Magruder, who wrote to John Jr. on December 2:

> They are shipping Bubbles down to me here—with a litter of pups due, thanks to your sister Ang and her lummox of a consort,—the sire is an unknown wonk! . . . and Agnes showed no remorse

at all—just the same as grandfather's gold watch chain [which Mougouch sold]. Of course they would be back on Union Square and Mother would have all the mess and trouble so why worry their precious selves! Only then, after it was a "fait accompli" they conceived the idea of—it would be "sweet and homey" for Popsicord to spend this Xmas eve mid-wifing Bubbles! can you tie that? . . . Sometimes I could wring Ang's neck!

Without telling her parents, young Esther Magruder married Paul Makanowitzky on January 15, 1944, at Langley Field, Virginia. The Gorkys and the Makanowitzkys got together from time to time, but the sisters were jealous of each other and the brothers-in-law were merely civil. Paul was not impressed with what he saw as Gorky's big-ego behavior at 36 Union Square. Gorky had a grudging respect for Paul. He was fascinated by Paul's musical scores; the notes, he said, were "dancing across the page." Later that winter, Gorky and Mougouch attended a concert at which Makanowitzky played the violin. His deft fingering prompted Gorky to remark: "He's too good. He should wear gloves that are two sizes too small."

In December 1943 the eminent Fifty-seventh Street art dealer Paul Rosenberg told Gorky that he would like to give him a show. He wanted thirty paintings as soon as possible, and he would give Gorky a monthly stipend, the amount of which remained to be determined. Gorky had recently sold two paintings, but, his mother-in-law reported, "he must get out of the $100 class into the $1000." Gorky's reaction to Rosenberg's desire to take him on was, she noted, typically wary: "Gorky is suffering the inevitable pains of feeling that he's in someone's hands but A. is handling that all right."

Gorky showed Rosenberg canvases that he had produced after visiting Schary in the summer of 1942, paintings like *The Pirate, Housatonic Falls,* and a version of *Waterfall.* Although he tended not to present his most recent works, he may have shown Rosenberg his Virginia drawings as well. "Gorky went up to Paul Rosenberg's gallery," Mougouch recalls, "and Rosenberg said that Gorky was the most 'aristocratic' painter in America and he wanted very much to handle him. 'You must let me be the captain of this ship. You just do the paintings and I'll steer your ship safely into port.' And Gorky clapped his little painter's hat on his head and collected his paintings and just left. Rosenberg wanted to be the boss man and Gorky wasn't planning that. Gorky came home. It was all over."

In early 1944 Gorky met André Breton, who had been in the United States since 1941 but whom Matta and others in the Surrealist circle had been reluctant to introduce to Gorky, feeling that Gorky was too rustic, not sufficiently sophisticated to be good company for Breton. Moreover, Breton spoke no English and Gorky did not speak French. It was Jeanne Reynal, then visiting New York from California, who finally decided that Gorky and Breton must meet. Jeanne wanted to meet Breton herself, so she asked Noguchi to officiate. The meeting between Gorky and Breton took place at a dinner organized by Reynal in a French restaurant in the small Hotel Lafayette on University Place, a cosmopolitan place where people played chess on marble-topped tables. As it turned out, Gorky and Breton were extremely compatible and their conversation, translated by Mougouch and Jeanne, was lively. "Gorky had found a soul mate," Mougouch says, "and Breton promised to come to see Gorky's work in the next day or so. Gorky and I danced all the way home."

When the date for Breton's visit was firmed up, Mougouch panicked. "I had never had a poet to dinner. What does one give a poet for dinner? We talked about it for hours." They racked their minds and came up with an idea for a poetic vegetable—artichokes. "I bought a lovely piece of Brie cheese. I walked all over New York getting our dinner. We had artichokes, rice pilaf, and a large Brie for dinner." Gorky insisted on making the studio even more spotless than it already was: "We scrubbed the darkest corners twenty times over but it couldn't have mattered if we had sat in the dust and eaten straw, it was all so emotional and exciting. Breton gave without measure, and this was what Gorky needed; Breton didn't, as Gorky said, 'miss the point.' He understood about all those childhood memories, all the mythology of Gorky's childhood, he didn't laugh or look embarrassed but instead made sympathetic noises and had tears in his eyes and was exquisitely polite, and Gorky and I nearly went up to heaven then and there with happiness."

During the meal, Gorky pulled a leaf off an artichoke, held it up and said to Breton, "Look! To me this is an owl." A year later, when Breton was helping Gorky invent titles for his paintings, Breton remembered the comment and decided that they should name a 1944 painting *The Leaf of the Artichoke Is an Owl*. Breton was, Mougouch remembers, "overwhelmed" by Gorky's paintings, works like *The Pirate*, *Waterfall*, and especially *The Liver Is the Cock's Comb* (Fig. 158), which Gorky had begun early in 1944. Breton later told Sidney Janis that *Liver* was "the most important picture done in America at that time," and he told Lionel Abel that Gorky was "the only painter in America" and that he didn't care for any of the others.

After dinner Breton asked about the wellsprings of Gorky's art, and he and Gorky talked about the importance of homeland. "André said art must spring from a source and that people who do not have a homeland do not contribute much to culture." Steeped in psychoanalytic theory, Breton also placed great emphasis on returning to childhood memories and fantasies, and this confirmed the direction Gorky's drawings and paintings had already taken. Beyond that, Breton endeared himself to Gorky and Mougouch by being entranced with Maro, who was now old enough to sit up straight in Gorky's huge hand and be promenaded around the room.

The exchange of letters between Mougouch and Jeanne Reynal from 1944 to 1946 is full of their excitement over Breton. The two friends gave each other news of Breton's estranged wife, Jacqueline Lamba, an accomplished Surrealist painter who worked in a manner similar to Matta's and who had recently left Breton for the sculptor and photographer David Hare. Mougouch kept Jeanne up to date on Breton's new love as well. She was a Chilean woman named Elisa Claro (née Binhoff), whom Breton had met in December 1943 and would marry in July 1945. From the evidence of the letters, Gorky and Mougouch's encounters with Breton were not always relaxed. Talking with Breton was intellectually demanding, language was a barrier, and there was an element of Old World formality. One of Jeanne Reynal's letters said the strain of being with Breton was "like a bath of molten steel."

Mougouch and Jeanne read and discussed everything by Breton that they could lay their hands on, and they seem to have shared an infatuation with him. Gorky was less interested. He didn't have the patience to read Breton himself, so Mougouch read snippets of Breton's writings to him. In a letter to Jeanne from the summer of 1944 she said: "do you think gorky wants to read all of breton not at all one or two phrases are beautiful to him but above all what he likes is breton the beautifully polite MAN who was so nice so much more than polite to encourage him that's all. In fact he dislikes to hear their theories or what happened and what they thought. He was very bored after a fashion with the Vases Communicants [*The Communicating Vessels*]."

Once Breton had befriended them, Gorky and Mougouch's social milieu became more sophisticated. Embraced by the Surrealist circle, Gorky felt in the thick of things, and the art world began to perceive him differently—less as a "has been" and more as an artist coming into his own. Late in 1944 Mougouch wrote to Jeanne: "And you know now if we go to an opening every body is so nice to us, they all come and say hello and speak so flatteringly to us even to me and I wonder if they don't see the goose pimples on my neck for two years ago we would stand like two toadstools in a field of mushrooms, so inedible to them. And gorky looks bewildered and says really has my painting changed that much, it has not. An ugly business and gorky can hardly be called a success yet, but people it seems are talking."

Despite the demands of family and social life, during the winter following his first Virginia summer Gorky was far more productive than he had been the previous winter. From that earlier period come only the Tate Gallery's *Waterfall*, one version or both of *The Pirate*, and the closely related *Abstract Composition*. From the winter of 1943–44 come a dozen marvelous canvases, works like *Golden Brown Painting, Virginia Landscape, One Year the Milkweed, Scent of Apricots on the Fields,* and *The Liver Is the Cock's Comb.* Gorky's heightened productivity points to his increased confidence. He knew that the fat portfolio of drawings he had brought back from Crooked Run had wonderful things in it and that he had found a style that was very much his own. Attention from Dorothy Miller, Paul Rosenberg, André Breton, and other art world luminaries was a tremendous boost. Moreover, in his new studio he could work without the distraction of a baby and all that that entailed.

In the canvases from the fall of 1943 through the spring of 1944 Gorky tried to translate the drawings he'd made the previous summer into paintings without losing the drawings' directness of response. Months later Mougouch wrote of Gorky's struggle in a letter to Jeanne: "isnt it funny that all last [spring] and even the winter before when he was agonizing over his drawings to recreate them exactly in paint and so stymied and every one would say but gorky you cant just reproduce, it cant be done and he would say yes in that tone of voice he gets when he knows what you mean but it doesnt register for him . . . well now at last he has come there himself but he *had* to break his heart trying the other

first!" Mougouch spoke of this struggle again in her 1949 letter to Ethel
Schwabacher:

> When he painted from his drawings it was different from drawing
> from nature because he was editing his own emotion and adding
> and using all his conscious knowledge of his art. This produced
> some wonderful paintings but he sometimes said he wished he
> could eliminate that art and make the painting as direct on the
> canvas as the emotion was within him in front of nature . . . he
> would like to eliminate the artistic and conscious selection . . . i
> think he did in some paintings, . . . he used that word lyricism you
> remember a great deal . . . the song of the plough, the song of the
> single person and the songs he liked were sighs deep expansion
> and suspension, be it in the human voice or in a drawing he *felt*
> these things he did not think anything though his intuition and
> erudition so to speak led him to very advanced intellectual con-
> ception.

A comparison between *Virginia Landscape* (c. 1943–44) and the untitled 1943 drawings on which it is based shows Gorky moving from paper to canvas by rendering his forms as mere touches of transparent color
in a fugue with thin black lines (Figs. 154 and 153). Some shapes that
are clearly defined by precise pencil lines in the drawings vanish entirely
in the painting. Other shapes lose their texture, color, and substance
and become evanescent wisps. In the drawings color is raucous and
highly physical, with areas of red crayon set aflame by yellows, greens,
blues, and blacks. In the painting color has an almost disembodied
delicacy.

Subject matter is much clearer in the drawings than in the paintings.
Stealing the scene in the drawings that led to *Virginia Landscape* is an
insectlike creature resembling a butterfly pupa or a milkweed pod, but
with what looks like a snake's head and a forked tongue. She stands in
the foreground slightly left of center displaying her podlike body, which
has a vertical slit down its center just like the seam that opens on milkweed when the dark seeds attached to the white fluff packed inside the
pod are ready to be released in autumn. The pod also suggests female
genitalia, and the drawings have various phallic forms, as well. In looking at Gorky's shapes we may see first an insect, then a plant, then a ser-

pent, and finally the sexual aspect becomes apparent. There is no fixed meaning: Gorky's multivalent shapes refer to fertility of all kinds— human, plant, insect, and animal.

When he developed the oil paintings based on his drawings, Gorky tried to re-create the drawings' long, graceful pencil lines by using a sign painter's liner or lettering brush. This is a brush with many bristles at the top (forming a kind of reservoir to hold paint), tapering down to a few longer bristles that can make long, thin unbroken lines. According to de Kooning, it was he who taught Gorky about the sign painter's brush. (The émigré painter Gabor Peterdi claimed the honor, too.) De Kooning said that one day he visited 36 Union Square and found Gorky cursing his inability to paint a long, thin line with his fat brushes. Astonished that his friend who was so knowledgeable about everything to do with art did not know about sign painter's liner brushes, de Kooning advised him to buy one. With his new brush in hand, de Kooning said, Gorky spent hours in "an ecstasy painting long beautiful lines." Mougouch tells another anecdote about Gorky and his sign painter's brush. Sometime in 1944 Serge Chermayeff sent his eight-year-old son, Peter, down to Union Square from his home at 301 East Twenty-first Street to ask Gorky if Serge could borrow the brush with which Gorky made his fine lines. Gorky gave Peter a fat brush and told him, "Tell your father to keep working until there are only two hairs left. Then I'll give him my brush."

Among the paintings from the fall of 1943 through the spring of 1944 are some, such as *Housatonic Falls* and *Golden Brown Painting* (Fig. 152), which continue the mode of the Tate's *Waterfall* and in which scrubbily brushed pigment covers most of the canvas. Variations on the same theme, *Housatonic Falls* and *Golden Brown Painting* both have a piling up of soft, vaguely anthropomorphic landscape forms that is very like the heaping up of curved mountain shapes in Kandinsky's *Improvisation No. 30* and in others of Kandinsky's compositions and improvisations from 1911 to 1913. Like Kandinsky also is the way pointed, sproutlike shapes are crossed by black lines at the top of Gorky's two paintings. In the lower left quadrant of both Gorky landscapes is a shape that moves upward on a diagonal that is similar to, and clearly developed from, the more obviously phallic shape in the Tate's *Waterfall*. It could be a boulder on which the waterfall cascades. Or it could refer to Kandinsky's blasting cannon in *Improvisation No. 30*. As with Kandin-

Fig. 100. Gorky, 1936

Fig. 101. *Self-Portrait*, c. 1936

Fig. 102. Corinne
Michael West, c. 1930

Fig. 103. Sketch of *Activities on the Field* (left side), north wall of model for Gorky's murals at Newark Airport (lost), 1936

Fig. 104. Fernand Léger, *The City*, 1919

Fig. 105. Gorky explaining mural sketch for *Activities on the Field* to Mayor Fiorello La Guardia and Harry Knight at the opening of the Federal Art Project Gallery, 7 East Thirty-eighth Street, 1935

Fig. 106. Gorky and Mayor La Guardia at the opening of *Murals for Public Buildings*, 1935

Fig. 107. Portrait of Leonore Portnoff, c. 1938–39

(*right*) Fig. 108. *Man's Conquest of the Air*, Aviation Building, New York World's Fair (lost), 1939

(*below*) Fig. 109. Sketch for Ben Marden's Riviera Club murals, 1940–41

Fig. 110. Mougouch, c. 1939

Fig. 111. *Portrait of Mougouch*, c. 1941

Fig. 112. Gorky and Mougouch, c. 1941

Fig. 113. Gorky, Mougouch, and Jeanne
Reynal at a photo booth in San Francisco, 1941

Fig. 114. *Bull in the Sun,* 1942

(*right*) Fig. 115. *Flowers in a Vase on Red Cloth,* 1942

Fig. 116. *The Pirate II,* 1942–43

Fig. 117. Roberto Matta Echaurren, *Inscape (Psychological Morphology No. 104),* 1939

Fig. 118. Portrait of Mougouch, pregnant, 1943

Fig. 119. Mougouch and Gorky on a beach in New Jersey, 1942

Fig. 120. Mougouch with Maro, spring 1943

Fig. 121. Gorky bathing Maro at Crooked Run Farm, Lincoln, Virginia, 1943

Fig. 123. Crooked Run Farm, 1943

Fig. 122. Gorky holding Maro, with Esther Magruder, at Crooked Run Farm, 1943

Fig. 125. *Composition II*, 1943

Fig. 124. *Portrait of Captain John Magruder*, c. 1943–44

Fig. 126. *Untitled*, 1944

Fig. 127. Gorky with
Maro and Mougouch,
1944

Fig. 128. Gorky dancing
at V. V. Richard and John
Magruder's wedding,
1944. John Magruder is
standing at far left.

Fig. 129. Gorky and Maro
moving from Roxbury to
Sherman, Connecticut,
1945

Fig. 130. Good-bye party for André Breton given by Matta Echaurren, New York, 1945. Standing, left to right: Bernard Reis, Irene Francis, Esteban Francis, Elena Calas, Gorky, Enrico Donati, Nicolas Calas. Seated, clockwise from front: Steffi Kiesler, André Breton, Mougouch, Max Ernst, Becky Reis, Elisa Breton, Patricia Matta, Frederick Kiesler, Nina Lebel, Matta Echaurren, Marcel Duchamp

Fig. 131. *Diary of a Seducer*, 1945

Fig. 132. *From a High Place*, 1944

Fig. 133. *From a High Place II*, 1946

Fig. 134. Gorky and Wifredo Lam, New York, 1946

Fig. 135. Gorky and his family, 1946

Fig. 136. *Fireplace in Virginia*, 1946

Fig. 137. *Fireplace in Virginia*, 1946

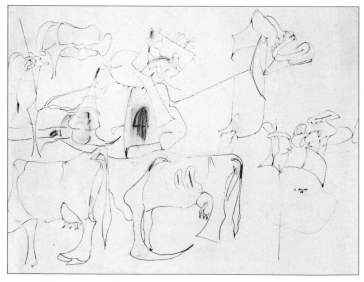

Fig. 138. *Drawing*, 1946

Fig. 139. Gorky with Maro and Natasha in Castine, Maine, 1947

Fig. 140. Mougouch in Castine

Fig. 141. *The Calendars* (lost), 1946–47

Fig. 142. *The Orators*, 1947

Fig. 143. Gorky in Sherman with Mme Enrico Donati, Marcel Duchamp, Maria Martins, and Frederick Kiesler, 1948

Fig. 144. The Glass House, 1948

Fig. 145. Gorky and family in the Glass House

Fig. 146. Gorky in his studio at the Glass House

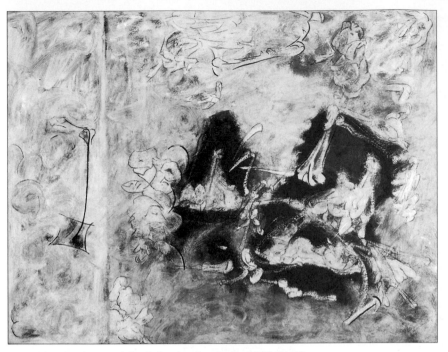

Fig. 147. *Dialogue of the Edge* (unfinished), c. 1947–48

Fig. 148. Last photograph of Gorky
(taken by Wifredo Lam outside the
Glass House), July 1948

sky's early improvisations, Gorky's images are not quite identifiable, but compared with Kandinsky Gorky is more abstract.

A second group of paintings that Gorky produced in the winter following his first Virginia summer is characterized by transparent veils of thin paint with much of the canvas left bare. Examples include *Virginia Landscape* (Fig. 154) and *Landscape*. In a third group of canvases, dated 1944 (some of these may be from the autumn following his second Virginia summer), the paint is similarly diluted with turpentine and equally runny, but more of the canvas is covered and the mood is more agitated. Among works in this category are *The Horns of the Landscape, The Leaf of the Artichoke Is an Owl,* and *One Year the Milkweed* (Fig. 156), the last of which was probably inspired by the milkweed bursting in the fall. A fourth grouping comprises more heavily pigmented paintings such as *Crooked Run, Scent of Apricots on the Fields,* and *The Liver Is the Cock's Comb,* in all of which Gorky's biomorphic forms cluster around the middle distance just as they do in the 1943 drawings.

The Liver Is the Cock's Comb, Gorky's largest canvas and one that many viewers feel is his masterpiece, was painted in April 1944. Like almost all his other paintings from this period it was based on a drawing from the previous summer (Figs. 158 and 159). Both the drawing and the painting celebrate nature's fecundity. Full of anatomical allusions, the drawing counterpoints precisely delineated shapes in pencil and ink against plumes of mostly primary color created by vertical stroking with wax crayons. The drawing's proliferation of delicate detail brings to mind Gorky's love for Persian carpets and for canon tables of Armenia (illuminated index pages in medieval Armenian Gospel manuscripts) (Fig. 52), but a more immediate source was Matta's drawings.

Whereas the drawings for *Virginia Landscape* are richer and denser in color than the canvas based on them, *Study for The Liver Is the Cock's Comb* is spare compared with the painting's sumptuous orchestration of full-bodied color. The colors Gorky chose for the plumes in the drawing remain the same in the painting—red, yellow, green, blue—but he added many mixed tones, with the result that color is at once raw, rich, and subtle. The painting's lower half is mostly earthy brown. Above an implied horizon, the blue, gray, and yellow background could refer to sky. Yet the landscape reference is less clear than it is in the study, in which the white of the paper and the transparent colors give a feeling of outdoor space and air. In the painting, on the other hand, most of the canvas is covered with opaque color, and planes set side by side close in space. Indeed, the division of the upper section of the background into colored planes recalls Gorky's Synthetic Cubist still lifes of 1937 and 1938. It is as if when he began to transfer his drawings into paintings Gorky transformed the imaginary landscape conceived in the Virginia fields into an interior stage.

On that stage he placed the same cast of characters that had appeared in the drawing, but the actors now seem to have learned their roles so well that they can improvise. A few shapes seem to be decipherable—a phallus, an orifice, an insect, apricots, and, at the painting's bottom edge, perhaps a recumbent dog (it could as well be a pile of paint rags). But again, no shape can be pinpointed as standing for any single object. *Liver* tantalizes the viewer with the suspicion that some drama is afoot, and, as we immerse ourselves in interpreting shapes as images, we also respond to the painting's beauty.

Many critics have seen liver shapes in Gorky's *The Liver Is the Cock's Comb.* Certainly the liver had some special meaning for Gorky, but I am not convinced that any liver is represented here. The statement he made about *Garden in Sochi* mentions the liver: "My liver is sick with purple." According to Gorky's nephew Karlen Mooradian, Armenians consider the liver to be the seat of the soul and the center of creative energy. Gorky specialist Nouritza Matossian notes that "my liver" is a term of endearment in Armenia. All this may be part of Gorky's meaning in this painting, but it is equally possible that its only impact was on his invention of a title. Mougouch says that one night at dinner when Gorky and Breton were discussing the way ideas of truth, honor, and courage differ in various cultures, Gorky, referring to courage, suddenly said: "The liver is the cock's comb."

When *Liver* was reproduced in Sidney Janis's *Abstract and Surrealist Art in America,* published in late 1944, it was accompanied by a quotation from Gorky that is so Surrealist in its ambiguity that it explains little: "The song of a cardinal, liver, mirrors that have not caught reflection, the aggressively heraldic branches, the saliva of the hungry man whose face is painted with white chalk." Mougouch feels that what Gorky was talking about was the images "in *his* mind" prompted by looking at his finished painting, "his alphabet, as it were. You *can see* all those things—

at least I can." The cardinal's strident song, or the flash of a cardinal glimpsed through branches, might be suggested by the bright red ovoid shapes. As often in Gorky's works, there appear to be avian creatures in the upper left and right. Indeed, fragments of birds: beaks, feathers, wattles, scrawny legs—maybe even the cockscomb of the painting's title— appear to be everywhere. But it must be remembered that Gorky said trees' foliage looked like feathers and that he painted birdsong without the bird.

William C. Seitz, in his catalog essay for the Museum of Modern Art's 1962 retrospective, wrote incisively about *Liver*: "What began as a landscape now has, in part, the effect of an interior enclosing a ritual performance by fantastic personages and mysterious objects." In his own statement about *Liver*, Gorky mentioned a man with a face whitened with chalk, which does indeed suggest some kind of ritual. Jeanne Reynal described *Liver* as having a "mask in the sky." On April 20, 1944, Mougouch wrote to Jeanne that Gorky had been working very hard on *Liver*, which she called "that huge canvas that you saw in the storeroom." She said that it looked "very live somehow like a world in the treetops that you are seeing from a treetop." Eight days later Jeanne wrote back asking about *Liver*: "Did Arshile feel satisfied when he painted that great canvas. God knows he well might. I'm glad its so successful. Did he really finish it in a week. Does he consider it finished? Or is the flight to the contrary a compulsion." (Jeanne refers to Gorky's endless reworking of the same canvas.) She wished she could buy the painting, but Gorky had already promised it to Jean Hebbeln, a young Sarah Lawrence graduate who, with her husband, the architect Henry Hebbeln, had been introduced to Gorky and Mougouch by the Chermayeffs.

The circumstance that led to Jean Hebbeln's acquisition of *The Liver Is the Cock's Comb* tells us something about the painting's euphoric color and dancelike movement and the masterful way in which Gorky composed all its notes into one splendid, pulsing harmony. Knowing that Mougouch had no money to buy clothes, Jean took her to Bonwit Teller to buy a fur coat. Mougouch asked Jean if she could have the money instead. "When I came home with a thousand dollars Gorky couldn't believe it. Our happiness absolutely exploded and then Gorky went and started to paint *The Liver Is the Cock's Comb* as a result of that gift of Jean's, which went boom like that, for no reason, nothing. It wasn't an exchange for a painting, nothing. He was so full of relief. I can't tell you what it is like to always be at the end of your tether. And when Gorky was doing this painting, he said, 'Give it to Jean.' And he gave it to her."

James Johnson Sweeny's "Five American Painters," published in *Harper's Bazaar* in 1944, included paragraphs on Gorky, Morris Graves, Milton Avery, Matta, and Pollock, all of whom were described as young, not widely known artists who addressed their art to nature. Sweeny proposed that Gorky's recent paintings showed "his realization of the value of literally returning to the earth," and he went on to call Gorky "one of the most promising talents in New York." He extolled Gorky's draftsmanship, his feeling for paint, and his understanding of contemporary movements in Europe. But until recently, Sweeny said, Gorky had been too dependent on other artists, and the "pounds of impasto" that Gorky had layered on his canvases bore witness to "a persistent lack of assurance or complete dissatisfaction with the work as it progressed." The following year, much to Gorky's chagrin, critic Clement Greenberg would discern in Gorky a similar insecurity, interpreting as weakness Gorky's refusal to make a clean sweep of art history.

Although each of the five painters received only one paragraph of Sweeny's attention, Gorky felt shortchanged, perhaps because Matta's paragraph was a tiny bit longer than his. He surmised that the other artists had been able to explain their work to Sweeny, whereas he had not. Mougouch recalls: "Gorky never could explain what he was doing. He could explain everybody else's paintings to people—I remember a gallery owner said to Gorky, 'I wish you'd come and hold forth on the work in my gallery every Saturday when the crowds come.'" Gorky's irritation was likely to have been directed also at the annoyingly up-and-coming Jackson Pollock. Sweeny had written a catalog essay for Pollock's first show at Peggy Guggenheim's Art of This Century in November 1943. Now Sweeny had chosen Pollock's *She-Wolf* as the only painting to be reproduced in color, whereas he included only a small black-and-white reproduction of a Gorky drawing. Even more galling, *She-Wolf* was soon purchased by the Museum of Modern Art.

In her April letter to Jeanne Reynal, Mougouch expressed her and Gorky's displeasure with Sweeny's article: "Did you get the *Harper's Bazaar*? Its such a wee drawing we were sort of disappointed but one always is—one feels there are flames belching from one's nostrils & the world says God bless you! Thinking you sneezed! The article too was just journalism & as Gorky said had he known Sweeney [*sic*] was so uninspired he would have talked himself up better . . . However people have been very enthusiastic & said that Gorky comes out very well in the article." Indeed he did come out well, for, like many later observers, Sweeny saw Gorky's recent drawings as an extraordinary breakthrough:

> Then last summer Gorky decided to put art out of his mind, the galleries of Fifty-seventh Street and the reproductions of Picasso, Léger, and Miró, and "look into the grass," as he put it. The product was a series of monumentally drawn details of what one might see in the heavy August grass, rendered without a thought of his fellow-artists' ambitions or theories of what a picture should be. And the result of this free response to nature was a freshness and personalization of idiom which Gorky had never previously approached, and a new vocabulary of forms on which he is at present drawing for a group of large oil paintings.

Taking Gorky literally, many writers since Sweeny have said that he drew what he saw when he lay in the grass, but, as Mougouch points out, Gorky was unlikely to have actually lain down in the fields—he was too afraid of snakes. In any case, he could get a close-up view of the life in the grass simply by using his imagination.

46

Cutting Down the Raphaels

✼

In April 1944 Mougouch took one-year-old Maro and went to visit her mother in Washington, DC. Upon her return home on April 19 she wrote to Jeanne Reynal that her week of rest had made her realize what an effort she made "to be a hausfrau. . . . Gorky the angel man cleared everything and stuck pretty flowers around and bits of paper with 'Will-come hom, my darling' on them and it felt like spring in my heart to come home to him." She told Jeanne that while in Washington she had seen her first lover, whom she had not seen since she left Shanghai. "How beautiful and fine and strong gorky is—but I must say the attraction beastly though it is, remains. I don't mind it must be hateful to be disgusted by oneself, even by one's worser self. I found myself feeling over and over how much I really do love gorky. I am so happy I do. Hello Jeanne I love you too."

Much of what we know about the following months comes from Mougouch's correspondence with Jeanne. In her April letter she said they would soon leave for Virginia and that Margaret Osborn would sub-let 36 Union Square. Just before leaving, Matta showed her his recent erotic drawings and possibly also his folio of eleven etchings of orgiastic scenes—cartoonlike couples in intricate sexual postures that are both cruel and absurd. On May 5 she wrote Jeanne:

Went to Matta's studio before leaving on the lure that he would give me [Breton's novel] Nadja—which he did. So I will read & send to you v. soon. He was sweet & a good boy & we sat & looked

& discussed his ideas. They are cockeyed if I may say—He be-
haves more & more like a spoiled boy who wants to masquerade
as de Sade. He has done some huge drawings v. well executed of
ladies & gents doing push push in a most ungentlemenly way
gents masturbating with one hand & slitting a throat with the
other all v. realistic—he was aching for me to be repulsed or
vomit but I couldn't react that strongly because the realism—
though not pornographic—was too graphic to move me anyway.
He then tried to tell me that this was man—man as he really
was—a cruel beast quite empty—I felt like saying my dear child
but did not . . . it's too recherché & not new nor mad—don't call
a flea an elephant—or vice versa—he speaks of wanting to live in
madness which is alright but not when turned on & off like a hot
water tap—if you are mad then something authentic comes out
& your madness drives you to death if you are conscious but
he wants to be mad like some girls want long hair—another
glamor—So different from our evening with Breton.

Mougouch also told Jeanne about a farewell dinner with "Papa Breton":

O what a beautiful man. I called him to say goodbye & he wanted
to come so we had a huge seignorial steak as planned with you &
then we all felt so happy we forgot to eat a specially good cheese I
bought for HIM. We just talked quietly—he looked again at G.'s
drawing with the idea of choosing one or two to be reproduced in
color in the next VVV. . . . Gorky's huge new canvas [*The Liver Is
the Cock's Comb*] was in the room & Breton was v. impressed with
it & spoke of it with great feeling & emotion. He said that Gorky,
and this interested us enormously, had inherited Lautrec. Not in
the style of Lautrec but that he was a kindred spirit his forms &
color were such as Lautrec might have come to. This was new to
Gorky & v. encouraging in the way he put it. And Breton meant it
as a great compliment. During dinner we giggled kiddishly on the
always hilarious subject of wives' parents. He told us such funny
stories of his first wife's parents & how they would say rubbing
their hands & what did you do today & he would say a few lines
were written etc—just like G. and Father. It was sweet to laugh at
such simple things with him. Then we talked of the country & lit-

tle brooks & G. & he swapped stories via me about stones & wal-
nuts & smells & Arshile was in a very poetic mood, & Breton
sensed that & really felt love for him I think. We spoke of sadness
& why & breton confessed his everlasting sadness & told of how
in his happiest moments with women even they would say but
you are sad & he would say no yet know that it was true. Gorky
shares this with him though he is wilder than B. and you know
Jeanne at this moment we all had tears in our eyes. It was a very
beautiful evening & very rare. He was very sweet to me too & said
for no reason at all that of all his friends he felt easiest to be translated by me because he knew enough english to know that I did
translate what was most important & with the proper feeling.
Ahem—with that pat on the back I plunged bravely on in the sea
of intangibles . . . then we got in to politics—the individual poet
vs. reality—etc—where would the new movement spring up—
Barcelona or Central America thinks B. some country that has
been touched but not broken by war or broken & sufficiently long
ago to heal He doesn't see himself returning to France but rather
to one of these countries. And so finally he left us—I forgot to say
that several times during the evening he & Gorky lept up &
clasped hands & once while I was putting Maro back to bed he
spoke to Gorky in English: such a strange sound! It was so banal
& ordinary his English I quite see how it pains him to speak. He
made us say we would write—O mercy me!—& tell little things
about Maro how she loved or what she saw—he said hardly a day
passed that he didn't think of that enchanted being as he calls
her—he played with her & made friends on the couch & adored
her little hat & Arshile's horses—of the horses he said that he
loved them, that they showed the same don a la vie [gift for life] as
G.'s large painting.

The horses in question are rocking horses carved out of wood with a
seat suspended between them for Maro to sit on. Although they are modeled on Greek bronze horses from the Geometric period that Gorky saw
in the Metropolitan Museum, they become, like his miniature Armenian carved plows, really a piece of sculpture whose sprightly forms share
the same vocabulary of shapes as his paintings. Gorky also built a cart for
Maro so that he could take her on walks. In Virginia he pulled the cart

into the fields where he drew, but Maro proved to be a distracting companion. "For God's sake, take her away!" Gorky would cry. "She has holes in her eyes! She wants all the flowers!"

Mougouch's and Jeanne's letters that spring and summer carry on a discussion about sexual freedom, human unhappiness, and intuition versus rationality. Much of the discussion comes out of their reading of Breton and their memories of conversations between Breton and Gorky. On May 5, for example, Mougouch wrote that Breton had agreed with Gorky on the subject of unhappiness. There were, as Gorky put it, "too many windows open." The result, according to Gorky, was that people no longer trusted intuition and that all of man's "secrets had been opened & aired even in sex there was responsibility imposed on him." In fact, Gorky did not approve when his friends discussed sex. Sex was meant to have mystery, and he was shocked, for example, when Mougouch did not close the bathroom door.

Mougouch's next letter to Jeanne (June 2) again raised the issue of the sadness that she felt Breton and Gorky shared. She discussed this sadness in relation to love's impermanence, a subject Breton had explored in conversation with her and Gorky as well as in *The Communicating Vessels*. Jeanne wrote back recalling an evening they had all spent together the previous spring. As the guests had risen from the dinner table at 36 Union Square, Breton had said: *"La femme change mais c'est toujours le même amour"* (The woman changes but it's always the same love). Jeanne said that Breton's agreement with Gorky on the issue of "open windows" had surprised her, "simply because I know of no one who has left so many [windows] open, and who insists on the 'porte battante.' " (The swinging door was presumably a metaphor for the coming and going of loves in Breton's life.) Jeanne went on to write of Gorky's more committed approach to love, and she suggested that Gorky was less sensuous than Breton and thus more willing to forgo new pleasures:

I think you are right that Arshile "has decided." He often spoke, and I wish I could remember just his words, but the sense was, that to run after a new love was to find only what you left in the old, and I think this applies to people like Isamu [Noguchi] who "run after" but not to voluptuaries like Breton who "find." For whom "on ne sort pas DU REVE" [one does not emerge from the dream]. Arshile is an ascetic and by his means "absence of" you quite probably reach the same conclusions as Breton who has "presence of " I think Breton is one of the most sensual people I have ever met. Any woman is bound to be affected by him . . . Most of the Surrealists are just little two penny cads like Matta and his poor little contribution to the "reve" and Dalí, masturbators but Breton is the real McCoy.

In subsequent letters Mougouch commented on Gorky's antirationalist approach, his stress on intuition, and his lack of self-awareness:

incidentally I must explain that g's reference to open windows was not in opposition to secrets disclosed or opened doors but in opposition to the general rationalist approach prevalent in modern society, the airing of all man not in the sense of discovery of new riches, new sources for progress, not in the freeing sense, but in the pretentious attempt to simplify and regularize, thus to bring duty into sexual relations, responsibility in the stultifying morally oppressive sense. Does that make more sense? I am sure he is not opposed to the open door, the glass house except that for instance he would say he has no secrets and he would never tell the things about himself that breton does simply because he does not give them that much importance *for him.* He is not analytical and doesn't know half of what happens to him. This fascinates and sometimes frightens me. Sometimes he seems thoughtless or ruthless but it is because he does not analyse, it's pure intuition that he functions on.

Mougouch ended her letter with a postscript that contradicted Jeanne's statement that Gorky was an ascetic. In speaking of Gorky's "absence of " compared with Breton's "presence of," Jeanne had probably meant absence of sensuality in relationship to women or infrequent engagement in sexual intercourse. In defense of Gorky, Mougouch argued that a man's sexual attraction to women was not the only measure of his sensuousness. Gorky, she said, had a sensuous relationship with the objects that he painted:

I don't agree with you that gorky is an ascetic. I think his intuition rests largely on sense perception. Maybe I'm wrong. I feel that his senses are very archaic, even primitive and v. strong, which would be explained by the high development of intuition. Is woman, the love of, etc. the only indication of sensuousness? Matta would not agree with me, but I feel that for a painter *all* things are objects sensed, whereas a poet is more apt to sense only those things that emotionally involve him. This is discussed in B's Amour Fou, I believe, B maintaining that the erotic emotion is the connecting link with inspiration. But to me this is the *poet's* prerogative and that's where Matta makes his mistake. His painting is for me also the explanation for the failure of surrealism to produce *painters*. Miró does not enter in—he *was* anyway.

During their first days in Virginia Gorky and Mougouch were full of plans to buy a home of their own. They had fallen in love with a nearby house and were planning "to creep up at nightfall because the owner has had no bids & there is a chancc if we do a too-expensive-for-us act that he'll come down in price . . . We had a lovely time in the wheatfield last night—it is too lovely here." Ten days later Jeanne replied by offering the Gorkys a long-term interest-free loan of up to two thousand dollars. If they wished they could repay the loan with four paintings. On June 2 Mougouch wrote back: "We were terribly touched by your plan for us but you know Jeanne I am worried that that house is much too far gone it is lovely but . . . we should try to find something a little nearer our condition as Serge [Chermayeff] would say, that Serge. It might as well be around here because it is just such hell to get g to move or look around o moan I do want to go to india and egypt before I die and spain and italy maybe." Mougouch described to Jeanne a room in the springhouse that she and Gorky had fixed up so that she could read and write and get away from her mother and sister:

Just a little square wooden house with a door and window but no door or window just the openings if you understand. G and I brought a cot down and fixed up a bench for a table and decided that this is the kind of house we want no more no less . . . A perfect sea of green wheat rolls up to the door so that the horizon is 4/5 of the way up . . . I do wish you were here to talk with because really you know gorky cant be bothered to discuss all these things [Breton's writings] with me and only wants to know the really succulent points and that takes a lot of digesting chez moi to be able to present them to him and then he does so make fun of me because he claims I am under the influence of [Breton] and of course I am but then he doesn't like me to know the little personal intimacies that b. rcvcals about himself!

In June she gave Jeanne news of Maro, who at fourteen months was crawling about on the lawn, most often naked in the sun. Gorky, she said, had gone through his elaborate prework ritual and was out in the Virginia fields:

Gorky has started his plunge and made several drawings one of which is a new start and I am anxious that he gets drowned and lost because I think wonderful things will happen. But it is fantastic the way he starts off. mr byrd or however he's spelt couldn't do more before an expedition to the north. G. must make special stretchers though he has a ton of ready made ones in every conceivable size, special little boxes for oddments that he never uses a great to do about sticks for snakes in special sizes! And then the poison ivy which he treats as an enemy army which must be disarmed and defeated before he can start drawing . . . o mougouch what a morning I had great puffing and panting look at this scar (shows me a little pimple) the most terrible sight I have ever seen . . . a huge field FULL of poison ivy . . . i killed it all made a path to walk through . . . I promise you Jeanne he will probably never go back to that field again this summer he will forget where it is! What can you do with such a man but just have patience I suppose. But how he loves all this he looks like a different person very brown and slim and youthful and when he has turned nine times around he will start and become someone else entirely sort of a depersonalized gorky.

In describing Gorky as "depersonalized," Mougouch caught something that she and Gorky believed was true of even the most self-revealing artists: immersed in his art, Gorky was closer to the thing he was making than he was even to himself. What emerged from under his pencil went beyond the individual self or personality: it was what he called "universal."

Her next letter, undated but probably written in July, suggests a change in their mood and a shift in the weather: "We both no longer wish to live here. First it is the future dust bowl of america, we are having a drought as bad as that one in 1930 when the cattle were just let loose to roam and find water, the crops are ruining, our garden we sweated over is turning to dust and Gorky begins to have enough of the landscape. That's a new development we may reach yet! Little Maro has the temper of a devil. But very sweetly now she expresses affection like a puppy, she rubs her face against ours and sometimes she takes your hand and lays her cheek in your palm and your heart bursts with joy." A major annoyance to both Gorky and Mougouch was the presence of her mother and seventeen-year-old sister Esther, who was pregnant and frightened for her bow-gunner husband, whose plane had been shot down and who was reported missing in action. It turned out that he was in a prison camp in Romania; when Romania capitulated in September 1944, he walked to Italy, where he was finally repatriated.

Young Esther had never felt comfortable in her brother-in-law's presence. Before she married and while she was studying ballet in New York, she occasionally brought a beau to 36 Union Square and Gorky would demolish him: "Once I brought a young man who was part of a jazz combo that was playing at the Village Vanguard. Before we left for his concert, Gorky took a piece of bread out of a bread basket and put it in the young man's pocket and said, 'Now you look properly dressed.'" Gorky was charmed by his pretty, blond ballet-dancer sister-in-law, but he was often critical. "I wanted to please but I couldn't," she recalls. "If I said I loved Debussy, he would say Debussy was a terrible composer. Mozart was greater than Beethoven, he said, because Mozart laughed and Beethoven cried. I loved Stravinsky, but Gorky said Stravinsky was old-fashioned and the *Sacre du Printemps* was 'pink and blue.' I could never get a grasp of what he did believe in, he was so clear about what he didn't believe in." Occasionally when Esther was alone with Gorky he was kind and gentle. Once he told her what it had been like to be a boy in Georgia. He said that when the shepherds came in at night the baby animals were placed closest to the fire. Then the men, then the children, then the women, and finally the larger animals.

As the summer went on, Mougouch's letters hint at loneliness: she could not always discuss her ideas and feelings with Gorky, and unlike him, she had no career on which to focus her energies. Several letters express a discontent with what she felt was her unproductive existence: "I am devoured with impatience at myself, at the absurd gap between what one can believe in and think and what one *does*. Do. What do I do." Just twenty-three years old, full of intelligence and energy, Mougouch was no longer satisfied with being a housewife. Once she had wanted to be a painter, but she had given that idea up. She now wished she could be a writer, and she even set up her typewriter in her springhouse refuge, but somehow, with a husband and child to look after, she never was able to find the time and discipline necessary to write or paint. She wanted, she said, "to lay an egg myself and when I get up and look, nothing there . . . humiliating."

Discontent sometimes deepened into depression. She spoke in one letter of the human "will to die" and her "savage desire to crack my head open again and again." In a late September letter she said that Breton had written and asked her "that horrible question about what do I do . . . o god. What do I do that is the question. If I could only earn some money I would write like kathleen norris . . . O well hell there is time and there are more important fishes to fry, how to live and propagate gorkys, paintings and infants though I know it would be better if I did more I don't so there." In an October letter Jeanne offered comfort: "Darlin' Mougouch you must not worry about what you are what you should be. When in doubt just look at Maro, look at A's painting. Do you not see the change there? You have had a part in this. These things are not to be sniffed at. If you really need to write, you will do it . . . Perhaps the proximity of your mother and sister makes you wonder. Well I assure and double reassure you that you have come a long way from that. This too is Arshile's merit. But it works interchangeably."

In early August Mougouch actually did earn some money by stripping the tassels off a neighbor's corn so that it could cross-pollinate. "I feel frightfully subdued from working 10 hrs a day in the cornfields detasseling corn but I made $60 in two wks. Which is more than I ever got for grinding that machine I call my brain! But I hate such physical labor for everything seems dulled except the boredom of those 10 hrs which is sharp as a knife."

Mougouch's feeling that she was doing nothing was exacerbated by Gorky's productivity. "He's a juke box," she wrote, probably in July. "Doing the most wonderful paintings again and always such terrific colour despite the absence of obsession. He is just using these new drawings as a base, the painting has pushed much further and developed . . . he has about 12 canvases some nearly finished though he feels all of them could be worked on indefinitely as usual. I hope you are going to like them, I HOPE so, my god!" On July 28 she wrote to her aunt Nathalie Campbell that "gorky is working ardently and making great progress." He had the "courage to take the hard road," she said, but there had been no break-through yet. In August she gave Jeanne further news of Gorky's work: "Gorky has been thrashing over two particular canvases & having now ravaged & worn them down like an angry sea he has left them to go out and draw—draw—draw. Today he is heart broken because the farmer has cut the weeds to let the grass grow for the cows & all looks too park-like for Gorky who loved the purple thistles & great milkweeds & ragweeds—Poor dear he always gets slugged—He stood on the hill watching the tractor down in the bottom land moaning 'They are cutting down the Raphaels.' "

Early in August Mougouch wrote to Jeanne that she was pregnant. "I am going to have another baby in April or March the Ides of March in-deed! Perhaps it is mad but it is what we both want—and very much. And think how economical: 1 cake 1 candle——!" Later that month her mother, seeing that she looked exhausted, suggested that Mougouch leave Maro and Gorky at Crooked Run and visit Serge and Barbara Chermayeff in Truro on Cape Cod. "It was the first time I'd been alone," Mougouch recalls. "On the train I had a wonderful feeling of total free-dom, feeling that no one was going to make me come back if I went away."

On August 28 she wrote Gorky from Truro:

Sirumem ? Poodoug Sweet darling I am having a lovely time—just swam across the lake and back again quick like a flash and felt so rested . . . I miss my two darlings awfully much I think of you every minute & hope you are well and miss me too a little bit. Do you think Maro does? I am just as glad you didn't come as you would have been bored with Serge & besides the food is all fried & Barbara walks along the beach and picks up a fish (dead) & that is breakfast—She even sticks leftover garbage in the soup like pan-cakes! We all tease her of course—Jean [Hebbeln, whose summer house was on the same pond] and I giggle as usual a good deal & Serge gets mad at that & won't let Barbara laugh . . . Everyone sends their love to you—they are so glad your paintings are going well—Jean & Henry send very special love to both of you—I suppose you had better give some of mine to mother but darling it is you above all else I love in the whole world—I kiss you my Poo-kouch—Your Mougouch xxxxxxx

On a stopover in Washington, on the way to or from Cape Cod, Mougouch's feeling of liberation and independence was heightened by a brief encounter with her former lover from Shanghai. The tryst reassured her about her own attractiveness and sexuality—being married to Gorky did not allow confidence in these matters to flourish.

An undated letter to Jeanne written about this time reflected on the relative contentment of her marriage, but it is hard not to hear an undertone of discontent in Mougouch's protestations of happiness: "I am in such a unique position for I am married to a man who is now *himself* a complete thing, there is not the same embroilment of embryos as in the case of young people. From this [comes] an independence & a reality that despite some things I am so god damned thankful for. But when I see the struggles & above all the false situations I begin to understand some things about change & dead skins that must be shed & by god marriage becomes a criminal institution that stunts too many growths. How little courage there is *to live*—How few dare!" As this outburst suggests, Mougouch's first infidelity to Gorky grew out of, and perhaps fostered, a fear that marriage—her marriage—might devolve into just such a "criminal institution."

Back at Crooked Run she wrote to Jeanne that her trip to the Cape had been "ill-fated." She had had a miscarriage a few days after arriving home:

o woe. I did so want that baby but there you are tit for tat from dame nature. It was rather a funny performance in retrospect as we were quite alone here without a car and really I did not know what was up until it became very reminiscent of giving birth. I gave a good old fashioned yelp and up to my room tore the 70 year old quaker gardener, a little negro boy [the housekeeper's grandson] who was helping him rake the lawn, complete with rake and last a crazy looking gorky bearing maro so that I had to hide in the closet. It was a back hills of virginny touch all right.

Eventually came the local doc who proceeded to raise my spirits with rabelaisian tales of birth and abortions in these very back hills. I never knew anything to make me laugh so from the belly though I ached in the heart. I hope I am caught in the wilds for my next birth, proper I hope. then we had no sooner removed the traces of this do than my marine brother and my father and mother all descended on us and they have only just left. Gorky and I both feel rather like a couple of pieces of driftwood just washed up on the beach, the roar of this past chaotic month is only just subsiding and leaving us curiously empty, a sort of Now, where am I feeling.

This really has been a bad luck summer, now the weather is queered, rainy, grey or too windy for g. to work outside and this is the time of year he likes best. Pray for good weather he has a lot of work to do yet. He has about twenty canvases that are, to my mind anyway, fit to exhibit [,] about 10 more in undone stages but he must have more drawings and more paintings if we are to have an exhibition this year because when we move back there will be the settling down, the worry, the finding of a studio or else of some rooms for us so he can work alone and all the abortive wastes of time that are [the] city. Right now I do not see how we can move back we are so broke. And yet we cannot afford to economize (o paradox) by staying here all winter because we don't sell anything here anyhow there is no place for g to work when it is cold. Those friends of ours [Henry and Jean Hebbeln] who own the painting you liked have bought a farm in n.y. state [actually Sherman, Connecticut] where it seems we are welcome but g. even balks at that because he is afraid of being cut off from any attention he might get [in Manhattan]. Even if we did eventually go out there we should have to be in n.y. until some arrangement is made if any is going to be made. Perhaps when pierre matisse sees these paintings he will take gorky. It is so hard to tell what kind of re- ception they will have because they are so new and so unlike any- thing else. There are two which he made the day your last letter came, he was so happy about the way you felt when you saw your own painting [a painting that Jeanne had purchased from Gorky] and all the things you said both of us felt so nice after reading your letter, so warm inside and he ran to the barn and out came

two canvases which I know or at least to me are the best of the lot
very strong but subtle in color, transparent color and very true
color not at all art colors, I cant describe them but they are very
complete paintings that came from him complete if you can see
what I mean . . . you probably could see but you cant read what I
drivel!

Mougouch went on about Gorky's recent work—some paintings were
very free, others were "very high colored" and "more worked on, different and less to my liking but still I know they are very good paintings."
She said Gorky would have been more productive if there had been people around who understood his work as Jeanne did and if he hadn't had
the irritation of his mother and sister-in-law—what she called "this constant bellyache."

In the fourth week of October Mougouch deposited Maro at her parents' house in Washington and went to the hospital to have a curettage.
Gorky stayed at Crooked Run. The curettage was, she wrote to Jeanne,
"such a cruel climax to this poisoned summer," and it was made worse
by her humiliation at being in debt to her mother, who paid her hospital
bills. "Gorky has been alone in the country, working & eating fried eggs
& oranges—& a pot of stuffed cabbage I made for him before leaving—
Poor darling—but he is better alone to work. I am dying to get back to
him." (Actually, Gorky had dined most evenings with Thomas and Mary
Taylor. In gratitude he gave them a drawing.) Jeanne wrote back at the
end of October and said she was sending a check and would continue to
send money for the next few months.

In the second week of November, distracted by preparations for departure, Mougouch wrote to Jeanne:

Life at the moment is me in the midst of chaos wondering
whether or not to transfer same to N.Y. . . . Do you think things
will happen in N.Y. for us? Hope is crashing & hanging in my
BRUST.

Gorky wants to send you a drawing but thinks perhaps best to
wait till we get home—He wants to send you the nicest & perhaps
he had better keep it for a bit to determine if it is the nicest . . .

Jeanne we were so glad to hear of your work. Gorky says good,
good & to your colours & their functioning he says It can, must be

done—it is what he wants to do & I say does . . . That you are using pale colours is wonderful—there you are in your most individual—Gorky saw great change in your drawing from the little sketch you sent he liked the variety & the search—this also he has found . . . Were this damn barn only weather proof! He has lost days simply because of rain & wind—It is such a wonderful place—around the walls he has his horse bones that we found last summer & hung on a fence to dry—& then these strange old rusty farm implements & bits of machinery & hayricks. & the pigeons who sit on the rafters & build [a] wall of their droppings beneath[.] it is a beautiful place.

While she packed, Gorky made up for time lost to inclement weather. Paying no attention to the fact that he was about to leave, he started a large new canvas that was bolder and sparer than anything he had yet done. To contend with this new work (*Painting*, now in the Peggy Guggenheim Collection in Venice), he had to feel, Mougouch said, "like a bonfire inside." She knew that Gorky's artistic breakthrough had come. Her letter ended with: "I must throw myself into a crate now but will write more coherently perhaps—from N.Y."

The paintings from the second half of 1944 are of several types, types that do not necessarily belong to different moments in time—Gorky was perfectly capable of working simultaneously in various modes. At one moment he covered his canvas with dense layers of lush, subtle colors, and at another he left it almost bare, placing on it only a few simple shapes and astringent colors that keep close to primary hues. In one group of paintings, some of which may be from spring 1944, he covered most of the canvas with colors so thinned by turpentine that they blurred and dripped. Examples are *How My Mother's Embroidered Apron Unfolds in My Life, The Leaf of the Artichoke Is an Owl, The Horns of the Landscape,* and *One Year the Milkweed* (Figs. 158 and 157). The paintings in this group are crowded with rounded shapes loosely drawn with a brush in black pigment that has been thinned to gray. Often these shapes have spots of color at their centers suggesting (as in the central womblike shape in the *Khorkom* and *Sochi* paintings) some primitive form of generation. In general, although a bird or insect might be decipherable here or there, the shapes do not join together to form distinct creatures. Rather one feels life pulsing all over the canvas. Perhaps part of the ambiguity of Gorky's shapes is the result of his looking at nature so closely. Like a face seen from the vantage point of a kiss, his shapes are out of focus and fragmentary. Certainly this feeling of intimate proximity is appropriate for *How My Mother's Embroidered Apron Unfolds in My Life*, which was prompted, he said, by the memory of pressing his face into his mother's lap while she told him stories. Here forms inspired by the Virginia landscape interlace with flowers and leaves on his mother's apron and with her folk tales. In *One Year the Milkweed*, we can imagine Gorky letting his imagination move so close to the bursting pods that the milkweed coalesced with his reverie: in the end, there was no division between inside and outside or between seeing and imagining. He painted both the milkweed in the field and the milkweed inside his head.

Another type of painting from 1944 is exemplified by *Love of a New Gun*, which, with its large amount of canvas left white and its tremulous, dilute, runny colors, recalls the slightly earlier *Landscape* acquired by Jeanne Reynal. Both paintings are among Gorky's most gentle. They have a feathery lightness, as if when he painted them he had been in a state of delight. *To Project, to Conjure* (Fig. 155) is similar in style but slightly denser—it is halfway between paintings like *How My Mother's Embroidered Apron Unfolds in My Life* and *Love of a New Gun*.

From 1944 come also a number of loosely painted canvases in which colors blur and blend and cover most of the surface. One of them, *The Sun, the Dervish in the Tree*, might, with its boot/butter churn image in the center, be a *Garden in Sochi* variant. As in several of the *Sochi* paintings, a bonelike shape with two lobes at its base penetrates the instep of the boot/butter churn shape. But unlike in most of the *Sochi* paintings, forms melt into an overall pulse of color. The slow drift of one color into another also recalls Thomas Wilfred's color organ, or Clavilux, which created quite a sensation when it was installed at Grand Central Station from 1933 to 1943 and which Matta, among others, greatly admired. Gorky would certainly have seen one of the public "lumia" recitals, in which constantly changing mists of color on a screen looked a little like an early Kandinsky set in motion. Gorky's melting and coalescing color in *The Sun, the Dervish in the Tree* also recalls Miró's transparent color veils. Miró is acknowledged also in Gorky's use of the dotted line and in the spidery motif set beside black and red spotches in the painting's upper right corner.

Gorky's *Water of the Flowery Mill* in the Metropolitan Museum (Fig. 160) is like a looser and even more lush and jubilant revisiting of *The Liver Is the Cock's Comb*. In both paintings a large, round-topped white shape loops up toward the canvas's upper edge, and in both paintings oval forms with clefts or with a spot of color at their center convey a feeling of abundance. In *Water of the Flowery Mill* several clusters of colored shapes, especially the yellow and brown grouping (with a green plume on top) on the right, are undeniably avian, especially if we think back to Gorky's hieroglyphs for birds in his *Khorkom* or *Garden in Sochi* series. The movement of color all over the canvas is like the flutter and chirping of birds in foliage and flowers. To wit, Gorky described the abandoned eighteenth-century mill near Crooked Run Farm that inspired the Metropolitan's picture this way to Julien Levy: "down the road, by the stream, that Old Mill, it used to grind corn, now it is covered with vines, birds, flowers, Flour Mill—Flowery Mill. That's funny! I like that idea." The experience of flowing water, flowers, stone, and reflection, together with the idea of transformation—wheat into flour and flour into bread—appealed to Gorky. Perhaps he linked the mill with the flour mills his mother took him to in Van.

Water of the Flowery Mill seems to have been based on a 1943 drawing like the untitled one in the Alan Stone collection (Fig. 153) in which Gorky transformed the minutia of nature—insects, flowers, worms, larvae, cocoons—into precisely delineated but not identifiable shapes and creatures. But in *Water of the Flowery Mill* shapes and colors take their cue from the watery subject: they run and flow like reflections in a mill pond. The creature with the yellow snake head and red and yellow pupae body in the center of the drawing reappears in the painting as the vertical orange form topped by a yellow oval "head."

Human beings must be genetically geared to spot creatures lurking in the bush. That same alertness makes us read images into Gorky's abstractions, and it prompted Gorky to see soldiers and peasant women in the clouds. Although he warned us not to put faces on his images, I see a woman lying forward with her hair falling over her face and her arms folded in front of her in the upper left corner of *Good Afternoon, Mrs. Lincoln* (Fig. 161). And if, obeying Gorky, I try to get rid of the image, it just keeps coming back. The drawing for *Good Afternoon, Mrs. Lincoln* makes the suggestion of a female, possibly a woman cradling something in her arms, even more explicit. Two biomorphs in the painting's upper right seem to be chatting in a landscape setting—the sky is pale blue and the earth below is tan. Between the biomorphs is a smaller creature—an offspring perhaps. It is, I think, legitimate to read these shapes as animate beings or even figures. They are, after all, not much more abstract than the humorous signs that stand for human beings in Miró's paintings.

A number of Gorky's drawings from the summer of 1944 leave much of the white of the paper showing. This group of drawings is simpler and sparer than the denser drawings from the previous summer, and the over-all effect is more graphic. Line is taut, swift, and wiry. The use of color and pencil shading is sparse. Yet Gorky worked in many ways at once, and some 1944 drawings are wildly rococo, full of soft sfumato and curling shapes that turn into Disneyesque creatures as Gorky's metamorphic imagination turns itself loose on cumulus clouds and feathery trees (Fig. 126). Of the drawings from this Virginia sojourn, Mougouch wrote to Jeanne in November: "When he works from nature there is always great truth in what he draws you feel the search & it cannot fail to communicate something—when he draws from memory at night or on rainy days the drawing is perhaps more bold but tends to be more ART you know what I mean, there is less truth, though often it makes a finer drawing it is less interesting especially for him."

The sparer type of drawing led to a new kind of painting of which *They Will Take My Island* and *Painting* (in the Peggy Guggenheim Collection) are examples (Figs. 162 and 163). Both were painted in Virginia in November, just before Gorky and Mougouch returned to New York. "Gorky works on as though we were not leaving in a few days," Mougouch wrote to Jeanne at the time, "& yesterday started a huge canvas, almost as big as the one in N.Y." The huge canvas (65¾ x 69¾ inches), called simply *Painting,* was the one she said he had to "feel like a bonfire inside to tackle." In *Painting* and in the canvases like *They Will Take My Island* that followed, Gorky struggled to find a new relationship between line and color. Perhaps the chill in the air and his imminent departure from Virginia forced him to make bold decisions.

With their mostly white backgrounds and their few spots of primary color floating quite free of line, the spare paintings from November 1944 looked so simple that Mougouch feared people would call them drawings. What Gorky had discovered was a means to keep the directness of

the drawings when he moved on to canvas. Line is less tentatively prob-
ing, less gentle and caressing than in earlier paintings. Bold, almost
fiercely bold, black lines zap across space. There is a headlong quality, as
if Gorky had been in a rush to explore his new ideas before heading
north. In *They Will Take My Island,* line's urgency parallels an urgency
of subject matter: on the right side of the canvas is what appears to be a
figure with her face turned skyward and one clawlike hand thrust up in a
gesture that testifies to Gorky's admiration for the weeping women with
sky-turned faces in Picasso's *Guernica*. A similar grieving woman appears
to the left in *From a High Place* (1944) (Fig. 132), a painting that may be
a kind of abstract self-portrait showing the artist (center) seated before his
easel (to the right).

Mougouch expressed her enthusiasm for Gorky's recent work in her
November letter to Jeanne. In some canvases, she said, he "used only
one tone of yellow blue red & black or gray in spots like this." (To give
Jeanne an inkling of what Gorky was doing, she drew a meandering line
and three color areas.) "And yet," she said, "what difference in the directions & planes v. fascinating to me for I look and see every kind of depth
all so much clearer than in cubism . . . so simple you know it looks especially as there are great areas of pure canvas I cant tell you how old fashioned & pointless seems a canvas all covered with brush strokes—of
course some will say 'but it is not painting' Shit on them."

Jeanne shared Mougouch's enthusiasm for the change in Gorky's
work. Months later, when she purchased *They Will Take My Island* and
it arrived at her home in Soda Springs, California, she wrote: "And it is
what Arshile had wanted to do for it has all the lightness and transparency of the drawings." Mougouch wrote back saying that she herself
loved *They Will Take My Island*: "Arshile too is v. proud & happy that
you have it—Sweeny, the boob & most everyone felt that it was the climax of the summer's work which it was—one of the last he did—it was
sort of a landmark to him & I have felt plenty bad that we had to move
back just as that was reached—like waking from a dream just before you
have solved the riddle—very hard to pick up again."

Of this new kind of painting, Gorky said, "any time I was ready to
make a line somewhere, I put it somewhere else. And it was always better." The simplification of means, together with line's independence
from color, would lead to the even sparer canvases of 1945 and 1946.

47

November and December
in New York

Getting settled at 36 Union Square in the late fall of 1944 was, as Mougouch had predicted, unsettling. Gorky was once again preoccupied with the search for a dealer—an onerous task, especially for an artist in his midforties who had not had a gallery show in nine years. Mougouch discovered that she was pregnant again. To complicate their lives even further, Jean Hebbeln gave them a ten-month-old English sheepdog, which they named Zango after the dog Gorky had had as a boy. Gorky sent Vartoosh snapshots of Maro and Zango and wrote, "This big dog belongs to Maro. His name is Zango. He reminds me of our own dogs." Gorky took great pleasure in the spectacle he created by dog walking—it was almost as good as taking Maro out in her grand English pram. "Having a dog has opened up a whole new life," he said. "I have a whole new group of friends. Now that I have a dog they come up and speak to me. I am perfectly respectable."

That winter Mougouch's brother, John, married a twenty-four-year-old art student named V. V. Richards. Having lost both his daughters to foreigners, Captain Magruder must have been happy about his son's choice. The bride was the daughter of a wealthy banker named August Richards. A photograph of the wedding reception, which took place in the Richardses' Fifth Avenue apartment, shows Gorky entertaining the guests by dancing an Armenian shepherd's dance (Fig. 128). With his longish dark hair, his Groucho Marx moustache, and his tweed jacket patched with leather at the elbows, he looks exotic. Men in pinstripes ignore him, but the groom in military uniform looks mildly amused and stout women wearing little hats watch Gorky with demure smiles. One even claps him on. With a cigarette dangling from the corner of his lips, Gorky holds one arm straight out—an Armenian Poseidon conquering the rough seas of Manhattan society. The other arm holds a large white handkerchief. The suspension and balance of his posture bring to mind the mobile poise of shapes' arrangement in his paintings. Gorky keeps his balance by the vector of his glance. His huge brown eyes seem focused on a place a few feet in front of his outstretched arm. Probably there was nothing located at that spot in space—the wedding guests wisely cleared the floor for Gorky's performance. The place on which his eyes are fixed was a location of Gorky's choosing. Similarly, when Gorky drew he established locations or points in space not according to what was actually there but according to where he imagined what he saw to be.

"He always took over completely," said Mougouch's younger sister Esther:

> He was doing a "Georgian" dance and he came over to August Richards's sister, a very formal elderly lady with her hair carefully put up in a great bun. She was plump with a big bosom. He danced over and came up behind her and started taking down her long dark hair. He took out her tortoiseshell comb and let her hair down. She was puzzled and uncomfortable, but she liked the attention. Afterward she went off and the maid helped her to put her hair back up. Gorky had no sense of other people. He could get away with this kind of behavior in some circles but not at a banker's house on Fifth Avenue. He had no sense of his audience.

Another wedding guest remembered that at some point in the festivities the bride organized a game of charades and Gorky, in order to act out some word—probably the word *hair*—went over to an unsuspecting female guest and took down her hairdo, his second assault on a woman's hair in a single evening!

Because her new husband, a Marine, had to return overseas, V. V. lived for a brief period as a paying guest at 36 Union Square. She recalls: "I paid seventy dollars a month for my room—the bedroom on the right off the passageway. They fed me as well. I boarded with Gorky and Mougouch the first year when Maro was a baby and Gorky had a studio across the street in an office building on top of Klein's department store." V. V. Rankine, as she is now called, treasures two memories of the time she spent with the Gorkys. The first was when she came home from Ozenfant's art school carrying a small and overworked canvas under her arm. Gorky asked her, "What did you do today, V. V.?" and when she showed him her painting, he said, "I appreciate the fact that you had the interest in this work to keep going into it, but next time, V. V., try and put a little more wonder in it." The other memory was of the day Mondrian visited Gorky's studio. After he came to live in New York in 1940, Mondrian met Gorky and they saw quite a bit of each other. "Gorky admired Mondrian's painting and he felt that Mondrian was a standard-bearer," Mougouch recalls. "Gorky also had a plot: he thought that Mondrian should marry my aunt Marion, because they both had tiny appetites." In Gorky's mind Mondrian stood for the tradition of European modernism and for the heroic persistence of abstract art, so a studio visit from Mondrian was a daunting occasion. According to V. V. Rankine, "Mondrian telephoned Gorky and said he wanted to come to Gorky's studio. Gorky was thrilled, but he felt that he could not take Mondrian to his new studio, because it was too small. So Gorky brought his paintings and his easel back to 36 Union Square and reset up his studio so that it wouldn't look like a living room. Before Mondrian arrived, Gorky said to me, 'I'll introduce you and you can shake hands, but then you must leave.' Mondrian came in his English pinstriped suit."

As winter began, Gorky did not feel sufficiently settled to paint. He continued his search for a gallery, and he sold a few paintings out of his studio. David Hare brought Peggy Guggenheim to look at his work and, though she did not offer him a show, she did buy *Painting* (Fig. 164), which Gorky had finished just before leaving Virginia. Mougouch wrote to Jeanne in December: "Peggy Guggenheim bought one of the latest largest pictures. She was crazy to have the one in janis's show [*The Liver Is the Cock's Comb*] but felt it was too large and everyone who has seen the one she bought thinks it much more advanced and interesting so you see our dear archangel we have a little money for the nounce and you must not rob your nest egg any more." Mougouch told Jeanne about their hopes that Gorky would find a gallery:

Everyday has either brought new promise or dashed a couple of our rosiest hopes and since we have been back it has been but waiting and buzzing.

Breton has been here several times, the last time I had thought to cook him my very best pilaff tossing in ½ lb. of butter and god knows what happened the rice was cook-resistant and the great poet had to eat his shashlik on a great hunk of bread! You can imagine how pleased gorky was . . . but he was so enthusiastic over g.s new work and we are to photograph one to be reproduced in some book he is doing . . . also Maro has 8 lines consecrated to her in Breton's new book on Eternal Youth written in canada this summer the first part of which it seems deals with women [*Arcanum 17*, published in 1945 with illustrations by Matta]. Very sweet. Eternal youth twould seem is Elisa his new woman whom he brings here. Kind of a buttonhead but rather charming in that way. Very different from jacqueline and don't imagine he will have much difficulty making her toe the line. The great joke is that she plays the piano or has and loves music [Breton hated music] so Breton is coming around just a bit o there is so much gossip my ears are full of it and it makes mc frightfully sad and I wish I did not have such ears as hear these things, gorky does not. And I think of you and I and all our romantic notions about the love of poets . . . things are not that way and yet strangely in essence perhaps they are and that is why details are untruthful something very pure is *felt* between people and then the details grow up and cover that . . . everyone, David [Hare] and everyone insists on telling us about Breton and his desire for power as though they would warn us but we feel safe because Gorky cannot speak french and we can never get too close. The danger is there though. I believe he [Breton] is a bit bothered that we are such friends with Jacqueline and David. However he spoke to [Pierre] Matisse for Gorky and this week that fellow is keeping us on tenterhooks waiting for his call . . . Pollock weaved in here yesterday to talk to gorky as a painter . . . you can imagine how *that* took then he insisted on using four letter words while gorky got greener and greener. He was drunk and I must say I was rather surprised for he seemed to lack any sensibility at all, sort of foolish he was.

Matta came today and he is going to make a new drawing for your friends which he declares will be better because he has only one of the old series which is like yours . . . He is very flush these days having found himself a young lady [Patricia Kane, who soon became Matta's wife and who subsequently married Pierre Matisse] with denghi [money] and anyway he makes quite a bit so he bought one of Gorky's new drawings. Nice of him.

Matta and David Hare persuaded Matisse, who was Matta's dealer, to come to look at Gorky's work. Pierre Matisse did not, however, offer Gorky a show. "Gorky showed him his whole portfolio of absolutely wonderful 1943 drawings from Virginia," Mougouch recalls. "But Matisse rejected Gorky. He asked Gorky such funny questions: 'Who are your buyers?' Well, Gorky had two buyers, Ethel Schwabacher and Mrs. Metzger. And Bernard Davis, who hadn't bought a painting in quite a long while. From Gorky's point of view, that was why he wanted a gallery— to collect patrons. If he had many patrons he wouldn't have needed a gallery." Gorky was miffed, and Matisse departed, unimpressed by Gorky's work. Later Gorky learned that Matisse had written to a friend that he found Gorky's work *"sur-chargée"*—overloaded, just too much.

By December Gorky and Mougouch had made a plan to leave New York at the turn of the year and go to Roxbury, Connecticut, where they had been offered the use of David Hare's house, studio, and car for nine months. "David's house is going to be wonderful as soon as I pull down the chintz and put the dainty mirrors and prettily framed prints up in the attic," she wrote to Jeanne. She was glad, she said, to get away from the "back-biting and opportunism" of the Manhattan art world.

We shan't be lonely. Two miles away is sandy calder and six yves tanguy who according to david and jacqueline is awfully nice. And david and j. will come out to see us. David is so in love with jacqueline and he says he thinks she is with him but for the present she won't marry again because she thinks marriage is a jinx now . . . I look forward with such joy [to a] whole year in the country *free* of family horror free of all the waste of energy which it is to move four times a year and this move won't count as we have not in the least settled here and gorky has not had the chance much to his disgust to start working . . .

we were glad to see noguchi in a pleasant mood though we have not seen him since.

On December 20, Gorky's search for a dealer came to an end when he signed a contract with Julien Levy, the dealer who had helped promote Surrealism in the United States and to whom he had shown his work in the early thirties. It was André Breton and Marcel Duchamp who convinced Levy to take Gorky on. Mougouch's girlhood friend the writer Eleanor Perényi, who worked for Levy in 1943 and 1944, may also have had a hand in his decision. She had become excited about Gorky's paintings when she and her mother, the novelist Grace Zaring Stone, visited 36 Union Square. "I rushed back to Julien Levy the next morning and said, 'I've got a wonderful painter for us!' Julien Levy said, 'Oh, who?' I said, 'Arshile Gorky.' 'Oh,' said Julien, 'he's not very good. He's very derivative. I'm not interested.'" Soon thereafter, however, Levy invited Gorky to join his gallery. Levy's own account of becoming Gorky's dealer put his reaction to Gorky's new work in a more positive light. He said that after he got out of the army Gorky came to see him and encouraged him to reopen his gallery: "The promise I had suspected in his early experiments seemed fulfilled."

Gorky was delighted to have his financial anxieties relieved by the guarantee of a monthly income of $175. And Levy promised him a show. On January 10, 1945, already ensconced in Hare's Roxbury farmhouse, Mougouch wrote to Jeanne about Gorky's new contract:

I have a strange hallucination that I have not told you of the contract with julien levy????? . . . anyway julien l. is all excited over g and feels he has felt that way ever since he first knew g.s work which was 15 yrs ago so he is also understanding of his old work. Its true you know he almost gave g. a show about 10 yrs ago but at the last minute got scared off quite why I cant make out. But he and his wife are so friendly and g. can talk to him quite freely and he will not dictate and though I do think he has the strangest dead romantic collection the very fact that g is so different from what he is in the habit of is a good thing . . . also he does I think know how to maestro things and that above all is what g. needs so that he can feel quite free just to paint and paint. Breton . . . is writing the forward [sic] to the catalogue and all this with the framing and printing has made it necessary to put off the show, originally scheduled for the first week in feb. until the end of feb or the first of march . . . The manipulations with julien are sort of dense to me but as I understand he owns so many paintings per annum plus so many drawings and we get a monthly dispensation of $175 and then after j. has sold enough to cover his annual outlay on g. we get 2/3 on every thing sold that does not belong to him. Not exactly lavish but it is steady and there is so much less in moral expense or spirit wrenching.

Gorky liked Julien Levy, but he did not like many of the artists that Levy showed. Moreover, he came to believe that Levy was unprofessional—sloppy about getting work seen and sold. Levy was often absent from his gallery, and sometimes during business hours the gallery was closed. Mougouch recalls that once she and Gorky went to the gallery and found Gorky's drawings spread all over the floor: "There was no space to walk and Jacob Beane who was secretary to Julien Levy at that time, was walking around over and on these drawings. Instead of Levy's choosing his paintings and giving the rest back, he never chose and so he did not give the rest back. Gorky said Julien hadn't tried to sell, because he did not want to pay Gorky more than the agreed upon stipend of $2,100.00 a year." Gorky was worse than Levy about keeping accounts, and he did not keep track of what paintings and drawings he sent to the gallery. As a result, it was never clear which works in the gallery belonged to Gorky and which to Levy. After a few seasons, Gorky became worried that, because the yearly ceiling was never reached, Levy now owned a large number of his works.

Gorky's complaints about Levy's lack of enterprise are borne out in a satire about Levy's gallery called "Art's Sake" that Eleanor Perényi published in the March 1947 issue of *Town and Country*. The piece is narrated by the assistant (Perényi) of an art dealer named Mr. Jellicoe, who is clearly meant to be Levy. The gallery is "in the doldrums." On its walls are paintings by a Russian artist who, being "the only surrealist who paints directly from nature," sounds very much like Gorky. No one is buying, so one day when Mr. Jellicoe has ignored a prospective buyer and gone out to lunch, his assistant says a few positive words about the show and makes a sale herself. When Mr. Jellicoe returns and learns that she has sold a painting for $350 to that "awful Babbitt," he is furious. The assistant knows that she will not be forgiven.

In preparation for Gorky's first exhibition at Julian Levy's, Breton offered to collaborate with Gorky on titles for his paintings. "You can't have a show without titles," Julien Levy had said. "People want to have a handle to pick paintings up with." Mougouch worried that it would be hard for Breton to understand the culture from which Gorky's subject matter sprang, and she wrote to Jeanne, "I think perhaps in the end g. will find his own titles though I think breton could help to bring them out." On New Year's Eve 1944, just before Gorky and Mougouch moved to Roxbury, André Breton came to 36 Union Square to work on titles. Breton told Gorky to say whatever came into his mind when he looked at his paintings, and as Gorky brought out one canvas after another, he talked about childhood memories connected to his imagery. When some phrase struck Breton as a possible title, he made a sign. If Gorky agreed that the title was suitable, Mougouch wrote it down. From Roxbury on January 10, Mougouch wrote Jeanne: "Breton came down new years eve and gorky told him something associated with or of each painting and breton with his marvelous incision picked those of g.s words which made a title. They are very nice I think, they are gorky not surrealism oder etwas [or something] and andré was very anxious to maintain that you know he did not want to make them surrealist." Evocative and elusive, the titles followed the Surrealist theory of titles, which, as Breton once explained, held that a title should leave a painting nameless in the sense that the title and the painting were two separate things.

The ten paintings presented in Gorky's first show at Julien Levy give an idea of the kind of title that came out of the session with Breton: *The Leaf of the Artichoke Is an Owl, One Year the Milkweed, Water of the Flowery Mill, The Sun, the Dervish in the Tree, The Horns of the Landscape, They Will Take My Island, The Pirate, Love of a New Gun, How My Mother's Embroidered Apron Unfolds in My Life.* Although he had not been present at the naming of Gorky's paintings, Levy, having spent "endless hours" discussing painting with Gorky, felt that he could offer "an approximation" of what Gorky said. When he included several of these approximations in his 1966 monograph, *Arshile Gorky*, he cautioned the reader not to assume too much from them—Gorky, he knew, did not want his imagery to be read in a literal way. Yet some of Levy's statements are overly literal, for example, the one associated with *Land-scape Table*: "No, the black spot is not Hitler's mustache. But imagine all those generals sitting before a map and carving the landscape as if it were food." What Levy wrote in connection with *The Leaf of the Artichoke Is an Owl* is a more probable distillation of Gorky's words: "One image leads to another, one wisdom leads to another when you look into it, like peeling an artichoke . . . the leaves lying in the plate like feathers . . . and of course the silhouette of an artichoke leaf is quite simply that of an owl."

PART XI

Gorky with Maro and André Breton in Roxbury, Connecticut, 1945

48

Roxbury

Early in January 1945 Gorky, Mougouch (nearly two months pregnant), and Maro, three months shy of two, moved to David Hare's house at 148 Good Hill Road between Roxbury and Woodbury. They rented 36 Union Square to Mougouch's sister Esther and sister-in-law V. V. Mougouch wrote to Jeanne on January 10: "We have rented the apt. . . . for a colossally huge outrageous sum which pleases me no end for I think extortion when practiced on ones own family which is addicted to degrading remarks about union sq, is really a fine thing. I feel like old mr. Scrudge or scrooge himself!" Not surprisingly, the landlord-tenant relationship was troubled. As it turned out, V. V. did not like living with Esther's three-month-old baby and she moved back uptown, leaving Esther with the problem of finding someone to share the rent. On June 4 Mougouch's father wrote to his son about the "grand bataille [great battle] of the studio . . . boy, it did wax bitter between the two poor little artistes [meaning V. V. and Esther] on one hand and those shylocks—the Gorkysteins, on the other." In the end, Mougouch's mother came to the rescue and made up V. V.'s share of the rent.

The move to Connecticut was by train. In the huge hall at Grand Central Station the sheepdog, Zango, bolted and Mougouch, bundled in a hand-me-down fur coat and clutching both Maro and Zango's leash, fell backwards and was pulled across the marble floor: "I had a full view of the stars painted on the waiting room ceiling." When Gorky returned from buying the tickets they all laughed at the disarray.

Upon their arrival, Gorky exclaimed about the beauty of the Roxbury train station, with its samples of local crafts displayed on the walls. The car David Hare had lent them was waiting in the parking lot. The only hitch was that Mougouch had not driven in a long time, and it was dark. Fearing for her family's safety on the snowy road, she made Gorky and Maro walk down the final hill.

Her January 10 letter to Jeanne told about their arrival:

> god you should have seen us the first day we arrived out here. We arrived at night and it snowed and snowed and the next day we had no bread no milk due to my idiocy so what must we do but set out for the roxbury general store with maro in the laundry basket nailed to two pieces of wood the idea being it was a sled. It took us three hrs to go and get back and of course by the time we had hauled her and a load of groceries up the huge hill the snow had quite melted and we could have gone in the car. But we did feel so good you know with our sheep dog bounding around gorky looking incredible in about three coats and two hats which were gradually heaped on maro who became nothing but a little red nose growing out of a welter of coats and cabbages.

Thanking Jeanne for sending money so that they could order warm country clothes from L.L. Bean, Agnes said she and Gorky felt "gay and goofy."

David Hare's house was a white clapboard Classical Revival structure set about twenty-five feet back from the road. Behind the house was a large barn that Hare had fixed up as a sculptor's studio. It had one long, narrow northeast window, and Gorky soon added another, but still he wasn't satisfied. The barn's cement floor was bad for his rheumatism, and, compared with the Virginia barn's rough board walls, the plasterboard walls made it feel, he said, like a big, white hangar. "He hated the barn also because David had a lot of machinery for making metal sculpture in it," Mougouch recalls. Gorky complained about the surrounding landscape, as well. Roxbury seemed less interesting than Virginia: "The trees were new growth and there were no waterfalls, no nearby river." Fortunately, Gorky was not working from nature. While in Roxbury he was busy transforming his Virginia drawings into paintings, and he was under pressure because his show was scheduled for March. "At David

Hare's house," Mougouch recalls, "Gorky was turning out paintings like butter cookies."

During their first days in Connecticut they fixed up the house and studio, putting all the bourgeois furniture and objects that they considered "pseudo surrealist junk" into the attic. Mougouch told Jeanne:

> gorky is so impressed with himself because he has a yellow couch in the studio he plans how you will come and discuss dieu sait quoi [God knows what] if not ingres! He thinks I am going to sit on it and read about David [the French painter Jacques-Louis David] to him you know that huge david book he has in french his pipe dream is that I translate it to him and it is so boring that I always go to sleep in the middle of the page so that in four years I have read him 10 pages . . . gorky is already so happy and eager to work. and that is all that matters. and never never do we want to live in the city again.

Their morning routine consisted of rising early and shoveling snow. Mougouch wrote in February: "Darling Jeanne Does Urban shovel lots & lots of snow? Gorky wants to know Its been so good for G's figgur — and he has no longer so many aches & pains partially due to long winter underwear I think." When Gorky took breaks from painting, they listened to music or read. Every day while Maro slept they walked in the forest, searching, Mougouch reported to Jeanne, for "subjects for gorky to work from when it gets warmer." They cleaned the house once a week or when guests were expected. The only really difficult chore was laundry. Gorky's winter underwear floating in a tub looked to Mougouch "big enough to sheathe an elephant!"

Mougouch's peasant-woman routine was motivated in part by an ethical view of the good life, a life lived close to the earth, exploiting no one else's labor, and determined by the seasons. Her effort to become Gorky's ideal wife amazed her father. "He thought I was a throwback to some ancestor or something. I worked in the garden. I did the wash. I plucked chickens and skinned rabbits. To do that I had to take lessons from a Polish lady who lived next door up the road on the hill. They were a very sweet Polish couple and during the war they gave us a beautiful piece of veal. And Gorky and I knew it was a calf that we had patted through the fence. We couldn't eat it. We cooked it and we looked at each other and we gave it to Zango."

Their life in Roxbury was solitary, but New York friends came to visit and they saw a few local Connecticut friends, including Alexander and Louisa Calder; Yves Tanguy and his American wife, the Surrealist painter Kay Sage; and André and Rose Masson. André Masson later said that Gorky was the only American painter he knew, and his son Diego Masson remembers Gorky coming to their house in New Preston, Connecticut. Masson's painting had a definite impact on Gorky. Both men were associated with Surrealism but separate from it. Both worked from a passionate observation of nature to create biomorphic semiabstractions. Gorky would have paid attention when Masson said, "I do not paint in front of but within nature." Masson's preoccupation with what he called "telluric" subject matter—themes of earth and germination, growth and metamorphosis—was similar to Gorky's fascination with fecundity. Even the shapes in Masson paintings of 1942–43 have much in common with Gorky's. For example, sprout/petal forms with their pointed tips filled in with color appear in both Masson's and Gorky's work, and both artists had a predilection for womblike shapes with suggestions of life burgeoning within.

Apart from the Tanguys, the friends they spent the most time with in Connecticut were the Calders, but Gorky never grew close to them:

> We saw the Calders about once a week, often with the Tanguys. The Calders were very sweet to me. Sandy Calder understood my relation to Gorky and its difficulty. Their daughters Sandra and Mary were especially sweet with Maro. But Gorky was not at ease with the Calders. He was jealous because of Sandy's success. He felt Calder didn't deserve it, that his work was all thanks to Miró. He thought Sandy was successful because he was married to Louisa who was a member of the James family, or because he was Sandy Calder and an American. He felt Calder had advantages that he did not have. Yet Calder gave nothing but pleasure to people and this was not in Gorky's aura—he couldn't understand it.
>
> When I was pregnant Sandy gave me his hand-woven striped trousers to wear with a beautiful buckle. Louisa had baskets of wool and was constantly knitting things. At meals Sandy's head would sink lower and lower. He snored. He would be sound

asleep except when his name was mentioned. Everyone else went on talking, and if he heard the word "Sandy," up his head went. He brought me a mobile to give to Gorky when he was sick. He gave us a painting and Gorky threw it away. He gave us a white stabile made of clay and Gorky did not like it. He gave me pins and earrings. Gorky had a very jealous character, and he did not appreciate this. If Gorky didn't understand someone, he would not trust them.

Calder recalled first meeting Mougouch when she and Jean Hebbeln came to his Manhattan workshop to buy a sculpture for Henry Hebbeln. "And then," Calder recalled, "I met Gorky with Hebbeln. And somehow I think I went down to see Mougouch and Gorky. They lived on Union Square." Remembering his visits with Gorky in Roxbury and remembering also his wife's efforts to find the Gorkys a house to buy, Calder said:

Somehow he seemed a little bit unhappy. Maybe it was his moustache. But I had a moustache once and I don't think I was unhappy . . . And we used to see them. As a matter of fact, Mougouch and my wife Louisa went out in search of a house for the Gorkys and they found a place. And my wife came back and said, "We have to sell out and buy this one." I said, "Uhhuh." But we didn't. Well, we were very good friends with Mougouch. But Gorky had a sort of plaintive side to him. He must have sung once or twice because I always associate that with him.

49

The Eye-Spring

Gorky's first exhibition at Julien Levy's small gallery at 24 East Fifty-seventh Street opened on March 6, 1945. A few days before the opening Gorky, Mougouch, and Maro took the train into the city and installed themselves in the Hotel Fourteen at 14 East Sixtieth Street, where Mougouch's mother was staying. On March 3 Esther Magruder wrote to her son: "The Gorkys flew into town on Wednesday with Maro in tow all done up in a fur coat handed on by the Chermayeffs—looking like a teddy-bear . . . doesn't talk yet . . . Gorky's show opens on Tuesday and there is a K T [cocktail] party at the gallery in P.M."

Preparations for the show were tense. As Julien Levy hung the paintings, Gorky watched with a wary eye. Levy's choice of frames—salmon-pink strips of wood—upset him. Gorky had hoped for gold, and André Breton had recommended that Levy frame two canvases with luxurious gold frames and two with simple wooden strips and leave two unframed, propped on easels. Gorky also felt that Levy could have selected a stronger show, but he said nothing. "We went and stood at the opening and nobody came," Mougouch remembers. Levy had not mailed the announcements on time:

We just waited there. Duchamp was there and Breton and my mother and Julien's wife, Muriel. And Mrs. Metzger and the Schwabachers were probably all there. Julien was half drunk. He was a heavy drinker and he always smelled of Roquefort cheeze. At the opening Gorky overheard Julien explaining his paintings to someone, and it made him so angry he went into a corner and started to sharpen his pencil. He was just horrified. Then he realized that Julien didn't really understand his paintings at all and was just backing him because he thought he would take off and he was getting Gorky for nothing.

In early April Mougouch wrote at length to Jeanne about the opening:

I guess to tell the truth it was a sort of dissapointment to us because we had both thought of something really good in the way of presentation he had everything paintings and andre's beautiful preface which he badly translated so many things that julien muffed like only printing a couple of hundred catalogues so that now there are no more when it is so important that everyone should have one but jeanne darling you must be very quiet about this because we have a years contract to live out and maybe more. Everyone said (except andre who told julien it was badly hung and framed and now thats a new swords point) it looked very beautiful and of course it couldn't help but . . . but all this made us very worried about the opening and we got there a bit late and drank a lot of cocktails furnished by an old friend of gorky's [Bernard Davis] and very soon gorky had that wild dishevelled look that I associate with our san francisco bouts remember that night in the spanish night club with isamu [Noguchi] and others when he told you I cared for nothing except clothes a sort of frantic undone but I'll-have-the-last-bitter-drop look that's how he looked by eight oclock. By that time julien had so tactfully and understandingly told him that the critics who had been there through the afternoon had been stonier and more unresponsive than he had ever known them that usually he could handle them and strike some responsive note in each one but this time there was a kind of blind opposition he had never in his career come up against were this [told] to marcel duchamp it would set him up for the evening but to gorky with his childlike dream that one day the critics will come and clasp him by the hand and say gorky we love you we have never done right by you forgive us etc well you know it was NOT the thing and then chermayeff of course with his the paintings are beautiful but old chap couldn't you have done

without the preface and above all the titles o well we just aint
made of the right metal tinplate is what we need I guess and then
my mother not knowing who was julien levy waltzing right up to
gorky talking to julien say[ing] what a pity he didn't hang ANY of
the best things at that point I think gorky just reached for the
pitcher of martinis o jesus my family. But despite what sounds
like a hiatus I think the show is a success from the people who
matter to us and I know the drawings are selling you know he
only showed last year's drawings none of this past summer because
of some crazy notion about the first being easier for the public to
understand and one painting is sold that is was sold the first day
and maybe more now o and killing story the next day gorky went
around in the morning and there in that narrow hall were [James
Johnson] sweeny [James Thrall] soby and [Alfred] barr . . . the lift
had bust! So the three brass hats puffed their way up four flights of
stairs and gorky made a rapid exit. It seems sweeny wanted two
paintings soby another two and barr that nasty barr wanted two
drawings so of course they went away undecided.

before the show sweeny had come around and chose four
paintings which he asked julien to put aside for some show that
might materialize under the heading unrecognized artists so stupid julien held back two of the most wonderful paintings and told
gorky about it when it was too late of course gorky would never let
himself be hung in such a show imagine unrecognized artists or
misunderstood or some such bunk and the most idiotic angle is
that for some fifteen years the museum has known gorky and in
every way except the public way they have made out to recognize
him do you get what I mean. I mean they are so insulting and so
gaga without rhyme or reason I mean they have known him all
along so why suddenly decide he is unrecognized . . . gorky makes
a poor moses in the bullrushes! Gorky has flatly refused to be in
such an exhibition . . .

well anyway at our opening pierre matisse asked us to come to
dinner on Thursday so we decided to sell my diamond pin and
just stay for three days and debauch which we did. Maro and
gorky went to the metropolitan museum in the morning and maro
shouted ge ge at the egyptian mummies to stand up and everyone
saw them walking down 57th street and maro looking like an elf

they were a great hit. We had supper with andre and elisa who is
awfully sweet and she just loves gorky I have come to like her very
much indeed and she has made andre very happy andre gave us
his manuscript for the preface and I am sending it to you to read
it is so different in french and then they took us to some party in
some people named reis house. [Bernard Reis was a lawyer and art
collector whose apartment on lower Fifth Avenue was a meeting
place for the Surrealists in exile. He was also Julien Levy's ac-
countant and treasurer of VVV.] they have many paintings and
the party was full of surrealists and most of whom were not on
speaking terms with andre. That was our social debut it seems and
gorky made a great hit with these people telling them about maro
for hours on end he can rave about that child endlessly and I
wonder how nice people are to be so responsive to every little
noise he says she makes this poor little horned toad that is coming
along had better be a boy . . . at this party andre had a loud verbal
fight with seligman while everyone looked on terrified while they
waved their pipes and pranced at each other and gorky just went
on talking about maro to the hostess how she said ge ge at the
moon quite unaware of any tension . . .

then the next night we went to matisse gosh he has such
lovely wonderful paintings . . . More or less the same people were
there andre and helion [French painter Jean Helion] but that
evening was very quiet and well behaved and matisse was so sweet
to gorky and maybe someday we can be with him he is not at all
cold at least he didn't seem so but he told jacqueline how much
he loved gorkys new painting but that he could not take everybody
o well and so ended our debauch on a very nice note really and
were we HAPPY to be home, how awfully glad we are that we are
not there those three days were just enough and THIS is life . . .
for us anyway I cannot conceive us ever living in the city again.

André Breton's "The Eye-Spring: Arshile Gorky" is perhaps the most
insightful essay ever written on Gorky. Gorky was delighted with it, and
it was soon reprinted as the final chapter in a new edition of Breton's *Surrealism and Painting*, first published in 1928. Although Gorky usually
hated to be interpreted and immediately became hostile if someone
claimed to understand what he was doing, Breton's essay pleased him,

no doubt because it is a poetic and imaginative work of art in itself. In his essay Breton warns the reader not to interpret Gorky's imagery too literally: Gorky, he says, thinks in analogies and all his forms are hybrids combining the seen with the felt and remembered. Thus, observed reality serves as a springboard to "profound states of mind" in which Gorky sees beyond appearances and beyond rationality to the superreal relationships between physical and mental structures. His art comes from the unconscious, the inner "spring" of the soul:

> The eye-spring . . . Arshile Gorky—for me the first painter to whom the secret has been completely revealed! Truly the eye was not made to take inventory like an auctioneer, nor to flirt with delusions and false recognitions like a maniac. It was made to cast a lineament, a conducting wire between the most heterogeneous things . . . The key of the mental prison . . . lies in a free unlimited play of *analogies* . . . One can admire today a canvas signed by Gorky, "The Liver is the Cock's Comb," which should be considered the great open door to the analogy world . . . Gorky is, of all the surrealist artists, the only one who maintains direct contact with nature—sits down to paint *before her* . . .
>
> Here is an art entirely new, . . . a leap beyond the ordinary and the known to indicate, with an impeccable arrow of light, a real feeling of liberty.

Before he wrote the essay, Breton had expressed concern that, since Surrealism was in a period of decline, his writing the preface might do Gorky more harm than good. Breton's apprehension was justified: Gorky's being taken up by the Surrealists made certain critics hostile. In the March 15, 1945, issue of *Art Digest*, Maude Riley vented her irritation at what she saw as the pretentious elitism of Breton's essay. She was annoyed with Breton's attribution of profundity to what she saw as Gorky's "incoherent 'accident' pictures," which were just a "debauch of emotionalism." As proof of Gorky's lack of control she pointed to his "running drips of turpentine."

More crushing, because it came from a highly respected critic, was Clement Greenberg's negative review in the March 24, 1945, issue of the *Nation*. It revealed Greenberg's distaste for Surrealism and his formalist preference for the kind of abstract art that came out of Cubism and moved toward flatness. Until recently, Greenberg said, Gorky had "stayed close to the most important problems of contemporary painting in the high style." But Gorky's long dependence on other artists made Greenberg suspect that he "lacked independence and masculinity of character." In Greenberg's view, Gorky's most recent paintings proved this suspicion right. Having cast aside Picasso and Miró, Gorky was now under the thumb of Kandinsky and Matta, that "prince of the comic-strippers." Gorky had been seduced by the Surrealists' worldly success. Given Gorky's high sense of honor and his fragile mixture of vulnerability and strength, Greenberg's suggestion that Gorky was weak, corrupted, and unmasculine wounded him. But Greenberg did not view Gorky as irredeemable. *They Will Take My Island* showed "promise," he said, and if Gorky was not a "first-rate artist," he was, in Greenberg's estimation, "a first-rate painter, a master of the mechanics and cuisine."

Edward Alden Jewell of the *New York Times* was more sympathetic to what he saw as a change in Gorky's style: "Gone are the larger, freer forms; forms that were clearly defined and, if related, detached. The expression now is fluid and lyrical, loosely weaving all-over designs that are intricate, spontaneous—in the nature of improvisations. And the gay warmth of his palette is like a flood of sunshine." Although Gorky was not greatly affected by good reviews, he was extremely touchy about bad ones. Mougouch's voice still has an edge of anger when she remembers Gorky's despair after reading Clement Greenberg's review: "I almost went and got a hammer and went after Greenberg. He said that Gorky had sold his soul to the devil. It was so humiliating and awful for Gorky and such a blow to him. And one year later, at Gorky's next exhibition, Greenberg ate his hat and said he'd been all wrong. But good reviews did not undo the wounding ones. Gorky never forgot. If anything could be twisted to make anything worse, Gorky managed to twist it."

Early in April Jeanne Reynal wrote to Mougouch saying she hoped Greenberg's essay would cause Gorky only "passing annoyance." That hope was dashed by Mougouch in her reply. For two months Gorky had, she said, been "paralyzed and agonized in a fever of self-criticism brought on by the suicidal attempt to see himself as others see him a terrible thing to see and for which I would gladly murder them one and all. He is unfortunately unable to dismiss them and julien has been a real sadist about sending out every piece of bad news and quite sliding over any good news." Only two paintings sold from the exhibition: *They Will Take My Island,* to Jeanne, and *The Leaf of the Artichoke Is an Owl,* to Wolfgang Schwabacher. As yet, Julien Levy had found no new patrons for Gorky.

50

Fearfully Linked with the Sun

※

In April 1945 André Breton and Elisa Claro spent three nights with
Gorky and Mougouch in Roxbury. Photographs Elisa took during a walk
in the woods show Gorky looking haggard and world-weary (p. 467). He
carries a battered straw basket and a walking stick; two-year-old Maro
rides on his shoulders. As is frequently the case in photographs, he is
smoking. Beside him, Breton, nattily dressed in proper shoes and a cor-
duroy jacket, holds, improbably, a pitchfork. Always aware of his leonine
looks, he thrusts back his shoulders, self-possessed.

Thanks to language barriers, Gorky's relationship to Breton was more
empathetic than intellectual. "When we see andré," Mougouch wrote to
Jeanne, "we do not really talk much. I am a little afraid to and you know
gorky doesn't really like to get philosophical." Yet during the visit Gorky
and Breton looked at Gorky's art books and discussed the idea of painting
with words. They talked also about Breton's soon-to-be-published book of
poems entitled *Young Cherry Trees Secured against Hares*, and Breton
asked Gorky to produce two black-and-white illustrations for the regular
edition and four hand-colored drawings for each of twenty deluxe copies.
Mougouch wrote to Jeanne in May: "There were two weeks of agony after Andre's visit here while Gorky strove to make 40 drawings for the "D"
[Deluxe ?] Edition of A's book . . . 'Shit' would ring across the field &
through the house but at last after using up $100 worth of paper he was
satisfied or worn out—I never know which & Andre was very pleased—
Each drawing is a little different but very fine & he was very glad in the
end that he had done them."

In the two drawings published in the regular edition, lines move across the paper with an eloquence and concision that predicts the taut linear configurations in paintings such as *Charred Beloved* and *Nude* from the following year (Figs. 167 and 168). Indeed, the frontispiece would serve as the basis for *Nude*. It is tempting to read both this drawing and the painting based on it as an abstract image of a woman lying on her back with her arms raised. The second drawing depicts a biomorphic creature with two *vagina dentata* heads and it recalls the personages in Miró's fantastical landscapes from the mid-1930s. If Gorky's two drawings do in fact allude to the female body, he was addressing the principal theme of *Cherry Trees*, most of whose poems relate to love and sex. One called "Freedom of Love" has imagery that is as metamorphic and hybrid as Gorky's. It begins: "My wife with the hair of a wood fire / with the thought of heat lightning, with the waist of an hourglass, with the waist of an otter in the teeth of a tiger . . . My wife with armpits of marten and of beechnut . . . with arms of seafoam and of riverlocks / And of a mingling of the wheat and the mill."

An April letter from Mougouch to Jeanne reported on Maro's second birthday, attended by Jacqueline Lamba and her daughter by Breton, Aube, on one of their regular weekend visits. Mougouch made a cake and they all decorated it with apple blossoms, rosebuds, and candles. "At the end of the meal it looked more like a scale model of shangri-la or maybe stalingrad after the siege." Despite Gorky and Mougouch's affection for Jacqueline, it pained them to hear her speak bitterly about Breton in front of Aube: "All I can say is may such a horrible nightmare never happen to us."

In May Gorky took part in two group shows, one of contemporary painting at the California Palace of the Legion of Honor in San Francisco, the other in New York at the 67 Gallery (at 67 West Fifty-seventh Street), opened by Howard Putzel in the fall of 1944, after he left his job as Peggy Guggenheim's assistant and adviser. Full of enthusiasm for what he saw emerging in New York, Putzel was one of the first to buy a Gorky. "He paid twenty dollars a month, but he simply had to have the picture," Levy said. In the May exhibition Putzel also included Masson, Matta, Miró, Arp, and Picasso, the Mexican Rufino Tamayo, and, among Americans, Pollock, Rothko, Baziotes, Motherwell, Krasner, Gottlieb, Hofmann, Richard Poussette-Dart, and Charles Seliger. Putzel called the show A *Problem for Critics*. The problem was how to characterize or name the kind of work being done by the Americans. "I believe we see real American painting beginning now," Putzel said, and he called it the "new metamorphism."

In May, before Breton and Elisa headed for Reno, where he would divorce Jacqueline and marry Elisa, they went to see Gorky and Mougouch a second time. Breton was planning to publish an American issue of a British Surrealist publication called *Message from Nowhere*, and he wanted Gorky, Matta, and perhaps Tanguy to contribute drawings. During the visit he encouraged Gorky and Mougouch to move to Paris. "We had such a gay time with them a week ago—planning to move, to Paris in the spring of next year," Mougouch wrote to Jeanne. "He says now that the war in Europe is over everything changes. Revolutionary activity recommences—no more coalition—I find this kind of talk very exciting like a child I guess because afterwards I poke Gorky for an answering glimmer & he looks at me quite blank for all my translating & I realize that actually we'll go back and stick some onions in the garden—nothing changes so quickly—for us anyway."

When Jeanne wrote back on June 27, she and Urban had just been traveling in the West with Breton and Elisa. Always quick to pass along news that might please Gorky, she reported that Breton had told her that Gorky would be "immediately appreciated" in Paris and that he would find there "all the stimulation of working not alone but among people who know what he is doing and will value it." Most encouraging to Gorky, she said that she had asked Breton whether he thought that Gorky's painting was "more important than anything we know of from reproductions of the work continuing in Paris and he said without a doubt. There is nothing new there just a repitition [*sic*] of everybodies [*sic*] known work. That Arshile had done something NEW."

In May Mougouch's sister Esther came to Roxbury for a few days, bringing her seven-month-old daughter, Sandra. Part of the purpose of her visit was to lend a hand: Mougouch had been ordered to stay in bed after symptoms that suggested danger of miscarriage. During Esther's visit there was a battle between David Hare's mother and his estranged wife's mother, the formidable Frances Perkins, secretary of labor under Roosevelt. The women came to divide the belongings of their respective offspring. Fearful that Mrs. Perkins would demand her share of the wedding presents, Mrs. Hare arrived first and hid her son's valuables in Mougouch's closet and under her bed. With an icebag on her huge belly, Mougouch was supposed to be a deterrent: her room was out of bounds. Mrs. Perkins turned up the next morning with a moving van, which she ordered backed up to the front door. Gorky, wearing his usual overalls and a lumberman's red-and-black-checked wool shirt, took Mrs. Perkins and Mrs. Harc around the house and listened as they squabbled over which wedding presents should rightfully go to whom and which objects were whose precious heirlooms. "It was terribly funny," Mougouch recalls, "because at one point Mrs. Perkins addressed Gorky as if he were one of the moving men. She said, 'Take this out to my van, please.' And Gorky said to her, 'Move it yourself, you old cow!'" She even tried to take a pot of oatmeal out of Gorky's hands as he was working in the kitchen. And, saying that of course she didn't want to disturb, she kept barging into Mougouch's bedroom to "glare with her gimlet eyes under my bed or in my face for a telltale expression—I kept right on with Dr. Holmes's Boston." At one point, Mougouch wrote to Jeanne, she "heard a great uproar downstairs from Gorky & E. [Esther] with loud expostulations from truck drivers & movers & Miss P. it seems they had even taken your mosaic." Since they had packed the mosaic in the front of the van it had to be returned by special messenger that night. "I don't believe I have ever witnessed such sordid goings on & more true to class behavior on the part of Miss P. Better proof of Herr Marx's concept of marriage in the capitalist world I can't imagine—& the most utter disregard of the gorky's belongings—I had to . . . [ask] Esther to sit on my shoes & clothes. The house is now furnished with two beds, a desk, 2 chairs 1 comfortable one & one table—the kitchen is OK."

Mougouch went on to send news of Maro: "Gorky spoils Maro outrageously so that I have to be constantly scolding him or her & of course when he had completely spoilt my hopes for a peaceful cup of coffee he vanishes to his studio leaving me to spank the creature . . . I get furious at Gorky for indulging her in a quite senseless way & then throwing up his hands with horror & calling her a nasty thing—Perhaps he will learn but more probably not & I shall have to play the role of the strict nanny." Jeanne was sympathetic: "Arshile," she wrote, "is just a skunk to play little goody two shoes leaving you the role of ogress always making the DONT'S." In another letter, however, Jeanne praised Gorky's domestic skills: "Arshile I know is the most wonderful nurse cook father husband and painter." The truth is that Gorky was both a doting and an impatient father. "All he could talk about was Maro," Mougouch says. "Maro would paint all over the walls with her shit and Gorky felt this was artistic. He read Freud." At parties Gorky would get Maro out of bed and parade her about in the palm of his hand. It wasn't long before Maro refused to stay in bed. "I used to lose my temper and smack her, and Gorky would smack her too. He had no worry about such matters." Although Gorky's studio was off-limits to Maro, she went out there anyway. "Once he chucked her out of the studio and she landed in a heap, fortunately in the grass. I saw her literally flying through the air. This bundle . . . I knew exactly what had happened. I lumbered out with my great pregnant belly across the field and I picked her up and dusted her off. She wasn't in the least upset. I don't think she cried at all. She wanted to go back into Gorky's studio."

In her June letter Mougouch told Jeanne that, though the weather had been rainy, Gorky was working well and the vegetable garden was equally productive. The garden was primarily Mougouch's responsibility, but her difficult pregnancy put the burden of caring for it on Gorky. "Oh, Zango!" Gorky would say when the vegetables were eaten by pests. "Why don't you kill a woodchuck, for goodness' sake?" But Zango would just look at Gorky and lie down. In another June letter, this one to Ethel Schwabacher, Mougouch said that Gorky was working hard: "Gorky has just gotten some new drawing paper & I see many canvases leaning against the studio in the sun—to whiten them you know—so there will follow now at last some good days of work I can tell it by the look in his eye—this past month he has done nothing but bemoan the weather & his terrible lack of talent—Are you so fearfully linked with the sun? If so my deep sympathy to wolf."

On July 4, 1945, Gorky wrote Vartoosh for the first time in many months:

My dearest Vartoosh:

Two days ago, I got your long awaited and sweet letter. But really, I wish you'd written more of yourselves and Moorad's present job. Any changes? I am seriously interested.

Happy to learn that you are fine, and Karlen has grown big and is doing well in school.

Now about ourselves. As you know, we were on the [Virginia]

farm with Agnes for nine months last year. I did a lot of painting and drawing, and all were well received in New York. We returned to New York and two months later came here [Roxbury]. We are staying at a friend's house that has a studio, at my disposal.

It's good here, and I am constantly working. The climate is just fine for Agnes and Maro. Agnes expects a baby early in August. Maro tries to speak out words and plays with her big dog, Zango. She picks flowers in the field, brings them to me in the studio, and wants me to show her books and offer her cookies. She says "Daddy poof! Gaga (meaning Zango) poof!, Mama poof!" and laughs. But when I ask her "Maro poof?" she says, "Daddy poof."

Yes, Agnes will have her baby late this summer. Her mother and the maid will come here for a month until Agnes comes home from the hospital.

We have another friend [Henry Hebbeln] here who owns a large farm, and we may go to stay with him in September, as our present landlord himself intends to live here. Otherwise, we shall return to New York.

I am enclosing a catalogue of my works on exhibit [in March]. Mr. André Breton, wrote a review of my works. He is a world famous French art critic, who writes about artists like Picasso.

The exhibit was held at Julien Levy Galleries, which usually houses rather serious works of art. All my paintings are to be shown at Julien Levy's this and probably next year. Beyond that, we shall renew our contract, if we agree on terms, that is how much he will pay me depends on the success my works will enjoy.

This is the first year that I am working without any financial worries. Mr. [Bernard] Davis has been very good to me too—he paid for and took care of the refreshments at the opening show. Mr. Levy sold seven [actually two] of my pictures . . . I have a few paintings which I believe will be well received in New York. However, I can't go to New York just yet. I may paint a new picture here, if I have the patience. [The translator omitted the following: "This is the first time I have written in Armenian for two years. I'm glad that Agapi and Satenik are well. Write to me immediately."]

Agnes has taken a few snapshots of Maro: I'll send you some, if they are good.

Agnes, Maro, and I send you our love

As ever,
Gorky

The offer of a roof over their heads from Henry and Jean Hebbeln, who had bought a farm in Sherman, solved the problem of where to go after David Hare returned to his Roxbury house in September. Gorky and Mougouch would rent the Hebbelns' farmhouse and barn after they were remodeled, and Henry Hebbeln would share 36 Union Square with them. Mougouch ended a late June letter to Jeanne about their plans with: "gorky is working so hard and too long of course like penelope he goes back to the studio at night and overdoes all his paintings till I could scream with rage how tiresome and utterly insane he is to go on doing the same thing every year I am only somewhat awed at the constancy with which the cycle is repeated but this is the month he should break through this miasma o life on a rolycoaster."

For all Mougouch's lament, the nine extant paintings from 1945 look fresh and direct, almost like drawings. *Diary of a Seducer* (Fig. 131) (the title, suggested by Max Ernst, comes from Kierkegaard's *Either/Or*) is the only painting that appears to have been worked on for long. The Roxbury paintings (Figs. 164 and 165) continue in the spare style developed just before Gorky left Virginia in the autumn of 1944, but the mood is slightly cooler and the tempo less impetuous. It is almost as if forms were suspended in some liquid medium—one thinks of the underwater ambience in contemporaneous Surrealist-inspired works by such New York School painters as Rothko or Baziotes. *Diary of a Seducer*'s protozoan shapes with radiating hairs, for example, recall the primal creatures that float in Rothko's *Slow Swirl at the Edge of the Sea* (1944). At first glance, Gorky's 1945 paintings seem to be more classically balanced than those of the previous year, but then, his deep knowledge of Cubism underlay even his most freely structured works.

As Gorky moved even further from the sensuous luxuriance of paintings like *Water of the Flowery Mill*, he exulted in putting line through its paces. Whereas the black lines in *Painting* and *They Will Take My Island* from 1944 were of various widths and had a kind of restless speed and a staccato dash to them, the lines in the 1945 paintings are less varied and have a more controlled grace. The black lines all appear to be approximately the same thickness, almost as if they were cut by a figure skater's blade. Gorky made these lines with the sign painter's brush that he had been experimenting with for several years and that he began to use regularly sometime early in 1945.

Line dives into or skims over thin color washes as it skirts around thicker patches of red, green, yellow, and black. Often the colored patches are ovals: sometimes they suggest an orifice and sometimes they are pinched along their contour to create a sprout/leaf/petal form. Compared with the shapes in the paintings like *They Will Take My Island* from the previous autumn, the shapes in the 1945 paintings are simple and self-contained. Although Gorky criticized Calder's sculpture as being too Miróesque, his own wiry black lines and his endlessly jostling equipoise might have been affected by seeing Calder's work. *Child's Companions*, for example, is like a painted mobile—it is as if Calder's shapes, having freed themselves from their attachment to wires and from the demands of gravity, have taken up positions to create an abstract landscape. In *Landscape Table* (Fig. 165), also from 1945, shapes seem to balance on a fulcrum, and in the lower right corner a grouping of shapes and lines resembles a small Calder stabile. But of course, the way Gorky's shapes float against a background of transparent, loosely brushed color is ultimately based on Calder's inspirer, Miró.

Gorky often placed a dominant shape so that it is cut off by the upper edge of his canvas. As a result, his forms seem suspended in shallow space. In four of the 1945 paintings, the shape that enters the canvas from the top is a dark rectangle; in two others it is a dark ellipse. The black rectangle in two closely related paintings, *Impatience* and *Good Hope Road* (also called *Hugging*) (Fig. 164), suggests the sooty interior of a fireplace—flamelike shapes seem to glow in its blackness. The rectangle in *Impatience* brings to mind the black vertical band from which the boot/butter churn hangs in the *Garden in Sochi* series: indeed, the rectangle's lower right corner touches the top of what might be a boot/butter churn motif. Both *Impatience* and *Good Hope Road* have, on the left, a grouping of shapes that can be read as a female figure, her bent arms raised over her head in an arch.

In calling a painting *Landscape Table*, Gorky made it clear that his paintings were both exteriors and interiors. As he moved from the Virginia drawings to oil on canvas in Roxbury, his spaces became shallow interiors. Sometimes they suggest a tabletop still life. Although the viewer can visualize the white background in *The Unattainable* as infinite extension, Gorky's line creates a delicate tracery that stays within the confines of a shallow space and, unlike Matta's line, never plunges into cavernous depths. Sometimes, as in *Diary of a Seducer*, Gorky evokes the mind's interior—like a Matta inscape. *Diary*'s soft, indeterminate shapes and meandering lines suggest a slow, anxious, dreamy state in which ideas, feelings, and memories float in and out of consciousness, now becoming hallucinatory images, now melting into the gray. Elaine de Kooning said that Gorky was always interested in what he called "the colors in the shade." The shade in this nearly grisaille painting seems touched with melancholy, as if sadness could block the sun.

Among the paintings that Mougouch watched Gorky struggling over in his Roxbury studio were two versions of his *Plough and the Song* series. (Those first versions are lost: according to Mougouch, two canvases from this series were destroyed in the fire in Gorky's studio the next year.) Given their title, we might assume that the *Plough and the Song* series had something to do with Gorky's memory of farmers singing as they worked in the Khorkom wheat fields. While Gorky was battling with this subject in August 1945, the Museum of Modern Art asked him to fill out a questionnaire. In answer to a question about the impact of his ancestry and background on his painting, he said that all his vital memories came from his childhood years: "These were the days when I smelled the bread, I saw my first red poppy, the moon, the innocent seeing. Since then these memories have become iconography, the shapes even the colors: millstone, red earth, yellow wheatfield, apricots etc." As in 1943, being in the country pried such images loose from the membrane of memory and set them floating before Gorky's mind and eye.

On August 8, 1945, in the Waterbury hospital, Mougouch gave birth to a girl, whom they named Yalda. They had expected a boy, and she was briefly disappointed. She wrote to both Jeanne and Ethel: "We have another skirt!" To Jeanne she said, "She is so strange & sweet with quite black hair & such long feet & fingers Gorky calls her his little pine tree & this is very much the situation—a rather straggly pine tree but so touching. She was born Aug 8 & I am milking her as gorky puts it." Yalda had a line of hair down her back and hair on her forehead. When Breton came to see her, he said politely, "the Little forehead is still not very well defined."

Two days before the baby arrived, an American bomber dropped a uranium bomb on Hiroshima and three days later, on August 9, a second, plutonium-type bomb was dropped on Nagasaki. Mougouch's letter spoke of the horror and irony of lying in a maternity ward and hearing about the bombing: "Sometimes I feel we are dinosaurs indeed there is another world where men breathe & breed disaster & death One wants to grip life by the scruff of the neck to assert its reality indeed more & more the *surreality* of OUR existence in this world—you know one *has* one hell of a nerve to make children especially the kind we seem to make or want to have sweet tender fierce & vulnerable." She said they planned to move to Sherman on the tenth of September. The farmhouse would not be ready: until the remodeling was finished they would have to live with the Hebbelns. Gorky, she said, "has some good work but it's a bad time to have to move."

For at least six months the new baby was still called Yalda. Finally, on a trip to New York, Gorky struck up a conversation with a man in a bar who informed him that Yalda in Hebrew meant girl, so he gave his daughter a Russian name, Natasha. The baby gained weight quickly and Gorky loved her earthy quality and her determination. Compared with the increasingly difficult two-and-a-half-year-old Maro, she was irresistible. In September Mougouch wrote to Jeanne: "Maro is presenting all the usual complications of growing consciousness—she is not at all an easy happy go lucky little child . . . just now its mommie or Dada all the day long."

As summer drew to a close, the prospect of packing and leaving Roxbury made Gorky anxious: "Gorky's short view is always a dim one," Mougouch wrote, "& at the moment he is cast down that we have to leave here—He is just working at a painting which he started when we first came out which had been a great problem to him & at last he feels it on the point of coming as they say of butter—This is always his most fruitful time of the year. Gorky & the apple trees & do hope with us that we have a fine autumn so that the lack of a proper studio will be offset by fine drawing weather."

PART XII

Gorky and his family with Zango, early 1946

51

Sherman

A photograph taken in the second week of September shows a barefoot Gorky, standing in front of a truck piled high with his and his family's belongings (Fig. 129). He is smoking during a break in the chore of packing up the Roxbury house and preparing to move to Sherman. Maro, now a thin girl with straight dark hair and an elfin but knowing beauty, is in his arms. As in the photograph taken with Breton half a year before, Gorky looks worn and gaunt.

The Hebbelns' home consisted of two small buildings joined by a communal living room; it looked, Mougouch thought, like "a huge bungalow." The Gorkys lived in one wing, the Hebbelns in the other. The situation was temporary, and Gorky was a man who longed for permanence—for his own farm, his own garden, for an island that no one could take from him. And the Hebbelns made bad housemates. Henry was mostly in New York living with a male lover, but he sometimes came to Sherman on weekends. Childless, married to a homosexual, and already deeply descended into alcoholism, Jean Hebbeln needed the Gorkys to share her home. "She wanted me to be there," Mougouch recalls. "She was in love with our whole setup."

Even before the Hebbeln farmhouse was ready, Gorky had the use of a makeshift studio in an outbuilding, and he soon got back to work. Mougouch's first letter to Jeanne after the move said, "G. has done some wonderful paintings going on [from] the one you have in that direction done the last month in Roxbury & Julien is very pleased so that thank a small mean god is that anyhow." The letter spoke also of feeling imprisoned by the Hebbelns, especially by Jean, who became jealous when she and Gorky saw their own friends and was therefore reluctant to lend them her car:

> We are completely at their mercy . . . They offer us what we want most in the world—a house & studio that can be ours forever if we want it—to buy it I mean—the ideal place for Gorky's work & up-bringing children. Isn't that monstrous opportunism when we feel as we do when she is drunk? O god dear Jeanne I wish I knew what was going to be what——I excuse us over & over again on the grounds that what counts more in our life is Gorky's painting & anything that can help him to freedom is worth any sacrifice but Art is LIFE & the life must never get separated—That's what I fear in short—are we compromising our life . . . I suppose we will stick it out—Our house wont be finished before January at least.

Soon after the move to Sherman, André and Elisa Breton stopped by and found Mougouch asleep and Gorky out walking in the hills with Maro. To make up for Gorky's absence, Mougouch produced tea in Jean Hebbeln's best tea set and Zango crashed into it and sent teacups flying. "I was so tired of this strain of living in other people's things," she told Jeanne. "I burst into tears & we all sat clucking at the misfortune for a few minutes then they made a speedy exit & I haven't seen them since!!" Fond though she was of Elisa, she noted that she sounded "like an echo of André." On the other hand, Mougouch herself often felt like a Gorky imitation: "I hardly dare open my trap about painting for instance because Gorky has gone through my pores as well as my head & it comes out shamelessly unadulterated Gorky though Gorky would be the first to deny that I could possibly talk like Gorky because he says I have the horrible Yankee or English or northern 'trick' of logic & you know how he hates the consecutive sentence much less thought! O poor dear me. I wish I weren't but I am to the point where even I can logic a Gorky idea!" A day or so after the tea set disaster, Gorky and Mougouch joined the Bretons at David Hare's Roxbury house. Their host was feeling the strain of being with Jacqueline's ex-husband. "David was sore as hell & the atmosphere was on the iron side but everyone put up brave chit chat—André was sick . . . & Elisa naturally wasn't too well & Gorky was suffering & I feel at these times a sort of claustrophobia of infirmities & art is life I feel too but the body . . . ?"

By Gorky's "suffering" she meant the blood in his stool and the pain in his anal area that his doctor attributed to hemorrhoids. Gorky had a constant complaint about constipation, as well. His doctor told him to take sitz baths. In her next letter (November 9, 1945) Jeanne recommended a bland diet, soaking in hot water and Epsom salts several times a day, and the use of a pain-relieving ointment: "Please don't tell Arshile that I mentioned all this for I do know and I respect his loathing of this sort of talk and that one knows about it too." Mougouch wrote back: "Gorky has been poaching in the dishpan alternately all day & declares himself much better—He felt so badly yesterday for he gets very frightened at the sight of blood that I was about to take him to the doctor whom poor man I had lambasted on the telephone he claimed G. was not a bad case at all so I said for gods sake if you can't take something out put something in or we shall both be in the looney bin."

Most of Mougouch's November letter is taken up with thanks for Jeanne's offer of two hundred dollars toward the purchase of a car. While in Sherman, Gorky tried unsuccessfully to learn to drive and, in his enthusiasm, pulled so hard on the emergency brake that it came off. In the middle of Mougouch's letter Gorky interjected a note of thanks to Jeanne:

Dear one it is so long ago we have not seen each other—Come to us this spring both of you—and how is your work. I have the stone picture [mosaic] you send to us. It is in my studio—

Thank you for all you have done for us—I shall write to Urban—Very soon next week when we are in New York—Jeanne—I am starting to work and when you are here I will show them to you—please come this spring and by then we will have our little house and you both can stay with us—

With my very love to you and Urban
Arshile

After Gorky returned his wife's pen, she wrote that he had "fled with confusion" because he had not written a letter in a long time.

As the autumn advanced, sharing the Sherman house with the

Hebbelns became less difficult: delirium tremens had frightened Jean into abstinence, and she was spending more time in New York. Gorky's career seemed to be on an upswing. Before leaving Roxbury, he had sent a group of his recent paintings to Julien Levy. Feeling they needed more work, he had withheld several of his more densely painted canvases, among them at least one version of *The Plough and the Song*. Mougouch's November letter to Jeanne said:

> Julien loves & adores the new paintings he told me today on the telephone & is forever hanging them on his walls—he also said there is an effort afoot to have six or eight gorkys in a room to themselves in some show the Modern Museum is putting on in the spring [*Fourteen Americans*, September 10–December 8, 1946] but he is not going to turn sommersaults until its definite so I haven't said anything to gorky because that mad house is so here today & gone tomorrow that it's not worth getting undone over them any more—But it would be nice—Julien wants to renew the contract & we are going in next week to discuss it—He has really been very good. Julien—not bothering Arshile about his work nor pushing him—Dear Joking Jesus how wonderful it will be when he has a studio really his own—I doubt if that will be before the spring but meanwhile this is not bad at all an excellent light.

They had not been to New York in months, she said, and didn't miss it. In Sherman they saw their new and near neighbors, the literary critic Malcolm Cowley and his wife, Muriel; the magic realist painter Peter Blume and his wife, Ebie; and the writer Matthew Josephson and his wife, Hanna. They also saw the Calders, the Bretons, and the Tanguys. Mougouch's November letter said that their visit with the Tanguys "was very gay & relaxed Tanguy is sweet you will like him I'm sure—He and gorky are killing together & very fond of each other really—the Abs [Bretons] haven't left yet for he is waiting for some money or something & very fulminating about the delay poor dear—We were given the S. & la P. [Breton's *Surréalisme et la peinture*] & I haven't yet really read it but it looks very marvelous & I see a night of translating ahead O dear."

Of the friendship with Yves Tanguy and his wife, Kay Sage, Mougouch recalls that "Tanguy was very charming and he would sing in my ear, but Gorky was never jealous of Yves." Sage, she said, was wonderful with Gorky, and Gorky felt protective of her because Tanguy was so rude to her, ignoring her and telling her to shut up. The well-brought-up Sage wanted everything to be perfectly arranged in her immaculately clean Colonial house—the right magazines on the coffee table, placed just so. Wanting to arrange her husband as well, she tried to transform Tanguy into a country squire by equipping him with a shotgun and rifle as well as a hunting cap and a shooting jacket from Abercrombie and Fitch. Tanguy resisted. Instead, with his robust humor amplified by alcohol, he told tales of his vagabond youth.

Although Mougouch spoke French and Gorky did not, Gorky remained the dominant personality in their social encounters with both expatriates and most Americans. He did not, however, engage in the endless conversations about art and the philosophy of art that he had enjoyed in the 1930s. Years later Mougouch wrote to Ethel Schwabacher: "As his painting flowered, the need for communication and creeds vanished—he no longer even cared to discuss painting or art and he cared not at all to hear another opinion. I don't mean mine, because we rarely differed seeing that he was me in painting he educated me completely but intuitively—or some way anyhow that left no footprints & I can never say now why I feel a painting etc. It just belongs or doesn't to this tree he planted in me!"

Gorky and Mougouch went to New York occasionally, and they were able to use 36 Union Square when the Hebbelns were in Sherman on weekends. In November Mougouch told Jeanne that she had not seen Noguchi in a year, but she had seen Matta: "Matta is still being the little blitz of the art world buying some wonderful paintings, Duchamp through dealers & giving everyone a pain in the ass—very strange little guy—He has a great hold on André & I can see why but I hate him because fundamentally he thinks André a silly old man & I can't help but wish on him the fate of Humpty Dumpty." It was probably sometime that fall that Gorky went to the city to deliver a lecture at the Architectural League, an event arranged by Henry Hebbeln. Mougouch stayed home to look after the children, but, she recalls, "when Gorky came back he was in cacahoots because he had the audience rolling in the aisles. Henry said it was an absolutely marvellous performance. Gorky gave the architects hell. He said that modern architecture was terrible: a fly on a wall could wreck a building. Walls, Gorky said, were only made for paintings."

On these trips to New York, Gorky saw a few exhibitions, especially those he was in. When, in November, his *Diary of a Seducer* was included in the 1945 Whitney Annual, he went to the opening. Toward the end of the evening he ran into the critic Harold Rosenberg, who greatly admired *Diary* and to whom Gorky was explaining the title when Clement Greenberg joined them. Apparently Gorky did not recognize Greenberg as the person with whom he had had a confrontation in the 1930s or as the writer of the negative review of his Julien Levy show the previous spring. After the opening Gorky joined the two critics at the Cedar Tavern at 24 University Place, and Greenberg began to hold forth about *Diary of a Seducer.* Gorky was infuriated. "Who the hell is this guy?" he asked. When he was told, he jumped up and said, "I'm going to kill him! That son of a bitch! That bastard, he said I was impotent! And here I am, a father of two children!" Greenberg defended himself by saying that he hadn't meant that Gorky was impotent. "I meant you were impotent as a painter!" Gorky said, "That's even worse!" And he picked up a sugar bowl to hurl at Greenberg.

Gorky's outbursts of aggressive behavior had been noted by friends since the 1930s. Balcomb Greene, for example, recalled giving a party at which Gorky responded to an insult from the drunken Pollock by shouting, "I am going to throw you out of the window!" He had to be restrained by friends. At a party at Pierre Matisse's the architect Le Corbusier, who had come to New York with plans for the United Nations headquarters, flirted with Mougouch. When he asked her where she was born and she said, "Boston," he said, "Ah, you must never say that. You should say you are from the Tierra del Fuego!" Seeing Gorky's darkening scowl, Breton warned off his compatriot by passing the edge of his flattened hand across his neck as he looked meaningfully at Gorky.

Mougouch wrote to Jeanne about a farewell dinner Matta and his wife, Patricia, gave for André Breton just before his December 4 departure for Haiti. It took place at a French restaurant that Enrico Donati, who was among the guests, remembers as La Parisienne on West Forty-sixth Street. A photograph of the party shows that the guests were mostly members of the Surrealist circle (Fig. 130). Standing between Elena Calas and Enrico Donati, Gorky looks grumpy, thin, and unwell. Twenty-four-year-old Mougouch, with her long brown hair, is seated between André Breton and Max Ernst; she looks ravishing, full of intelligent if slightly impudent vivacity. Apart from the Gorkys and Nicolas and

Elena Calas, the married couples in the photograph include Bernard and Becky Reiss, Esteban and Irene Francis, and Frederick and Steffi Kiesler. Max Ernst, Nina Lebel, and Marcel Duchamp appear to have come to the party alone.

After dinner the guests sat around the table and played the Surrealist game of Truth or Consequences or *Le jeu de la verité*, in which players take turns at being asked embarrassing questions, usually involving love and sex. Those interrogated must answer truthfully or accept the consequences, which could be even more embarrassing—for example, they might be told to kiss someone in the room, preferably someone else's spouse, or, when these games got out of hand, they might be told to pretend to masturbate in public. Mougouch was asked, "What part of a woman's body do you kiss most attentively when making love to her?" She blushed and said she didn't know. Gorky glowered. Sensing trouble, Breton, who always played master of ceremonies at these events, announced, *"Passons!"* He then patted Mougouch's hand and the players went on to the next victim. At the end of the evening came another sort of Surrealist game—Matta absconded without paying the bill. As Mougouch wrote to Jeanne, "We were all suddenly asked to pay the bill—André was in a rage from start to finish but I began to think they just love to be outraged."

That autumn Gorky and Mougouch saw the Schwabachers from time to time. Late in 1945 Mougouch wrote to thank them for Wolfgang's check and for a "care package" of clothes, blankets, and toys. With this "unexpected windfall," she said, they were going to buy Gorky a "much needed suit poor darling his things are so out at the elbows people are convinced he affects it as a style." They planned to go into the city and wanted the Schwabachers to dine with them at 36 Union Square. "Gorky is much much better," Mougouch wrote, and were he not "freezing in his studio" due to a delay with the heat he "would be very happy." In fact, he was anxious: between his poor health, the move to Sherman, and the problems with getting into his newly renovated studio, Gorky had not been as productive as he wished. He was especially worried about having enough work for his spring exhibition. On January 9, 1946, Mougouch wrote to Jeanne: "Julien is bleeding him constantly for more paintings but meets a sort of passive resistance made possible by our remoteness from New York another advantage of living in the country."

Mougouch confided her concerns about Gorky's relationship with Levy in another letter to the Schwabachers. Gorky had meant to give Wolfgang a call about his legal arrangements with the gallery but had put it off because he found the whole issue too confusing, and, Mougouch explained, "he really didn't know what to say." Gorky had asked Levy for more money to cover the expense of materials, and Levy had given him a hundred dollars but no permanent raise. Because they had been snowed in, Gorky had not been able to take his new work into the gallery. "Then also he was unhappy about his work & didn't really feel anything was fit to take to Julien so he felt he was not in any position to press his point. I only hope Julien is not in a pet. He was very anxious to get a new lot of paintings before the New Year and he hasn't."

Gorky and Mougouch spent Christmas 1945 in Sherman. David Hare and Jacqueline and her daughter, Aube, came over on Christmas Eve. The countryside was heavy with snow, and Aube made a Santa Claus snowman for Maro. A Christmas package from the Schwabachers was full of secondhand treasures: a coat for Gorky, a hat for Mougouch, toys for the children. The day after Christmas Mougouch and her daughters flew to Washington to visit her parents. Gorky was pleased to have some time to work, as she put it, "unmolested by children," and she would have a well-deserved rest. She wrote to Jeanne on January 9: "Darling G. I left with Jean & Henry & work. I hope he has been able to catch up a bit on all the time lost in the past 4 months. I don't go back until the 20th & I have wild hopes to move into our house sometime in Feb. . . . This is a horribly dull letter but I feel sort of dispersed—I always do when I leave Gorky as though the center of my life just wasn't there a very bad sign I suppose." While she was in Washington, Gorky wrote Mougouch two letters:

Mouguch
my very darling
I love you I love you. It has been so long time. I miss you and ever
    Darling Maro and Yalda.
I have been working very hard I will come to New York when you
    are there

Julien has send his check, but we have very many bills this month.
Dearest you are so dear to me—.
Kiss Maro and Yalda for me.
I kiss you my very Dear love your
Arshile

Mougouch my Darling

Henry has gone to New York and his darling Wife sleeps all day and night?

But I am doing some very good paintings

So if you can arrange with your doctor to see you next Monday, Henry will drive to New York with the car and me and my pictures.

Please darling pay the rent.—I love you Dear Dear sweet hart and kiss Maro and Yalda

With much love

52

Phoenix

✹

On January 16, 1946, the outbuilding that served as Gorky's Sherman studio burned to the ground. Twenty days later, as if to minimize the extent of the disaster, Gorky opened a letter to Vartoosh with casual family news—Mougouch and Maro had had colds, Natasha was growing fast. Then he said:

> Vartoosh dear, ten days ago a fire starting in the chimney of my studio in Sherman, Connecticut, destroyed everything I had there: paintings, drawings, sketches, and books, all were burned to ashes, not a thing was salvaged. Well, it's too great a loss for me, and I don't wish to write about it any longer, as I don't want you to worry about it too.
>
> We are well, and I am still working.
>
> Dear Vartoosh, I have hopes that some day we shall have more time, both you and me, to get together; perhaps we shall come to visit you.
>
> Maro has grown, she speaks and dances now. Can you make or have made to order a Caucasian costume for Maro? I shall gladly pay the cost.
>
> About that picture. Send me the measurements of the inside of the frame, not the outer wide side. The truth is, I had started on the picture long ago, last summer, but that too is in ashes now.

He told his sister that Ethel Schwabacher had found him a place to work and Wolfgang had given him five hundred dollars, "so that out of even such a thing something new can grow." His exhibition scheduled for February 25 was postponed until April, since "all the paintings were lost." He closed his letter with reassuring news about his career: "A few days ago a famous writer of France wrote me a letter saying that he wanted to write about me and wants me to send some studies or rather photographs of my studies. And, as you know, I have a contract here with the best gallery in New York so that every year I give 12 paintings to them, and every year they give me [an income and an exhibition]. So you must not worry about us. We are well."

Mougouch was in New York when the studio burned. She had left the children in Washington with her parents while she came to Manhattan to see her dentist. Gorky had planned to meet her at 36 Union Square on Monday, January 21, when he had arranged to deliver paintings to the Julien Levy Gallery. But the fire changed all that. Two hours after the flames were extinguished, Jean Hebbeln reached Mougouch by phone and told her what had happened. Mougouch then spoke with Gorky over the telephone, and the hollowness of his voice filled her with despair. They agreed to meet in the city the next day.

The fire was caused by the pot-bellied wood stove, which Gorky had bought for twenty dollars, and which was installed too close to a wooden beam and with no asbestos around the chimney. Gorky, with his passion for fire, had the stove burning too hot.

When he first noticed the smoke he thought it came from his cigarette. When he finally realized that his studio was on fire he panicked. Perhaps he connected the fire with the story of his grandmother's burning of his family's ancestral church. He acted as if he were under a curse: instead of calling the fire department or informing Jean that the studio was burning, he went to get water from the kitchen of the Hebbelns' house and carried it in a pail up to the studio. "He spent half an hour being a donkey. He walked right past Jean and said nothing about the fire. After the third trip through the living room with the third bucket of water, Jean asked, 'What's happened, Gorky?' 'Studio on fire,' he said. He had been afraid to tell her. He felt such shame. Jean then called the fire department. Gorky was a donkey in moments of crisis. His moves were totally erratic."

Gorky's close neighbor Malcolm Cowley came over and watched the fire. Gorky was, Cowley said, "tragic." The fire department was doing the best it could, but it was too late. Another immediate neighbor, Peter Blume, recalled:

> We went to the fire to see what we could do. This was before they really had a well-trained fire department in Sherman . . . In those days they had an old fire engine and they really didn't know how to make it work . . . Gorky just kept banging his forehead on the ground, banging, banging and saying his whole life's work was in there, that he had lost everything he'd ever done.

Mougouch's January 1946 letter gives a vivid picture of the catastrophe:

> Darling Jeanne
>
> Anything that follows is an understatement: on Wednesday Jan 16th Gorky's studio in the country burned to the ground. Everything was lost. I was in New York at the time having left the kids in Washington for a few days while I dealt with dentists— Then this happened. Gorky smelled some smoke but he was working with great passion & thought it was his cigarette! Only Paul Bunyan can top that—next thing he knew the roof was in flames—losing his head utterly he ran to the house for a pail of water but they say that he didn't really say the studio was burning down—Whatever happened the tragedy came in that he tried to save the burning building instead of hauling out everything he could—you can imagine his terror & panic & none of those people there are quick enough they just stood & watched it burn while Gorky rushed madly in shutting the door behind him so they'd have to haul him out of the smoke—he managed to rescue a hammer, a screwdriver & a box of powdered charcoal.
>
> He sobbed & cried all this while poor dear & I got the news 2 hrs later Gorky sounded so hollow I think my heart broke & I waited all night in fear until I could see him the next morning—I went to Peggy [Osborn]—she was so kind to me—

Gorky's deadened tone on the telephone had filled Mougouch with dread, but, she recalls, "when I saw him, he was not dejected at all.

There was an element of relief—why, I can't tell you." She wrote to Jeanne: "Gorky even says he feels a new freedom from the past now that it is actually burned like you feel when you are young and there is no past so things could be worse." The day after the fire, when Gorky came into the city and met Mougouch at 36 Union Square, he told her, "It's all right. I've got it all inside me. I can go on painting." He was, she remembers, "happy and almost laughing. We went to a bar and had drinks. It was jolly. I told him that Ethel Schwabacher had called to say that she had a friend with a ballroom he could use as a studio."

Two years later, during an interview with a newspaper reporter, Gorky recalled his feeling of liberation. He said that his art materials and paintings had burned but "sometimes it is very good to have everything cleaned out like that, and be forced to begin again." Gorky was obsessed with cleaning—cleaning himself, cleaning his studio, cleaning his canvases by scraping them down and starting over. Losing his paintings in the fire was a forced expurgation of the past—it prepared a space for renewal. Mougouch's January letter continued:

> When he walked into the studio the next morning he was wonderful—he has been wonderful ever since He says it is all inside him, the painting on his easel, the one he was working on during the fire is still burning in his mind & he only wants to get to work immediately—I suppose that this thing is so terrific he does not quite grasp it & if he can just work he can fill up some of the vacuum before he realizes it—all the drawings of these past 3 yrs except for some few at Juliens—about 20 canvases & then his easel that easel was like golgotha to me & his palettes his books not all of them but the ones he cared most about—I don't know Jeanne its pretty ghastly—
>
> But as calamities go it has its exhilerating sides—Gorky is a most awesome phoenix and the people my God utter strangers have been so kind. Little Bayard O. [Margaret Osborn's son] who's back from the wars & Peggy's man John Marshall appeared with a very decent sized easel they had combed the streets to find. That's one of the drawbacks its so hard to replace anything. Then a dame Yclept Hochschild who heard thru a friend of a friend offered him the use of her penthouse ballroom until a studio turns up—or possibly if he likes working there he can stay until April

when we will move back to the country—The emergency being over. He may find it impossible to work freely there—its very beautiful 17 floors high with a terrace all around looking over the park the city the reservoir a hollywood set in fact & he is to be quite alone & undisturbed as its only this room in a tower.

The day after the fire Mougouch went to Sherman, packed up their belongings, and took them to 36 Union Square. She and Gorky were both relieved to be free of their arrangement with the Hebbelns. "I can't tell you what a state of moral & physical exhaustion we were in from four months of that really rotten atmosphere," she told Jeanne. Having installed themselves in Manhattan, they went to Washington to collect Maro and Natasha from the Magruders' home. Their visit was extended because Mougouch came down with the flu. "I feel perfectly miserable knowing I'm keeping Gorky in Limbo," she told Jeanne, "but he is so far quite delighted to be with the children after nearly a month of separation—Maro's radiance when Gorky is with her is really phenomenal—that child is such a bundle of complexes & complication as to make me feel at times quite inadequate to bring her up."

Whereas Mougouch's letter to Jeanne said that about twenty canvases had been lost, a letter she wrote to Ethel Schwabacher four years later said that Gorky had lost "roughly at least 15 canvases painted in the year 1945 . . . all the work of our 9 months in Roxbury and 3 months in Sherman. 2 excellent paintings of the Song and Plough theme. 3 or 4 portraits of me done over a period of 4 years and perhaps 6 paintings on which he worked intermittently for five or six years. (realistic head and flower paintings). The rest were along the lines of Jeanne's *They will take my Island* . . . Anyhow the total loss in the fire was about 27 paintings." Fortunately, some of Gorky's Roxbury paintings had been sent to Julien Levy, and Gorky had not brought all his Virginia drawings to Connecticut, leaving some of them safely stored at 36 Union Square. Although Mougouch told Jeanne that Gorky had rescued only "a hammer, a screw driver, and a box of powdered charcoal" from the burning studio, she recently said that Gorky had also removed "a few paintings and the photograph of himself with his mother." Peter Blume, in his eyewitness account of the fire, said that Gorky had "gotten a number of things from the studio."

Soon after moving back to 36 Union Square, Gorky the phoenix began to paint in the borrowed penthouse. Indeed, the horror of the fire seemed to propel him, or perhaps, as he said, some of the lost work survived in his memory and hands. By the time his exhibition opened in April this blaze of creativity had produced enough canvases to fill the gallery. Indeed, it was a kind of blaze. Many people have compared Gorky's creative process to fire: "He had that fire, that burning," said Max Schnitzler. "His mind blazed with a fiery river of ever-varying images," said Ethel Schwabacher. Mougouch had observed that he needed to "feel like a bonfire inside" in order to forge ahead in his art, and Gorky himself used a fire metaphor when he said the painting he had been working on when the fire broke out was still burning inside his head.

Although Mougouch's letter to Jeanne said that Julien Levy had been very supportive after the studio fire, he did ask Gorky, "What will I put in your show?" To prepare for his April exhibition, Gorky headed for his penthouse studio early each morning with a picnic lunch consisting of soup, sandwiches, and fruit. Mougouch's February 5 letter said:

> We are so busy starting over again that we forget that this is *gone* — but even this realization carries its lift—strange how man is equipped—Gorky is working very hard. I send him off in the morning with his lunch pail so that he wont have to come down from his tower until dark. Surely the only man who goes off to work in a penthouse ballroom toting his lunch in a little black pail—a sky miner—He's strangely happy. The Ballroom will do till we find something else—its very far—101st St & 5th but the people have been very nice & leave him entirely to himself . . . You shall see Jeanne Gorky will have quite a few things by the time you come East its amazing how he feels like working—I don't believe I have ever seen him so free about his work its just the right time that's all & nothing can stop him — & when its not just the right time nothing on earth can help him.

During these months Gorky produced *Delicate Game*, *Nude*, and three versions of *Charred Beloved*, all paintings in which his masterful yet graceful line skates across the canvas to create shapes that are even sparer than those in the paintings from the previous year. *Delicate Game* is very like *Child's Companions* from 1945, but, with its spots of red, yellow, green, and black intermingled with an exquisite tracery of line, it is more laconic. The linked shapes of *Nude*, based on one of the drawings Gorky made for Breton's *Cherry Trees*, bring to mind the fantastical anatomies created in the Surrealist game of Exquisite Corpse, in which each player adds a portion of a figure to a communal drawing without being able to see what the previous player has drawn. Gorky's vertically linked shapes also recall the way Tanguy created tall, cairnlike creatures by stacking one stony shape on top of another.

All three versions of *Charred Beloved* (Figs. 166 and 167) have richly brushed backgrounds that here and there come forward and cover the shapes defined by thin black lines that look continuous but that, seen close up, reveal that, after making a few feet of line, Gorky had to lift his sign painter's brush from the canvas and reimmerse it in liquid paint. In *Charred Beloved I* the ash-colored ground is made warm and glowing by a sublayer of orange and yellow. Given the title, one can assume that this painting alludes to the studio fire. Smoky texture, a flamelike ellipse, and cindery tones suggest, if not fire itself, the memory of fire. But although *Charred Beloved* is, like most of Gorky's other paintings, tinged with sadness, its simplicity and lightness also recall Gorky's feeling of release. A linked series of shapes rises from a charred "foot," gashed with red, to two forms that look like bird's heads (one upright, the other hanging), to a fluttering kite shape in the upper right corner. The upward movement suggests the idea of transcendence—perhaps something like the phoenix in Gorky that so astounded Mougouch with its regenerative force. As Jeanne wrote in her first letter after the fire: "It's not given to everyone to die in life and spring braver more sure than ever."

Gorky and Mougouch were glad to be back at 36 Union Square. For a while they slept in the studio because Henry Hebbeln was still using the bedroom, but he was there very little and was looking for an apartment of his own. Whether they would return to Sherman or not, they left up in the air. "Gorky knew he had foolishly burned the studio down. He knew if he'd told Jean it was on fire, it might have been saved. The Hebbelns were good about it, but after the fire Gorky had a feeling of such guilt that he didn't really want to go back to Sherman. And then Jean was so drunk and she and Henry were having such trouble in their marriage, and somehow we just blanked it out and thought we ought to go it alone."

Gorky's guilt soon turned into hostility toward Jean. "We have lately begun to feel," Mougouch wrote to Jeanne on February 5,

> that we must not go back to Sherman . . . Somehow Gorky has come to hate Jean & there is a strange feeling though it is all underneath—of hatred very ugly somewhere . . .
>
> If we don't go back then we must decide what we can do—we could perhaps stay in the city for the next year & then next spring go to Paris—But we cannot just go to the country for the summer as Gorky says he cannot endure this constant moving . . . As for money we shall manage thanks to everyone thanks above all to you & we hope that Julien may get something out of insurance which he has applied for to help a little later on.

Financial support came also from a circular that Chermayeff sent to Gorky's friends to raise money for him. In addition, Wolfgang Schwabacher secured a thousand-dollar grant for Gorky from the New-Land Foundation, an organization that raised money for refugees from Nazi terror and that he was president of. (Schwabacher sent five hundred dollars on March 19, the balance to be paid in six months.)

Mougouch's description of Gorky's repressed and "ugly" hatred for Jean Hebbeln is one among a number of signs that she was beginning to recognize her husband's dark side. His behavior often had an edge of violence. Although she acted amused by his heaving Maro out of his Roxbury studio and onto the grass, she feared the effect of Gorky's anger on the children. "He used to upset me about it—he used to say things," she recalls. In her January letter to Jeanne she said, "I know now how very bad it is for them to be dragged through our moods & be exposed too much to the heat of the many Gorky explosions—its all right perhaps later when they can get it into a general pattern but so young its horribly frightening for them—& Gorky & I shriek as you know & control would be worse—so I am going to try her in a nursery school for a while." Jeanne, who would soon come to New York to live, wrote back on February 5: "I don't think violence is such a shock to children especially when they see as well the making up. If it had ALL been that way but it isn't and children are pretty aggressive too."

5 3

A Tree Cut Down

✺

Despite the pains in his abdomen and the blood in his stool, Gorky worked long hours to get ready for his show. He seemed to exult in the challenge. As Mougouch said in her February letter to Jeanne, when he was working well nothing could stop him, and "when its not just the right time nothing on earth can help him." These words would soon prove prophetic. Beginning with the studio fire, his luck turned. Until the end of his life, Gorky would be cursed by disasters that paralleled the terrors of his youth: the end mirrored the beginning.

On March 5, 1946, after several days of tests, Gorky underwent a colostomy at Mount Sinai Hospital in New York. The pain and bleeding that his doctor at Columbia-Presbyterian had brushed off as caused by hemorrhoids turned out to be symptoms of rectal cancer: "Gorky had been ill for the last year," Mougouch recalls. "In Sherman he had been bleeding badly. I saw blood in the toilet and was horrified. There was a lot of blood in his stool. I called the doctor and said something was wrong. The doctor said, 'It's normal with hemorrhoids. Your husband is a hypochondriac.'" In fact, Gorky had suspected something was seriously wrong but had put the idea out of his mind. After the fire he was con-sumed by work—nothing could stop him. Raphael Soyer remembered meeting Gorky on Fifty-seventh Street and hearing about his plan to do a series of large drawings. "He was sick," Soyer recalled, "and told me he had lost a lot of blood. He was quite worried, but at the same time very enthusiastic about his work."

Gorky finally went to see Harry Weiss, a doctor who had cured him in the 1930s when his right hand had become paralyzed and partially numb from lead poisoning. "And Dr. Weiss rang me and said, 'Come to Mount Sinai,'" Mougouch recalls. "He said, 'Your husband is going to need your smile. Bring his pajamas and a toothbrush. Gorky is going to the hospital now.'"

Mougouch was with Gorky just before the operation: "He was miserable. I waited while he was operated. It took a long time. Afterward he was unconscious. I had to go back to the children." On the evening after the operation, she wrote to Gorky: "My only ever darling I just called the hospital & finally you are out of the operating room & they say your condition is fairly good—this tells me nothing of course for what I want to ask about is the light the look in your adored eyes." In language made ardent by the crisis, Mougouch went on to say that she loved him more than ever. Her fervor in this and other letters was true to what she felt at that moment, when all she wanted in the world was to reduce her husband's pain and to restore his confidence in his manhood.

Three days later, in a letter to Jeanne Reynal, she spoke of her welling up of love in response to Gorky's disaster:

Gorky has had a successful operation for cancer. It was localized in the rectum & they are pretty sure or at least very optimistic that it may never return . . . He had the very best surgeon, several doctors were there, 2 of them friends of ours & they have told me it was a very fine piece of surgery—Jesus what an expression—They had to remove his rectum, open his belly, examine his intestines for any traces, & open him a hole on the side of his belly to make up for what they had to take away. O Jeanne. But they assure me he will get used to this arrangement & will be able to live quite normally. If the cancer does not reappear for 5 years they consider him fairly safe. He has been told it was a tumor. I couldn't bear to have him know the other thing yet because you see it may never reappear & must he live with fear of something which perhaps will never happen? He will have enough it seems to me with just this rearranged body business. I saw him yesterday for an hour & he is doing very well rapidly getting better though naturally any messing in the gut is ghastly pain—But his spirit seemed very beautiful to me, he only wants to get well & out of there & back to life and his work & I am going to somehow arrange to go back to

Sherman as soon as it is safe for him because he loves it there & it will be warm soon & he'll be able to work outside & perhaps we can manage to build him a very simple studio. This is all in the future but somehow one's mind races to something like this some sort of doing that will make him happy. I love him so, I wish this had happened to me, I love him more than I have ever dreamed it was possible to love and still it is not possible to take this thing on to me. But he must not know about it, he must not have fear that is all I care about so strongly that I won't let myself fear either. He is so beautiful, so strong & healthy, he has lost 20 lbs though & must get them back quickly. His show will still take place. There will only be about 6 paintings & a few drawings but that is plenty last time there were too many.

Gorky was in Ward Q at Mount Sinai Hospital for about two weeks. After the operation he was, Mougouch recalls, "like a tree cut down." Although she had hoped to conceal from Gorky the nature of his illness, he eventually learned that what had been removed was not just a benign tumor. Later tests showed that the cancer had not returned. Nevertheless, he lived in fear of a recurrence: at the time of his operation, the survival rate over a five-year period was only 26 percent. The worst problem was Gorky's image of himself as maimed. Reared on a farm where a man's strength was his means of survival, Gorky had always been enormously proud of his strong body. "He used to compare himself to a lion," Mougouch recalls, "but later, when he was diminishing, he did not walk as fast as me."

Mougouch visited Gorky whenever she could find a babysitter. When she could not get to the hospital, she bolstered his spirits by sending notes. A March 8 note said: "I know you were straining while I was there. Please don't strain at all I love you my dear one & if you can't talk I love only to look at you only forgive me that my eyes filled with tears when I saw you in pain. They wont next time because I know that is no help to you."

Ethel Schwabacher visited Gorky at Mount Sinai and recalled how moved he was by the way the men in the neighboring beds bore their pain. She admired the mobile that Calder had brought Gorky, and she learned of other friends' generosity as well. Mougouch's great-aunt had sent a check, Jeanne had sold securities so as to be able to give him five thousand dollars, and Mina Metzger, with Ethel's help, had managed through connections at Mount Sinai Hospital to have Gorky treated free of charge.

Between visits to the hospital, carrying food, letters, and drawing materials so that Gorky could work while convalescing, Mougouch looked after the children, prepared a room for Gorky to work in after he came home, and saw friends. To her surprise, his absence was liberating. The burden of Gorky's changeable moods was lifted. She did not have to worry about keeping the children out of his way:

> I had two weeks on my own with the children. It was all so easy. No one was angry with the children. Gorky's temper had been short because he was ill and everything got on his nerves. I saw an old flirt. He took me to Delmonico's and it was so different from what I was used to. He was very good-looking, possibly bi-sexual. He came and went as if I had needed something sweet and had it. When Ethel Schwabacher saw me she looked at me very suspiciously and said, "You are looking absolutely wonderful!" She meant, "What's the matter with you. Why aren't you looking absolutely drawn apart?" I wasn't drawn apart because for the first time in my life with Gorky I was taking it easy. I'd only been alone once before, when I took the train to Cape Cod and had that wonderful feeling of total freedom.

Just before Gorky left the hospital, he was given a list of people, such as the postmaster general, who had undergone colostomies and were nevertheless leading full and active lives. Gorky was supposed to feel heartened, but he wasn't. A decade later Mougouch looked back:

> Courage, they say, look at the postmaster general . . . what poet, what painter who had spent the years of his life removing all the fat from his nerves, who had allowed no skin of habit to deaden the slightest sensation, whose one desire is to be vulnerable beyond what he knows of himself, is interested in courage? Gorky had no interest in that way out. He had one reality only, and that was *in* . . . [Coping with his "rearranged body"] was a deadly bat-

tle, a total, willful, crazy exhausting of Arshile Gorky, a crucifixion, golgotha every other day. What love, what friendship, what
"artistic" recognition could touch him now?

Gorky slowly recovered some of his former strength, but he was, as
Mougouch said, "disgusted by his operation." He had always been
squeamish. Armenians were brought up to be wary, fastidious, and modest, and Gorky was all these things. His obsession with cleanliness was
shared by many Armenian genocide survivors. In his memoir *Black Dog
of Fate*, the Armenian American poet Peter Balakian recalled his father's
endless hand washing: "Sometimes it seemed that the whole physical
world made my father squeamish . . . In all of this germ madness there
seemed to be some deeper, more pervasive anxiety being expressed . . .
For my grandparents' and parents' generation, perhaps the world was a
place conspiring to kill you . . . As my grandmother said to me as I lay on
my bed recovering from measles, 'Sleep with one eye open; know the
evil eye.' " Gorky slept as if with two eyes open.

In the ablutions connected with his stoma (the orifice in his abdomen that replaced his anus), Gorky was, Mougouch says, fanatical:

> He was incredibly driven to push everything to its very screaming
> limit. He was terribly puritanical. Having a colostomy was simply
> awful for him. Gorky was not at ease with bodily functions. There
> was nothing I could do to convince him that I did not find the
> hole in his side disgusting, and for ages he wouldn't go out at all
> because he was afraid of oozing. Most of the time he wouldn't
> wear a bag. He just wore a bandage that he ripped off every day
> and it ripped the hairs out of his tummy. He would lie in the bath-
> tub every day or so and give himself an enema and clean himself
> out. The skin around the hole became like a vulva. It was soft. Af-
> ter the enema, he put on the adhesive tape again. He weakened
> himself from these ablutions.

Gorky's moral and physical exhaustion unbalanced him. "After the operation he became totally paranoid. In the last two years he didn't want to
see other artists because he felt they were stealing all his ideas. . . . I
didn't realize that I would not be able to convince him that what had
happened to his body was all right. His manhood was so terribly as-

saulted by the operation and his already jealous temperament became totally impossible."

Friends who saw Gorky after the operation were shocked to see how thin and changed he was. He looked hunched over, shrunken, and sick, said his former student Revington Arthur, who spotted Gorky on Fifty-seventh Street. "He was wearing this blue sailor cap, you know a mackinaw coat, and he was just dragging his feet along. He looked like he could fall down any minute. I followed him for a while just in case he did fall . . . I could have stood directly in front of him and I don't believe he would have noticed me. He was preoccupied." Soon after Gorky came home from the hospital, Gaston de Havenon paid him a visit. "He told me about wearing a little bag and felt OK," de Havenon remembered. "After a while I felt that Gorky was not as happy and optimistic as before—and the present situation had no doubt created complications in his sex life and relationship." Sometime that spring Marny George saw Gorky and found him mellowed. In 1951, shortly before her own death from colon cancer, she recalled the meeting in a letter to James Thrall Soby: "He was the same. 'We never change' he had said. 'No, we never change,' I admitted, blushing miserably remembering a hundred beastly things I had done, 'but we can become what we are.' . . . His violence was gone, there was a quiet, other-worldliness about him (but others can tell of this)."

When Yenovk Der Hagopian went to see Gorky he heard noises coming from the place on Gorky's abdomen where the doctors had attached a bag. "Pardon me, pardon me," Gorky kept saying, but Hagopian could not figure out the reason for the apology. "What kind of an aristocrat have you turned into?" he asked. "What is this 'pardon me' business?" Gorky answered, "Priest's son, don't you know?" and with tears in his eyes he told Hagopian about his operation. When Hagopian began to cry, Gorky grabbed the legs of his chair and lifted his old friend high in the air. "And he shook me. Had he let go, my head would have been broken." "Don't you dare cry!" Gorky shouted. "Don't you dare cry!"

Gorky's rage finally exhausted itself and Hagopian was able to ask him why he hadn't been told about the operation. Gorky replied, "Is it a wedding to which I must send you an invitation?" Gorky lay down on a sofa to rest and the two old friends drank wine. "Come tomorrow," Gorky said. "We'll go to an Armenian restaurant." The following evening Gorky ignored doctor's orders and ordered a rich Armenian meal. "Manuk, you don't have permission to eat such food," Hagopian warned. "Babam, whatever you eat, I'll eat," said Gorky. "Whatever is going to happen, let it happen. Today we are together."

After dinner Gorky and Hagopian returned to Union Square and lay on the floor and talked about Van. Hagopian asked, "Why did it happen?" Not wanting to discuss his illness, Gorky said, "Priest's son, now I have a studio. Come there and sit and draw. You take one end of the room and in the other end I'll draw." Hagopian said he had no easel and no money to buy art materials, and Gorky opened up a trunk filled with tubes of paint. "Who is going to use all this?" he asked. "Don't worry about such things. I'll bring another easel."

About this time Gorky told Lionel Abel about his cancer operation and said, "Well, maybe I'm like Job." Being Job's wife became increasingly difficult. The following December Mougouch sought help from Dr. M. Esther Harding, a Jungian analyst who had been treating her great-aunt Marion Hosmer for twenty years. Gorky's behavior was becoming more and more unpredictable. Often his irritability flared into violence. Ethel Schwabacher wrote of the marital strains: "Though the operation had been a major one, it had not actually affected his sexual potency; but, due to the traumatic nature of the experience, he did, in effect, become temporarily impotent. And the tensions arising from this condition drove him into moody states of anxiety and anger." While it is true that Gorky's shame about the hole in his side gave him an aversion to physical intimacy, his sexual problems did not begin with the colostomy. According to many of the women who were close to him, Gorky had never been at ease with sex. He suffered from premature ejaculation. Mercedes Matter said, very discreetly, that Gorky had "problems." As we have seen, Corinne Michael West's diary notes suggest that she and Gorky did not have a sexual relationship and their attempts at one ended in frustration. Sirun Mussikian had a great deal of difficulty luring Gorky into bed, and when she finally did he bit her.

Perhaps because of the feelings of inadequacy that come with premature ejaculation, Gorky's lovemaking was at best sporadic. This was especially confusing for Mougouch, who, being young and inexperienced, assumed there must be something wrong with her. Gorky did not disabuse her of this idea. Like many partially impotent men, he wanted his wife to believe that he would perform better with a different partner. "He used to say that had I been a lady from his part of the world and if he had touched me with his finger I would have been in perfect ecstasy. I would have shaken like a jelly. Instead I felt like jello that did not gel. I became very friendly with Dr. Weiss and I asked him, 'Can you tell by looking at me or by examining me whether I am normal? I am worried I'm not.' He said, 'You know, you can't expect Gorky to be a truck driver.' " Early in her marriage, when Mougouch had gone to a woman gynecologist for birth control, the doctor had asked her how often she and her husband made love. When she told the doctor how infrequently, the doctor exclaimed, "He must have a mistress!"

The Sky Miner's Haul

※

On April 9 Gorky's exhibition opened at the Julien Levy gallery. The brochure listed twelve paintings and reprinted Breton's essay of the previous year. All the paintings were of the spare style in which Gorky's breathtaking line held a dialogue with strokes and shapes in primary colors. Just as Mougouch had feared, the paintings exhibited—two versions of *Charred Beloved, Nude,* and *Delicate Game,* plus paintings from 1945 such at *The Unattainable* and *Child's Companions*—looked to some viewers like tinted drawings. The painter John Ferren came to the opening and asked, "Isn't it a little little?" And Gorky responded, "It may be, but it's all that I do now."

Several critics missed the layered and scumbled color of Gorky's earlier work. One, probably Maude Riley, who had been so negative about Gorky's 1945 show, complained about the difficulty of decoding Gorky's paintings. Another said, "Gorky's trend of late has been toward disconcerting meagerness of statement." Others were less negative, but nearly all took a tone of condescension. The *Herald Tribune* (May 12) said the paintings were "confidently designed" and "sensitively brushed" but that, while Gorky was aiming at an "abstract Symbolism in the manner of Matta," his ideas were "not altogether or readily communicable without the aid of a catalogue." A more sympathetic reviewer opined that "waywardness, wit and elegance combine in the work of Arshile Gorky, now on view in the Julien Levy Gallery, to make attractive wall decorations . . . His elegance blooms like a peach tree in spring . . . Gorky is a sort of a Debussy among painters." A favorable piece in the *New York Sun*

(April 20, 1946) suggests that Julien Levy was up to his old game of concocting explanations for Gorky's paintings and offering them to bewildered viewers. The pictures were, the reviewer said, "packed with implications" but hard to divine: "The one called *Landscape Table*, for instance, was done from nature in an open autumn field, with thoughts about Hitler and world politics competing in the artist's mind with impressions of the attacks of crows on the neighboring corn. This interpretation, I confess, I owe to Mr. Levy. I might not myself have 'got' it. My preferred picture is the one called *Hugging*, but Mr. Levy did not tell me who was hugging who, and I just liked it as a picture."

The most important review was Clement Greenberg's in the *Nation* (May 4, 1946). As usual, Greenberg played king of the art world, praising with one hand—Gorky had "digested" his influences and produced "some of the best modern painting ever turned out by an American"—and withdrawing approval with the other (he was among those who regarded the recent paintings as "essentially tinted drawings"). Reading between the lines, one might feel that Greenberg was exasperated with Gorky for not being more like Pollock. He wanted Gorky to paint flatter and tougher, to risk ugliness and go beyond European tradition. Pollock, in Greenberg's view, deflected art history, whereas Gorky, lacking Pollock's bold inventiveness, merely added to that history his own personal note. Gorky was thus not an artist of "epochal stature." Instead he was "a lyrical, personal painter." If Gorky could accept these limitations, Greenberg suggested, he would "soon acquire the integral arrogance that his talent entitles him to." At that point he might "paint pictures so original that they will look ugly at first."

Although Gorky was pleased by Greenberg's change of heart, it is easy to imagine his annoyance at Greenberg's tone. It was all very well to be patted on the back for lyricism and painterly instinct, but to be faulted for not being sufficiently brave or inventive to produce an "eruption into the mainstream," as Greenberg felt Pollock had done, must have stung. Mougouch recalls that by the time Greenberg recognized Gorky's stature, Gorky was "more and more indifferent toward what people said," but he continued to long for recognition. Of the public indifference to his art de Kooning said: "That's why he had such a sad time, somehow, because he could have gotten something out of it. I don't mean that he ought to get rich, but he could have come to the state of mind that he was very much appreciated."

Gorky certainly never got rich, but 1946 turned out to be a good year for sales. Julien Levy sold *Good Hope Road* for $500 and *Charred Beloved I* for $720. *Impatience* went to Yves Tanguy and Kay Sage for $350, and Jeanne Reynal bought *Delicate Game* for $275. This was the last good year. During Gorky's lifetime, Levy managed to sell only one other painting.

A photograph of Gorky taken by Irving Penn for *Vogue* magazine in May or June of 1946 shows Gorky and the Cuban Surrealist painter Wifredo Lam seated on ice cream parlor chairs pulled up to a round café table on which lie what look like a pencil and a piece of charcoal (Fig. 134). Gorky is elegantly dressed in a tweed jacket and gray flannel trousers that he had bought on an excursion to Brooks Brothers with Mougouch and Jeanne. But on his feet he wears, as he often did, sandal-like shoes. His face is drawn from illness. He had been unable to work during his convalescence, and he was once again experiencing abdominal pains, which frightened him but turned out to be nothing grave. The art critic and lecturer Rosamund Bernier, who arranged the photo shoot, said that Gorky looked "very down." In the weeks that followed, Gorky and Mougouch saw quite a bit of Lam. Just before leaving for Crooked Run in July, she wrote to Jeanne about how much she and Gorky liked Lam's purity and sweetness: "Gorky thinks he is adorable too & claims he used to be like that before America made him bitter . . . He is coming to dinner tonight then I don't suppose we shall see him again which is sad . . . He is like a delicious plum or a honydew melon—! My god so different from all the surrealists."

Shortly before their departure, Gorky was photographed again, with his family (Fig. 135). He and Mougouch dressed up the children and took them to the Twenty-third Street studio of his old friend the Albanian-born Gjon Mili, a photographer for *Life*. Gorky wrote Vartoosh: "A few days ago a friend of mine, who happens to be a famous photographer, took some pictures of the children. I have not seen the proofs yet. Will send you some pictures." He also took pictures of Gorky alone (p. 1). In Mili's portraits Gorky wears the same clothes he'd worn when posing for Penn. He looks less ravaged than he had a month or so earlier, but his eyes are equally sad. As in several other photographs, it is clear that Gorky wanted his hands to be noticed. In one shot he holds a cigarette and touches his right eyebrow with the tip of his thumb as if it helped him to think—as if he were touching his "eye-spring." Mili said of his friendship with Gorky: "Gorky was the only person I ever met who liked both Uccello and Seurat . . . I am orthodox and since both Armenians and Albanians had been under Mohamedan Turkish domination, our outlook on life was somewhat the same."

Although Gorky and Mougouch's immediate plan was to spend the summer and early fall in Virginia, their long-term plans were still up in the air. They could not face going back to live with the Hebbelns. In any case, the farmhouse renovation was not completed. They looked at a few possible houses in Connecticut. They even considered buying a converted barn plus sixty-five acres in Dublin, New Hampshire, but nothing seemed quite right. "You know in a way gorky is so right to be so caring," Mougouch wrote to Jeanne. "There just has to be that love in whatever he does." In mid-July she told Jeanne that they would go to Virginia at the end of the week and would stay as long as they could, "for gorky has to do some drawing or he & I will die." She ended her letter with news of an argument between Gorky, Bayard Osborn, Bayard's new wife, and his mother, Margaret: "We had the inevitable Shakespeare argument Gorky holding out that he was a rehashed pedant against a wall of Osborns & by god she [Bayard's new wife] took gorky's stand—more than I have the courage to do—They took Zango which is a sad but huge relief."

Just before heading south, Mougouch and Gorky found a summer tenant for the Union Square studio, a young architect named Anne Tredick. "I heard there was a studio for rent," she recalls, "and I went down and met Gorky. He told me if I rented it I must scrub the oak parquet floor once a week and use Clorox bleach. The floor was a light tan color. He did not want it waxed. It took two hours every Saturday morning. At the end of the summer Gorky was pleased about how well I kept the floor. I paid fifty-five dollars a month. I already owned a Gorky drawing bought for me by an architect friend at an auction benefit at the AIA/Architectural League of New York City." Anne Tredick (now Anne Dickey) had in fact met Gorky two years earlier at an auction to raise money for the war effort. She remembers him singing an Armenian song, "a gentle song at first, ending in a great cry of horror." To her he seemed a tragic figure: "Once I met him in the street and Gorky said, 'Please tell Alfred Barr to buy one of my paintings.' Gorky was desperate for funds. Alfred said curtly, 'We already have a Gorky or two.' "

55

Third Virginia Summer

Late in July Gorky and Mougouch packed the children and themselves into an army Jeep that Commodore Magruder loaned them and headed for Crooked Run. Although the heat was oppressive, they wore coats to prevent sunburn. Mougouch remembers the terror of driving through the Holland Tunnel with her convalescent husband, a three-year-old, and a nearly one-year-old, plus their pile of baggage, in an open Jeep. Even though it went only forty-five miles per hour, they loved the Jeep and the spectacle they made in it. "If they are cheaper next year we may get one," Mougouch wrote to Jeanne. During the trip, the children sat on a mattress in the back and Gorky sat on an air cushion given to him by Frederick Kiesler. As they drove through Bucks County, they longed to stop and look for a house to buy, but, wrote Mougouch, "we were at our wits end and g just had the strength to get here."

During the early part of their final summer at Crooked Run they had the house to themselves, and Gorky was happy to be back in a place where he had worked so well in the past. But when the Magruders returned from vacation, life grew tense. "My father was back from the war. During the earlier summers, my mother was the minority and we were more the boss. Now we were the minority. There were too many people in the house. My sister was in and out. Gorky had no real studio." The barn that had served Gorky as a studio in 1943 and 1944 had itself burned down, so Gorky drew in the fields and in bad weather worked in a room over the garage.

Gorky's August 12 letter to Vartoosh said:

My dearest Vartoosh:

We received your long awaited dear letter. But such sad news—your foot in that condition . . .

We thought we were going to have a home in Connecticut this summer, but that damned fire ended all hopes. Agnes and I were planning to have you and Karlen with us during the summer, but that too is a thing of the past. As for us visiting you, that's quite impossible, because I have to get to work and do a lot of painting. You know, even after leaving the hospital, I was unable for a long while to do any work. Thank you all the same, my darling. I am feeling much better now. We and the children are staying on Agnes' mother's farm. Her parents are spending their vacation in Canada.

Maro is a big girl now and looks like an angel. She resembles our mother so much. Natasha is already a year old, and is very curious about things. She eats well, is able to stand up by herself, and even says da-da . . .

Very glad that Karlen is growing and is doing so well in school . . .

Do not worry about me, dear, because I have a wife like Agnes, I am really very fortunate. She sends to all of you her true love. She wishes to thank you for the stockings and is sorry that you had that accident. She wants you to take a good rest and hopes that Moorad is a better cook than I am.

Will you write me how you prepare dough for bread and also for *gatah*? A few days ago Agnes and I tried to bake some; it tasted like everything but gatah.

Warm kisses and love from the four of us to all of you. Kisses to Karlen and Moorad.

Always loving you,
Gorky

Mougouch's first letter to Jeanne from Virginia expressed Gorky's and her feeling of relief at having returned to the farm:

Dear sweetheart Jeanne that was a lovely letter we read it at lunch and gorky went so indian as to scoop the inside out of his sweet potato and leaving the strange shape of the skin intact I found it afterwards when I was scooping the garboonya and he says it was the influence of your letter . . .

we just slept and lay in the sun for the first few days watched the sun go down and come up and the birds flying about with all that delicious awakening of one's sensibilities that you have when you are getting well from an operation some little core in you is battered about and bruised like hell in the city and when it stops—suddenly—then slowly and magically the tiniest little nucleus begins to form again inside you so slowly but it is of such sweetness this feeling that I think I have plumbed the depths of the old saw its so nice to bump your head against the wall etc. What is there about this country that does suit us I suppose it is simply the familiar and also it is very restful to us at this time to just come to this house which we know so well and have it all to ourselves and just work and rest no involvements no rent a jeep and trailer at our disposal it is very lucky it came when it did g. was beginning to feel great pain in the same old place and he and the doc were worrying which gave me some nightmares but it has almost disappeared and I think it was exhaustion depression and standing too much on his feet because even I feel where they hacked out the baby if I get tired and stand too much. And he looks so much younger he is already like natasha brown as an indian they brown much quicker than maro and I and he is so happy drawing and already has 21 little sketches nothing but something you know and more than he had in a whole year in conn. There is some richness in just this little valley that does seem to inspire him . . . but we would any day settle for bucks county and somehow I must try to arrange in the fall some house hunting in those parts.

She went on to discuss the role of the woman artist, a subject she and Gorky had discussed with Breton. Unlike Breton, who felt that a woman should be inspired by "her man" and that that, in turn, would inspire the man, Gorky thought that there should be a specifically female art and that it was a mistake for women artists to imitate men. Mougouch ended her letter with: "Gorky sends you his very dearest love he is busily scratching away saying he is doing the most interesting and instructive work for himself just scratching color on a pad so the beginning is the same anywhere but aren't you happy to be home at last home being any-where you work with love."

It was probably August when Mougouch next wrote Jeanne: "Gorky is drawing feverishly & discovering new things—he has a huge portfolio of drawings already & some are extraordinary—he says he hasn't found what he wants to paint yet but there is still time & also he really doesn't have any place to work—to paint I mean." Drawing as if his life de-pended on it, Gorky produced some of his most impassioned images. Many of the hauntingly painful configurations in the 1946 drawings would reappear transformed in the rich and powerful paintings of the following year. Hour upon hour he sat on his stool and drew what the fields brought to his imagination. The process helped to put distance be-tween him and the twin disasters of 1946: for all the anger and agony contained in his swift and cutting line, these drawings were also an affir-mation of life.

Mougouch told Jeanne she thought they would stay in Virginia until the end of November:

Thru Nov. is still some time & perhaps it is better to go back to N.Y. then anyway—I don't think we can live too isolated either anymore. When Gorky gets these waves of depression which he has always had to a degree but which are now pretty demoralizing because all this bizness [the enemas Gorky gave himself because of his colostomy] we have to go thru every other day takes it out of him physically and spiritually—its pretty difficult to help him out of it all alone & the stimulation & warmth of other people makes a great difference to both of us.

Toward the end of the summer, they left the children with a babysit-ter and took a quick trip to New Milford, Connecticut, where they stayed with Kay Sage and Yves Tanguy in order to look at a house that the Tan-guys thought might suit them. The house turned out to be all wrong, but they fell in love with a nearby farm. After enjoying the process of imag-ining themselves living there—thinking about where they would picnic and where Gorky would paint, they talked to a bank about a mortgage, made an offer of $15,000, and rushed back to Virginia to retrieve their daughters from the home of the babysitter: "I left them with a dreadful looking harlot in Lincoln & they are alive but that's about all—They both have upset stomachs & nasty blotches all over them & Gorky is full of recriminations that I didn't let him see the creature before we left—wise me. We did have great fun being off alone together & Gorky does feel very well & was so happy—which is mostly because his work is going well." The possibility of spending some months in Paris was still alive. However, Mougouch wrote, "the Tanguys had heard from the Matisses & other friends that Paris is not so hot—a very false & quite mad esprit de luxe—a stifling intellectual atmosphere of each little group beating its drums behind closed café doors with no air in between & opportunism rampant."

Around this time, Mougouch wrote to thank Wolfgang Schwabacher for the second installment of the New-Land Foundation grant. She said it would help with "our one big aim—a house" where Gorky could work in peace. Gorky was, she said, "working like a madman—a happy one. I tore 50 drawings away from him to send to Julien—it took him 2 whole days of muttering & puttering to make up his mind to send them & now he comes home exclaiming I must write to Julien to tell him they are nothing for only today has he discovered etc etc." In her next letter to Jeanne, Mougouch said they might use part of the grant to finance a visit to France that would last no more than two months because Gorky couldn't work in temporary situations:

> It takes ages for him to get acclimated & because of this operation it is not good for him any more to have too much time—He really wants to live very simply among friends & work—He feels he has his best work to do & it eats him not to be able to—I think he would like to go to France see & meet some people & things then come back here & reflect—Because I think he is a reflective person not so much action it doesn't much matter where he lives as long as he is free & quiet—his action is entirely in the painting.

The Gorky family made a brief trip to New York to attend the September 10 opening of the Museum of Modern Art's *Fourteen Americans*, in which Gorky had a room of his own. Organized by Dorothy Miller, the show was in part a substitute for the exhibition conceived in 1943 that was to have contrasted contemporary American realists and abstractionists and that finally comprised only figurative painters. Among the artists in the present show whom Miller had invited and then disinvited in 1943 were Gorky, Theodore Roszak, and Irene Rice Pereira. Other abstractionists included were Hare, Motherwell, Noguchi, and Mark Tobey. Gorky and Mougouch were not impressed with the museum's choice of participants, and they continued to feel that the museum's behavior toward artists was irresponsible. Gorky's friend Saul Steinberg agreed: "What happened was we were in the same show at the Museum of Modern Art, a show called 'Fourteen Americans.' We both sort of sneered at these things, at the museum. We didn't quite believe that they knew what they were doing or that they were important. They were like people who jump on a bandwagon."

The room devoted to Gorky looked splendid. It was hung with eight paintings, including the more finished version of *The Artist and His Mother*, and three drawings. The catalog reprinted part of Breton's essay and a brief biography propagating the usual misinformation about Gorky's birth and education. Mougouch remembers all the guests at the opening sitting around in a circle, the women on one side, the men on the other, "like a French wedding." Afterward there was a party on a terrace, at which she talked to Matta. "I was there with the children. Natasha was a year old. I was still milking her. 'Can't you give me a little bit of milk?' Matta asked. He was *always* trying something on with me, but it was out of the question." Matta was not easily discouraged. At the party he said to Mougouch, "Promise to ring me if you ever feel like seeing me." It is clear from Mougouch's letters that, though she was charmed by Matta, as everybody else was, she found him rather silly. The note of scorn in her remarks about Matta may have been prompted by her recognition of the rivalry between Gorky and his much younger, much jollier, and much more successful friend. Matta's confidence, facility, and skin-deep originality irked Gorky, especially as the art critics never stopped commenting on how much Gorky had learned from Matta. Mougouch's disdain may also have been self-protective, a shield against Matta's endless seductiveness and her own susceptibility to it.

Gorky's inclusion in *Fourteen Americans* was his first major and official recognition in New York. He was gratified by the honor, but, as Ethel Schwabacher wrote, "the success seemed inconclusive to Gorky, as it was not followed by a warm response to his paintings from the general public. He told me he thought that full recognition might well come only after his death as it had with so many of the great artists who had been ahead of their time."

Critical reaction to *Fourteen Americans* was negative and sales were discouraging. A few of the museum's trustees and staff members bought works from the show, but no one chose a Gorky. Gorky received little (and mixed) critical attention, but some encouragement came from Clement Greenberg, who wrote in the *Nation* that half of the participants were artists on whom "the fate of American art depends at the moment," and among these important artists he cited Gorky.

Mougouch's late summer and early fall letters to Jeanne spoke of Gorky's and her wish to find a house in Connecticut or go to Paris. Either way, Gorky must keep on "wallowing in the volupté of drawing." He had been "living in the fields," she said, and he was "feeling happier in his work than ever before." But now the weather in Louden County had turned: "no wind but a strange worried greyness, a disturbed feeling in the pit of the stomach." Even so, Gorky was "so on fire with his drawing he can't lie in bed at night—what will I do with him in the rain—some knockout pills would be good—Don't see much hope of getting him away from here before we have to leave anyway." An October 6 letter from Jeanne encouraged the Gorkys to go to Paris. Breton had told her that Gorky was "the one artist for whom he would do something in Paris."

On October 15 Mougouch wrote to Wolfgang Schwabacher that Julien Levy had said nothing about collecting the insurance money for the loss of Gorky's paintings in the fire. "Gorky doesn't want to ask such questions until he has some paintings behind him for moral strength." The problem was that Gorky wasn't painting: the light in his studio over the garage was bad and he didn't feel free to make a mess. Also he had no easel. Instead he was drawing. It was the only thing he enjoyed, and months of being unable to work after his cancer operation had made him more single-minded than ever. "Gorky drowns himself in work—work so sure and independent, so true that I feel quite shaken at times."

In the early autumn evenings, Gorky would sit by the fire in the low-ceilinged living room and draw. Much to Mougouch's annoyance, he borrowed her onionskin writing paper. "It was hard to get this paper in Virginia. He would grab my pad. He'd write 'To my Mouguch' on the drawing because it was on my paper." Her description of Gorky as "so on fire with his drawing" that he couldn't sleep is borne out in the drawings' impetuous mood. His fast-moving hand left marks that seem driven by inner crisis.

The so-called *Fireplace in Virginia* drawings (Figs. 136 and 137), done on Mougouch's 11-by-8½-inch letter paper, usually have two abstract figures set on either side of a roundish shape, sometimes outlined with dots. This shape has been interpreted as a palette, but it could also be the round opening of a *tonir*. Perhaps these family gatherings by the fire triggered memories of the Adoians' clannish closeness during the long Anatolian winters. In one drawing the central oval seems to be offered by a kind of bone figure on the left to a creature on the right, which looks like a conflation of an insect, a human being, and a rocking chair. This hybrid, with large feet that resemble rockers or ice skate blades, appears in many of the *Fireplace in Virginia* drawings. Sometimes it appears twice. A similar creature turns up in a study for *The Calendars* (1946–47) (Fig. 141) and, less clearly, in the painting *Making the Calendar* (1949). Mutant versions of these two figures sit at either end of a table laid with what looks like cutlery, wine glasses, and dishes (the oval becomes a platter) in *From a High Place II* (1946) (Fig. 133). Given the blue and green bands of this painting's background, the table is outdoors (a "landscape table"). As with Matisse's self-portrait with his wife entitled *Conversation* (1908–09), the domestic scene seems fraught with tension. In at least two drawings associated with the *Fireplace in Virginia* series, the central oval is missing, but there is instead a long, horizontal bonelike figure, which Ethel Schwabacher saw as a "recumbent figure of a man" and which could be the first idea for the prone figure in *The Orators* (1947) (Fig. 142).

In some *Fireplace in Virginia* drawings, insectlike creatures seem to surround the central motif as if it were indeed a *tonir*. On the left there is a creature with a kind of dragonfly body, antennae, and a spiky mouth. It appears to sit on its haunches so that its body forms a diagonal very like the insect figure seen on the right in *Agony* and in the *Pastoral* series, both 1947 (Figs. 175 and 171). This creature, though aggressive, looks stooped and maimed. It is difficult not to interpret it as an expression of Gorky's feeling of physical impairment and diminished masculinity.

Most of the drawings from the summer of 1946 were done out of doors (Figs. 136–138, 174, 176, and 178). In them Gorky explored themes that would reappear in his 1947 paintings. Some of the more carefully worked out drawings from 1946, especially ones that are squared up with grid lines so that they could serve as studies for paintings, seem as refined as ever. But many of the drawings from the third

Virginia summer seem anxious and irascible. As the viewer's eye travels over a drawing's surface, the terrain it covers is no longer seductive, soft, or feathery. Instead it is full of shapes that might prick, little points that look cruel instead of playful or sprightly, as they might if drawn by Miró. Gorky's once mellifluous line turns into brusque scribbles as his hand cuts back and forth, back and forth, across the paper.

In the drawings from the two earlier Virginia summers, Gorky's exuberant response to nature's fertility merged with his sensuous delight in creating shapes and in using ink, pencil, and crayon in the richest possible way. Yet even in these earlier drawings, voluptuousness mixed with pain, wit with menace. In 1946 pain becomes paramount. His line now has claws, his personages look freakish and tortured, his shapes are weapons. A lethal-looking shape that resembles a crossbow or a flying bat appears in many drawings. Yet, as Mougouch insists, "he did not set out to draw or paint agony. When he looked at trees he saw battles and conflict. *Menace* was a word he used a lot, and *battle*. He was interested in the opposition of one shape to another."

An October 22 letter from Mougouch to Ethel Schwabacher spoke of her and Gorky's autumnal melancholy: "We are drowned in the sweet sadness of the last weeks here—The days seem so short so suddenly and though we have loved every minute of it its as though we must love these days almost desperately, its sweeter than it ever has been, the air so clear all the ripeness of the gold corn and the burning of leaves and the blue blueness of the sky make you sad with longing to hold back what passes but it passes like a beautiful stranger in a 19th century novel." Three days before leaving Virginia, Gorky wrote to Vartoosh about family matters: Maro could talk; Natasha could stand and even dance; he and Mougouch were "contemplating a trip to Paris next Spring. Our great friend the world famous poet André Breton, who had written so well of me, wants us to visit Paris." Gorky spoke also of his drawings: "This summer I finished a lot of drawings—292 of them. Never have I been able to do so much work, and they are good, too." Not only did he have to make up for lost time, he was in a race against mortality. But he saw that these new drawings were full of possibilities and that he could go on for years developing paintings from them.

Mougouch had written to Breton on October 6 telling him of Gorky and her hopes of coming to Paris. She said that Gorky's health had improved and that if he was happy he could put up with any kind of living conditions. What he needed was to lead a simple life. A small house near Paris would be just right. Gorky and she felt like gamblers: would Breton throw the dice for them? At the moment, she reported, Gorky was immersed in nature, drawing like a madman in the fields. He had told her that nature "entered his head and closed his ears," presumably meaning that his art was a dialogue no longer with other art but with nature. The idea of closed ears suggests not only Gorky's concentration but also his isolation as he focused on nothing but his work. On November 4 Breton answered Mougouch's letter. Gorky and she should come to Paris, he said. Paris needed Gorky. Parisian air would do him good. With Duchamp, Breton was organizing a Surrealist exhibition for the following year and he wanted Gorky to participate.

In her final letter to Jeanne before Gorky's and her departure for New York on November 20, Mougouch said:

> gorky hasn't done any paintings he has drawn & drawn That's what he wanted to do like drinking at a spring—he can paint all these next months—we are going to live a very withdrawn life when we get back save pennies & energy. G. only wants to work. Julien Levy is upset—he wanted two paintings for the Whitney annual—Gorky feels so calm so certain that even the fact that Julien's tithe is nearly due & Julien upset doesn't bother him at all—he doesn't even know J. is upset—I should be in a tizzy if it weren't for what you have done for him because if Julien wants to end contracts he can because all that matters is the calm passion of gorky he is full of work—there can be no disaster.

PART XIII

Gorky in Castine, Maine, 1947

56

Gorky and the Surrealists

Gorky returned to 36 Union Square in the fall of 1946 eager to get back to painting after a summer of drawing, but the exigencies of family and city life interfered. His daughters were underfoot. Maro, now three and a half, was miserable at the local nursery school; spinal problems kept Mougouch lying under a borrowed sunlamp for several days—ultraviolet rays remained a cure-all in the Gorky family.

Finally Gorky rented a studio across the street in the building belonging to Klein's department store. It was small and inexpensive but had good light and the children couldn't get at him. Late that autumn, Mougouch wrote her final letter to Jeanne, who was about to move from California to New York City: "And New York is so disintegrating untill you get proper stranglehold on it. We haven't gone out at all—only quietly seeing a few people but even so—Kiesler we saw—poor thing he seems insane at times & o the jealousy that seeps in—We saw No Exit [by Jean Paul Sartre] . . . 25th rate bila bila."

The notion of going to France—possibly with Jeanne and Urban and David and Jacqueline—was still alive, if somewhat daunting. Gorky needed to be sure of finding a place to work, for, as Mougouch put it to Jeanne, "none of you Creators like limbo." Moreover, Matta had said that New York was more alive than Paris and had more of a sense of possibility. Paris, Matta reported, was depressing: "No freedom of movement no café sitting unless its *your* café, poaching on anyone else's preserves is spying, all energy left is spent in talk talk, v. difficult to find a place to work, much less live & as for Gorky's imperious plumbing out of the question . . . [Pierre] Matisse is down on France, Tanguy & all of them really—Unless you are a communist you haven't a chance."

Gorky had not started painting yet, she said, and not much was happening in terms of organizing a show because Julien Levy was preoccupied with marital difficulties and, although he wanted Gorky to deliver paintings to the gallery, he didn't even want to see the drawings from the past summer. An added pressure came from Margaret Osborn's request that Gorky design a cover for her novel. "He is breaking his bones over that," Mougouch wrote. "As soon as he feels he has to suit some publisher's taste or even hers Gorky is stymied & rightly so . . . I should have prevented his ever getting involved—only if he does manage to wring out something that'll do he will feel so much happier because of that desire to *sometimes* be able to give what someone needs not just what one has—its very human especially when you realize how greatly he had been given to." The problem was that when Mougouch read Osborn's book out loud to Gorky he grew bored and stopped listening.

Although his doctor found no signs of a recurrence, Gorky worried, and he kept asking people what they knew about cancer. The children got on his nerves; he and Mougouch fought. Any sign of ebullience in her conversations with men piqued Gorky's jealousy. She felt caged. The more she tried to sort out her psyche with Dr. Harding, the more intent she grew on finding the kind of inner freedom that she thought might help her relationship to Gorky.

In the late fall Gorky was given the manuscript for the Surrealist critic and poet Nicolas Calas's preface and introduction to the catalog of a group exhibition that Calas was organizing for the Hugo Gallery at 26 East Fifty-fifth Street. The show, first called *X-Centric Art* but later renamed *Bloodflames*, would be presented the following March. It would include, besides Gorky's *Nude*, work by Lam, Matta, Noguchi, Hare, Helen Phillips, Gerome Kamrowski, and Jeanne Reynal, plus "boomerang frames" by Kiesler, who would also turn the gallery into a kind of sculpture by painting the walls, ceiling, and floor. Disliking Calas's text and the name *X-Centric Art*, Gorky arranged to meet with Calas. Whether Calas changed his essay after hearing Gorky's criticisms is not known. Much of what Calas wrote was mumbo jumbo, but he expressed several ideas that were part of the intellectual combustion that fed the invention of Abstract Expressionism. He stressed, for example, magic and animism, hybrid creatures, and art as risk, as liberating force, as a "reaching toward the unseen." What he wrote about Gorky is almost as elusive and allusive as the paintings he was attempting to capture. Yet Calas's insistence on the sense of emptiness in Gorky's paintings rings true: "Gorky," he said, "raises vacancy to the level of a positive aesthetic element. . . . What fearful emptiness of feeling and what lack of satisfaction interrupted the course of lines only to be resumed further on."

Gorky remained ambivalent toward the Surrealist context in which his paintings had been received since the beginning of the war. Possibly part of his standoffishness had to do with disappointment. Breton's 1945 essay had been the high point of his critical acclaim. Breton had encouraged him to come to Paris, but after he left New York even Breton thought better of the idea. "Breton said that apartments with good plumbing were too expensive," Mougouch recalls. "I think he was afraid we'd be dependent on him."

On January 12, 1947, Breton sent Gorky a copy of the prospectus for *Le surréalisme en 1947: Exposition international du surréalisme,* a show that he and Duchamp were organizing for the Galerie Maeght in Paris and in which he wanted to include Gorky. He added a note asking for Gorky and Mougouch's news and saying he hoped they would come to Paris in time for the show's July opening. But Gorky was wary: "You don't drag a donkey onto ice twice," was his response. He sent *How My Mother's Embroidered Apron Unfolds in My Life* to the show. After that he heard nothing more from Breton about the possibility of his having a one-man exhibition in Paris. "Gorky was waiting for accolades," says Mougouch. "That Breton did not say loud and clear that Gorky was the most fascinating artist he'd met in the United States was a disappointment." Worse still was Breton's assertion sometime later that there were no painters in America. As Ethel Schwabacher later recalled, "Breton doubtless did not have any idea of the effect that this comment could have on a man of Gorky's sensitivity. I do not believe that he knew how isolated Gorky felt himself to be."

When he married and especially after he moved to Connecticut, Gorky changed his circle of friends. Many of his companions from the Depression years felt that he had abandoned them in favor of the Surrealists. Looking back, Mougouch believes that Gorky distanced himself from old friends thanks partly to his removal from the city and partly to the sufficiency of having a family. But there was also his increasing paranoia: he felt that other painters were copying him or trying to outmaneuver him professionally. He called them "snakes in the grass" or "throat-cutters." This attitude made his company increasingly difficult, and he became further isolated. His isolation was noted by Balcomb Greene in his 1951 essay on Gorky:

> Because of his spectacular appearance, he easily became a celebrity. He was better known than his paintings were. He had separated himself from the unknown artists, lost the feeling of belonging with his artistic equals . . . It is little wonder that Gorky's Celebrated Personality became very early an extension of him—hard offensive points which stood out all around him, frequently spikes to hurt others . . . One evening I was invited to the apartment of an important European architect who had just arrived in New York. Gorky was present. This architect, of Russian birth, asked us the names of American painters whose work should be seen. Gorky replied sharply that Americans couldn't paint. Our host seemed embarrassed. I denounced Gorky at once, comprehensively. It was the end of our friendship.

Another reason Gorky stopped seeing his friends from the 1930s was that he preferred to keep company with people who had not witnessed his struggles during the previous decade, people who had never heard him called the "Picasso of Washington Square." The Surrealists came on the scene at the moment when his long apprenticeship flowered into a highly original style of his own. And when they welcomed Gorky into their inner sanctum, he felt that he was at last joining the mainstream of Western art.

Noguchi saw little of Gorky after the mid-1940s: "When he became successful and had a show at Julien Levy's I almost stopped seeing him altogether. He became one of the boys . . . He was a success, in a different grouping. I knew them. They took him over like a pet doll." De Kooning said he stopped seeing Gorky after Gorky was swept into the world of "those Connecticut Puerto Ricans." In a similar vein, Stuart Davis wrote in 1957: "Long after I had ceased to have contact with him, he got mixed up with a swarm of migrant Surrealists who fixed him up pretty good in more ways than one." Davis's scathing tone may have been part of an anti-Surrealist backlash that occurred in some intellectual circles in the mid-1940s, a time when the Surrealist movement was clearly in decline.

Although Gorky was flattered to be taken up by the Surrealists, he also liked to keep them and the art world in general at arm's length. His reclusive attitude is glimpsed in a remark that Edwin Denby heard him make sometime after the colostomy. Denby ran into Gorky with the de Koonings at a diner on Sixth Avenue across from Eighth Street: "Well, I went in and joined them. Cup of coffee, sitting there. And I said that I had just read in the newspaper that, after the war was over, there were 175,000,000 more people alive in the world than there had been before it started. And Gorky looked at me with his marvelous eyes and he said, "That is the most terrible thing I have heard."

Since his cancer operation, Gorky had pulled away not only from friends but from his Armenian family as well. "He feared Vartoosh's deep concern for his health. He did not want her to know how he felt, how he had changed . . . I think he knew she would be worried sick if she saw him and it would have driven him mad," says Mougouch. He wrote his last letter to his sister, his first in months, in the spring of 1947. The curtness of his note suggests that he felt writing letters stole time and energy that he needed for painting: "Dear Vartoosh, don't worry about us, we are well, we really felt very bad when we heard that this winter was so hard for you and we are happy that you are well. We have not heard from Agapi nor Satenik and surely they too have their problems. Write again soon, with warm embraces, missing you, your Gorghi."

Gorky's new friends did little to dispel his bitterness or his feeling of isolation. Indeed, Lillian Kiesler said that her husband came to regret having introduced Gorky to the Surrealists. Gorky was, she said, "like a magical Armenian suddenly finding himself in the toughest, most sophisticated circle in the world, the most literate circle in the world . . . It was like falling out of grace, falling out of innocence with, I would say, its advantages and disadvantages." The atmosphere the Surrealists created put enormous pressure on people with whom they came in contact. To be accepted, people had to be original, playful, outrageously imaginative. They had to take risks, live life to the limit, follow their own personal morality, one that went beyond conventional moral scruples. In a period when divorce was frowned on, the Surrealist group had affairs and divorces with impunity. In 1943, for example, Jacqueline Lamba left Breton for David Hare, David Hare left Susanna Wilson for Jacqueline, Max Ernst left Peggy Guggenheim for Dorothea Tanning, and when Matta's wife, Anne, gave birth to twin boys, Matta left her and took up with the heiress Patricia Kane, who later left him for Pierre Matisse. Noguchi became involved with Matta's ex-wife Anne. Free love was a subject in the air. With his Eastern ideas about fidelity in marriage, Gorky found it hard to condone his friends' behavior.

Jeanne Reynal said that at parties where the French Surrealists were present, Gorky steered the conversation away from gaiety to serious discussions of art. "Gorky felt the Surrealists played games, flirting with death, dicing with people's emotions," Mougouch recalls. "But this did not stop him from being amused by talking to people like Dorothea Tanning, and he admired Max Ernst. He was not close to Ernst, but he had all of Ernst's books. And he liked Ernst's poetic titles. He did not want to be Ernst's friend. He didn't understand the Surrealists' fascination with sexual perversion."

Margaret Osborn saw Gorky's association with the Surrealists as a destructive force:

When he moved to Sherman, he was plunged into a closed world, one which, in important ways, was foreign to him. He had none of the language of the worldly, none of their cynicism. He was meant to plane it alone, and now belonged to a club . . . He was simple, where his companions were complicated, and complicated in ways they had little patience with . . . He was, in spite of the devotion of some friends, defenseless in surroundings of such sophistication, of such fast knowledge, and with these the playful Surrealist cult of Sadism, dangerous to the vulnerable in the hands of the thoughtless or malicious.

One playful but not at all malicious Surrealist whom Gorky met in the winter or spring of 1947 was Joan Miró. Miró arrived in New York with his wife and daughter in February 1947 and he stayed in the United States for eight months working on a mural commission for the dining room of the new Terrace Plaza Hotel in Cincinnati. When Gorky saw the mural, either at Miró's studio or at the Museum of Modern Art, where James Thrall Soby arranged for a viewing, he was disappointed. He had imagined it would be simpler, with only three black shapes. He said that he preferred to think of Miró's mural the way he had pictured it in his mind's eye. Sidney Janis remembered Gorky pointing out aspects of Miró that were "distasteful to him" at a Buchholtz Gallery exhibition: "He showed how Miró arrived at his form which was supposed to be spontaneous, and pointed to little evidences of charcoal beneath the paint on the outer edges."

Whatever reservations Gorky had about Miró's new work, when he and Miró met they got on well. Miró told Gorky that Gorky was the only American painter who really understood what Miró was doing, and it is true that most American adaptations of Miró's biomorphism are heavy-handed. A letter Mougouch wrote to her great-aunt Nathalie on April 8, 1947, said: "Gorky is hard at work and feeling happier about it at long last, I think. He had had some rather wonderful compliments paid him of late. They want to bring out a book on him [Ethel Schwabacher was talking about writing a monograph] and Joan Miró is here for a visit (doing a mural in a Cincinnati hotel). Speaks of G. as the only painter in America."

That spring the Gorkys gave a dinner party in Miró's honor. Mougouch recalls that quite a large group came. Jeanne and Urban, Margaret Osborn, and the Schwabachers were included, and there was also José Luis Sert, the architect of the dining room for which Miró was producing his mural. Carlos and Sally Montoya came as well. "Montoya played the guitar and his wife unfortunately insisted on dancing flamenco dances. Miró and Gorky danced all over the studio and Sert danced with them. The three men were very funny. The two Spaniards were so short they came up to Gorky's elbows." Miró and Gorky sang their native songs and everyone drank from a glass *porrón*, a wine decanter with a long spout.

A decade later Ethel Schwabacher recollected that 36 Union Square was immaculate—Gorky had scrubbed the floor that morning—and the table was laid with many different Armenian dishes. "After supper we sat about the enormous low table [actually a model's stand]. Gorky offered wine in a bottle and without glasses. With reversed hand and arm bent sharply at the elbow he raised the flask to his lips, and tilting his head back, drank deeply from the curved spout. Then he passed the flask. No one could manage it, the wine spilled, faces were dripping, laughter mixed with the wine. Gaily Miró took the flask, sat straight, his legs firmly planted wide apart, then with a gesture of bravado and virtuosity, accomplished the feat. Waves of applause greeted him." Although Schwabacher remembers the gaiety, there was an undertone of sadness in Gorky's "wailing" songs. Mougouch says that "after the cancer operation Gorky took a very dim view of most everything. Nothing excited him. Even the fact that Miró said he was the best artist in America didn't help. Not at all. Nothing really got through. Nothing anyone could do could make up for the terrible things done to him."

When he was not at his easel and immersed in the landscape of memory, Gorky became more and more unhappy. "Gorky was entirely painting," Mougouch observes. "I mean I fitted in and so did the children as long as they fitted in and were not too much trouble. Distractions from painting were intolerable." Gorky's behavior toward his family was volatile. When he was angry, he forgot that his daughters were small children, and he was physically rough. "He shouted at Maro. Maro did that normal thing of wanting to poke Natasha's eyes out or bump her on the head. Gorky's attitude was to grab Natasha away and hold her on high and glare at poor Maro, saying, 'Do you want to kill your little sister!?' " Another time when Maro was doing her best to torture her sibling, Gorky picked her up and threw her across the room. Five minutes later he would spoil her. In one of his rages Gorky, who loved animals, picked up a cat and threw it against a wall. The cat survived, but Mougouch was afraid that he might do the same to one of the children.

Her letters hint at her growing malaise. "More and more our marriage was just about my engagement with Gorky's painting," she recalls. "But I loved *him*. I had been playing doppelgänger to Gorky, making life possible for him. I wasn't having any fun. The laughs were getting fewer and farther between." Gorky's disapproval was deflating. He made Mougouch feel insufficient as a woman and as an intellect. "Gorky even made me feel it was a mistake for me to be Anglo-Saxon. This did not help my confidence." Sexual problems were not discussed. Feeling maimed by the colostomy, Gorky took out his rage and humiliation on his family. His jealousy was worse than ever. Convinced that satisfaction in work might lift his spirits, Mougouch focused on Gorky's career.

She confided her troubles to her analyst, who said, "Stop thinking about Gorky. Find out who you are." Dr. Harding suggested that Mougouch keep a diary of her dreams. Mougouch's identity struggles must have been trying for Gorky, who needed a woman to mold herself according to his Armenian ideal. The more she looked for strength and affirmation apart from him, the more Gorky's suspiciousness grew. The more impossible he became, the more he drove a wedge between them.

5 7

Castine

In the summer of 1947, Mougouch spent nearly four months visiting her great-aunt Marion Hosmer on the coast of Maine. It would be good, she reasoned, for the children to be away from the city's heat. More important, Gorky needed a stretch of time to work without interference. With his family away, he could give up the rented studio he disliked and paint again at 36 Union Square. That these months away might come as a relief to Mougouch went unspoken. On June 4, leaving Gorky with a large supply of preaddressed postcards in the hopes that he would write, Mougouch and the children boarded a train for Bangor. Her aunt met them at the station and drove them to her summer home overlooking the water at Castine.

Mougouch's letters to Gorky from Castine are unfailingly solicitous of his health and happiness and full of encouragement for his work. She tried to give him a picture of where she was and what she and the children were doing and feeling. To assuage Gorky's financial anxiety, she dutifully told him how little money she was spending on food. Gorky's letters to Mougouch are shorter and less informative, but they, too, are tender. His poor command of English reminds one why he borrowed other writers' words in his earlier correspondence with Mougouch and Corinne. His first letter, undated but postmarked June 7, said:

My darling Mouguch (galupcheg)
How lownly is with out you and the little ones you are in my hart every moment of the day. I hop you did not have to hard of

time in the train how is [it] there? Here rains every day I am working very well don't you worry about me my sweet one. Have received you telegram and the lovely curds.

I love you all Kiss my Maro and love your galupcheg

Hello to Aunt Marion.

On June 8 Mougouch wrote to Gorky: "Dear darling—It's so strange to be writing to you but I suppose I shall get used to the idea—it's hard to realize that you aren't with us and can't know what we are doing."

Later that month Jeanne, who was now living in New York and seeing a good deal of Gorky, wrote to Mougouch:

We do all miss you so and Arshile is so touching about you and what you mean and how he misses you and he does of course terribly but he is working and very well and it's a pleasure to see him like that. The drawings are beautiful and I think he is finding a great satisfaction in their magnitude. He does not show them to anyone and so I feel very honored that I have seen them. A painting too he showed one from before your departure which is even in its present state extraordinary.

Last night the Calas came here and arshile and then we just takled that is meant to be talk but I guess it was really tackle. Dear A. was out to do everyone down on all scores politics Saint Freud everything. it was quite fun I thought . . . Last week the Levys came and they were very sweet and we shall see them tonight but alas A will not be there for it is [his] night with his guts [his enema]. All this entertaining for A. Its rather sweet though i expect it just bores him really.

A few days later Mougouch wrote to Gorky about Jeanne's enthusiasm for his new work: "Everything that comes from your beautiful hand seems touched with magic that sings in my chest." She told him how Maro reminded her of him: "Her little mouth falls out sometimes with a full roundness that is so like your mouth when you are quite oblivious—like an expectant little animal the way you look sometimes when you make love to me." Although she made clear that she did not want him to interrupt his work, in this and several other letters Mougouch begged Gorky to come to Maine. He wrote back: "Mougouch I love to come I want so much to put my arms about you and kiss you all over and hold my little one's in my arm's. Perhaps I will be able to come when I do some painting's you know."

Gorky's letters to Mougouch over the next two months continued to say that, although he wanted to join her in Maine, he could not because of work. He told her about friends he'd seen: Jeanne and Urban, Ethel Schwabacher, Mina Metzger, the Hebbelns, Noguchi, Pierre and Teeny Matisse, Nicolas Calas, Julien and Muriel Levy, Dr. Weiss, and Marcel Duchamp. He had run into Lionel Abel at a party and, as was his habit, Gorky had extolled Stalin and deprecated Shakespeare. Abel countered by saying that Stalin knew nothing about Shakespeare or about art. Gorky came back with the idea that if Stalin had chosen a career in art he would have ended up on Fifty-seventh Street along with other successful painters.

Gorky invariably told Mougouch that he was working "day and night" and working well. In the early part of the summer he made preparatory drawings for paintings. On July 5 he wrote: "Also I just this afternoon finish a very large drawing. (from the Schwabacher's drawing) it is very large one about 80 × 102 inches, and it looks very good. I am to begin to paint coming Monday. I am sorry my darling for not writing to you sooner. as you see I had to finish that drawing." A week later he wrote that he was still making large studies for paintings. Presumably he meant squared-up preparatory drawings, of which there are several for the paintings he would produce later that summer.

The enormous drawing that Gorky referred to in his letter is *Summation*, now in the Museum of Modern Art. By rubbing the paper with pastel and charcoal, Gorky created a gray, fluid ambient: it is as though we are floating in the liquid depths of the Jungian unconscious. *Summation*'s cast of characters, drawn in pencil, comes out of the various themes explored in his Virginia drawings. Gorky seems to have gathered together all his imaginary beings for their final curtain call. But he never made the same shapes or creatures twice: they mutate and metamorphose from drawing to drawing, from drawing to painting, and from painting to painting. When Gorky showed *Summation* to Ethel that summer, he said: "There is my world."

Several letters mention sales. Ethel Schwabacher bought his drawing for *Summation*. On July 12 he said that Jeanne Reynal told him she wanted to buy one of his new drawings, and she did in fact acquire the squared-up drawing for *The Betrothal.* Another sale that Gorky reported to Mougouch was of his early painting *The Antique Cast* to Mina Metzger for $1,200. After the 20 percent commission to Levy, Gorky received $960.

By July 16 Gorky had embarked on an extraordinary series of paintings. His letter of that date says: "Mouguch I have been painting every day and now want to paint a picture every day . . . Now as I was painting my darling please pray to God so I can do some good paintings. I have been reading Delacroix Journal, he writes well thinks well and like's pictures but wrong." Two days later he wrote: "I am working very hard and the paintings are not so bad." On August 18 he said: "I have been working very well—and making very many painting's I wish you could see them. But when you return I want my harvest too be very big and good . . . I have to work and free myself with my work—. You are with me my darling with out you I could not [word deleted] go on working."

Jeanne kept Mougouch informed about Gorky's progress. On July 19 she wrote: "A is of course very much in the 'throws,' the drawings were very beautiful that he made and now he is painting, if he is really getting at something that is eating him all will be well. he does not show anything now and so one cannot know." On August 2, recognizing that the paintings from the summer of 1947 were among Gorky's most poignant and powerful works, Jeanne assured Mougouch that Gorky's painting was going well.

Now that he was caught up in the momentum of work, Gorky was even less willing to go to Maine. Mougouch wished he would come for Natasha's birthday on August 8, but he wrote on July 28: "I have so much work to do before Julien comes back in September if I am not there darling you know my hart is there with you and the baby's—; my little Natasha she will be two years old, and her dady is not there; you my mouguch have to take my part too." On Natasha's birthday he wrote: "Sweet hart Mouguch. My sweet hart. I love you. Please don't feel badly that I did'nt come over—and be with you and see the baby's—forgive me my love . . . Think of me and think I am there at Natashas birthday-party, and singing with you—My darling please forgive this letter I just had my bath."

Gorky did go to Maine the day after Natasha's birthday. Snapshots of him in bathing trunks lying on the beach beside his daughters show a thin, tired, not particularly happy man (Figs. 139 and 140 and p. 553). In one he is drawing. In another he sits beside the small folding easel he had given to Maro along with a real wooden paint box. Of his five-day visit Mougouch recalls: "He did not really want to come. He couldn't stand to be away from his work for long, and he hated being away because of not having his own bathtub. When Gorky came to Maine we were asked to dinner at Dr. Baker's and his wife. They were neighbors and had been nice to me. Gorky behaved very rudely. He contradicted them. He was bored and did not like stuffy Maine WASPs." Gorky got on better with Marion Hosmer, who understood him and, to his delight, called him a "water carrier," which she said was a Jungian term meaning that Gorky brought his imagery up out of his depths.

He and Mougouch took walks, picnicked, and swam. After he left, she reminded him in a letter of their having gone together "down by the big rock" at sunset. What was most pleasing to her were their conversations about art:

> This week in Castine was the one time when Gorky explained things to me. He'd sent me up a box of watercolors and crayons and a pad. I have a drawing that is partly by me and partly by Gorky. He explained to me how everything in your picture had to be in relation to something through tension, a relationship of tension between whatever part of the object you were looking at— say, a part of that tree—and something else that was equally strong, like a cloud. I can't describe it, but at the time I was quite aware of it, and suddenly when he said that and he did it on my drawing it took on a completely different life. As though you were almost working with wires between shapes. The shapes, in their placement, were all in a relationship, with a tautness. It had to do with the placing of it and the shape of it and the relation of that shape to that other shape. None of these relationships were accidental. They are very tense.

The evening she put Gorky on a train back to New York, Mougouch wrote to him and drew a cartoonlike picture of a moustachioed Gorky on the train and herself and the children on the platform waving goodbye: "O we do miss you so & tonight is so like last night only there are no arms, no great tender loving face looking down at me." Three days later she wrote that she hadn't had a chance to "explode any more landscapes," which suggests that Gorky had used this term in their recent conversations about drawing from nature. She ended her letter with wifely admonishments: she had paid his art-supply bill; he should get his trousers cleaned, eat steak, brush his teeth morning and night, not drink too much coffee, and send her a kiss.

Her next letter (August 21) closed with a wish that their relationship could be happy. Indeed, several of Mougouch's letters hint that there was something missing in their marriage. She spoke, for example, of her feeling of exhilaration at being in nature, of feeling more fully alive than ever before. In another August letter she said: "But still my sweet love I love you with the same love and I would we were free in that love and lived closer to that feeling—surely it is the attitude that creates the atmosphere surely my love and your love can transcend the miserable barriers built by modern life.xxxx Sweet Arshile Do you love me—I love you so greatly that sometimes it almost seems not you nor I At other times all you then again all I . . . Your Mougouch"

In Gorky's first letter to Mougouch after his return from Castine he once again borrowed from and paraphrased Gaudier-Brzeska's love letters. He wrote: "I am so blessed by the day when the great sun guided me to you. I press you to me with all my force. and only your love enables me to work." His next letter (undated) thanked her for photographs she had sent: "I love the pictures of you, they are beautiful of you—I just love them and keep looking at them and talk to them most of the day when I am not working." He had been, he said,

working all day and most of the night . . .
 I am beginning to see the promised land.
 last week I was also depressed.
 —Mouguch my sweet but don't you be depressed . . .
 as yet I have not seen anyone. I just want to work, and my work is going so well now, with new excitement;
 I have been reading What is Existentialism? by William Barrett.
 (and) Modern Women;—"The Last Sex."
 —galupcheg don't be angry about this letter; This dreadful letter. I have been working so hard that my head goes round—and round . . .
 I kiss you passionately, my sweet Mouguch on your lovely

mouth and your lovely eyes I fold you to me in gentle affection
and hope that you will not be so depressed.

With all my love
Pook.

Mougouch wrote back: "I am so overjoyed that you see at last the
promised land—That a beautiful land is promised you there can be no
doubt." A letter postmarked September 4 said she had had the rest she
needed and was ready to come home: "I long to live with you again & be
near you & cook for you and talk with you & just see you come and go
with your wonderful rhythmical walk—I sometimes hear one of your
songs, just a sound of your voice and I wonder how I have lived four
months without it & then these months seem like a period of sleep."
Gorky's next letter told of going to the Metropolitan Museum to see Picasso's portrait of Gertrude Stein and Ingres's self-portrait, but what he
had really admired that day was Persian art: "The persians art is great, I
feel compelled to tell you this my Mouguch because it pleases me so
much. I adore those sick and lovely persian civilisation which reveals
there ancient custome's to me, which is deeply impregnated with my
own."

As the time for Mougouch's return drew closer, Gorky wrote: "Two
more weeks, and then my darling's are coming back to me. Oh what a
happy day. for me that will be . . . I have been working very hard and
well and have got a lot of pictures and have been looking for a place to
work in. I do hope that I will be able to find one . . . mouguch my sweet
hart, I just had my bath and you know how stupid it makes me . . . please
mouguch forgive my stupid letter." Mougouch wrote on September 15:
"Do you realize in little more than 2 weeks we shall be home—O
darling I have missed you—too long—longer than these few months—
for a long long time—I only hope I'll be able to live a little more true to
myself—Ah I'm a lazy son of a gun . . . xx Mouk"

Despite her saying how much she was looking forward to seeing
Gorky, Mougouch's last letters betray anxiety about her return. Where
will they live? Will she be able to hold on to the feeling of wholeness
that four months on her own had given her? One note said she was looking around Castine for a studio for Gorky for the following summer. In
another she suggested that she and the children might break their return
journey with a visit to her uncle Henry Hosmer in Concord, near

Boston. She hoped Gorky would join them and together they would visit his relatives in Watertown and museums in Boston. Gorky wrote back: "I must say I can't come to Boston. Because I am working, you know. And have so many a many thing to do here . . . I can't come because I am painting and have so much cleaning to do."

Mougouch says that Gorky forbade her to stop in Concord. If he said this in so many words in a letter, it is lost. In late September he did write to say how urgently he wanted her to come home:

Mouguch my only love

I want you all back, with kisses and love and flowers, and clean house, and some paintings and many many kisses and embraces and clasp my beloved wife flower of my hart and light of my eyes come back come back to my arms I love you and I love our two sweet little girls come back I want you. I miss you terribly it has been such a long time!

I have been reading your sweet letters over and over again and they are wonderful my dearest. I love you I love you. My mouguch. I have been working all day and cleaning the house by night. yes working and dreaming for your coming home my dear. Oh what a happy day that will be for me come back. I want you dear love. I think I have found a place to work in I hope so—I am to see tomorrow or next day. it is round 10th st.

Had dinner with Julien few day ago. They were very sweet. they send there love to you.

I think we will waite and talke about Jean and [the possible purchase of] her farm house when you come back darling. Now it is Sunday night and am all alone and out side of my window's someone sings a sad song and my dreamy brow is burning with flames I want to press you and my little girls to my warm bosom. I kiss you and kiss your lovely body my love and kiss my little darlings for me I wait for you.

Pook

My love to Aunt Marion.

This is Gorky's last letter from the summer of 1947. Mougouch, the children, and Aunt Marion stopped over in Concord, and when Aunt Marion returned to New York one day before her niece, Gorky told her that when Mougouch came home he would beat her. Aunt Marion was shocked. Calmly she set him straight: "In this country, dear Gorky, men do not beat their wives!"

Gorky did not come to meet Mougouch and the children when they arrived at Grand Central Station: "When we walked in the door of 36 Union Square the children were terribly pleased to see Gorky. But after the summer in Castine, Gorky was cold and angry. He took it out on me for a bit. I was given hell for not returning straight away. I lived in total fear of him."

The problems that Mougouch had escaped by going to Castine were waiting for her. Chief among them was the question of where they were going to live. Gorky had still not found a separate studio, nor had he found a nursery school for the girls. Their home was soon overflowing with domesticity. Mougouch eventually put the children in a small private school on Fourth Avenue and Irving Place, which meant that Gorky had his 36 Union Square studio to himself for several hours each day, and she had a little freedom. But not enough—after four months of independence in Castine, being subject to Gorky's will and moods was even more difficult than before.

The gravest problem that fall was Gorky's increasing inability to work. He had written to Mougouch that he hoped to have a wonderful "harvest" of paintings finished by the time she returned, and he did. Working day and night he had produced masterpieces—two versions of *The Betrothal*, *Agony*, *The Plough and the Song*, *The Limit*, *Summation*, *Pastoral*. The twenty or so paintings from that summer were indeed his "promised land."

PART XIV

Gorky in the Glass House, January 1948

58

The Glass House

✵

Just before Christmas 1947, Gorky, Mougouch, and the children moved to the the Glass House, as the Hebbelns' remodeled farmhouse has come to be known. The plan to go abroad was abandoned once and for all because of the difficulty of finding an appropriate living space in Paris. Gorky and Mougouch also gave up the idea of buying a house — the houses they liked were always too expensive. "And then Gorky began to get more and more agitated," she recalls. "I hoped it was a question of time before he would be all right. I was a hopeless optimist. But he was not at all optimistic, and when we got into the Glass House he was filled with gloom and despair. He was always more gloomy in winter."

Aunt Marion joined them at the Glass House that first Christmas. Gorky cut down an evergreen and they decorated it with tinsel streamers. Four-year-old Maro looked with wonder: "Who hung worms on the Christmas tree?" she asked. Two days after Christmas, Gorky's father died. Sedrak's last days had been sad. Having been forced to leave the room he rented from a Providence shoe salesman, he had moved in with his son Hagop. They fought, so he checked himself into the local hospital, stopped eating, and died about ten days later. According to Vartoosh, who always protected Gorky and did not hesitate to rearrange the facts in such a way as to put her older brother in a better light, Gorky was not told about his father's death. Other family members recall that Satenik informed him, probably by telegram. Gorky did not respond, and when his father's estate was being settled he made no claim on it. Only Hagop's two sons attended their grandfather's funeral at Providence's

North Burial Ground. Although Gorky was not close to his father, his failure to help him in his last years must have added to Gorky's depression. No doubt it also brought home to him his estrangement from his Armenian family. Gorky said nothing about his father's death to Mougouch. He could not, for he had led her to believe that the last time he had seen his father was when Sedrak rode off into the mist along the shore of Lake Van. As a result, Mougouch says, he couldn't grieve, and his pain turned him in upon himself.

The Glass House in Sherman was an 1803 post-and-beam farmhouse that Henry Hebbeln had gutted to create an eight-room home with a sophisticated combination of old and modern. On the south gable end a huge curtain of glass replaced the clapboards and let sun pour in. Floors were pegged chestnut, and here and there a chestnut post was left freestanding. Rooms were on three levels connected by a steep open staircase that seemed to float in space. The gabled attic became a master bedroom sheathed on one side with glass.

On January 15, *Life* magazine photographers came to shoot a photo essay about Hebbeln's renovation. Mougouch wrote to Ethel Schwabacher: "Life Magazine is underfoot today & tomorrow—They are doing the house & how we live in it.—any plugs for Gorky will be purely incidental—except that everyone will think we live in great style—which we do—we are so lucky." On February 16, *Life* ran "Old House Made New," which included a full-page photograph taken at night from outside the house looking in through the glass wall (Fig. 144). Gorky, wearing his red-and-black-checked wool shirt and his Navajo vest, sits in the living room with Natasha on his lap. Mougouch, Maro, and a guest are on the left. The photograph reveals what for Gorky was wrong with this house: it was too open and too modern. Even though the glass wall looked out on nothing but nature, darkness seemed to be looking in. Another photograph shows Gorky sitting hunched over on an uncomfortable platform-style sofa. He looks lonely and sad as he stares out at the snow. In yet another shot, he and his daughters sit around the dining table on stools designed by Alvar Aalto (Fig. 145). As Mougouch, looking young and beautiful, carries in the meal, Gorky bends his head forward as if he were saying grace, which he certainly wasn't. His bowed head suggests the weariness and isolation of depression.

Mougouch came to realize that Gorky should never have been uprooted from 36 Union Square. He needed the familiarity of the place where he had painted for seventeen years and where he had invented himself as an artist. He needed a milieu, the feeling of belonging to a community of artists—even if he no longer saw those artists, their proximity helped define who he was. "The Sherman house did not fit either of us," she recalls. "It just wasn't us. It was not something you could burrow comfortably into. It had no cozy corners." Gorky did not feel at home with the Glass House's modern furniture, pieces chosen by the architect so that they had no binding personal history. And the long, narrow studio that had been a woodshed and that was attached to the west side of the house didn't feel right to Gorky, either. He and Mougouch had fixed it up, but it was cramped, and he surely mourned the studio up on the hill where he had painted until he burned it down. His new studio was about thirteen feet wide and twenty-four feet long, with one long, high window along the north wall. It had a cement floor, which he covered with old Oriental rugs, and it was sheathed with white wallboard between exposed beams. A photograph of Gorky taken that winter shows him before his easel, brush in one hand, palette in the other (Fig. 146). As he stands back to look at his canvas his brow is deeply furrowed. He wears his favorite painting clothes—the checked wool shirt, the vest, and the tight-fitting blue woolen cap that he wore even in summer. He is thin but not fit: his shoulders look narrow and his stomach, once so hard that he challenged friends to hit it, looks soft.

During these dark months Gorky talked about suicide. More than once he walked off into the woods carrying a rope. Knowing that Gorky would not harm himself in front of his children, Mougouch would send them after him, saying, "Run! Daddy's going to make a swing for you!" But Gorky's protectiveness went only so far. Elena Calas recalled his bringing a rope along on a walk and asking Maro to choose a suitable tree from which he could hang himself: "I told him he should not talk about such things in front of a child."

Not long after the *Life* article appeared, Gorky ran into Barnett Newman at a party in the city given by Matta and Patricia. Gorky and Newman had a long acquaintance but were not close, and in recent years Newman had come to think of Gorky as "the white-haired boy of Breton and the Surrealists." Newman was talking to Baziotes when Gorky arrived. Not recognizing Newman, Gorky asked him who he was. "Well, you know who I am," Newman replied. "I'm Barney Newman. Who are you?"

And I said, "I was glad to see you as the first American artist to be featured in *Life* magazine." This had never happened before to that extent . . . And I added, "I'm very happy because this was an achievement because we were all underground." And he said, "Yes, but didn't I look sad? Didn't I look unhappy?" So I said, "Well, I really didn't notice that. I thought you looked sort of quiet." And then Gorky said, "To hell with *Life* magazine. The important thing is life! What interests me is my two daughters and not all this nonsense about the art world." And so we had quite an animated conversation in relation to certain [concepts] where we definitely agreed. And then Gorky got light-veined. I don't remember exactly how it came up. I may have asked him indirectly. "You know how I came to this country?" Gorky said. And he told this sarcastic story which I have a feeling he made up on the spot. "Well, when I was a young boy in Armenia, my mother used to take me to church. And every time I went to church, I was always struck by the fact that the devils were all black and the angels were all blonde. Then later I heard that in the United States, all the girls are blonde. So I figured they were angels. So I came to this country." So we had kind of a very good time. And I thought the story was fantastic. What a man.

Money problems followed the Gorky family to Sherman. "We had $175 a month," Mougouch recalls. "Our rent was $55. There was electricity and telephone. The children went to a private school. We bought a car with Jeanne Reynal's money. I drove the children to school." But the worst problem was that Gorky had worked so hard in the summer of 1947 that he had exhausted himself and felt he had nothing left inside. Gorky had cleaned himself out, scrubbed the surfaces of his soul, just as he scrubbed his studio floor or cleansed his body inside and out. As he had said in one of his letters to Mougouch, painting that summer had been a kind of liberation or catharsis. He had taken in his "harvest." Now he was paralyzed. "That whole winter he was suicidal," say Mougouch:

He was saying he had nothing to paint, he couldn't paint. There was nothing to paint about. He didn't like the landscape in Sherman. He could no longer turn to his drawings from the summers in Virginia as a source for painting. He'd exhausted them, used them to the limit. He wanted to cover the canvas again and go further. He wanted to do more paintings like *The Orators*, which is covered with quite dense paint, but he couldn't. He did a lot of scumbling. He had two ways of working: one was dense, the other was thin. He liked to work in the denser way, as in paintings like *The Plough and the Song*—he'd paint and scrape and repaint. But he couldn't do that and keep the immediacy of his drawings. Maybe Gorky had painted himself into a corner. Maybe he felt he hadn't solved his problem. He'd finished with the thin, runny paintings. Now he was finished with the denser paintings. There are many unfinished canvases like *The Apple Orchard* from this period. He'd run out of steam. In the summer of 1947 he went to the limit with *The Limit*. He had to go on to something else. I think he was mortally ill. He was mortally wounded and that summer he had pushed himself too far.

Mougouch kept hoping that Gorky's mood would lift. She took him for walks and tried to get him interested in drawing the landscape, but the clouds, the shadows on snow, the spaces between branches no longer prompted invention. "He needed something new," she says. "He couldn't get anything out of the Connecticut landscape. He walked with me for hours, looking for a subject in nature. Every day he asked me for a subject. He was desperate to be in contact with something, no matter what." She suggested that he draw or paint the human form. "He agonized about the human figure and about its absence in his work. I wanted Gorky to go back and try portraiture. I offered to sit for him." He tried to paint Mougouch, but he found he could no longer paint from life. Nothing seemed worth painting. Depression made everything seem impossible and futile. He told Matta that he wanted to make his painting more connected with reality. "One of the last things Gorky said to me," Matta recalled, "was that he wanted to get some kind of human reference in his work." But, increasingly disconnected from nature and from people, Gorky could not paint a connection he did not feel. The forms and colors he placed on canvas lacked conviction.

Being an artist was crucial to Gorky's self-respect. Shushan had insisted that her only son live up to his priestly ancestors: if Gorky could not paint he was nothing. When he visited Raphael Soyer in 1948, his old friend saw his anguish: "In a particularly melancholy mood he pointed to a newly stretched bare canvas and said, 'This is art, anything done to its surface in color or charcoal will destroy its innate beauty.' In other words, he reached a point of no art."

"Gorky's depression was invasive," Mougouch recalls. And it was catching. The newfound feelings of wholeness and vitality that she had discovered in Castine were slipping away. Now that she was living in Sherman, she no longer had the emotional support of Dr. Harding. "I only had Gorky." It took all her strength to keep acting cheerful and doing her job of being the perfect artist's wife. Every day when she drove the children to and from school in the newly acquired secondhand Pontiac station wagon, she passed a lake. "I felt I wanted to step on the accelerator and go into the lake," she says. "I couldn't see any way out."

She was finding it harder and harder to reach Gorky. Pain, anger, and distrust cut him off from others. He didn't want to go anywhere for fear that he could not control his bowels. He hated the noises that came out of his bowels. Once when they were driving back to Sherman from the city, he suddenly burst. Mougouch stopped the car. They got out and she tried to help him. She didn't mind, she said. He pushed her away and, shouting and waving his arms, walked off into the trees. As the weeks went by he became more and more closed to his wife's solicitude. He wanted to be left alone. He did not want her to help him clean his stoma. He did not want to be touched. Julien Levy's wife, Muriel, saw Mougouch's predicament: "I'm sure that Gorky was punishing her for his illness. They had a miserable time. It was too bad because of the children."

That spring Marion Hosmer fell ill. Mougouch wanted to spend time with her, but Gorky wouldn't let her go to New York. He was suspicious even when she took the car to the local market. One March day Aunt Marion told Mougouch that if she didn't come to see her quickly it might be too late. Gorky refused to let Mougouch leave the Glass House, and Marion Hosmer died without her favorite niece saying good-bye. Even more upsetting than his jealousy was the way Gorky would suddenly be overcome by rage at the children, mostly at Maro, who was vociferous and demanding and constantly wanted to get into his studio. One day Maro was sitting on the living room sofa cutting hearts out of red paper, perhaps to make a valentine. While she worked on the hearts, she kept playing the same children's song over and over on her toy gramophone: "Tom Pearce, Tom Pearce, lend me your gray mare, all-along, out-along, down-along, lea." Gorky finally came out of his studio and broke the record to pieces.

According to one of Mougouch's upbeat letters to Ethel and Wolfgang Schwabacher, this one written on January 15, Gorky was working: "Our house is perfectly sweet if somewhat noisy. We are so very anxious to have you with us for a weekend . . . We go to bed very early 9:00 PM or 8:30 if you like Eat very simply—its so like fairyland in the snow . . . Gorky is painting." Much of her letter was about Gorky's contract with Julien Levy. They often consulted Wolfgang Schwabacher on business matters:

> Some months ago Julien told Gorky he was going to give him a raise $25 a month—but now it appears it isn't really a raise since he is demanding more pictures to cover it—Then G. told him he must have some money for material & Julien agreed to another $50 a month—supposedly for material—it seems that means more paintings too or whatever pro rata means—Well anyway its all rather hopeless & as the money is very nice to have we can't complain I guess. But do you think some inquiry ought to be made about which 12 paintings & what 30 drawings per annum at what rate have been taken by the gallery so far? Gorky doesn't keep count & neither do I but I could if I should (with difficulty because Julien is so hard to pin down). All I know is that to date he has the works—all of everything except a few drawings & we never know what if anything is sold & how would one unless they were numbered.

There were two French galleries, she said, that wanted to give Gorky a show. One wanted to work with Julien, the other without. "Julien was just here for the weekend but we didn't like to broach such subjects."

Show at Julien Levy

⁂

Gorky's art had been having quite a bit of exposure over the course of the last year. On February 18, 1947, *Arshile Gorky: Colored Drawings* opened at the Julien Levy Gallery. The show stayed up only about a week, and a *New York Times* reviewer pronounced the drawings "rather slight" and "non-objective. There is evidence of command of line but to what purpose is considerably less clear." A reviewer for *Art Digest* wrote that Gorky had drawn "the more intimate parts of a flower" and "the productive end of a cow" in a "rather loose manner and occasionally touched up with a spot or two of bright watercolor. It is a highly personal, acutely concentrated kind of doodling and quite intriguing. One feels, rather than 'sees,' what he is getting at." That same year the Whitney, the Museum of Modern Art, the Art Institute of Chicago, and the California Palace of the Legion of Honor included him in group shows. In a January 15, 1948, letter to her great-aunt Nathalie Campbell, Mougouch said that Gorky had received his "first decent enthusiastic review" from Clement Greenberg. Reporting on that winter's Whitney Annual, Greenberg had singled out Gorky's *The Calendars* (1947) (Fig. 141) as "The best painting in the exhibition and one of the best pictures ever done by an American." But again Greenberg honored with one sentence and humiliated with the next. Gorky's work, he said, was an "end product" that added nothing new to the history of art. The long time Gorky had taken "to arrive at himself" and his "chronic diffidence in the face of Parisian art" had finally paid off, and he now expected Gorky to produce "masterpieces." Greenberg's accolades didn't change Gorky's

Fig. 149. *Garden in Sochi*, 1941

Fig. 150. *Garden in Sochi*, c. 1943–47

Fig. 151. *Waterfall*, 1942–43

Fig. 152. *Golden Brown Painting*, c. 1943–44

Fig. 153. *Untitled*, 1943

Fig. 154.
Untitled, c. 1943–44

Fig. 155. *To Project, to Conjure*, 1944

Fig. 156. *One Year the Milkweed*, 1944

Fig. 157. *How My Mother's Embroidered Apron Unfolds in My Life*, 1944

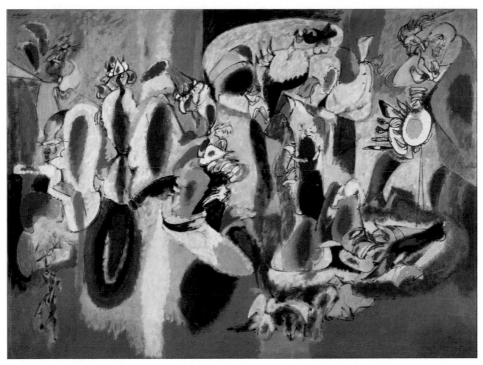

Fig. 158. *The Liver Is the Cock's Comb*, 1944

Fig. 159. Study for *The Liver Is the Cock's Comb*, 1943

Fig. 160. *Water of the Flowery Mill*, 1944

Fig. 161. *Good Afternoon, Mrs. Lincoln*, 1944

Fig. 162. *They Will Take My Island*, 1944

Fig. 163. *Painting*, 1944

Fig. 164. *Good Hope Road II* (also called *Pastoral* or *Hugging*), 1945

Fig. 165. *Landscape Table*, 1945

Fig. 166. *Charred Beloved I*, 1946

Fig. 167. *Charred Beloved III*,
1946

Fig. 168. *The Plough and the Song,* 1947

Fig. 169. Study for *The Plough and the Song,* 1944

Fig. 170. *The Betrothal II*, 1947

Fig. 171. *Pastoral*, 1947

Fig. 172. Study for *Pastoral*, 1946

Fig. 173. *The Limit*, 1947

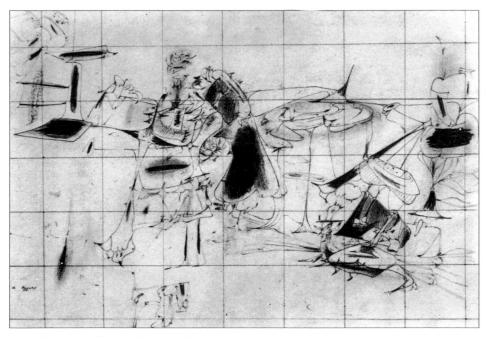

Fig. 174. Study for *The Limit*, 1946

Fig. 175. *Agony*, 1947

Fig. 176. Study for *Agony I*, 1946–47

Fig. 177. *Dark Green Painting*, c. 1948

Fig. 178. Study for *Dark Green Painting*, 1946

Fig. 179. *Unfinished Painting*, c. 1947–48

Fig. 180. *Last Painting*, 1948

mood. "At the end of his life Gorky gave up caring about his reputation," Mougouch recalls. "He knew his 1947 paintings were good. He just didn't know where to go from there."

At the end of February 1948, Gorky and Mougouch drove into New York for the opening of an exhibition of Gorky's paintings at Julien Levy's gallery. They stayed, as was now their custom, in Jeanne's brownstone on West Eleventh Street, a house full of a rich variety of objects: kachina dolls and primitive masks, as well as sculptures by Ernst, Calder, and Noguchi and paintings by Lam, Ernst, Enrico Donati, William Stanley Hayter, and, of course, Gorky. Then there was that thorn in Gorky's side, Jackson Pollock's *Magic Mirrors*. Jeanne herself set the standard for "upper bohemian" attire, decking herself out in Mexican-style peasant skirts and an array of American Indian silver and turquoise jewelry. Her home was a meeting place for artists and intellectuals, a place where friends dropped in and stayed for dinner.

At the opening, Ethel Schwabacher observed, "Levy, quick, dark, subtle, willingly interpreted Gorky to those who came . . . Many people milled around; their words drifted: 'too like Miró . . . obscure . . . extreme . . . Gradually the confused state of the naïve spectators and the biting innuendoes of the acknowledged artists and critics must have overwhelmed Gorky." The paintings included in Gorky's fourth Julien Levy show were all from 1947. Most had been painted during that summer of intense work when his family was in Maine.

The following day Gorky and Mougouch arrived for lunch at the Schwabachers' apartment in an unhappy mood. Gorky was distressed by the way the guests at his opening had, like Levy, tried to explain the imagery in his paintings. Ethel tried to comfort Gorky by giving her own, more purely visual response to his art. She sent Gorky and Mougouch home with a box of hand-me-downs and a canary—the latter an apt gift for someone sunk into depths as dark as a coal mine. The next day, back in the Glass House, Mougouch wrote to thank Ethel for the gifts and to tell her how much she appreciated her understanding of Gorky's painting:

Ethel you don't know how it did our battered morale good to hear you talk about how you looked at Gorky's painting. We were just finding out how most people don't, even ones whom we thought didn't go symbol snatching and it was a rude shock to us both. I'm convinced there still are a few people above ground who love painting as painting not as a sop for gossip and pathology and it is more of such people that Gorky should see.

Though just now he doesn't care about anything but to work on some fresh canvas and really give himself over to painting. We haven't seen a single criticism about his show which is just dandy.

In Ethel's view, Gorky's unhappiness, his "variability of mood and a certain impatience," was exacerbated by his feeling misunderstood by his audience. An actual example of Gorky's being misunderstood—or making himself incomprehensible—is a chance meeting he had with de Kooning and Milton Resnick shortly after his exhibition opened. Resnick recalls:

We met Gorky in the park and we said to him that we'd seen his show and it was very good. Gorky liked it that we appreciated him. Then he said, "I'm going home. Why don't you take a walk with me?" We kept walking and then Gorky said, "You know when I was painting those paintings I would think of where to put a line and at the moment when I painted the line, I'd put it somewhere else. And it was always better than it would have been if I'd put the line where I thought it would be." Then he looked at de Kooning and said, almost fiercely, "No eyes, no eyes." De Kooning got upset. He thought Gorky was insulting him. Then Gorky said, "Never mind, never mind," and he ran away. De Kooning said, "He thinks I put eyes in the picture like an illustrator. He thinks I'm an illustrator." I didn't think that Gorky meant that. He was talking to both of us. I think Gorky meant his [own] paintings were not anatomical, not figurative. Bill and I went to Bill's studio and we talked about Gorky—he was so good with his brush. I looked at Bill's paintings. I said to Bill, "So much drawing on the top and little on the bottom." Bill said, "I don't care what you think, great art is great illustration."

More misunderstanding came from the critics. An *Art News* reviewer saw Gorky's work as an extension of Matta's and said: "Gorky's little masks, books, dogs and figures are spotted among the hot reds and yellows to give a gay, decorative effect which is sometimes marred by sloppy technique." Sam Hunter's unenthusiastic review appeared in the *New York Times* on the day of the opening. Hunter approved of Gorky's thinner, more transparent paint surface, but he saw it as a stepping down of energy. Although he found Gorky's color "oversweet," he compared it to "a brilliant run in music . . . The most durable impression is of a testimony of labor, with all the wipings, erasures, tentative sallies and retreats of form left standing."

Clement Greenberg's more favorable review in the *Nation* mixed misunderstanding with acute visual perception. The Schwabachers sent the clipping to Gorky, and Mougouch wrote Ethel that the piece was "amazing." No doubt Greenberg's formalist approach, his lack of interest in "symbol-snatching," pleased Gorky. Even better, Greenberg said Gorky was "the equal of any painter of his own generation anywhere." He commended Gorky for his brush handling, draftsmanship, solidity, and sensuousness. "On the face of it," Greenberg wrote, "Gorky is a complete hedonist, deeper in his hedonism than almost any French painter . . . his primary impulse to paint lies in the enjoyment of art itself." Although he was squeamish and chaste about bodily matters, Gorky was a voluptuary when it came to putting pigment on canvas. Tense lines and searing colors may communicate the painter's self-critical, self-denying, anxious nature, but if you look closely at how his paintings were made, stroke by stroke, line by line, you can see Gorky lavishing all his sensuality on the materials and processes of art. For all that, Gorky's impulse to paint surely came from a deeper and more passionate source than Greenberg's notion of "the enjoyment of art itself."

Although he still discerned the influence of Matta and Miró, Greenberg said Gorky had gone beyond both these models and had "at last" arrived at himself. Compared with Matta, he said, Gorky possessed "a plenitude of painterly qualities such as Matta himself appears incapable of." In comparison with Miró, Gorky was, in Greenberg's view, more advanced in that he identified his background more closely with his canvas surface. He accomplished this melding by "scumbling or washing in his pigment transparently over large areas, or by varying color in narrow gradations from one area to another." But Greenberg held the carrot of his approval always just in front of Gorky's nose. This time his carp was that Gorky should move his whole arm when he painted, not just his wrist or elbow. Greenberg clearly still wanted Gorky to be more like Pollock, and he again suggested that Gorky had yet to paint "his greatest pictures."

Gorky was sufficiently happy with Greenberg's review to put the critic's past insults behind him and to offer him a drawing. Greenberg recalled that he chose a good one and subsequently sold it for a high price. Despite Greenberg's praise, Levy sold only one painting out of the February 1948 show, *Soft Night*, for $700.

Compared with the attenuated, spare paintings of 1945 and 1946 such as *The Unattainable* and *Charred Beloved*, the 1947 paintings are dense and rich. In the earlier works tensile black lines make swift and exquisite trajectories between spots or areas of diaphanous color. By contrast, in *The Calendars* and in the other sensuously layered canvases of 1947, line is once again given the job of defining shapes, and shapes have a suggestion of volume. There is a greater emphasis on painterly process, a return to scumbling as opposed to smooth, transparent washes of color. Planes are overlaid with several different colors so that earlier colors show through. As opposed to the feeling of openness and suspension seen in the 1945 paintings, Gorky has returned to the firm planar structure of works like *The Liver Is the Cock's Comb* of 1944. His imagery is now set in a shallow space defined by seven or eight color planes and by verticals and diagonals that suggest the walls and floor of an interior, perhaps the corner of a room with an up-tilted floor. The flat color areas also recall the Synthetic Cubist planes that created a sheltered, closed-in space in Gorky's paintings of the second half of the 1930s such as *Enigmatic Combat*. The feeling of closeness is further emphasized by the way all the shifting planes and the clusters of shapes finally reside on (or orient themselves to) the surface of the canvas.

Many of the paintings from 1947 reveal a heightened tension, a tautness that is sometimes painful. This is in part because they are based on the irascible Virginia drawings from the summer of 1946. In both the drawings and the paintings based on them, lines and forms are stretched to the snapping point. Skeletal figures, some of which are made up of a concatenation of vertically stacked shapes (probably influenced by Tanguy), look like a nightmarish vision of surgical equipment.

When he praised *The Calendars* at the Whitney Annual, Clement Greenberg recognized that with this painting Gorky had hit his full stride. For all the delicate beauty of 1946 paintings like *Charred Beloved*, the densely brushed and firmly orchestrated canvases of 1947 are fuller, more generous, and more resonant with feeling. What the imagery portrays hardly matters. The viewer responds to groupings of shapes, to tensions between abutting planes, to Gorky's caressing brush, and to the odd, mostly muted colors—lavenders, yellows, gray-green, and orange.

Canvases like *The Calendars*, which have richly layered and scumbled paint and a structure of colored planes, represent only one direction that Gorky's art took in 1947. Other canvases are softer, more open and fluid. They have thin veils of translucent color that often drips and bleeds into the adjacent color. Much of the canvas is left bare so that space seems to breathe more freely. Often these more diaphanous paintings are variations on a theme. In 1947 Gorky created several series, each with one or two densely painted versions (probably the initial works in the series) and a few versions in which the paint is thinned with turpentine. *The Calendars* has two thinner variations: *Making the Calendar* and *Days, Etc.*, both signed and dated 1947 and both using the same imagery as the principal denser version but embedding that imagery in transparent veils of turpentine-thinned pigment. In both of the thinly painted versions, the imagery is ambiguous and seems to melt into the painterly process. In *Days, Etc.* so much of it is washed away that it can hardly be identified. The one image that remains clear is the sumptuous reclining nude in the upper left. Art historian Harry Rand sees the shape within the rectangle in *The Calendars* and its sequels as a pinup girl on a calendar. I suspect that the nude is a painting within a painting, perhaps in homage to Matisse's *Red Studio*, a work that Gorky adored. Gorky told Julien Levy that *Days, Etc.* was related to *The Calendars*: "There is that poem by Paul Eluard—'Days, like fingers, twist their battalions'—but I think that is too long."

The Plough and the Song series, perhaps the most intricately worked-out and iconographically intriguing sequence of paintings Gorky ever painted, was based on a drawing from the summer of 1944 now in the Allen Memorial Art Museum at Oberlin College (Figs. 168 and 169). If, as Mougouch says, two versions of the *The Plough and the Song* were lost in the 1946 studio fire, then Gorky had produced the first two paintings in this series by the end of 1945. That he waited until late in 1946 to take up the theme again is explained by the disruption caused by the fire and his cancer operation. His months of recuperation in the city were followed by a summer and fall of nonstop drawing in Virginia. Probably the earliest extant version of *The Plough and the Song* was begun in New

York in December 1946. The versions in the Milton Gordon and Ober-lin collections were almost certainly from the summer of 1947.

With the first drawing for *The Plough and the Song*, all the basic elements are present. The changes Gorky made from one work to the next in the series, which consists of three drawings and three paintings, are minor alterations in texture, light, and color. There is so much excitement in the painterly process that the viewer forgets that Gorky started with a kind of blueprint. He took the final squared-up drawing and transferred it to three separate canvases that are similar but not identical in size. This procedure is not unlike the way in the early 1930s he traced the composition of one finished drawing onto the next sheet. At that earlier time, the cautiousness of this approach was stultifying. In 1947 his use of a squared-up drawing as a starting point for several canvases was liberating: with the organization of forms set and given, Gorky could luxuriate in the process of laying down strokes of color. His creative energies continued to be engaged on the deepest level, for the meaning of his paintings was embedded as much in the abstract qualities of shape, texture, and color as in imagery.

The biggest changes in T*he Plough and the Song* series take place between the 1944 drawing and the two later drawings, which are probably from 1946 and 1947. Gorky moved the tall, bony figure on the left forward and the central imagery back, thus creating more space at the bottom of the picture and leaving room for the color plane seen in the lower right corner of each painting. This plane, like the two rectangular planes in the upper register of *The Calendars*, both asserts the flatness of the canvas and creates a window into another space or scale. In the two densely painted and scumbled versions of *The Plough and the Song*, the imagery comprises a series of linked shapes that seem suspended between the rectangle in the lower right corner and another rectangle in the upper left. In the thinly painted version (now in Oberlin) the imagery seems to float and dissolve in a liquid field of yellow, suggesting an ecstatic melding.

The subject of *The Plough and the Song* appears to be a celebration of fertility—earthly, human, and artistic. As Gorky sat on his stool under the hot Virginia sun and gazed with rapt attention at the fields, he thought back to the wooden ploughs used on his family farm in Armenia and to the songs the farmers sang as they ploughed. The largest section of the plough, the moldboard, designed to push aside earth as the ploughshare furrows the earth, is an upside-down version of Gorky's favorite boot/butter churn motif. In both the *Garden in Sochi* and *The Plough and the Song* series, this shape creates a base or plinth for creatures or personages made up of vertically linked shapes. In some drawings, this "foot" appears as a kind of skid.

The shapes in *The Plough and the Song* are easy to read because there is little overlapping and contours are razor-sharp. Moreover, the imagery is very much the same from drawing to drawing and from one painting to the next. A conflation of landscape forms with forms that suggest the interior of the body, it seems to picture the fertile earth as a metaphor for human procreation—perhaps even as a parallel to artistic creation. Yet, just as Gorky would have wished, the imagery has baffled everyone who has studied it. In his 1954 essay on *The Plough and the Song*, William C. Seitz said: "Exact identification of its elements is of course impossible; each of us will see them differently, and we shall all miss personal meanings which the artist wished to keep hidden." Seitz saw a tall figure on the left, and he called the ring of small black dots an "ovary," inside of which was the "directly-observed anatomy of a flower." But he bore in mind Gorky's frequent quip, "I never put a face on an image," and wisely refrained from identifying forms in any fixed way. In seeking Gorky's meaning, Ethel Schwabacher let her poetic imagination run free—perhaps too free. But since she knew Gorky well and captured the mood of his paintings, we must respect her poetic license: "In *The Plow and the Song* we find the sun-warmed fertility of the earth, plow-turned the sheltering bone, the winding birth passage and spacious exit chambers out of which the seed passes into space . . . The vertical image combines metaphors of plow, flower and bone, its base rooted in the moist field; its center is elaborated with suggestions of seed and leaf; its upper half, enveloped by the warm orange ochre earth, is raised in a pregnant gesture."

Mougouch wrote to Ethel Schwabacher in December 1949: "There are some drawings which I can actually see as a certain place, the fundamental arrangement of shapes in nature serving as a base. The song and the plough is of a field that goes up from the barn or what was the barn. There is no waterfall the intestinal shape or whatever you call it (maro called it a big worm to Gorky's delight) was a collapsed haystack . . . haystack field and sky are the elements."

I do not see a haystack in the *Plough and the Song* series, but a field is easy to imagine and, in the version in the Art Institute of Chicago, there appears to be sky. The wheat-colored ground in the Milton Gordon version (Fig. 168) has vertical strokes that suggest wheat growing or heat rising from the field. It seems reasonable to identify the tall concatenation of shapes on the left as a figure, probably male; in the upper right is a female torso very like the female nude in *The Calendars*. The male is bony and full of sharp protrusions. The female is lobed, fleshy, and voluptuous. In two versions of *The Plough and the Song* she is flesh-color or pink. Other shapes in the painting suggest male and female genitalia, perhaps some primal coupling. Where the tubular shape that rises on a diagonal from left to right makes contact with the oval that Seitz called an ovary, it suggests the miracle of conception. The sexual theme, so dear to the Surrealists and especially to Matta, is handled as always with discretion. Gorky maintains a kind of innocence. Even when he draws a phallic or vaginal shape, he offers alternative readings: the shape could also be a flower, a mushroom, or some kind of protozoan.

The feeling of earthy growth under the summer sun suggested by *The Plough and the Song* is replaced in *The Limit* (Fig. 173) by a sense of absence that echoes through a vast, cool, blue-gray space. Gone are the forms generating forms in a great visceral huddle. Shapes are now isolated from each other. Small Miróesque spots of color—red, blue, green, yellow—fall away from the larger forms and become particles of matter floating in space. The feeling of boundlessness brings to mind Gorky's determination to get rid of the horizon line, something he learned from Miró and Matisse. "When he did a landscape he didn't want a horizon in there," Mougouch says. "He adored Miró's sense of suspension. He liked Matisse's *Red Studio*, in which everything is suspended with perfect placement and related only to itself. Gorky achieved this feeling of suspension marvelously in *The Limit*."

Two figures are intimated in *The Limit* but not defined, for much of the imagery seen in the squared-up 1946 drawing on which the painting is based (Fig. 174) vanishes beneath the painting's gray ground. One figure, probably male, wearing some kind of black hood, stands in the center facing leftward. Like the figure on the left in many of the *Fireplace in Virginia* drawings, his arms are outstretched. His phallic body has a lobed base that brings to mind the black vertical in the *Garden in Sochi* series. The other figure, created by the group of shapes in the upper left corner, appears to be a seated female.

Gorky covered the whole canvas with a gray ground on top of which he painted a veil of white scumbles that descends from the painting's left and upper margins. This veil creates a cloud screen that serves as a *repoussoir* to push the gray ground back. As a result, the gray suggests infinite extension, a chilling emptiness that Nicolas Calas saw as central to Gorky's content. A similar apprehension of endless void prompted Gorky's friend de Kooning to fill up canvases like *Asheville* (1948) and *Excavation* (1950) with heaving fragments of figures and objects. De Kooning's 1949 statement about infinite space seems to reflect the feeling of emptiness conveyed in Gorky's *The Limit*: "In Genesis, it is said that in the beginning was the void and god acted upon it. For an artist that is clear enough. It is so mysterious that it takes away all doubt. One is utterly lost in space forever. You can float in it, fly in it, suspend in it and today, it seems, to tremble in it is maybe the best or anyhow very fashionable. The idea of being integrated with it is a desperate idea." In *The Limit* Gorky does indeed tremble in vast space. What he said, according to Julien Levy, about this painting seems right: "I have been so lonely, exasperated and how to paint such empty space—so empty it's the limit!"

The loneliness, the feeling of emptiness, and even the exasperation are all present, if suppressed, in the painting. The vestiges of imagery— an oval here, a loop or a slit there—have a pathos that distinguishes them from their source in Miró. Miró's suspended spots of color are buoyant and often funny, whereas Gorky's shapes seem signals of loss. Nicolas Calas captured something of this sadness when he wrote in his *Bloodflames* catalog: "Gorky is in incessant pursuit of the isolated, or rather, of that line or color which will become isolated by achieving independence. A blue detached from the night, a red withdrawn from the flesh, a curve formed out of the resistance of the branch to the gale, the bitterness that ossifies the lip after the smile has faded away, the weight of the bones felt after the embrace has been unlocked—that which remains and is worthy of lasting is recalled and lauded."

To turn from *The Limit* to the Museum of Modern Art's *Agony* (Fig. 175) is to turn from chilly vastness to a closed space made unbearably hot by reds and red browns, glimmers of yellow and white—the colors of fire. The imagery, defined by black lines that are sometimes submerged beneath the red ground, consists of an insectlike creature with a phallic body, large feet, and two lines for legs, bending toward a taller skeletal creature on the left. Between them is a dangerous-looking contraption consisting of a rectangle with pinched contours suspended from a hooked line weighted at its base by a rounded black triangle. This contraption creates a mood of tension—one false move and the pinched rectangle will whip forward as if it had been held back by a spring. The creature looks like a cross between a feathered fetish and (as William Seitz pointed out) a dentist's chair. That the creature with its orifice and red tongue or phallus is human is suggested in one of the drawings from around 1946 in which its ribs are revealed. Its pelvic area is decorated with feathers, perhaps inspired by Jeanne Reynal's collection of Hopi Indian kachina dolls, which often sport feathers. This and the other skeletal figures that populate Gorky's 1946 drawings and the paintings based on them probably derive from Matta's totemic personages of the mid-1940s, which in turn are based on ethnographic sculptures from New Ireland. Some viewers see the personages in *Agony* as relating to Gorky's colostomy. Others might detect sexual difficulties, marital conflicts, or even Gorky's jealousy. Although we will never know what Gorky intended, the painting does seem to present a confrontation between two characters, probably male and female.

The Orators (Fig. 142), another of the great paintings from the summer of 1947, has been described by Ethel Schwabacher, Julien Levy, and Harry Rand as a testimonial to the death of Gorky's father. Levy purported to quote Gorky on *The Orators*: "My father's death, and everybody making big orations while a candle gutters out like a life. I didn't love my father very much, but I know about Armenian funerals." Although this "quotation" would seem to clinch the matter, Levy, as we have seen, was promiscuous about applying his own meanings to Gorky's paintings. The problem with seeing *The Orators* as inspired by Sedrak's funeral is that Gorky's father did not die until December 1947, several months after the painting was almost certainly finished. If indeed *The Orators* refers to a funeral oration, it is more likely that Gorky was remembering the funeral of his maternal grandmother Hamaspiur Der Marderosian in the mountain village of Ermerur in 1910. On the other hand, the painting could simply be a recollection of Armenian funerals in general.

Or it could have nothing to do with funerals: Gorky told Mougouch that the title had to do with the orators who stood on soapboxes in Union Square waving their arms as they railed against inequities. He must have been obfuscating: if the idea for *The Orators* came from soapbox orators, why is there a clearly identifiable recumbent figure surrounded by agitated figures? Perhaps the recumbent man is a patient, not a corpse. *The Orators* might depict, albeit in abstract terms, Gorky's memory of lying helpless on an operating table while doctors and nurses hovered over him. Similarly, some of the imagery in *Agony* suggests a nightmare vision of a medical apparatus. When Marny George, having herself undergone a colostomy, saw Gorky's 1947 paintings with their bodies and body parts all gone askew, she wrote to James Thrall Soby: "How many personal symbols in the last paintings have an unbearable clarity for me!"

In the summer of 1947 Gorky made three versions of *The Betrothal* (Fig. 170). The first two have dense, scumbled grounds. The third, which Gorky gave to the International Rescue Committee in January 1948, has delicately drawn shapes that, like the shapes in the Oberlin version of *The Plough and the Song*, seem to dissolve into the thinly painted and loosely brushed ground. *The Betrothal* has been interpreted and reinterpreted. Julien Levy wrote that it was influenced by Duchamp's 1912 *Bride*, a painting in which human anatomy is similarly transformed into abstract shapes and that Gorky saw hanging in Levy's apartment as early as 1937, when he remarked on its elegance and exclaimed: "For a man who rejects painting . . ." Ethel Schwabacher said that *The Betrothal* was about "the wooing and drawing together of the sexes," and she saw the creature on the left as a horse and rider inspired by the prancing horse and rider in Uccello's *The Battle of San Romano*, which Gorky had copied in a sketch. I see the *Betrothal* as a ceremony having to do with marriage—not a modern marriage but one that seems medieval and that includes, on the left, an equestrian bride wearing a wreath or a crown and, following her to the right, a helmeted male. The figures' armored appearance brings to mind not only Uccello but also the mounted saints carved in relief at Akhtamar. More immediate inspiration might have come from the caparisoned horses and soldiers dressed for battle in the Metropolitan Museum's armor room, a place where Gorky often pulled out his sketch pad. Perhaps the *Betrothal* series is based on memories of traditional Armenian weddings in which the groom would ride to fetch his bride in a procession, accompanied by the music of a drum and a horn. In some villages the family came to collect the bride while the groom waited at the church. The bride would then be brought to him on a horse amid a procession of singing and rejoicing family members. After the ceremony, when the groom led the bride to his family's home, he was allowed by Turkish law to carry a sword to protect his wife from Kurds.

For all the apparent fanfare, *The Betrothal* is not celebratory. The members of the wedding move like soldiers on their way to battle. Lines are painfully precise, almost brittle in their tautness. If one thinks of Gorky's lines as nerves, one could say that in this painting his nerves were stretched to their limit. Indeed, *The Betrothal* is one of the least sensuous and least tender of Gorky's paintings from the summer of 1947.

Pastoral (Fig. 171) and *Terra Cotta*, both from that same summer, are more lighthearted outdoor (possibly barnyard) scenes. Both depart radically from the tense and painful 1946 drawings (Fig. 172) on which they are based, and both move in the direction of painterly spontaneity and simplification of form. Vivid in the drawings but barely decipherable in the paintings is a female creature with feet that look like rockers. To the right is a masculine-looking creature that looks part insect and part bird. Like the personage on the right in *Agony*, it has a phallic projection. As in *Agony*, too, it seems to embody Gorky's painful preoccupation, after the colostomy, with bodily functions and sex. But, as Gorky moved from drawing to painting, subject matter gave way to painterly process. The ground color, a transparent wash, now took an active role, cutting out and leaving in reserve shapes that remain the white of the canvas. Underdrawing is no longer evident and a fluid, seemingly relaxed movement of the brush takes precedence over draftsmanship. Whatever snippets of drawing exist are done with thin paint flowing from a medium-width brush.

Pastoral and *Terra Cotta* suggest the catharsis or release that Gorky told Mougouch he hoped would come through painting during the summer of 1947. Yet that feeling of ease was the product of hours of discipline: Gorky drew the theme of *Pastoral* so many times that he memorized it; this endless rehearsal allowed the paintings to look as fresh as improvisations. When Jeanne Reynal wrote to Mougouch in Castine in August 1947, she may have been thinking of paintings like *Pastoral* and *Terra Cotta* when she said, "It is always amazing to me that out of his anguish he always emerges with something that makes no mention of same. What he has painted is like a butterfly or many butterflies lovely fragile & depersonalized. Or perhaps he has concretized the ephemeral nature of man which is to lay its eggs & go its way."

Gorky's body of work comes to a magisterial conclusion with the paintings from the summer of 1947. After that he struggled and failed to regain his stride. Only once, in *Dark Green Painting* (c. 1948) (Fig. 177), a gloomy canvas based on one of his more complex and prickly 1946 drawings (Fig. 178), was he able to touch the achievement of the previous summer's work. With its somber greens and blacks enlivened by small patches of ocher and lavender, this painting evokes evening sunlight sifting through hemlock branches. During a wintry walk in the Sherman woods with Ethel Schwabacher, Gorky pointed to the evergreens and said, "Yes, it was this green that found its way into the painting, and the red-brown of the fallen pine-needles." But *Dark Green Painting* may just as easily be an interior with figures and objects caught in the light of an evening fire. Either way, the light is fading and it brings on a mood of reverie in which the flux of perceptions, memories, and feelings coalesces into semirecognizable configurations that then dissolve, disperse, or metamorphose into a new set of relationships. I might see, for example, a man in *Dark Green Painting*'s center, perhaps a camouflaged self-portrait, for just to the left is an oval that suggests a palette. But the next moment this grouping of shapes turns into something else entirely.

As he tried to find something and some way to paint in the fall of 1947 and the winter and spring of 1948, Gorky kept scraping and repainting canvases from the previous summer. One of them, a second version of *The Limit*, which is unsigned, untitled, and apparently unfinished, belongs with a small number of canvases that Gorky labored over and abandoned during the unhappy months that followed his family's return from Maine. This group of paintings, which also includes *Painting* (Fig. 179), several versions of *From a High Place*, and *Dialogue of the Edge* (Fig. 147), is highly abstract and evidence of process is left emphatically visible. From this late period come also a number of small, brusquely painted abstract canvases, some of which have primitive signs very like those seen in Adolph Gottlieb's pictographs of the 1940s (but probably deriving from Miró).

The painterly handling seen in Gorky's 1948 canvases comes close to Abstract Expressionism, which was just then getting off the ground. Full of chasms and crevices, *Dialogue of the Edge* and *Painting*, for example, have something of the mood of crisis conveyed by the swirling brush strokes opening into a dark abyss in Jackson Pollock's 1953 *The Deep*. Nothing is securely set in space. Shapes look as if they are about to be devoured by the tidal sweep of color. It is possible that Gorky was trying to escape his obsession with control and his search for perfect beauty. Perhaps he was forcing himself to take risks, to venture into rough terrain that verged on ugliness. But, like almost everything else Gorky's brush touched, the late unfinished paintings remain elegiac and tender. The pale lavenders and grays that nearly cover the imagery in *Painting* are as poignant as ash and embers in a dying fire.

"*Red Painting* and so-called *Last Painting* (Fig. 180) were the only ones finished that winter of '47–'48," Mougouch recalled. *Red Painting*, which seems to depict an interior with a recumbent female, appears to be an effort toward joy. By contrast, *Last Painting* is entirely bleak. Its red, green, and yellow strokes and its swaths of black appear to have been made in a rush of anger and despair. Yet, for all the painting's expressionistic vehemence, its imagery was not invented during the painterly process: indeed, *Last Painting* is, according to Jim Jordan, really a version of *From a High Place*. As in *Theme for From a High Place*, there appear to be three schematic figures and possibly a smaller fourth one just above the green oval. The dominant figure (on the left) looks like an angry white owl. With vertical slits for eyes, a beak for a nose, and a right hand raised in a fist, it seems an omen of death. In his monograph on Gorky, opposite the color plate of *Last Painting*, Julien Levy placed two quotations from Chekhov's story *The Black Monk*. Levy maintained that for several weeks prior to his death Gorky had been asking Mougouch to read and reread this story to him. Mougouch does not remember reading *The Black Monk*, though she says she may have read Chekhov and she did read a lot of Ibsen to Gorky. Levy probably invented the connection between *Last Painting* and the Chekhov story, but it is a nice parallel, for the specter of death in the tale catches *Last Painting*'s apocalyptic mood. In any case, *Last Painting* is a terrifying testimony to Gorky's state of mind. As the death figure rushes forward, black and white strokes close out hope.

60

No More Ploughs

⚸

On March 5, 1948, the *Sunday Republican Magazine*, a local Waterbury paper, published a piece about Gorky entitled "A Painter in a Glass House." It was one of a series of profiles of Connecticut artists written by the Calders' friend Talcott B. Clapp. Clapp came to interview Gorky, but he did not see much of Gorky's work, because the 1947 paintings were on exhibit at Julien Levy. Exaggerating to make a better story, Gorky told his visitor that everything painted before 1947 had been destroyed in his studio fire. In spite of his gloom, Gorky appears to have warmed to his interviewer: Clapp's quotations capture Gorky's humor and contradictoriness as well as his ability to play the maestro even in the worst of circumstances. Gorky offered the usual misinformation about his background. "Although Gorky was born in Russia," Clapp wrote,

he is what he calls "an early American." He dislikes being called a foreigner and says he is more like one of the first settlers because he can appreciate the advantages of being in America to a far greater extent than those who were born here "by lucky accident." He has always made his home in the East and went to college at Brown for a while. Once when he and Mrs. Gorky decided to see what the West Coast looked like, they got as far as the Mississippi when he felt he was too far from home and wanted to come back. Since then they have never strayed far from Connecticut.

Gorky told Clapp that he always donned his blue woolen cap before starting to paint: it was as essential a part of his equipment as a brush or an easel. When Clapp suggested photographing him at work in his studio, Gorky, perhaps feeling fraudulent because of his painter's block, refused. "It would be like taking a picture of me with my pants down," he said. "When you take a picture of a business man at his desk with shelves of books behind him, do you think he has read all of them? It would be the same with me if you took my picture surrounded by canvases. Do you think I would be worthy of all that material?"

He had been painting all his life, Gorky told Clapp, but he still knew nothing about painting: "It would be a sad thing for an artist if he knew how to paint—so sad. An artist paints because it is a challenge to him— it is like trying to twist the devil. If you overcome it, there is no sport left. I don't even like to talk about painting. It is impossible to talk about painting because I don't know what it is. If I knew what it was I would get out a patent and then no one else would be able to paint." Up to this point Gorky had spoken quietly and, Clapp said, "cautiously." Now, when Clapp asked him how long it took him to finish a painting, Gorky caught fire:

> I don't like that word, "finish." When something is finished, that means it's dead, doesn't it? I believe in everlastingness. I never finish a painting—I just stop working on it for a while. I like painting because it's something I can never come to the end of. Sometimes I paint a picture, then I paint it all out. Sometimes I'm working on 15 or 20 pictures at the same time. I do that because I want to— because I like to change my mind so often. The thing to do is to always keep starting to paint, never finish painting.

Gorky stood up and began to pace. He walked over to a small painting on canvas that was propped on the windowsill. "The oldest girl did this. She paints like a little bird. And this other, the young one did. See, she paints on both sides of the canvas. She is more like a passionate plumber. I wish I could paint as freely as they do. There is a gravity of playfulness in their work. If they could only keep it—but they will lose it as they grow older."

Gorky went on to give Clapp a glimpse into his creative process:

"When I feel tired and discouraged and I lie down on the sofa, then I think of the simplest thing I can—a piece of string—and I go in and paint it. That's the way to keep painting—to create something inside that makes you want to recreate it." Suddenly Gorky stopped speaking and looked over at Clapp: "What are you doing, taking down everything I say? You're just like a sponge. Newspapermen in New York are just like steel—nothing you say sinks in to them. They are strong and they shine and reflect rather than absorb. Strength is the most miserable quality you can have. You must be elastic, like rubber, to take everything in; then let it out and take your own shape again."

The conversation moved on to the countryside, which, Gorky said, constantly revealed some new aspect of its beauty. "You don't recognize it [beauty] when you are looking for it, and you won't find it by looking in a magazine. It's right here in the moon, the stars, the horizon, the snow formations, the first patch of brown earth under the poplar. In this house we can see all those things. But what I really miss are the songs in the fields. No one sings them any more because every one has become a little businessman. And there are no more plows. I love a plow more than anything else on a farm." At this point Mougouch spoke in praise of their house, how the sun flooded it in winter so that they needed to use heat only at night. "The children love it because it's just like a playhouse to them. But then, of course, it's a playhouse for us, too."

Friends' reminiscences of Gorky that spring portray him in a dour mood. Calder said: "I remember when they were having a hard time, maybe it was six months before he died. They came over to Roxbury. I was there and my mother was there, but Louisa wasn't. He was having a terrible time getting those paint coat rags, and I didn't help him very much. And he gave me a drawing." Raoul Hague had lost contact with Gorky for several years when, in 1948, they met and had a drink in a bar in midtown Manhattan. "And he started talking to me about his operation. I had not heard about it and because I often joked with him over the years, I thought that he was exaggerating and that there had really never been an operation, that he was putting me on. And when we parted I was laughing. And he bent his head down. I'm tortured by it to this day because I didn't realize until too late that he was serious. He was telling the truth. It hurts me still." About this time Gorky's former student Revington Arthur ran into Gorky on Madison Avenue: "He was hardly recognizable—he shuffled, had shrunk physically, and was obviously racked with illness." One evening in spring 1948, Conrad Marcarelli met Gorky at the Jumble Shop: "We had a beer and something to eat. We were talking about old times. And I said that I was going to Europe in a few days. And he remarked, 'That's what I ought to do. Get the hell out of America.' That was a few months before his death." A photograph taken in Sherman on May 23, 1948 (Fig. 143), shows an emaciated Gorky attempting to act happy in the company of Duchamp, Surrealist sculptor Maria Martins, Mrs. Enrico Donati, and Frederick Kiesler. Although his mouth smiles, his eyes remain bleak.

In spite of the increasing misery of her life with Gorky, Mougouch's letters to the Schwabachers were invariably cheerful. Early in 1948 she wrote: "We are in a sparkling world of snow & icicles & we so hope you will get out for a weekend while it looks so fresh—& is such fun." Around March 25 she wrote again:

> Its wonderful out here now, the children live in mud holes and blissful dirt & I run around with the rake and the broom wanting to balayer [French for sweep] the whole countryside—anything rather than stay indoors where I ought to be shaking out moths & washing grey windows. Gorky is scraping and painting furiously, erupting now and then from his little studio to hug someone then rushing back in. When are you *all* coming out?
>
> We are coming in ourselves this Thursday and we would want to have a chance to see you if it is possible? Could we have lunch together on Friday. I would suggest dinner Thursday night but we bed down at Jeanne Reynal's and have a feeling we really ought to dine with them . . . I can hear the first frogs singing tonight. O. Golly.

Gorky and Mougouch did go into the city in late March, and Ethel accompanied them back to Sherman. During her visit, Gorky took her for a walk and he invited her to use his studio as she had when she was his student. It seems that in moments of despair he wanted another person working alongside him. Feeling life's precariousness, he no longer needed to hoard art materials but instead offered to share his stash with friends. A few years later, in her pioneering biography of Gorky, Ethel recollected the visit:

We arrived in Sherman at night, stopped at the village store to pick up some groceries and then continued up the winding steep road to the Glass House . . . After dinner we sat around the fire for a short time looking at a catalogue of Giacometti. In the morning Gorky invited me into his studio, which was small and square, with a large north window. An old stove in the corner heated it and also dried the children's clothes. Gorky begged me to work. When I declined he showed me several of his paintings. Then he again asked me to work. He seemed to feel lonely, desperately in need of communication.

After a little we walked out into the icy world. Snow covered the rolling hills. We walked in back of Natasha, and as we walked Gorky smiled proudly. "She is a healthy girl. Look how solidly she plants her feet on the path." . . . As we looked at the white snow a strange breath of icy wind seemed to shake Gorky. I could not help feeling that the whiteness invaded him with a sense of emptiness and finality; now that the sun was sinking it was bitter cold. In the great living room of the Glass House the children Maro and Natasha were laughing and shouting. Gorky went in to them. Seating one on either knee, he gave them the toys he had brought from the city.

It might have been during this visit to Sherman that a plan was hatched for Ethel to write a book about Gorky. Mougouch was to help by asking Gorky questions and taking notes on his answers. On May 17, after seeing the Schwabachers in the city, Mougouch wrote to Wolfgang thanking him for his advice on their Glass House lease: "Both Gorky & I enjoyed our visit with Ethel and came away so stimulated by her work & her talk of the work we should do and I see it (her plan) as a great important effort to crystalize thoughts and action into communicable form." Gorky was indeed delighted that Ethel would write a monograph on his art, but he told her he didn't want all the details of his life recorded. He suggested that she model her book on Robert Melville's *Picasso: Master of the Phantom*, a fifty-two-page book published in London in 1939. It was from this book that Gorky took (and used in his Newark murals statement) the quotation from Rimbaud about the poet's job being to define the "multiplication of progress" in the time in which he lived. "Gorky used to love the Melville book on Picasso," Mougouch recalls, "because he felt that the best way for an artist to explain another artist was to let their own imagination start to work in response to the artist's work."

Melville's idiosyncratic and highly imaginative paean to Picasso often sounds as if he were writing about Gorky. Melville spoke, for example, of his own "bitterness and depression" as he tried to free himself from Picasso, who seemed to have occupied the entire territory of art. His passion for Picasso had, he said, been sufficient to "bankrupt whatever personal vision I possessed," a phrase Gorky may have had in mind when he told his artist friends that, thanks to Picasso, "we are all bankrupt."

61

Peeled Onion

✼

On June 1, 1948, Gorky and Mougouch gave a party to celebrate her twenty-seventh birthday. The Cowleys, Blumes, Calders, Josephsons, and Tanguys were among the guests. Gorky made an enormous bonfire—one of those nearly out-of-control fires that seemed to leap from some buried hearth in his soul. He lay the marinated and skewered lamb on the fire and when it was cooked they ate at a table set up in the grass on the south side of the house. "We danced to the music of a gramophone," Mougouch recalls, "and then I danced by myself in the vegetable garden. I remember whirling around with a lunatic pleasure in dancing by myself."

As Mougouch danced, Gorky watched with a disapproving eye. Her beauty, youth, and giddy energy were in terrible contrast to his maimed body. She was the farthest thing from the modest, compliant Armenian bride whom he had pictured only a decade or so earlier in *Portrait of Myself and My Imaginary Wife*. He turned to his mother-in-law, who had come up from Virginia for the birthday, and complained that Mougouch was a flirt. Esther Magruder had noticed Gorky's increasing irritability and gloom as well as his possessiveness. She came to her daughter's defense: "Well, you know, Gorky, you do keep Agnes on a very short leash. She's an American girl, born and bred, and they are used to a certain amount of independence. I think you ought to let her do a little more of whatever she wants to do."

After the party, Mougouch and Esther decided that the children

should accompany Esther home to Virginia. The atmosphere in the
Glass House was too tense. With the children out of the way, there
would be fewer explosions, and Mougouch and Gorky might be able to
sort out some of their problems. Gorky had never liked to talk about
problems, and in the last year he had become increasingly uncommu-
nicative. His negativity and occasional violence were driving the wedge
between Mougouch and him deeper and deeper. Without the children
watching and listening, Mougouch could try to smooth things over. At
the very least she would have a few weeks of much-needed freedom. In
the end the children's trip to Virginia was postponed for a few weeks so
that it would coincide with their grandfather's birthday.

Mougouch was understandably restless. Her marriage had never
been sexually fulfilling; now she was finding it emotionally stifling as
well. "Gorky was isolating me from his life. He was wrapped in silence
all those last months. There was no way of getting into it." His remoteness made her long for intimacy. For years she had fended off Matta's
flirtatiousness. Now his naughty-boy behavior began to attract her: Matta
was accessible and playful, whereas Gorky was remote, dark, and saturnine.

A few days after the birthday party, Matta came to the Glass House
for the weekend. Later he confessed that he had fallen in love with
Mougouch on one of the many weekends that he spent at the Glass
House. Perhaps it was that first weekend in June. After everyone had retired for the evening, Matta noticed that, because of its angle, the open
window to Gorky and Mougouch's attic bedroom reflected their bed. As
Matta told the story, he saw Mougouch's reflection reflected on the window of the floor below. While it is unlikely that any window opened in
such a way that Matta could have seen via reflections up into Gorky and
Mougouch's bedroom, it made a good story. Matta must have gone outside, stood in the grass, and looked up. He was smitten.

Dr. Harding had asked Mougouch to keep a diary of her dreams. Although the diary's tone is anything but confessional, Mougouch sometimes wrote her thoughts about events. After Matta's visit, her diary entry
for June 7 says nothing to indicate any amorous relationship with Matta.
On the contrary, it talks about ideas that had come up in conversation.
But it certainly reveals a fascination with Matta's ideological pursuits,
plus a bit of womanly compassion, as if she felt she could rescue Matta
from his misguided superficiality. She wrote:

Matta was here this weekend & we enjoyed him—we talked a great deal about his magazine Instead [a broadside produced by Matta and Lionel Abel in 1947 and 1948] & always reverted to his central theme the creation of a new myth—the *word* which will release a new flow of enthusiasm & energy—Gorky & I tried to make clear our feeling that these things are not consciously planned nor are they even apt to be recognized when they happen by any group of socalled intellectuals, consciously striving to hit the jackpot as it were—But as usual we were really talking on two planes none of us adhering to a single plane . . . It is Surrealism that Matta would supersede with a new reawakening of the same spirit of poetry . . .

If only I felt more sure of myself—sure of what it is that I am opposing in Matta's effort. Certainly he is stimulating if only in this provocative way of stirring you to formulate your opposition. But then 9/10 of the disagreement arises from the difference in our lives, our attitudes. He lives almost as a public man. His great effort seems concentrated on solving or rather proving the validity of his own anguish in world terms—if *he* could spring the lock that hides the secret of our times . . . I feel sorry for him & wish in one way we could work with him—but I don't trust him . . . it is too often a very superficial enthusiasm—too quick his recognition—& his own desire for greatness could so easily blind him to the truth & lead him to embrace the easy superficial way.

And yet, within a few days, she had taken Matta as a lover.

Mougouch's memory of her liaison with Matta makes it seem just a passing fling. "I bolted on June 17, the morning after this horrid experience with Julien Levy and Gorky," she recalls. Julien Levy had come to dinner at the Glass House, bringing with him a bottle of whiskey. Although Gorky was not a drinker, when he drank he did so without caution, and this particular evening both men had a great deal to drink. After dinner they sat in the living room talking about the role of the artist's wife. She should be like a barn door, they decided, or like a barn into which the artist backed his cart, or, even better, like a horse pulling a cart driven by the artist. "Julien did not see me as a human being at all," Mougouch recalls. When she asked him why he flirted with other artists' wives—Patricia Matta or Dorothea Tanning, for example—and did not flirt with her, Julien said: "But you are a national monument." "These things," says Mougouch, "this and the comment about the barn door, were like hammer blows—down, down dog! I began to see that I was just supposed to be a support person to keep Gorky oiled so he could produce paintings for Julien Levy. I was so angry I left the room in tears."

The next morning she left the house:

> I packed a tiny suitcase. I told Gorky I was going away, but I didn't tell him where. I had a local girl who used to baby-sit for the children. I got her to come early and to leave when the children went to bed. I said to Gorky, "I'm going away for a couple of days." I said I'd be back on Sunday. After I left I rang up Matta. It was perhaps the worst thing I ever did, but I did it. The affair with Matta ruined my life in one zip. But if I'd stayed, Gorky's violence would probably have driven me away anyhow, as he got worse and worse.
>
> I got into my car and drove down to the village. I rang up Matta and said: "Do you really want to meet me somewhere? I'm going to be on the Saw Mill River Parkway at such and such a mileage." And he was there. I went away with Matta for two days and came back and felt completely reborn. I felt I had been given a gift to make me strong and patient and loving with my family. I felt very softened and deeply protective of Gorky. I felt completely capable of bottling up my problems. I had no intention of flying off. I felt so completely that I had somebody in my life that I could feel something with that I hadn't felt for a long while. It was terribly exciting. I felt a new strength. I felt that somebody had loved me and I could go on forever. It was as though some angel were guiding me. I could deal with anything now. And I felt that Gorky would never know.
>
> I told no one, but I don't know that Matta was discreet. I assumed he would be. Matta knew I did not want to leave Gorky, that I had no intention of continuing to see him alone. But I have been told by others that Matta was even boastful.

Mougouch and Matta met at the agreed-upon milepost, and she left her car behind some bushes and climbed into Matta's car. They drove to the Hudson River, took a ferry across, and went on to Matta's house at

Sneden's Landing. Upon her return home, she did not discuss where she had been, and Gorky asked no questions. Either his powers of denial or his need to keep his home together made him keep silent. Mougouch recalls: "Gorky did not know who I'd been with. But maybe he guessed. Julien Levy later told me that Gorky had discovered that I'd taken my diaphragm. It was usually in the cupboard where I kept it in a toilet case. Gorky did not make a scene immediately because he couldn't in front of the children."

Many people learned about their love affair, and many were disapproving. Gorky's old friend David Margolis, for example, says that though he did not see Gorky when he was living in Sherman, he often heard about him through Mischa Reznikoff. "When she started fooling around with Matta it was devastating," Margolis recalls. "When I saw Mischa Reznikoff, I'd say, 'Did you hear from Gorky?' And Reznikoff told me that Gorky's wife was having an affair with Matta. Gorky told Reznikoff that he was going to commit suicide. Mischa was very angry. He told me this many times while the affair was going on, so it must have lasted for some time."

Matta's version of events is elusive. He said he saw less of Gorky and Mougouch after they moved to Roxbury in 1945 and more of them again when they returned to the city after the 1946 studio fire. "When Gorky got very ill I kept coming for weekends," Matta recalled. Matta's sense of fun and the evident pleasure he took in women must have been a wonderful relief for Mougouch, and he said they came to care for each other deeply. He believed that part of their bond arose from their similar backgrounds. "Mougouch was very lost among these people in the art world," Matta said.

> She was brought up differently from Gorky. She was like a cousin to me. We spoke the same language. We were "tweedy" and the others were "oily." Mougouch and I had the same education. Before Gorky became ill, they sometimes came to my house in Sneden's Landing. Our children were the same age. Gorky and Mougouch's daughters would come to Sneden's Landing and see my sons. But when Gorky was ill my place was not comfortable enough for him, and I would visit them. The relationship with Mougouch became very strong for her. She was fantastic with Gorky, because he was very ill and had to do—things to do

with the colostomy. She was like a disciple to Gorky. She was very devoted to him . . . Gorky was sweet and fragile and moving. He had an inferiority complex.

Shortly after Mougouch returned from her two days with Matta, she took Maro and Natasha to Crooked Run for their grandfather's birthday: "My mother's idea was to get the children out from under me. She had seen that Gorky was nervous and irritable and difficult when she came up for my birthday. She thought it would be good for me to have a little time without the children. While I was away in Virginia, Julien Levy said he would look after Gorky and he and Muriel could have him for dinner."

Levy was true to his word. On June 26 Gorky spent the day with the Levys. As they were driving him home, their car skidded and rolled onto its side as they came down the hill where Route 67 descends into New Milford. Gorky's neck was broken. In his 1977 memoir, not an entirely reliable piece of reportage, Levy described Gorky's visit. That morning Levy had taken Gorky to a farm, where they enjoyed the smell of cow dung and watched a cow with her calf. Levy thought visiting a farm would ease Gorky's tension, perhaps bring back happy boyhood memories. They surveyed the fields and hemlock groves near Levy's house. It was all very bucolic, and in better times Gorky surely would have regaled Levy with some story about his homeland, but Gorky was not to be comforted. "I hope you are happy, Julien," he said. "I am not. Mougouch is leaving me."

"Mougouch? Oh, no!" Levy cried.

"I read from her diary last night. What can I do?"

The writer B. Blake Levitt, who helped Levy prepare his memoir for publication, recently added a few details to this story in an article for the *Litchfield County Times.* Levitt remembered that, fearing a libel suit, he and Levy cut a section of the manuscript that said that Gorky had told Julien that he had read Mougouch's diary and that it contained "details of her affair and intentions to divorce." What Gorky said to Levy about Mougouch's diary and what Levy wrote about what Gorky said probably have little basis in fact. Mougouch says that her diary contained nothing about affairs or plans. "I had never hidden my diary from Gorky. It was about my dreams and my own selfish troubles. Gorky was never interested." In any case, Gorky's feeling of abandonment that accompanied his depression could have made him perceive himself as abandoned even if he wasn't. And Levy's memoir was affected by his anger at Mougouch over her liaison with Matta. Moreover, to assuage his own guilt at having caused Gorky's broken neck, he wanted to paint a picture of Mougouch as the woman who drove Gorky to despair.

When Gorky told Julien Levy about Mougouch's leaving, Levy could think of nothing more comforting to say than: "Let's face reality. You are just beginning your own greatness. Nothing should diminish that. Let's go and drink to that. Let's go, or we'll be late for lunch." The Levys had been invited to a luncheon party in Ridgefield at the home of the prominent Freudian psychoanalyst Allan Roos. Most of the guests were psychiatrists and their wives. The plan was that Roos would give Levy a boxer puppy, and Levy was looking forward to the event. Gorky gave his cheerful friend a dubious look and asked: "Would you like I should also get a dog for a friend?" Then he lapsed into silence, and neither the lively conversation nor the lunch changed his melancholy demeanor. Meanwhile, Levy was having a good time talking with the distinguished doctor Sándor Ferenczi about the role of the unconscious in artistic creation. Normally this topic would have engaged Gorky, but now he remained aloof, isolated in the stranglehold of wordlessness that sometimes afflicts people with depression.

Levy recalled that during the afternoon Roos drew him aside and said: "Your companion is depressed."

"He has reason to be," Levy answered, "real reasons, not imaginary."

"Perhaps he should have help."

"It's been offered," Levy said, thinking back to the time after Gorky's cancer operation when Mougouch told him that she and Jeanne Reynal had tried to persuade Gorky to see a Jungian analyst. Mougouch had warned Levy: "Don't dare mention analysis to him. The very idea throws him into a rage."

After lunch Gorky and Levy packed the puppy into the car and drove back to the Levys' home in Bridgewater. Julien asked Gorky to stay for supper, but Gorky was reluctant—all he wanted was to go home in case Mougouch called. Levy's memoir says that Gorky did not know where she was. Possibly he suspected that she had left the children with her parents at Crooked Run and then gone to meet the lover with whom she had vanished only nine days before. Having persuaded Gorky to stay, Julien began to prepare a steak dinner, but a thunderstorm cut the electricity, and the stove was electric. When the telephone went dead, too, Gorky became frantic. Finally they decided to take the steak over to the Glass House and cook it in the fireplace.

Levy's telling of the events that followed appears to be an attempt at self-exoneration. As he drove through the night rain, he glanced at Gorky:

> I met his eyes and felt suddenly pervaded by a sense of more than ordinary gloom, of uncanny desolation. Who was this other black presence who seemed to be exuding darkness over all of us like a tangible substance? Yet this was just a trick of the night silhouetted against lightning.
>
> We were starting down Chicken Hill when the skid began, slowly and relentlessly . . . The few seconds were so slow, vivid, and out of time . . . I myself was not driving as fast as the rain. I slowly, gently, and with great caution pressed the brakes. But it was too late. Everything for hours past seemed to have been too late. Especially the answers to Gorky's question, which repeated itself again and again in his eyes. "What shall I do?" I felt again the sad fatality, that shape of blackness, presaged and as the road sharply turned, that darkness left the car, struck audibly, against the clay bank, and the pine trees and, passing through them vanished like smoke. [Here Levy is taking off from a passage in Chekhov's "The Black Monk." The monk, Chekhov says, appeared like a black pillar, "flew across the river, struck inaudibly against the clay bank and pine trees, and, passing them, vanished like smoke."]
>
> I almost pulled the car out of its skid, but not in time. The front wheels narrowly missed a roadside post, the back wheels sideslipped, perhaps only three or four inches, enough to hang up the hub for a moment. The car jolted, then as it stopped it turned slowly over on its left side. Gorky fell heavily against me and I felt a cracking pain in my shoulder. The puppy started an endless frightened yelping from somewhere in the back seat, from which Muriel scrambled, unharmed.

Muriel Levy's version of the story is slightly different: "Julien was drunk. He had a bottle of wine in the car to take to Gorky's for dinner. It was

5:30 p.m. I was in the back seat with the new puppy. Gorky was in front next to Julien, who was talking and driving. Oh God, Julien was the world's worst driver and he'd had a lot to drink that day."

Three days after the accident and after she had visited the place where the accident occurred, Mougouch wrote to Ethel Schwabacher: "Actually it is a very dangerous hill, one even I creep down on winter days in second gear and as nearly as I can make out Julien was going a little too fast on a wet night on a hill with a bad crown and they caught the hub of the wheel in the post marking a culvert on the side of the road . . . and Gorky sitting on that side got the worst of it . . . Julien can perambulate with his collarbone and Muriel Levy had some black eyes and some bruises but nothing serious."

When people living nearby heard the crash, they came and helped lift the passengers and the injured puppy out of the car's uppermost door. At first it appeared that no one was gravely hurt, but as a precaution someone drove Gorky and the Levys to New Milford Hospital, where Julien was interviewed by a state trooper and where both he and Gorky had X rays taken. Levy's X ray showed that he had a broken collarbone. Gorky seemed to be fine. While Levy's shoulder was being taped, Gorky became impatient. Determined to get home lest he miss a call from Mougouch, he found someone to drive him to Sherman. As he left, Levy said: "If Mougouch phones, tell her you need her. Call me in the morning."

The following day Gorky called Julien to say that he had a terrible headache and was feeling "lonely and depressed." Kay Sage drove the Levys and the boxer puppy to the vet (the dog had a torn ligament) and then picked up Gorky and took him back with them to Bridgewater. "Well, Muriel," Gorky said as he greeted the Levys, "we could all be angels now." When they arrived at the Levys' house, Gorky was agitated. "Get me to New York," he pleaded, presumably because he thought Mougouch might be there. Kay Sage and Yves Tanguy tried to make him keep still. "He was quiet during lunch," Levy recalled, "then he put through a call to Virginia, trying without success to reach his wife. He wanted Mougouch back." At this point the hospital telephoned to say that Gorky's X rays had been reexamined and that his neck was broken— he had fractured vertebrae as well as a broken clavicle. Kay drove Gorky to the hospital, where he spent the next nine days in traction.

Kay called Mougouch and told her what had happened. "I was in

Virginia not long," Mougouch recalls, "when I had this telephone call from Kay Sage saying Gorky was in the hospital with a broken neck. I took a plane to New York. Matta picked me up at the airport and drove me to Connecticut. He left me at New Milford Hospital and went to wait at a café nearby." When she saw Gorky Mougouch was alarmed:

> He was in traction and he was completely berserk. They had to set his collarbone but when he got back up he discovered that his right arm was completely awful. I guess the nerves of the right arm had gotten messed up somehow, and his arm was semiparalyzed. He couldn't lift it. So he saw this blackest despair. The nurses all said he was impossible: "You'll have to take him home," they said. And I said, "I can't take him home. He's in traction." They said, "He won't let us do anything to him." They wanted to give him an enema. He refused. They said, "Now, Mr. Gorky, be brave." He said, "Why on earth should I be brave? I've spent my whole life making myself tremble like a leaf at whatever happens, and now you want me to be like an unpeeled onion. I have no more skins." They told me all this and they said he was a very sick man. Gorky couldn't take it—this state. He couldn't bear being in traction with a colostomy. His feelings of privacy were assaulted. He hated having somebody else touch him there. Having somebody do anything to him was awful for him. He was terrible to the nurses. He was a very bad patient. The nurses all looked at me as if it were a great sorrow to be Gorky's wife.

Delirious and terrified by hallucinations, Gorky called out for Dr. Weiss. Mougouch telephoned Weiss, who said, "The morphine probably doesn't agree with him. I will put him on something else. Give me the nurse." Mougouch fetched the head nurse and Gorky, having been injected with a tranquilizer, finally fell asleep. "I stayed so long holding Gorky's hand that I fell asleep, too," Mougouch recalls. At one point she lay down under Gorky's bed, as if lying there she could draw the pain downward and out of him. "I woke up when the nurses came in to do something." Now that Gorky was sleeping she was able to leave. "I went out and I suppose Matta drove me back to the house or to the railroad, where I'd left my car when I flew with the children to Virginia." After she retrieved her car, Matta returned to New York City and she spent the night with the Tanguys because she was too upset to be alone in the Glass House.

Mina Metzger and Dr. Harry Weiss came out from the city to see Gorky in the hospital. "According to the doctors in the New Milford hospital and Dr. Weiss," wrote Ethel Schwabacher, "Gorky had every reason to expect a full recovery from the purely physical effects of the broken vertebrae within a few months." Three days after the accident Mougouch wrote to the Schwabachers:

> Gorky is coming along, agonizing as the process is and I am constantly surprised at how well he looks with this incredible apparatus around his head and his enormous brown hands folded on his chest. . . . But darling gorky is in hell just now though the doctor assures us it wont last tell that to Dante when you see this man on a hot night with his tummy and 2" of flannel pad around his ears, chin and face drawn back by a 25lb weight. He no longer is plagued by horrible visions on the ceiling which nearly drove him mad the first two days and he is regaining the use of his right hand so a great deal of torment has been allayed. And he seems to be very comforted to just have me in the hospital near him which nearly breaks my heart as I am so conscious of my inability to share his pain. O well, it will be oaver soon and thank god it was no worse.
>
> Julien says I must get a lawyer and get as much money as I can from his insurance people without putting him in jail! Sordid as this seems, to translate a pain into money if it will help gorky I am going to do as he says. And it has occurred to me that the twelve weeks he has to spend in a collar will be less tedious if something very happy is going on around him. And that would be a studio off from the house. If we can get enough money from the insurance for that project I think Gorky would be terribly happy.

Mougouch said that to cover the down payment on the Hebbeln house, which she and Gorky were hoping to buy, she was trying to sell the house in Castine bequeathed to her by her great-aunt Marion:

> I feel certain that that house [in Castine] will never be useful to us and I hope to get $5000 for it. Bradbury [a New Milford

lawyer] is going to try to get the estate to take a $12,000 mortgage and we would have 94 and some odd dollars a month for 15 years plus taxes and insurance to pay for this house. That is what we pay now in rent and this way at least we will have something to show for it . . . and it will mean a lot to Gorky's state of mind and that is all that really counts so that actually the house will be worth more than the $16,800 we will be paying for it. Please my dear wise frinds say you approve!

Gorky sends you his dearest love and thanks you for your concern about him and I shall be waiting very anxiously for your reaction to all this. My fondest love to Brenda and Chris [the Schwabachers' children] and the both of you.

This does not sound like the letter of a woman who had made up her mind to leave her husband. On the contrary, Mougouch did everything she could to ease Gorky's suffering, including bringing him home-cooked meals because he refused to eat the hospital food and reading aloud to relax him into sleep. As usual when things got difficult, her mind turned to housing: everything would be better, she thought, if only they had a house of their own.

In his memoir Julien Levy recalled Mougouch's driving him to visit Gorky in the hospital. (He could not drive because of his broken collarbone.) Perhaps it was during this car ride that Levy suggested Mougouch sue his insurance company. This may also have been the occasion when Levy told her that the accident was Gorky's fault. It was, he said, Gorky's black, self-destructive will that caused him to lose control of the car and run into the post.

Levy noticed during his visit that it was so hot that the white enamel hospital walls were perspiring. Gorky lay with a leather chin strap tied to a winch to immobilize his head and keep his neck stretched. He called it "a rack of torture" and submitted to it only by force. To give Mougouch and Gorky time alone, Levy wandered around talking with the interns. One of them told him that Gorky had said he was a "famous genius" and that the hospital staff should "make way for the throngs" that would come to visit him. The intern tapped his head and asked Levy if the patient was indeed a genius. Levy replied that Gorky quite possibly was but that it was his own secret.

Peter and Ebie Blume also came. With his head pulled back, his arms out, and weights hanging down on all sides to stretch his neck and keep his vertebrae apart, Gorky "looked like Christ in a crucifixion," Peter observed. Gorky had often been told he looked like Jesus, but this was the first time he was compared to the crucified Christ. Margaret Osborn saw his agony as well. Gorky called her from the hospital and complained that the doctors refused to give him morphine. She happened to have some morphine for her back pain and she drove to New Milford to give him some. She found him in an iron bed with a strap under his chin that ran back through the bars of the headboard. "He was harnessed and immobile and I had always seen him moving and up. And he was in a very bad state of mind, angry and unhappy and tormented and in considerable pain . . . I came away thinking, Gorky was crucified."

On July 5, exhausted and demoralized, Gorky was released from the hospital. The indignity of being helpless and having nurses trying to give him an enema through the opening in his abdomen had been more than he could bear. Now he was sent home wearing a large leather and metal collar to support his neck. To him it was humiliating and it kept him awake at night. The attic bedroom was like an oven. Some nights Gorky moved downstairs and slept on the sofa. Still he couldn't sleep. The pain went on and on. Sleeping pills didn't work. The sound of his groans could be heard upstairs.

Mougouch recalls: "After the accident, everything was awful as far as Gorky was concerned. Everything just collapsed. When he came home he had to wear his leather collar. He hated it. When he was lying down he'd take it off. His arm was not getting better. He was in misery about the arm." These misfortunes plunged Gorky into a depression darker and more total than ever before. It was as though all the horrors of his childhood swarmed out from someplace deep inside him. "The fire, the cancer, the broken neck were the external facts," Mougouch says, "but Gorky always had all these tragedies within him; his depressions were black and monumental, everyone was 'a snake in the grass'; there was death and hatred and self-destruction in a great flow of black lava. All this long before anything actually happened. The fire was awful, but I have never seen Gorky so strong, so calm, so free. The paintings, he said, were all in him. He would make better ones. But the cancer operation and the car accident, that was different."

The broken neck would not be the final blow. Gorky was distressed over his failing marriage as well. His being an invalid brought his wife to his side, but it did not give him a position of strength. Ethel Schwabacher wrote: "The rising fury of obsessive doubts and consuming jealousy that tormented him in the form of 'horrible visions' as he lay brooding in the hospital now threatened to overwhelm him totally."

For a week or so after he was discharged from the hospital, Gorky and Mougouch were alone together in the Glass House. The Magruders kept the children in Virginia so that their daughter could devote herself to Gorky's care. During their week alone, Mougouch played nurse, read to Gorky, and cooked the limited foods he could eat—starches and meat, no vegetables and no spices, because they irritated his stomach. He was in pain. He sweated into the neck brace and it chafed his skin.

> I can remember arranging a place in the sun for Gorky to lie under a tree where his head would have a rest so he could take his collar off. I had hoped things were getting better between us. He hadn't asked any questions and I hadn't given him any answers. I missed the children and one of the things that froze my heart was that, when I told Gorky that I missed them terribly, he said, "Yes, but you see, maybe the children . . ." Then there was a silence and he said, "I don't care if they come back or not." I said, "You don't care if they ever come back?" He said, "Absolutely not." I suppose he was buttoning up all his hatred for my betrayal and it was spinning out onto the children. Then I thought, well, they must come back.

After Maro and Natasha's return, Julien Levy came for a visit. His recollection of Gorky is oddly sanguine, meant perhaps to diminish the accident's psychological harm: "In his home, the Hebbeln House in Sherman, he seemed happy, surrounded by his children, cared for by his wife, and preparing canvases to paint again. He looked like some barbarian warrior in the strange armor of his leather and steel neckbrace, and he showed me a model of an arbalest he was carving." Levy must have seen the crossbow that resembled a dead bird that Gorky made about this time. For all its whimsy—it has strings attached to look like feathers and a trigger that doubles as a penis—the bow seems an omen of death. It is unlikely that Levy was correct in his memory that Gorky was preparing canvases. "He couldn't have painted," Mougouch says. "He couldn't raise his arm."

Although he was beginning to regain the use of his right arm, progress was slow. Peter Blume recalled: "He was depressed after the break of his neck for fear that he would not be able to paint . . . Everybody kept saying, 'Of course you're going to paint again.' But I don't know if that convinced him." There was one positive sign: Gorky was learning to draw with his left hand, and he told Blume that sometimes what he produced seemed "more truthful" than what he drew with his right hand. A young artist who visited the Glass House at the time recalled Gorky's discomfort: "That brace. I cannot get it out of my head. It was not Gorky I saw there—in that lovely house—with all those clever people. It was a man, in some way demoted; Gorky's ghost."

Among the people who visited Gorky were Helena and Wifredo Lam. Gorky had gone into the city for a checkup with Dr. Weiss. Mougouch stayed home with the children. Jeanne Reynal recalled that she had agreed to drive Gorky back to Sherman, but she felt nervous about being alone in the car with him because he had come to her house after his doctor's appointment in a state of emotional disarray. Perhaps Weiss had given him bad news about his health. In any case, Jeanne said she asked Helena and Wifredo to accompany her to Sherman.

Helena remembered the event differently. She said that Noguchi called her and Wifredo one morning to ask them to join him and Gorky on the drive to Sherman. Noguchi picked Gorky up and drove to Pierre Matisse's East Seventy-second Street apartment, where the Lams were staying that summer. "When they arrived at our house," Helena recalled, "Gorky told the doorman to ring and ask us to come to the window, as he did not want to come up. When we looked out we saw Gorky standing on the sidewalk, sad and dejected, constantly squeezing a small black rag-type doll in his hand. Wifredo and I were perturbed by Gorky's looks but hoped that the drive with Noguchi and ourselves would animate him." Gorky's right arm was stiff, she remembered. "It hung down, he couldn't move it."

In the car Gorky made an effort to talk about painting with Wifredo, but mostly he was subdued. When they reached Sherman, he asked Noguchi to stop for a minute at the local store. He wanted to buy candy for Maro and Natasha. Helena went into the store with him and bought some chocolates for herself. When she tried to pay, Gorky would not let her. He gave her a dark look and said, "Helena, what does it matter who pays? Nothing matters anymore, soon all will be over anyway."

Mougouch came to the door to greet her guests wearing a long white skirt that accentuated her slenderness and grace. Helena observed how much in love with her Gorky was. The group sat in the sunny living room, and Mougouch offered food, tea, and whiskey. Gorky was silent. Mougouch put on a record of an American version of a Yiddish song made popular by the Andrews Sisters. As she served her friends she sang along:

> Bei mir bist du schoen, please let me explain
> Bei mir bist du schoen means you're grand
> Bei mir bist du schoen, again I'll explain
> It means you're the fairest in the land
>
> I could say bella, bella, even say wunderbar
> Each language only helps me tell you how grand you are
> I've tried to explain, bei mir bist du schoen
> So kiss me, and say you understand.

Mougouch began dancing around the room. "She was in another world," Helena Lam recalled. "She wanted to go on being happy." Gorky, perhaps sensing that she was not dancing with him in her mind, flew into a rage and told her to stop. "Why?" Helena asked. "She is a beautiful young woman and has to have some outlet." Gorky grumbled something that Helena could not hear. After this he became "listless and depressed." On the drive back to the city Helena said to Jeanne: "It must be difficult for that young girl because she wants to have fun and her husband won't let her." Jeanne explained that Mougouch and Gorky were having a hard time and that, together with his other troubles, their conflict put him in a state of despair.

Indeed, being alone without the children had done nothing to improve their relationship, and after the children returned, tensions heightened. Maro remembers lying in bed at night listening to her parents fight. One night she woke Natasha up and made her accompany her upstairs to their parents' bedroom. What the girls, five and nearly three, saw was their parents naked and Gorky leaning over their mother as if he were about to hit her. When he caught sight of his small daughters in the light of the doorway, he lowered his arm, got up, and put them back to bed. This scene imprinted on Maro's memory as an image of violence. But Maro may have misread her father's intent.

Margaret Osborn observed: "He had a considerable masochism; with it he punished himself and those close to him." Summoning her indomitable optimism, Mougouch tried to bolster Gorky's morale, but with each passing day his depression and anger made her realize that this was a battle she could not win. "No logic, no behavior pattern could pertain," she remembers. "In the end I became like someone grabbing for a raft." Several years later she recalled in a letter to Ethel Schwabacher:

> It was only in the last two years that I felt the weight and pressure of your trust and I guess a lot of people's assumption that I would be able to manage our lives wisely so that Gorky's work would not be interrupted and his mind left free of worry. And it was a long struggle and possibly a wrong one before I realized that it was not one but three lives at stake and do you realize that this was not clear to me until 2 months before gorkys death, that until that time I still hoped to not disturb him. I was ignorant and dumb wasnt I! Until the end I was still snatching at any straw that fell our way, money or a house then a studio that would create the security he needed and relax his inner tension so that the[n] our problems could be solved more sanely and safely. The accident put an end to that effort, of that there can be no doubt . . . whether it would have failed anyway everyone but me seems to know. Perhaps I have said all these things to you before but can you hold it against me that I would seek again and again to show you that our feeling for you was of love, that our life, the small part that I may have been in his life all considered, that it was what it seemed to be, it was love and painting and roses and thorns and dark and light, all the things that get lost in a survey of facts and analysis.

62

Darkness Spreads over My Soul

On Thursday evening, July 15, Gorky's determination to control his jealous rage collapsed. "Gorky got terribly drunk," Mougouch recalls. "Maybe I said I was going upstairs to bed. Then he came up and broke everything up. He behaved like a loony. He threw paintings out the window. I tried to stop him. Matta had, over the years, given me presents and given Gorky presents. These Gorky tore up." He turned not only on Matta's drawings but also on some American Indian necklaces with turquoise and bears' teeth that Jeanne Reynal had given Mougouch and that she kept hanging from the top corner of her dressing-table mirror.

Mougouch tried to calm Gorky, but he pushed her away and she stumbled and fell down the stairs. "He beat me up and threw me down the stairs. I was horrified for the children. They had been put to bed but they awoke. Gorky realized that he was doing something terrible to the children. He rushed into their bedroom and sat on Maro's bed. Both children sat bolt upright and started to cry. He said, 'My little darlings, you must realize I'm an artist and artists sometimes have to act a bit crazy. That's why I'm like this now. Do you understand?' Maro said, 'No, I don't!' "

At this point, Mougouch left the house. "The sight of me made him crazy," she explains. Through the immense glass wall on the south side of the house she watched what Gorky was doing inside. She saw him sitting on the chair beside the telephone table on the second-floor stair landing with his daughters on his lap. Later she found out that he was telephoning friends and telling them that she was leaving him and that she had gone to get the police.

Assuming that Gorky would not be violent in front of the children, Mougouch finally went back inside, climbed the stairs, and put Maro and Natasha back to bed. To allay their fears, she read to them. "Then I came downstairs to deal with Gorky. By now he had exhausted himself. He was lying on the floor in the dark." She knelt and removed his neck brace. She washed his face and put a pillow under his head. The two of them lay side by side in the moonlight that poured in through the wall of glass.

> I spent all night calming him down. I told him absolutely every-thing quite truly and frankly. I had not wanted him to know about Matta. But I realized that he had sniffed it out. Gorky said he would digest it. I told him why I'd gone off with Matta, and that the strain of marriage was almost more than I could bear, and that he treated me like a barn door, and that I couldn't stand it. And I thought after this that we were on a new plateau. We talked all night long. I thought he understood that I loved him and had no intention of leaving him. He asked me if I loved Matta and I said yes but that I loved Gorky more. I thought everything was okay. I told him the reason I'd gone off with Matta. I told him I would not go again. I said that Matta didn't want me to leave him, that Matta loved him deeply and Matta had a wife—Patricia. Gorky did not know that Patricia was carrying on an affair with Pierre Matisse. Gorky loved Matta and Matta really loved Gorky.

The following day, weary after a sleepless night, Gorky and Mougouch drove into New York City. Each had a doctor's appointment, she with a dermatologist to remove a mole on her forehead and he with Dr. Weiss for a checkup. They packed the children into the back of the car, and Gorky sat in the front beside Mougouch. She questioned him about why he had brought his heavy Irish walking stick, but he was eva-sive. She dropped Gorky at Dr. Weiss's office at Seventy-eighth Street and Park Avenue, then drove to the Village to deposit the children at Jeanne Reynal's. From there she went to her doctor's appointment, and when it was over, she telephoned Matta. "I called Matta to tell him not to come to see us in Sherman that weekend—that Gorky knew about our affair. Matta told me he had just come in from Central Park, where he'd met Gorky, and he said: 'You've got to go to Gorky's doctor. Gorky's quite mad.' Matta told me not to return with Gorky to Sherman. He said Gorky was dangerous."

Apparently Gorky had telephoned Matta from the Glass House while Mougouch was putting the children in the car. He had asked Matta to meet him on the hill just south of the Metropolitan Museum. After his appointment with Dr. Weiss, Gorky went to Central Park, met Matta, and threatened to kill him. "I'm going to beat you up," he said, raising his walking stick with his one functioning arm. "I'm going to give you a good beating. You are very charming, but you have interfered with my family life." Holding the stick high, he went on: "Besides, whatever your talents, you don't understand work. Like the Soviet Union. You don't understand it." As he went after Matta with his stick, the nimble Matta ducked and dodged and begged Gorky to desist. Finally, either worn out or worried about his injured neck, Gorky gave up.

According to the story Matta told friends, he and Gorky then sat side by side on the grassy slope. They embraced and wept and talked. Gorky said, "You have no idea how difficult she is, Matta." He asked Matta if he loved Mougouch and Matta said he did, but he reassured Gorky that he did not intend to live with her. "She's not going to leave you," Matta said. "She's not going to live with me." Then Gorky began to rant about Stalin: "The whole trouble is that none of you believe in Stalin." At this point Matta decided that Gorky had lost his mind.

Following Matta's advice, Mougouch went to see Dr. Weiss:

I told him everything. I told him I'd had a two-day fling and that Gorky had discovered it. I told him what had happened the night before. He knew, he said: "I've been watching him and he's been going down under." He said he had seen it in Gorky's painting. Gorky was "sinking into darkness." He said that with such pain, any man would go down under. Gorky was insane. I was like someone grabbing for a raft. Fatherly and kind, Dr. Weiss was that raft. Dr. Weiss said: "Yes, I found Gorky very disturbed. He'll beat you up. He'll kill you all. It's very dangerous and I have to save the lives I can save. I'm sending you to your mother's.

I'm going to call up the airport and get you and the children tickets."

When Mougouch expressed fear that, if she and the children left, Gorky would kill himself, Weiss said, "What do you want me to do? Put him in a straitjacket?" What she had done with Matta, he said, could not be undone: "Gorky is never going to forgive you."

Mougouch persuaded him to give Gorky a sedative. When he had seen Gorky a few hours earlier, Weiss had in fact given Gorky tranquilizers, but knowing what Gorky would face when he discovered his family gone, he telephoned Jeanne Reynal and asked her to pick up a prescription for a stronger dose. He instructed her to put Maro and Natasha in a taxi and send them up to his office. He arranged for Mougouch and the children's flight to Washington, and he called the Magruders to inform them that they were on their way. "I'm sending your daughter down to you," he told Esther. "Be good to her. She has suffered a lot." When the children arrived, Mougouch climbed into their taxi and Weiss saw them off. Her parents were there to meet them at the Washington airport.

On July 18, two days after she arrived at Crooked Run Farm, Mougouch wrote to Ethel and Wolfgang Schwabacher explaining her departure. If the letter contains some note of self-justification—for example, her citing Weiss's advice, the children's well-being, and Gorky's need to be free as reasons for her leaving—it is also a cry from the heart. After Gorky pushed her down the stairs, she knew she had to get away to keep from going under herself. Weiss gave her permission to save herself, a permission she needed, for she was a person who refused to accept defeat. What she wrote to the Schwabachers was:

Dear Ethel & Wolf
    I am sure by now you must have heard something from Gorky and whatever it was it must have been a great shock to you both. I am sorry that I myself can tell you nothing that will lighten your so kind & generous hearts—but only add to the dread weight of this final disaster. That it must be final I know not only from my own heart by now wrung quite bloodless but from the advice of Doctor Weiss. There is everything & nothing to explain for the words look so cold & short & it has been a very long & passionate

struggle which I can no longer make especially as there are two hopeful little girls involved. Dr. Weiss is coldly objective though I know he has a warm understanding but he tells me from his standpoint the situation looks untenable & I *know* I can no longer hold on.

Gorky's mental condition is serious, has been for several years and I have been dreadfully wrong in trying to pretend otherwise. What lucidity & energy he can regain must go to his painting. The children & I are too great a drain & responsibility. You know I have loved him and tried to fill his need—but now I cannot.

At the moment he is in no shape to make any decisions regarding the children nor do I know what we will be able to do with the future, even as to where we should live. I have written our tenant in the studio explaining the necessity of Gorky having it back, if for no other reason to try to establish a sense of continuity in his tormented world & later when I see how things go I must find a job & make a home for the girls. But as I say, Gorky is going through such a total turmoil that all plans are futile. I came down here without even a toothbrush on the advice of Doctor Weiss who warned me that this kind of situation can create the most serious psychic trauma in the life of a child and must be halted immediately. I think in a few days or a week I will take them up to Castine until I can come to some understanding with Gorky.

As to why I have never given you any inkling of what was going on I can only say that I thought the problem purely personal & a question of my adjusting to him & that I never conceived of life as easy & that if we failed it was because I had failed—a fatal case of inflation alas, for this thing is far beyond me now, and all his friends with all their warmth & affection can only help him if he can help himself.

Believe me, my heart has been totally engaged even to the exclusion of my instinctive nature and if I could have I would have spared him this but my love was not strong enough I guess.

I shall always be devoted to you & grateful beyond words & thank God I know you love him.

Agnes.

When Gorky arrived at Jeanne Reynal's West Eleventh Street house late that afternoon and found his wife and children gone, Jeanne was there to comfort him. She gave him the sedative Dr. Weiss had prescribed, but it didn't seem to have any effect. He refused to lie down. Instead he kept going in and out of the house. Gorky spent the next three days and nights wandering around, telephoning or dropping in on old friends, including some that he hadn't seen in a long time. He was drinking heavily and he barely slept. Jeanne thought he was acting in a psychotic manner and did her best to soothe him, but he did not trust her, for he felt that she had conspired with Mougouch in betraying him. At one point she persuaded him to lie down, but when he struggled to remove his neck brace with his left hand and she tried to help him, he pushed her away. "Only a wife can do that," he snarled. The ministrations of women had become anathema to him. He had become untouchable.

The day Mougouch left him, Gorky spent the night at Jeanne's. The next day he phoned Ethel and Wolfgang to discuss the lease of the Sherman house. They invited him to come and visit them on their farm in Pennington, New Jersey, but Gorky said he would rather go back to the Glass House. "I am very unhappy," he said. "My home is broken up." The shock of losing his family must have brought back wrenching childhood memories. Like the loss of his physical integrity, it was, Schwabacher wrote, "insupportable." When Gorky called Mina Metzger, she likewise invited him to come and stay at her apartment. She and Dr. Weiss would find him a psychiatrist, she said. Indeed, with the help of Muriel Levy it was finally arranged for Gorky to see Dr. Allan Roos in four days. Gorky declined Mina Metzger's invitation. All he wanted was to go home. Next he called Margaret Osborn and told her that Mougouch had abandoned him. He asked if she would drive him to Sherman, but her severe back problems made that impossible.

In his wanderings, Gorky went to see Reuben Nakian, who was out. Gorky then walked over to Gaston de Havenon's house at 7 East Eighth Street on the corner of MacDougal. By now it was the middle of the night. He rang the bell over and over, but no one answered. He walked around the corner to Noguchi's studio on MacDougal Alley. Noguchi was awakened by a voice: "Isamu! Isamu! Isamu!" "I thought I was dreaming," Noguchi said, "and then the calling came again like a song."

He went to the gate to find Gorky weeping and holding a colored papier-mâché bird. "Nobody loves me," Gorky said. "I am so unhappy. Nobody loves me: even my friend Gaston, to whom I wanted to give this bird, will not open his door after I rang and rang his bell for a long time." Noguchi took Gorky by the hand, led him into his studio, and tried to ease his agitation. Sometime later Noguchi told de Havenon about the bird that Gorky had made for him, but when de Havenon went to Noguchi's studio to retrieve it, it was nowhere to be found.

On the evening of July 18, Gorky turned up at Jeanne Reynal's door. Catching sight of him through the window, she thought he looked insane and she was afraid to let him in. From the other side of the glass he raved and gesticulated at her. He would come back to haunt her, he said as he slouched off into the night. He went to Noguchi's studio a second time. Again he called out from the gate. This time he sounded like a wailing drunkard, and it was a long while before Noguchi got out of bed. One story has it that Gorky spent the whole night on Noguchi's doorstep because Noguchi had been so worn out and exasperated by Gorky's histrionics that he decided to pretend he wasn't home. In Noguchi's written account, dawn had not yet broken when the doorbell woke him up. He went through the garden to open the gate, and there he found his old friend "gaunt and pale" and weeping. In his hands were two old and dirty rag dolls that Maro and Natasha had left behind at Jeanne's when they took the taxi to the airport. "This is all I have. This is all I have left," Gorky said. "Noguchi, I am done." They went inside and talked for a long while. Gorky asked Noguchi to drive him to Connecticut. "He looked and sounded so distraught that I was afraid to take him up. I tried to talk him out of it, to calm him down, but he was insistent."

Noguchi surmised that Gorky had sought him out because he was "a fellow immigrant out of his past." Like many of Gorky's other friends, Noguchi blamed Gorky's current distress on the sophisticated milieu that had pulled him in, played with him, and hurt him in the process:

> He felt he had been abandoned . . . He felt that people who had pretended to be his friends were not his friends. He felt that he had been completely abandoned, betrayed by his friends, his wife, this one and the other, that people were laughing at him and they had no further use for him because he had this operation . . . He is the classic example of a tragic hero, the one that is crucified.

Maybe he felt he had this role to play . . . The society people had taken him up, used him and then abandoned him . . . They were only interested in him as a successful hero, not as a tragic hero.

Finally Noguchi agreed to drive Gorky to Sherman. On the way out of town they stopped at Dr. Weiss's office because Gorky wanted to see him. Noguchi waited in the car. When Gorky returned he was upset. "They want to do a lobotomy on me!" he said. He himself was beginning to question his sanity, Noguchi recalled. "When he was worried about having a lobotomy, he thought, 'Well, maybe I am a little cuckoo.' " Gorky was terrified that he'd be put in an asylum. Although lobotomies were performed in the 1940s, Gorky probably misunderstood what Weiss said or meant. Perhaps Weiss made some overly dramatic comment like the one he had made to Mougouch about putting Gorky in a straitjacket. Nervous about being alone with Gorky in the car, Noguchi asked Wifredo Lam to come along. Later he was glad he had taken this precaution: on the way to Sherman Gorky became so violent that they had to stop the car.

Back in Connecticut that afternoon, the three men walked among the apple trees and, to his companions, Gorky seemed happy to be home. They called Saul Schary, who lived about six miles from Sherman but had not seen Gorky in years. Schary agreed to come over and offered to pick up something to eat on his way. While waiting for him, they sat outside and, perhaps as a distraction or to change the mood, Lam took photographs of Gorky seated on the lawn, leaning against a makeshift plywood back rest (Fig. 148). Two cots that Mougouch had set out so that she and the convalescent Gorky could lie in the sun are visible in the background. The Hebbelns' wirehaired dachshund can just be made out on the right. Gorky wears what look like woolen trousers—strange given the July heat. No doubt this was what he had been wearing when he drove into the city for his doctor's appointment three days before. He is naked above the waist. His chest and arms are thin but well-formed. He leans his head against his right hand and rests his chin on the huge leather neck brace. His expression is one of deepest quietude, as if he had given up hope. He is in the middle of a field, surrounded by sunshine, but his eyes are shut. He is forty-eight years old and he is closing out the world.

"Why don't you give Mougouch a call?" Noguchi suggested.

Gorky was reluctant, but Noguchi kept urging him. "I thought there might be a reconciliation. He kept saying she had left him, and this and that about Matta, and I kept on saying, 'It's not true.' You know how people will grab onto straws. So he called her . . . and he turned around [afterward] and said, 'No good, no good.' "

Hoping that looking at his paintings would bring Gorky back to life, the four artists (including Schary) went into his studio. There they found stacks of unfinished canvases, and as they looked, Gorky did become more like his old self. Peter Blume turned up and joined them in the studio. Now that Gorky had these two neighbors to look after him, Noguchi felt that it would be safe for him and Lam to leave. After they left, Gorky spoke with Blume and Schary about his fear that because of his injured arm he would never paint again. No matter how much encouragement Gorky's friends proffered, Gorky was convinced that everything was hopeless.

When his friends had gone home, Gorky continued the barrage of phone calls that he had begun in New York. Either this night or the next, he called Mougouch. She offered to come back to Sherman. Gorky told her she need not worry. He would "act like a man." She would be free.

The following morning David Hare called to invite Gorky to lunch. Gorky declined, but they talked for some while about Cubism, and Hare thought that Gorky sounded rational. At the behest of Julien Levy, Mougouch's sister Esther came out from the city to see if she could help. She found Gorky in a desperate state. "He was weeping. There was no one to care for him. He thought he smelled. There was this man in agony and I didn't know what to do for him." He told Esther that he wanted his children. Esther telephoned Crooked Run to ask Mougouch to call Gorky, but, in her recollection, her mother told her to mind her own business and did not put Mougouch on the phone.

That evening after dinner Saul Schary returned and spent a few hours with Gorky. "He was upset, I could see that. His eyes—Gorky had dark eyes—there was a curious kind of blue glaze over them. And his face was kind of splotched, red and white, and he was very agitated." Gorky told Schary his troubles. "And he just had nothing to live for anymore. It's as simple as that." He showed Schary a book about Leonardo da Vinci that Mougouch had given him for his birthday. They examined it plate by plate. Suddenly he changed the subject: "You know, Schary, I made a terrible mistake getting in with these Surrealist people. The husbands sleep with each other's wives. The wives sleep with each other. And the husbands sleep with each other. They're terrible people. I never should have let Mougouch get mixed up with them."

After Schary left, or perhaps even before, Gorky began drinking heavily. It was about 11:00 p.m. He continued his telephone calls to old friends and acquaintances. Julien Levy was a recipient of one call. He thought Gorky sounded crazy. Gorky asked him, Levy recalled, for "the address of a good charwoman, only incidentally telling me that his wife was no longer with him and that she had taken the children." Another time Levy remembered the phone call differently: "He called me up and said would I know the address of any good call girl in Sherman or in Bridgewater, that he was lonely and his wife wasn't home. And I said, 'Oh, come on, Gorky. Don't talk like that. I've never heard you talk nonsense like that.' [I told him] he'd got plenty of friends and he was great. There were lots of girls who were in love with him. So it was a kind of weird message."

During his hours of telephoning, Gorky called Kay Sage to cancel a lunch appointment set for the next day. The plan had been for Sage to get Gorky together with Dr. Allan Roos. Now, he said, he could not come to lunch, because he was "going on a long journey." Concerned, Sage called Levy and told him that Gorky was calling all his friends and asking each one for a different favor. Julien told Sage that Gorky's conversation with him had been equally bizarre. Indeed, the idea of Gorky's asking for help was odd—Gorky was not the kind of person who asked friends for help. But maybe, Sage said, "He's just raving, maybe he's drunk." In any case, it was the middle of the night—too late for her to drive to Sherman. She would call Peter Blume, who lived next door. Maybe he would go over. But he didn't.

The following morning Schary called Gorky to ask if he could come and pick up a pair of distance glasses that he had taken off when they were looking at the Leonardo book the night before. Gorky said he would have them ready for him. Schary drove to the Glass House, entered by the screen door, which was always open, and found Gorky hunched over the telephone. "Yes, my dear," Gorky said. "No, my dear." Then, "Good-bye, my dear," and he hung up. "He was in a very disturbed way when I got there. And he turned toward me, with my glasses in his hand, and said, 'Schary, Mougouch has left me. And my life is over. I'm not going to live anymore.'" Schary delayed his departure as long as he could. He tried to persuade Gorky that he had everything to live for: his children, his painting. His work was beginning to sell. Gorky was unconvinced. "Don't worry, Schary. I am going to act as a man does." After an hour or so Gorky said, "Schary, would you please leave. I have to do something." Thinking that Gorky meant he had to attend to his bowels, Schary agreed to go. Gorky accompanied him out to his car. "And I got in the car and he came around and picked up my hand, which was on the car, and he took it in both of his large hands, kissed it, and said, 'Good-bye, Schary.'" When Gorky turned and walked back toward the house, Schary noticed something strange; "Gorky had a slouch when he walked. But this particular morning after he left me, he walked with very rapid short steps into the house. As though he'd definitely made up his mind to do something and he was going to do it."

When Saul Schary left Gorky that morning, he went to Peter and Ebie Blume's house to tell them that Gorky was threatening suicide. He asked Peter to go over with Ebie and try to cajole Gorky out of his bleak state of mind. Blume was in the middle of shaving. He said, "Oh, he's been talking about it for twenty-five years. He wouldn't do it." Schary warned: "Peter, if he's ever gonna do it, he's gonna do it now, because he's got plenty of reason to."

Having said good-bye to Schary, Gorky called Mougouch again. In the last few days, to allay their daughter's agitation, the Magruders had insisted that Mougouch stop sitting by the telephone and come for a drive. "There was one day when they drove me around, and I remember the agony of being in the car away from the telephone." But she did not miss Gorky's call on the morning of July 21. He told her he was going to take his bath. After that he would "free her and free himself." When she talks about these days, Mougouch's voice becomes constricted, almost as if her vocal cords cannot give sound to this memory: "He told me, 'I'm going to kill myself. I'm going to hang myself.' I said, 'Don't. I'll come back. I am coming back.' He said, 'Don't come back. I've read your diary and I'm going to free you.' He said it quite nicely." She repeated her offer to return to the Glass House, but Gorky abruptly hung up. Mougouch tried to call Gorky back, but he didn't answer.

Full of dread, she waited. She felt certain that Gorky would carry out his threat. "I sat by the telephone and then Peter Blume rang. Gorky had hung himself."

Soon after Schary had returned home that morning, the phone rang. It was Peter Blume calling from the Glass House to ask whether Gorky was with him. He and Ebie had searched the house and Gorky was nowhere to be found. Meanwhile Kay Sage called Gorky's other close neighbors, Malcolm and Muriel Cowley. Muriel answered the phone. Kay asked her to check on Gorky. "Don't go alone," she said. Malcolm and Muriel drove to the Glass House and went inside. No one was there. They went over to the Blumes' to confer. Blume recalled that by this time it was almost noon. "So we all went over, that is, Malcolm, Muriel and Ebie, my wife. We got into Malcolm's car. . . . So Malcolm and I, when we got there, at first started looking all through the house for Gorky." In Gorky's studio there was a painting on the easel. It was, Blume recalled, light in color, and Gorky had slashed it with a knife. They moved on to the barn, where they found a rope dangling from the rafters. In preparing for his suicide, Gorky had apparently considered various possible sites. They also found several lengths of rope lying in the grass near trees and above a knoll, and there were ropes with nooses hanging from the wood-shed door and from the apple tree behind the house.

Leaving their wives in the house, Blume and Cowley searched the surrounding area. They walked about half a mile to a waterfall in a gorge thick with hemlock. Blume's account continued:

Malcolm and I went up to the waterfall and the road sort of pe-tered out and we had to stumble around in there. And we looked all over, thinking that he might possibly try to hang himself from one of the overhanging trees, because I thought that he had sort of a profound interest in the waterfall. And because it was so far re-moved from everything else, I thought this might be the place where he might choose to commit suicide. But he wasn't any-where around. So we started wandering and came to a little road where the uranium prospector [from whom the Hebbelns had bought the property] had placed a stone crusher for construc-tion. Gorky had two dogs, a dachshund and a huge dog as big as a horse. [The dogs belonged to the Hebbelns.] And when we saw this little dog barking as we came up, we knew this was where Gorky was and that's how we found him.

Malcolm Cowley remembered it this way:

On our return from the gorge, Gorky's dog ran out from a side road and began barking at us. We turned and followed the dog, which immediately stopped barking and trotted ahead of us. He led us to an old shed. The French would call it a hangar. That is, it was open on one side. And inside the shed, Gorky's body was hanging, looking like wax, his feet only a few inches from the ground. His shirt had slipped up and his pants had slipped down, and you could see the bandage around his abdomen.

Gorky was hanging in a shed that stood on a rise in the woods several minutes' walk from the Glass House, not far from where his studio had been until he burned it down. Today the shed is gone, but the foundation stones remain. Just in front of where the shed once stood the land drops away, and on the ground below are metal beams sunk in concrete and some large stones that may be the foundation for the stone-crushing machinery. Blume continued:

We found him hanging from the rafters right in this little shed next to the stone crusher . . . It was an open shed right next to the stone crusher and surrounded by a lot of junk . . . I saw . . . little dangling bits of rope around, hanging from rafters . . . He had strung this clothesline over the rafters, had made a noose, and then stood on the box, just an ordinary box, which he kicked out from under him when he let himself down. And actually, when he was hanging, his feet could almost have touched the ground. He was so close because the rope, which was just a single clothesline, had become very much distended, quite stretched out by the weight of his body. There wasn't any double loop. It was just thrown over . . . Right next to the body was an old crate that a picture could have come in. Not a very big one, perhaps about 20 × 40 inches. And Gorky had written a note on that, "Good-by my loves." . . . In white chalk. And apparently when the state troopers came around, just before they cut him down, they were looking all over for the chalk. But presumably Gorky just wrote the note and threw the chalk away. The chalk wasn't to be found anywhere. And the troopers were looking for it because they wanted to be sure that it was a suicide and not a homicide . . . The

[neck] harness was right there at his feet. He was wearing jeans and a white shirt. Gorky committed suicide in the morning.

According to Malcolm Cowley's memory, Gorky had stood on an empty champagne case:

This shed, built by an eccentric rich man named Young, was moderately full of empty wine cases, empty wooden wine cases. Gorky had stood on one of them to knot the rope and then had kicked the case out from under him. Over nearer the wall another case was standing up, and on that Gorky had written a message in chalk. Peter's memory and my memory differ about what he had written on this. I remember distinctly the words written in chalk, "Good-by all my loved." And at that point, it seemed to me, the chalk had broken because there were two tiny nubs of chalk lying on the ground behind, beside this wine case standing on its side. There was nothing to do at that moment except to telephone the state police, which we did.

The next day the *New York Times* ran an obituary:

GORKY'S COUSIN ENDS LIFE
Artist Hangs Himself in Barn on His Connecticut Place
Sherman, Conn., July 21

Arshile Gorky, a painter with a studio in the Spring Lake district of this town, hanged himself today in a barn on his property after telephoning a neighbor and one of his art students that he was going to take his life. He was 45 years old.

Mr. Gorky was born in Russia and was a first cousin of Maxim Gorky, the writer. He came to this country in 1924 and formerly was on the faculty of the Grand Central School of Art in New York, where he also had been a student.

Commodore Magruder accompanied Mougouch back from Virginia to Connecticut and to the funeral parlor in New Milford where Gorky's body had been taken. Mougouch went alone into the room where he lay. "He looked absolutely wonderful. He did not look maimed. He wore his Indian vest and his red-and-black-checked shirt. They left me in the room with him for a long while. I remember kissing him." She and her father then went to look for a minister. Although Gorky did not believe in God or in the church, she explains, he would have wanted a funeral. "We went from one minister of the cloth to another trying to get someone to speak over his body. My father was marvelous: we'd sit down in a minister's office and when we came to the point that it was a suicide, they would say, 'I'm sorry, we can't perform a service for a suicide.' My father would say, 'Thank you very much. Good evening, sir,' and we'd march out and to the next one."

Finally an Episcopal minister from Roxbury, a Father Day, agreed to perform a brief ceremony outside the church in Sherman. Gorky's sisters and their husbands and a few friends—Jeanne and Urban, Noguchi, Saul Schary, and the Lams, Calders, Cowleys, Levys, and Blumes—gathered at the little cemetery beside the small white colonial church opposite the Cowleys' house. Gorky's grave was on the side of a grassy hill. All dressed in black, his Armenian sisters huddled together, confused and disappointed that there was no church ceremony. Satenik's daughter Florence remembered Mougouch walking across the grass carrying a bouquet of flowers. She wore a scoop-necked black dress and sandals, and she looked very beautiful. Gorky's relatives were all weeping, Mougouch recalls, "and suddenly they started coming toward me as if they were going to envelop me in tears. My father put his arm out to stop them. They hated my father for that." Vartoosh remembered embracing Gorky's old friend the house painter whom Gorky called Master Bill. They both wept, and he asked Vartoosh who all the strangers were, for he did not see Gorky's friends from the 1930s among the mourners.

Julien Levy described the funeral in his memoir: "The skies darkened and it started to rain, first a drizzle but soon a chilling downpour. We stood huddled on a hillock somewhat removed from the grave, the Blumes, Saul Schary and I. Yves and Kay [Tanguy] had not come. 'I don't take much stock in funerals,' said Kay." When all the mourners had gathered, Father Day led them downhill to the grave and read the brief service. After the assembled guests threw the first earth into the grave, Mougouch insisted that the grave be filled in. Perhaps she felt that Gorky should not be left alone in an unfinished grave exposed to the stormy sky.

Perhaps she needed that feeling of finality that comes with the filling in of earth. The gravediggers grumbled. The rain did not abate and people began to drift away toward their cars. "The few who remained fixed by her widow's commanding stare waited for the last spadeful to fall and the last sod to be placed. The grave was then stamped down by Mougouch." Before it was edited to remove libelous details, Levy's manuscript had said that Mougouch did a little dance on the grave. Levy chose to see her tamping down the earth as an act of callousness, a dance. What she was doing was settling her husband into the earth; it was like tucking in the blankets around a sleeping child. "I wanted to get into the hole with Gorky," she says.

A strange and mournful prose poem—almost a suicide note—written out in Armenian in Gorky's often illegible hand was found among his papers after he died:

> In this world there is no place for me
> They promise promise and do not fulfill their promises
> because of the myths
> which surround my persona—
> Why promise if they cannot keep their word
> I came because they asked me. The world is full of fire and
> troubles with
> what pain
> I have come to understand this melancholy fire [three illegible
> words] which
> came in the early morning
> painfully I at last conclude that this life means nothing and is
> only a painful
> withdrawal.
> The rays of nocturnal light make my soul ache as they did
> when my blue
> hopes and my poor cat died [?]
> This night is alive, and yet at the same time my soul cries out in
> suffering as darkness spreads over my soul—
> It is dead and the night of suffering has devoured my soul

> ———

> As I grow older my wisdom grows, comforts me, and expands—

The dreams of attaining exceptional skill with my talent came to me long ago but now are sleeping. Written approval has come to me — (who [one illegible word, followed by a cancelation]

    This night is come and during this terror my brain must continue to labour

    How can we, or rather I [unfinished]

——

——

    I come with my weary soul in terror of madness, appearing to be outward-looking and mythical only from outside.

——

For all the obscurity and seeming distraction of these lines, there was one thing about which Gorky was unambiguous. That was his absolute commitment to art. He knew himself through painting, and that is how he wanted others to know him. Almost a decade after he died, when Mougouch found out that he was Armenian and that his father had not vanished from his life forever after giving him a pair of red slippers, she wrote: "No joy, no black despair ever wrung from him the admission that he was born Vostanig Adoian: he was the painter Arshile Gorky to the very limit of his life, of his love, his entire personality a pure creation of the will to paint. No desire, no temptation could ever stand in the way of his painting, not even the temptation to drown in the cold water of Boston's Charles River: suddenly, out in the middle and ready to die, he remembered — what about painting? — and swam swiftly to shore. He was very young then, but he never changed."

❧ PART XV ❧

63

Aftermath

Gorky's death sent shock waves through the New York art world. In many artists' minds Gorky stood for what it meant to be a modern painter— poverty, hard work, neglect, suffering, together with the conviction that painting was worth the battle, that art could be a civilizing and liberating force for humanity. His suicide enhanced his mythic stature. But not every artist saw it as a tragic gesture. His old competitor Jackson Pollock said to Clement Greenberg: "Why give a lot of bastards a chance to say 'I told you so'? And you don't sort of take others with you, scarring them like Gorky did with that note when he hung himself, 'Goodbye, dears' or some shit. The guy always did talk too much." De Kooning was kinder. Like most of Gorky's friends, he attributed Gorky's death to the cumulative effect of a series of blows:

> He lived an irregular life and had his own rhythm. He didn't have it rosy. There's no doubt about it. He was too advanced to be appreciated in his time. Then he had that terrible ailment, then he got in an accident. Before that the barn burned down and he lost a lot of paintings. And he was in that plaster cast [the leather neck brace]. It was too much for a human being, just too much. And he had always been a perfectionist . . . But I tell you one thing, some of his paintings will be much better than some of the ones by Picasso, Matisse, El Greco. A lot of them will be better than a lot of those great masterpieces.

An August 29, 1948, letter from Jeanne Reynal (who was then visiting Mougouch in Castine) to Ethel Schwabacher urged her to write Gorky's biography and offered insight into Gorky's frame of mind in the period before his death. Although Jeanne loved Gorky, she saw the barriers that made him increasingly difficult in his last years:

> This was part of his unloving nature; that everyone was a Judas and a deceiver. That he was alone is of course a fundamental truth with all its variants of not aloneness love family friendship and the great not aloneness of his art. You know he did want everything both ways, to be alone & yet have every [illegible word] of not alone, this ambiguity was at the very core of his horrible last days when I think he could be said to be insane, O my [he] *lived* so, seeing all, until his head would break to write of this life, galloping to its end, out from this center, is a superhuman task.

Jeanne's emphasis on Gorky's mistrust, which she saw as caused by childhood trauma, makes one realize how devastating was his feeling of being forsaken when Mougouch took the children and left. His jealousy, which began well before they married, finally pushed his wife to fulfill his fears. And since she was a crucial part of Gorky's invention of himself and essential to his sense of finally belonging in a place, losing Mougouch was catastrophic. Painting was, of course, his mainstay, but painting had abandoned him, too. In a state of creative paralysis, and with his family gone, he felt his world fall apart. Yet, although present misfortunes precipitated his suicide, depression surely was the principal cause. And it is likely that his hanging himself had almost as much to do with horrors witnessed as a child as with his current anguish.

A letter from Mougouch to Ethel Schwabacher written three and a half years later, when Mougouch was remarried to John C. Phillips (an artist and my father), was, like Jeanne Reynal's letter, meant to help Ethel with her Gorky monograph. Mougouch tried to explain why she had never told Ethel about the problems she and Gorky were having. Gorky had, she said, a "conception of dignity and privacy" that made it "IMPOLITE and irrelevant" to reveal personal difficulties. He did not want friends to know his weaknesses. Mougouch saw in Gorky "the fundamental desire to escape human involvement that has made of many an artist's life a much more tortured and lonely struggle than even Gorky's."

This separateness, this desire not to be known, was, she said, "directly traceable to his background and the fact that he was a refugee and hated it, was an oriental and denied it because it made him more refugee." Mougouch tried to give Ethel some understanding of her marriage and why she had had to leave it:

> When I went to Dr. Weiss to ask his advice and help because I re-
> alized that it was quite beyond my personal scope, I told him of
> the hideous jealousy and violence and he said there was no love
> between us. It is true that finally after seven years of sexual frustra-
> tion the erotic love situation on my side at least was practically im-
> possible but my god there was love, quite enough to break a heart
> . . . The kind Jungian analyst that I sought help from in the spring
> of 1947 wrote me after Gorky's death that I had loved him as
> much as he would let me and i have listened and read about
> artists and others who don't really want love and happiness and its
> all true but my god he did love me and he let me love him. there
> is no end to the yes and no of every aspect of our life.

After Gorky's death Mougouch left the Glass House and temporarily moved in with Jeanne Reynal. Gorky's paintings and all their possessions were put in storage when she turned the lease to 36 Union Square over to the young architect who had been subletting the studio for several years. Most of Gorky's painting materials she gave away. His palette went to the painter Bayard Osborn, who had so generously rounded up an easel to replace the one lost in the studio fire. She took Gorky's stockpile of canvas, high-quality drawing paper, and tubes of oil paint back to the art-supply store, for she needed money. Julien Levy's monthly payments ended with Gorky's death, and her allowance from her father was only a hundred dollars a month. Help came when the suit against Julien Levy's insurance company finally gave her $8,500. It would have been more, but Mougouch had to accept a reduced amount because the insurance company's lawyers learned about her love affair with Matta and this weakened her case. A December 9, 1948, letter from Mougouch to Ethel and Wolfgang Schwabacher said that the trial was off and that she had settled out of court for $11,000: "So the girls and I are richer by $8,500." Presumably her lawyer took $2,500.

In early August Mougouch and the children went to Castine with

Jeanne and Urban. Matta joined her there for a few days at the end of the month. He was now separated from his wife, and that autumn he lived in an apartment off Madison Avenue loaned to him by Leo Castelli. "Matta and I saw each other while I was staying at Jeanne's. I felt loved by Matta, which held me up." Jeanne condoned the liaison because she knew how thwarted and unhappy her friend had been in her marriage. "Jeanne's attitude was that we should toast love. When Matta came down to pick me up for dinner on our first meeting after Gorky's death, she got out a bottle of champagne." Nevertheless, Mougouch felt her and her daughters' lives were in ruin. "How could Gorky leave me and his children? Was he right to punish me so?"

It was perhaps on their way back from Castine that Mougouch and Matta stopped in Cape Cod. They stayed in Truro, where Matta and various other Surrealists had spent the summer of 1942 in a house on the dunes rented from my father. My father recalls returning home and hearing music playing. He went inside and there were Matta and Mougouch dancing. Not long before, my father had met Mougouch at a party given by Serge Chermayeff in New York. Chermayeff had asked him to be kind to her because she had recently lost her husband and was very sad. Having found Mougouch exceedingly attractive, my father was delighted to meet her again in Cape Cod. At first he thought she had come to see him, but soon he realized that she was there with Matta. The men vied for Mougouch's attention and the afternoon was full of laughter.

While Matta helped sustain Mougouch's spirits in the immediate aftermath of Gorky's death that autumn, he himself suffered an emotional collapse. Patricia left him when she heard about his infidelity. He discovered that she had been having a long affair with Pierre Matisse. "There was a fight between Matta and Patricia and Pierre Matisse, who was Matta's dealer," Mougouch recalls. "Pierre Matisse and Patricia took Matta's paintings away. He was without a house, without a wife, without anything. Jeanne bought a painting from Matta at this time so that he would have enough money to go to Chile." Equally painful, many of Matta's artist friends blamed him for Gorky's suicide and would not speak to him. As she watched Matta becoming more and more miserable, Mougouch realized that their relationship could not have a future:

> I went to see Duchamp. I said, "Don't you think it's too much for Matta?" Duchamp said, "Of course you can't live with Matta."

Duchamp felt it was too much responsibility for Matta. Matta had, after all, left his wife Pajarito when she gave birth to twins. How was I going to put two more children around his neck? I also felt that we would spend the rest of our lives with this terrible ghost. Duchamp asked me, "Have you ever lived alone?" He said, "I think you should go somewhere with the children and paint or write." I felt I had to get Matta out of town because of the accusations and the fight with his wife and Matisse. The house fell down around our heads. I had the idea that Matta must go to Chile to see his mother and father. I took him to the airport and I remember watching him go. I stood by the fence and waved to him and cried and cried, as I had never cried in my whole life.

Matta visited his parents in Chile, and then went on to Paris. By this time, a close friend reported, he was "close to a nervous breakdown." He phoned Breton and the Surrealists in Paris to explain his behavior. He said his affair with Mougouch could be attributed to "the unrestrained pursuit of desire," something that the Surrealists professed to esteem. After all, Matta argued, didn't the Surrealists revere the Marquis de Sade? Had not Breton written in *The Second Surrealist Manifesto* that "the simplest Surrealist act consists in going, revolver in hand, into the street and firing as many shots as possible at random into the crowd"? Breton would have none of these arguments. He called Matta a "murderer" and hung up on him. On October 25, 1948, the Surrealists issued a statement excommunicating Matta from the Surrealist pantheon—the reason, "intellectual disqualification and moral turpitude."

Eleven years later, at a kind of happening entitled the *Execution of the Testament of the Marquis de Sade*, Matta was reinstated. Some two hundred members of the Parisian haut monde and intelligentsia stood in a semicircle, their mood made suitably solemn by a tape recording of Breton reading from Sade's *Justine* against the background sound of an erupting volcano. An artist dressed as a devil came onto the stage dragging a black coffin with an erect penis poking through its lid. A woman undressed him, revealing a body covered in black paint, and the devil then grabbed a red-hot iron and branded the word *Sade* on his heart. "Who is next?" he asked, and the tipsy Matta, happy to be back in Breton's company, rushed forward, bared his chest, and branded his left breast.

By the end of the year Mougouch and Maro and Natasha sailed for Naples with my father. He and Mougouch were married the following year.

Before she left for Italy, Mougouch attended Gorky's memorial exhibition, which opened in mid-November at the Julien Levy Gallery. The show included eight paintings, one from 1934 and the rest from the 1940s. Sam Hunter, who had given Gorky's show such a negative review ten months earlier, wrote in the *New York Times*: "Altogether the impression is of an extraordinarily delicate, tactile talent that had blossomed to full intensity."

Gorky had always wished for the favorable opinion of Henry McBride, whom he considered the dean of American art critics. Having for the most part ignored Gorky when he was alive, McBride now wrote in the *Sun*:

> The tragic and shocking death by suicide last summer of Arshile Gorky is recalled by a memorial show of paintings by this artist in the Julien Levy Gallery. The effect of these highly stylized, sumptuous paintings upon the observer now is accusatory, naturally. One asks oneself why this had to be, why quicker help could not have been proffered, for it is evident the man had great talent and equally certain that a vast amount of anguish preceded the suicide. Fortunately for Gorky's memory all the pictures now shown are lent by collectors who will know how to value them. Such canvases as the 'Soft Night' and the 'Garden in Sochi' must rank among the best American productions to date in the modern vein.

Clement Greenberg (who lent a drawing to the show) wrote in the *Nation* that "American art cannot afford Gorky's death, and it is doubly unfortunate that it came at a time when he was beginning to realize the fullness of his gifts, giving promise of a production whose quality would surpass anything he had done so far." He said Gorky was one of the few artists "qualified to represent American art to the world."

Art News ran a short review in December 1948 and the following month published Willem de Kooning's poignant letter to the editor:

Sir:

In a piece on Arshile Gorky's memorial show—and it was a very little piece indeed—it was mentioned that I was one of his influences. Now that is plain silly. When, about fifteen years ago, I walked into Arshile's studio for the first time, the atmosphere was so beautiful that I got a little dizzy and when I came to, I was bright enough to take the hint immediately. If the bookkeepers think it necessary continuously to make sure of where things and people come from, well then, I come from 36 Union Square. It is incredible to me that other people live there now. I am glad that it is about impossible to get away from his powerful influence. As long as I keep it with myself I'll be doing all right. Sweet Arshile, bless your dear heart.

Yours, etc.
Willem de Kooning
New York, N.Y.

Three months after Gorky's memorial show opened, Julien Levy closed his gallery. In a 1979 interview he gave the reason: "I was very depressed by the suicide of Arshile Gorky. I got a psychological malaise from the fact that as soon as he was dead, his prices started to go up. A demand for his work occurred instantly. I hadn't been able to get collectors to look at it while he was alive, and now they came running in trying to own a Gorky while they could still get one." Gorky's prices have been rising ever since, and now when the occasional canvas from the 1940s appears on the market its value is placed in the millions. But while Gorky's paintings are more and more treasured, they seem to have been pursued by the same bad luck that Gorky felt plagued him and that he attributed to his grandmother's burning of the family church. *The Orators* was badly damaged in a fire in 1961, and in the same year *The Calendars*, acquired by Nelson A. Rockefeller in 1950, was destroyed in a fire in the Executive Mansion in Albany. A few years later, approximately fifteen paintings and drawings were lost in a plane crash near Jamaica. Allan Stone, a New York art dealer who has a passion for Gorky's paintings, says that strange things happen to Gorky's canvases—for no ostensible physical reason they fall off the wall.

6 4

Fame

꼭

After his death, as he had hoped—and, in his more confident moments, expected—Gorky took his place in the tradition of Western art. He was celebrated in a number of exhibitions. Reviewers looked favorably on his work, and collectors upped the ante. In 1950 he was given a show at the Samuel Kootz Gallery, and Weldon Kees wrote in the *Nation*: "There is little painting of our time to match the richness, sensuousness, and elegance of the last canvases of Arshile Gorky, at Kootz . . . Perhaps Gorky, now that he is safely dead, will receive the recognition denied him when he was in a position to care." In *Partisan Review*, Clement Greenberg said that the Kootz exhibition was "the most brilliant and consistent show by an American artist" he had ever seen and that Gorky was a "better handler of brush and paint than anyone he was radically influenced by, including Picasso and Miró." He went further: Gorky was "one of the great painters of his time and among the very greatest of his generation. This, of course, makes his absence all the more tragic."

The 1950 Venice Biennale brought Gorky official recognition. Half of the American Pavilion was dedicated to a first-generation modernist, John Marin. The other half showcased six contemporary American painters. Alfred Barr chose Gorky, de Kooning, and Pollock. Alfred Frankfurter, U.S. commissioner for the Biennale, was more conservative in his choices: Hyman Bloom, Lee Gatch, and Rico Lebrun. Further renown came in January 1951, with Gorky's full-scale retrospective at the Whitney Museum, which traveled to Minneapolis and San Francisco. Ethel Schwabacher wrote the catalogue essay and Lloyd Goodrich contributed a biography. Most reviews were favorable. The *New York Times* (January 7, 1951) compared Gorky's work to Alban Berg's Violin Concerto, Eliot's "The Wasteland," and Dostoevsky and James Joyce.

One exception to the general chorus of praise came from Emily Genauer. In the *New York Herald Tribune* (January 7, 1951) she called Gorky a blatant imitator, and she seemed particularly piqued by what she called his "near-canonization by a small but influential group of art-world impresarios who . . . are already hailing him as the greatest painter America ever produced . . . The only thing worse than the idolatry of second-rate artists while they're living is idolatry of them after they're dead." Genauer's review incited the fury of the New York art world. Soon after it appeared she was seated at a dinner party next to a well-known playwright whom she greatly admired. Convinced that Gorky was the greatest American painter of the century, he suddenly turned on her and asked: "Why do you flay dead dogs?"

Gorky's death, the first of a series of untimely deaths among New York School painters, marked the end of one era and the beginning of the next. Gorky died, everyone said, at the peak of his powers (they were not aware of the creative paralysis of his last ten months). His work was a liberating force for those who followed. The Whitney retrospective, the first major museum show devoted to an artist of Gorky's generation, made other American artists realize that they, too, were coming into the public eye. That Gorky's work, life, and death haunted his artist colleagues was demonstrated in their need to gossip about him, to reinvent as a hero the man who had, even in his lifetime, created his own legend.

In February 1951 this need to talk about Gorky prompted *Homage to Gorky,* a symposium at the two-year-old Artists' Club (also called the Eighth Street Club) at 39 East Eighth Street. Addressing the question of Gorky's influences, Lloyd Goodrich took issue with Emily Genauer's review. "Only prejudice and malice," he said, "could fail to see the creative power of these works." Gorky was, he said, "learning the language of modern art, as a musician learns by composing variations on themes by other composers . . . His own artistic nature was so rich, so deeply sensuous, so healthily physical, so much in love with pigment and color, line and form, that everything he touched, even in his most obviously influenced works, was himself."

Gorky's most enthusiastic supporters were painters. During his lifetime he was admired by a small group of artists, including some of the future Abstract Expressionists, most notably de Kooning. After his death, his fame spread. The Abstract Expressionist Adolph Gottlieb, who had been more of an acquaintance than a friend, wrote in his essay for the catalog of Gorky's 1950 Kootz Gallery exhibition: "For him, as for a few others, the vital task was a wedding of abstraction and surrealism. Out of these opposites something new could emerge, and Gorky's work is part of the evidence that this is true . . . Here is style in the best sense of the word. Here is true *alla prima* painting, the ultimate in craftsmanship in any period and any style." Even Jackson Pollock became an admirer. In January 1951, he wrote about Gorky's Whitney memorial show in a letter to his friend the artist Alfonso Ossorio: "Gorky's show opened yesterday—it's really impressive and wonderful to see an artist's development in one big show. More than 90 percent of the work I'd never seen before—he was on the beam the last few years of his life. The catalogue doesn't have enough reproductions in it, but will send you one anyway."

During the 1950s a younger generation of New York artists not only venerated Gorky but learned to paint by studying his work. By 1955 Hilton Kramer could write: "If any single figure may be said to preside over the abstract painting of the younger generation in America today with the status of a master, it is the late Arshile Gorky." Emily Genauer, who continued to think of Gorky as a *pasticheur*, noted in her *New York Times* review of Gorky's 1955 drawing show at the Sidney Janis Gallery: "It is extraordinary how this artist, ever since his suicide, . . . has been growing into a legend. Hordes of young painters, I am told, have been pouring into the gallery since the morning the show opened, as reverently as if Gorky were the new Van Gogh."

From Gorky young artists learned the pleasure and passion of moving a brush loaded with pigment across canvas: they learned that the paint itself, spreading in transparent veils, layered, scumbled, drawn out in long thin lines, dripped or bursting in plumes, could be a vehicle for the communication of feeling. From him also they learned to loosen Cubist space and to create ambiguous depths. Beyond that, they learned that living and painting are identical—paintings define the artist. Both first- and second-generation Abstract Expressionists were inspired by Gorky's achievement. Milton Resnick, for example, said: "I would rank Gorky as the finest American artist." And sculptor Philip Pavia insisted: "Gorky was the star of that world! I went to his studio many times . . . Gorky did drip paintings before Jackson came along, but people can't admit how big an influence Gorky was on him—I don't know why."

Looking at Gorky's great paintings and drawings from the 1940s, critics and art historians have had difficulty pinpointing his historical position. Most writers rightly see him as a transitional figure mediating between European modernism—especially Cubism and Surrealism—and Abstract Expressionism. Some see him as closer to Surrealism and some as closer to Abstract Expressionism. On the Surrealist side is Robert Melville, whose book on Picasso Gorky so admired. He calls Gorky's art "the lovely swan song of the Surrealist movement" and views Gorky as "a forerunner of the new American painting, not a contributor to it." Similarly, William Rubin concludes his 1963 Gorky article with: "One felt that if Gorky was indeed a Janus figure facing backward to the European tradition and forward to the New American Painting, then only the eyes that looked back were in focus."

Although Surrealism played a role in the liberation of his art, Gorky was not a Surrealist. He shared the Surrealist stress on poetry, childhood memories, sex, and pain—the last two often linked. As in Surrealism, his shapes and creatures and his apparently improvisatory lines were intended to evoke impulses from the unconscious and to create a mood of enigma. But although Surrealist ideas about automatism helped Gorky let his paint run and drip, even when he incorporated accident into his painting, he consciously directed which accidents he would allow to remain. Another difference between Gorky and the Surrealists is that Gorky moved from a starting point in nature toward abstraction. He was busy penetrating the mystery of what he saw on this earth; he did not hanker after the realm of the *au delà*. Unlike the Surrealists, he had no scorn for aesthetic and moral values. He was convinced of the nobility of craftsmanship. These traditionalist values and his reverence for art history were at odds with the Surrealist notion of a revolution in consciousness. He did not want to take art to the brink of non-art in order to find a "sur-reality" in which the dream and reality are one. Instead his genius was to create beauty by the most natural joining of reality and dream.

Among those who see Gorky as part of the Abstract Expressionist group is Harold Rosenberg, who describes Gorky as a "typical hero of

Abstract Expressionism." Gorky's work was, says Rosenberg, "almost a visual metaphor of the digestion of European painting on this side of the Atlantic and its conversion into a new substance." Likewise, Hilton Kramer sees Gorky as "one of the pioneers of Abstract Expressionism."

Although Gorky shared certain freedoms with the Abstract Expressionists, he was not one of them. The principal quality that he shared with Abstract Expressionists such as de Kooning and Pollock was his communication of emotion through the sensuous process of painting. He insisted both on the concrete fact of pigment on canvas and on each colored stroke as a carrier of feeling. Like his contemporaries who went on, after his death, to create the first independent and original painting style in the United States, Gorky believed that his abstract forms and colors held momentous contents. Like Rothko and Newman, he felt his subject matter was tragic, primal, and universal. But, compared with those of the Abstract Expressionist painters, Gorky's images had a more obvious starting point in nature, and though the general look of his paintings was generated by the act of painting, his images were not. His paintings were more refined, less headlong than theirs. Most were preceded by several studies. In addition, his scale was that of traditional easel painting; he did not aspire to the gigantic scale associated with Abstract Expressionism. The broad strokes and monumental color areas of, say, Franz Kline or Mark Rothko seem to press forward toward the viewer and to move beyond the boundaries of the framing edge. The arena for Gorky's smallish shapes and personages, on the other hand, is not the canvas itself, as in Abstract Expressionism. Rather it is a carefully set up, stagelike space that is ambiguous without being limitless.

Gorky died too soon to see the Abstract Expressionists invent their mature styles. With his demise, other American artists were able to free themselves from something that he himself never relinquished—a reverence for European tradition. New York School painters could be brasher and more risk-taking than Gorky because they held up Paris no longer as an ideal to yearn toward but rather as a marker from which to push off. By the end of the 1940s, New York artists began to recognize that a new American art was emerging, and they increasingly saw that the most exciting postwar art was being created not in Paris but in New York.

In the second half of the 1950s, Europeans began to see this too. The reputations of artists like Gorky began to grow abroad. The French were resistant. Resenting their loss of artistic hegemony, they tended to take a dim view of the new American painting. When Gorky's work was shown in *Regards sur la peinture américaine* in 1952 (at Paris's Galerie de France) and in the various exhibitions that the Museum of Modern Art circulated in Europe in the 1950s, the French were, in the main, supercilious and judged Gorky a Miró imitator. The Italian response to American art and to Gorky was more sympathetic, perhaps because no hegemony was threatened. In 1957 the Italian painter Afro wrote a paean to Gorky in the catalog for Gorky's 1957 exhibition at the Galleria dell' Obelisco in Rome:

> The first time I went to America, in 1950, I saw several paintings by Gorky. Standing before them, I immediately sensed his greatness and realized that I was entering a world of original and highly distinctive imagery: an imagination, a palette, a febrile dream possessed only by Gorky . . . Gorky's paintings gave me courage. Fearless, passionate, and full of love, he taught me to look for truth without false modesty, . . . to search only within myself, where images are still embedded in their obscure origins—unwitting and sincere . . . There is a desperate innocence in his eye, a will to love, a consuming awareness of pain in the world.

When the Museum of Modern Art presented a Gorky retrospective in 1962, Gorky's place among the masters of Western art was secure: as art historian Robert Rosenblum put it, "At his best, Gorky can rival and, I believe, even surpass the finest of Miró—which is to say that he is one of the major painters of our century." But by this time Gorky's work was no longer a major influence on young painters. The upcoming generation was intrigued with the cooler approaches offered in pop art, color field, and hard-edge abstraction.

In recent years several writers, beginning with Gorky's nephew Karlen Mooradian, have wanted to situate Gorky in art history as an Armenian. But, just as the Dutch immigrant de Kooning and the Russian immigrant Rothko are considered American artists, so Gorky, having lived and developed as a painter in this country, is American. He may never have felt like an American; very likely he wished he could belong to the School of Paris. Art, he believed, was an expression of its time and place, but it also had to go beyond topicality to explore the constants buried in the human psyche. "Art is always universal," he said.

Although his art has a European refinement, and although his true subject matter was his memory of Armenia filtered through present observation and feeling, Gorky was quintessentially American in his polyglot melding of many cultures and in the way his feelings of dislocation and exile gave urgency to his reinvention of his self. Today Gorky is generally thought of as one of the most important American painters. In reviewing the first half of the Whitney Museum's centennial exhibition, *The American Century: Art and Culture 1900–1950*, the poet and *New Yorker* art critic Peter Schjeldahl wrote: "For greatest American artist of the first half of the twentieth century, I nominate Arshile Gorky . . . He counted for the most in the most tragic way. . . . He conveyed the possibility of local world-class painting to all the fledging Abstract Expressionists. He made works that give and give, feeding himself into them as if into flames."

Gorky's paintings come straight out of his life, and their poignancy is searing. But they will always keep their mystery, for Gorky was both a genius of self-expression and a master of concealment. By his sustained giving, Gorky fed himself into the flames, but he never explained the fire.

NOTES

SELECTED BIBLIOGRAPHY

ACKNOWLEDGMENTS

INDEX

Notes

※

PROLOGUE

3 "I don't like that word": Talcott B. Clapp, "A Painter in a Glass House," p. 6.

4 "It would be a sad thing": Ibid.

4 "the eye-spring": André Breton, "The Eye-Spring: Arshile Gorky," in *Arshile Gorky*, exhibition brochure, Julien Levy Gallery, n.p.

4 "the equal of any painter": Clement Greenberg, "Art," *Nation*, March 20, 1948, pp. 331–32.

5 "Gorky just kept banging": Malcolm Cowley, interview by Karlen Mooradian, 1966.

1: CHARAHAN SURP NISHAN

10 Centuries of living as a subject: Armenians believed that their sufferings were God's punishment, their destiny, or *jagadakeer*, which translates literally as "what is written on the forehead" (Susie Hoogasian Villa and Mary Kilbourne Matossian, *Armenian Village Life before 1914*, p. 144).

10 "Beat not on my doors": Karlen Mooradian, *Arshile Gorky Adoian*, p. 107 (hereafter AGA). Karlen Mooradian, the author of two books and many articles on Gorky, was Gorky's nephew. His work on Gorky is invaluable, especially his compilation of interviews entitled *The Many Worlds of Arshile Gorky*. The tapes of these and other interviews by Mooradian are in the Gorky/Mooradian Archive at the Eastern Diocese of the Armenian Church of America. His accounts of Gorky's family history, however, are not always reliable. Most of Mooradian's information came from his mother, Vartoosh Mooradian, Gorky's youngest sister, who was still a child when she left Turkish Armenia. Moreover, Vartoosh was, as Gorky's widow, Agnes Fielding (Mougouch) put it, "in love with Gorky," and she had powerful reasons for casting him in a favorable light. Either because of those reasons or because

her memory was faulty, Vartoosh did not always tell a story the same way twice. Karlen Mooradian learned from his mother, for example, that Charahan Surp Nishan was a grand edifice with ten windows, six interior columns, and an "opulent dome." In fact, the church was about twenty by twenty feet square and its tiny cupola, supported by two piers, had only four small windows. Mooradian said the church was embellished with "dozens of gold incense chandeliers" and with splendid frescoes depicting "Armenian royalty and religious scenes" (*AGA*, p. 102). This is part of his and Vartoosh's aggrandizing imaginations. The dark church interior was much too humble to have been adorned with frescoes.

10 Arshile Gorky would look back: Karlen Mooradian believed that Gorky saw in his grandmother's rejection of the Christian God a return to pagan beliefs, many of which continued to thrive through the sixteen centuries of Armenian Christianity.

10 "I think our lives": Typed note inserted in one of Gorky's art books, quoted in Matthew Spender, *From a High Place: A Life of Arshile Gorky*, p. 243.

11 "the black one, the unlucky one": Notes from Mina Metzger interview with Vartoosh Mooradian, December 1948.

11 His companions assumed: Milton Resnick, telephone interview by author, March 15, 1999.

11 "I am not a man burdened": Mooradian, *The Many Worlds of Arshile Gorky*, hereafter *Worlds*), p. 192.

2: ARMENIANS IN OTTOMAN TURKEY

12 In *The Decline and Fall of the Roman Empire*: Christopher J. Walker, *Armenia: The Survival of a Nation*, p. 19.

14 Van's governor spent his time: Ibid., p. 125. The quotations from the British vice-consul come from reports to the British Foreign Office, FO 881/5168, p. 17.

14 The judge imposed this penalty: Clarence D. Ussher, *An American Physician in Turkey: A Narrative of Adventures in Peace and in War*, p. 148.

14 As a result: The English traveler Noel Buxton, a liberal member of Parliament who visited Russian Armenia and the eastern provinces of Turkey in 1913, wrote: "We found many Kurd families installed in an Armenian village, the ejected population being crowded into the remaining houses. Other peasants had been notified to give up their houses, by a fixed date, to Kurds still occupying their summer tents" (Noel Buxton and Harold Buxton, *Travels and Politics in Armenia*, p. 117).

14 "All have been ransacked": Ibid., p. 110.

14 The loyal *millet*: As the French ambassador at Constantinople, Paul Cambon, wrote in 1894: "As a result of telling the Armenians they were plotting, the Armenians finally plotted; as a result of repeating to them that Armenia did not exist, they finally believed in the reality of its existence, and thus, in a few years, secret societies were formed which exploited to their advantage the

vices and faults of the Turkish administration and which spread throughout all Armenia the idea of national consciousness and independence (Yves Ternon, *The Armenians: History of a Genocide*, p. 48).

15 The Hunchaks went further: In 1862, the same year that the Armenians in the mountain town of Zeitun in Cilicia revolted against Turkish cruelty, there was an uprising of twenty thousand Armenians in Van. Ten years later, recognizing that conditions had not improved, forty-six Vanetzis (people from Van) took an oath to dedicate themselves to the cause of Armenian liberty and formed the Union of Salvation, the first revolutionary society in Turkish Armenia. Its founding charter stated: "Gone is our honor: our churches have been violated. They have kidnapped our brides and youth; they take away our rights and try to exterminate our nation . . . Let us find a way of salvation . . . If not we will soon lose everything." In 1878 came the formation of the Society of the Black Cross, which aimed at the protection of unarmed Armenians from unjust taxation and looting. (The quotation is from the *Livres jaune*, document 6m, p. 12, in *Documents diplomatiques: Affaires armeniennes. Projets de reformes dans l'empire Ottoman, 1893–1897*, published as *Livres jaune*, Paris, 1897. Quoted in Williams, *Armenia*, p. 73.)

3: KHORKOM

16 "How much butchery": *Anthology of Armenian Poetry*, ed. and trans. Diana Der Hovanessian and Marzbed Margossian, pp. 122–23.

16 Gorky's father may have been: Matthew Spender, "Arshile Gorky's Early Life," in *Arshile Gorky: The Breakthrough Years*, exhibition catalog, Modern Art Museum of Fort Worth, p. 29.

16 Sixteen-year-old Shushan: Mooradian, AGA, pp. 104–06.

17 Prudian and all his male: Spender, *From a High Place*, pp. 13–14.

17 In 1899: Khorkom means "barn guest." Legend has it that the name commemorates a victory in one of Armenia's countless wars when warriors from Khorkom raided the neighboring town of Artemid and abducted the women and killed the men. Centuries later the men of Artemid attempted revenge but lost again. After locking them in a pen meant for animals, the men of Khorkom cut their throats and renamed Khorkom after its victory over its "barn guests" (Mooradian, AGA, pp. 111–12).

18 The boats used for such: Ussher, *American Physician*, pp. 120–21.

18 Like most other peasant families: Shushan's daughter Akabi said that her stepfather, Sedrak, had a *khan* (warehouse) in Constantinople for import and export. Given the difficulty of traveling from Khorkom to Constantinople, this seems unlikely.

18 Sedrak Adoian's offspring: Ruth McCulloch, notes from an interview with Vartoosh Mooradian, Whitney Museum of American Art, Artist's File. According to family legend, the Adoians were descended from a fifth-century knight called Adom. But Karlen Mooradian and his mother were apt to invent grand genealogies for their family. In his two books on Gorky, Karlen,

for example, calls Shushan "Lady Shushan," when in fact what was left of Armenian aristocracy on the Anatolian plateau was wiped out in the thirteenth century (Mooradian, *AGA*, p. 109).

18 "We were always with our mother": Satenik Avedisian, letter to Mina Metzger, March 31, 1949.

19 In addition, she had lived: There is a family rumor that the Turk who raped Shushan left her with child. It has been hinted that Satenik, Shushan's third daughter, was not Sedrak's but the child of the Turk (Agnes Fielding, known as Mougouch), interviewed by author; unless otherwise stated, all future quotations from Agnes Fielding, who was married to Gorky from 1941 to 1948, come from my series of interviews with her between 1994 and 1999 in London).

19 As the English traveler: H.F.B. Lynch, *Armenia: Travels and Studies*, vol. 2, p. 92.

19 Besides his older sister: According to Krikor's son Ado and according to Karlen Mooradian, Sedrak was the oldest brother (Mooradian, *Worlds*, p. 81, and *AGA*, p. 112). Matthew Spender, on the other hand, believes that Krikor was the eldest (*From a High Place*, p. 10).

19–20 One American missionary: Donald E. Miller and Lorna Touryan Miller, *Survivors: An Oral History of the Armenian Genocide*, p. 233.

20 After they were weaned: Villa and Matossian, *Armenian Village Life*, p. 27.

20 Gorky's older sister, Satenik: Satenik Avedisian, letter to Mina Metzger. If Satenik was born in 1901, her birth would have come two years after her parents married. Since Armenian village wives tended to have children as soon as possible (it improved their status within their husband's extended family), it seems likely that Satenik was born a year or so earlier.

20 Gorky is said to have: Ibid. If there were any more formal records of the Adoian children's births or baptisms, they would probably have been written in the family Bible or recorded in the local church, and such documents would have been lost during the 1915 massacres. Years later Gorky's brother-in-law Moorad Mooradian told Gorky's widow, Mougouch, that "due to starvation and terror and raids and politics, those people [the Armenians] never did know when they were born or when they died or where" (Agnes Gorky Phillips [later Agnes Fielding], letter to Ethel Schwabacher, December 28, 1949).

20 His 1936 recollection: Arshile Gorky, "My Murals for the Newark Airport: An Interpretation," p. 13.

20 The usual date given: Arshile Gorky, letter to Vartoosh Mooradian, October 28, 1940, in Mooradian, *AGA*, p. 265. In preparing their biographies of Arshile Gorky, Nouritza Matossian and Matthew Spender independently discovered that many of Gorky's letters published by Karlen Mooradian are fakes. Mooradian invented these letters, perhaps because he wanted to present Gorky as an Armenian rather than an American artist. He may also have felt that Gorky's critical neglect in the United States could be rectified if Americans had, direct from the artist, a way of understanding his art. In general, the parts of the published letters that speak about art or about Gorky's at-

tachment to Armenian culture are not written by Gorky. In an appendix Matossian lists the letters alleged to be by Gorky for which no originals exist (*Black Angel: A Life of Arshile Gorky*, pp. 496–97).

21 In 1942 Gorky wrote: Arshile Gorky, letter to Dorothy Miller, June 26, 1942.

21 A sculptor friend once: Thomas Hess, *Abstract Painting: Background and the American Phase*, p. 108.

21 Very likely the nineteen- or: There are several other arguments for a date of around 1900 for Gorky's birth. In all photographs Gorky looks much older than he would have been had he indeed been born in 1904. In a photograph of him and his mother taken in Van City in 1912 he looks at least twelve. In photographs from the 1930s he appears worn and with the creased brow of a man approaching middle age. In addition, if Gorky had been born in 1904 he would have been six when he left Khorkom to go to live in Van City in 1910. The activities Gorky talked about having enjoyed in Khorkom—swimming far out into Lake Van, riding into the mountains to join shepherds, whittling shepherd's flutes, and climbing tall poplar trees to steal eggs from nests—are not the kinds of things most six-year-olds can do. If, as Gorky's sisters recall, he was unable to talk until he was about six and only after that attended the village school in Khorkom (Armenian children did not begin school until they were six or seven), he must have been older than six when he left Khorkom for Van.

When the Adoian family moved from the old city of Van to Aikesdan in September 1910, Gorky became, according to Karlen Mooradian, the best friend of Karlen's father, Moorad Mooradian, born in 1896. If this close friendship existed, it supports the idea that Gorky must have been older than six when he moved to Aikesdan; it is unlikely that boys of six and fourteen would have been best friends.

If he had been born in 1904, he would have been only eleven during the siege of Van City and during the subsequent trek over the mountains to Russian Armenia in 1915. What is known about his activities during the siege and about his life as a refugee make him sound older than that. A final reason for believing that Gorky was born around 1900 is that several of his boyhood friends were born about that time. Gorky's close friend in Khorkom, Yenovk Der Hagopian, for example, was born in 1900.

21 Karlen Mooradian felt: Karlen Mooradian, "The Unknown Gorky," p. 52.

21 Studies of Armenians: Miller and Miller, *Survivors*, p. 158.

22 Gorky became vehement: Esther Brooks, interview by author.

22 A few years later the head: G. C. Raynolds, "Report of the Village Work in the Van Field, Turkey," 1909–1910, American Missionary Reports.

22 In April 1908: Ussher, *American Physician*, pp. 126–29. As Ussher tells it: "With automatic pistols they kept several companies at bay until reinforcements came, when they took refuge in a house on the corner, and for two hours kept the Turks at a distance of two hundred yards. In front of the house was a five-gallon can of dynamite which one of the soldiers, engaged in carrying off the munitions, had discreetly set down in the middle of the road before he ran away. Finally a bullet struck it and the explosion that followed

shattered windows in the neighborhood and threw to the ground every one within a block or two." Both the Armenians and the Turks thought the explosion was an enemy cannon or bomb, and both sides fled.

23 "In some cases horseshoes": Buxton and Buxton, *Travels and Politics*, pp. 43–44.

23 Years later Satenik: Karlen Mooradian tells a different story, which he must have learned from his mother, Vartoosh. He says that Sima was still living and attending boarding school when Shushan took her three youngest children to live in Van City in 1910. That year, he says, Sima fell ill and her death threw Shushan into a depression, which deeply affected Gorky (AGA, p. 124).

23 Of her oldest half sister's: Satenik Avedisian, interview by Karlen Mooradian.

23 If a farmer could not: Kertzo Dickran, *Varak*, pp. 61–62; quoted in Matossian, *Black Angel*, pp. 19–20.

23 "They had faces like": Matossian, ibid., p. 20.

23 As Hagop told the story: Spender, *From a High Place*, p. 19.

24 All Turkish subjects: Before the Young Turk revolution of 1908, Turkey did not recognize the right of its subjects to emigrate, and it was extremely difficult to obtain permission to leave the country. *Teskeres*, or special visas permitting travel from the Turkish interior to the coast, were costly and difficult to obtain. In 1899 the sultan prohibited emigration entirely. But Armenians continued to leave their native land by bribing the authorities. In 1908, when the new Turkish constitution lifted the travel restriction, the cost of passports and passage was greatly reduced. Now not only wealthy Armenians but also many farmers and laborers could afford the voyage. In the fiscal year 1908, 3,299 Armenians went to the United States despite the well-publicized depressed economic conditions there (Robert Mirak, *Torn between Two Lands: Armenians in America, 1890 to World War I*, p. 52).

24 At what was called: Young Turk officials actually attended services at the Armenian church to honor the Armenians massacred by Abdul Hamid's henchmen in 1895–96 (Walker, *Armenia*, p. 181).

24 The revolution had changed: Ussher, *American Physician*, p. 148.

24 There were attacks: Ussher wrote (Ibid., pp. 163–64):

> The massacre in Van was planned for the 26th. Bands of Turks armed with daggers were to be ready at the head of each street in the bazaar or market; at the appointed moment they were to close the gates of the market and, passing quietly without outcry or pistol shot from shop to shop, they were to kill all the Armenians, allowing none to escape and warn others. Having thus disposed of nearly all the able-bodied men, they were to raise the cry that the Armenians in the Gardens [Aikesdan was also called the Gardens] were attacking the Turkish women there in the absence of their protectors, and, enlisting the help of the unsuspecting soldiers, they were to rush out into the Armenian quarters and begin a slaughter which, they bound

themselves by an oath, should last three days; after that they would divide the spoil.

When day dawned on the 26th of April so violent a blizzard was raging that the Armenians did not attempt the three-mile walk from their homes to the bazaar in the walled city, and thus were frustrated the plans for a massacre on that day.

25 The Adoians' home was an exception: Spender, *From a High Place*, pp. 5–6.
25 Years later when Gorky wished: Agnes Fielding, interview by author.
26 When it was time to eat: To this day in the mud brick, dirt-floored village houses in eastern Turkey, now taken over by Kurds, the cylindrical fireplace dug in the earth is the center of family life. An older woman is in charge of baking bread, and younger women and children gather around. The assignment of the various chores connected with bread making depends on family hierarchy. In ascending order of social importance, the flour is kneaded, then handed to the next woman, who shapes it and places it on a pillow. The most important woman takes the round, flat uncooked loaves and slaps them onto the upper sidewall of the *tonir*, in the bottom of which the perpetual cow-dung fire burns. *Lavash* is removed with tongs and piled up or handed out to the waiting family members—sometimes topped with crumbly cheese.
26 Like earth and water: Villa and Matossian, *Armenian Village Life*, p. 129.
26 "My smoke has died down": Ibid., pp. 33–34.
26 When the villagers returned: Ibid., p. 137.
27 "I tell stories to myself": Julien Levy, *Arshile Gorky: Paintings, Drawings, Studies*, p. 34.
27 It was she who assigned: Mooradian, AGA, p. 112.
28 Pears were hung: Mooradian, *Worlds*, p. 81.
28 He also had a sheepdog: Ibid.
28 The other was the *gutan*: Villa and Matossian, *Armenian Village Life*, p. 43.
28 At New Year in some parts: Ibid., p. 135.
29 An American consular report: Mirak, *Torn between Two Lands*, p. 15. The quotation that follows is from Mirak, p. 20.
29 In a letter written: Mooradian, AGA, p. 255. Mooradian also gives the words to another plowing song that Vartoosh used to sing and that he claims to be the source for the title of Gorky's painting series *The Plough and the Song*. He prints the song, called "*Gutani Yerk*," on p. 159 of AGA. Among Gorky's papers is a song in the Vanetzi dialect and penned by Gorky. In the song a peasant sings praises to his beautiful plow, on which life depends. The farmer says he places his hand on the plow, asks for a blessing from the holy cross, and asks the plow to open deep-cut furrows, for which the farmer will make the plow his "true partner." "As one we'll work, as one we'll dwell, and high and low as one god haul."
29 "And there are no more": Clapp, "A Painter in a Glass House," February 9, 1948.

4: BOYHOOD

30 "She was a modest lady": Mooradian, *Worlds*, p. 88.

30 To his wife in the 1940s: Agnes Fielding, interview by author.

30 "Learn your lessons": Mooradian, *AGA*, p. 117.

31 "Her prayers were so ardent": Agnes Gorky Phillips (later Fielding), letter to Ethel Schwabacher, December 28, 1949. Agnes Gorky's letters to Ethel Schwabacher are in the Whitney Museum Library. Agnes Fielding (or Mougouch), as she is now called, kindly gave me copies of these letters.

31 "And so she wanted Gorky": Mooradian, *Worlds*, p. 32.

31 "It was on a high slope": Satenik Avedisian, interview by Karlen Mooradian, 1966.

31 Satenik remembered the time: Ibid.

32 The priest, Der Hagop: Mooradian, *Worlds*, pp. 79–80.

33 "Each lad would spit": Ibid., p. 88.

33 Ado remembered that scattered: Ibid., p. 78.

33 "At that time, all we knew": Ibid., p. 136.

33 Recognizing Gorky and: Ibid., pp. 136–37. Although the American missionaries said that the villagers in the Van area were too poor to own Bibles, Shushan is thought to have possessed an illustrated one handed down to her from her father.

34 These they would take: Ibid., p. 79.

34 "During those gatherings": Matossian, *Black Angel*, p. 30. The quotation is from Paregham Hovnanyan's unpublished memoir written in Armenian and translated by Nouritza Matossian.

34 "Let his flesh be yours": Matossian, *Black Angel*, p. 25.

34 "I don't know what": Ibid., p. 26.

35 Gorky maintained that he drew: Elaine de Kooning, "Gorky: Painter of His Own Legend," p. 40, and Arshile Gorky, letter to Dorothy Miller.

35 "His hand would even move": Akabi Amerian, interview by Karlen Mooradian.

35 Satenik remembered her: Satenik Avedisian, interview by Karlen Mooradian.

35 When he insisted on drawing: Spender, "Arshile Gorky's Early Life," p. 32.

35 When Ado gave the correct: Ado Adoian, interview by Karlen Mooradian, 1966.

35 In one of them he drew: This and the following drawing are illustrated in *Gorky: Drawings*, exhibition catalog, M. Knoedler & Co., Inc., p. 32.

35 Another shows a small: Illustrated in Mooradian, *Worlds*, p. 238, and in *AGA*, p. 158. Mooradian invents titles and subjects for Gorky's works. This drawing he identifies (wrongly, I think) as representing himself, his mother, Vartoosh, and his father, Moorad Mooradian.

35–36 Other memory images depict Khorkom's agrarian life: Illustrated in Mooradian, *Worlds*, pp. 235–36.

36 "Though but a year older": Ibid., p. 83.

36 "One should play hard": Ibid.

36 To protect his head: Ado Adoian, Mooradian, *Worlds*, p. 84.

36 Once when his companions: Mooradian, Ibid., p. 85.

36 Gorky was probably older: Mary Burliuk, "Arshile Gorky."

36 In later life, Gorky delighted: Elaine de Kooning, "Gorky: Painter of His Own Legend," p. 41.

36 One is that Sedrak and Krikor: Akabi said that Gorky was eight years old when this happened. Since Sedrak left Armenia in 1908, this means that Gorky must have been born at least as early as 1900. Gorky told his wife the same story.

37 As she moved toward: Gorky's sister Satenik told it differently: "As far as I can remember, Gorky didn't speak until he was about six years old—we don't know why, he had no illness that prevented him from speaking. He always drew pictures on the sand and did a great deal of wood carving. My mother engaged a tutor who then lived with us, to teach him to speak. About three months after this tutor came to live with us, he took Gorky to a nearby cliff and pretended he was going to leap off. This had its intended effect upon Gorky, for it frightened him into speaking. The first word he spoke was 'Alkoura,' which doesn't mean anything. Gorky later named a painting 'Alkoura' " (Satenik Avedisian, letter to Mina Metzger). In Akabi's version of the story, Gorky did not begin to talk until after an episode in which he disappeared after a swim and his family thought he might have drowned. When Gorky finally came home and found his family in a state of alarm, he said "Yes hos em," meaning "I am here" (Akabi Amerian, interview by Karlen Mooradian, 1964). In yet another telling, Gorky's tutor tried to frighten Gorky into speaking by saying, "I will beat you up if you do not behave." Gorky grabbed a stick and ran upstairs to the roof. When his cousin tried to take the stick away, Gorky hit him, whereupon Kevork pretended he was hurt and cried, "Al gou lam" ("I am crying"). Gorky began to cry too. He ran downstairs shouting, "Al gou lam!" His mother and sisters were amazed—Gorky was uttering words. Over the years, through constant retelling, "Al gou lam" became "Alkoura" or "Argula." Argula is a nonsense word that Gorky used for the title of a 1938 painting, one of the first in the Garden in Sochi series.

37 And Gorky said his first: Agnes Fielding, interview by author. In a letter to Ethel Schwabacher written on October 24, 1950, she said that argula was Gorky's first word and that when she lived with Gorky "his world as he described it was built around these images and names."

37 Kevork Kondakian: Of Krikor's abuse, Gorky's cousin and former tutor recalled: "This was a very unfortunate thing in the family and Manoug [also spelled Manuk] got impressed by that and he never forgot. As a child he couldn't speak at all (Kevork Kondakian, interview by Karlen Mooradian, 1965).

5: THE DEPARTURE OF SEDRAK ADOIAN

38 In 1906, just about the time: 1908 is the date that Sedrak Adoian's daughters said he left Turkish Armenia, but he is listed in the Ellis Island records on a ship manifest for the St. Laurent, which arrived in New York on December 28, 1906. Its point of departure was Le Havre, France. Sedrak gave his age as thirty-five. If he was indeed born, as his family said, in 1863, he would

have been forty-three when he emigrated to America. On the ship manifest he gave his place of residence as Batumi (Batum), Russia. (The Ellis Island records spell it "Batsuni.")

According to Vartoosh, Sedrak Adoian left home to avoid being drafted into the Turkish army, which would, she said, have forced him to fight fellow Armenians. But this view of Sedrak's reason for leaving seems spurious: until September 1909 Armenians and other non-Muslim Turkish subjects could not serve in the Ottoman army; Muslims did not want to fight their holy wars with the help of infidels. Christians paid a *bedel*, or exemption fee. Moreover, Armenians would not have been required to fight Armenians until the First World War, when the Turkish army, including Armenian recruits, fought Russian soldiers and Armenian volunteers, men who had emigrated from Turkey to Russian Armenia.

39 Krikor's younger son: Matossian, *Black Angel*, p. 40.
39 In an enormous, elaborately: The photograph is in Mooradian, AGA, p. 105.
39 After presenting Gorky with: Ibid., p. 119.
39 "Gorky had a thousand": Agnes Gorky Phillips (later Fielding), letter to Ethel Schwabacher, December 28, 1949.

6: AKHTAMAR

40 On certain religious: The small cruciform church consisted of a central square room under a pyramidal dome plus a semicircular apse and a tiny chapel. According to Gorky's mother's family legend, Charahan Surp Nishan was built in the fifth century after the men in the family returned from battling the Persians to discover that one of their daughters had disappeared. A dream told them that she would be returned if they built a church. The church was built and the girl reappeared. Because of its miraculous powers the church became a pilgrimage site.
40 "They gave us a room": Satenik Avedisian, interview by Karlen Mooradian.
41 "And Tamar's lover": Hovhaness Toumanian, "Akhtamar," *Anthology of Armenian Poetry*, pp. 160–62.
42 "She didn't see him": Matossian, *Black Angel*, p. 40.
43 Kevork Kondakian recalled: Kevork Kondakian, interview by Karlen Mooradian.
43 "Since then these memories": Museum of Modern Art, Department of Painting and Sculpture, Arshile Gorky, Collection File, Artist Records, August 1945.

7: TO VAN

47 The trip of some twenty: American Missionary Reports. The report of the Van Medical Mission for June 1, 1910, to June 1, 1911, says: "Travel in some regions is almost nil because of certain Kurd out-laws who have murdered and robbed a number of Armenians." One government official who did try to stop the brigandage in Van province was fired from his job and called a *giavour*, a Christian infidel.

48 It was in fact the one: Including the inhabitants of Aikesdan, which means the vineyards and which was really an extension of the city, Van had some fifty thousand inhabitants, three-fifths of whom were Armenians. Within the massive walls that enclosed the old city lived 2,500 Armenians and 1,250 Turks. Although a few streets were mixed, Armenians and Turks lived in different quarters. Christians and Muslims had commercial relations, but they kept their distance from each other. The covered market was in the hands of the Armenians.

48 Henry Morgenthau: Henry Morgenthau, *Ambassador Morgenthau's Story*, p. 293.

48 H.F.B. Lynch, for example: Lynch, *Armenia*, vol. 2, p. 38.

48 Fear and suspicion: Ibid., p. 85.

49 "It makes my heart bleed": Elizabeth Barrow, letter to Dr. James L. Barton, American Missionary Reports.

49 He saw a copy: Lynch, *Armenia*, vol. 2, p. 95.

50 "Mother begged him": Matossian, *Black Angel*, p. 49.

51 Gorky is said to have: Mooradian, AGA, p. 133.

8: THE AMERICAN MISSION AT VAN

53 Boys entered the school: Jane Yarrow, the wife of the school's superintendent, taught there alongside some nine to eighteen Armenian teachers (their number increased as the school grew). In late 1910 or early 1911, when Gorky entered the school, there were 352 students and eleven Armenian teachers. By February 1915, two months before the siege of Van and four months before the missionaries and the Armenian population of Van were forced to flee, there were over one thousand students.

54 "Please, help Manoug": Arshag Mooradian, interview by Karlen Mooradian, 1965.

55 "Gorky took it by the reins": Satenik Avedisian, interview by Karlen Mooradian.

55 "Couple of times he did": Yenovk Der Hagopian, interview by Karlen Mooradian. Gorky's childhood friend Paregham Hovnanyan gave a similar picture of Gorky's aggressiveness and his conflicted nature. Gorky was "a very deep boy and very good," Hovnanyan said. "When he did naughty things, he did them secretly. He didn't show them to anyone. He beat the boys, he beat us" (Matossian, *Black Angel*, p. 24).

55 "I wish I was a dog": Satenik Avedisian, interview by Karlen Mooradian.

9: MASSACRES

57 Meanwhile, conscription took: Armenians who had paid the military exemption fee and who did not want to leave their homes and farms were forced into service. But many others enlisted willingly, for they still thought of themselves as loyal Ottoman subjects, and they were eager to defend the empire. A quarter of a million Armenians registered in the army.

57 On October 7: Grace Higley Knapp, letter to Dr. Barton, American Missionary Reports.
58 "Many fainted where they": Ussher, *American Physician*, p. 216.
58 Gorky's aunt Yeva was part: Matossian, *Black Angel*, p. 503, n. 11.
58 "Mummy said this aloud": Ibid., pp. 61–62.
58 In December, full of: My discussion of the fighting in the Caucasus is largely drawn from Walker, *Armenia*, pp. 198–200.
58 Forced to retreat: The Turkish government maintained that Armenian soldiers were deserting the Turkish army and crossing the border into Russia to join the Russian army. No doubt some of these Armenians had only recently fled from Turkey, but others had gone to Russia years earlier. Enver Pasha also claimed that the Armenian civilians in the battle area had served as spies and had secretly helped the Armenian volunteers.
59 "They had to spend practically": Henry Morgenthau, *Secrets of the Bosphorus*, pp. 198–99.
59 Onnig Mukhitarian, in his memoir: Onnig Mukhitarian, *An Account of the Glorious Struggle of Van-Vasbouragan*, part 1 of *The Defense of Van*, pp. 3–4.
59 "When he appeared in Van": American Missionary Reports.
60 "A feeling of despondency": Rushdouni's letter is reprinted in the English *Blue Book* presented by Lord James Bryce and Arnold Toynbee in *The Treatment of the Armenians in the Ottoman Empire*, Documents Presented to Vinount Grey of Falloden, London, J. Causton and Sons, 1916, p. 15.
61 "By the next morning": Elizabeth Barrows Ussher, letter to friends at home, May 8, 1915, American Missionary Reports. This "letter" is really a chronicle of events at Van in the spring of 1915. Some parts of it are called "notes from my diary."
61 "Every available covered spot": Ibid.
62 "If the rebels dare": *La défense héroïque de Van*, p. 5.
62 "Everybody, whether old or young": Mukhitarian, *Account*, p. 23.
62 "Groups of young men": Ibid.
63 "This land will belong": Haig Gossoian, *The Self Defense of Armenians in the Historic City of Van*, part 2 of *The Defense of Van*, p. 18.
63 "I won't leave one": Ussher, *American Physician*, p. 237–38.
63 This procedure was repeated: Morgenthau, *Ambassador*, p. 297. Dr. Ussher said that it was not on April 15 but on April 19 that the twenty-five hundred men of Akantz, the second-largest town on the lake, were taken in groups of fifty with their hands tied behind them to the banks of a river and killed.
63 The women and children: Ussher, *American Physician*, p. 265. The most detailed non-Armenian eyewitness account of the massacres in Van comes from Grisell M. McLaren and Myrtle O. Shane, two American nurses stationed in Van City: "On April 19, 1915, a general massacre of the Armenians was planned . . . soldiers and Kurds, in some instances taking cannon with them, attacked the smaller towns and villages of the province and met with little resistance because most of the able-bodied men had been drafted into the Sultan's army and those who were left had very little ammunition. Fifty-five

thousand men, women and children were slaughtered (Vahakn N. Dadrian, *German Responsibility in the Armenian Genocide: A Review of the Historical Evidence of German Complicity*, p. 31; the quotation is originally from Grace Higley Knapp, *The Tragedy of Bitlis*, p. 15).

64 Their killers, a detachment: Rafael de Nogales, *Four Years beneath the Crescent*, pp. 60–65. Nogales may have shifted the timing of events to make a better story. An American missionary nurse reported that in the middle of May 1915, when their boat stopped at Ahktamar, they learned that the previous day Turkish soldiers had killed one or more priests and some of the orphan boys living on the island. The Turks had also desecrated the church, throwing vestments and other ecclesiastical articles on the floor, stealing silver crosses, and tearing the silver off miters.

64 Coming closer, Nogales: Ibid.

64 The next day Elizabeth: Elizabeth Barrows Ussher, letter.

64 "I forebear to describe": Ussher, *American Physician*, p. 238.

64 In his postwar report: Dadrian, *German Responsibility*, p. 34.

64 In Ambassador Morgenthau's view: Morgenthau, *Ambassador*, pp. 296–97.

64 "If any Moslem protect": Ussher, *American Physician*, p. 244.

65 The procedure that Turkish: Morgenthau, *Ambassador*, p. 297.

65 For example, a Turk: Mukhitarian, *Account*, p. 70.

65 Ernest Yarrow told of babies: S. Arartian, "Récit du missionaire en chef americain Monsieur Yaro" (Ernest Yarrow's account), published in *Arev*, an Armenian journal, in Baku, July 16–29, 1915; reprinted in *La défense héroïque de Van*, p. 8.

10: THE SIEGE OF VAN

66 Two armed Armenian men: *La défense héroïque*, p. 6.

66 Although the *vali*: Elizabeth Barrows Ussher, letter.

66 Austrian vice field marshal: Dadrian, *German Responsibility*, p. 32.

66 "Most were praying, frozen": Mukhitarian, *Account*, p. 38.

67 Their arsenal consisted: Gossoian, *Self Defense*, p. 13. The number of troops and ammunition vary according to the writer.

67 He had ordered them: *La défense héroïque*, pp. 44–45.

67 "Tongues of fire piercing": Mukhitarian, *Account*, p. 42.

67 In moments when the firing: Nogales, *Memoirs of a Soldier of Fortune*, p. 270. See also *Four Years*, p. 72.

68 "On the fourth day": Gossoian, *Self Defense*, pp. 29–30.

68 The Aikesdan Armenians set: According to the American missionaries, it was Ernest Yarrow who organized the task forces. Dr. Ussher noted that the Armenians had no experience with organization and that "Mr. Yarrow organized a government with a mayor, judges, police, and board of health." Grace Knapp said Yarrow "soon had everything in smoothly running order, with everyone hard at work at what he was best fitted to do. A regular city government for the whole city of thirty thousand inhabitants was organized. . . .

The town had never been so well policed before" (Ussher, *American Physician*, p. 251, and Grace Higley Knapp, *The Mission at Van: In Turkey in War Time*, p. 37).

68 "They took ammunition to": Matossian, *Black Angel*, p. 68.

68 "We had even planted flowers": *Ararat*, Fall 1971, p. 10.

68 These trips worried: Mooradian, *AGA*, p. 135.

68 If, as Vartoosh maintained: *Ararat*, Fall 1971, p. 10.

69 One of the scouts' more dramatic moments: Ussher, *American Physician*, p. 271.

69 Extolling the bravery of the defenders: Morgenthau, *Ambassador*, p. 299.

69 "A fiery amazon with flying": Mukhitarian, *Account*, p. 62.

70 "Each house was a fortress": Nogales, *Four Years*, p. 80.

70 "While the shrapnel was raining": Bryce and Toynbee, *Treatment of the Armenians*, p. 65.

70 "At night they created": Mukhitarian, *Account*, pp. 52–53.

70 "Before the trouble began": Elizabeth Barrows Ussher, letter.

71 On April 25 over ten thousand: Ibid.

71 "Sunday morning, April 25": Ussher, *American Physician*, p. 266.

71 "Their hands and feet were blistered": Elizabeth Barrows Ussher, letter.

72 The newcomers, Mukhitarian recalled: Mukhitarian, *Account*, p. 74.

72 "Still others told of their": Ibid., p. 91.

72 On May 8 the Armenians: Different reports give different dates for the burning of Varag Monastery. Dr. Ussher said he saw it burning on April 30. Ernest Yarrow said the fire was on April 26. Onnig Mukhitarian said it happened on May 8.

73 "All are hungry, footsore": Mukhitarian, *Account*, p. 90.

73 "Several of our refugees had": Ussher, *American Physician*, p. 262.

73 "We became so used to": Knapp, *Mission at Van*, p. 38.

73 If a single shot was fired: Ibid., p. 36. In fact, armed Armenians were not allowed to enter the compound and wounded Armenian soldiers were refused entry to the American hospital. Dr. Ussher did, however, treat Armenian soldiers at hospitals set up by the Armenian defense outside the mission.

74 He gathered as much produce: Matossian, *Black Angel*, p. 73.

74 By the fourth week of the siege: Ussher, *American Physician*, p. 275.

74 "We became a 'city all' ": Knapp, *Mission at Van*, p. 39.

74 There was, said Dr. Ussher: Ibid., p. 277.

11: OUR FATHERLAND

76 "Sometimes the smoke and cinders": Letter from Elizabeth Barrows Ussher, Van, to her home in Connecticut, May 30, 1915, American Missionary Report 27–28.

76 "The castle rock, the symbol": Gossoian, *Self Defense*, p. 59.

76 "The whole city was awake": Knapp, *Mission at Van*, p. 40.

76 "A magnificent blaze it made": Ussher, *American Physician*, p. 282.

76 In what Gossoian described: Gossoian, *Self Defense*, p. 58.

76 "It would require the brush": Mukhitarian, *Account*, p. 116.

77 Wells were filled with: Ussher, *American Physician*, p. 283.

77 Inside were the charred corpses: Matossian, *Black Angel*, p. 75.

77 "As they sat there on the hillside": Grisell M. McLaren, "Under the Crescent," American Missionary Reports.

78 The cannon thundered: Mukhitarian, *Account*, p. 120.

78 The Armenian defenders lined: Elizabeth Barrows Ussher, letter.

78 "We are today celebrating": Mukhitarian, *Account*, p. 123.

78 The Armenians of Aikesdan: Ussher, *American Physician*, p. 288. The old city was never rebuilt. Modern Van is located in what was formerly Aikesdan. Amid the grass-covered mounds that were once homes in the walled city, only two mosques remain standing. One has been rebuilt; the other escaped the Turkish cannonball.

79 "We understood what they": Matossian, *Black Angel*, p. 77.

79 "The greater part of it": Herr Spöerr; letter published in the German journal "Sonnenoufgang," October, 1915. Reprinted in James Bryce and Arnold Toynbee in *The Treatment of the Armenians in the Ottoman Empire*.

12: FLIGHT INTO RUSSIA

83 The Armenians were to take refuge: Russian Armenia's Armenian population was partly made up of the descendants of between sixty and ninety thousand Turkish Armenians who, in 1829, had followed the withdrawing Russian army westward. Another part of the population was made up of the Armenians fleeing Ottoman oppression later in the nineteenth and twentieth centuries.

83 "Many . . . carried everything they": Ussher, *American Physician*, p. 304.

83 "We took nothing but a few": Mooradian, *Worlds*, p. 80. According to Vartoosh, the flight from Van began on June 15, but, even if one takes into account the difference between the Julian and the Gregorian calendars, this is wrong.

84 "But all of us walked": Ibid.

84 The Adoian family followed: Akabi Amerian, interview by Karlen Mooradian.

84 "I'm not leaving him": Matossian, *Black Angel*, p. 80.

84 Dr. Ussher's memoir says: Ussher, *An American Physician*, p. 307.

85 The river was in flood: American Missionary Reports.

85 "It was a race for life": Knapp, *Mission at Van*, p. 45.

85 "But thousands struggled on": Ussher, *American Physician*, pp. 311–12.

86 "We slept at night a little": Matossian, *Black Angel*, p. 80.

86 A cloud of soft volcanic: Souren Aprahamian, *From Van to Detroit*, p. 65.

86 "Many thousands died of dysentery": Ussher, *American Physician*, pp. 313–14.

86 "We lacked water, so we": *Ararat*, Fall 1971, p. 11.

86–87 "We had read about it": Ibid., p. 10.

87 It was, said Dr. Ussher: Ussher, *American Physician*, p. 317.

87 The family was afraid she might: Akabi said that Yeva and Nevart died of cholera in Etchmiadzin, but Aharon Der Marderosian's daughter Abisag Der

Marderosian Sarkisian said that Yeva died of starvation at Igdir and that Nevart made it safely to Yerevan, where she bore a son, Gurken, and where in 1918, after sleeping outside for three months, she died of starvation, dehydration, and childbirth (Abisag Der Marderosian Sarkisian, interview by Karlen Mooradian).

13: YEREVAN

89 Ernest Yarrow compared: Ernest A. Yarrow, "Winter Relief in the Caucasus," December 15, 1919, American Missionary Reports.

89 For several days the Adoians: Karlen Mooradian writes that they spent several nights sleeping in front of the church (*AGA*, p. 141). Akabi said they slept outside only for one night (Akabi Amerian, interview by Karlen Mooradian).

90 "You were allowed to eat": Matossian, *Black Angel*, p. 86.

90 Vartoosh, who worshiped: Vartoosh Mooradian, letter to Ethel Schwabacher.

90 "You might learn something": Matossian, *Black Angel*, p. 88.

91 Like many other adolescent boys: Agnes Fielding, interview by author.

91 "But Gorky continued sketching": Vartoosh Mooradian, letter to Ethel Schwabacher. It is interesting that in this letter Vartoosh suggests that Shushan did not encourage Gorky's drawing, whereas Vartoosh's conversations with her son, Karlen Mooradian, give the impression that Shushan was gratified by Gorky's artistic inclination.

92 "She said she would not go": Matossian, *Black Angel*, p. 88.

92 "Why did she send me away": Spender, *From a High Place*, p. 42. According to Akabi, Shushan said that she would join her daughters in the United States later. It was Akabi who finally persuaded her sister to leave (Akabi Amerian, interview by Karlen Mooradian).

92 "She was sitting there": Spender, *From a High Place*, p. 43.

92 "It gave us hope": *Ararat*, Fall 1971, p. 11.

94 And after March 1918: The American relief workers made efforts to leave relief activities in the hands of responsible Armenians (American Missionary Reports, letter from Ernest Yarrow, December 15, 1919, American relief activities in the Caucasus, Historical Memoranda, 1919, Microfilm Unit 5, reel 717, vol. 25E, 1910–1919).

95 "It wasn't politics": Matossian, *Black Angel*, p. 94.

14: FAMINE

96 "When she became ill": *Ararat*, Fall 1971, p. 12.

97 In the bitter cold: Ibid.

97 Sometimes they were reduced: David Marshal Lang, *The Armenians: A People in Exile*, p. 115.

97 "The skeleton-like women and children": Richard Hovannisian, *The Republic of Armenia*, pp. 127–28.

97 "For heaven's sake hurry": Ibid., p. 134.

98 "Mother could not work": *Ararat*, Fall 1971, p. 12.

98 Since she was too weak: Although Vartoosh Mooradian told her son, Karlen, that just before Shushan Adoian died she was dictating a letter to Sedrak Adoian, on another occasion Vartoosh remembered differently. She told Ethel Schwabacher that her mother was dictating a letter to Akabi and Satenik, who were living in Watertown, Massachusetts. See Vartoosh Mooradian's letter to Schwabacher.

98 His mother said: Mooradian, *Worlds*, p. 31.

98 "Her head fell": *Ararat*, Fall 1971, p. 12. In her letter to Ethel Schwabacher, Vartoosh Mooradian said that after their mother died in their arms, "There we were, Gorky and I, two helpless, confused little orphans who did not know what to do, where to turn for help. We both ran out crying and screaming in despair. . . . We felt so lonely and forsaken in this cold world."

98 "I don't know which cemetery": Matossian, *Black Angel*, p. 100.

98 Gorky always wished his mother: *Ararat*, Fall 1971, p. 13.

98 Other times, perhaps out of shame: Agnes Gorky Phillips (Agnes Fielding), letter to Ethel Schwabacher, December 28, 1949, Agnes Fielding personal archive. Gorky told his wife that when his mother died he was twelve and his sister was about nine.

99 "C. D. Ussher": A photocopy of Dr. Ussher's letter is in Matthew Spender's papers, Whitney Museum Library.

101 Instead they were given: *Ararat*, Fall 1971, p. 14.

102 "We were both crying": Matossian, *Black Angel*, p. 115.

103 "This is called chocolate": Ibid., p. 118.

15: WATERTOWN AND PROVIDENCE

107 For a century the town: In 1816 there were about eight hundred Armenians living in Watertown. Fourteen years later there were over thirty-five hundred, and in the third quarter of the nineteenth century Watertown's population doubled. In addition to Armenia, people came from Ireland, Italy, and Greece.

108 Watertown's most important employer: In 1896, Hood Rubber Company's founding year, the company employed several Armenian bachelors living in nearby Brighton. In 1898 one of a group of about ten houses that stood close to the factory became a boardinghouse for twenty Armenian Hood Rubber employees. Other Armenians working there commuted from various Boston suburbs. By 1902 Hood had about four hundred Armenian employees, and at the peak of Armenian immigration (1908 to 1914) some five hundred Armenians worked there.

109 Sedrak Adoian lived at 207: His youngest son, George Adoian, said Hagop was born between 1884 and 1886.

109 The hardships he had borne: George Adoian, interview by author.

109 "His wife, Heghine, was": Matossian, *Black Angel*, p. 120.

109 "No," said Sedrak: Ibid., p. 122.

110 "But Gorky visited often": *Ararat*, Fall 1971, p. 15.

110 "I am going to be a painter": Matossian, *Black Angel*, p. 123.

110 When Gorky replied: Agnes Fielding, interview by author.

110 Later he would tell people: Arshile Gorky, letter to Dorothy Miller.

111 On other occasions he said: Ethel Schwabacher, *Arshile Gorky*, p. 28.

111 "I knew that [he wasn't Russian]": Mischa Reznikoff, interview by Karlen Mooradian.

112 "They'll arrest you": Matossian, *Black Angel*, p. 124.

112 "The courage to do anything": Kevork Kondakian, interview by Karlen Mooradian.

112 After work Akabi and Gorky: Matossian, *Black Angel*, p. 128.

113 "I love you anyway": Spender, *From a High Place*, p. 56.

113 "He loved to sing Armenian": Matossian, *Black Angel*, p. 128.

113 In the fall of 1921: According to Mischa Reznikoff, the Technical High School was a preparatory school for Brown University's School of Engineering (Schwabacher, *Arshile Gorky*, p. 28). This may help explain why Gorky later claimed to have attended Brown.

113 According to Vartoosh: Vartoosh Mooradian, letter to Ethel Schwabacher.

113 "But if I had a wife": Satenik Avedisian, interview by Karlen Mooradian.

114 Vartoosh said he was fired: Mooradian, *Worlds*, p. 36.

114 "He stared at me": Matossian, *Black Angel*, p. 144.

115 The policeman had the last: Mooradian, *Worlds*, pp. 54–55.

16: THE YOUNG MASTER

116 At some point in 1922: Will Barnet, interview by author, New York, December 27, 1994.

116 "One day we had a very": Norris C. Baker, letter to Arshile Gorky, November 9, 1946.

116 To learn oil painting: Gorky may also have copied El Greco and Van Dyck, possibly from actual works in museums or possibly from reproductions. These copies were later lost in the fire in Akabi's Watertown house (see Spender, "Arshile Gorky's Early Life," p. 33).

116 She recalled that Gorky washed: Katherine O'D. Murphy, interview by Karlen Mooradian, and Katherine Murphy, letter to Ethel Schwabacher, August 30, 1952, Whitney Museum, Artist's File.

117 In Boston, Vartoosh recalled: *Ararat*, Fall 1971, p. 15.

117 "Then she eloped": Matossian, *Black Angel*, p. 130.

117 "You're gonna bring the house": Ibid, p. 131.

117 When he came to he insisted: Liberty Miller (also called Azaduhi Amerian), interview by Karlen Mooradian, August 26, 1972.

118 "He was laying the groundwork": Will Barnet, interviewed by author. Barnet, a student at the Boston Museum School in those years, did not meet Gorky until after Gorky moved to New York. But in Boston he heard about Gorky through a Boston Museum School student named John Hussian, an Armenian from Van who lived in Watertown and was married to Gorky's second cousin, Mariam Melikian. (Mariam had been part of Gorky's party traveling

from Yerevan to Ellis Island in 1919, and her grandfather Vartan Adoian was Gorky's paternal grandfather's brother.)

118 Furious, the manager put: Matossian, *Black Angel*, p. 138.

118 "He said to me": Mooradian, *Worlds*, p. 32.

118 "He was so accomplished": Ethel Cooke, interview and correspondence with Karlen Mooradian.

118 He played with the possibility: Harold Rosenberg, *Arshile Gorky: The Man, the Time, the Idea*, pp. 41–42.

118 "Arshile" is thought to be: Matthew Spender has recently suggested that since Gorky first spelled his first name "Arshel" (actually Arshele), the name might come from the Armenian word *aysaharel*, which means "possessed by an evil spirit" or "blown by an evil wind" (Spender, *From a High Place*, p. 60).

119 Once he swam out into: Agnes Fielding, interview by author.

119 "You have to be strong enough": Mooradian, *Worlds*, p. 60, n. 23.

119 "I must have been born": Schwabacher, *Arshile Gorky*, p. 114.

119 Vartoosh remembered that when: Mooradian, *Worlds*, pp. 31–32.

119 According to Ethel Cooke: Ethel Cooke, interview and correspondence with Karlen Mooradian.

119 But mainly he learned by: Meyer Schapiro, "Introduction," Schwabacher, *Arshile Gorky*, p. 11.

120 "But his genuine talent": Stuart Davis, "Arshile Gorky in the 1930s," p. 58.

120 Connah was using Sargent's: Ethel Cooke, interview and correspondence with Karlen Mooradian.

120 "Well, she rubs into me": Ibid.

120 From Gorky's Boston years: Katherine Murphy, letter to Ethel Schwabacher.

121 Ethel Cooke said the photograph: In Cooke's memory, the photograph was taken in 1924 on one of Gorky's visits to the New School of Design just after he moved to New York.

122 When he was accused of: Will Barnet, interview by author.

122 "So I gave him $10.00": Diane Waldman, essay in Guggenheim Museum, *Arshile Gorky: A Retrospective*, 1981, p. 16.

122 "He caught the universal": Arshile Gorky, "Fetish of Antique Stifles Art Here, Says Gorky Kin," p. 17.

123 New York was the liveliest: Mooradian, *Worlds*, p. 37.

123 When he said good-bye: Katherine Murphy, letter to Elaine de Kooning, July 29, 1951, and Katherine Murphy, letter to Ethel Schwabacher. In Karlen Mooradian's interview with Katherine Murphy, he noted that she said: "If I don't become a great artist, I don't know what I'll be. A cook, maybe." Probably Mooradian mistook the word *crook* for *cook*.

123 Akabi, like Vartoosh, would: Spender, *From a High Place*, p. 33.

17: THE EARLY YEARS IN NEW YORK

127 He had a reasonable command: Jacob Kainen, interview by author, July 29, 1995.

127 "He was completely conscious": Davis, "Arshile Gorky in the 1930s," p. 179.

127 Gorky began life in New York: Jim Jordan and Robert Goldwater, *The Paintings of Arshile Gorky: A Critical Catalogue*, p. 94, n. 2 (hereafter Cat. Rais.).

127 In September 1926 he lived: Nathan I. Bijur, letter to Mrs. David Metzger, November 1949.

128 "The year of the Wall Street Crash": Davis, "Arshile Gorky in the 1930s," p. 179.

128 "When we try to do that": *Ararat*, Fall 1971, p. 15.

128 A few years later, when he: Davis, "Arshile Gorky in the 1930s," p. 179.

128 "When I went to say good-bye": Stergis M. Stergis, interview by Karlen Mooradian.

129 "It was a work of art": Raphael Soyer interviewed by Karlen Mooradian, Diocese of the Armenian Church of America.

129 "The question of how he acquired": Davis, "Arshile Gorky in the 1930s," p. 178.

129 Mariam Davis, the Armenian-born: Mariam Davis, interview by her nephew Earl Davis (Stuart Davis's son) on behalf of the author, June 1996. Mariam Davis's sister-in-law Roselle Davis recalled: "It was assumed that he did not have the same economic stress that the others [artists during the Depression] did. Because he had someone who was able to pay his rent and provide him with food" (Roselle Davis, interview by Karlen Mooradian, May 3, 1966). Raoul Hague said that someone named Vanderberg was the "first woman who supported Gorky" (Raoul Hague, interview by Karlen Mooradian).

129 Written in red ink: David Dearinger, conversation with author, December 1999.

130 "I'm afraid I still thought": Mooradian, *Worlds*, pp. 197–99, and Mark Rothko, interview by Karlen Mooradian. The quotations from Rothko that follow are from the same sources.

130 But Gorky may have studied: Jordan, Cat. Rais., pp. 18–19.

130 "He had a wild, poetic": Mooradian, *Worlds*, pp. 197–99.

131 He taught the antique class: The school's other departments were illustration, design, interior decoration, and sculpture. One of the Grand Central School's catalogs, probably for fall 1926, states that the school's approach is not academic or avant-garde but "thoroughly modern and individual." The school's ideal was that "a thorough technical training may be secured without prejudicing the mind of the students in favor of any particular creed of art, leaving them free to express their own individuality without undue influence from their instructors" (Museum of Modern Art Library, Artist's File).

131 "You'd think it was by Fechin": Stergis M. Stergis, interview by Karlen Mooradian.

131–132 "It had been arranged that": George Yphantis, letter to Jim Jordan, 1969, in Jordan, Cat. Rais., p. 133, n. 1. The New School of Design had recently changed its name to the New England School of Design.

132 "I'm going to paint you": Liberty Miller, telephone interview by author, January 18, 2002, and interview by Karlen Mooradian.

132 It was a ridiculous waste: Varsik Avedisian Berberian, interview by Karlen Mooradian, September 8, 1965.

132 "Then it was too high": Satenik Avedisian, interview by Karlen Mooradian, trans. from the Armenian by Nouritza Matossian, *Black Angel*, p. 208.

133 "He carried a little sketchbook": Varsik Avedisian Berberian, interview by Karlen Mooradian.

133 On visits to Niagara Falls: Spender, *From a High Place*, p. 77.

133 "It was quite a price": Ethel M. Cooke, interview by Karlen Mooradian.

134 "The gallery didn't want nothing": Stergis M. Stergis, interview by Karlen Mooradian.

134 Knowing how much Gorky: Haroutune Hazarian, interview by Karlen Mooradian.

134 "The young Russian hears": Gorky, "Fetish."

18: APPRENTICE TO THE MASTERS

136 When Gorky set about to paint: Arshile Gorky, "Garden in Sochi," June 26, 1942.

136 When the light was gone: Diane Waldman, essay in *Arshile Gorky*, p. 21.

136 A 1926 painting of nudes: The painting of nudes is now lost, but it is reproduced in a blurry illustration in the Grand Central catalog from about 1926–27.

137 "And then he'd take the stuff": Stergis M. Stergis, interview by Karlen Mooradian.

137 Several of Gorky's Cézannesque: The list of books in Gorky's library compiled by Matthew Spender (and deposited in the Archives of American Art, Washington, DC) includes another volume by Meier-Graefe, *Cézanne und sein Kreis*, Munich, 1922. Other books on Cézanne listed as being in Gorky's library are: Fritz Novotny, *Paul Cézanne*, New York, 1937; a Skira book on Cézanne published in 1939; and *Paul Cézanne*, Munich, 1912. Spender also made a list of reproductions that Gorky owned, among them *Pommes sur un Table*, *Le Fumeur*, a portrait of Mme Cézanne, and a landscape of Estaque.

138 "It was his imagination": Mischa Reznikoff, interview by Karlen Mooradian.

139 It was written by the Armenian: Spender, *From a High Place*, pp. 73–74. Spender believes that Gorky took the English translation from Alice Stone's anthology of Armenian poetry published in Boston in 1917. Gorky changed the line breaks, omitted the word "is" after "soul," wrote "dawn" instead of "down" after "raining," and used a comma instead of a period before "perhaps."

140 "upon them from on high": Arshile Gorky, "Thirst," *Grand Central School of Art Quarterly*, November 1926, reprinted in Ethel Schwabacher, p. 21.

141 Indeed, as Jim Jordan observes: See Jordan's long essay, "The Paintings of Arshile Gorky: New Discoveries, New Sources, and Chronology," Cat. Rais., pp. 21–22. Gorky probably saw a reproduction of this portrait in the 1927 issue of *Cahiers d'Art*. He also must have seen it in Wildenstein & Company's

Loan Exhibition of Paintings by Paul Cézanne under the Auspices of Mrs. Chester Dale, which opened in New York on January 28, 1928.

141 "At other times, he raised": Harold Rosenberg, *Arshile Gorky: The Man, The Time, The Idea,* p. 46.

141 "How could there be anything fine": Gorky, "Fetish," p. 125.

141 "When I finish, it's going": Matossian, *Black Angel,* p. 157.

142 As in Gauguin's *Self-Portrait:* To give his sitters an extra alertness, Matisse, too, sometimes used this device of setting one eye slightly askew. Gorky picked up on the idea in his very Matissean *Portrait of a Girl* (c. 1928). Here the girl's black, almond-shaped eyes are set at an angle like those of Matisse's *Yvonne Landsberg* (1914) or like Matisse's own eyes in his 1918 *Self-Portrait.*

142 "Are you mad": Rosenberg, *Arshile Gorky,* p. 16.

142 "He worked like a madman": Mischa Reznikoff, interview by Karlen Mooradian.

142 "I have a portrait": Stergis M. Stergis, interview by Karlen Mooradian.

142 Gorky's first reaction was anger: Shnorig Avedissian, interview by Karlen Mooradian.

19: TEACHING

144 "There were, in fact, wars": Mooradian, *Worlds,* pp. 92 and 94–95.

144 To allow a student: Hans Burkhardt, essay in *Arshile Gorky: Paintings and Drawings, 1927–1937, in the Collection of Mr. and Mrs. Hans Burkhardt,* exhibition catalog, 1963.

144 "But I'll let you do it": Colin Gardener, "Interview with Hans Burkhardt," p. 105.

145 "Perhaps one out of 50,000": Hans Burkhardt, interview by Paul J. Karistrom, November 25, 1974.

145 "But he was a force": Max Schnitzler, interview by Karlen Mooradian, 1966.

145 "His teeth were spaced": Revington Arthur, interview by Karlen Mooradian, May 5, 1966.

145 Gorky would bring records: Carol Bernard Hoffman, "The Subject: In or Out?" unpublished manuscript, Archives of American Art, Hans Burkhardt papers.

145 Once he invited a Hungarian: Rosenberg, *Arshile Gorky,* p. 45.

145 "You signed up for a class": Revington Arthur, *op. cit.*

146 "Yeah, sure, Sis": Helen Austin, interview by Harry W. Anderson, February 22, 1979.

146 "In order to paint": Mel Lader, essay in *Arshile Gorky: Works on Paper,* exhibition catalog, 1992, p. 20.

146 He would insist that: Warren McCulloch and Rook McCulloch, interview by Karlen Mooradian, 1966.

146 "If you draw a horse": Karlen Mooradian, "The Philosophy of Arshile Gorky," p. 53. The quotation that follows is from the same source.

146 Another time she was painting: John M. McGregor, "Arshile Gorky's Agony: The Phallus and the Flame," p. 6.

146 Once he reprimanded an overly: Herluf Svenningsen, interview by Karlen Mooradian.

146 He told Murch not to use: Daniel Robbins, *Walter Murch: A Retrospective Exhibition*, Rhode Island School of Design, Providence, 1966, pp. 21–23.

147 "And so of course my attitude": Ethel Schwabacher, interview by Colette Roberts for the Archives of American Art.

147 Gorky would take Ethel's: Ethel Schwabacher, interview by Ruth Bowman, January 17, 1976.

147 The result was a storm: Emily Mason, conversation with author, February 10, 2000.

147 "He would practically do it": Ethel Schwabacher, interview by Ruth Bowman.

147 When Mischa Reznikoff studied: Mooradian, "Philosophy of Arshile Gorky," p. 58.

147 "If you just make the shape": Mooradian, *Worlds*, p. 211.

148 Shortly thereafter it was purchased: Besides the tulip still life, Nathan Bijur also bought *Still Life of Flowers* and *Still Life, Egg Plants* (both 1928) and two portraits of young women, *Portrait of a Girl* (c. 1927) and *Portrait of Mougouch* (c. 1928). Gorky told Bijur that he had painted *Portrait of a Girl* while he was studying in Paris, but the painting almost certainly depicts one of Gorky's Armenian relatives in Watertown. The Bijurs' teenage daughter Jean (now Jean Weiss) accompanied her father to Gorky's Saturday classes at the Sullivan Street studio (Jean Bijur Weiss, letter to Matthew Spender, March 7, 1994, Matthew Spender papers, Whitney Museum, Library).

148 "Look to nature": Mooradian, "The Gardener From Eden," p. 6.

148 A series of snapshots: Reproduced in Appendix II in Phyllis Rosenzweig, *Arshile Gorky: The Hirshhorn Museum and Sculpture Garden Collection*, p. 47.

148 "While working he would suddenly": Mina B. Metzger, unpublished memoir of Arshile Gorky, January 6, 1949.

148 He also took students to: During its first year the Museum of Modern Art exhibited some of the European modernists that the American vanguard longed to know better. The opening show included works by Cézanne, Gauguin, Seurat, and Van Gogh. Two and a half months later the museum put on *Painting in Paris*, which included fifteen Picassos, eleven Matisses, plus works by de Chirico, Léger, and Miró.

149 "There was tenderness, cruelty": Schwabacher, *Arshile Gorky*, pp. 111–12, and Ethel Schwabacher interview by Ruth Bowman. The quotations from Gorky that follow are from the same two sources.

149 She agreed to pay that amount: Agnes Fielding, interview by author.

150 Recognizing his poverty: Ethel Schwabacher once told Gorky, "I'd like to buy a painting from you which would cover your next month's rent." She gave him fifty dollars and said, "Give me whatever you'd like in return." Gorky gave her two paintings, and she told him that she knew they were worth much more than fifty dollars and that she would try to sell one and give him the money. "I sold one of them to a teacher at Dalton School for $25 more" (Ethel Schwabacher, interview by Ruth Bowman).

150 "You could have picked up": Gardener, "Interview with Hans Burkhardt," p. 105.

150 "I know he appreciated it": Burkhardt, essay in *Arshile Gorky: Paintings and Drawings, 1927–1937*, n.p.

150 "They'd bother the hell out": Mooradian, *Worlds*, pp. 204–05.

20: *THE ARTIST AND HIS MOTHER*

151 Saul Schary, however, said: Saul Schary, conversation with Lloyd Goodrich, director of the Whitney Museum. The conversation took place on July 5, 1950, about the time the Whitney acquired *The Artist and His Mother* from Julien Levy. In the Whitney Museum's file of documents on *The Artist and His Mother* a typed page of information about the painting includes Saul Schary's story as told to Lloyd Goodrich on July 12, 1950.

151 A November 1942 letter: Agnes Fielding, conversation with author, 1976, and Agnes (Mougouch) Gorky, letter to Mrs. John Magruder, November 9, 1942.

151 The pencil drawing on which: The drawing entitled *The Artist and His Mother* is in the National Gallery of Art, Washington, DC. The National Gallery owns the version of the finished portrait that is closest to this drawing.

152 "There was something sad": Bruce Hooton, "One Who Saw First: Major Gorky Show," p. 5 (The manuscript for this April 1, 1981 interview with Willem de Kooning is in the Archives of American Art, Washington, DC).

152 "In the 1930s to be an Armenian": Richard G. Hovannisian, *The Armenian in History and Literature*, p. 217.

154 "The very first painting": Revington Arthur, *op. cit.*

154 Saul Schary said that when he: Robert Reiff, *A Stylistic Analysis of Arshile Gorky's Art from 1943–1948*, p. 7, n. 1.

154 Yet, given the fact that: A similar story told by de Kooning to Bruce Hooton (Hooten, "One Who Saw First") sounds more plausible. De Kooning maintained that when Gorky was commissioned to paint his Riviera Club murals in 1940 he had trouble proceeding from his drawings to the mural and asked De Kooning's advice. While the study for *The Artist and His Mother* proves that Gorky knew very well how to square up a drawing, it is possible that transferring something conceived in small scale to the large scale of a mural was a problem for him.

155 All the tension that this: In the struggle between the mother's centered magnetism and the boy's ambivalence, Shushan wins out in the end. Not only does Gorky incline toward his mother, but her face, though it appears at first to be absolutely frontal, turns ever so slightly toward her son. This turn is suggested by subtle deviations from her face's nearly perfect oval and by the way her right eye is higher than her left and by the shadow on the right side of her nose. The tension between mother and son in *The Artist and His Mother* recalls the tension between father and daughter in a portrait that Gorky greatly admired, Balthus's portrait of Miró and his daughter in the Museum of Modern Art.

156 Over a period of several years: Saul Schary, conversation with Lloyd Goodrich.

156 "He felt that scrubbing his floor": Mooradian, "Gardener from Eden," p. 8.
156 "You are living someplace": Willem de Kooning, interview by Karlen Mooradian, 1966.
156 "In case the art market": Frederick Childs, interview by Karlen Mooradian, 1967.
156 He also loved the immaculate: According to Matthew Spender's list in the Archives of American Art, Gorky owned reproductions of Bronzino's Lucrezia Panciatuchi, Maria di Medici, Eleonora of Toledo, and *Portrait of a Man*.
157 Picasso's huge, dark Iberian: Gorky seems to have looked hard at two other of Picasso renderings of young men: the younger of the two boys in Picasso's 1905 *Family of Saltimbanques* has an awkwardness similar to Gorky's own in his portrait of himself with his mother, and the position of the young acrobat's black slippered feet is also close. Something of the earnestness tinged with sadness of the youth in Picasso's *Boy Leading a Horse* (1905) reappears in Gorky's self-portrait. In this Picasso the shapes of the background color left in reserve by the horse's and the boy's legs have an extraordinary vitality. Gorky tried to achieve the same thing in the space between mother and son in the Whitney's *The Artist and His Mother*.
157 In his 1936 essay: Gorky, "My Murals for the Newark Airport: An Interpretation." Having looked at so many sources for Gorky's double portrait, one almost forgets that most of the composition was based on the 1912 photograph. A contemporaneous photograph (reproduced in *La défense héroïque de Van*) offers a different kind of shock. Captioned "Armenian woman combatant from Chatakh" (an alternative spelling of Shadakh), it shows a woman with a veil holding a gun in her right hand; her left arm rests on the shoulders of a boy who looks about twelve. This boy is every bit as serious and unsmiling as the young Gorky, a reminder that part of the feeling of sadness that emanates from Gorky's two versions of *The Artist and His Mother* comes from the desperate political realities for Armenians in Turkey at that time.

21: PORTRAIT OF MYSELF AND MY IMAGINARY WIFE

158 With her long, wavy brown hair: Alma Perry, interview by author, June 1995.
159 "The model was beautiful": Mercedes Carles Matter, interview by author, August 1, 1997.
159 All the students in the life: Joseph Solman, interview by author, December 18, 1999.
159 Sirun had a look: Roselle Davis, interview by Karlen Mooradian.
159 She called him: Sirun Mussikian (Ruth March French), interview by Karlen Mooradian, and Mussikian, correspondence with Mooradian, 1965–81 in Mooradian, *Worlds*, pp. 223–24, nn. 42 and 49. Unless otherwise noted, all quotations from Sirun Mussikian come from these sources.
160 He opened the door to find: Mischa Reznikoff, interview by Karlen Mooradian.
162 Gorky's *Portrait of a Woman*, based: Jordan, Cat. Rais., no. 40.
162 "It just seemed that his love": Roselle Davis, interview by Karlen Mooradian.

163 "That was the difficulty": Agnes Gorky Phillips, notes written in the late 1950s after the publication of Ethel Schwabacher's *Arshile Gorky* (1957), Agnes Fielding, personal archive.

164 "He took her everywhere": Matossian, *Black Angel,* p. 173.

164 "Gorky was holding her hand": Liberty Miller, telephone interview by author.

165 "He said she was heartless": Matossian, *Black Angel,* p. 180.

166 Her relief at being away: Joseph Solman, interview by author.

166 "Next thing I knew": Mariam Davis, interview by Earl Davis. Sirun Mussikian pursued a career in acting and married twice, first to a professor and second to the California architect Gregory Ain.

167 "That was the end": Raoul Hague, interview by Karlen Mooradian.

167 Dreading the emptiness: Yenovk Der Hagopian, interview by Karlen Mooradian.

167 The distance that Gorky put: This painting could have been begun earlier, but the date Gorky wrote in the upper left corner is wrong. He often misdated his canvases.

167–168 "He said his one wish": Mina Metzger, unpublished memoir. Helen Sandow concurred: "Gorky was a homebody. He had the reputation of being a bohemian and I don't know why, because I said to my husband, 'You know what he needs? He needs a wife and a couple of children.' He wanted what every bourgeois man wants" (interview by the author, May 30, 1995).

168 *Portrait of Myself and My Imaginary Wife*: Melvin Lader draws a parallel between Gorky's head and Picasso's *Head of a Sailor* (1907), which has somewhat similar primitivistic features and is similarly bowed ("Graham, Gorky, de Kooning, and the 'Ingres Revival' in America," p. 99, n. 32).

168 In addition, Gorky's greenish: Gorky loved Grünewald and owned a 1936 edition of William Fraener's *Matthias Grünewald.* Some visitors to Gorky's studio remembered seeing a reproduction of Grünewald's Isenheim altarpiece on the wall.

168 Drawing himself up to his full: Mariam Davis, interview by Earl Davis.

168 "And he really was quite": Mooradian, *Worlds,* p. 123.

168 "Here comes Jesus Christ": Satenik Avesidian, interview by Karlen Mooradian.

169 Gorky shared with his countrymen: One of these photographs is reproduced in Morgenthau, *Ambassador,* p. 300.

22: THE CAFETERIA PEOPLE

170 "The difference that strikes": Poindexter Gallery, *The Thirties: Painting in New York,* n.p.

170 Concurring, sculptor David Smith: David Smith, "Notes on My Work," p. 44.

170 Of their alienation he observed: Garnett McCoy, ed., *David Smith,* p. 85.

170 "The focus was on French": Bruce B. Glaser, "Jackson Pollock: An Interview with Lee Krasner," p. 37.

171 "They are not stupid": Raoul Hague, interview by Karlen Mooradian.

171 "But it never bothered Gorky": Mooradian, *Worlds,* pp. 131–32.

171 Having been a prominent member: In the first decade of the twentieth century Burliuk had exhibited with Mikhail Larionov and Natalie Goncharova. In 1912 Kandinsky invited him to show with the Blue Rider group. The Russian futurist poet Vladimir Mayakovsky was a friend and Burliuk wrote lectures and manifestos with him. Possibly Burliuk introduced Gorky to Mayakovsky. Gorky told his second wife that he had met the poet, which, if true, would have been in the summer of 1925, when Mayakovsky was in New York living near Washington Square. Gorky might also have met him through a friend called Hugo Gellert for whom Mayakovsky posed for a portrait drawing to illustrate an article by the Communist journalist Mike Gold. From Gorky's point of view, Mayakovsky cut a poor figure because he fainted after pricking his finger on a pin in his pocket. (This detail may give credibility to Gorky's story—Mayakovsky's father had died of septicemia after pricking his finger with a pin.) See Spender, *From a High Place*, p. 69 and note on p. 382.

171 "He talked very little about": Mariam Davis, interview by Earl Davis.

172 "They keep asking me": Helen Sandow, interview by author.

174 "They look like college": Matthew Spender, interview with Dorothy Dehner, November 20, 1993, Matthew Spender papers.

174 "You f—ing little rug peddler": Peter Schjeldahl, "The Great Gorky," and Schjeldahl, telephone conversation with author, January 2002.

174 "Sometimes we were embarrassed": Mooradian, *Worlds*, pp. 113–14.

174 At exhibition openings he'd: Ibid., pp. 161 and 163.

174 Gorky had "no feelings": Spender, *From a High Place*, p. 101.

175 Gorky said "That's silly": Mooradian, "Gardener of Eden," p. 7.

175 He took the magazine: Spender, *From a High Place*, p. 98.

175 "He got the point": Willem de Kooning, interview by Karlen Mooradian.

176 De Kooning remembered Graham: Anecdote told to the author by Dore Ashton, 1973.

176 During the 1930s Gorky and Graham: Julien Levy, foreword to *Arshile Gorky: Paintings, Drawings, Studies*, exhibition catalog, Museum of Modern Art, 1962, p. 7.

176 Gorky confessed: Julien Levy, interview by author, 1973.

176 "Certainly they admired each": Jacob Kainen, "Remembering John Graham," p. 30.

176 Gorky and Graham would talk: Hedda Sterne, interview by author, New York City, 1973.

177 "After a while," said Kainen: Kainen, "Remembering John Graham," p. 25.

177 "The sculpture seems routine": Jacob Kainen, interview with author.

177 "We were the cafeteria": Willem de Kooning, telephone conversation with author, December 1972.

177 They were recognized as: James T. Valliere, "De Kooning on Pollock," p. 603.

177 In December 1931 Graham wrote: John Graham's December 28, 1931, letter to Duncan Phillips is quoted in Spender, *From a High Place*, p. 84. The letter is in the Duncan Phillips papers at the Archives of American Art.

177 Their vibrant interchange: Of all the Manhattan vanguard in those Depression years, Graham's work is closest to Gorky's, but parallels can also be drawn between Graham and de Kooning, and certain paintings by Jackson Pollock show his link with Graham as well.

177 From the evidence of the work: The most vivid example of the exchange of influence between Gorky and Graham is seen in Graham's *The White Pipe* of 1930 (New York University art collection) and Gorky's *Still Life* of 1929 (Jordan, Cat. Rais., no. 73). Both paintings depict that favorite Cubist motif, a clay pipe. Graham's pipe with two lobes swelling from its base is similar to the central biomorphic shape (probably a conflation of a boot/butter churn) in Gorky's 1929 *Still Life*.

177–178 All three artists took their cues from Picasso: Besides the obvious interchange in the three artists' Ingres-inspired portraits of the later 1930s and early 1940s, there are a number of paintings and drawings from the late 1920s to about 1937 that show Gorky and Graham looking over each other's shoulders. Graham's Surrealistic ink drawings with biomorphic shapes and with areas of light and dark created by changing the density of the crosshatching are similar to Gorky's ink drawings. Graham's *Portrait of Elinor Gibson* (1930), in the Phillips Collection in Washington, bears some resemblance to Gorky's *Portrait of Vartoosh* (c. 1933–36) in the Hirshhorn Museum, but the connection comes largely from the mutual influence of Picasso.

178 All the combustive issues: Both de Kooning and Lee Krasner testified to the affinity between Graham's ideas and the later practice of the Abstract Expressionists. Krasner said Graham's ideas were "not concretized, but in the air," and de Kooning likewise insisted that Graham's ideas as expressed in *System and Dialectics in Art* reflected the climate of thought and feeling in the downtown art world of the 1930s (Lee Krasner, conversation with author, December 1972, and Willem de Kooning, telephone conversation with author).

178 "They thought the same": Agnes Fielding (then Agnes Phillips), letter to author, December 9, 1972.

178 In 1942 Graham said: Sidney Janis, *Abstract and Surrealist Art in America*, p. 54.

179 Only painting, he said: John Graham, *System and Dialectics in Art*, p. 207.

179 "In a perfect composition": Ibid., p. 20.

179 The organization of forms: Ibid., pp. 19, 56.

23: COPY ART AND IMITATE NATURE

180 Gorky came back with: Rosenberg, *Arshile Gorky*, p. 66.

180 Levy promised a show: Levy, foreword to *Arshile Gorky*, p. 7.

180 He made the borrowed: Kainen, "Memories of Arshile Gorky," p. 97.

180 Moreover, his unabashed borrowings: Schapiro, introduction to Schwabacher, *Arshile Gorky*, p. 11.

180 He insisted that he had: Raphael Soyer, *Self-Revealment: A Memoir*, p. 100.

181 Gorky countered: John Ferren, quoted in Poindexter Gallery, *The 30's: Painting in New York*, n.p.

181 To his friend the painter: Balcomb Greene, "Memories of Arshile Gorky," p. 109. This article was written in January 1951 for *Magazine of Art* but not used. It exists in manuscript form in Gorky's Artist's File in the Whitney Museum of American Art Library. It was finally published in *Arts Magazine* in March 1976.

181 One of Gorky's favorite: Peter Busa, notebooks, p. 9.

181 To a young abstract painter: Thomas B. Hess, *Abstract Painting: Background and the American Phase*, p. 108.

181 He then pulled out: Kainen, "Memories of Arshile Gorky," pp. 96–98.

181 In front of Picasso's: Waldman, essay in *Arshile Gorky*, p. 27, and Joseph Solman, interview by author.

181 Turning away from the painting: Metzger, memoir of Gorky.

181 Harold Rosenberg posited the idea: Rosenberg, *Arshile Gorky*, p. 63.

182 "Somehow," de Kooning said: Ibid., p. 66.

182 "Somebody like André Breton": Hooten, "One Who Saw First," p. 5.

182 "Nowadays, you don't work": Saul Schary, interview by Karlen Mooradian.

182 "Since I, as a son": Milton Resnick, quoted in Mooradian, *Worlds*, pp. 192–93.

182 He had several one-person: In 1927 a retrospective of Matisse's work was mounted at the Valentine Dudensing Gallery. The Valentine Gallery showed him in 1929 and in 1931 the Museum of Modern Art gave him a major exhibition.

183 In *Still Life with a Horse* (1928): Jordan, Cat. Rais., no. 47.

183 From now on, Gorky's vision: André Breton, *Surrealism and Painting*, p. 200.

184 It is as though: Among the books and periodicals owned by Gorky (and included by Spender in his list of books in Gorky's library) is a fifteen-page catalog written by Waldemar George and entitled *Picasso, dessins* (Paris, 1926). Spender has suggested that the image in the larger of the two 1929 still lifes (indeed at 47" × 60" it was clearly intended to be a major opus) may have come from this catalog of Picasso's drawings. The catalog, which belongs to Spender's wife, Gorky's eldest daughter, Maro, is full of Gorky's fingerprints.

184 In both these still lifes: Both versions of Picasso's *Seated Woman* were reproduced in a 1927 issue of *Cahiers d'Art*.

184 As Jim Jordan notes, Gorky: Jordan, Cat. Rais., p. 31.

184 The larger of Gorky's two: Waldman, *Arshile Gorky*, p. 25. Jim Jordan proposes that the painting also draws on Braque's collage *Musical Forms (Guitar and Clarinets)* of 1918 (Cat. Rais., pp. 34–35).

186 Gorky told friends that: Jordan, Cat. Rais., p. 38.

186 In several of Gorky's paintings: Gorky could have seen Miró as early as 1926, when the Spaniard was included in the Brooklyn Museum's "International Exhibition of Modern Art." Miró was also visible at the Gallery of Living Art and in a number of group shows, including two at the Museum of Modern Art in 1930. Also in 1930 the Valentine Gallery mounted Miró's first one-man show in New York. Then, starting in 1932, Pierre Matisse gave Miró yearly or biannual exhibitions.

186 Indeed, the dog seems: The dog also brings to mind a creature from another Miró painting, the hare in *Landscape* of 1927.

187 He drew incessantly and on: Marny George, letter to James Thrall Soby, March 15, 1951.

187 "Always keeping my hand": Sidney Janis, *An Exhibition of 35 Selected Drawings from the Late Work of Arshile Gorky,* October 24, 1959, n.p.

187 "And then he'd draw a profile": Mooradian, *Worlds,* p. 150.

187 "Now," he explained: Mooradian, "Philosophy of Arshile Gorky," p. 57.

187 "How about Ingres": Kainen, "Memories of Arshile Gorky," p. 98. Kainen appears to have adapted this "memory" from Mary Burliuk's memoir, "Arshile Gorky."

188 These themes, as set: Joseph P. Ruzika, "Introduction to the Plates," *Arshile Gorky and the Genesis of Abstraction: Drawings from the Early 1930s,* exhibition catalog, Princeton University Art Museum and Stephen Mazoh Gallery, New York, 1994, p. 1.

188–189 In Gorky's work of the 1930s: Rosenberg, *Arshile Gorky,* p. 72.

189 Gorky's image was based: For a complete discussion of these sources, see Ruzika, "Introduction to the Plates," p. 2.

190 In works like *Metamorphosis:* Paintings by Masson were reproduced in *Cashiers d'Art* in 1929 and 1931. Gorky would also have seen Masson's work in exhibitions such as the Wadsworth Atheneum's *Newer Super-Realism.* This was the first major Surrealist show in this country, and, after closing in Hartford, it moved to the Julien Levy Gallery in January 1932. Masson had a one-man show at Pierre Matisse in 1933. Beyond that, his *Cock Fight* (1930), with its whiplash line creating semiabstract free-form creatures, hung in the Museum of Living Art at New York University.

190 Yet another source was Picasso's: Waldman, *Arshile Gorky,* p. 29.

191 In Picasso, Graham wrote: Graham, *System and Dialectics of Art,* p. 96.

191 All three are derived from: The derivation from Giorgio de Chirico was first noted by Waldman, *Arshile Gorky,* p. 31. The word *Enigma* appears in de Chirico's *Fatal Temple* over the fish-shaped kitchen mold in the lower right. *Nostalgia,* too, is a word that de Chirico used in several other titles. In calling his drawings *Nighttime, Enigma, and Nostalgia,* Gorky might also have been encouraged by his friendship with John Graham, who frequently used the word *enigma* and who in *System and Dialectics of Art* described Picasso's work as "nostalgic and enigmatic."

191 Elaine de Kooning recalled his reaction: de Kooning, "Gorky: Painter of His own Legend," p. 64.

192 "There are mines of gold": Arshile Gorky's letters to his wife are in her personal archive.

192 According to the Gorky myth: Schwabacher, *Arshile Gorky,* p. 50.

192 "Has the subject any special": Curatorial files, Museum of Modern Art. Quoted in *Arshile Gorky: Paintings and Drawings, 1929–1942,* exhibition catalog, Gagosian Gallery, New York, 1998, p. 60.

193 "He had that uncanny": Mooradian, *Worlds,* p. 176.

24: ANOTHER CUP OF COFFEE, ANOTHER PIECE OF PIE

197 "Gorky swept in with his": Greene, "Memories of Arshile Gorky," pp. 108–10.
197 Stuart Davis recalled that: Davis, "Arshile Gorky in the 1930s," p. 58.
198 "Like all such skylight affairs": Ibid.
199 "Yes that was the way": Mooradian, *Worlds*, p. 129.
199 "You had the feeling about Gorky": Ibid., p. 61, n. 25.
199 "He used to call people": *Ararat*, Fall 1971, p. 51.
200 "In a city as nomadic": Margaret Osborn, "The Mystery of Arshile Gorky: A Personal Account," *Art News*, February 1963, p. 58.
200 As Suzanne La Follette wrote: Suzanne La Follette, "The Artist and the Depression," p. 265.
200 Gorky had always had: Schwabacher, *Arshile Gorky*, p. 59.
200 "You will see much of this": Mougouch Phillips (later Agnes Fielding), letter to Patricia Passloff, in Poindexter Gallery, *The 30's: Painting in New York*, n.p.
200–201 "And I thought the best": Ethel Schwabacher, interview by Ruth Bowman.
201 He would give de Havenon: Gaston T. de Havenon, "Reminiscence of Gorky."
201 "And he posed his hands": Mooradian, *Worlds*, p. 205.
201 "He goes out and begs": Willem de Kooning, interview by Karlen Mooradian. Unless otherwise noted, all quotations from Willem de Kooning come from this interview.
201 "Gorky had gone to bed": Letter from Will Barnet, May 1, 1980, quoted in Waldman, *Arshile Gorky*, p. 25. It seems more likely that the cheese Will Barnet spoke of was part of a still life setup. Gorky made only two known collages (both cheeseless). One is a drawing on the *Cubist Standing Figure* theme (c. 1930–31). The other is a small, Picasso-inspired *Still Life* (c. 1934–35) with a label from a sandpaper wrapping affixed to its surface (Jordan, Cat. Rais., no. 126).
202 She said, "I'm not making": George Adoian, interview by author. The story was told to Adoian by an artist named Albert Gold who lived in Greenwich Village and was a friend of Gorky's.
202 "In all, we probably went": Mooradian, *Worlds*, p. 170.
202 Gorky listened quietly: Mercedes Carles Matter, interview by author.
203 "He always had the last": *Ararat*, Fall 1971, p. 49. See also Mooradian, *Worlds*, p. 129.
203 "It was literally the center": Mooradian, "Gardener from Eden," p. 5. Margaret Osborn summed up Gorky's personality with these words: "Arshile Gorky, was in his personal habits, an aristocrat, in his emotions, a romantic, and in his splendid intellect, unclassifiable. But the most salient thing in him, one that fused many disparate attributes, was his unswerving devotion to art, not an attitude, nor a self-consciousness, but an endeavor in which he was primarily and constantly engaged" (Osborn, "Mystery of Arshile Gorky," p. 43).
203 "Really it can be hit any": Warren McCulloch, interview by Karlen Mooradian, and Mooradian, *Worlds*, pp. 168–69.

203 Gorky welcomed challenges: Davis, "Arshile Gorky in the 1930s," p. 57.

203 Once at a party he gave: Mooradian, *Worlds*, p. 204.

204 "He was very sensitive": Ibid., p. 123.

204 "As far as he was concerned": Mooradian, "Gardener from Eden," p. 8.

204 Finally he yelled: Peter Busa, interview by Karlen Mooradian, 1973.

204 "O yes, Gorky was strong": Mooradian, *Worlds*, p. 172. The painter Aristodimos Kaldis had another tale about Gorky's bellicosity. Late one evening a group of artists were having supper at a Fourteenth Street cafeteria when an argument broke out about the relative importance of painting and sculpture. The "easily excitable Gorky . . . got so mad he got up and says to some stranger, 'Oh, I feel like spitting at you.' The stranger threatened to beat Gorky up, but Gorky demurred: 'Look, now I have a girlfriend and I don't want there to be a black eye. I want to marry.' " Friends separated the sparring men. The following afternoon Gorky came to Kaldis's studio to meet Louis Schapiro, a possible patron from Rockport, Massachusetts. Schapiro arrived accompanied by the older painter Abraham Walkowitz, known for his Expressionist views of Manhattan and for his Rodin-inspired drawings of Isadora Duncan. It was clear that Walkowitz wanted to introduce Schapiro to his own artist friends. "Gorky couldn't stand him," Kaldis recalled. "And he said that he [Walkowitz] copies Redon. And of course the other guy retorted that you [Gorky] copied Picasso and everybody else, how dare you" (Aristodimos Kaldis, interview transcript, Matthew Spender papers, Whitney Museum of American Art Library).

204 Raoul Hague recalled that: Ibid., p. 172.

204 For all his love of roughhousing: Mirak, *Torn between Two Lands*, p. 138.

205 "We used to get loaded": Mischa Reznikoff, interview by Karlen Mooradian.

205 "Gorky became aware of this": Davis, "Arshile Gorky in the 1930s," p. 57.

205 Although his speaking voice: Mooradian, *Worlds*, p. 155.

205 "He sure had terrific style": *Ararat*, Fall 1971, pp. 51–52. The quotation that follows is from the same source.

205 "He could have taken": Spender, *From a High Place*, p. 102.

206 "You have to remember": Mooradian, *Worlds*, p. 174.

206 Jacob Kainen said: Kainen, "Memories of Arshile Gorky," p. 98.

206 With a few drinks: Mooradian, *Worlds*, p. 204.

206 "What's wrong with cow": Kainen, "Memories of Arshile Gorky," p. 96.

207 "He might become very abrupt": Mooradian, *Worlds*, p. 191.

207 Once Gorky wrote that he: Arshile Gorky, statement about *Garden in Sochi*.

207 Kainen once noted that: Jacob Kainen, interview by Avis Berman.

207 Her restaurant, said Reuben Nakian: Mooradian, *Worlds*, p. 175.

207 "He was sort of Papa": Poindexter Gallery, *The 30's*, n.p.

207 Smith remembered designer Frederick: McCoy, *David Smith*, p. 86.

207 "The Jumble Shop was a place": Ibid., pp. 189–90.

208 "I don't want it": Arpenik Karebian, interview by Karlen Mooradian, July 22, 1966.

208 His favorites starred: Mooradian, *Worlds*, p. 205.

208 "Soon a succession of outraged calls": Kainen, "Memories of Arshile Gorky," p. 97.
208 "Gorky saw things differently": Raoul Hague, interview by Karlen Mooradian, and Mooradian, *Worlds*, p. 149.

25: FERVENT SCRUTINIZER

209 "No interesting touch or": Schapiro, "Introduction," Schwabacher, *Arshile Gorky*, p. 11.
209 "He was the best informed": Peter Busa, interview by Jack Taylor, c. 1972.
210 "People who didn't meet him": Elaine de Kooning, "Gorky: Painter of His Own Legend," p. 39.
210 Will Barnet recalls standing: Will Barnet, interview by author.
210 "After a time Gorky stepped": Kainen, "Memories of Arshile Gorky," p. 98.
210 Not surprisingly, the guards: Mooradian, "Philosophy of Arshile Gorky," p. 55.
210–211 "The Renaissance discovered chiaroscuro": Schwabacher, *Arshile Gorky*, p. 16.
211 "This sort of analysis": Kainen, "Memories of Arshile Gorky," p. 97.
211 Among Gorky's collection: The photograph of Poussin's *The Triumph of Bacchus* on which Gorky and Graham drew is reproduced in Spender, *From a High Place*, p. 96.
211 "We used to hit": John Gruen, *The Party's Over Now*, p. 244.
211 In 1939, when Picasso's: Metzger, unpublished memoir of Gorky.
211 His friends were as amazed: Gorky had books on Italian Renaissance painting (Giotto, Uccello, Masaccio, Pisanello, Carpaccio, Raphael, Leonardo da Vinci, Michelangelo, and Titian, for example). He owned volumes on Bosch, Grünewald, Rembrandt, and Turner, and on Goya, El Greco, Claude Lorrain, David, Ingres, Corot, Daumier, Manet, Degas, Renoir, Bonnard, Toulouse-Lautrec, Cézanne, Van Gogh, and Seurat. His books on twentieth-century art included monographs on Douanier Rousseau, Modigliani, Picasso, Braque, Gris, Matisse, Léger, Klee, Kandinsky, Miró, de Chirico, and Dalí, plus various volumes on Surrealism and on Russian modernism. Also in his library were books on Japanese screens, Oceanic and African art, Catalonian art, Coptic and Islamic textiles, Islamic miniatures, Russian primitives, and Greek sculpture. On the practical side, he owned, and spent a lot of time looking at, Max Dorner's *The Materials of the Artist*, published in 1937. He also kept up with recent art developments, and his library included many issues of such journals as *Cahiers d'Art, Verve, L'Art d'Aujourd'hui, Formes, Camera Work, The Arts, Axis, Abstraction-Création Art Non-Figuratif, Omnibus, Creative Art*, and *Art Digest*. In addition, he had a vast collection of reproductions ranging from a Roman terra-cotta to ancient Armenian embroidery and from Simoni Martini to Cranach to Brancusi.
212 Margolis was impressed: Mooradian, *Worlds*, p. 164.
212 "You can have it for": Ibid., pp. 215–16.
213 On his long late-afternoon: Mooradian, "Philosophy of Arshile Gorky," p. 52.

213 Raoul Hague recalled that Gorky: Mooradian, *Worlds*, p. 149.

213 When he saw the hooded: Kainen, 'Memories of Arshile Gorky," p. 97.

213 Sometimes Gorky's outbursts: Mooradian, "Philosophy of Arshile Gorky," p. 52.

213 When Holger Cahill introduced: Irving Sandler, telephone conversation with author, January 24, 2002.

213 Lillian Olinsey (later Lillian Kiesler): Frederick Kiesler had arrived in the United States in 1926, and he soon had a job designing an avant-garde cinema on Eighth Street near the Whitney Studio Club. According to Lillian Olinsey Kiesler, he and Gorky met through John Graham, whom she called the "self-appointed missionary for introducing similar souls to each other." For one of his interiors, she recalls, Kiesler designed a glass-topped table with aluminum legs and attached underneath it was a painting by Gorky. Around 1929 Gorky arranged for Kiesler to give a series of lectures at the Grand Central Art School.

213 "Both of them were passionate": Lillian Olinsey Kiesler, interview by author, April 9, 1999.

214 "Gorky called it the real": Mooradian, *Worlds*, pp. 159–60.

214 They agreed that nature was: Fritz Bultman, interview by author, New York, March 18, 1973.

26: EXHIBITIONS

215 "In spite of his derivative style": Alfred H. Barr, letter to Karlen Mooradian, March 30, 1966.

216 A Braque-inspired *Still Life*: Nathan I. Bijur, letter to Mina Metzger, November 1949.

216 He never saw Neumann: Reiff, *Stylistic Analysis of Arshile Gorky's Art*, p. 127, n. 3.

217 *Fruit* (c. 1928–29) was: The Downtown Gallery's papers are in the Archives of American Art. The Gorky entries are quoted in Jordan, Cat. Rais., p. 179.

217 In addition, George McNeil: George McNeil, "American Abstractionists Venerable at Twenty," p. 64.

217 Knowing that Gorky: Davis, "Arshile Gorky in the 1930s," pp. 57–58.

218 "He made his vision clear": Arshile Gorky, "Stuart Davis," pp. 213, 217. Reprinted in Diane Kelder, ed., *Stuart Davis*, pp. 192–94. Kelder eliminates one line. After "How could they ever have understood Cubism or the art of the twentieth century?" she misses the line that says: "How could they even conceive of the elements that go into the making of art?"

219 "We kidded about it a lot": Davis, "Arshile Gorky in the 1930s," p. 58.

219 Gorky owned several issues: Entitled *Objects* and dated 1932, it now belongs to the Museum of Modern Art.

219 The gallery was directed by: Dorothy Miller, interview by Karlen Mooradian, 1967. Gorky's second wife, Agnes Magruder (Mougouch), would corroborate what Miller said. In 1956 she wrote: "A lot of Gorky's paintings of the late

20's and perhaps some early 30's disappeared along with some character with a gallery in Philadelphia" (Poindexter Gallery, *The 30's*).

220 Kiesler's observations were the most perceptive: The remainder of Kiesler's note reads:

> Unswerving, critical reason seeks the quintessence of Picasso-Miró, drunkenly to absorb them only to exude them again in deep slumber, after such feast.
>
> This Caucasian stranger, having just quenched his hunger and thirst, is ready to shoulder down the doors into land of his own—for those who wait without the threshold.
>
> The genius of Asia celebrates his marriage to the spirit of Europe.
>
> Such an event is rare.
>
> We are fortunate to be witnesses.
>
> Tourists of the American, Asiatic and European Continents are invited.
>
> Tickets free and tickets at popular prices. All depends on you.
>
> The earlier you come, the longer your pleasure will last.

The Mellon Galleries exhibition brochure is in the library of the Museum of Modern Art.

220 While in Philadelphia, he visited: For Gorky's work purchased by Bernard Davis, see Jordan, Cat. Rais., nos. 65, 66, 75, 77, 79, and 80.

220 It took place on February 28: The show was chosen by a jury of seven that included Holger Cahill, Alfred Barr, and painter George Biddle. Gorky contributed a painting called *Organization No. 4* (1931), a 1932 drawing called *Nighttime of Nostalgia*, and his 1931 lithograph *The Kiss*.

221 *New York Times* critic: *New York Times*, December 30, 1933, p. 11.

221 A year later, in February 1935: Gorky showed four works in the Whitney's abstraction show, three named *Composition* and one titled *Organization*. (At this stage in his career, Gorky preferred the most abstract titles.) Among other younger participants were Gorky's friends Byron Browne, Balcomb Greene, and John Graham.

221 This prompted the younger: McNeil, "American Abstractionists Venerable at Twenty," p. 64.

222 Gorky's two still lifes in the Guild's: *New York Times*, October 13, 1935, p. 19.

222 In November 1935 Gorky signed: The Guild Art Gallery agreed to present at least one one-man show and to include him in group shows. It took a commission of one-third of the gross sales. The arrangement lasted a year. At the top of the original contract is a note that Margaret Lefranc wrote in 1981: "The Julien Levy Gallery offered Gorky a contract with a stipend of about $25.00 weekly. As we could not match that and we knew Gorky had financial difficulties, we released him of this contract." Julien Levy apparently offered to represent Gorky late in 1936 or early in 1937, but he did not in fact show him until 1945. Further evidence of Levy's early offer is a 1945 letter from

Gorky's second wife, Agnes Magruder (Mougouch), saying that around 1935 Levy almost gave Gorky a show but at the last minute he got scared off. (Agnes Gorky's letters to Jeanne Reynal are in her personal archive.)

222 Gorky would introduce Anna: Matossian, *Black Angel*, pp. 242–43. The quotations from Anna Walinska come from Matossian's 1992 interview with her.

222 The Guild's press releases: Guild Art Gallery Papers, Archives of American Art, Washington, DC.

222 A few days later when: Spender, *From a High Place*, p. 139.

222 They wrote to Alfred Barr: Anna Walinska and Margaret Lefranc, letter to Alfred H. Barr, November 20, 1935, Guild Art Gallery Papers.

223 Gorky's show of eighteen: The brochure for Gorky's *Abstract Drawings* show listed fourteen untitled works, as well as *Nighttime Nostalgia* (owned by Martin Janis), *Composition* (in the collection of Sidney Janis), *Detail for Mural* (which belonged to Alfred Auerbach), and *Enigmatic Triptych* (which was loaned by William Muschenheim, an architect whom Gorky might have met through Kiesler and who with his wife, Lisa, became a friend and patron).

223 The *New York Times* called: The *New York Times* piece came out on Sunday, December 22, 1935. All the press clippings for Gorky's show at the Guild Art Gallery are in the Guild Art Gallery Papers.

223 Perhaps on the recommendation: The drawing was later given by the Société Anonyme to the Yale University Art Gallery. Dreier had, in fact, become interested in Gorky's work five years earlier, when she herself added his name to the list of artists to be included in the Société Anonyme exhibition that inaugurated the New School. And, two years before she purchased the Gorky drawing, she had shown her interest in him when Burgoyne Diller and Werner Drewes proposed to her the idea of making a portfolio of prints to publicize the work of abstract artists. Besides Diller, Drewes, and Gorky, the other artists involved in the print project were Alexander Calder, David Smith, Joseph Albers, John Graham, Harry Holtzman, and Paul Outerbridge. An agreement was reached to produce forty portfolios, half of which would be given to major museums and collectors, but the portfolio was never produced (*The Société Anonyme and the Dreier Bequest at Yale University: A Catalogue Raisonné*, p. 21).

224 When they finished eating: Spender, *From a High Place*, p. 143.

225 "In 1934 John Graham": Kainen, "Memories of Arshile Gorky," p. 96.

225 Among progressive-thinking students: Mooradian, *Worlds*, p. 159.

225 Lee Krasner remembered Gorky: Ibid., p. 191.

225 Gorky put the matter: Cynthia Joyce Jaffe, "Reuben Nakian."

225 Although most of them: Dore Ashton, *The New York School: A Cultural Reckoning*, p. 10.

226 They felt that unless it: Mooradian, *Worlds*, p. 128.

226 "Old world, yes": Ibid., p. 144.

226 The first of these was: Funded by Harry Hopkins's Civil Works Administration, the PWAP cost about $1,312,000 and it employed about 3,700 artists to decorate new public buildings with murals. The PWAP's purpose, according to its national director, Edward Bruce, was "to employ artists to make a picto-

rial representation of the American scene for the embellishment of public buildings" (Gallery Association of New York State, *New Deal for Art*, p. 4). In principle, artists were supposed to be free to address the American scene in any way they wished. In practice, most artists realized that they were expected to work in a representational mode. The other two early relief projects were the Treasury Relief Art Project (TRAP) and the Treasury Section of Painting and Sculpture. TRAP cost $833,784 and employed about 446 people, 75 percent of whom were on relief, to produce art for existing public buildings. The Treasury Section cost about $2,571,000 and, after holding anonymous competitions, it awarded fourteen hundred contracts for murals and sculptures for new government buildings.

226 "My intention is to create": National Archives Record Group 121, Entry No. 117, Box 4. Quoted in Francis V. O'Connor, "The Economy of Patronage," p. 95.

226 Gorky's attempt to combine: Like Gorky, Stuart Davis seems to have protested too much when he argued that abstract art not only reflected modern life but fostered social progress (Stuart Davis, "Abstract Painting Today," in Francis V. O'Connor, *Art for the Millions*, pp. 126–27).

226 The following month Gorky named: The January 17, 1934, progress report is on deposit in the Archives of American Art, roll DC 113, frames 287–289. Gorky may have been given advice on possible mural locations by Frederick Kiesler, whose job it was to find appropriate sites.

227 Indeed, as Ethel Schwabacher: Schwabacher, *Arshile Gorky*, p. 48.

227 Gorky never painted *1934*: Francis O'Connor surmises that Gorky was dropped from the PWAP because his studies proved too abstract for the conventional taste of PWAP administrators Juliana Force and her assistant, Lloyd Goodrich, who was later to become a Gorky champion. O'Connor's surmise is given credence by Goodrich's memory of a meeting of museum people and critics at the Whitney Museum on the evening of April 10, 1933. The subject under discussion was subject matter versus abstract form in painting, specifically in painting produced by artists working on government mural projects. Even though no artists had been invited to speak, Gorky was in the audience, and when he heard Goodrich say that representational painting was the best way to communicate human values, he stood up and made a pitch for abstraction. He said that abstract paintings were better suited to modern architecture and that they had the same kind of geometric underpinnings as representational paintings. When it became clear that Gorky had a great deal more to say, Goodrich cut him short. At the time Goodrich felt that Gorky was not being serious, but years later, as he thought about what Gorky had said, he saw that it had merit. "I never should have talked like that to an artist," Goodrich reminisced. "I've always felt badly about it" (Spender, *From a High Place*, pp. 111–12, and Avis Berman, *Rebels on Eighth Street*, p. 376).

27: MARNY GEORGE

228 "He shied away from girls": Raphael Soyer, interview by Karlen Mooradian, 1966.

228 A group of young people: Mrs. Chaim Gross, interview by author, February 1996.

229 "He used to call them": Mariam Davis, interview by Earl Davis.

229 His method of courtship: Elaine de Kooning, interview by Karlen Mooradian, 1965.

229 De Kooning remembered: Willem de Kooning, interview by Karlen Mooradian.

229 "One fell in love": Mooradian, *Worlds*, p. 148.

230 "And I hope that when": Mooradian, *Worlds*, p. 155.

230 "Hell! I don't like": Mischa Reznikoff, interview by Karlen Mooradian, 1966.

230 A love affair, which: Taylor Stoehr, letter to author, January 10, 1995. Stoehr learned of this while working on a book on Paul Goodman, with whom Cerille Miller later became involved.

230 Sometime in the 1930s: Barbara Hale (Mrs. Robert Beverly Hale), conversation with author, June 1995. Barbara Hale said that Rene Oakman was related to her husband, Robert Beverly Hale.

231 "And one day a lovely": Marny George, letter to James Thrall Soby, March 15, 1951.

231 Mischa Reznikoff remembered: Mischa Reznikoff, interview by Karlen Mooradian.

231 At a cocktail party: Spender, *From a High Place*, p. 119.

231 "Here are my grandmother's": Mischa Reznikoff, interview by Karlen Mooradian.

232 "At the wedding I": Helen Sandow, interview by author.

232 "He had felt he could": Schwabacher, *Arshile Gorky*, p. 61.

233 "He had all these": Willem de Kooning, conversation with Allan Stone. Remark repeated to the author in conversation, November 1994.

234 Instead he flew into: Agnes Fielding, interview by author.

234 In the mid-1940s: Julien Levy, letter to Ethel Schwabacher, May 1950.

235 Vartoosh was pregnant: Mooradian, *Worlds*, p. 47.

235 He laughed, held his nephew: Ibid., p. 44.

235 "My husband has no work": Matossian, *Black Angel*, p. 256.

236 "Poor Bill felt so": Mooradian, *Worlds*, pp. 47–48.

236 "I asked for a yogurt": Marjorie Housepian Dobkin, conversation with author, May 10, 2000.

236 Her voice was endlessly: Agnes Fielding, interview by author.

236 "That's when she became": Matossian, *Black Angel*, p. 237.

237 In August he enrolled: The largest of the New Deal art relief programs, the Federal Art Project was part of the Works Progress Administration (WPA), which between 1935 and 1943 hired three million people, only 2 percent of whom worked on cultural projects—others did all kinds of work, including building roads, dams, bridges, airports, hospitals, libraries, sewers, and playgrounds.

237 These connections probably explain why: Because Diller was a passionate advocate for abstract art, the mural division in New York City supported a relatively large number of abstract artists—among them Stuart Davis, Byron Browne, Ilya Bolotowsky, and de Kooning. (De Kooning was on the project for only a year; as a noncitizen, he had to resign.)

238 "O, that guy really knows": Mooradian, *Worlds*, p. 155.

238 The man in the photograph": Agnes Fielding told me this story. The expression "cross cucumber" comes from Spender, *From a High Place*, p. 205.

28: CORINNE

239 In the spring of 1935: Patricia Margaret Richmond, "Michael West: Paintings from the 1940s and 1950s." Richmond said that Gorky and Marny George met in the winter of 1933, but that is unlikely because Corinne Michael West recalled that they had both been divorced, and Gorky did not marry and divorce Marny George until 1934.

239 When her marriage failed: She is listed as Corinne West on the class roster of Hofmann's evening class at the Art Students League for 1932–33. Fellow students in the class included Burgoyne Diller, Harry Holtzman, Leo Lances, George McNeil, Lillian Olinsey (later Kiesler), Mercedes Carles (later Matter), Irene Pereira, Louise Nevelson, and Hazel Smith. She is also listed in the afternoon class, along with some of the same fellow students plus Betty Parsons and Albert Swinden.

239 In notes written decades: Corinne Michael West, "Notes, Gorky." This is a spiral notebook full of notes on Gorky written in 1977, 1978, and 1988. I am grateful to Stuart and Roberta Friedman for allowing me to read Corinne Michael West's papers, which are in their personal archive in Granite Springs, NY. All quotations from Corinne Michael West come from this notebook unless otherwise noted.

240 His paintings were *tremendous*: In a subsequent entry she edited this thought. She said: "Then when Hofmann began painting and showing at the Kootz gallery—such wonderful pictures I was torn between the two. After this experience came Pollock. . . . But Hofmann and Gorky were the basis."

241 In order to impress: Corinne Michael West, notes on Gorky written at the request of Ethel Schwabacher, Whitney Museum of American Art, Artist's File.

242 "When I was there": Corinne Michael West said that the portrait was probably sold to Edmund Greacen, director of the Grand Central School of Art.

243 Gorky told Peter Busa: Peter Busa, notebooks, p. 7.

243 She probably moved: It has been written that Corinne Michael West moved to Rochester with her parents, but it seems more likely that she joined her parents later. Moreover, her notes mention that she borrowed her father's car and drove with Gorky from New York City, where she was living, to Philadelphia for the September 1935 opening of Gorky's exhibition at the Boyer Galleries.

243 "He finally gave me two": On August 3 Gorky sent Corinne a telegram: "Darling taking train Wednesday will arrive Thursday 8 AM. Please have breakfast with me love Arshile."

243 "We planned to marry": West, "Notes on Gorky."

244 "I miss you terribly": Arshile Gorky, letters to Corinne Michael West.

244 The fourth and longest: The passage that Gorky borrowed from Breton and Eluard's *The Immaculate Conception* (translated by Samuel Beckett) is called "Simulation of General Paralysis Essayed" and is one of five "attempted simulations" of various psychotic states in which the authors tried to find out whether a poet might use the language of insanity without losing his mental equilibrium.

244 In his second letter: He wrote:

> My precious love
> Thou my great one whom I adore beautiful as the whole earth and the most beautiful stars of the earth that I adore thou my great woman adored by all the powers of the stars beautiful with the beauty of the thousands of millions of queens who adorn the earth the adoration that I have for thy beauty brings me to my knees to beg thee to think of me I am brought to my knees I adore the ["Simulations" says "thy"] beauty think of me thou my adorable beauty my great beauty whom I adore I roll the diamonds in the moss loftier than the forest whose most lofty hair of thine think of me
> — forget me not my little woman when possible at ingle-nook or the sand of emerald — look at thyself in my hand that keeps me steadfast on the whole world so that thou mayest recognize me for who I am my dark-fair woman my beautiful one my foolish one think of me in paradise my head in my hands.

245 The first is Eluard's: Actually Eluard's poem is called "L'Amoureuse," or "Woman in Love," and it comes from the collection *Mourir de ne pas mourir* (1924):

> She is standing on my lids
> And her hair is in my hair
> She has the colour of my eye
> She has the body of my hand
> In my shade she is engulfed
> As a stone against the sky
>
> She will never close her eyes
> And she does not let me sleep
> And her dreams in the bright day
> Make the suns evaporate
> And me laugh cry and laugh
> Speak when I have nothing to say.

245 Years later, in a letter: Corinne Michael West, letter to Ethel Schwabacher, 1954, in Schwabacher, *Arshile Gorky*, p. 64.

245 Corinne's sister Faith said: Spender, *From a High Place*, p. 155.
246 Schwabacher recalled the end: Schwabacher, *Arshile Gorky*, p. 64.

29: LYRICAL MAN

247 Some months later Gorky: Yenovk Der Hagopian, interview by Karlen Mooradian.
248 "All we spoke about": Mooradian, *Worlds*, p. 176.
248 Around 1936 or 1937: Ibid., p. 164.
248 "Four dollars was a": David Margolis, interview by author, November 6, 1997.
248 "And pretty soon he drew": Ibid.
249 "So we all went": Mooradian, *Worlds*, pp. 113–14.
249 "And when we went out": Ibid.
249 The McCullochs' middle child: David McCulloch, conversation with author, March 28, 2002.
249 "That's why he found it": Mooradian, *Worlds*, pp. 167–68.
249–250 The result of this endeavor: When the stone head was exhibited in Gorky's memorial show in 1948 it was titled *Sculptured Head* and dated 1932.
250 "We started one but": Mooradian, *Worlds*, p. 138.
250 He went back about eight: Ibid., p. 204, Saul Schary, interview by Karlen Mooradian, 1965.
251 "And he would love": Greene, "Memories of Arshile Gorky," pp. 108–10.
251 "And this he could": Mooradian, *Worlds*, pp. 107–08.
251 When Gorky discovered that: Lewis Balamuth, "I Met A. Gorky," pp. 2–3.
252 Gorky shouted back: Joseph Solman, interview by author.

30: THE ARTISTS' UNION AND THE AMERICAN ABSTRACT ARTISTS

255 In the early 1930s: Soon there were artists' unions in cities across the country. Their principal function was to serve as collective bargaining agencies for artists employed on government art projects. They fought for expansion of those projects, and they struggled to prevent conservative congressmen from reducing annual appropriations. They also worked to broaden the audience for American art. To this end, the New York City Artists' Union pushed for the formation of a municipal art gallery, which was inaugurated by Mayor La Guardia on January 6, 1936, and it published *Art Front*, whose first editor was Stuart Davis.
255 "It took four men": Stuart Davis, interview by Harlan Phillips, 1962, pp. 318–19. I am grateful to Earl Davis for permission to read this transcript.
256 "He loved creating": Rosalind Bengelsdorf Browne, interview by Karlen Mooradian, 1966.
256 After listening for a while: Dorothy Dehner, interview by Garnett McCoy, 1966, p. 21. Quoted in Spender, *From a High Place*, p. 129.
257 "Gorky was a touching": Bernarda Bryson Shahn, telephone conversation with author, June 4, 1997.

257 Gorky gave several lectures: Mooradian, *Worlds*, p. 113. In a photograph of Gorky and de Kooning taken around 1935, a small painting of half an apple is propped on Gorky's easel. Jim Jordan surmises that Gorky used the apple painting (which he cut from a larger canvas and attached to a piece of wood) as a tool to illustrate his ideas about Cubism.

257 "I wanted Gorky with me": Greene, "Memories of Arshile Gorky," pp. 109–10.

258 "And so it was a very": Willem de Kooning, interview by Bruce Hooten, pp. 15–16.

258 Since it was Gorky: Mercedes Carles Matter, interview by author.

259 "Our friendship terminated": Davis, "Arshile Gorky in the 1930s," p. 58.

259 "He wasn't a joiner": Mariam Davis, interview by Earl Davis. Stuart Davis's final break with Gorky may also have been related to Gorky's lack of enthusiasm for the Artists' Congress (Greene, "Memories of Arshile Gorky," p. 110). Greene found Gorky's attitude toward social issues "supercilious" and "playful." It was, he said, "a period in which orthodoxy of political views was spreading like cancer. Gorky declaiming like a prophet about plastic qualities in paint was in a sense a beacon to innumerable Union 'followers.' . . . I'm sure that his absolute allegiance to quality in a world of art and his own personal devotion to the act of painting kept him from being distrusted or disliked—except on the higher managerial levels . . . It was a time of paper organizations with their letterheads of sponsoring celebrities, issued one every minute—publicity throwaways, and nothing else. Gorky declined such advertising."

260 Their purpose, as one critic: Quoted in Irving Sandler, *The Triumph of American Painting: A History of Abstract Expressionism*, p. 23.

260 As George McNeil recalled: McNeil, "American Abstractionists Venerable at Twenty," p. 64.

260 With the idea of setting: Besides Gorky, Holtzman, Lassaw, McNeil, Bengelsdorf, Browne, Swinden, Burgoyne Diller, and Balcomb and Gertrude Greene, there were de Kooning, Giorgio Cavallon, Mercedes Carles, Josef Albers, Bolotowsky, A. N. Christie, Werner Drewes, Ray Kaiser, Paul Kelpe, Leo Lances, Alice Mason, George L. K. Morris, John Opper, Esphyr Slobodkina, Richard Taylor, R. D. Trumbull, Vaclav Vytlacil, and Wilfred Zogbaum.

261 "After a while, the bunch": Mooradian, *Worlds*, pp. 109–10. In "American Abstractionists Venerable at Twenty," George McNeil remembered Gorky's playing teacher a little differently:

> With his extraordinary magnetism and drive, Arshile Gorky argued, cajoled and threatened for a dynamic manifesto type of movement. He proposed that everyone paint an electric-bulb, a piece of string and only one other object in red, black and white. At the next meeting, when these paintings were to be criticized (mainly by Gorky), only two or three works were brought in. Characteristically, Gorky did not submit a painting. During the ensuing clamor, Gorky admit-

ted that he was to be the leader; he was roundly rebuked, and he then dramatically walked out of the studio and the group. However, though he never exhibited with the A.A.A. [American Abstract Artists], Gorky continued to fraternize with individual members.

Mercedes Carles said that Gorky told everyone to paint a red, black, and white painting but that "no one did, and so Gorky resigned and left. He wanted the American Abstract Artists to become an art movement" (Mercedes Carles Matter, interview by author).

261 "But first you have to": Mooradian, *Worlds*, p. 110, and Susan C. Larsen, "The Quest for an American Abstract Tradition, 1927–1944," in Museum of Art, Carnegie Institute, *Abstract Painting and Sculpture in America*, p. 36.

262 Gorky and de Kooning were: The group's prospectus, issued later that month, said that the American Abstract Artists hoped to improve the situation for the abstract artist "(1) by providing a center for the exchange of ideas, the comparison of works, the clarification of new tendencies or directions etc., and (2) by giving the individual artist the chance to exhibit his own work at a minimum of expense" (Larsen, "Quest for an American Abstract Tradition," p. 36).

262 The opening night was a: McNeil, "American Abstractionists Venerable at Twenty," p. 65.

262 Mercedes Matter recalled: Mercedes Carles Matter, interview by author.

· 262 "The only difference is": Karlen Mooradian in *Worlds* transcribed Bolotowsky's words as "we all steal from the masses," but, given the context of what Gorky was saying, he clearly misheard.

262 "Flat things irritated": Quoted in Larsen, "Quest for an American Abstract Tradition," pp. 29–30.

262 Harry Holtzman expressed: Sandler, *Triumph of American Painting*, p. 26, n. 27.

263 "The uptown people were": Mercedes Carles Matter, interview by author.

51: THE NEWARK AIRPORT MURALS

264 Burgoyne Diller recalled: Burgoyne Diller, interview by Harlan Phillips, p. 34.

264 Accompanied by Davis, Gorky: As Diller recalled in an undated note written to help Ethel Schwabacher with her Gorky monograph, Gorky's Floyd Bennett Field mural was intended to be "a montage of photo enlargements and painting designed by Gorky." Wyatt Davis's contribution was, Diller said, the provision of "photographic material of planes, plane parts—hangars and like material." Gorky's collage study incorporating Davis's photographs is lost but recorded in a photograph. See *Murals without Walls*, p. 58.

264 Barr responded the following: McMahon's letter and Barr's response are in the Whitney Museum of American Art, Artist's File.

265 Reviewing the show: Undated clipping in the Guild Art Gallery Papers.

265 "After the applause": Edwin Denby, untitled essay in Poindexter Gallery, *The 30's*, n.p.

265 The most reliable source: Whitney Museum of American Art, Artist's File.
265 Gorky explained that he'd been: Peter Busa, interview by Jack Taylor.
266 Soon after this encounter: Francis V. O'Connor, "Arshile Gorky's Newark Airport Murals," in Newark Museum, *Murals Without Walls*, p. 24.
266 Years later, Burgoyne Diller: Burgoyne Diller, interview by Harlan Phillips, p. 34. Floyd Bennett Field was a pet project of the mayor's, and after Gorky and La Guardia's confrontation, it was out of the question as a site for Gorky's mural. Diller said:

> There wasn't too much of a debate on it [Gorky's mural proposal] before we presented it to the mayor for his approval because Floyd Bennett Airport was his baby. We felt we really—the Commissioner of Docks had approved it, everybody had approved it all along the line, but then we went to see La Guardia at the opening of the first Federal Art Gallery in New York City. It was on 39th [actually 38th] Street. He came in with a group of his commissioners. It was all very impressive. He stood in front of Gorky's mural sketches and said, "Well, this is Tammany Hall politicians." So the Commissioner of Docks called me the next day and he said "You heard him?" I said, "Yes, the project is dead, because of La Guardia's baby."
> . . . We picked up the pieces, keeping the same theme, discarding the idea of using the photographs at all, but having Gorky utilize the motif, because at the time this was not alien to what he would be interested in doing. He never was completely a nonobjective painter, although he got really interested in this. Then we made preparations hoping to get a mural at Newark Airport, and it was accepted there, in spite of La Guardia, and we put it up in a more forward-looking environment.

In his note for Ethel Schwabacher, Diller said, "La Guardia's comment 'If this is art I am a Tammany hall politician' was enough to have the project dropped by the Dept. of Docks—in charge of La Guardia Airport." He surely meant Floyd Bennett Field. In fact, according to the *Herald Tribune*'s report, the mayor's comment about being a Tammany politician was made in response not to Gorky's mural study but to a mural study by abstractionist Albert Swinden.

266 By the end of January 1936: O'Connor, "Arshile Gorky's Newark Airport Murals," pp. 21–22.
266 "He was doing too much": Ibid., p. 206.
266 Sometime in late spring: Mariam Davis, Wyatt Davis's widow, recalls that the assignment for Wyatt and Gorky to make a photomural together didn't work out because "Gorky decided he wanted the painting without the photographs. He didn't tell Wyatt. Wyatt had made lots of photo blowups of engines and tools for the mural. Gorky didn't want any of the photographs. He got the painting all slicked up and finished it. But Wyatt took all the photographs he had taken and made a mural for the Newark Airport. They gave

him a wall. It's in an alcove. Wyatt was mad at Gorky for a while, but when he got the assignment for his photographic mural he decided it was just as well."

266 By August 1936 his designs: Most of the Newark Art Commission's members were conservative in their approach to art, but fortunately for Gorky two important members were sympathetic to modernism. On September 30 the *Newark Evening News* reported: "Judging from unofficial accounts the meeting last month of sponsors and Federal Art heads at which the murals were tentatively accepted must have been worth the price of admission. Faced by the superior art background of such judges as Miss Beatrice Winser, director of the Newark Museum, and Dr. Frank Kingdon, president of Newark University, airport officials voiced their disapproval with such preliminaries as 'I don't know anything about art but. . . .' "

266 "That unleashed the devil": "Poverty, Politics and Artists: 1930–1945," p. 99.

267 By mid-September, when: The museum showed the *Activities on the Field* panel, the scale model of the Administration Building foyer, and eight photographs illustrating the derivation of Gorky's semiabstract shapes.

267 The *Newark Evening News* reported: September 30, 1936. The idea of removable murals was in the air for, as Frederick Kiesler's December *Art Front* article entitled "Murals without Walls: Relating to Gorky's Newark Project" noted, the reason Gorky and other FAP muralists made murals that were really oil paintings on canvas affixed to walls was that the murals could be moved if the building was torn down.

267 It is inappropriate to wait: Olive M. Lyford, letter to Alfred H. Barr, October 2, 1936, and Alfred H. Barr, letter to Olive M. Lyford, October 14, 1936.

267 Perhaps to create a better: The three-page typed fact sheet is in the Newark Museum Library. After several paragraphs of curriculum vitae, complete with the usual misinformation about birth and education, the statement says:

> *Philosophy of Painting*: Gorky's ideas are very interesting and based on an apparently wide knowledge of painting and esthetics. His method is perhaps inclined to be mystical; but he is aware of the complex problems, technical, formal and social, confronting the artist today. In his mural he has sought to express his concern with these problems.
>
> These problems fundamentally, from Gorky's point of view, revolve around the question of space. This is space not in a Kantian metaphysical sense, but in the sense that in the plastic arts a form, a shape, an object, must logically occupy a given space. The predominant concern of the painter, therefore, from this point of view, is to achieve this occupation of space by an object by means proper to the medium of painting.
>
> From this point of view, also, sheerly technical considerations are of secondary importance. How, asks Gorky, can an artist give himself exclusively to problems of grinding pigment or using an air-brush or some kind of new paint, when the all-obsessing problem of form in

space has not been solved? This means in his case that he is not interested abstractly in materials. Yet he *is* interested in technic [sic] as a method of creating form. And he adds, how can one separate method from the artist's intention and creation?

In his designs for the Newark Airport, Gorky has concerned himself with forms derived from aviation and from the airplane. But since scientific invention is ever changing, he does not wish to use these forms in a literal spirit, because the airplanes of today will be obsolete in a few years, but a mural should certainly be able to speak to people of the future in a language above the purely topical idiom. So it is the forms of an airplane in an abstract and essential mood which Gorky has utilized in his designs, wings seen as almost straight lines, as they actually look when viewed in profile, a rudder, an aileron, an instrument board, a wheel, a lamp, a cylinder, insignia from the under-wings and from the fuselage, all distilled to their ultimate expression.

With these forms he seeks to occupy the space given him, the walls allocated to the mural. These spaces are rectangular, they are two dimensional, they are solid constructions of masonry. And the artist must not violate their essential function, which is a supporting and protecting one. Therefore his design must not seem to break through the wall or to shatter the wall; his design must really occupy the space it is intended for and not seek to move outward in a three-dimensional disruptive way.

Yet since the artist has a theme, "Aviation," he must create more than the inanimate forms of his subject matter; he must create also the mood of aviation, of flying. This mood is suspension in space, the sense of objects floating in space. And moreover this mood is bound to be colored by that thing which differentiates the 20th century from the 19th, the technical and scientific integrations involved in the machine. This differentia Gorky calls "the operation of our time." And he amplifies this by explaining how the original material is lost through this operation, as the linen or raw silk of the wing's fuselage becomes not a textile but a sustaining member of the heavier-than-air flying machine. For this it is necessary, he states, to have a dialectical organization of forms so that "the beautiful miracle of our times, the miracle of the engineer, of the scientist, of the artist" may be fully realized in the painting. Here obviously those qualities of his being which made him study to be a civil engineer express themselves. [Gorky told the author of the fact sheet that he had studied civil engineering at Brown University.]

The intellectually stimulating aspect of Gorky's equipment for painting this mural is suggested when he quotes Heraclitus as writing that a part is more beautiful than the whole. Here indeed is the keynote of abstract painting, this insistence that metonymy is a legitimate device of the painter as it is of the rhetorician. This quality of Gorky's mind is again revealed when he speaks enthusiastically of

Hogarth's "Analysis of Beauty" as being the forefather of modern painting. And one understands more of his principles when he mentions his heroes in painting, Paolo Uccello, Ingres, David, Picasso.

From this it is evident that Gorky is a modern painter. He himself explains, when queried as to what prizes he has won, "Do modern painters ever win prizes at the salons?" But what is "modern"? In an obvious sense modern is cubist or abstract. But there is more to the modern spirit in painting than a style. This Gorky insists on. Actually he would say that "modern" means a certain way of looking at life in this transitional period. It means observing the outside world which surrounds the artist, but observing it not in terms of memory, nostalgia or association, but in terms of its own forms and textures. This means that the modern painter does not go back to Piero della Francesca for his inspiration, or his organization of form; instead he uses the discoveries "of our ancestors, [such] as Picasso" to continue that exploration of experience which is the artist's function. "How," asks Gorky, "can I understand those men of another century when I can't even understand the world today?"

268 Cavallon's principal contribution: Elena Cimenti, "Giorgio Cavallon: 1932–1960," pp. 46–47. I am grateful to Elena Cimenti for translating the lines in her dissertation that discuss Gorky.

268 "I remember one morning": Thomas B. Hess, "Arshile Gorky Flies Again."

268 "Every time, he found": Giorgio Cavallon, interview by Karlen Mooradian, 1966.

268 Naturally, he beat out: Arnold Blanch, interview by Dorothy Seckler, June 13, 1963.

268 Indeed, they were affixed to the wall twice: The adhesive was probably the same plastic glue that did not adhere properly when used for Edward Laning's Ellis Island mural in fall 1935. In his memoir about the WPA mural projects, Laning said that Raphael Doktar, the project's technical supervisor, rejected as too old-fashioned Laning's suggestion that they use white lead adhesive for mounting his mural. Doktor told the technical crew to use a new plastic adhesive. When the plastic adhesive dried it left bumps and hollows in the canvas. Laning's remaining panels were affixed with lead glue instead (Edward Laning, "The New Deal Mural Projects," in O'Connor, *The New Deal Art Projects*, p. 96).

268 In August 1937 Gorky: Arshile Gorky, letters to Vartoosh, trans. Haig Partizian. In fact, Gorky did not have to paint the murals again.

269 "She'll soon be O.K.": Partizian translation. I have used Partizian's translation except where other translations have greater clarity.

269 Texaco's red star logo: Jim Jordan, "The Place of the Newark Murals in Gorky's Art," in Newark Museum, *Murals without Walls*, p. 63, n. 6.

269 Gorky was asked to: Karal Ann Marling, *Wall-to-Wall America: A Cultural History of Post-Office Murals in the Great Depression*, Minneapolis, 1982, p. 48.

270 The *Newark Ledger* had the last: Newark Museum, *Murals without Walls*, p. 39. All these newspaper clippings are on file at the Newark Museum Library.

270 During World War II: In 1972 Ruth Bowman, then curator of New York University's art collection, began to search for the lost murals. The discovery of a thread from one of the canvas panels protruding from a nail hole led to the recovery of two of the ten panels. The other eight panels are thought to have been detached from the wall, rolled up, and stored. One Newark employee told Ruth Bowman that he saw the panels being taken to the local dump (Ruth Bowman, conversation with author, 1995).

271 In November 1936 Gorky: *Art for the Millions* was finally published in 1973 by Boston's New York Graphic Society. Francis V. O'Connor was the editor. Gorky's essay exists in holographic draft. Its graceful and clear prose suggests that Gorky sought editorial assistance. A much-edited version was prepared by the WPA/FAP. The editor, probably the editor of the whole report, Emanuel M. Benson, eliminated several paragraphs from the beginning of Gorky's essay—no doubt he found Gorky's description of an Armenian Lenten calendar too poetic and way off the point. Benson added an introduction, a kind of press release, whose ideas appear to be drawn from the 1936 fact sheet on Gorky and his mural now in the Newark Museum Library.

271 Taking the object out: Gorky, "My Murals for the Newark Airport."

274 "The enormous becoming normal": Ibid. The quotation from Arthur Rimbaud comes from his letter to Paul Demeny, May 15, 1871. The original reads: "Le poète définirait la quantité d'inconnu s'éveillant en son temps dans l'âme universelle: il donnerait plus que la formule de sa pensée, que l'annotation de sa marché au Progrès! Enormité devenant norme, absorbée par tous, il serait vraiment un multiplicateur de progrès!" (quoted in O'Connor, *Art for the Millions*, p. 73, n. 2). The version of Gorky's essay published in *Art for the Millions* is close to the holograph manuscript (discovered after the publication of *Art for the Millions*), except that it has been lightly edited, probably by Emanuel Benson.

274 For his murals' subject: Olive Lyford's report laid out the murals' subject matter—the history of aviation. The photomurals planned for the large second-floor foyer would depict "forms which have evolved from aerodynamic limitations; in other words, with the advent of the science of aviation, new forms came into being." Lyford went on to outline the themes to be portrayed. Gorky would follow her outline in choosing his subject matter, which he described as: "The early development of forms considered by inventors from the earliest records, to the successful flight of the first plane. Modern developments showing the phases through which plane design has passed since the first plane was built, to the present. The mechanics of flying: the instruments, characteristic forms of airplane construction and flying, including related sciences such as meteorology and communication. The activities on the field showing all general daily routine in active life as seen about Newark Airport" (O'Connor, "Arshile Gorky's Newark Airport Murals," pp. 21–22).

275 In addition, Gorky surely saw: The press release for Gorky's first lecture at the

Guild Art Gallery on November 24, 1935, said that the lecture was arranged in response to the "interest aroused by the recent exhibition of the works of Fernand Léger at the Museum of Modern Art." If Gorky talked about Léger in his lecture, he undoubtedly saw Léger's show.

275 The lamppost that bisects: Jordan, Cat. Rais., p. 61.

275 The bracing example of: Waldman, *Arshile Gorky*, p. 38.

275 Elaine de Kooning recalled: de Kooning, "Gorky: Painter of His Own Legend," p. 40.

276 "He used oil paint": Frederick T. Kiesler, "Murals without Walls," p. 10.

276 *Organization* is based on: Indeed, Gorky knew *Painter and Model* intimately, for once when he was baby-sitting for the Janises' sons, the youngest boy drew on it. Carroll Janis (b. 1931) remembers making chalk marks over an area of black in the lower right corner of the painting. Recently he recalled: "It wasn't a scribble. It was adding color to the lower part of the painter's chair where Picasso had had color, but the color was suppressed under black and white." Lovingly Gorky cleaned Carroll's marks off the canvas (Carroll Janis, conversation with author, February 1999).

277 "That's worth a lot of money": Mooradian, *Worlds*, p. 140.

277 To his old friend: Max Schnitzler, interview by Karlen Mooradian.

277 To Rose's astonishment, Gorky: Spender, *From a High Place*, p. 150.

277 Other artists were admiring: Mooradian, *Worlds*, p. 155.

278 Gorky squeezed out paint: Davis, "Arshile Gorky in the 1930s," p. 57.

278 "See the excitement": Raoul Hague, interview by Karlen Mooradian.

278 David Smith remembered: From David Smith's journal in the *Archives of American Art Journal*, April 1968.

278 "He used to walk away": Mooradian, *Worlds*, p. 165.

278 "He fought it, he burned": Ibid., p. 208.

279 "The issue about physical": Greene, "Memories of Arshile Gorky," p. 110.

279 "Coat after coat": Willem de Kooning, interview by Karlen Mooradian.

280 We do not know what kind: Waldman, *Arshile Gorky*, pp. 44–45. The Picasso drawing in the collection of Mr. and Mrs. Victor Ganz is illustrated as figure 35.

32: "DEEPER AND PURER WORK"

282 "Ever your affectionate": Marderosian and Kucuikian translation.

282 "As I had written to you": In February 1937 a photograph of Gorky working on his Newark murals was published in *Architectural Record* to accompany an article by Frederick Keisler entitled "An Architect in Search of. . . ."

282 "Yes, I did sell two": The painting Gorky sold to Ethel Schwabacher could have been one of four paintings from this period that she acquired in the second half of the 1930s. Among these are two small canvases from about 1936–37 that explore the same theme. One is entitled *Battle at Sunset with the God of the Maize*, the other is untitled (Jordan, Cat. Rais., nos. 150 and 151). She and her husband also bought the version of the *Khorkom* series that is now in the Anderson collection and a variant called *Composition*, also

called *Still Life* (1936–38), and a small untitled abstraction related to the Sochi theme (c. 1937–38).

283 "With love and kisses": Partizian translation.

283 "There was an unresolved": Isobel Grossman, "If Memory Serves," in University of Texas at Austin, *Arshile Gorky: Drawings to Paintings*, pp. 11–12.

284 On the morning of May 12, 1937: Marderosian and Kucuikian translation.

284 He told his sister: Mooradian, *Worlds*, pp. 251–252.

284 Schwabacher wrote to Gorky: Whitney Museum of American Art, Artist's File.

284 The following August, Gorky: Mooradian, *Worlds*, p. 255.

284 Conflicts between father and son: Spender, *From a High Place*, pp. 177–78.

285 "She ran away": Partizian translation.

285 "Oh, I miss you": Partizian translation.

285 In a January 1, 1938: Marderosian and Kucuikian translation.

286 "I tell him": Mooradian, AGA, pp. 253–55.

286 The series is based: That these drawings evolved out of *Nighttime, Enigma and Nostalgia* can be seen by looking at two transitional drawings, one in graphite on paper, c. 1932–34, the other, c. 1933 to 1936, done in black and brown ink, with the cross-hatchings blurred with an ink wash (Princeton University Art Museum and Stephen Mazoh gallery, exhibition catalog nos. 33 and 32).

287 They are lighter in: Gorky wrote "A. Gorky 36" on the front of the canvas and "Gorky/1930–1936" on the back of the canvas. The latter inscription probably reflects the long period during which he kept reworking *Image in Khorkom*.

287 Instead it is a separate: If Gorky got the idea for the black lines from the lines that indicate tears in Picasso's 1937 series of weeping women, and if the Albright-Knox version of *Khorkom* is indeed c. 1936, then Gorky must have added the black lines after the Albright-Knox version was mostly finished. Gorky's New Year's Day 1938 letter to Vartoosh indicates that he was still making changes on this painting.

288 "But I have to finish": Partizian translation.

289 Art historian William Rubin: William Rubin, "Arshile Gorky, Surrealism, and the New American Painting," p. 379.

289 Sources in Picasso's 1934: Ibid. and Jordan, Cat. Rais., p. 323.

289 "I desire to create": Mooradian, AGA, p. 255.

289 "It required considerable time": Ibid., p. 257.

289 In *Summer in Sochi, Black Sea*: The painting also closely resembles three paintings on the theme of *Battle at Sunset with the God of the Maize*, (all c. 1936 or 1937).

290 Mougouch said of *Apricots*: Jordan, Cat. Rais., p. 364.

290 They recall the women: Three other paintings confirm the interpretation. The first is an untitled 1939 painting in Stephen Mazoh's collection in which a figure with a curved, upraised arm and a wide head closely resembles the figure on the left in *Argula*. Above her is a semiabstract bird head and tail just like the one in the upper left corner of *Argula*. The second ex-

ample is an untitled oil on cardboard (Jordan, Cat. Rais., no. 225). Agnes Fielding recalled that "Gorky made many of these paintings, which he called 'Valentines,' on the boards placed inside shirts returned from the laundry. He gave them away to people who came to dinner (or when we went out!). These were kept by the door on a shelf where they could easily be reached as he was saying good night." In this particular "valentine," the two female figures flanking a boot/butter churn recall Miró's personages in his molten landscapes of 1935 to 1936 (see, for example, Miró's *Nocturne* in the Roland Penrose collection). As in the *Garden in Sochi* series, the boot/butter churn hangs from a vertical entering from the top of the picture, and a ball is poised above one of the boot/butter churn's pointed ends. The third example that confirms the identification of the figures in *Argula* as female, is *Composition* (c. 1939–41, Jordan, Cat. Rais., no. 226). The two figures and the bird from *Argula* reappear on either side of a boot/butter churn-cum-ball that is suspended from the top edge of the painting. The boot/butter churn now takes on its typical *Garden in Sochi* shape and, as in that series, it has a feathery embryonic creature inside. The woman on the right, who holds the line that attaches the ball to the boot/butter churn, now has curious legs that have metamorphosed out of what was a kind of bird head/chariot in *Argula*.

291 As a result, images: Gorky had known about Byzantine mosaics ever since his months in Constantinople when he was nineteen or twenty. Russian icons he knew through books. The murals he saw in churches in Van did not have gold: vestiges of murals at Akhtamar and Varag were, even in Gorky's time, mostly faded blues and reds.

33: ARMENIAN PORTRAITS

292 "You could tell as": Mooradian, *Worlds*, p. 175.

292 "And he knew he was": Ibid., pp. 139–40. It is possible that Karlen Mooradian changed the wording in the transcripts of his interviews in order to make Gorky seem more articulate about his attachment to his Armenian heritage. In listening to the tape of Mooradian's interview with Raoul Hague, for example, I did not hear Hague saying: "He had tears in his eyes when he spoke of Van. . . . Because he had Van in him," but this is what Hague says in Mooradian's transcript of his interview in *Worlds* (p. 148). Any of the following quotations from *Worlds* may have been edited or rewritten by Mooradian. The Diocese of the Armenian Church in America has granted only limited access to Karlen Mooradian's taped interviews.

292 "He was uprooted by": Aristodimos Kaldis, interview by Karlen Mooradian, 1966.

292 "His images were always": Isamu Noguchi, interview by Karlen Mooradian, 1966. See also Mooradian, *Worlds*, p. 181.

292 "You felt it all": Mooradian, *Worlds*, p. 151.

293 When he talked about his: Ibid., p. 132, and Hooton, "One Who Saw First," p. 4.

293 "Why should he worry": de Kooning, interview by Bruce Hooton, April 1, 1981.

293 "Somehow, you felt that he": Ibid., p. 195.

293 Jacob Kainen saw another side: Jacob Kainen, interview by Avis Berman, 1982, and Kainen, "Memories of Arshile Gorky," p. 98.

293 In Harold Rosenberg's view: Rosenberg, *Arshile Gorky*, pp. 92–93.

294 Vartoosh, who sat for him: Mooradian, *Worlds*, p. 41.

294 *Portrait of Vartoosh*: Mooradian, *Worlds*, p. 45.

294 "I was often with Gorky": Willem de Kooning, interview by Harold Rosenberg, *Art News*, September 1972, reprinted in Rosenberg, *De Kooning*, p. 49. Gorky's emphasis on pink and flesh color was shared by de Kooning, whose portraits of the late 1930s and early 1940s owe much to Gorky in the way parts of the anatomy—especially the shoulder and arm—are separated out and become almost abstract. De Kooning's abstractions of 1938 to 1941 were influenced by Gorky as well. The swooping curvilinear shapes in his *Elegy* (c. 1939), for example, are close to Gorky's shapes in the *Garden in Sochi* series of the late 1930s and early 1940s. And, like Gorky, de Kooning produced portrait drawings inspired by Ingres. His *Self-Portrait with Imaginary Brother* (c. 1938) is closely related to Gorky's several contemporaneous studies for *The Artist and His Mother*. Perhaps de Kooning took the idea of the imaginary companion from Gorky's *Portrait of Myself and an Imaginary Wife*. In any case, the relationship between the taller and the smaller brothers in de Kooning's drawing seems to reflect the fraternal relationship between Gorky and de Kooning in those years.

295 Gorky was delighted to see: Matisse's *Laurette in a White Blouse* was dated 1916 and called *Lorette* in the exhibition catalog.

296 This may be a spoof: David Burliuk's painting *In Moses Soyer Studio* is reproduced in *Color and Rhyme*, 1945.

296 "A gentle fellow, actually": Mooradian, *Worlds*, p. 212.

296 "How he kept it in": Ibid, p. 99.

296 On one of his visits: Raphael Soyer, *Homage to Thomas Eakins*, p. 146.

297 "I may someday": Mooradian, *Worlds*, p. 100.

297 De Kooning once observed: de Kooning, interview by Karlen Mooradian.

297 Soon after they met: Kainen, "Memories of Arshile Gorky," p. 97. See also Kainen, "Posing for Gorky: A Memoir of the New York Master," and Kainen, interview by Avis Berman.

298 He told Kainen how: Kainen, "Memories of Arshile Gorky," p. 96. See also Kainen, "Posing for Gorky," and interview by Avis Berman.

298 He held his big palette: Kainen, interview by Avis Berman.

298 Mougouch said that she: Jordan, Cat. Rais., p. 247.

298 "I caught a last glimpse": Kainen, "Memories of Arshile Gorky," p. 97.

299 "When I come there, my dear": Marderosian and Kucuikian translation. Gorky probably refers to the drawing of his mother now in the Art Institute of Chicago.

299 Ethel Schwabacher got it right: Schwabacher, *Arshile Gorky*, p. 36.

34: THE END OF THE DECADE

301 A still life of Gorky's: According to his curriculum vitae he had a one-man show at the Boyer Gallery in November, but the show probably did not take place. No record of it exists, and though Boyer had opened a gallery in New York in December 1936 with a show that included Gorky, he soon went into debt and his gallery disappeared.

301 "The students looked at him": Mooradian, *Worlds*, pp. 161–62 and Conrad Marcarelli, interview by Karlen Mooradian, 1966.

301 In his April 18, 1938, letter: Marderosian and Kucuikian translation.

302 Although Parisians were enthusiastic: James Thrall Soby, "Does Our Art Impress Europe?" *Saturday Review of Literature*, August 6, 1950, p. 143.

302 But James Johnson Sweeny: James Johnson Sweeny, "L' art contemporain aux Etats-Unis," *Cahiers d'Art* 13 (1938): 51, 63.

303 "Her father didn't think": Helen Sandow, interview by author.

303 "And now I understand": Spender, *From a High Place*, p. 191.

303 "A romance": Matossian, *Black Angel*, p. 287.

303 "I mean it was right": Willem de Kooning, interview by Karlen Mooradian.

304 But Hague knew better: Raoul Hague, interview by Karlen Mooradian.

304 In Giorgio Cavallon's view: Cimenti, "Giorgio Cavallon," p. 47. Gorky's window was a "severe abstraction" using "facets of black and extremely primary colors," recalled Peter Busa, who, along with the abstract painter Jean Xercon, was assigned to paint a mural in another part of the chapel. When the priest in charge at Rikers Island saw the cartoons for Busa's mural, which Busa described as an altarpiece, he asked Busa to paint in the haloes. Busa refused, and his project never saw completion. Gorky's project may have collapsed for similar reasons, or perhaps it was not finished because, as Cavallon said, Gorky drank so much when Leonore Gallet left him that he could not focus on his work (Peter Busa, interview by Karlen Mooradian, and interview by Jack Taylor, p. 11; see also Browne, "The American Abstract Artists and the WPA Federal Art Project," p. 235).

304 "He suffered a lot": Giorgio Cavallon, interview by Karlen Mooradian.

304 There were several uncompleted: A commission for murals in a restaurant was secured for Gorky by the architect William Lescaze. The subject, Agnes Fielding recalls, was either Moors or Turks, and Gorky made gouache studies, but the project fell through. Another project is recorded only in a statement that Gorky made about a proposed mural that is in Agnes Fielding's personal archive. The statement is dated 1939 and it is written in awkward capital letters with two words crossed out: " 'Concise statement of project' To attempt to evolve a form of abstract painting free from foreign influences; to reveal in new designs, form and color the sources of American cultural traditions; to interpret in abstract form the art and customs of the American Indian, the pioneer, the ranch, farm and folk-life in this country." Gorky would have had to go against his deep-seated belief in cultural internationalism to have concocted such a statement. To be "free from foreign influences" was hardly the goal of this worshiper of European tradition. His attempt to sound

like one of the regionalists who were so successful in the Depression years suggests how desperate artists were to secure public art commissions.

304 Gorky's earliest mention: Partizian translation. The Marderosian and Ku-cuikian translation reads: "I'll draw [paint] a portrait and after that a big mu-ral which if it works will be very beautiful."

304 "I am always thinking": Partizian translation.

305 "So, I've been working": Partizian translation.

305 In late February 1938: Marderosian and Kucuikian translation.

305 In May Gorky's mural proposal: In securing the World's Fair commission Gorky was helped by Burgoyne Diller, who, with Holger Cahill and Audrey McMahon, was very much involved with art at the fair. Diller extolled Gorky's work to the architect William Lescaze, who was himself already a Gorky admirer, having seen Gorky's work in exhibitions and at Newark (William Lescaze, letter to Wolfgang Schwabacher, January 13, 1949). Ca-hill recommended a liberal approach to art and architecture. Art at the fair, he said, should give a picture of American art's development and show how industry had improved the quality of American life.

By 1937 the WPA/FAP had made specific recommendations, among them that artists on the project decorate various state buildings at the fair. The theme of the fair as stated in a booklet put out by the Publicity Depart-ment in 1939 was: "To contribute to A Happier Way of American Living by demonstrating how it can be achieved through the growing interdependence of men of every class and function, and by showing the things, ideas and forces at work in the world which are the Tools of Today and with which the better World of Tomorrow is to be built" (Olive Lyford Gavert, "The WPA Federal Art Project and the New York World's Fair, 1939–1940," in O'Con-nor, *The New Deal Art Projects*, p. 250). If Gorky had to concoct statements along these lines to accompany his proposals for murals at the World's Fair, it must have been a struggle.

305 "Your loving brother, Gorky": Partizian translation.

306 "The bank already knew that": Partizian translation.

306 "Dear Murad as you know": Arshile Gorky, letter to Moorad Mooradian, c. May 1939. Marderosian and Kucuikian translation.

306 "That will be much better": Marderosian and Kucuikian translation.

306 At this point, with the United States: In 1942 the WPA became the Graphic Section of the War Services Division. Mural painters were put to work de-signing and executing camouflage patterns for tanks and ships, and graphic artists made posters. Finally in 1943, with the country focused on the war ef-fort and with the economic recovery that accompanied its entering the war, the project was liquidated.

306 He asked Holger Cahill: To Max Weber, he wrote on October 21, 1939:

> Dear Mr. Weber
>   With a warm clasp of your hand, may I ask your kind permission to use your name as a reference in applying for a fellowship of the Guggenheim Foundation?

I do not know anyone whose approval of my work, has been a greater source of hope and encouragement than yours. Therefore I am taking this privilige of asking you to offer a recommandation for me should it be requested.

I remember with fondness the day we spent together at the museum — and I have read, and re-read with profound emotion the beautiful book of your poems and wood cuts wich you sent me. I feel deeply honored to have the rare privilege of possesing it.

Will you answer me?

Yours, in all sincerity
Arshile Gorky

307 When the World's Fair opened: *World's Fair 1939: Painting and Sculpture in the World of Tomorrow.*

307 When the young Agnes Magruder met him: Mougouch Phillips (Agnes Fielding), letter to Patricia Passloff in Poindexter Gallery, *The 30's.*

307 In one of his letters to Vartoosh: Arshile Gorky, undated letter to Vartoosh Mooradian, probably 1939.

308 "Towards the end of the 30's": Mougouch Phillips, letter to Patricia Passloff.

308 "Only afterward I was told": Dorothea Tanning, *Birthday Party,* p. 73.

309 "Your loved brother Gorghi": Marderosian and Kucuikian translation.

309 "My dear I have to tell you": Spender, *In a High Place,* p. 193.

309 "I too feel lonely": Marderosian and Kucuikian translation. Karlen Mooradian dates the letter July 1, 1939.

310 "He was being a bit funny": Mooradian, *Worlds,* pp. 106–07.

310 "That's all I want to say": Raoul Hague, interview by Karlen Mooradian, and Mooradian, *Worlds,* pp. 149–50.

310 "Suddenly Bill was on the floor": Elaine de Kooning, interview by Karlen Mooradian.

310 "Gorky had not spoken": Poindexter Gallery, *The 30's.*

312 "I have one of them left": Isamu Noguchi, interview by Karlen Mooradian.

312 "I don't know if he": Matossian, *Black Angel,* p. 289. The Isamu Noguchi Foundation has photographs of two versions of the collaborations produced that night. (Both originals are now lost.) One drawn in crayon and ink on a 17⅝ by 23 inch sheet of paper had two ominous dark trapezoids with eyes and bird legs overlaid on a background of swirling lines. The other (signed by the three artists but closest to Gorky in style) had six biomorphic creatures floating in a dark space.

312 When they finished drawing": Gaston de Havenon, "Reminiscence of Arshile Gorky."

312 It was, Soyer recalled, to be a single figure: Mooradian, *Worlds,* pp. 212–13.

55: A LANGUAGE FOR ALL TO UNDERSTAND

313 "This Friday I'll see": Marderosian and Kucuikian translation.

314 Mrs. Muschenheim was hospitalized: Matossian, *Black Angel,* p. 282.

314 "Such is life": Partizian translation.

314 Through Noguchi and Willie: Willem de Kooning, interview by Bruce Hooton.

314 "I really worked hard": Schwabacher, *Arshile Gorky*, p. 78.

315 Planned for the 1939 season: Undated newspaper clipping printed on the exhibition panel for the Newark Museum's *Museums without Walls*. I am grateful to Ruth Bowman for lending me the exhibition panels.

315 A black janitor watched: Spender, *From a High Place*, p. 212.

315 He also helped Gorky: Willem de Kooning, interview by Bruce Hooton.

315 According to de Kooning: Hess, "Arshile Gorky Flies Again."

315 "He right away went": Willem de Kooning, interview by Bruce Hooton.

315 Gorky's Ben Marden murals: According to the Riviera Club's architect, Louis Allen Abramson, to whom Gorky gave the sketches, the murals followed these studies closely (Jordan, Cat. Rais., p. 391).

316 The mural to the right: In the gouache with the beige background, the beige has flaked away in many places, revealing blue underneath. Presumably Gorky originally planned a blue background for both murals.

316 Years later, Gorky pointed out: Letter from Jeanne Reynal quoted in Brown University, *Graham, Gorky, Smith, and Davis in the Thirties*.

317 "Certainly we all dream": Malcolm Johnson, "Café Life in New York," *New York Sun*, August 22, 1941, p. 15. Quoted in Schwabacher, *Arshile Gorky*, pp. 78–79.

317 Already in the 1940s: Schwabacher, *Arshile Gorky*, p. 78.

317 Warren McCulloch remembered: Mooradian, *Worlds*, p. 168.

36: MOUGOUCH

321 "They're so strong": Edvard Lieber's notes on a conversation with Elaine de Kooning, in Lieber, letter to author, May 9, 1998. I am grateful to Mr. Lieber for giving me excerpts from his notes that contain anecdotes about Gorky.

322 The meeting took place: According to Elaine de Kooning, Agnes (soon to be renamed Mougouch) already knew both Fred Schrady and his girlfriend, Kay Mason, and she had been invited to Schrady's party and planned to go. According to Mougouch, she had not met Schrady, and de Kooning took her to the party as his guest.

323 "More important for his life": Schwabacher, *Arshile Gorky*, p. 84.

325 "You had the feeling": Peter Ruta, interview with author, October 28, 1997.

37: COHABITATION

330 "Gorky galupchig have you been": Gorky had finished the Ben Marden mural in March. Agnes may have been referring to a commission for a mural in a restaurant secured for Gorky by an architect friend (possibly William Lescaze). "Besides William Muschenheim," Mougouch recalls, "there was another architect with a French name who lived just off Gramercy Park. He

and his wife wined and dined us once a month. We'd be given steak. I think he commissioned a mural in a restaurant. Gorky's *Three Figures by the Sea* was a study for it, but it was rejected. It didn't pass muster." The "explanation" that Mougouch mentions in her letter probably refers to Gorky's statement about his Ben Marden murals to Malcolm Johnson, whose piece on the murals would appear in the *New York Sun* on August 22, 1941.

331 At this point Gorky's letter: Gorky's letter continues with paragraphs borrowed (with a few alterations) from Gaudier-Brzeska.

The beasts had a curious effect on me, which I haven't hitherto experienced. I have always admired them, but now I hate them the dreadful savagery of these wild animals who hurl themselves on their food is too horribly like the ways of humans, what moved me most was a group of four chimpanzees.

They were very like primitive man, they walked helping themselves with their hands, and looked like old men, their backs all bent, they discussed things in little groups, shared their food with dispute but with much wisdom—the strongest giving bread and carrots for the oranges and bananas belonging to the others. Its most depressing to thus see our own origin—depressing not because we sprang from this, but that we may easily slip back to it. Our knowledge is great, but how empty! How ephemeral! So small a thing, and we lose all. We no longer know chemistry as did the men of the Italian renaissance, and it will be a long while before we rediscover their secrets. Art comes instinctively to us, but it is so uncertain. I have in front of me photographs of all Picasso's best works. The more I admire them the further I feel myself removed from all art, it seems so easy, so limited! We are part of the world creation, and we ourselves create nothing. Our knowledge allows us to make use of all the forces already in existence—our art to interpret emotions already felt. A big war, an epidemic, and we collapse into ignorance and darkness, fit sons of chimpanzees. Our one consolation is love, confidence, the embracing of spirit and of body. When we are united we think neither of outer darkness nor of animal brutality. Our human superiority vibrates through our passions, and we love the world—but how insignificant we really are, and how subject to universal law! Mere midgets in the wide universe, but masters of our particular planet. Oh Mouguch, Mouguch, how strange it all is in my memory, I compare the slender springing grace of a lovely man with the hairy mass of monkey flesh.

The mastery of an energetic head, full of individual character, with the stupid masks of chimpanzees who can scarcely raise the beginnings of a smile, these comparisons are so terrible, so formidable, in the mind; for if the blind masses of humanity, which always persecute their pioneer spirits, had the desire, or rather the power, then would our tall and erect stature be bent, and we should be covered with hideous fur; the grass would grow over our finest works, and we should return to bestiality.

These wicked people who are so ignorant, we hate them, don't we love? These brutes who have eyes for nothing save their animal passions, who think only of eating, who fight each other and wallow in dirt. Foul disgusting fellows who only crush people of our own kind, whose instinct is for beauty, for ideas and for reflection, sweet dear, I am so blessed in being able to have you, blessed be the day when the great sun guided me to you. Without your love I should have been flung into an outer darkness, where bones rot, and where man is subject to the same law as beasts—final destruction, the humiliation of extinction.

331 Some critics, such as Hilton Kramer: Hilton Kramer, "The Case of the Purloined Image."
332 "He was a pain in the ass": Willem de Kooning, interview by Karlen Mooradian.
333 "Dear Vartoosh": Spender, *From a High Place*, p. 211.
334 Most of the rest of Gorky's letter: Gorky's letter went on using Gaudier-Brzeska's words.
335 "They all took his ideas": Aristodimos Kaldis, interview by Karlen Mooradian.
336 "She was in and out": Agnes Phillips, letter to Ethel Schwabacher, February 9, 1952.

38: SAN FRANCISCO

339 "Always loving you all": Mooradian, *AGA*, pp. 269–71.
339 Besides this sale and the two: The two paintings purchased by Jeanne Reynal were *Image in Khorkom* and the smaller of the two large 1929 still lifes with the boot motif (Illustrated in Jim Jordan's Cat. Rais. 148 and 73). Jeanne also acquired *Tracking Down Guiltless Doves*, c. 1938–39 (which is closely related to the painting Dorothy Miller bought), a Sochi variant called *Composition*, c. 1939–41, and *Enigmatic Combat*, 1937 (Cat. Rais. 220, 226, and 176). Probably it was about this time that Margaret Osborn bought the highly Picassoid *Head Composition*, 1938 (Cat. Rais. 211), which had been exhibited in the Whitney Annual in January and February of 1940.
340 "He was always elaborating": Isamu Noguchi, interview by Karlen Mooradian.
340 He would say: Mooradian, "Philosophy of Arshile Gorky," p. 60.
340 "Gorky was always educating me": Isamu Noguchi, interview by Karlen Mooradian.
343 "Wild and witty": Jeanne Reynal, interview by Karlen Mooradian, 1965.
344 When he overheard Varda: Spender, *From a High Place*, p. 223.
345 "With many kisses to all": Partizian translation.
347 Suddenly he saw: Dorothy Miller, who with her husband, Holger Cahill, visited San Francisco that summer, must have been thinking of the same sculp-

ture when she said that Gorky took a piece of wood about two feet long, "and he started to carve it until it got thinner and thinner until it ended up like a Giacometti. Except that Gorky sculpted that long before Giacometti had made those things [Giacometti's thin figures began during World War II]. Gorky just carved it way down to a very, very thin human figure" (Mooradian, *Worlds*, p. 171).

348 "I forgot to write": Partizian translation.

348 Among the many people whom: Barbara Chermayeff, interview by author, September 3, 1993.

39: MARRIAGE

350 "He was happy to see me again": Manuel Tolegian, interview by Karlen Mooradian, 1982.

351 Holger Cahill visited: Dorothy Miller, interview by Karlen Mooradian.

351 It quoted Gorky's aim: Review by Emilia Hodel, *San Francisco News*, August 17, 1941, Whitney Museum of American Art, Artist's File. The other newspaper clippings are also in the Whitney's Artist's File.

352 "The two of us send": Mooradian translation.

353 Mougouch was twenty: On September 15, two days after his wedding, Gorky wrote to Vartoosh and Moorad on a postcard from the Storey County courthouse: "We just got married and are sending our love to you. Mougouch and Gorky."

354 "With affectionate greetings": Marderosian and Kucuikian translation.

355 "Later, Gorky and Agnes walked": Mooradian, *Worlds*, pp. 49–50.

355 "Now give Mr. Chaliapin": Matossian, *Black Angel*, p. 315.

355 "But I gave him $15": Mooradian, *Worlds*, p. 50.

357 "He always wrote that he": Ibid.

40: GARDEN IN SOCHI

359 The sequence of the three: Ethel Schwabacher, Harold Rosenberg, and William Seitz placed the highly Miróesque yellow-ground version (now in a private collection in Italy) first. They put the white-ground *Sochi* that belongs to the Museum of Modern Art second, and the green-ground *Sochi*, also in the Museum of Modern Art, third. The green-ground version is the only one for which we have a definite date—the first days of October 1941. William Rubin, basing his argument on Gorky's development from Picasso's Cubism to "conceptions closer to Surrealism," reversed the order, placing the green-ground 1941 version first, the yellow-ground version second, and the "painterly" white-ground version third ("Arshile Gorky, Surrealism, and the New American Painting," p. 383). Rubin saw the green-ground *Sochi*'s heavy, gritty paint surface and its shapes cut out by the ground color as characteristics of Gorky's Synthetic Cubist paintings of the second half of the 1930s. He hypothesized that Gorky painted the yellow-ground version under the immediate stimulus of the Miró retrospective at the Museum of

Modern Art in the late autumn and winter of 1941–42—thus a little later than the green-ground *Sochi*. The yellow-ground version's thinner paint surface linked it, he said, with Gorky's later work. In the white-ground *Sochi*, Rubin saw painterly handling, shallow depth, and line's independence from color as qualities that emerge in Gorky's mature style. He therefore assigned it to the end of 1943 or possibly as late as 1946 or 1947. All these hypotheses make very good sense and are based on close observation of the paintings in question.

In my 1972 master's thesis on the *Garden in Sochi* series, I attempted to establish a chronology for the series by tracing the development of shapes and images from one painting to the next, starting with *Khorkom*. Because the green-ground *Sochi*'s shapes are closer to those in the *Khorkom* series and because the arrangement of downward-pointing bird head cum tail feathers on the left comes out of two earlier versions of the *Sochi* theme—*Argula* and *Composition* (Jordan, Cat. Rais., nos. 218 and 236)—I agreed with Rubin and placed the green-ground version first. Moreover, the biomorphic creature on the left in the green-ground *Sochi* has more in common with the wispy figures in *Argula* and *Composition* than does the more full-bodied biomorph in the same location in the yellow-ground version. Also, the tall, pointed shape that pokes into the green-ground *Sochi* from the canvas's bottom edge recalls similar shapes in the same location in *Argula* and *Composition*.

Another reason to place the green-ground *Sochi* first is that the yellow-ground *Sochi* is closer to the final white-ground version, in which the central black vertical has a two-lobed base. This feature appears to have its origin in the way the descending black band in the green-ground *Sochi* (and in *Argula* and *Composition*) stops short at one of the boot/butter churn's points or sprouts. With his genius for reinventing shapes from one painting to the next, Gorky may have decided to combine into a single shape the black band and the two lobes of the green ground that cut into the top of the boot/butter churn. Together, these shapes form the black band with a lobed base. Other possible sources for the black band's lobed base are the lobed biomorphic shapes in Miró's paintings of around 1933 or the low-relief designs on Armenian *khatchkars*, many of which depict the holy cross with a two-lobed base. Two-lobed shapes also appear in many of Gorky's drawings from the early 1930s, where they refer to breasts or buttocks.

359 Thus the blatantly: Jordan, Cat. Rais., pp. 80–81.

360 When Gorky fetched: Spender, *From a High Place*, p. 241.

360 The museum would pay Gorky: Agnes Fielding remembers the museum's acquisition of the green-ground *Garden in Sochi* somewhat differently: "The Museum of Modern Art swapped the *Garden in Sochi* for a painting that Ethel Schwabacher had given them and which Gorky wanted like a hole in the head, because he had about five of that series. Gorky was quite shocked by this."

360 "It is very difficult for me": Arshile Gorky, letter to Dorothy Miller.

362 "Let my illness stay behind": Villa and Matossian, *Armenian Village Life*, p. 129.

363 Perched above the "females": Perhaps they are storks. In Armenia cranes and storks were much revered, and as a boy Gorky had a special love for them.

363 Its burst of radiant yellow: Levy, *Arshile Gorky*, p. 23.

41: CAMOUFLAGE

366 "You now are my only hope": John and Esther Magruder's letters are in the personal archive of Mougouch's nephew Malcolm Magruder. I am grateful to him for making them available to me.

367 Gorky wrote to Vartoosh: Partizian translation.

368 "Gorky suggested chopping holes": Peter Busa, notebooks, p. 35.

368 "I don't have a problem": Peter Busa, interview by Karlen Mooradian.

368 "Ruined the whole morning": Peter Busa, interview by Jack Taylor, p. 10.

368 "Always loving you": Mooradian translation (Mooradian misdates the letter October 28, 1940).

369 He read every book: Mooradian, *Worlds*, p. 168.

369 "And then after that we organized": Mooradian, *Worlds*, p. 188.

369 "A fantastic kind of Paradise": Betty Parsons, interview by Paul Cummings, 1969, pp. 36–37.

370 "Then we had a big": Mooradian, *Worlds*, p. 156.

370 For the drawing class: According to Schwabacher, Gorky's class was finally dissolved because of insufficient enrollment (*Arshile Gorky*, p. 82).

370 Gorky would say: The models seem to have included Peggy Guggenheim's daughter, Pegeen, who at the time was broke (Jacqueline Bogard Weld, *Peggy: The Wayward Guggenheim*, p. 319).

370 "Because he was trying to keep": Betty Parsons, interview by Paul Cummings, p. 36.

370 Another method Gorky had: Waldman, *Arshile Gorky*, p. 263.

370 "He didn't like anything": Mooradian, *Worlds*, pp. 188–89.

372 There was some truth: Miller and Miller, *Survivors*, p. 5.

373 "He thought they were the best": Agnes Phillips, notes written in the late 1950s.

375 "She actually became so much": Raphael Soyer, interview by Karlen Mooradian.

375 "She was a socialite": Peter Busa, interview by Karlen Mooradian.

375 "He showed me love": This and the quotation that follows are from Matossian, *Black Angel*, pp. 328 and 358.

42: SURREALISTS IN EXILE

379 "Dictation by thought": Rubin, essay in Museum of Modern Art, *Dada, Surrealism, and Their Heritage*, p. 64.

380 The Julien Levy and Pierre Matisse: In 1942 the Pierre Matisse Gallery, which had been showing Miró for years and which in 1935 gave Masson a show, mounted *Artists in Exile*. This exhibition included fourteen artists who had come to live in the United States: Eugene Berman, Breton, Chagall,

Ernst, Léger, Lipchitz, Masson, Matta, Mondrian, Ozenfant, Seligman, Tanguy, Pavel Tchelitchew, and Ossip Zadkine. Julien Levy had put on a Surrealist group show in 1932 (the same show as *Newer Super-Realism*, presented in 1931 at the Wadsworth Atheneum), and over the next decade he exhibited numerous Surrealists, including Ernst, Tanguy, and, in 1940, the recently arrived Matta. Among other Surrealists or artists connected with Surrealism to whom Julien Levy gave shows were Eugene Berman (1932), Man Ray (1932), Joseph Cornell (1932), Charles Howard (1933), Pavel Tchelitchew (1933), Dalí (1933, 1934, 1937, and 1939), Giacometti (1935), Magritte (1936), and Wolfgang Paalen (1940).

380 With its imaginative layout: Levy included a selection of writings by Lautréamont, de Sade, Rimbaud, Freud, Breton, Eluard, and Dalí, all printed on paper in different pastel shades. The book also reproduced works by Ernst, Duchamp, Miró, Tanguy, de Chirico, and Picasso, among others.

380 Levy recalled, "When my book": Julien Levy, *Memoir of an Art Gallery*, p. 284.

380 Gorky actually owned a copy: Among other books on Surrealism that Gorky possessed are Dalí's *L'amour et al memoire*, Waldemar George's *Giorgio de Chirico*, and Breton's second and enlarged edition of *Le surréalisme et la peinture*.

380 Levy's definition of Surrealism: Levy, *Surrealism*, p. 3.

381 Levy's book quoted from a lecture: Ibid., p. 7.

381 Gorky must also have been: Gorky may have met Dalí through Julien Levy at the 1939 World's Fair, where Dalí's Surrealist pavilion, called Dream of Venus, featured a large aquarium in which ten bathing beauties were to swim against a background of the ruins of Pompeii, play on a soft, undulating piano, warm themselves at an underwater hearth, or milk a cow. When one of the project's backers insisted that the bathers wear rubber mermaid tails, Dalí, claiming that his art was being compromised, wrote a manifesto spoofing the Declaration of Independence and had copies of it dropped from an airplane over Manhattan. The manifesto said: "Man is entitled to the enigma and simulacrums that are founded on these great vital constants: the sexual instinct, the consciousness of death, the physical melancholy caused by time-space." He called on contemporary artists to let "loose the avenging thunder of your paranoiac inspiration" (Martica Sawin, *Surrealism in Exile and the Beginning of the New York School*, pp. 77–78).

381 On those frequent occasions when: Mooradian, *Worlds*, p. 107.

381 "Dalí told him to pick": Peter Busa, interview by Jack Taylor.

381 Gorky answered: Lillian Orlowsky, telephone interview with author, October 3, 1999.

382 Early in 1941 he went: Sawin, *Surrealism in Exile*, p. 156.

382 In his introduction he encouraged: Ibid., pp. 159, 161–62.

382 Indeed, Onslow Ford recalled: Ibid., p. 158, and telephone conversation with Onslow Ford, Winter, 2002.

382 In Julien Levy's opinion: Levy, *Memoir*, p. 285.

382 "But I echo very softly": Ibid., p. 284.

382 "All my life her stories": Levy, *Arshile Gorky*, p. 34.

383 "You know, I really feel like painting": *Ararat*, Fall 1971, p. 48.

383 "We all laughed": Provincetown Art Association and Museum, *Life Colors Art: Fifty Years of Painting by Peter Busa*, p. 51.

383 Matta described his relationship: Levy, *Arshile Gorky*, p. 24.

384 "Having heard Matta laugh": Lionel Abel, *The Intellectual Follies: A Memoir of the Literary Venture in New York and Paris*, p. 45.

385 "That's how I did it": Sawin, *Surrealism in Exile*, p. 167.

385 Once he tried to explain: Ibid., p. 29.

386 As the critic and art historian: Schapiro, "Introduction," in Schwabacher, *Arshile Gorky*, pp. 12–13.

386 The Americans, Pavia said: "Poverty, Politics and Artists: 1930–1945."

386 "We have tried to help": Sawin, *Surrealism in Exile*, p. 70.

387 "It is to a great degree": William S. Rubin, *Dada and Surrealist Art*, p. 342.

387 "I am particularly impressed": Museum of Modern Art, *Jackson Pollock*, p. 32.

388 At the crowded opening: Peggy Guggenheim, *Out of This Century: Confessions of an Art Addict*, p. 230.

389 When Gorky brought his paintings: Peter Busa, notebooks, p. 30.

389 What Pollock meant: Jeffrey Potter, *To a Violent Grave: An Oral Biography of Jackson Pollock*, p. 61.

389 He knew that Gorky was: Peter Busa, interview by Karlen Mooradian.

389 When things calmed down: Peter Busa, notebooks, p. 30.

389 "Gorky just answered him": *Ararat*, Fall 1971, p. 50.

390 "All are priced with great": James E. B. Breslin, *Mark Rothko: A Biography*, p. 160.

390 "He has been too busy": Samuel M. Kootz, *New Frontiers in American Painting*, p. 49.

390 "I kneel down before this artist": Badrik Selian, interview by Karlen Mooradian, October 15, 1966.

391 "It looks good": Marderoisan and Kucuikian translation.

392 "Picasso," Graham wrote: Dorothy Dehner, foreword to Graham, *System and Dialectics of Art*, p. xx.

392 After Graham's conversion from: Most of Graham's friendships with artists cooled after his apostasy. De Kooning, who kept up with Graham, recalled that when Graham visited his studio in the late 1950s he would sit with his back to de Kooning's canvases because "it made him sick to see all that struggle going on." Yet as he stood up to leave, Graham would reassure de Kooning: "I don't have to look at it, Bill. I know it's good" (Fritz Bultman, interview by author).

43: *WATERFALL*

393 "He just stood on the rock": Mooradian, *Worlds*, p. 204.

393 Schary and his wife kept: *Waterfall*, pencil and crayon on paper, 14 9/8" × 11 3/8" (1942), is illustrated as fig. 18 in *Arshile Gorky: The Hirshhorn Museum and Sculpture Garden Collection*, 1979.

394 Eight months after his visit: Arshile Gorky, letter to Vartoosh Mooradian, Feb. 17, 1943, in Spender, "Letters and Documents," p. 53. This letter is one of fourteen Gorky letters that Vartoosh Mooradian loaned to Ethel Schwabacher when she was at work on her biography. They were translated by Partizian.

395 "He was very naïve": Agnes Gorky Phillips, letter to Ethel Schwabacher, December 28, 1949.

396 "He was inspired by the flowers": Jordan, Cat. Rais., p. 380, n. 1.

397 The nearly abstract painting appears: Mooradian, *Worlds*, p. 204.

397 Kandinsky was highly visible: Probably Gorky first saw Kandinsky's paintings when they were exhibited in the Blue Four exhibition at New York's Daniel Gallery in 1925 and at the Société Anonyme in 1926 and 1927. In 1936 he must have seen Kandinsky's work at J. B. Neumann's New Art Circle (where he himself had shown work), or he could have seen it at the Nierendorf Gallery in 1937 and 1941.

397 . . . his library contained various works: In Gorky's library are fifteen pages from M. T. H. Sadler's introduction to Kandinsky's *The Art of Spiritual Harmony*. Gorky also owned Will Grohmann's *Kandinsky*, published by *Cahiers d'Art* in 1930, and the exhibition catalog of Kandinsky's 1945 memorial show in New York.

398 In Levy's view, Gorky's: Levy, *Arshile Gorky*, p. 26.

401 In December she wrote: Among the disinvited were Gorky, Theodore Roszak, Irene Rice Pereira, David Hare, Robert Motherwell, Noguchi, and Mark Tobey (Museum of Modern Art, *Museum of Modern Art at Mid-Century*, p. 65).

401 "I am doing very lovely personal": Partizian translation.

402 "Always your loving brother": Ibid.

402 "A friend of my mother moved": Burliuk, "Arshile Gorky," pp. 1, 2.

404 A 1942 ink drawing: The Gorky drawing is illustrated in the 1949 issue of *Color and Rhyme* in which Mary Burliuk's reminiscence appears.

404 "I loved him": Hirshhorn Museum and Sculpture Garden, *The Golden Door: Artist-Immigrants of America, 1876–1776*, p. 195.

405 Shortly before or after Hirshhorn's: Hirshhorn Museum and Sculpture Garden, *Arshile Gorky: The Hirshhorn Museum and Sculpture Garden Collection*, p. 8. See also Jordan, Cat. Rais., p. 237.

406 "And so we are happy": Mooradian, *Worlds*, pp. 279–80.

406–407 (Nazarbekian visited Gorky): Another possible reason for choosing the name Maro was Toumanian's long romantic poem "Maro," which Gorky surely knew. It tells the story of a nine-year-old village girl who is given in marriage to a shepherd whom she hates and leaves. Because of the shame this brings on the family, her father beats her and throws her out of the house. Maro wanders in the mountains, falls into a valley, and dies. If indeed Gorky had this poem in mind when he named his daughter, the choice seems odd.

44: VIRGINIA

415 His understanding of Esther was: Agnes Gorky Phillips, letter to Ethel Schwabacher, December 28, 1949.

417 "He used to make those little": Ibid.

419 He would tell stories: Asa Moore Janney, interview with author, July 29, 1996.

419 "I'm inventing, just like you": Thomas E. Taylor, interview with author, July 28, 1996.

419 "He said that he came out": Asa Moore Janney, interview with author.

419 Gorky loved to tell about the time: Thomas E. Taylor, interview with author.

419 (Actually, Gorky stole this story): Raoul Hague, interview by Karlen Mooradian.

420 But Gorky knew that: In the summer of 1944 Gorky gave the Taylors a drawing as a gift for their having fed him dinner every night during a week in which Mougouch was away.

421 "I'm drawing the space between": Malcolm Magruder, conversation with author, July 28, 1996.

421 "Like a little world down there": Robert Jonas, interview by Mooradian, *Worlds*, p. 152.

421 When James Johnson Sweeny wrote: Sweeny, "Five American Painters," p. 122. (Karlen Mooradian, who sometimes tampered with his interviewee's words, might have altered what Robert Jonas said in order to conform to Sweeny's article.)

425 "That's about all the news": Mougouch's younger sister (now called Esther Brooks) remembers that the first encounter between Gorky and Paul Makanowitzky had taken place earlier that year at 36 Union Square:

> I brought Paul to meet Gorky and Paul started speaking Russian and Paul began to ask questions—how could Gorky be related to Maxim Gorky, because Gorky was an assumed name. Paul was highly literate and well-educated. The relationship between Paul and Gorky didn't take. They had nothing in common. Paul thought Gorky was a joke, but not as a painter. It was all the razzmatazz at the Union Square studio, the trying to create an image, that was antipathetic to Paul. Our worlds were very different. Paul and I lived in the music world and Gorky and Mougouch were in the world of painting. When Paul spoke Russian to Gorky during that first meeting, Gorky became belligerent and sort of aloof and he made us feel uncomfortable and he faked his way through it by taking out a copy of a painting by Ingres and saying that Ingres was the best painter, and he put the reproduction upside down on the wall and Paul felt why can't you look at Ingres right side up?

45. *THE LEAF OF THE ARTICHOKE IS AN OWL*

427 "She said she had not enough": Peter Ruta, interview by author.

427 "Kurt Valentine liked Gorky": Mooradian, *Worlds*, p. 171.

428 "I simply can't work": Ibid., pp. 172–73.

431 Breton later told Sidney Janis: Sidney Janis, interview by Karlen Mooradian, 1965, and Matossian, *Black Angel*, p. 369.

431 One of Jeanne Reynal's letters: Jeanne Reynal, letter to Mougouch Gorky, April 14, 1945.

434 (The émigré painter Gabor Peterdi): Sawin, *Surrealism in Exile*, p. 331. Another commentator about Gorky's adoption of the sign painter's brush was none other than Clement Greenberg, who said he remembered Gorky pulling from his pocket a round-headed bristle brush that he had worn down to a point. When Gorky dipped such brushes in paint, "they'd come out like a little tuft point that he would paint with, holding the brush between forefinger & thumb and he'd get this fine line. Then the round-headed brushes became quite common" (Karlen Mooradian, "The Wars of Arshile Gorky," p. 6).

434 With his new brush in hand: Rosenberg, *Arshile Gorky*, p. 68. Although de Kooning said that he gave Gorky this technical tip at a time when Gorky was heavily influenced by Miró, it seems more likely that Gorky learned about the sign painter's brush in the winter of 1943–44, two or three years after his fascination with Miró had subsided.

434 "Then I'll give him my brush": Ivan Chermayeff, conversation with author, December 2, 1998, and Peter Chermayeff, conversation with author, summer 1997.

434 Variations on the same theme: Gorky's continued interest in Kandinsky is suggested in a letter Jeanne Reynal wrote from her home in Soda Springs, California, on April 12, 1944, shortly after she and Urban had stayed with the Gorkys at Union Square. Jeanne told Agnes she had sent Gorky a color reproduction of Kandinsky's *Improvisation No. 30* (1913) in the Art Institute of Chicago: "He has the picture already, the one with the cannon, but I thought his [reproduction] was not in color."

436 According to Gorky's nephew: Diane Rosenberg Karp, "Arshile Gorky: The Language of Art," pp. 55–56.

436 Gorky specialist Nouritza Matossian: Matossian, *Black Angel*, p. 353.

436 When *Liver* was reproduced: Janis, *Abstract and Surrealist Art in America*, p. 120. Apparently Sidney Janis's first efforts to find a publisher met with rejection. With the encouragement and support of a group of artists gathered at Gorky's studio, Janis finally persuaded Jeanne Reynal's brother to publish the book. The book also served as a catalog for a traveling show that Janis organized in conjunction with the San Francisco Museum of Art. In November and December 1944 the show, which included Gorky's *The Liver Is the Cock's Comb*, was mounted in New York's Mortimer Brandt Gallery on Fifty-seventh Street, and it traveled to Cincinnati, Denver, Santa Barbara, and San Francisco.

437 Jeanne Reynal described *Liver*: Jeanne Reynal, letter to Mougouch Gorky, April 19, 1944.

46: CUTTING DOWN THE RAPHAELS

441 "We just talked quietly": In her letter Mougouch must have been referring to a planned fifth issue, which did not appear. The fourth and last issue of the Surrealist magazine *VVV* was dated February 1944, and no work by Gorky appears in it. It has a red cover with a huge *vagina dentata* drawn by Matta, and the reproductions are mostly in primary colors. Mougouch told Jeanne that Gorky's colors were "far too subtle & varied" for the silk-screen method that *VVV* usually used and that Duchamp was trying to find another printing technique.

442 Although they are modeled: For a fuller discussion of Gorky's whittling and sculpture, see my "The Sculptures of Arshile Gorky."

456 It is, I think, legitimate to read: In his catalog essay for Gorky's 1962 retrospective at the Museum of Modern Art, William C. Seitz was rightly perplexed by Gorky's imagery: "Should the levitated bodies at the right of *Good Afternoon, Mrs. Lincoln* be read as odd personages meeting in conversation? Toward the upper left: did Gorky envisage a long-haired female figure leaning forward and gesturing with truncated arms over a gnarled landscape? One cannot say without prior knowledge, for no two spectators will decode Gorky's allusions in the same way" (Museum of Modern Art, *Arshile Gorky*, p. 33).

457 "And it was always better": Waldman, *Arshile Gorky*, p. 57.

47: NOVEMBER AND DECEMBER IN NEW YORK

459 Another wedding guest remembered: Peter Brooks (who later became Esther's second husband), conversation with author, October 23, 1999. Brooks insisted that the two hair disassemblies were separate incidents, not one event remembered differently.

460 Gorky asked her, "What did you do": V. V. Rankine, interview by author, May 4, 1995.

462 Matta and David Hare persuaded Matisse: When, toward the end of their time in Virginia, Agnes had written to Jeanne about Gorky's career, Jeanne had answered (October 4, 1944): "Do you think Rosenberg will not come through? Matisse of course is less interested in 'sales' I guess he is better. Somehow one lost a little faith in Rosenberg with all his money makers." Given Gorky's dismissal of Paul Rosenberg the previous winter, it is curious that Rosenberg was still considered a possible dealer for Gorky's work.

463 Soon thereafter, however, Levy: Eleanor Perényi, interview by author, October 13, 1995.

463 He said that after he got out: Julien Levy, foreword in Museum of Modern Art, *Arshile Gorky*, pp. 8–9.

463 Gorky was delighted to have: The December 20 letter of agreement between Levy and Gorky said:

> Confirming our verbal agreement, I am enclosing herewith a check for $350 as an advance on twelve monthly payments of $175 each,

commencing on January 1st, 1945. (I understand that you wish these payments irregularly, more in advance at this time and less over the summer, but totaling $2100 by January 1946.) . . . The gallery agrees that after gross sales to our account reach $3000, additional sales for the year, will be credited to the account of the artist (less 1/3 commission to the gallery) whether the paintings sold at that time belong to the artist or to the gallery inventory. If the paintings belong to the gallery inventory, another one will be substituted in its place. In other words after the gallery's gross proceeds have reached $3000 the artist has a share of all the further profits during the year.

465 Evocative and elusive: Abel, *Intellectual Follies*, p. 49.

48: ROXBURY

472 Their life in Roxbury was: It is possible, although unlikely, that Gorky had met the Massons during his summer visit to Saul Schary in 1942. Probably he met them through either Calder or Tanguy after he moved to David Hare's.

472 Gorky would have paid attention: Levy, *Arshile Gorky*, p. 30.

473 "He must have sung once": Mooradian, *Worlds*, p. 118.

49: THE EYE-SPRING

478 In his essay Breton warns: Breton wrote: "Easy-going amateurs will come here for their meager rewards: in spite of all warning to the contrary they will insist on seeing in these compositions a still-life, a landscape, or a figure instead of daring to face the *hybrid* forms in which all human emotion is precipitated. By 'hybrids' I mean the resultants provoked in an observer contemplating a natural spectacle with extreme concentration, the resultants being a combination of the spectacle and a flux of childhood and other memories, and the observer being gifted to a rare degree with the grace of emotion" ("The Eye-Spring," in Julien Levy Gallery, *Arshile Gorky*).

478 Here is an art entirely new: Ibid.

478 Before he wrote the essay: Levy, *Arshile Gorky*, p. 21.

479 "And the gay warmth of his palette": Edward Alden Jewell, "Art Old and New," *New York Times*, March 11, 1945, sect. X, p. 8. Other reviews appeared in the *Herald Tribune*, March 11 (clipping in Agnes Fielding's personal archive), *Art News* (March 15, 1945, p. 24), and the *New Yorker* (March 17, 1945, p. 77). Gorky's friend Gaston de Havenon recalled having spoken to the art critic at the *New Yorker*, on Gorky's behalf, but the critic said he was "not ready for that kind of work yet" (Gaston de Havenon, "Reminiscence" of Gorky).

50: FEARFULLY LINKED WITH THE SUN

482 "He paid twenty dollars a month": Quoted in Weld, *Peggy: The Wayward Guggenheim*, p. 331.

483 "I believe we see real American painting": Sawin, *Surrealism in Exile*, p. 368.

486–487 "As ever, Gorky": Partizian translation. The lines that Partizian omitted come from the Marderosian and Kucuikian translation.

487 *Diary of a Seducer* (whose title): Levy, *Arshile Gorky*, p. 35, and Schwabacher, *Arshile Gorky*, p. 104. If there were other much revised and many-layered canvases, they must have been among those lost in a studio fire the following year.

489 Elaine de Kooning said that Gorky: de Kooning, "Gorky: Painter of His Own Legend," pp. 63–66. I do not see the connection made by Elaine de Kooning between Gorky's *Diary* and Jacques-Louis David's *Mars Disarmed by Venus*. De Kooning writes that Gorky based his composition closely on the shapes and spaces in this particular David. In my view, *Diary* has more to do with Miró's modulation of gray washes in *The Birth of the World* (1925) than with any earlier masterpiece. Whatever its sources, *Diary* is an independent work and Gorky was proud enough of it to send it to the Whitney Annual, where it was titled *Journal d'un séducteur*.

489 "Since then these memories": Museum of Modern Art, Arshile Gorky Collection File.

51: SHERMAN

496 "O dear": Breton gave Gorky the expanded French version of his *Le surréalisme et la peinture*, which incorporated the essay he had written on Gorky for the Julien Levy brochure. The book was published by Bretano's in April 1945. What Breton was "fulminating" about was the delay in his plan to leave for a lecture tour of Haiti and the French West Indies, after which he would go home to Paris.

497 Instead, with his robust humor: Levy, *Memoir*, pp. 267–68.

498 "Who the hell is this guy": Harold Rosenberg, interview by Karlen Mooradian, 1966.

498 Balcomb Greene, for example, recalled: Mooradian, *Worlds*, p. 146.

498 It took place at a French: Enrico Donati, interview by author, December 3, 1998.

499 Mougouch was asked, "What part": Spender, *From a High Place*, p. 301. The story is told slightly differently in Matossian, *Black Angel*, p. 383.

52: PHOENIX

502 "The truth is, I had started": Partizian translation.

503 "We are well": Marderosian and Kucuikian translation.

504 "Gorky just kept banging": Mooradian, *Worlds*, pp. 105–06.

505 He said that his art materials: Clapp, "Painter in a Glass House," p. 6.

506 Peter Blume, in his eyewitness: The fire and Gorky's loss became part of the Gorky mythology, a mythology that was, even then, growing quickly as Gorky stories circulated and recirculated among young painters. The second-generation Abstract Expressionist painter Milton Resnick, for example, said that Gorky had thought about saving his paintings but "then he realized that if he took anything, he'd have to take not what belonged to him, but what belonged to the man from whom he rented the house. So in honor he took nothing. Just walked out and watched the whole house burn" (Mooradian, *Worlds*, p. 195).

507 Many people have compared: Mooradian, *Worlds*, p. 209.

507 "His mind blazed with a fiery river": Schwabacher, *Arshile Gorky*, p. 17.

53: A TREE CUT DOWN

510 "He was quite worried": Mooradian, *Worlds*, p. 212.

512 Nevertheless, he lived in fear: Spender, *From a High Place*, p. 306.

514 "What love, what friendship": Agnes Phillips, notes written in the late 1950s.

514 In his memoir *Black Dog of Fate*: Peter Balakian, *Black Dog of Fate*, pp. 87–88.

515 "He was preoccupied": Mooradian, *Worlds*, pp. 96–97.

515 "His violence was gone": Marny George, letter to James Thrall Soby, March 15, 1951.

515 "Pardon me, pardon me": Yenovk Der Hagopian, interview by Karlen Mooradian.

516 About this time Gorky told: Abel, *Intellectual Follies*, p. 52.

516 "And the tensions arising": Schwabacher, *Arshile Gorky*, p. 134.

54: THE SKY MINER'S HAUL

518 And Gorky responded, "It may": Agnes Fielding, interview by author.

518 One, probably Maude: Copies of this review and the others quoted here were collected by Ethel Schwabacher and are now in Gorky's Artist's File in the Whitney Museum of American Art.

519 "My preferred picture is the one": This criticism and the two that follow come from Ethel Schwabacher's notes on reviews of Gorky's shows. Her notes are in the Whitney Museum.

519 "I don't mean that he ought to": Willem de Kooning, interview by Bruce Hooton.

520 *Impatience* went to Yves Tanguy: Spender, *From a High Place*, p. 309.

520 The art critic and lecturer Rosamund Bernier: The idea for the photograph of Gorky and Lam had been Bernier's: "In May 1946 I began working for *Vogue*, and I suggested to Penn the idea of photographing these two artists together—they were such opposite types. The photograph was not made for any particular purpose. We went to Gorky's studio, where he lived with Mougouch, but the photograph was taken outside. Gorky and Lam knew of each other and they respected each other as artists, but they had no common

language and Lam was very vague and very shy (conversation with author, March 14, 1998).

521 Mili said of his friendship: Mooradian, *Worlds*, p. 65, n. 41.

521 "I already owned a Gorky": Anne Tredick Dickey, interview by author, July 14, 1997.

55: THIRD VIRGINIA SUMMER

523 "Always loving you, Gorky": Partizian translation.

527 Gorky and Mougouch were not impressed: Besides the abstract contingent, there were artists who worked in expressionistic but representational modes and there were genre painters. Also included was Saul Steinberg, who even then worked in a caricatural drawing style all his own.

527 "They were like people who jump on a bandwagon": Mooradian, *Worlds*, pp. 214–15.

527 It was hung with eight: Besides *The Artist and His Mother*, the museum selected its own green-ground version of *Garden in Sochi*, plus *Water of the Flowery Mill*, *The Unattainable*, *Landscape Table*, *Diary of a Seducer*, *Child's Companions*, and *Nude*. The three drawings were *Anatomical Blackboard* (1943) and two pencil drawings from 1944 entitled *The Backbone of My Ancestor Was Far Away* and *The Visible Monument-Soft*, both loaned by a Mrs. Peggy Rohde.

527 "He told me he thought that full recognition": Schwabacher, *Arshile Gorky*, pp. 123–24.

528 Gorky received little (and mixed): Greenberg, "Art," *Nation*, Nov. 23, 1946, p. 594.

529 In at least two drawings: Schwabacher, *Arshile Gorky*, p. 118.

530 "Never have I been able to": Partizian translation.

530 But he saw that these new drawings: Mooradian, "Philosophy of Arshile Gorky," p. 55.

530 Mougouch had written to Breton: Agnes Gorky, letter to André Breton, October 6, 1946, Bibliothèque Littéraire Jacques Doucet, Paris. Quoted in Spender, *From a High Place*, p. 314.

531 With Duchamp, Breton was organizing: André Breton's letter to Agnes Gorky is in her personal archive.

56: GORKY AND THE SURREALISTS

537 Yet Calas's insistence on the sense of emptiness: Hugo Gallery, *Bloodflames*, pp. 7–8.

537 But Gorky was wary: Agnes Gorky Phillips, notes written in the late 1950s.

537 As Ethel Schwabacher later recalled: Schwabacher, "Further Thoughts on Gorky."

538 "It was the end of our friendship": Greene, "Memories of Arshile Gorky," p. 110.

538 "They took him over like": Noguchi, interview by Karlen Mooradian.

538 De Kooning said he stopped: Spender, *From a High Place*, p. 341.

538 In a similar vein, Stuart Davis: Stuart Davis, "Handmaiden of Misery," p. 17.

538 Davis's scathing tone may have: See, e.g., Klaus Mann and Peyton Boswell, quoted in Martica Sawin, *Surrealism in Exile*, p. 293.

539 "And Gorky looked at me": Edwin Denby, interview by Karlen Mooradian, 1966.

539 "Write again soon, with warm": Spender, *From a High Place*, p. 320.

539 "It was like falling out": Mooradian, *Worlds*, p. 160.

540 Jeanne Reynal said that at parties: Jeanne Reynal, interview by Karlen Mooradian, in Mooradian, "Philosophy of Arshile Gorky," p. 55.

540 "He was simple, where": Osborn, "Mystery of Arshile Gorky," p. 59.

541 "He showed how Miró": Ethel Schwabacher, notes on a conversation with Sidney Janis, January 12, 1949.

541 Miró told Gorky that Gorky: Reiff, *Stylistic Analysis*, p. 223.

542 "Waves of applause greeted him": Schwabacher, *Arshile Gorky*, pp. 122–23.

542 The cat survived, but Agnes: Anna Hamburger, conversation with author, March 21, 1998.

57: CASTINE

544 His poor command of English reminds: Mougouch's letters to Arshile Gorky and Arshile Gorky's letters to Mougouch are in her personal archive, London. I have left Gorky's faulty spelling and grammar.

546 Gorky came back with the idea: In his last years Gorky's unswerving devotion to Stalin often got him into skirmishes. Another time, when the conversation turned to Stalin's insistence that the city of Kars be returned to Armenia, which to many American Russia watchers seemed an ominous sign, Gorky came out with, "But Stalin is right! It's ours." Both these conversations are reported in Spender, *From a High Place*, pp. 322, 329–30.

546 The enormous drawing that Gorky referred: There are two 1946 studies for *Summation*; the one done in crayon and pencil in the Whitney Museum belonged to the Schwabachers. The other was acquired by Sidney and Harriet Janis and given to the Museum of Modern Art. The final version of *Summation* (also in MoMA), done in pencil, pastel, and charcoal on paper mounted on composition board, has a few touches of color but the general impression it gives is of a painting in grisaille.

546 When Gorky showed *Summation* to Ethel: Schwabacher, "Further Thoughts on Gorky."

549 "and only your love enables me": Gaudier-Brzeska wrote: "Sweet dear, I am so blessed in being able to love you, and blessed be the day when the great sun guided me to you; without your love I should have been flung into an outer darkness. . . . Dear, dear love, I press you to me with all my force, and only your help enables me to work. I thank you, dear Sun, lovely Star, for having created women and men that we may be united."

58: THE GLASS HOUSE

555 Gorky did not respond: Reiff, *Stylistic Analysis*, p. 123. George Adoian gave this information to Reiff in conversation.

557 Elena Calas recalled his: Spender, *From a High Place*, p. 352.

558 What a man: Mooradian, *Worlds*, pp. 179–80.

559 "He was desperate to be": Agnes Phillips, annotations to her copy of Ethel Schwabacher's recently published biography of Gorky. Quoted in French in Matthew Spender, "Origines et développement de l'oeuvre dessiné de Arshile Gorky," in Museé Cantonal des Beaux-Arts, *Arshile Gorky: Oeuvres sur papier, 1929–1947*, p. 43, n. 31.

559 "One of the last things Gorky": Matta, conversation with Peter Busa, in Provincetown Art Association and Museum, *Life Colors Art: Fifty Years of Painting by Peter Busa*, p. 53.

560 "In other words, he reached": Raphael Soyer, *Diary of an Artist*, p. 268.

560 He pushed her away and: Spender, *From a High Place*, p. 352.

561 Gorky finally came out: Ibid., p. 348.

59: SHOW AT JULIEN LEVY

562 That same year the Whitney: *The Calendars* was shown in the Whitney's 1947 winter painting annual and a 1947 drawing in its March 1948 *Annual of Sculpture, Watercolors and Drawings*. That spring (1947) Gorky's 1932 *Objects* was included in the Museum of Modern Art's *Drawings in the Collection of the Museum of Modern Art*. In November 1947 the Art Institute of Chicago included *The Sun, the Dervish in the Tree* (1944) in its *Abstract and Surrealist American Art*, and the California Palace of the Legion of Honor included his *Nude* (1946) in its *Second Annual Exhibition of Paintings*. Finally, in January 1948 Gorky showed a drawing entitled *The Betrothal* in the Whitney's sculpture, watercolor, and drawing annual.

562 Reporting on that winter's Whitney: Greenberg, "Art," January 10, 1948, p. 52.

563 At the opening, Ethel: Schwabacher, *Arshile Gorky*, pp. 136–37.

563 The paintings included in Gorky's: The paintings in Gorky's 1948 show at Julien Levy were: *Soft Night, Agony, The Calendars, Making the Calendar, The Betrothal I* and *II, The Orators, The Beginning—Pale Grey, The Limit, The Opaque, Pastoral II, Year after Year, Four P.M.,* and *The Plough and the Song. Summation,* Gorky's huge drawing, hung in Levy's office but was not an official part of the show.

564 In Ethel's view, Gorky's unhappiness: Schwabacher, *Arshile Gorky*, p. 138.

564 "Bill said, 'I don't care what' ": Milton Resnick, interview by author, June 1999.

564 An *Art News* reviewer saw: *Art News*, March 1948, p. 46.

565 Although he found Gorky's color: Clipping in Whitney Museum of American Art, Artist's File.

565 The Schwabachers sent the clipping: Greenberg, "Art," March 20, 1948, pp. 331–32.

567 Much of the canvas is left: Among the more thinly painted canvases of 1947 are a third version of *The Plough and the Song, Making the Calendar, Days, Etc., Study for Agony, Theme for Plumage Landscape, Plumage Landscape, Year after Year,* a third version of *The Betrothal, Anti-Medusa, The Opaque, Pastoral, Terra Cotta,* and *Summer Snow.*

567 *The Calendars* has two thinner: In his fascinating but misguided study of Gorky's iconography, art historian Harry Rand rightly traces the imagery of *The Calendars* (1946–47) to the *Fireplace in Virginia* drawings of 1946. Rand maintains that Gorky's subject in these drawings and in *The Calendars* is home and family. That may be true, but Rand goes too far in identifying shapes and groupings of shapes as representations of specific realities—he spots, among other things, all four members of the Gorky family, a dog, a lamp, and other furnishings, including a pinup calendar and a calendar with a fledgling bird. I cannot find much of the imagery Rand describes.

　　In Rand's view, Gorky was a "modern history painter . . . a visual diarist . . . a realist, an illuminator . . . who used a coherent system of signs." I see Gorky as a highly personal abstract painter who often verged in the direction of semiabstraction and whose signs, symbols, and shapes stand for one thing at one time and for something else at another. Gorky did not think in the literal way that Rand suggests. He did not see an object and then proceed to obfuscate or disguise it. Rather he saw objects as full of visual and metamorphic possibility, so that one image might have several referents. Equally important, Gorky was very much a formalist: what he put on canvas or paper was largely determined by aesthetic concerns. Here and there he let the lines and shapes suggest an object, but not necessarily the object that had prompted the line or shape to begin with.

　　For all that, Rand's persistence in attempting to decode Gorky's symbolic language is understandable. While Gorky set himself up as an abstract painter and hated having people read images into his work, he also invited viewers to look for images by deliberately creating nearly recognizable shapes. When people asked what his paintings represented, he would reply, "See what you want!" Knowing that the spectator's attention would be heightened by seeing shapes that looked identifiable, Gorky pulled the viewer into his art by hinting at objects and dramas, and he held the viewer by keeping those objects and dramas a mystery.

569 Yet, just as Gorky would have wished: Even Harry Rand was stumped by *The Plough and the Song's* iconography: He said the painting was so advanced in its earliest examples that no comprehensive identification of its forms currently seems possible." Rand, *Arshile Gorky: The Implication of Symbols,* p. 219).

569 In his 1954 essay on *The Plough*: William C. Seitz, "Arshile Gorky's 'The Plough and the Song,' " p. 7.

569 But since she knew Gorky well: Schwabacher, *Arshile Gorky,* p. 128.

571 "The idea of being integrated": Willem de Kooning, paper delivered at *Subjects of the Artist: A New Art School,* February 18, 1949. Quoted in Thomas B. Hess, in Museum of Modern Art, *Willem de Kooning,* p. 15.

571 What he said, according to Julien: Levy, *Arshile Gorky*, p. 35.

572 *The Orators*, another of the great: Schwabacher, *Arshile Gorky*, p. 128.

572 Levy purported to quote: Levy, *Arshile Gorky*, p. 35.

572 The problem with seeing: Rand, *Arshile Gorky: The Implication of Symbols*, p. 159.

572 If indeed *The Orators* refers: *Ararat*, Fall 1971, p. 5, and AGA, pp. 108, 151. Mooradian says that *The Orators* was painted before Gorky's father died and that "Gorky in his Armenian correspondence several times refers to Lady Hamaspiur's funeral in Armenia as the source for *Orators*" (notes to pp. 167, 151). Mooradian's information is, however, often inaccurate.

573 *The Orators* might depict: Several drawings on Mougouch's letter paper from 1946 depict an assembly of insectoid creatures not unlike the "mourners" in *The Orators* (see A. *Gorky: Drawings*, figs. 17 and 18). Two studies for *The Orators* from about 1946–47 show a reclining man surrounded by eight or nine monstrous mourners or hospital attendants. As with many of Gorky's creatures, there is a cartoonish aspect to their fearsomeness, especially the tallest monster, who stands on the left at the foot of the bed or bier and appears to be adjusting some kind of cloth over the dead man's (or surgery patient's) thighs. In the studies the mourner on the near side of the bed and closest to the recumbent figure's head sits on what looks like a chair of modern design. In the painting only two clearly identifiable figures remain.

573 When Marny George, having herself: George, letter to James Thrall Soby.

573 Julien Levy wrote that it was influenced: Levy, *Arshile Gorky*, pp. 31–32.

573 Ethel Schwabacher said that *The Betrothal*: AGA, pp. 128, 131.

574 After the ceremony, when the groom: Villa and Matossian, *Armenian Village Life*, pp. 82–83.

575 Indeed, during a wintry walk: Schwabacher, *Arshile Gorky*, pp. 139–40.

576 "*Red Painting* and so-called": Jordan, Cat. Rais., p. 359.

576 Yet, for all the painting's: Ibid., p. 541.

576 Levy maintained that for several: Levy, *Arshile Gorky*, pp. 9–11, and Levy, *Memoir*, p. 291.

60: NO MORE PLOUGHS

579 "And he gave me a drawing": Mooradian, *Worlds*, p. 119.

579 "It hurts me still": Ibid., p. 151.

579 About this time Gorky's former: Revington Arthur, letter to Ruth Bowman, 1978.

580 "That was a few months before": Mooradian, *Worlds*, p. 163.

581 "Seating one on either knee": Schwabacher, *Arshile Gorky*, pp. 139–40.

582 His passion for Picasso had: Robert Melville, *Picasso: Master of the Phantom*, p. 1.

61: PEELED ONION

583 "I think you ought to let": Agnes Fielding, interview by author.

587 "He told me this many times": David Margolis, interviewed by author.

587 He said he saw less of Gorky and Mougouch: Roberto Matta Echaurren, interview by author, June 3, 1993.

588 On June 26 Gorky spent the day: Julien Levy, interview by Stephen Robeson Miller, December 16, 1972, Archives of American Art. I am grateful to Lisa Jacobs for sending me a copy of this interview.

588 "Mougouch is leaving me": Levy, *Memoir*, p. 288. The quotations that follow are from pp. 289–91.

588 Levitt remembered that, fearing: B. Blake Levitt, "Another View of Arshile Gorky," p. 5.

590 "I felt again the sad fatality": Levy, *Arshile Gorky*, p. 10.

591 "Oh God, Julien was the world's worst": Matossian, *Black Angel*, p. 456.

591 The following day Gorky called Julien: Levy, *Memoir*, p. 288.

591 "Well, Muriel," Gorky said: Matossian, *Black Angel*, p. 457.

591 Kay drove Gorky: In a 1972 interview Levy gave a slightly different version of the story. He said that after the accident he brought Gorky back to his house in Bridgewater and called Kay, who immediately came to lend a hand. Gorky was, said Levy, "very anxious to get home to hear what his phone call would be. And he complained of a very bad headache while Kay was here, so Kay insisted that it shouldn't be overlooked, that he should be stopped by at the New Milford hospital to get a check on why he had such a bad headache." Levy said he didn't remember whether Kay drove Gorky home or to the emergency room, or whether Gorky spent the night at the Levys' and Kay drove him to the hospital in the morning. "At any rate, they discovered that he had a fractured neck and had to put him in traction, so he never did get home from that trip" (Levy, interview by Stephen Robeson Miller).

593 "According to the doctors in the": Schwabacher, *Arshile Gorky*, p. 140.

594 It was, he said, Gorky's black: Levy told Karlen Mooradian that he lost control of the car because he was distracted by the hypnotic expression on Gorky's face (Mooradian, "The Wars of Arshile Gorky," p. 8).

594 Levy replied that Gorky quite possibly: Levy, *Memoir*, p. 287.

594 With his head pulled back: Mooradian, *Worlds*, p. 105.

595 "I came away thinking": Ibid., p. 188, and Margaret Osborn, interview by Karlen Mooradian.

595 "But the cancer operation": Agnes Gorky Phillips, notes written in the late 1950s.

596 Ethel Schwabacher wrote: Schwabacher, *Arshile Gorky*, p. 142.

596 "He looked like some barbarian warrior": Levy, *Memoir*, p. 292.

597 "But I don't know if that": Mooradian, *Worlds*, p. 102.

597 "It was a man, in some way": Osborn, "Mystery of Arshile Gorky," p. 59.

597 "It hung down, he couldn't": Matossian, *Black Angel*, pp. 461–62.

598 "Nothing matters anymore, soon all": Helena Benitez, *Wifredo and Helena*, p. 185.

598 "She wanted to go on being": Matossian, *Black Angel*, p. 462.

598 After this he became "listless": Benitez, *Wifredo and Helena*, p. 185.

598 On the drive back to the city: Matossian, *Black Angel*, p. 462.

599 When he caught sight of his: Spender, *From a High Place*, p. 362.

599 Margaret Osborn observed: Osborn, "Mystery of Arshile Gorky," p. 58.

599 "Perhaps I have said all these things": Agnes Phillips, letter to Ethel Schwabacher, February 9, 1952.

62: DARKNESS SPREADS OVER MY SOUL

602 "You don't understand it": Abel, *Intellectual Follies*, p. 53. This version of the story was told by Matta to Lionel Abel shortly after Gorky's death.

605 "My home is broken up": Schwabacher, *Arshile Gorky*, p. 144.

605 "I thought I was dreaming": de Havenon, "Reminiscence of Gorky."

606 One story has it that Gorky: Katherine Kuh, interview by Matthew Spender, in *From a High Place*, p. 368.

606 "Noguchi, I am done": Isamu Noguchi, *Isamu Noguchi: A Sculptor's World*, p. 30.

606 "I tried to talk him out": Karp, "Arshile Gorky: The Language of Art," p. 37.

606 Noguchi surmised that Gorky: Noguchi, *Isamu Noguchi*, p. 30.

607 "They were only interested in him": Isamu Noguchi, interview by Karlen Mooradian.

607 Later he was glad he had: Spender, *From a High Place*, p. 369.

607 Schary agreed to come over: Isamu Noguchi, interview by Karlen Mooradian.

608 "So he called her . . . and": Ibid. Gorky may have dialed and got no answer, for Mougouch says that after she left for Virginia she only received one phone call from Gorky. But, from the evidence of people who were with Gorky on his last days, Gorky called Mougouch more than once.

608 "There was this man in agony": Matossian, *Black Angel*, p. 469.

609 "I never should have let": Saul Schary, interview by Karlen Mooradian, and Mooradian, *Worlds*, p. 206.

609 Gorky asked him, Levy recalled: Levy, *Arshile Gorky*, p. 10.

609 "So it was a kind of weird": Julien Levy, interview by Stephen Robeson Miller. Levy's memoir offers another version of the telephone conversation: "Late in the evening of July 20, 1948, Gorky telephoned. 'Can you get me a woman?' he abruptly asked. . . . He explained that what he was searching for was occasional companionship, female; occasional cooking, female; occasional sympathy, female. . . . The glass house was too desolate alone. . . . I suggested he try to sleep, and in the morning we would think of something, someone" (Levy, *Memoir*, pp. 292–93).

609 Now, he said, he could not come: Dorothy Miller, letter to Robeson Miller, February 8, 1976. Ethel Schwabacher, notes on a telephone conversation with Holger Cahill.

609 But he didn't: According to some reports, Gorky's phone call to cancel lunch with Kay Sage took place in the morning, and it was then that she called Peter Blume.

609 Then, "Good-bye, my dear": Saul Schary, interview by Karlen Mooradian.

610 "As though he'd definitely made up": Ibid.
611 "So we all went over": Mooradian, *Worlds*, pp. 103–05.
611 They also found several lengths: Ibid., p. 119.
613 "Gorky committed suicide in the morning": Ibid., p. 104.
613 "good by all loved": Cowley thought that, had the chalk not broken, Gorky would have written, "Good-by my loved ones." Julien Levy's version of what was written on the crate has become the official one. He seems to have combined Blume's "loves" with Cowley's "loved." He said Gorky wrote: "Goodbye My Loveds" (Levy, *Arshile Gorky*, p. 9).
613 "He came to this country": *New York Times*, July 22, 1948, p. 23.
614 Vartoosh remembered embracing Gorky's old friend: Mooradian, "Wars of Arshile Gorky," p. 8.
615 "The grave was then stamped down": Levy, *Memoir*, p. 294.
615 Before it was edited to remove: Levitt, "Another View of Gorky."
616 "I come with my weary soul": Spender, *From a High Place*, p. 194. The Whitney Museum of American Art has a different translation of this poem.
616 "He was very young then": Agnes Gorky Phillips, unpublished notes.

63:AFTERMATH

619 "The guy always did talk": Potter, *To a Violent Grave*, p. 266.
619 "A lot of them will be": Mooradian, *Worlds*, pp. 132–33.
621 Presumably her lawyer took: To support Agnes's legal case, various art-world notables were asked to write letters attesting to Gorky's stature. On August 19, Monroe Wheeler of the Museum of Modern Art wrote to Agnes's lawyer, H. B. Bradbury, in New Milford that Gorky was "one of the most distinguished painters of his generation in this country." Dorothy Miller wrote: "As to the regard and esteem in which Gorky was held in the art world, I place a high value on it. Leading American critics and progressive museums have placed him, I should say, among the dozen to twenty most important American painters of the generation born shortly after 1900." Clement Greenberg's tribute was just what was needed:

> Arshile Gorky's death was an incalculable loss to American art. Gorky was among the four or five most important painters alive in this country at the time he died. I would also say that he was one of the most important painters of his generation anywhere in the world and would have more than held his own in Paris, London, and Rome. . . . Nobody else is doing what he was and nobody else will show us what direction American painting may have taken in certain of its aspects had Gorky lived longer.

> On December 9, The *New York Times* ran a piece on the settlement:

> Mrs. Agnes Magruder Gorky agreed today to accept $11,000 from Julien Levy, New York art gallery owner, in settlement of a $20,000

damage suit arising from the death of her husband, Arshile Gorky, the Russian-born artist. Mr. Gorky was a cousin of Maxim Gorky, the writer.

Mrs. Gorky contended that her husband's suicide last July 21 was attributable to injuries suffered a month earlier when Mr. Levy's automobile, in which he was a passenger, was involved in an accident. The artist became melancholy and morose as a result of the injuries, she asserted, and his mental depression caused him to take his life.

The settlement was announced by counsel as a jury was being selected in Superior Court to try the case.

The letters and the *Times* clipping are in the Whitney Museum of American Art, Artist's File.

623 "I stood by the fence": Gossip among the Paris Surrealists had the story differently: Marcel Jean's letter to Kiesler (April 20, 1949) said Matta had left Mougouch.

623 By this time, a close friend: Abel, *Intellectual Follies*, p. 54.

623 Had not Breton written in: Quoted in Abel, *Intellectual Follies*, p. 47.

623 On October 25, 1948, the Surrealists: Mark Polizzotti, *Revolution of the Mind: The Life of André Breton*, p. 557.

623 "Who is next?": Ibid., p. 606.

624 The show included eight paintings: The exhibition brochure lists the following works: *White Abstraction* (1934), the green-ground version of *Garden in Sochi*, borrowed from the Museum of Modern Art (1941), *The Liver Is the Cock's Comb* (1944), *The Pirate* (listed as 1945 but in fact painted between 1942 and 1943), *Delicate Game* (1946), *Good Hope Road* (1945), *Impatience* (1945 but listed as 1946), *Soft Night* (1947 but listed as 1948), and the *Sculptured Head* from 1932 in Mina Metzger's collection. A group of drawings was borrowed from various collectors.

624 "Altogether the impression is": *New York Times*, November 21, 1948. The clipping is in the Whitney Museum, Artist's File.

624 "Such canvases as the": Whitney Museum, Artist's File.

624 He said Gorky was: Greenberg, "Art," December 11, 1948, p. 676.

625 "I hadn't been able to get": Judith Parker, "Art to Me Is Almost a Religion" (interview with Julien Levy), *Harvard Magazine*, September–October 1979, p. 44.

64: FAME

626 In 1950 he was given a show: Weldon Kees, "Art," *Nation*, April 8, 1950, pp. 333–34.

626 "This, of course, makes his absence": Clement Greenberg, "Art Chronicle," pp. 512–13.

627 Convinced that Gorky was the greatest: Emily Genauer, "Gorky, Now Legend, in Week's New Shows," *New York Times*, October 2, 1955. Whitney Museum of American Art, Artist's File.

627 Gorky was, he said: Lloyd Goodrich's text is in the Whitney Museum, Artist's File.

628 "The catalogue doesn't have enough": Museum of Modern Art, *Jackson Pollock*, p. 57.

628 "Hordes of young painters": Genauer, "Gorky, Now Legend."

628 And sculptor Philip Pavia insisted: Potter, *To a Violent Grave*, p. 100.

629 He calls Gorky's art: Robert Melville, " 'The New American Painting' at the Tate," *Arts*, April 1959, p. 18.

629 Similarly, William Rubin concludes: Rubin, "Arshile Gorky, Surrealism, and the New American Painting," p. 38.

630 Gorky's work was, says Rosenberg: Rosenberg, *Arshile Gorky*, pp. 13–14.

630 Likewise, Hilton Kramer sees: Hilton Kramer, "Tragedy of Life and Art," p. 117.

630 Gorky died too soon to see: As Meyer Schapiro put it, "Pollock and Rothko and Gottlieb and de Kooning were people who found themselves only after the death of Gorky. They received a stimulus from Gorky. I think all of these people were stimulated by the presence of Gorky without necessarily imitating him. Gorky's independence and great knowledge and seriousness all contributed something" (Mooradian, *Worlds*, p. 202).

631 "There is a desperate innocence": Afro, "Arshile Gorky," trans. and rpt. in Palazzo delle Esposizioni, *Arshile Gorky: Works on Paper*, p. 12.

631 When the Museum of Modern Art presented: Robert Rosenblum, "Arshile Gorky," p. 33.

632 "He made works that give and give": Peter Schjeldahl, "American Pie: The Whitney's Empty Blockbuster," p. 96.

Selected Bibliography

✺

BOOKS ON GORKY

A. *Gorky: Drawings.* New York, 1970.

Jordan, Jim M., and Robert Goldwater. *The Paintings of Arshile Gorky: A Critical Catalogue.* New York and London, 1980. Abbreviated Cat. Rais.

Lader, Melvin P. *Arshile Gorky.* New York, 1985.

Levy, Julien. *Arshile Gorky: Paintings, Drawings, Studies.* New York, 1966.

Matossian, Nouritza. *Black Angel: A Life of Arshile Gorky.* New York, 1999.

Mooradian, Karlen. *Arshile Gorky Adoian.* Chicago, 1978. Abbreviated AGA.

———. *The Many Worlds of Arshile Gorky.* Chicago, 1980. Abbreviated Worlds.

Rand, Harry. *Arshile Gorky: The Implication of Symbols.* Berkeley and Los Angeles, 1991.

Reiff, Robert. *A Stylistic Analysis of Arshile Gorky's Art from 1943–1948.* New York, 1978.

Rosenberg, Harold. *Arshile Gorky: The Man, the Time, the Idea.* New York, 1962.

Schwabacher, Ethel. *Arshile Gorky.* Pref. Lloyd Goodrich. Introd. Meyer Schapiro. New York, 1957.

Spender, Matthew. *From a High Place: A Life of Arshile Gorky.* New York, 1999.

BOOKS ON RELATED TOPICS

Abel, Lionel. *The Intellectual Follies: A Memoir of the Literary Venture in New York and Paris.* New York, 1982.

Ashton, Dore. *The New York School: A Cultural Reckoning.* New York, 1973.

Benitez, Helena. *Wifredo and Helena: My Life with Wifredo Lam, 1939–1950.* Lausanne, 1999.

Berman, Avis. *Rebels on Eighth Street.* New York, 1990.

Breslin, James E. B. *Mark Rothko: A Biography.* Chicago, 1993.

Breton, André. *Surrealism and Painting*. Trans. Simon Watson Taylor. New York, 1972.

Graham, John. *System and Dialectics of Art*. Annot. and introd. Marcia Epstein Allentuck. Foreword Dorothy Dehner. Baltimore, 1971.

Gruen, John. *The Party's Over Now*. New York, 1967.

Guggenheim, Peggy. *Out of This Century: Confessions of an Art Addict*. New York, 1980.

Hess, Thomas B. *Abstract Painting: Background and the American Phase*. New York, 1951.

Janis, Sidney, *Abstract and Surrealist Art in America*. New York, 1944.

Kootz, Samuel M. *New Frontiers in American Painting*. New York, 1943.

Levy, Julien. *Memoir of an Art Gallery*. New York, 1977.

———. *Surrealism*. New York, 1936.

McCoy, Garnett, ed. *David Smith*. New York, 1973.

Meier-Graefe, Julius. *Paul Cézanne*. Munich, 1923.

Melville, Robert. *Picasso: Master of the Phantom*. London, 1939.

Museum of Modern Art. *The Museum of Modern Art at Mid-Century: At Home and Abroad*. New York, 1994. Includes Lynn Zelevansky, "Dorothy Miller's 'Americans' 1942–63."

Noguchi, Isamu. *Isamu Noguchi: A Sculptor's World*. New York, 1968.

O'Connor, Francis V., ed. *Art for the Millions: Essays from the 1930s by Artists and Administrators of the WPA Federal Art Project*. New York Graphic Society, Boston, 1973.

———, ed. *The New Deal Art Projects: An Anthology of Memoirs*. Washington, DC, 1972.

Polizzotti, Mark. *Revolution of the Mind: The Life of André Breton*. New York, 1995.

Potter, Jeffrey. *To a Violent Grave: An Oral Biography of Jackson Pollock*. Wainscott, NY, 1985.

Rosenberg, Harold. *Willem de Kooning*. New York, 1973.

Rubin, William S. *Dada and Surrealist Art*. New York, 1968.

Sandler, Irving. *The Triumph of American Painting: A History of Abstract Expressionism*. New York, 1970.

Sawin, Martica. *Surrealism in Exile and the Beginning of the New York School*. Cambridge, MA, 1995.

Soyer, Raphael. *Diary of an Artist*. Washington, DC, 1977.

———. *Homage to Thomas Eakins*. South Brunswick, NJ, 1966.

———. *Self-Revealment: A Memoir*. New York, 1967.

Tanning, Dorothea. *Birthday Party*. San Francisco, 1986.

Weld, Jacqueline Bogard. *Peggy: The Wayward Guggenheim*. New York, 1986.

EXHIBITION CATALOGS OF GORKY'S WORK (BY DATE)

Mellon Gallery. *Arshile Gorky*. Notes by Holger Cahill, Stuart Davis, and Harriet Janowitz. Philadelphia, 1934.

Julien Levy Gallery. *Arshile Gorky*. Essay "The Eye-Spring: Arshile Gorky" by André Breton. Trans. Julien Levy. New York, March 1945.

Kootz Gallery. *Selected Paintings by the Late Arshile Gorky.* Essay by Adolph Gottlieb. New York, March 28–April 24, 1950.

Whitney Museum of American Art. *Arshile Gorky, Memorial Exhibition.* Essay by Ethel Schwabacher. New York, 1951.

Sidney Janis Gallery. *An Exhibition of 35 Selected Drawings from the Late Work of Arshile Gorky.* Text by Sidney Janis. New York, October 24, 1959.

Museum of Modern Art. *Arshile Gorky: Paintings, Drawings, Studies.* Essay by William C. Seitz. Foreword by Julien Levy. New York, 1962.

La Jolla Art Center. *Arshile Gorky: Paintings and Drawings, 1927–1937, in the Collection of Mr. and Mrs. Hans Burkhardt.* Essay by Hans Burkhardt. La Jolla, CA, February 21–March 21, 1963.

Tate Gallery. *Arshile Gorky: Paintings and Drawings.* Introd. Robert Melville. London, 1965.

M. Knoedler & Co., Inc. *Gorky: Drawings.* Essay by Jim Jordan. New York, 1969.

University of Maryland. *The Drawings of Arshile Gorky.* Pref. George Levitine. Foreword by William H. Gerdts. College Park, 1969.

University of Texas at Austin. *Arshile Gorky: Drawings to Paintings.* Essays by Isobel Grossman, Hayden Herrera, Karlen Mooradian, Harry Rand, Alice Baber, Jim M. Jordan, Ethel Schwabacher, and Reuben Nakian. Austin, 1975.

Newark Museum. *Murals without Walls: Arshile Gorky's Aviation Murals Rediscovered.* Essays by Francis V. O'Connor, Frederick T. Kiesler, Ruth Bowman, and Jim Jordan. Newark, 1978.

Hirshhorn Museum and Sculpture Garden, Smithsonian Institution. *Arshile Gorky: The Hirshhorn Museum and Sculpture Garden Collection.* Essay by Phyllis Rosenzweig. Washington, DC, 1979.

Solomon R. Guggenheim Museum. *Arshile Gorky: A Retrospective.* Essay by Diane Waldman. New York, 1981.

Museé Cantonal des Beaux-Arts. *Arshile Gorky: Oeuvres sur papier, 1929–1947.* Essays by Erika Billeter, Bernard Blistene, Konrad Oberhuber, Matthew Spender, André Breton, and Frank O'Hara. Lausanne, 1990.

Palazzo delle Esposizioni. *Arshile Gorky: Works on Paper.* Essays by Melvin Lader and Afro. Rome, 1992.

Stephen Mazoh Gallery. *Arshile Gorky and the Genesis of Abstraction: Drawings from the Early 1930s.* "Introduction to the Plates" by Joseph P. Ruzika. Essays by Matthew Spender and Barbara Rose. New York, 1994.

Gagosian Gallery. *Arshile Gorky: Late Paintings.* Interview with Willem de Kooning. New York, 1994.

Modern Art Museum of Fort Worth. *Arshile Gorky: The Breakthrough Years.* Essays by Dore Ashton, Michael Auping, and Matthew Spender. Fort Worth, TX, 1995.

Gagosian Gallery. *Arshile Gorky: Paintings and Drawings, 1929–1942.* Essays by Donald Kuspir, Melvin Lader, and Matthew Spender. New York, 1998.

——. *Arshile Gorky: Portraits.* Essays by David Anfam and Matthew Spender. New York, 2001.

EXHIBITION CATALOGS ON RELATED TOPICS

Brown University. *Graham, Gorky, Smith, and Davis in the Thirties.* Providence, 1977.

Gallery Association of New York State. *New Deal for Art.* Essay by Marlene Park and Gerald E. Markowitz. Hamilton, NY, 1977.

Hirshhorn Museum and Sculpture Garden. *The Golden Door: Artist-Immigrants of America, 1876 1776.* Essays by Daniel J. Boorstin and Cynthia Jaffee McCabe. Washington, DC, 1976.

Hugo Gallery. *Bloodflames.* Essay by Nicolas Calas. New York, 1947.

Museum of Art, Carnegie Institute. *Abstract Painting and Sculpture in America.* Ed. John R. Lane and Susan C. Larsen. Pittsburgh, 1983.

Museum of Modern Art. *Dada, Surrealism, and Their Heritage.* Essay by William S. Rubin. New York, 1968.

——. *Willem de Kooning.* Essay by Thomas B. Hess. New York, 1968.

——. *Jackson Pollock.* Essay by Francis V. O'Connor. New York, 1967.

National Gallery of Art. *American Art at Mid-Century: The Subjects of the Artist.* Washington, DC, 1978. Includes Eliza E. Rathbone, "Arshile Gorky: The Plough and the Song."

Poindexter Gallery. *The Thirties: Painting in New York.* Ed. Patricia Pasloff. New York, 1956.

Provincetown Art Association and Museum. *Life Colors Art: Fifty Years of Painting by Peter Busa.* Provincetown, MA, 1992.

JOURNALS: SPECIAL ISSUES ON GORKY

Ararat. Ed. Karlen Mooradian. Fall 1971.

Arti Visive, Summer 1957.

Arts Magazine, March 1976.

ARTICLES ON GORKY

Alloway, Lawrence. "Gorky." *Art Forum,* March 1963, pp. 28–31.

Ash, John. "Arshile Gorky: How My Mother's Embroidered Apron Unfolds in My Life, 1944." *Artforum,* September 1995, pp. 78–80.

Ashton, Dore. "Arshile Gorky, peintre romantique." *XXè Siècle,* June 1962, pp. 76–81.

——. "New York Commentary." *Studio International,* Feb. 1970, pp. 73–74.

Balakian, Peter. "Arshile Gorky and the Armenian Genocide." *Art in America,* February 1996, pp. 58–67, 108–09.

Balamuth, Lewis. "I Met A. Gorky." *Color and Rhyme,* April 29, 1949, pp. 2–3.

Brach, Paul. "Gorky's Secret Garden." *Art in America,* October 1981, pp. 122–26.

Burliuk, Mary. "Arshile Gorky." *Color and Rhyme* 19 (1949): 1–2.

Clapp, Talcott B. "A Painter in a Glass House." *Sunday Republican Magazine* (Waterbury, CT), February 9, 1948, p. 6.

Davis, Stuart. "Arshile Gorky in the 1930s: A Personal Recollection." *Magazine of*

Art, February 1951, pp. 56–58. Rpt. in *Stuart Davis*. Ed. Diane Kelder. New York, 1971.

——. "Handmaiden of Misery." *Saturday Review*, December 28, 1957, pp. 16–17.

de Kooning, Elaine. "Gorky: Painter of His Own Legend." *Art News*, January 1951, pp. 38–41, 63–66.

de Kooning, Willem. Letter to the editor. *Art News*, January 1949, p. 6.

Fitzgerald, Michael. "Arshile Gorky's 'The Limit,' " *Art Magazine*, March 1980, pp. 110–15.

Goldwater, Robert. "The Genius of the Moujik." *Saturday Review*, May 19, 1962, p. 38.

Goodrich, Lloyd. "Notes on Eight Works by Arshile Gorky." *Magazine of Art*, February 1951, pp. 59–61.

Greenberg, Clement. "Art." *Nation*, March 24, 1945, pp. 342–43.

——. "Art." *Nation*, May 4, 1946, pp. 552–53.

——. "Art." *Nation*, November 23, 1946, p. 594.

——. "Art." *Nation*, January 10, 1948, p. 52.

——. "Art." *Nation*, March 20, 1948, pp. 331–32.

——. "Art." *Nation*, December 11, 1948, p. 676.

——. "Art Chronicle." *Partisan Review*, May–June 1950, pp. 512–13.

Greene, Balcomb. "Memories of Arshile Gorky." *Arts Magazine*, March 1976, pp. 108–10.

Herrera, Hayden. "The Sculptures of Arshile Gorky." *Arts Magazine*, March 1976, pp. 88–90.

——. "Arshile Gorky's Self-Portraits: The Painter by Himself." *Art in America*, March–April, 1976, pp. 56–64.

——. "Gorky's Distant Likenesses," *Art in America*, November 2002, pp. 148–151.

Hess, Thomas B. "Arshile Gorky Flies Again." *New York Magazine*, September 12, 1977, pp. 84–89.

Hooton, Bruce. "One Who Saw First: Major Gorky Show." *Art/World*, April 18–May 16, 1981, p. 5 (interview with Willem de Kooning).

Jordan, Jim M. "Arshile Gorky at Crooked Run Farm." *Arts Magazine*, March 1976, pp. 99–103.

Kainen, Jacob. "Memories of Arshile Gorky." *Arts Magazine*, March 1976, pp. 96–98.

——. "Posing for Gorky: A Memoir of the New York Master." *Washington Post*, June 10, 1979.

Kiesler, Frederick T. "Murals without Walls: Relating to Gorky's Newark Project." *Art Front*, December 18, 1936, pp. 10–11. Rpt. in Newark Museum, *Murals without Walls*, p. 31.

Kramer, Hilton. "The Case of the Purloined Image." *New York Times*, June 25, 1981, sec. C, p. 15.

——. "Tragedy of Life and Art." *Art and Antiques*, October 1995, p. 117.

Levitt, B. Blake. "Another View of Arshile Gorky." *Litchfield County Times*, August 6, 1999, p. 5.

McGregor, John M. "Arshile Gorky's Agony: The Phallus and the Flame." *Express*, Summer 1981, pp. 5–6.

Miller, Jo. "The Prints of Arshile Gorky." *Brooklyn Museum Annual* 6 (1964–65): 57–61.

Monte, James. "The Life and Work of Arshile Gorky." *Museum Magazine*, July–August 1981, pp. 42–47.

Mooradian, Karlen. "Arshile Gorky." *Armenian Review*, Summer 1955, pp. 49–58.

——. "The Gardener from Eden." *Ararat*, Winter 1968, pp. 3–13.

——. "The Philosophy of Arshile Gorky." *Armenian Digest*, September–October 1971, pp. 52–74.

——. "The Unknown Gorky." *Art News*, September 1967, pp. 52, 53, 66–68.

——. "The Wars of Arshile Gorky." *Ararat*, Fall 1983, pp. 2–16.

O'Connor, Francis V. "The Economy of Patronage: Arshile Gorky on the Art Projects." *Arts Magazine*, March 1976, pp. 94–95.

O'Hara, Frank. "Art Chronicle." *Kulchur*, Summer 1962, pp. 55–56.

Osborn, Margaret. "The Mystery of Arshile Gorky: A Personal Account." *Art News*, February 1963, pp. 42–43, 58–61.

Riley, Maude. "The Eye-Spring: Arshile Gorky." *Art Digest*, March 15, 1945, p. 10.

Rose, Barbara. "Arshile Gorky and John Graham, Eastern Exiles in a Western World." *Arts Magazine*, March 1976, pp. 62–69.

Rosenblum, Robert. "Arshile Gorky." *Arts Magazine*, January 1958, pp. 30–33.

Rubin, William. "Arshile Gorky, Surrealism, and the New American Painting." *Art International*, February 25, 1963, pp. 27–38. Rpt. in Metropolitan Museum of Art, *New York Painting and Sculpture: 1940–1970*. New York, 1970, pp. 379–83.

Schapiro, Meyer. "Gorky: The Creative Influence." *Art News*, September 1957, pp. 28–31, 52.

Schjeldahl, Peter. "The Great Gorky." *Village Voice*, May 13, 1981.

Seitz, William C. "Arshile Gorky's 'The Plough and the Song.' " *Allen Memorial Art Museum Bulletin* 12 (1954): 5–15.

Sweeny, James Johnson. "Five American Painters." *Harper's Bazaar*, April 1944, pp. 122, 124.

Sweeny, Jim. "Arshile Gorky's Drawings." *Ararat*, Spring 1996, pp. 30–37.

Vaccaro, Nick Dante. "Gorky's Debt to Gaudier-Brzeska." *Art Journal*, Fall 1963, pp. 33–34.

ARTICLES ON RELATED TOPICS

Art in America, v. 53, August–September, 1965, Special Issue: The Artist Speaks, woven from documents from the Archives of American Art, "Poverty, Politics and Artists, 1930–1945."

Carson, Ruth. "Bright Side Out." *Colliers*, January 28, 1939.

Gardener, Colin. "Interview with Hans Burkhardt." *Arts Magazine*, p. 105.

Glaser, Bruce B. "Jackson Pollock: An Interview with Lee Krasner." *Arts Magazine*, April 1967, p. 37.

Herrera, Hayden. "John Graham: Modernist Turns Magus," *Arts Magazine*, October 1976, pp. 100–105.

———. "Le Feu Ardent: John Graham's Journal," *Archives of American Art Journal*, No. 2, 1974, pp. 6–17.

Kainen, Jacob. "Remembering John Graham." *Arts Magazine*, November 1986, pp. 25–31.

La Follette, Suzanne. "The Artist and the Depression." *Nation*, September 6, 1933, p. 265.

Lader, Melvin P. "Graham, Gorky, de Kooning, and the 'Ingres Revival' in America." *Arts Magazine*, March 1978, pp. 94–99.

McNeil, George. "American Abstractionists Venerable at Twenty." *Art News*, May 1956, p. 64.

Parker, Judith. "Art to Me Is Almost a Religion." *Harvard Magazine*, September–October 1979, p. 44 (interview with Julien Levy).

Perényi, Eleanor. "Art's Sake." *Town and Country*, March 1947, pp. 126, 198, 200.

Schjeldahl, Peter. "American Pie: The Whitney's Empty Blockbuster." *New Yorker*, May 17, 1999, p. 96.

Smith, David. "Notes on My Work." *Arts Magazine*, February 1960, p. 44.

Valliere, James T. "De Kooning on Pollock." *Partisan Review*, Fall 1967, p. 603.

ARTICLES BY ARSHILE GORKY

"Fetish of Antique Stifles Art Here, Says Gorky Kin." *New York Evening Post*, September 15, 1926, p. 17. Original newspaper clipping in Whitney Museum of American Art, Artist's File. Rpt. in Harold Rosenberg, *Arshile Gorky: The Man, the Time, the Idea*, pp. 123–26.

"Thirst." *Grand Central School of Art Quarterly*, November 1926. Rpt. in Ethel Schwabacher, *Arshile Gorky*, p. 21.

"Stuart Davis." *Creative Art*, September 1931, pp. 213, 217. Rpt. in Diane Kelder, ed., *Stuart Davis*, New York, 1971, pp. 192–94.

"My Murals for the Newark Airport: An Interpretation, 1936." First version of this essay rpt. in Francis V. O'Connor, *Art for the Millions*, pp. 72–73. Also rpt. in Newark Museum, in *Murals without Walls*, pp. 13–16.

Artist's questionnaire about *Argula*, 1941. Museum of Modern Art, Artist's File.

"Garden in Sochi." Essay written on June 26, 1942, at the request of the Museum of Modern Art. Typescript in the Museum of Modern Art, Artist's File. Rpt. in Ethel Schwabacher, *Arshile Gorky*, p. 66.

"Camouflage." *Grand Central School of Art Course Announcement*, 1942. Rpt. in Harold Rosenberg, *Arshile Gorky*, pp. 133–35.

LETTERS BY ARSHILE GORKY

Letters to Vartoosh and Moorad Mooradian (in Armenian). Arshile Gorky/Mooradian Archive, Eastern Diocese of the Armenian Church of America, New York City. A selection of these letters, translated by Haig Partizian for Ethel Schwabacher are in the Whitney Museum of American Art, Artist's File. Gorky's letters were also translated by Ani Marderosian and Piero

Kucuikian for Matthew Spender. Copies of these translations are in the Matthew Spender Papers, Whitney Museum of American Art. A selection of Gorky's letters were translated and published by Karlen Mooradian in *Arshile Gorky Adoian* and *The Many Worlds of Arshile Gorky*, but Mooradian fabricated many of these letters.

Letters to Corinne Michael West. Stuart and Roberta Friedman, personal archive, Granite Springs, NY.

Letter to Max Weber, October 21, 1939. Archives of American Art.

Letter to Dorothy Miller, June 26, 1942. Museum of Modern Art, Artist's File.

Letters to Mougouch Gorky. Agnes Fielding, personal archive, London.

DOCUMENTS

Notes and correspondence of Agnes Gorky Phillips (Agnes or Mougouch Fielding) are listed under "Agnes Gorky."

American Missionary Reports. Papers of the American Board of Commissioners for Foreign Missions: The Near East. The American Missionary Reports are on microfilm in the Zohrab Center of the Eastern Diocese of the Armenian Church in New York City and in Houghton Library, Harvard University.

Arthur, Revington. Letter to Ruth Bowman, 1978. Newark Museum Library, Artist's File.

Austin, Helen. Interview by Harry W. Anderson, February 22, 1979. Interview notes in Harry Anderson's personal archive.

Avedisian, Satenik. Letter to Mina Metzger, March 31, 1949. Whitney Museum of American Art, Artist's File.

Baker, Norris C. Letter to Arshile Gorky. November 9, 1946. Collection Maro Gorky. Photocopies in the Whitney Museum of American Art, Artist's File, and the Archives of American Art.

Barr, Alfred H. Letter to Olive M. Lyford, October 14, 1936. Whitney Museum of American Art, Artist's File.

———. Letter to Audrey McMahon, December 3, 1935. Whitney Museum of American Art, Artist's File.

———. Letter to Karlen Mooradian, March 30, 1966. Vartoosh Mooradian Papers, Eastern Diocese of the Armenian Church of America.

Bijur, Nathan I. Letter to Mina Metzger. November 1949. Whitney Museum of American Art, Artist's File.

Busa, Peter. Interview by Jack Taylor, c. 1972. Transcript in Christopher Busa's personal archive, Provincetown, MA. The transcript is also in the Archives of American Art, Peter Busa Papers.

———. Notebooks. Christopher Busa, personal archive, Provincetown, MA.

Cimenti, Elena. "Giorgio Cavallon: 1932–1960." Diss., University of Venice, 1992.

Diller, Burgoyne. Letter to Ethel Schwabacher. November 1949. Whitney Museum of American Art, Artist's File.

Ellis Island records, ship's manifest. American Family Immigration History Center. Passenger records are available at www.ellisislandrecords.org.

Fact sheet on Gorky and his Newark mural project. Newark Museum Library.

George, Marny. Letter to James Thrall Soby, March 15, 1951. Whitney Museum of American Art, Artist's File.

Goodrich, Lloyd. Notes on a conversation with Saul Schary, July 5, 1950. Whitney Museum of Modern Art, archive information about paintings in the collection.

Gorky, Agnes. Letter to author, December 9, 1972.

——. Notes written in the late 1950s after the publication of Ethel Schwabacher's *Arshile Gorky* (1957). Agnes Fielding, personal archive, London.

——. Letters to Arshile Gorky. Agnes Fielding, personal archive, London.

——. Letters to Nathalie Campbell. Agnes Fielding, personal archive, London.

——. Letters to Jeanne Reynal. Agnes Fielding, personal archive, London.

——. Letters to Esther Magruder. Agnes Fielding, personal archive, London.

——. Letters to Ethel Schwabacher. Whitney Museum of American Art, Artist's File.

Grand Central School of Art, New York. Catalog for 1926–27. Whitney Museum of American Art, Artist's File.

Guild Art Gallery Papers. Archives of American Art.

de Havenon, Gaston T. "Reminiscence of Gorky." Handwritten manuscript in the Archives of American Art.

Herrera, Hayden. "Garden of Fantasy: Arshile Gorky's Garden in Sochi." Master's thesis, Hunter College, 1972.

Jaffe, Cynthia Joyce. "Reuben Nakian." Master's thesis, Columbia University, n.d. A portion of this thesis is in the Newark Museum, Artist's File.

Karp, Diane Rosenberg. "Arshile Gorky: The Language of Art." Ph.D. diss. University of Pennsylvania, 1982.

Lescaze, William. Letter to Wolfgang Schwabacher, January 13, 1949. Whitney Museum of American Art, Artist's File.

Levy, Julien. Letter to Ethel Schwabacher, May 1950. Whitney Museum of American Art, Artist's File.

Julien Levy Gallery. Contract with Arshile Gorky, 1945. Agnes Fielding, personal archive, London.

Lieber, Edvard. Notes on a conversation with Elaine de Kooning, in Lieber, letter to author, May 9, 1998.

Lyford, Olive M. Letter to Alfred H. Barr, October 2, 1936. Whitney Museum of American Art, Artist's File.

Magruder, John, and Esther Magruder. Letters. Malcolm Magruder, personal archive, Virginia.

McCulloch, Ruth. Notes from interview with Vartoosh Mooradian. Whitney Museum of American Art, Artist's File.

McMahon, Audrey. Letter to Alfred H. Barr, December 2, 1935. Whitney Museum of American Art, Artist's File.

Metzger, Mina B. Unpublished memoir of Arshile Gorky, January 6, 1949. Whitney Museum of American Art, Artist's File.

———. Notes from interview with Vartoosh Mooradian, December 1948. Schwabacher Papers, Whitney Museum of American Art, Artist's File.

Mooradian, Vartoosh. Letter to Ethel Schwabacher. Whitney Museum of American Art, Artist's File.

Murphy, Katherine. Letter to Ethel Schwabacher, August 30, 1952. Whitney Museum of American Art, Artist's File.

———. Letter to Elaine de Kooning, July 29, 1951. Museum of Modern Art, Department of Painting and Sculpture, Arshile Gorky, Collection File, Museum of Modern Art, Artist's File, August 1945.

New School of Design. Catalog, n.d. Museum of Modern Art, Artist's File.

Reynal, Jeanne. Letters to Agnes Gorky (Mougouch). Archives of American Art.

———. Letter to Ethel Schwabacher, August 29, 1948. Whitney Museum of American Art, Artist's File.

Richmond, Patricia Margaret. "Michael West: Paintings from the 1940s and 1950s." Master's thesis, Columbia College and George Washington University, 1995.

Schwabacher, Ethel. Interview by Ruth Bowman, January 17, 1976. Transcript in Newark Museum, Artist's File.

———. "Further Thoughts on Gorky." Unpublished text written for Isobel Grossman, 1974. Whitney Museum of American Art, Artist's File.

———. Notes on a telephone conversation with Holger Cahill. Schwabacher Papers, Whitney Museum of American Art, Artist's File.

———. Notes on a conversation with Sidney Janis, January 12, 1949. Whitney Museum of American Art, Artist's File.

Spender, Matthew. Interview with Dorothy Dehner, November 20, 1993. Matthew Spender Papers, Whitney Museum of American Art.

———, comp. "Letters and Documents."

Stoehr, Taylor. Letter to author, January 10, 1995.

Weiss, Jean Bijur. Letter to Matthew Spender, March 7, 1994. Matthew Spender Papers, Whitney Museum of American Art.

West, Corinne Michael. "Notes, Gorky." 1977, 1978, 1988. Corinne Michael West Papers, Stuart and Roberta Friedman, personal archive, Granite Springs, NY.

———. Notes on Gorky written at the request of Ethel Schwabacher. Whitney Museum of American Art, Artist's File.

BOOKS ABOUT ARMENIAN HISTORY AND CULTURE

Aprahamian, Souren. *From Van to Detroit*. Ann Arbor, 1993.

Arlen, Michael J. *Passage to Ararat*. New York, 1975.

Balakian, Peter. *Black Dog of Fate*. New York, 1997.

Bournoutian, George A. *A History of the Armenian People*. Vol. 2. Costa Mesa, CA, 1994.

Bryce, James, and Arnold Toynbee. *The Treatment of the Armenians in the Ottoman Empire*. London, 1916.

Buxton, Noel, and Harold Buxton. *Travels and Politics in Armenia*. London, 1914.

Dadrian, Vahakn N. *German Responsibility in the Armenian Genocide: A Review of the Historical Evidence of German Complicity.* Watertown, MA, 1996.

La défense héroïque de Van. Trans. M.G. Édition de la Revue *Droschak.* Geneva, 1916.

Hartunian, Abraham H. *Neither to Laugh nor to Weep: A Memoir of the Armenian Genocide.* Trans. Vartan Hartunian. Cambridge, MA, 1968.

Hovanessian, Diana Der, and Marzbed Margossian, eds. and trans. *Anthology of Armenian Poetry.* New York, 1978.

Hovannisian, Richard G., ed. *The Armenian Genocide.* New York, 1992.

——, ed. *The Armenian in History and Literature.* Malibu, 1981.

——. *Armenia on the Road to Independence, 1918.* Berkeley, 1967.

——. *The Republic of Armenia.* Vol. 1: *The First Year, 1918–1919.* Berkeley, 1971.

Illustration armenienne: 1901–1906. Keghouni, photographic review published by the Mkhitarian Order, Venice, St. Lazars, compilation of various issues from 1901–06.

Knapp, Grace Higley. *The Mission at Van: In Turkey in War Time.* Privately printed, 1915.

——. *The Tragedy of Bitlis.* New York, 1919.

Lang, David Marshal. *The Armenians: A People in Exile.* London, 1981.

Lynch, H. F. B. *Armenia: Travels and Studies.* 2 vols. 1901; rpt. New York, 1990.

Mandelstam, Osip. *Journey to Armenia.* Trans. Sidney Monas. San Francisco, 1979.

Miller, Donald E., and Lorna Touryan Miller. *Survivors: An Oral History of the Armenian Genocide.* Berkeley, 1993.

Mirak, Robert. *Torn between Two Lands: Armenians in America, 1890 to World War I.* Cambridge, MA, 1983.

Morgenthau, Henry. *Ambassador Morgenthau's Story.* New York, 1918.

——. *Secrets of the Bosphorus.* London, 1918.

Mukhitarian, Onnig, and Haig Gossoian. *The Defense of Van.* Trans. Samuels S. Tarpinian. Michigan, 1980. Mukhitarian is the author of part 1, *An Account of the Glorious Struggle of Van-Vasbouragan.* Gossoian is the author of part 2, *The Self Defense of Armenians in the Historic City of Van.*

Nalbandian, Louise. *The Armenian Revolutionary Movement: The Development of Armenian Political Parties through the Nineteenth Century.* Berkeley, 1963.

Nogales, Rafael de, *Four Years beneath the Crescent.* New York, 1926.

——. *Memoirs of a Soldier of Fortune.* New York, 1932.

Ternon, Yves. *The Armenians: History of a Genocide.* Trans. Rouben C. Cholakian. Delmar, NY, 1981.

Ussher, Clarence D. *An American Physician in Turkey: A Narrative of Adventures in Peace and in War.* Boston, 1917.

Villa, Susie Hoogasian, and Mary Kilbourne Matossian. *Armenian Village Life before 1914.* Detroit, 1982.

Walker, Christopher J. *Armenia: The Survival of a Nation.* 1980. Rev. ed. London, 1991.

Williams, W. Llewellyn. *Armenia: Past and Present. A Study and a Forecast.* 1916. Rev. ed. London, 1990.

INTERVIEWS BY AND CONVERSATIONS WITH THE AUTHOR

Adoian, George. Interview. Cranston, RI, July 21, 1997.
Ashton, Dore. Conversation. New York City, 1973.
Barnet, Will. Interview. New York City, December 27, 1994.
Bernier, Rosamund. Conversation. New York City, March 14, 1998.
Brooks, Esther. Interview. Dublin, NH, October 23 and 24, 1999.
Brooks, Peter. Conversation. Dublin, NH, October 23, 1999.
Bowman, Ruth. Conversation. Truro, MA, 1995.
Bultman, Fritz. Interview. New York City, March 18, 1973.
Chermayeff, Barbara. Interview. Truro, MA, September 3, 1993.
Chermayeff, Ivan. Conversation. New York City, December 2, 1998.
Chermayeff, Peter. Conversation. Truro, MA, 1997.
Combe-Martin, Michel. Interview. New York City, November 24, 1999.
Davis, Mariam. Interview by Earl Davis on behalf of author. June 1996.
Dearinger, David. Conversation. New York City, December 1999.
de Kooning, Willem. Telephone conversation. December 1972.
Dickey, Anne Tredick. Interview. Truro, MA, July 14, 1997.
Dobkin, Marjorie Housepian. Conversation. New York City, May 10, 2000.
Donati, Enrico. Interview. December 3, 1998.
Fielding, Agnes (Mougouch). Interviews. London, 1994–99.
Gross, Mrs. Chaim. Interview. February 1996.
Hale, Barbara. Conversation. Springs, Long Island, June 1995.
Hamburger, Anna. Conversation. New York City, March 21, 1998.
Janis, Carroll. Conversation. New York City, February 1999.
Janney, Asa Moore. Interview. Lincoln, VA, July 29, 1996.
Kainen, Jacob. Interview. Chevy Chase, MD, July 29, 1995.
Kiesler, Lillian Olinsey. Interview. New York City, April 9, 1999.
Krasner, Lee. Conversation. New York City, December 1972.
Levy, Julien. Interview. Bridgewater, CT, 1973.
Magruder, Malcolm. Conversation. Middleburg, VT, July 28, 1996.
Margolis, David. Interview. New York City, November 6, 1997.
Mason, Emily. Conversation. New York City, February 10, 2000.
Matta Echaurren, Roberto. Interview. Paris, June 3, 1993.
Matter, Mercedes Carles. Interview. Bridgehampton, NY, August 1, 1997.
McCulloch, David. Conversation. Old Lyme, CT, March 28, 2002.
Miller, Liberty. Telephone interview. January 18, 2002.
Orlowsky, Lillian. Telephone interview. October 3, 1999.
Perényi, Eleanor. Interview. Stonington, CT, October 13, 1995.
Perry, Alma. Interview. New York City, June 1995.
Rankine, V. V. Interview. Washington, DC, May 4, 1995.
Resnick, Milton. Telephone interview. New York City, March 15, 1999, and June 1999.
Ruta, Peter. Interview. New York City, October 28, 1997.
Sandler, Irving. Telephone conversation. January 24, 2002.
Sandow, Helen. Interview. New York City, May 30, 1995.

Schjeldahl, Peter. Telephone conversation. January 2002.
Schwabacher, Christopher. Interview. New York City, June 17, 1993.
Shahn, Bernarda Bryson. Conversation. New York City, June 4, 1997.
Solman, Joseph. Interview. New York City, December 18, 1999.
Sterne, Hedda. Interview. New York City, 1973.
Stone, Allan. Conversation. New York City, November 1994.
Taylor, Thomas E. Interview. Hamilton, VT, July 28, 1996.

TAPED INTERVIEWS BY KARLEN MOORADIAN:
Eastern Diocese of the Armenian Church of America (transcripts of
thirty-seven of these interviews are published in Karlen Mooradian, *The Many
Worlds of Arshile Gorky,* Chicago, 1980.)

Ado Adoian, 1966.
Akabi Amerian, 1966.
Azad Adoian, 1966.
Revington Arthur, 1966.
Satenik Avedisian, 1965.
Shnorig Avedissian, 1966.
Will Barnet, 1967.
Varsik Avedisian Berberian, 1965.
Ilya Bolotowsky, 1973.
Peter Blume, 1966.
Rosalind Bengelsdorf Browne, 1966.
Peter Busa, 1973.
Alexander Calder, 1966.
Giorgio Cavallon, 1966.
Frederick Childs, 1967.
Ethel Cooke, 1966.
Malcolm Cowley, 1966.
Roselle Davis (Mrs. Stuart Davis), 1966.
Elaine de Kooning, 1965.
Willem de Kooning, 1966.
Edwin Denby, 1966.
John Ferren, 1966.
Balcomb Greene, 1966.
Yenovk Der Hagopian, 1965.
Raoul Hague, 1966.
Haroutune Hazarian, 1965.
Sidney Janis, 1965.
Robert Jonas, 1966.
Aristodimos Kaldis, 1966.
Arpenik Karebian, n.d.
Lillian Olinsky Kiesler, 1966.
Kevork Kondakian, 1965.
Lee Krasner, 1966.

Conrad Marcarelli, 1966.
David Margolis, 1966.
Warren McCullough and Rook McCulloch, 1966.
Dorothy Miller, 1967.
Liberty Miller (also called Azaduhi Amerian), August 26, 1972.
Arshag Mooradian, 1965.
Vartoosh Mooradian, 1965–66.
Sirun Mussikian (Ruth March French), 1972.
Reuben Nakian, 1966, 1980.
Barnett Newman, 1966.
Isamu Noguchi, 1966.
Margaret Osborn, 1965.
Betty Parsons, 1966.
Milton Resnick, 1966.
Jeanne Reynal, 1965.
Mischa Reznikoff, 1966.
Harold Rosenberg, 1966.
Mark Rothko, 1967.
Abisag Der Marderosian Sarkisian, 1964, 1965.
Meyer Schapiro, 1966.
Saul Schary, 1965.
Max Schnitzler, 1966.
Badrik Selian, 1966.
Stergis M. Stergis, 1966.
Raphael Soyer, 1966.
Saul Steinberg, 1966.
Herluf Svenningsen, 1966.
Manuel Tolegian, 1982.
Erhard Weyhe, 1966.

INTERVIEWS IN THE ARCHIVES OF AMERICAN ART,
SMITHSONIAN INSTITUTION

Blanch, Arnold. Interview by Dorothy Seckler. June 13, 1963.
Burkhardt, Hans. Interview by Paul J. Karistrom. Los Angeles, November 25,
    1974.
Davis, Stuart. Interview by Harlan Phillips. 1962.
Dehner, Dorothy. Interview by Garnett McCoy. 1966.
de Kooning, Willem. Interview by Bruce Hooton. April 1, 1981.
Kainen, Jacob. Interview by Avis Berman. 1982.
Levy, Julien. Interview by Stephen Robeson Miller. December 16, 1972.
Parsons, Betty. Interview by Paul Cummings. 1969.
Schwabacher, Ethel. Interview by Colette Roberts. 1965.

Acknowledgments

✻

For her careful reading of my manuscript and for the many hours she spent digging into her memories and her archives, I want to thank Arshile Gorky's widow, my godmother, Mougouch Fielding. This book could not have been written without her encouragement and help. I owe a large debt of gratitude to Penny Ferrer for going over an early draft of my manuscript chapter by chapter and helping me to clarify its structure. My daughter Margot Herrera brought her keen editorial skills to bear upon the first few chapters, thus enabling me to go on writing with her advice in mind. At the Wylie Agency, Zoë Pagnamenta read my manuscript and her enthusiasm was heartening.

Several art dealers have been enormously generous in providing photographs of Arshile Gorky and his works. Jill Weinberg of the Lennon Weinberg Gallery lent me many color transparencies; the Gagosian Gallery lent numerous photographs as well. The Knoedler Gallery had copies made of photographs in its archive. Jason McCoy and Stephen Mazoh also lent photographs. Many museums and private collectors were helpful in rounding up photographs and in giving me permission to reproduce works by Gorky in their collections. They are named in the art acknowledgments, and I extend my thanks to all of them. The Whitney Museum of American Art and the Solomon R. Guggenheim Museum let me look through their Gorky archives, for which I am grateful. Two publishers have been generous in their loans of photographs: I am especially indebted to Bob Abrams and Abbeville Press for lending me a large group of photographs of Gorky's paintings. Eric Himmel at Harry N. Abrams kindly provided a color transparency of one of Gorky's *Garden in Sochi* paintings. Sotheby's Inc lent transparencies, as well.

I thank the staffs of the Archives of American Art in New York and Washington, DC, for their help. The librarians at New York's Museum of Modern Art, the Whitney Museum, and the Newark Museum were unstinting in their cooperation. Aram Arkan at the Zorab Library of the Diocese of the Armenian Church of America directed me toward many publications on Armenian history. Artists

Rights Society and Art Resource deserve thanks for their efficiency and goodwill in the gathering of photographs of artworks. I would like to acknowledge the John Simon Guggenheim Memorial Foundation for granting me a fellowship that financed a trip to Gorky's birthplace in Eastern Turkey. My gratitude goes also to the Bogliasco Foundation for inviting me to the Liguria Study Center for six weeks of concentrated work.

Many individuals have contributed to the making of this book. Gorky's daughters Maro and Natasha Gorky and Maro Gorky's husband, Matthew Spender, kindly lent photographs. Mougouch Fielding's nephew Malcolm Magruder loaned letters and gave me a tour of Crooked Run Farm, where Gorky made so many of his best drawings. Two Gorky scholars, Jim M. Jordan and Melvin P. Lader, were hugely generous in their help. Novelist Peter Sourian lent me many books on Armenian history and culture, and his intelligence and humor propelled me through moments of discouragement. Stuart Davis's nephew Earl Davis kindly interviewed his aunt Mariam Davis on my behalf. Stuart Friedman provided me with copies of many documents in the Corinne Michael West Archive. Karekin Arzoomanian and Vartan Gregorian were thoughtful in their efforts to open avenues of Gorky research. The many interviewees who shared with me their memories and thoughts about Gorky are listed in the Bibliography. Their contribution to my book is large, and I am deeply indebted to them.

At Farrar, Straus and Giroux I wish to thank Jonathan Galassi for his astute first reading, and Roslyn Schloss for her copy editor's expert eye. Finally, I owe a huge debt of gratitude to my editor, Lorin Stein, whose formidable literary intelligence and excellent judgment made my biography of Gorky a much better book.

Index

Aalto, Alvar, 556
Abdul Hamid II, Sultan, 14, 15, 24, 640*n*
Abel, Lionel, 384, 431, 516, 546, 585
Abramson, Louis Allen, 314, 690*n*
Abstract Expressionism, 292, 316, 380, 382, 536, 628–30, 632, 662*n*, 704*n*
Abstraction-Création Art Non-Figuratif, 219, 260, 667*n*
Académie Julien, 131
Adoian, Ado (Gorky's cousin), 30, 32, 33–36, 91, 93, 283, 309, 638*n*
Adoian, Azad (Gorky's cousin), 39, 91, 94–95, 236, 294
Adoian, Baidzar (Gorky's aunt), 38, 42, 43
Adoian, Charles (Gorky's nephew), 109
Adoian, Dawn (Gorky's niece), 112
Adoian, George (Gorky's nephew), 109, 111–14, 201–2
Adoian, Hagop (Gorky's half-brother), 19, 21, 23, 38, 39, 103, 109–14, 133, 164, 284, 555
Adoian, Krikor (Gorky's uncle), 15, 19, 30, 32, 36–39, 42, 43, 47, 55, 79, 638*n*, 643*n*
Adoian, Lucille (Gorky's niece), 112, 164

Adoian, Manouk (Gorky's grand-father), 19, 22, 28
Adoian, Misak (Gorky's uncle), 15
Adoian, Nanig (Gorky's grandmother), 19
Adoian, Oughaper (Gorky's half-sister), 19
Adoian, Rus (Gorky's cousin), 38, 79
Adoian, Satenik (Gorky's sister), *see* Avedisian, Satenik
Adoian, Sedrak (Gorky's father), 22, 31, 35, 36, 40, 43, 63, 99, 103, 109–12, 284, 285, 637*n*, 651*n*; birth of children of, 20, 638*n*; death of, 555–56, 572, 709*n*; emigration to America of, 38, 42, 107, 643–44*n*; estrangement of Gorky from, 114, 616; marriage of Shushan and, 17–20; money sent by, 39, 42, 49, 50, 92, 100; photograph of family sent to, 54, 152; remarriage of, 113, 133
Adoian, Shushan (Gorky's mother, née Der Marderosian), 9, 12, 40, 47, 49–51, 159, 232, 637*n*, 642–44*nn*, 650*n*; and Akabi's marriage, 42–43; ambitions for Gorky of, 30–31, 118, 150, 559; birth of children of, 20,

Adoian, Shushan (*cont.*)
638*n*; bread baking by, 229–30;
death of, 98–100, 651*n*; death of
eldest daughter of, 23, 640*n*; education of children of, 34, 35,
53–54; emigration of husband,
38–39, 133; murder of first husband of, 16–17; photography of
Gorky and, 54–55, 152, 402; portraits of, 41, 46, 141, 151–57,
167, 187, 199, 283–84, 297, 299,
301, 527, 658*n*, 659*n*, 686*n*,
705*n*; remarriage of, 17–20; in
Russia, 89–92, 96–98; during
World War I, 58, 64, 68, 74, 84,
86–88
Adoian, Vartan (Gorky's great-uncle),
653*n*
Adoian, Vartoosh (Gorky's sister), *see*
Mooradian, Vartoosh
Adoian, Vosdanig, *see* Gorky, Arshile
Afro, 631
Aghayan (author), 34
Ain, Gregory, 660*n*
Albers, Joseph, 670*n*, 676*n*
Albright-Knox Art Gallery (Buffalo),
211, 217, 287, 684*n*
Alexander, Nohrabed, 34
Allied Artists of America, 131
Alpert, Anne, 384, 540
Amerian, Akabi (Gorky's half-sister,
née Prudian), 55, 56, 86, 101,
103, 117, 172, 284, 285, 333, 486,
539, 637*n*, 643*n*, 649*n*; birth of
son of, 54; childhood of, 9, 16,
19, 23, 26, 27, 35; emigration to
America of, 92, 650*n*; at Gorky's
funeral, 614; marriage of, 42–43,
49; portrait of, 294; in Russia, 89,
90; in Watertown, 108–10,
112–13, 132, 152, 164, 235,
651*n*, 652*n*; during World War I,
68, 84, 87
Amerian, Azaduhi, *see* Miller, Liberty
Amerian, Gurken (Jimmy), 54, 68, 84,
92, 108, 235

Amerian, Mkrdich, 42–43, 49, 56, 92,
101, 103, 108–10
Amerian, Sushik (Florence), 108
Amerian, Thomas, 108
Amerian, Varsik (Lillian), 108
American Abstract Artists (AAA), 170,
260–63, 677*n*
American Board of Commissioners for
Foreign Missions, 56
American Federation of Art, 283, 284
American Ministry of Relief, 101
American Mission at Van, 18, 22, 23,
43, 53, 59, 61, 71, 73–77, 79, 85,
90, 100, 110; Reports of, 56, 94,
644–45*n*
American Music Hall, 317
American Relief Committee, 90, 91,
94
American Scene painting, 180, 215
Amirkhanian, Lusi, 19
Anrep, Boris von, 336
Arabs, 12
Aram (Dashnak leader), 62
Ararat, Legion of, 77
Architectural League, 497, 521
Architectural Record, 282, 683*n*
Armenakan Party, 4
Armenian Relief Organization, 119
Armenians, 9–10, 12–30, 34, 35, 38,
41, 42, 47–51, 55, 226, 640*n*,
645–46*nn*, 659*n*; in America,
107–8, 113–14, 118, 139, 159–
69, 651*n*; autonomous nation of,
94–95; genocide of, 57–66, 80,
85, 94, 119, 367, 372, 373, 514,
646–47*nn*; insurrection against
Turks of, 66–80; portraits of,
294–300; as refugees, 83–94; in
Russia, 95–100, 118, 234, 236,
649*n*
Armory Show, 144
Arp, Jean, 216, 482
Art d'Aujourd'hui, L', 667*n*
Art Center, 216
Art Digest, 478, 562, 667*n*
Art Front, 259, 266, 275, 675*n*, 679*n*

Arthur, Revington, 144–46, 154, 515, 579–70
Art Institute of Chicago, 355, 562, 570, 686n, 700n; *Abstract and Surrealist Art in America*, 707n
Artists' Club, 627
Artists' Committee of Action, 255–56
Artists' Congress, 259, 676n
Artists' Union, New York City, 170, 255–57, 259, 266, 268, 675n
Art for the Millions, 271, 682n
Art News, 564, 624–25, 702n
Arts, The, 667n
Arts Club of Chicago, 211
Art Students League, 159, 174, 217, 225, 241, 325, 350, 673n; "Art Exhibition for the Benefit of Armenian War Relief," 390
Art of This Century gallery (New York), 380, 388
Arvas, Ibrahim, 64
Assyrians, 12
Auerbach, Alfred, 670n
Austin, Helen, 145
Austin, Nathaniel, 145
Avedisian, Florence (Gorky's niece), 614
Avedisian, Sarkis, 108, 132
Avedisian, Satenik (Gorky's sister, née Adoian), 18, 23, 55, 58, 108, 132, 164, 168–69, 333, 486, 539, 638n, 651n; birth of, 20, 643n; childhood of, 9, 35, 40; education of, 49, 90; emigration to America of, 92; and father's death, 555; at Gorky's funeral, 614
Avedisian, Varsik (Gorky's niece), 132–33
Avedissian, Shnorig, 142–43
Avery, Milton, 438
Axis, 667n
Azeris, 99

Bach, Johann Sebastian, 173
Baghdasarian, B. Hohannes, 54

Bagratuni, Ashot, 15
Baker, Norris C., 116
Balakian, Peter, 514
Balamuth, Lewis, 250
Balkan wars, 24
Balthus, 658n
Bard, Phil, 257
Bardik, Vart, 33
Barnes Foundation, 220, 366
Barnet, Will, 118, 201, 210, 652n, 665n
Barr, Alfred H., 178, 181, 215–16, 222, 264, 267, 360, 476, 521, 626, 669n
Barrows, Elizabeth, *see* Ussher, Elizabeth
Bartlett, Dr., 407
Barton, James L., 56
Batum, Treaty of, 94
Bauhaus, 261
Baziotes, William, 388, 482, 487, 557
Beane, Jacob, 464
Becker, Blanche, 157
Becker, John, 210
Beckett, Samuel, 245, 674n
Beethoven, Ludwig van, 173, 447
Bengelsdorf, Rosalind, 174, 248–49, 256, 257, 260, 676n
Berbian, Mr. and Mrs. Michel J., 363
Berg, Alban, 627
Berle, Adolf A., Jr., 265
Benson, Emanuel M., 682n
Berman, Eugene, 695n, 696n
Bernier, Rosamund, 520, 704n
Biddle, George, 669n
Bierderman, Charles, 302
Bijur, Jean, 231, 657n
Bijur, Nathan I., 16, 148, 216, 219, 231, 657n
Binhoff, Elisa, *see* Breton, Elisa
Blanch, Arnold, 268
Bloom, Hyman, 626
Blume, Ebie, 496, 583, 594, 610, 611, 614
Blume, Peter, 5, 496, 504, 506, 583, 594, 597, 608–14, 704n, 711n, 712n

Bolotowsky, Ilya, 250, 260–62, 274, 309–10, 673n, 676n
Bolsheviks, 93
Bonnard, Pierre, 667n
Bonte, C. H., 220
Bosch, Hieronymus, 210, 667n
Boston Museum of Fine Arts, 112, 116, 117, 122, 131–33, 137, 248; School of, 652n
Boston Public Library, 248
Bowes, Major, 370–71
Bowman, Ruth, 682n
Boyer, C. Philip, 219–20, 224
Boyer Galleries (Philadelphia), 221, 224, 242, 673n
Boyer Gallery (New York), 224, 225, 687n
Bradbury, H. B., 712n
Brancusi, Constantin, 250, 667n
Brandt, Mortimer, Gallery (New York), 700n
Braque, Georges, 157, 183, 187, 212, 216, 223, 241, 243, 352, 392, 667n; *Musical Forms (Guitar and Clarinets)*, 663n
Brest-Litovsk, Treaty of, 93
Breton, André, 4, 183, 448, 463, 467, 482, 486, 527, 528, 530–31, 537, 557, 695n, 696n, 702n; arrival in New York of, 380; Connecticut visits of, 481, 483, 494, 496; de Kooning on, 182; introduction to Gorky of, 430–32; at Levy Gallery exhibition opening, 474; marriages and divorces of, 431, 483, 540; Matta and, 385, 497–99, 623; Mougouch on, 163, 436, 441–44, 446, 465; on role of women artists, 524
  works: *Amour Fou*, 445; *Arcanum 17*, 461; *The Communicating Vessels*, 443; *The Immaculate Conception* (with Eluard), 244, 674n; *Nadja*, 440; *The Second Surrealist Manifesto*, 623; *Surrealism and Painting*, 477–78, 496, 696n,
703n; *Surrealist Manifesto*, 379; *Young Cherry Trees Secured Against Hares*, 481, 482, 508
Breton, Aube, 482, 500
Breton, Elisa (née Binhoff), 431, 461, 481, 483, 494, 496
Breton, Jacqueline (also called Jacqueline Lamba), 431, 461, 462, 482, 483, 494, 500, 535, 540
British Purchasing Company, 400–401
Bronzino, Il, 156, 242, 298, 659n
Brooklyn Museum, 663
Brooks, Esther, *see* Makanowitzky, Esther
Brooks, Peter, 701n
Brown, John Nicholas, 212
Browne, Byron, 248–49, 260, 669n, 673n
Brown University, 111, 241, 360; School of Engineering, 652n, 680n
Bruce, Edward, 670n
Brueghel, Pieter, 212
Bryson, Bernarda, 256–57
Buccholtz Gallery, 541
Buffalo Fine Art Academy, 217
Bultman, Fritz, 214
Burkhardt, Hans, 144, 148, 150
Burliuk, David, 175, 335, 402, 404, 661n; *In Moses Soyer Studio*, 296, 686n
Burliuk, Mary, 402, 403, 698n
Burrows, Carlyle, 223
Busa, Peter, 204, 209, 210, 243, 335, 367–68, 375, 381, 383, 388–89, 687n
Buxton, Harold, 23
Buxton, Noel, 23, 636n

Cahiers d'Art, 137, 177, 181, 189, 190, 302, 655n, 663n, 664n, 667n, 698n
Cahill, Holger, 202, 213, 220, 237, 306, 351, 669n, 688n, 692n
Calas, Elena, 498, 557
Calas, Nicolas, 498, 536–37, 545, 546, 571

Calder, Alexander, 216, 290, 388, 472–73, 488, 496, 512, 563, 577, 579, 583, 614, 670n, 702n

Calder, Louisa, 372–73, 496, 577, 579, 583, 614

California Palace of the Legion of Honor, 562; *Second Annual Exhibition of Paintings*, 707n

California School of Fine Arts, 344

Cambon, Paul, 636n

Camera Work, 667n

Campbell, Nathalie, 389, 394, 418, 449, 541, 562

Caniff, Milt, 424

Carbee, Scott, 116

Carles, Arthur B., 258

Carles, Mercedes, *see* Matter, Mercedes

Carnegie Institute, 131

Carpaccio, Vittore, 667n

Carson, Ruth, 307

Castelli, Leo, 622

Cavallon, Giorgio, 267–68, 279, 302, 304, 676n

Cézanne, Paul, 123, 135–41, 144, 145, 154, 158, 159, 161, 162, 180, 181, 297, 361, 390, 396, 417, 655n, 667n; in Barnes Foundation collection, 220; Cubism and, 138–39, 182–83, 250; landscapes by, 136; Museum of Modern Art exhibition of, 657n; portraits by, 21, 151; still lifes by, 136, 153; use of color by, 298; watercolors by, 138

   works: *Boy with a Skull*, 138; *Le Fumeur*, 655n; *Louis Guillaume*, 141; *Pommes sur un Table*, 655n; *Self-Portrait with Beret*, 139

Chagall, Marc, 695n

Chaliapin, Boris, 355

Chamberlain, Neville, 311

Chardin, Jean-Baptiste-Siméon, 396

Chase, William Merritt, 121, 130

Chase School, 121

Chekhov, Anton, 576, 590

Chermayeff, Barbara, 348, 400, 437, 449, 474

Chermayeff, Peter, 434

Chermayeff, Serge, 348, 375, 405, 434, 437, 445, 449, 474, 509, 622

Chicago, University of, 165

China Today, 325, 330, 332

Chirico, Giorgio de, 252, 657n, 667n, 696n; *The Fatal Temple*, 191, 664n

Chodorow, Eugene, 264

Chooligan, Felix, 121

Chopin, Frédéric, 173

Christians, 12, 24, 32, 240, 636n, 644n, 645n; iconography of, 153–54; Turkish persecution of, 14, 16–17, 56, 59, 63, 64, 67

Christie, A. N., 676n

Cickovsky, Nick, 296

Cincinnati Civic Theater, 239

Circle, 260

Civil Works Administration, 670n

Clapp, Talcott B., 577–79

Claro, Elisa, *see* Breton, Elisa

Claude Lorraine, 667n

Cloisters, 302

Cole, Jim, 419

Colliers magazine, 307

Color and Rhyme, 403, 686n, 698n

Combe Martin, Elsa, 321, 325

Combe Martin, Michael, 325, 327

Communists, 94, 164, 172, 237, 238, 255–58, 311, 312, 373, 374, 394, 425, 536, 661n; Chinese, 321, 324, 325, 329, 332

Congregational Church of America, 53

Congress, U.S., 238

Connah, Douglas John, 116, 119–21, 123, 129

Cooke, Ethel M., 118–21, 133, 653n

Copley, John Singleton, 157

Cornell, Joseph, 696n

Corot, Camille, 167, 667n

Cowley, Malcolm, 5, 496, 504, 583, 611–14, 712n

Cowley, Muriel, 396, 583, 611, 614
Cranach, Lucas, 667n
Creative Art, 217, 667n
Cronin, Frank, 120
Cubism, 173, 182–89, 207, 242, 248,
    288, 291, 301, 369, 388, 487, 608,
    628, 668n, 676n; abandonment of
    grid of, 316, 364; of American Ab-
    stract Artists, 263; in Armory
    Show, 144; Cézanne and, 138,
    182–83, 250; cloisonné, 279, 289;
    and Creative Art article, 217, 218;
    Greenberg and, 479; Krasner and,
    208; of Newark Airport murals,
    270, 271, 274; of older mod-
    ernists, 221; of still lifes, 220, 290,
    295, 662n; Surrealism and, 192,
    271, 379, 382, 629, 693n; Syn-
    thetic, 181, 183–85, 218, 255,
    289, 436, 566, 693n

Dabrowsky, Ivan, see Graham, John
Daily Worker, 374
Dalí, Salvador, 335, 344, 380, 381,
    444, 667n, 696n
Daniel Gallery (New York), 210, 698n
Dashnak Party, 15, 22, 23, 38, 40, 62,
    99, 114
Daumier, Honoré, 667n
David, Jacques-Louis, 471, 667n, 681n;
    Death of Socrates, 209; Mars Dis-
    armed by Venus, 703n
David of Sasun (epic), 48
Davis, Bernard, 192, 201, 220, 230,
    232, 234, 235, 242, 291, 313, 335,
    462, 475
Davis, Bette, 373
Davis, Irmagard, 230
Davis, Mariam, 129, 166, 168, 171,
    228–29, 233, 259, 654n, 678n
Davis, Roselle, 159, 161, 162, 168,
    204, 654n
Davis, Stuart, 120, 127–29, 159, 192,
    197, 203–5, 220, 221, 225, 226,
    255, 276, 293, 304, 671n; and

Corinne Michael West's affair
    with Gorky, 242; Creative Art arti-
    cle on, 217–19; de Kooning and,
    175; Eggbeater series by, 173,
    185; Graham and, 171, 177, 179,
    392; Léger and, 222; Magazine of
    Art article by, 219; and Marny
    George's marriage to Gorky, 231;
    New York exhibitions of, 216–17,
    392; political engagement of, 259,
    675n, 676n; proto-pop paintings
    by, 214; and Sirun Mussikian's af-
    fair with Gorky, 161, 163; on Sur-
    realists, 538; Sweeny on, 302;
    Union Square studio described
    by, 198
Davis, Wyatt, 129, 171, 196, 264–66,
    275, 677n, 678n
Debussy, Claude, 447
Degas, Edgar, 122, 667n
Dehner Dorothy, 174, 256, 392
de Kooning, Elaine (née Fried), 191,
    199, 202–3, 209, 210, 310, 321,
    322, 335, 489, 539, 690n, 703n
de Kooning, Willem, 152, 171, 187,
    221, 225–26, 236, 278, 310, 519,
    538, 628, 631, 673n, 676n, 714n;
    American Abstract Artists and,
    262, 676n; in Artists' Union,
    257–58; Art News letter to editor
    from, 624–25; attitude toward
    originality of, 181–82; beginning
    of friendship of Gorky and,
    174–75; Denby and, 170, 539;
    Graham and, 176, 177, 392,
    662n, 697n; childhood tales told
    by Gorky to, 293; on Gorky's
    death, 619; on Gorky's female pa-
    trons, 233; on Gorky's painting
    methods, 156, 279, 297; on
    Gorky's politics, 332; on Gorky's
    social behavior, 202–3, 205, 207,
    229; on Lenore Gallet's affair with
    Gorky, 303; marriage of, 199; on
    Metropolitan Museum pilgrim-
    ages, 209; misunderstandings

between Gorky and, 564; Mougouch and, 321–23, 333, 335; Pollock and, 389; portraits by, 295, 299, 300, 686n; and Riviera Club murals, 315, 658n; sign-painter's brush used by, 434, 700n; Surrealists and, 383; in Venice Biennale, 626; during World War II, 367
  works: *Asheville*, 571; *Elegy*, 686n; *Excavation*, 571; *Self-Portrait with Imaginary Brother*, 686n
Delacroix, Eugène, 547
Demeny, Paul, 682n
Denby, Edwin, 170, 265, 310, 549
Dewey, Thomas E., 265
Dickey, Anne (née Tredick), 521
Diller, Burgoyne, 237, 264, 266–67, 670n, 673n, 676–78nn, 688n
Disney, Walt, 343, 424
Djemal Pasha, 25, 56
Doktar, Raphael, 681n
Donati, Enrico, 498, 563
Donati, Mrs. Enrico, 580
Dorner, Max, 667n
Dostoevsky, Feodor, 627
Downtown Gallery (New York), 216–18
Dreier, Katherine, 216, 223, 670n
Drewes, Werner, 261, 670n, 676n
Dro, General, 77, 78, 99
Drum, General, 367
Duchamp, Marcel, 216, 463, 474, 499, 531, 539, 546, 580, 622–23, 696n, 701n; *Bride*, 573
Duncan, Isadora, 159, 666n
Durand-Ruel Gallery (New York), 137, 210
Durlacher Gallery (New York), 211
Duveneck, Frank, 121

Ede, H. S., 244
Eliot, T. S., 627
Eluard, Paul, 229, 245, 383, 567, 696n; *The Immaculate Concep-*

tion (with Breton), 244, 674n; *Mourir de ne pas mourir*, 674n
Engels, Friedrich, 354, 380
Enver Pasha, 24, 56, 58, 59, 646n
Ernst, Jimmy, 384–85
Ernst, Max, 334, 363, 379, 380, 384, 386–87, 487, 498, 499, 540, 563, 696n; *The Kiss*, 190; *Night of Love*, 190
Expressionism, 216, 260, 262, 279, 397, 666n; *see also* Abstract Expressionism
Exquisite Corpse, 508

Fascism, 310
Fauve, 182
Fayum mummy portraits, 157
Fechin, Nicolai Ivanovich, 131
Federal Art Gallery (New York), 678n
Federal Art Project (FAP), 170, 202, 225, 237–38, 264–71, 274, 275, 278, 306, 672n, 682n, 688n
Federal Bureau of Investigation (FBI), 238, 369, 374
Feininger, Lyonel, 304
Félix, Fernando, 166
Ferenczi, Sándor, 589
Ferragil Gallery (New York), 133
Ferren, John, 181, 518
Fielding, Agnes, *see* Gorky, Mougouch
First Municipal Art Exhibition (New York), 220–21, 230
Force, Juliana, 223, 226–27, 671n
Formes, 667n
Fortune magazine, 399–400
Forum Gallery (New York), 220–21, 230
Fraener, William, 660n
Francis, Esteban, 499
Francis, Irene, 499
Frankenstein, Alfred, 351–52
Frankfurter, Alfred, 626
Freed, William, 381
Frelinghuysen, Suzy, 263
French, Ruth March, *see* Mussikian, Sirun

Freud, Sigmund, 485, 696n
Freudianism, 178, 598
Frick Collection, 148, 156, 258
Fried, Elaine, see de Kooning, Elaine
Fry, Roger, 137
Fuller, Buckminster, 207, 335, 336, 339, 385, 399

Gagik Ardsruni, King of Armenia, 41
Gainsborough, Thomas, 210
Galerie de France (Paris), 631
Galerie Maeght (Paris), 537
Gallatin, Albert E., 128, 148, 189, 207, 223, 263, 274
Galleria dell' Obelisco (Rome), 631
Gallet, Leonore, 302–4, 308, 687n
Garabedian, Kertzo Dickran Der, 99–102
Gardener, Isabella Stewart, Museum (Boston), 116
Gatch, Lee, 626
Gaudier-Brzeska, Henri, 244, 331, 334, 549, 691n, 706n
Gaugin, Paul, 657n; Self-Portrait, 142; Where Have We Come From? What Are We? Where Are We Going?, 248
Gellert, Hugo, 661n
Genauer, Emily, 223, 224, 265, 627, 628
George, Marny (Gorky's first wife), 187, 230–34, 240, 245, 349, 515, 573, 673n
George, Waldemar, 663n, 696n
German Mission, 53, 79
Giacometti, Alberto, 581, 693n, 696n
Gibbon, Edward, 12
Giotto, 667n
Gogh, Vincent Van, 142, 657n, 667n
Gold, Manny, 330
Gold, Mike, 661n
Goncharova, Natalie, 661n
Goodman, Paul, 672n
Goodrich, Lloyd, 226–27, 358, 360, 626–27, 658n, 671n

Goodyear, A. Conger, 310
Gordon, Milton, 568
Gorky, Arshile: Abstract Expressionism and, 628–30, 632, 714n; aggressiveness of, 203–4, 666n; American Abstract Artists and, 260–64, 676–77nn; anti-Semitism of, 372–73; art book collection of, 211–12, 667n, 698n; art studies of, 116–21, 129–31; in automobile accident, 588–97, 710n; birth of, 20–21, 638n, 639n; birth of children of, 405–8, 489–90, 698n; bohemian circle of, 170–73, 661n; breakup of marriage of, 598–609, 620; Breton and, 163, 430–32, 441–43, 465, 467, 481–83, 494, 498–99, 530–31; Calder and, 472–73; cancer of, 495, 510–16, 536, 539, 579–80; Cézannesque painting approach of, 136–41, 250; in Chicago, 354–57; childhood of, 9, 12, 21–22, 25–40, 43, 47–52, 292–93, 403–4, 643n; correspondence of Mougouch and, 192, 329–34; courtship of Mougouch and, 322–23, 325–29; creative process of, 277–79, 422–23, 444–45, 679–81nn; on cross-country trip with Noguchi, 337–43; dancing of, 204–5, 458–59; daughters' relationship with, 427–28, 442–43, 484–85, 493, 494, 509, 535, 542, 552, 557, 560–61; Davis article by, 217–19; decides to become artist, 111–12; de Kooning's friendship with, 174–75; depression of, 37, 557–60; drawings by, 187–92, 417, 420–26, 432–35, 446, 448–49, 462, 528–30 (see also specific titles under works); early years of marriage of, 366–67, 370–75; education of, 34–36, 49–50, 53–55, 90, 110–11, 113,

645*n*; emigration to America of, 99–103; fabrication of personal history by, 21, 39, 43, 111, 119, 134–35; family background of, 15, 16, 635–38*n*; fatalism of, 11, 310; Federal Art Project and, 237–38; fire in studio of, 3–5, 502–7, 528, 704*n*; first marriage of, 230–34, 673*n*; funeral of, 613–15; galleries frequented by, 210–11; at Glass House, 555–61, 577–81, 583–84, 596; Graham and, 174–79, 392, 662*n*; in group shows, 215–17, 220–21, 224–25, 281, 285, 301–2, 358, 360, 389–91, 401, 482, 498, 526–28, 536, 626–27, 631; Hare's Roxbury house rented by, 462, 463, 469–72, 483–86; *Harper's Bazaar* article on, 438–39; introduced to Mougouch, 321–22, 690*n*; Kiesler and, 213–14, 668*n*; landscapes by, 136, 137 (*see also specific titles under* works); lectures by, 219, 252, 281–84, 497, 683*n*; Léger and, 217, 222–23, 349, 402–3; letters to Mougouch from, 192, 329–34, 500–501, 544–46, 549–51, 691–92*n*; Levy as dealer for, 463–66, 474–77, 486, 496, 499–500, 507, 518–20, 536, 562–63, 566, 624–25, 669–70*n*, 701–2*n*; loneliness of, 307–9, 620–21; love affairs of, 142, 158–67, 228–30, 239–46, 258–59, 302–4, 308, 673*n*, 674*n*, 687*n*; in Maine, 547–48; Makanowitzky and, 425, 429, 699*n*; marriage of Mougouch and, 353–54, 365–66, 693*n*; Matta and, 383–87; Miró and, 540–42; Mondrian and, 460; and mother's death, 97–99, 651*n*; and Mougouch's affair with Matta, 584–89; moves to New York, 123, 127, 132; mural projects of,

226–27, 237, 264–76, 304–7, 314–17, 362, 364, 658*n*, 671*n*, 677–80*nn*, 682*n*, 687*n*, 688*n*, 690*n*; museum pilgrimages of, 209–10, 248; name change of, 118–19, 633*n*; one-man shows of, 219–24, 337, 344, 351–52, 465, 474–80, 486, 518–20, 562–66, 624–26, 631, 669*n*, 670*n*, 687*n*; perceptive sensitivity of, 192–93; photograph of mother and, 54–55, 152–54; Picasso's influence on, 180–91, 663*n*; politics of, 255–59, 311, 549, 676*n*, 709*n*; Pollock and, 388–89, 461; portraits by, 42, 132–33, 137, 181, 182, 284–85, 294–98 (*see also specific titles under* works); poverty of, 160–61, 200–203, 233, 301, 313–14, 366, 399, 657*n*; prose poem by, 615–16; in Providence, 109–11; rejection of originality by, 181–82; restaurants frequented by, 205–8; in Russian Armenia, 89–93, 96–97, 650*n*; in San Francisco, 344–52, 354; at Schary's country house, 393–94; sculptures by, 249–50, 347, 442, 693*n*; self-portraits of, 120–21, 139–42, 145, 182, 188, 217, 245, 294, 297–300; sexual problems of, 160, 516–17, 542, 584; sign-painter's brush used by, 434, 700*n*; still lifes by, 137, 138, 182–85, 302 (*see also specific titles under* works); suicide of, 608–13, 619, 622, 624, 711–13*nn*; Sullivan Street studio of, 127–29; summer vacations of, 248–51; Surrealists and, 379–83, 387–88, 536–40, 629, 696*n*; symposium on, 627; Tanguys and, 496–97; teaching career of, 123, 129, 131, 134, 144–51, 161, 202, 203, 368–70; Union Square studio of, 197–200; Vartoosh in New

Gorky, Arshile (*cont.*)
York with, 142–43, 234–37, 247;
at Virginia farm, 408–9, 411,
413–21, 425–26, 442–43,
445–53, 520–25, 528–30; *Vogue*
photograph of Lam and, 520,
704–5*n*; in Watertown, 107–9,
112–15, 132, 164–65, 167, 247;
during World War I, 58, 60,
67–69, 72, 74, 77, 79, 84–88;
during World War II, 310–12,
366–70
works: *Abstract Composition*, 432;
Abstraction with Palette, 186, 234;
Activities on the Field, 253, 267,
269, 272, 275, 679*n*; *Aerial Map*,
271, 274; *After Khorkom*, 288;
Agony, 286, 529, 552, 571–74,
707*n*; *Anatomical Blackboard*,
424, 705*n*; *The Antique Cast*, 181,
224, 547; *Anti-Medusa*, 708*n*; *The
Apple Orchard*, 559; *Apricots*,
289–90; *Argula*, 290–91, 358,
359, 684–85*n*, 694*n*; *The Artist
and His Mother*, 41, 46, 141,
151–57, 167, 187, 199, 283–84,
297, 299, 301, 527, 658*n*, 659*n*,
686*n*, 705*n*; *Aviation*, 265–66;
*The Backbone of My Ancestor Was
Far Away*, 705*n*; *Battle at Sunset
with the God of the Maize*, 683*n*,
684*n*; *The Beginning—Pale Grey*,
707*n*; *The Betrothal*, 42, 286, 547,
552, 573–74, 707*n*, 708*n*; *Blue
Figure in Chair*, 186; *Boy with
Head on Mother's Lap*, 8; *Bull in
the Sun*, 391; *The Calendars*, 529,
562, 566–68, 570, 625, 707*n*,
708*n*; *Charred Beloved*, 582, 507,
508, 520, 566; *Child of an Indumean Night*, 405; *Child's Companions*, 488, 508, 518, 705*n*;
Column with Objects, 188, 227;
Composition, 279, 290, 359,
669*n*, 670*n*, 683*n*, 685*n*, 692*n*,
694*n*; *Composition II*, 428; *Composition with Head*, 279, 292*n*;
Composition with Vegetables, 183;
Crooked Run, 435; *Cubist Standing Figure*, 188, 189, 665*n*; *Dark
Green Painting*, 575; *Days, Etc.*,
567, 708*n*; *Dead Bird*, 250; *Delicate Game*, 507–8, 518, 520,
713*n*; *Deposition*, 154; *Detail for
Mural*, 670*n*; *Dialogue of the
Edge*, 575–76; *Diary of a Seducer*,
487, 489, 498, 703*n*, 705*n*; *Early
Aviation*, 273, 274; *Ecorché*, 188;
Enigmatic Combat, 288–89, 351,
566, 692*n*; *Enigmatic Triptych*,
670*n*; *Fireplace in Virginia* drawings, 529, 570, 708*n*; *Forms*, 223;
Four P.M., 707*n*; *From a High
Place*, 457, 575, 576; *From a High
Place II*, 529; *Fruit*, 217; *Garden
in Sochi* series, 31, 42, 184,
288–91, 307, 316, 339, 358–64,
387, 391, 396, 436, 453–55, 488,
569, 570, 624, 685*n*, 686*n*,
692–94*nn*, 705*n*, 713*n*; *Golden
Brown Painting*, 432, 434; *Good
Afternoon, Mrs. Lincoln*, 455–56,
701*n*; *Good Hope Road*, 488, 520,
713*n*; *The Head*, 390; *The Horns
of the Landscape*, 435, 453, 465;
Housatonic Falls, 429, 434; *How
My Mother's Embroidered Apron
Unfolds in My Life*, 382, 453,
454, 465, 537; *Hugging*, 488; *Image in Khorkom*, 188, 286–87,
360, 684*n*, 692*n*; *Impatience*, 488,
520, 713*n*; *Improvisation*, 216;
Khorkom series, 191, 286–91,
294, 351, 358, 398, 453, 455,
683*n*, 694*n*; *The Kiss*, 186, 669*n*;
Lady in the Window, 130; *Landscape*, 435, 454; *Landscape Table*,
466, 488, 519, 705*n*; *Last Painting*, 576; *The Leaf of the Artichoke
Is an Owl*, 430, 435, 453, 465,
466, 480; *The Limit*, 155, 552,
559, 570–71, 575, 707*n*; *The*

Liver Is the Cock's Comb, 430–32, 435–38, 441, 455, 460, 566, 700n, 713n; *Love of a New Gun*, 454, 465; *Making the Calendar*, 529, 567, 707n, 708n; *Man's Conquest of the Air*, 307; *Manikin*, 217; *Mechanical Aspects of Airplane Construction*, 265; *Mechanics of Flying*, 270, 271, 273, 274; *Modern Aviation*, 273; *Nighttime, Enigma, and Nostalgia* series, 167, 188–92, 218, 219, 221, 223, 227, 276, 279, 286, 316, 664n, 684n; *Nighttime Nostalgia*, 670n; *Nighttime of Nostalgia*, 669n; *1934*, 226–27; *Nude*, 482, 507, 508, 518, 536, 705n, 707n; *Objects*, 707n; *Objects with Ecorché*, 227; *One Year the Milkweed*, 432, 435, 453, 454, 465; *The Opaque*, 707n, 708n; *The Orators*, 43, 529, 559, 572–73, 625, 707n, 709n; *Organization*, 235, 276–77, 279, 290, 669n; *Organization No. II*, 279; *Organization No. 4*, 669n; *Painter and Model*, 217, 683n; *Painting (1936–37)*, 279–80, 284, 290, 302; *Painting (1944)*, 454, 456, 460, 487; *Painting (1947–48)*, 575, 576; *Park Street Church*, 122–23; *Pastoral* series, 286, 529, 552, 574, 707n, 708n; *Pears, Peaches, Pitcher*, 137; *The Pirate*, 394, 398–99, 429, 430, 432, 465, 713n; *The Plough and the Song* series, 29, 489, 496, 552, 558, 567–70, 573, 641n, 707n, 708n; *Plumage Landscape*, 708n; *Portrait of Ahko*, 294–95, 351, 391; *Portrait of George Yphantis*, 131–32; *Portrait of a Girl*, 656n, 657n; *Portrait of Jacob Kainen*, 297–98; *Portrait of Master Bill*, 299; *Portrait of Mougouch*, 657n; *Portrait of Myself and My Imaginary Wife*, 41, 167–69, 191, 583, 686n; *Portrait of Vartoosh*, 294, 295, 297, 298, 351, 662n; *Portrait of a Woman*, 162; *Reclining Nude*, 162; *Red Painting*, 576; *Scent of Apricots on the Fields*, 28, 432, 435; *Sculptured Head*, 713n; *Self-Portrait* (c. 1923–24), 120–21; *Self-Portrait* (c. 1926–27), 140; *Self-Portrait* (c. 1928; Guggenheim Collection), 141; *Self-Portrait at the Age of Nine*, 140, 141, 145; *Shenandoah Landscape*, 428; *Soft Night*, 566, 624, 707n, 713n; *Still Life* (1928), 138, 182, 183, 662n; *Still Life* (c. 1930–31), 186; *Still Life* (c. 1931–33), 186; *Still Life* (c. 1934–35), 665n; *Still Life* (c. 1936–38), 684n; *Still Life, Egg Plants*, 657n; *Still Life with Flowers*, 182, 657n; *Still Life with Horse*, 183; *Still Life with Palette*, 185; *Still Life with Pears*, 183; *Still Life with Skull*, 138, 181; *Still Life on a Table*, 279; Study for *Agony*, 708n; Study for *The Liver Is the Cock's Comb*, 435; *Summation*, 546, 552, 706n, 707n; *Summer Snow*, 708n; *Summer in Sochi, Black Sea*, 289–90, 390, 684n; *The Sun, the Dervish in the Tree*, 454, 465, 707n; *Sunset in Central Park*, 186; *Terra Cotta*, 574, 708n; *Theme from a High Place*, 576; *Theme for Plumage Landscape*, 708n; *Three Figures by the Sea*, 691n; *They Will Take My Island*, 413, 456–57, 465, 479, 480, 487, 488, 506; *To Project, To Conjure*, 454; *Tracking Down Guiltless Doves*, 290, 692n; *The Unattainable*, 489, 518, 566, 705n; *Virginia Landscape*, 421–22, 432, 433, 435; *The Visible Monument-Soft*, 705n; *Water of the Flowery Mill*, 455, 465, 487, 705n; *Waterfall*, 394, 397–98,

Gorky, Arshile (*cont.*)
429, 430, 432, 434; *White Abstraction*, 713*n*; *Year after Year*, 707*n*, 708*n*

Gorky, Maro (daughter), 426, 442, 460, 474, 484, 485, 487, 490, 500–502, 530, 545, 555, 558, 581, 586, 610, 663*n*, 698*n*; birth of, 405–8; and breakup of parents' marriage, 598–601, 603–6, 608, 609, 620; Breton and, 431, 461, 467; and Calders' daughters, 472; during cancer treatment hospitalization, 511, 513; dog given to, 458; grandparents and, 405, 440, 452, 474, 506, 583–84, 588, 589, 596; in *Life* magazine photograph, 556; in Maine, 544, 547–48, 621–22; and Matta's sons, 587; at Metropolitan Museum, 476; in nursery school, 535, 552; Gorky's rages against, 509, 542, 560; in Roxbury, 469–71, 486; talk about suicide to, 557; in Union Square studio, 427–28; at Virginia farm, 408–9, 413–16, 420, 425, 443, 447–49

Gorky, Maxim, 119, 134–35, 162, 164, 182, 220, 613, 699*n*, 713*n*

Gorky, Mougouch (née Agnes Magruder; later Agnes Phillips and Agnes Fielding; Gorky's second wife), 21, 39, 110, 151, 181, 191, 226, 319, 321–28, 355, 363, 572, 577, 581–82, 616, 638*n*, 643*n*, 651*n*, 668–69*n*, 687*n*, 699*n*, 700*n*, 704*n*, 705*n*, 709*n*; abortion undergone by, 350–51; in analysis, 516, 536, 542–43, 583; and automobile accident, 591–97; at Schary's country house, 393–94; at Virginia farm, 413–21, 425–26, 445–53, 520–25, 528–30; birth of daughters of, 405–8, 489–90; breakup of marriage of, 598–609; Breton and,

163, 430–32, 436, 441–44, 448, 461, 465, 481–83, 494, 498–99, 524, 530–31, 537; at brother's wedding, 458–59; Calders and, 373; during cancer treatment, 510–14; in Chicago, 354–57; cross-country trip of, 337–43; on Depression-era poverty and isolation, 200, 307–8; descriptions of Gorky by, 205, 326; dinners for art dealers hosted by, 427; domestic difficulties of, 427–28; early years of marriage of, 366–67, 370–75, 517; family background of, 323; at Glass House, 555–61, 579–81, 583–84, 596; on Gorky's first marriage, 234; at Gorky's funeral, 613–15; and Gorky's suicide, 610; on Graham, 178; Hare's Roxbury house rented by, 462, 463, 469–72, 483–86; Hebbelns and, 437–38, 473, 487, 493–97, 508, 509, 521; insurance payment to, 621, 712–13*n*; introduced to Gorky, 321–22, 690*n*; Lam and, 520; Léger and, 402–4; letters from Gorky to, 192, 329–34, 500–501, 544–46, 691–92*n*; Levy and, 463–64, 474–77, 479–80, 499–500, 518, 563, 585–86, 670*n*; in Maine, 544–52, 574, 620–22; at Makanowitzky concert, 429; marriage of Gorky and, 352–54, 693*n*; Matta and, 384–86, 440–41, 445, 462, 527, 584–89, 621–23; Miró and, 541–42; miscarriage of, 450–52; and outbreak of World War II, 367; paintings discussed by, 290, 298, 358, 359, 361, 405, 422–23, 433, 456–57, 530, 562–63, 567, 576, 684–85*n*, 694*n*; parents' response to marriage of, 365–66; politics of, 324, 325, 332, 354; portraits of, 297, 350–51; pregnancies of, 394–96, 399–402,

450, 469, 483–84; remarriage of, 620, 624; in San Francisco, 344–52, 354; Schwabachers and, 563–65, 569, 580–81, 599, 620–21; on sign-painters' brush, 434; similarities among Marny, Corinne, and, 240; social circle of Gorky and, 334–36; on Stalinism, 256; and studio fire, 5, 502–8; Surrealists and, 386–89, 540, 609, 701n; on Sweeny's article, 438–39; Tanguys and, 496–97, 525–26; V. V. and, 459–60; Vartoosh and, 236, 355–57, 539, 635n

Gorky, Natasha (briefly named Yalda; daughter), 500–502, 530, 535, 558, 581, 586, 610; birth of, 489–90; and breakup of parents' marriage, 598–601, 603–6, 608, 609, 620; during cancer treatment hospitalization, 511, 513; grandparents and, 506, 583–84, 588, 589, 596; in *Life* magazine photograph, 556; in Maine, 544, 547, 621–22; and Matta's sons, 587; and mother's remarriage, 624; in nursery school, 552; Gorky's rages against, 542, 560

Gossoian, Haig, 67–68, 76

Gottlieb, Adolph, 260, 389, 482, 575, 628, 714n

Goya, Francisco, 242, 667n

Graber, Nathan, 148

Graham, John, 171, 174, 176–79, 207, 211, 221, 223, 225, 278, 662n, 668n, 670n, 697n; American Abstract Artists and, 262; Hofmann and, 214; New York exhibitions of, 175, 217, 389, 392, 669n; on Picasso, 191; portraits by 295, 299 works: *Portrait of Elinor Gibson,* 662n; *System and Dialectics of Art,* 178, 662n, 664n; *Studio,* 178–79; *The White Pipe,* 662n

Grand Central School of Art, 130–31, 134, 144–49, 151, 158, 161, 225,

360, 613; camouflage class at, 314, 368–70; catalogs of, 154, 654n; lectures at, 241, 668n; models at, 159; *Quarterly* of, 139

Grand Central Station (New York), Clavilux installation in, 454

Graves, Morris, 438

Greacen, Edmund, 130, 314, 368

Great Depression, 11, 160, 170, 177, 178, 192, 200, 204–5, 208, 212, 225, 235, 259, 284, 295, 300, 307, 399, 537, 654n, 662n, 688n

Greco, El, 133, 210, 619, 652n, 667n

Greeks, 12; ancient, 442

Greenberg, Clement, 4, 204, 478–79, 498, 519, 528, 562, 565–66, 619, 624, 626, 700n, 712n

Greenberg, Herman A., 234

Greene, Balcomb, 181, 197, 213, 226, 229, 251, 257, 278–79, 309, 314, 498, 538, 669n, 676n

Greene, Gertrude, 251, 314, 676n

Gris, Juan, 217, 241, 667n

Grohmann, Will, 698n

Gross, Chaim, 228

Grossman, I. Donald, 283–84

Grossman, Isobel, 283–84

Grünewald, Matthias, 168, 361, 660n, 667n

Guggenheim, Pegeen, 695n

Guggenheim, Peggy, 207, 334, 380, 382, 388, 460, 482, 540, 695n; Collection, 453, 456

Guggenheim Foundation, 306, 688n

Guggenheim Museum, 397

Guild Art Gallery (New York), 221–24, 669n, 683n

Hagopian, Parsegh Der, 101

Hagopian, Yenovk Der, 33, 55, 101, 114–15, 132, 163, 167, 247, 250, 292, 515–16, 639n

Hague, Raoul, 167, 171, 187, 197, 204, 208–10, 213, 303–4, 579, 654n, 685n

Hale, Barbara, 672n
Hale, Robert Beverly, 672n
Halpert, Edith, 216
Hals, Frans, 116, 121; *Malle Babbe*, 130
Hamidiyes, 57
Harachtimagan, 139
Harding, M. Esther, 516, 536, 542, 560, 584
Hare, David, 388, 431, 460–63, 469–71, 483–84, 487, 494, 500, 527, 535, 536, 540, 608, 702n
Harper's Bazaar, 421, 438–39
Hartley, Marsden, 221
Havenon, Gaston de, 201, 302, 303, 311–12, 396, 515, 605, 606, 702n
Hawthorne, Charles, 129
Hayter, William Stanley, 563
Hazarian, Haroutune, 134, 390
Hebbeln, Henry, 437, 450, 473, 490, 494, 496, 500, 506, 521, 546, 593, 596, 607; Architectural League lecture arranged by, 497; Connecticut farm purchased by, 451, 486; farmhouse remodeled by, 555, 556, 611; homosexuality of, 493; shares Union Square studio, 487, 508
Hebbeln, Jean, 449–50, 487, 490, 494, 497, 500, 506, 521, 546, 593, 596, 607; alcoholism of, 493, 496; Calder and, 473; Connecticut farm purchased by, 451, 611; dog given to Gorkys by, 458; gift of painting to, 437–38; Gorky's hostility toward, 509; and studio fire, 503, 508
Helion, Jean, 477
Henri, Robert, 121
Heraclitus, 680n
High Museum of Art (Atlanta), 363
Hirshhorn, Joseph H., 404–5
Hirshhorn Museum, 294, 295, 298, 393, 398, 404, 433, 662n
Hitler, Adolf, 310, 311, 372, 519
Hofmann, Hans, 179, 204, 213, 214,

225, 239, 241, 258, 324, 335, 381, 482, 673n
Hogarth, William, 681n
Holtzman, Harry, 260, 262, 670n, 673n, 676n
Hood Rubber Company, 108, 114, 115, 117, 247, 651n
Hooton, Bruce, 658n
Hoover, Herbert, 200
Hopkins, Harry, 670n
Hopkins, Miriam, 343
Hosmer, Esther, *see* Magruder, Esther
Hosmer, Harriet, 323
Hosmer, Henry, 366, 550
Hosmer, Marion, 407, 427, 516, 544, 545, 548, 551–52, 555, 560, 593
Housepian, Moses, 236
House of Representatives, U.S., 367
Hovannisian, Richard G., 152
Hovnanyan, Paregham, 645n
Howard, Charles, 344, 696n
Hugo Gallery, 536
Hunchak Party, 15, 172, 406, 637n
Hunter, Sam, 565, 624
Hussian, John, 132, 652n

Impressionism, 122, 123, 130, 210
Ingres, Jean-Auguste-Dominique, 149, 178, 179, 186–88, 242, 260, 262, 336, 361, 417, 471, 662n, 667n, 681n, 686n, 699n; brush strokes of, 209; Pach's book on, 308; Picasso and, 151–52, 188; portrait of *Mme d' Haussonville*, 156, 294, 298; portraits by, 210, 258, 294, 295, 298; self-portrait of, 156, 550
International Rescue Committee, 573
Iowa, University of, 324
Iron Winding Company, 110, 284
Ishkhan (Dashnak leader), 62, 94
Issahakian (author), 34
Ittihad ve Terakke Jemieti (Committee of Union and Progress), 23–24, 58, 64

Janis, Carroll, 683*n*
Janis, Harriet, 186, 220, 231, 232, 240, 276, 282, 283, 427, 436, 706*n*
Janis, Martin, 211, 670*n*
Janis, Sidney, 186, 211, 220, 231, 232, 240, 276, 283, 321, 427, 541, 628, 670*n*, 700*n*, 706*n*
Janney, Asa Moore, 418, 419
Jeu de Paume (Paris), 301, 303
Jevdet Bey, 59–64, 66, 70, 72–75
Jewell, Edward Alden, 221, 222, 479
Jews, 158, 170, 372–73
Johnson, Malcolm, 317, 691*n*
Jonas, Robert, 229, 292, 369, 421
Jones, Buck, 208
Jordan, Jim, 141, 184, 359, 576, 663*n*, 676*n*
Josephson, Hanna, 496, 583
Josephson, Matthew, 496, 583
Joyce, James, 627
Jungianism, 178, 516, 548, 589

Kachaturian, Simon, 87
Kahlo, Frida, 347
Kainen, Jacob, 176–77, 181, 187, 197, 206–8, 210, 211, 213, 225, 293, 297–98
Kaiser, Ray, 676*n*
Kaldis, Aristodimos, 205, 229, 237–38, 277–78, 292, 335, 369, 666*n*
Kamrowski, Gerome, 536
Kandinsky, Wassily, 215–18, 360, 397, 434–35, 454, 479, 661*n*, 667*n*, 698*n*; *Improvisation No. 30*, 434, 700*n*
Kane, Patricia, *see* Matisse, Patricia
Karebian, Arpenik, 208
Kaths, Karl, 324
Katz, Leo, 308
Keaton, Buster, 302
Kees, Weldon, 626
Kelder, Diane, 668*n*
Kelekian, Alice, 355
Kelekian, Hampartzoum, 101
Kelekian, Sedrak, 101

Kelekian, Vergine, 101
Kelpe, Paul, 676*n*
Kemalists, 99
Kerensky, Alexandre, 93
Khojabedian, Vanno, 390
Kierkegaard, Søren, 487
Kiesler, Frederick, 207, 213–14, 220, 222, 387, 499, 522, 535, 580, 668–71*nn*; articles on Newark Airport murals by, 275–76, 281, 679*n*; 683*n*; galleries designed by, 388, 536
Kiesler, Lillian (née Olinsey), 213–14, 225, 539, 668*n*, 673*n*
Kiesler, Steffi, 499
Kingdon, Frank, 679*n*
Klee, Paul, 216, 667*n*
Kline, Franz, 630
Kling, Joe, 183
Knapp, Grace Higley, 57, 73, 74, 76, 85, 647*n*
Knoedler Galleries (New York), 133–34, 210
Kondakian, Kevork, 37, 43, 112
Kondakian, Yeghus, 19, 20, 26–28, 37, 38, 47, 79
Kootz, Samuel M., 389–90, 626, 628, 673*n*
Kramer, Ethel, *see* Schwabacher, Ethel
Kramer, Hilton, 331, 628, 630
Krasner, Lee, 170, 207–8, 225, 389, 392, 482, 662*n*
Kurds, 9, 14, 15, 18, 22, 24, 28, 47, 48, 52, 57, 60, 64, 65, 84–86, 641*n*, 644*n*

Lader, Melvin, 162, 660*n*
La Farge, John, 335
La Farge, Oliver, 341
La Follette, Suzanne, 200
La Guardia, Fiorello H., 220, 255, 265–66, 675*n*, 678*n*
Lam, Helena, 597–98, 614
Lam, Wifredo, 520, 536, 563, 597, 607, 608, 614, 704*n*

Lamba, Jacqueline, *see* Breton, Jacqueline
Lane, James, 223
Lances, Leo, 673*n*, 676*n*
Laning, Edward, 681*n*
Larionov, Mikhail, 661*n*
Lassaw, Ibram, 260, 676*n*
Laurens, Albert Paul, 131
Laurent, Robert, 325
Lautréamont, Le Comte de, 419, 696*n*
Lawson, Ernest, 122
Lebel, Nina, 499
Lebrun, Rico, 626
Le Corbusier (Charles-Edouard Jeanneret), 275, 383, 498
Lefranc, Margaret, 222, 224, 669*n*
Léger, Fernand, 218, 258, 390, 400, 423, 439, 667*n*, 696*n*; *The City*, 275; in Museum of Modern Art exhibitions, 657*n*, 683*n*; Gorky's murals inspired by, 274; in New York, 217, 222–23, 402–4; in San Francisco, 349; in Sidney Janis collection, 211
Lenin, V. I., 93, 162, 235, 258, 354
Leonardo da Vinci, 608, 609, 667*n*
Leonardo da Vinci School, 301
Lescaze, William, 305, 307, 687*n*, 688*n*, 690*n*
Levitt, B. Blake, 588
Levy, Edgar, 221
Levy, Julien, 180, 234, 382, 455, 477, 480, 493, 496, 499, 509, 528, 546, 551, 560, 567, 571, 573, 587, 625, 710–13*nn*; attitude toward Mougouch of, 585–89; in automobile accident, 588–91, 593, 594, 596, 710*n*; 712–13*n*; as Gorky's dealer, 463–64, 496, 499–501, 506, 520, 526, 531, 547, 561, 566, 621, 658*n*, 669*n*, 701*n*; at Gorky's funeral, 614–15; and Gorky's suicide, 608, 609, 711*n*, 712*n*; Graham and, 176; explanations of Gorky's work by, 398–99, 572, 576; monograph on

Gorky by, 465–66; *Surrealism*, 244, 245, 380, 381
Levy, Julien, Gallery, 176, 503, 505; closing of, 625; Gorky exhibitions at, 4, 465, 474–76, 482, 486, 498, 507, 518–19, 538, 562–63, 624, 703*n*, 707*n*, 713*n*; Matta exhibitions at, 383, 387, 424; Perényi's satire about, 464–65; Surrealists and, 210, 380, 664*n*, 696*n*
Levy, Muriel, 474, 546, 560, 588, 590–91, 605, 614
Life magazine, 324, 520, 556, 558
Limon, José, 167
Lipchitz, Jacques, 696*n*
Litchfield County Times, 588
Litvak, Anatole, 341
Living Art, Gallery of, 128, 189, 663*n*
Lyford, Olive, 267, 274, 682*n*
Lynch, H.F.B., 18, 48–49, 88

MacAgy, Douglas, 344
Macy's department store, *Contemporary American Painting* exhibition at, 389
Magazine of Art, 219
Magritte, René, 696*n*
Magruder, Esther (née Hosmer; Mougouch's mother), 323, 329, 366, 394, 399, 407, 421, 425, 469, 608; and breakup of Gorkys' marriage, 602, 603, 610; correspondence of, 151, 355, 400–401, 428, 474; first meeting of Gorky and, 333; gift of painting to, 420; grandchildren and, 405, 440, 452, 474, 506, 583–84, 588, 589; Virginia farm of, 408, 413, 415–17, 421, 445, 447, 522
Magruder, Esther (Mougouch's sister), *see* Makanowitzky, Esther
Magruder, Commodore John Holmes (Mougouch's father), 323–24, 329, 333, 394, 415, 419, 421, 428–29, 469, 471; and breakup of

Gorkys' marriage, 603, 610; first
  meeting of Gorky and, 366; at
  Gorky's funeral, 613–14; grand-
  children and, 405, 452, 506, 584,
  588, 596; portrait of, 324; Virginia
  farm of, 408–9, 522
Magruder, John Holmes, III
  (Mougouch's brother), 366, 394,
  400, 405, 408, 425, 428, 450,
  458–59, 469, 474
Magruder, V. V. (née Richards, later
  Rankine; Mougouch's sister-in-
  law), 458–60, 469
Magruder, Agnes, *see* Gorky,
  Mougouch
Magvich, Louis, 419
Majestic Theater (Boston), 117
Makanowitsky, Esther (née Magruder;
  later Brooks), 22, 366, 416, 425,
  428, 429, 445, 447, 459, 469, 483,
  484, 522, 608, 699n, 701n
Makanowitsky, Paul, 366, 425, 429,
  699n
Makanowitsky, Sandra, 483
Mallarmé, Stéphane, 405
Manchester Guardian, 60
Manet, Édouard, 396, 667n
Mannerists, 156
Manoogian, Hmayag, 62
Manukian, Aram, 78
Mao Zedong, 324
Marcarelli, Conrad, 301, 580
Marden, Ben, 314–17, 325, 359, 362,
  364, 391, 658n, 690n
Marderosian, Abisag Der (Gorky's
  cousin), 649–50n
Marderosian, Aharon Der (Gorky's un-
  cle), 43, 53, 54, 79, 91, 96, 98, 99,
  133, 649n
Marderosian, Gurken Der (Gorky's
  cousin), 650n
Marderosian, Hamaspiur Der (Gorky's
  grandmother), 9–11, 572, 625,
  636n
Marderosian, Moses Der (Gorky's
  uncle), 10, 18, 79, 133

Marderosian, Nevart Der (Gorky's
  aunt), 87, 649–50n
Marderosian, Nishan Der (Gorky's
  uncle), 9–10
Marderosian, Sarkis Der (Gorky's
  grandfather), 9, 50
Marderosian, Yeva Der (Gorky's aunt),
  49, 58, 87, 649–50n
Margolis, David, 212, 248, 249, 278,
  311, 587
Margules, De Hirsh, 311
Marin, John, 626
Marshall, John, 505
Martini, Simoni, 667n
Martins, Maria, 580
Marx, Karl, 235, 258, 354, 484
Marx Brothers, 117
Marxism, 178, 392
Masaccio, 667n
Mason, Alice Trumbull, 147, 676n
Mason, Kay, 690n
Masson, André, 184, 279, 380, 482,
  664n, 695n, 696n, 702n; *Cock-
  fight*, 128, 664n; *Combats*, 289;
  Metamorphosis, 190
Matisse, Henri, 135, 149, 157, 181,
  208, 215, 222, 297, 380, 396, 619,
  667n; linear drawings by, 187;
  New York exhibitions of, 182–83,
  392, 657n, 663n; odalisque paint-
  ings by, 398; in Sidney Janis col-
  lection, 211; windows in paintings
  by, 153
  works: *Conversation*, 529; *Jazz*, 391;
  Laurette in a White Blouse, 295,
  686n; *Red Studio*, 567, 570; *Self-
  Portrait* (1906), 141–42, 656n;
  Woman with a Veil, 162; *Yvonne
  Landsberg*, 656n
Matisse, Patricia (née Kane), 462, 498,
  540, 557, 585, 601, 622, 623
Matisse, Pierre, 461, 476, 498, 526,
  536, 546, 597, 701n; gallery of,
  210, 380, 387, 663n, 664n, 695n;
  Patricia Kane Matta and, 462,
  540, 601, 622

Matisse, Teeny, 546
Matossian, Nourtiza, 436, 638*n*
Matta, Anne (née Alpert), 384,
    540
Matta Echaurren, Roberto, 334,
    383–86, 394, 395, 397, 431,
    440–41, 445, 527, 535, 540, 557,
    559, 564, 592, 696*n*; abstract sym-
    bolism of, 518; *Arcanum 17* illus-
    trated by, 461; arrival in America
    of, 379, 380; Breton and, 430,
    461, 483, 497–99, 622, 623; cir-
    cle motifs of, 423; drawings by,
    417, 425–26, 435, 62; Grand
    Central Clavilux installation ad-
    mired by, 454; Greenberg on,
    479, 565; inscapes of, 489;
    Mougouch's affair with, 584–89,
    600–603, 608, 621–23; New York
    exhibitions of, 383, 424, 482, 536,
    696*n*; Reynal's criticism of, 444;
    sexual narratives of, 424, 570;
    Sweeny on, 438; totemic person-
    ages of, 572
Matta, Patricia, *see* Matisse, Patricia
Matter, Mercedes (née Carles), 159,
    258–59, 262, 263, 516, 673*n*,
    676*n*, 677*n*
Matther, Frank Jewett, Jr., 219
Mattox, Charles, 172
Matulka, Jan (artist), 217
Mayakovsky, Vladimir, 394, 661*n*
Maynard, Ken, 208
Mayne, Nick, 200
Mazoh, Stephen, 684*n*
McBride, Henry, 624
McCulloch, David, 249
McCulloch, Rook, 172, 249
McCulloch, Warren, 204, 249, 317,
    369
McLaren, Grisell, 77, 646*n*
McMahon, Audrey, 264–66, 686*n*
McMillen Gallery (New York), 392
McNeil, George, 217, 255, 258, 260,
    262, 673*n*, 676*n*
Medes, 12

Meier-Graefe, Julius, 137–39, 144,
    655*n*
Melikian, Arax, 85, 92, 99
Melikian, Azniv, 92
Melikian, Mariam, 85, 99, 132, 652*n*
Mellon Galleries (Philadelphia), 219
Melville, Robert, 581–82, 629
Memling, Hans, 242
Message from Nowhere, 483
Metropolitan Museum of Art (New
    York), 148, 150, 168, 209–10,
    326, 372, 442, 455, 476, 550; ar-
    mor room of, 573; Byzantine Sec-
    tion of, 242; Cézannes in, 137;
    Fayum mummy portraits in, 157;
    Hals in, 130; Ingres in, 156; Ori-
    ental carpets in, 49, 149; Poussins
    in, 175; Rodin Gallery of, 136;
    Vermeers in, 149
Metzger, Mina, 167, 172, 181, 204,
    236, 249, 313, 331, 335, 338, 546,
    605; and Gorky's cancer treat-
    ment, 513; de Kooning and, 333;
    at Levy Gallery exhibition open-
    ing, 474; paintings purchased by,
    240, 302, 401, 462, 547, 713*n*;
    studies with Gorky, 147–50, 202,
    282, 386; Vandercooks and, 374
Michelangelo, 155, 189, 667*n*
Mili, Gjon, 520–21
Miller, Cerille, 230, 672*n*
Miller, Dorothy, 21, 202, 204, 219–20,
    339, 351, 360, 390, 391, 401, 427,
    432, 526, 692*n*, 712*n*
Miller, Liberty (Gorky's niece, née
    Azaduhi Amerian), 17, 42, 108,
    109, 115, 117, 132, 146, 164,
    302–3
Milton, John, 49
Miró, Joan, 157, 181, 215, 218, 352,
    390, 391, 423, 439, 456, 479, 565,
    626, 631, 663*n*, 667*n*, 669*n*,
    700*n*; Balthus's portrait of, 658*n*;
    Catalonian themes of, 291; faces
    in gouaches by, 363; fantastical
    landscapes of, 482, 685*n*; murals

influenced by, 274, 316, 364; in Museum of Modern Art exhibitions, 657n, 663n, 693–94n; in New York, 540–42; painting technique of, 190; protozoan creatures of, 184; sense of suspension of, 570; use of color by, 122, 454, 488, 571

works: *The Birth of the World*, 703n; *Dog Barking at the Moon*, 128, 186; *The Farm*, 359; *Landscape*, 664n; *Painting*, 280; *The Siesta*, 280; *Still Life with Old Shoe*, 362

Modigliani, Amedeo, 250, 667n

Mondrian, Piet, 260, 262, 276, 352, 460, 696n

Monet, Claude, 122, 159

Mongols, 12

Monticelli, Adolphe, 130

Montoya, Carlos, 541

Montoya, Sally, 541

Montross Gallery (New York), 210, 260

Mooradian, Arshag, 54, 110

Mooradian, Karlen, 19, 21, 121, 436, 631, 639n, 641n, 642n, 650n, 653n, 685n, 709n, 710n; birth of, 235, 236; books and articles on Gorky by, 635–38n; childhood of, 283–86, 295, 321, 338, 345, 354, 355, 365, 396, 401, 485; family stories told by Vartoosh to, 16, 17, 68, 118, 636n, 640n, 651n

Mooradian, Moorad, 117, 164, 165, 238, 242, 294, 295, 339, 355, 396, 401, 485, 638n, 639n, 641n; correspondence of, 29, 268, 286, 306, 314, 315, 345, 353–54, 365, 406, 693n; in New York, 234–36; Stalinism of, 172, 192

Mooradian, Vartoosh (née Adoian), 16, 17, 31, 34, 54, 114, 118, 123, 399, 636n, 637n, 640n, 641n, 644n, 651n; birth of, 20; birth of son of, 235, 236; in Boston, 345; in Chicago, 281, 354–57; childhood

of, 42, 50, 54, 58; correspondence of, 29, 217, 268–69, 281–86, 288, 289, 299, 301–9, 313–15, 333, 338–39, 345, 347–48, 352–54, 357, 365, 367, 368, 371, 391, 393–94, 396, 401, 406, 458, 485–87, 502–3, 522–23, 530, 650n, 684n, 693n, 698n; devotion to Gorky of, 112; emigration to America of, 99–103; and father's death, 555; and father's remarriage, 113; financial help from, 197; gift of painting to, 186, 189; at Gorky's funeral, 614; marriage of, 117; in New York, 142–43, 160, 234–37, 247, 294; in Philadelphia, 242; portraits of, 284–85, 295, 297, 299, 351, 642n; in Russian Armenia, 89–93, 96–99; snobbery of, 395; Stalinism of, 172, 192; in Watertown, 108–10, 139, 164–65; during World War I, 68, 79, 84, 86–87, 649n

Moore, Henry, 316

Morgenthau, Henry, 48, 59, 63, 69

Morris, George L. K., 263, 676n

Motherwell, Robert, 388, 482, 527

Moudoyan, Krikor, 98, 101

Mozart, Wolfgang Amadeus, 173, 447

Mukhitarian, Onnig, 59, 62–63, 66, 69–70, 72, 76–77, 648n

Munich School, 121

Murch, Walter, 146

Murphy, Katherine, 116, 120–23, 653n

Muschenheim, Art, 314

Muschenheim, Lisa, 240, 313, 314, 670n

Muschenheim, William, 240, 304, 313, 314, 335, 365, 367, 670n, 690n

Museum of Modern Art (New York), 43, 178, 301, 338, 489, 541, 562, 631, 657n, 712n, 713n; acquisition of Gorky's works by, 192,

Museum of Modern Art (*cont.*)
360, 438, 546, 571, 706*n*;
Gaudier-Brzeska show at, 331;
Goodyear's retirement from, 310;
Gorky retrospective at, 437, 701*n*;
Dalí lecture at, 381; Léger retrospective at, 275, 683*n*; Matisse
show at, 663*n*; Miller as curator
at, 21, 202, 339, 390; Miró retrospective at, 693–94*n*; opening
of, 148; Picasso show at, 181;
Sidney Janis collection shown
at, 211; Sweeny and,
302
    exhibitions: *Drawings in the Collec-*
tion of the Museum of Modern
Art, 707*n*; *Fantastic Art, Dada,*
Surrealism, 380; *Fourteen Ameri-*
cans, 401, 496, 526–28; *New*
American Acquisitions, 291; *New*
Horizons in American Art, 225,
267; *New Rugs by American*
Artists, 390–91; *Painting in Paris*,
657*n*; *Twelve Contemporary*
Painters, 428; *Twentieth-Century*
Portraits, 295, 391; *Works by 46*
Painters and Sculptors under 35
Years of Age, 215–16
Museum of Non-Objective Painting,
    see Guggenheim Museum
Muslims, 12, 16, 24, 56, 59, 63–65,
644*n*, 645*n*
Mussikian, Sirun, 159–68, 171,
185, 191, 192, 230, 516,
660*n*

Najarian, Heghine (Gorky's sister-in-
law), 109, 112
Nakian, Paul, 247
Nakian, Reuben, 193, 206, 207, 225,
247–48, 292, 335, 605
Nation, The, 200, 478–79, 519, 528,
565, 624, 626
National Academy of Design, 21, 129,
159

National Gallery (London), 157
National Gallery of Art (Washington,
D.C.), 151–55, 210, 658*n*
Nazarbekian, Avetis, 172, 406–7
Nazarbekian, Maro (née Miriam Var-
danian), 172, 406
Nazism, 311, 509
Neininger, Urban, 344, 345, 352, 353,
413, 495, 535, 541, 546, 614, 622,
700*n*
Nelson, Randolph, 245
Neumann, J. B., 216, 698*n*
Nevelson, Louise, 673*n*
New American Painting, 629
Newark Airport, murals for, 157, 179,
237, 243, 245, 264–76, 304, 307,
317, 678*n*, 680*n*, 682*n*, 683*n*
Newark Art Commission, 264, 266,
270–71, 679*n*
Newark Evening News, 267, 679*n*
Newark Ledger, 269, 270
Newark Museum, 267, 679*n*
New Art Circle Gallery (New York),
216, 698*n*
New England Butt Company, 284
New-Land Foundation, 509, 526
Newman, Barnett, 557–58, 630
New School for Social Research, 216,
252, 382, 670*n*
New School of Design, 116, 118–20,
131; New York branch of, 123,
129, 653*n*
New York *Daily News*, 372
New Yorker, The, 702*n*
New York Evening Post, 134–35
New York Graphic Society, 682*n*
New York Herald Tribune, 223, 265,
518, 627, 702*n*
New York Mirror, 372
New York Post, 372
New York Public Library, 138
New York School of Art, 121
New York School painters, 177, 178,
214, 487, 627, 630
New York Sun, 316–17, 518–19,
624

New York Times, The, 221–23, 369, 389, 479, 562, 565, 613, 624, 627, 628, 712*n*

New York University, 173, 275, 664*n*, 682*n*; Library, 128

New York World Telegram, 223, 224, 265

New York World's Fair (1939), 304–7, 317, 364, 688*n*, 696*n*

Nicholas II, Czar of Russia, 93

Nierendorf Gallery (New York), 698*n*

Nikolaev, General, 78

Nogales, General Rafael de, 63–64, 66, 70, 73, 647*n*

Noguchi, Isamu, 156, 292, 336, 385, 443, 475, 497, 546, 563, 597, 689*n*; during breakup of Gorkys' marriage, 605–8; cross-country trip with, 337–43, 346; Fuller and, 335; at Gorky's funeral, 614; in Hugo Gallery *Bloodflames* exhibition, 536; Marden mural commission arranged by, 314; in Museum of Modern Art *Fourteen Americans* exhibition, 527; and outbreak of World War II, 311, 312; Surrealists and, 387, 430, 538, 540

Novotny, Fritz, 655*n*

Oakman, Rene, 230, 672*n*

Oberlin College, Allen Memorial Art Museum, 567, 568, 573

O'Connor, Francis V., 671*n*, 682*n*

Olinsey, Lillian, *see* Kiesler, Lillian

Omnibus, 667*n*

Onslow Ford, Gordon, 380, 382, 384

Opper, John, 676*n*

Orlowsky, Lillian, 381

Orozco, José Clemente, 189

Osborn, Bayard, 505, 521, 621

Osborn, Margaret (Peggy), 199–200, 335–37, 341, 440, 504, 505, 521, 536, 540, 541, 595, 599, 605, 665*n*, 692*n*

Ossorio, Alfonso, 628

Ottoman State Bank, 101

Outerbridge, Paul, 670*n*

Ozenfant, Amédée, 275, 460, 696*n*

Paalen, Wolfgang, 696*n*

Pach, Walter, 308

Parade (ballet), 255

Paris, School of, 3, 122, 181, 211, 215, 385, 387, 397, 631

Parker, Dorothy, 343

Parsons, Betty, 369, 370, 673*n*

Partisan Review, 204, 626

Pavia, Philip, 386, 628–29

Penn, Irving, 520, 704*n*

Pennsylvania Academy of Fine Art, 224

Pereira, Irene Rice, 527, 673*n*

Perényi, Eleanor, 463, 464

Perkins, Frances, 483–84

Perry, Alma, 158

Persians, 12

Pétain, Marshal, 349

Peterdi, Gabor, 434

Petit, George, Galérie, 189

Philadelphia Inquirer, 220, 221

Philadelphia Museum of Fine Arts, 234

Phillips, Collection, 662*n*

Phillips, Duncan, 177

Phillips, Helen, 536

Phillips, John C., 620, 622–24

Picasso, Pablo, 11, 135, 149, 157, 215, 223, 241, 281, 297, 352, 361, 387, 390, 417, 423, 439, 479, 619, 626, 666*n*, 667*n*, 669*n*, 681*n*, 684*n*, 696*n*; birthday of, 21; Breton and, 486; in *Cahiers d'Art,* 302; catalog of drawings of, 663*n*; Cubism of, 144, 182–86, 189, 208, 279, 364, 693*n*; Davis and, 217, 218; Graham and, 176–79, 191, 392, 662*n*, 664*n*; Ingres and, 151–52, 187, 188; Melville's book on, 581–82, 629; Gorky's murals

Picasso, Pablo (*cont.*)
  influenced by, 274; neoclassical
    women of, 167, 232; New York
    exhibitions of, 180, 181, 211, 482,
    657*n*; portraits by, 295, 550; still
    lifes by, 243, 665*n*; use of color by
    122, 683*n*; weeping women series
    by, 287–88
  works: *Boy Leading a Horse*, 659*n*;
    Bullfights, 289; *Crucifixion* draw-
    ings, 190; *Dinard—Design for a
    Monument*, 189; *The Dreams and
    Lies of General Franco*, 424; *Fam-
    ily of Saltimbanques*, 659*n*; *Figure
    au bord de la mer*, 189; *Girl before
    a Mirror*, 289; *Guernica*, 211,
    308, 457; *Harlequin*, 186, 255;
    Head of a Sailor, 660*n*; *Lysistrata*,
    400; *Mandolin and Music Stand
    (Musical Instrument)*, 184; *Painter
    and Model*, 186, 276, 289; *Painter
    with a Model Knitting*, 190; *Red
    Tablecloth with Plaster Cast*, 214;
    Seated Woman, 181, 184, 186,
    190, 663*n*; *Self-Portrait* (1906),
    128, 299; *The Studio*, 276, 277;
    The Three Musicians, 181, 186,
    274; *Women Playing at the Edge
    of the Sea*, 280, 290, 291
Piening, Peter, 399–400
Piero della Francesca, 681*n*
Pisanello, 667*n*
Pissarro, Camile, 122
Pollet, Joseph, 404
Pollock, Jackson, 170, 387–89, 392,
    461, 482, 498, 519, 565, 619, 626,
    628, 629, 662*n*, 673*n*, 714*n*; *The
    Deep*, 575; *Magic Mirrors*, 563;
    She-Wolf, 438
Pomiankowski, Vice Field Marshal,
    66
Pop Art, 214
Postimpressionism, 215
Poussette-Dart, Richard, 482
Poussin, Nicolas, 175, 336; *Triumph of
    Baccus*, 211

Princeton University, 219; Art Mu-
    seum, 188
Prohibition, 203
Protestants, 53, 54
Prudian, Akabi (Gorky's half-sister), *see*
    Amerian, Akabi
Prudian, Sima (Gorky's half-sister), 16,
    18, 23, 53, 640*n*
Prudian, Tomas, 16–17, 19
Public Works of Art Project (PWAP),
    226–27, 237, 317, 670*n*, 671*n*
Puget, Pierre, 136
Purists, 275
Putzel, Howard, 382, 482–83
Puvis de Chavannes, Pierre-Cécile,
    248

Ruffi, 16, 34
Rand, Harry, 567, 572, 708*n*
Rankine, V. V., *see* Magruder, V. V.
Raphael, 209, 210, 667*n*
Ray, Man, 696*n*
Raynolds, G. C., 85, 90, 91
Red Army, 95, 312, 372
Red Cross, 73, 85
Redon, Odilon, 424, 666*n*
Reid, Whitelaw, 387
Reiff, Robert, 216
Reinhardt Gallery (New York), 137
Reis, Becky, 499
Reis, Bernard, 477, 499
Rembrandt, 187, 667*n*
Renaissance, 122, 153, 157, 210–11,
    667*n*
Renoir, Auguste, 122, 667*n*
Resnick, Milton, 293, 564, 628, 704*n*
Reynal, Jeanne, 316, 336, 337, 339,
    343, 413, 418, 456, 457, 589, 597,
    598, 621–22; during breakup of
    Gorkys' marriage, 601, 603, 605,
    606; Breton introduced to Gorky
    by, 430; in California, 336,
    334–48, 350, 352; correspon-
    dence of Mougouch and,
    431–32, 438, 440–53, 456, 457,

460–65, 469–71, 475–77, 479, 481–84, 489, 493–500, 504–7, 509, 511–12, 521–26, 528, 531, 535, 545, 574, 700n, 701n; financial help from, 452, 495, 513, 558; gifts to Mougouch from, 600; at Gorky's funeral, 614; in Hugo Gallery *Bloodflames* exhibition, 536; kachina doll collection of, 563, 572; on *The Liver Is the Cock's Comb*, 437; at Miró dinner party, 541; New York brownstone of, 563, 580; paintings and drawings purchased by, 336, 351, 451, 454, 480, 520, 546–47, 692n; and Schwabacher's biography, 620; at Surrealist parties, 540; at wedding of Gorky and Mougouch, 352–53

Reznikoff, Mischa, 111, 138, 142, 147, 158–60, 175, 187, 205, 207, 221, 230–32, 252, 587, 652n

Rhode Island School of Design, 111

Richards, August, 458, 459

Richards, V. V., *see* Magruder, V. V.

Richmond, Patricia Margaret, 673n

Riley, Maude, 478, 518

Rimbaud, Arthur, 274, 581, 682n, 696n

Rivera, Diego, 347

Riviera Club murals, 304, 314, 325, 658n, 690n

Robinson, Edward G., 302

Robinson, Colonel James, 241

Rochester Arts Club, 243, 244

Rockefeller, John D., 217

Rockefeller, Nelson A., 625

Rockefeller Center (New York), 220

Rodin, Auguste, 666n; *The Poet and the Model*, 136; *The Thinker*, 181

Rohde, Peggy, 705n

Romans, 12

Roos, Allan, 589, 605, 609

Rose, Herman, 277

Rosenberg, Harold, 141, 181–82, 188–89, 197, 293, 429, 432, 498, 629–30, 693n, 701n

Rosenblum, Robert, 631

Roszak, Theodore, 527

Rothko, Mark, 129–30, 141, 260, 388, 389, 482, 630, 631, 714n; *Slow Swirl at the Edge of the Sea*, 487

Rousseau, Henri, 667n

Rubin, William, 289, 629, 693n

Rushdouni, Y. K., 60, 70

Russian Revolution, 90–94

Russians, 77–79, 83–87, 118

Ruta, Peter, 325, 427

Sacco, Nicola, 256

Sade, Marquis de, 439, 623, 696n

Sadler, M.T.H., 698n

Sage, Kay, 380, 496–97, 520, 525–26, 583, 591–93, 609, 611, 614, 710n, 711n

San Francisco Chronicle, 344, 346, 352

San Francisco Examiner, 351

San Francisco Museum of Modern Art, 337, 344, 347–49, 351–52, 700n

San Francisco News, 351

Sandow, Alexander, 172–73, 231, 252, 369

Sandow, Helen, 172–73, 231–32, 303, 660n

Santillo, Lorenzo, 239–40, 242

Sarafian, Akabi (Gorky's step-mother), 115

Sargent, John Singer, 120, 159

Sarian, Oksen, 369

Sarkisian, Abisag (née Der Marderosian), 649–50n

Saroyan, William, 201

Sartre, Jean-Paul, 535

Schapiro, Louis, 666n

Schapiro, Meyer, 120, 180, 209, 386, 714n

Schary, Saul, 150, 182, 206, 266, 302, 394–95, 607–11; on *The Artist and His Mother*, 151, 154–56, 658n; country house of, 250, 393, 397, 399, 429, 702n; at Gorky's

Schary, Saul (*cont.*)
  funeral, 614; mural for Marden
  by, 315; portrait of Gorky by, 201;
  during World War II, 367
Schjeldahl, Peter, 632
Schnitzler, Max, 145, 277, 278, 507
Schrady, Fred, 322, 690*n*
Schwabacher, Ethel (née Kramer),
  210, 227, 503, 507, 527, 563–64,
  569, 572, 573, 575, 596, 605, 626,
  651*n*, 693*n*, 695*n*, 706*n*; biography of Gorky by, 39, 356, 541,
  581, 620–21, 677*n*, 678*n*, 698*n*;
  on Breton, 537; correspondence
  of Mougouch and, 395, 415,
  422–24, 433, 485, 489, 497, 499,
  500, 506, 530, 556, 561, 563–65,
  580, 581, 591, 593, 599, 603–4,
  620–21, 643*n*; Corinne Michael
  West and, 240, 243, 245, 246; on
  Depression-era poverty, 192,
  200–201; dinners hosted by, 335;
  on *Fireplace in Virginia* drawings,
  529; and Gorky's cancer treatment, 512–13, 516; at Levy
  Gallery exhibition opening, 474;
  and Maro's birth, 408; at Miró
  dinner party, 541; Mougouch described by, 323; painting donated
  to Museum of Modern Art by,
  360, 694*n*; paintings and drawings
  purchased by, 282, 284, 288, 386,
  462, 546, 657*n*, 683*n*; on *Self-
  Portrait*, 299–300; studies with
  Gorky, 146–50, 158, 202
Schwabacher, Wolfgang, 308, 503,
  509, 565, 605, 706*n*; correspondence of Mougouch and, 499,
  500, 526, 528, 561, 580, 581, 593,
  603–4, 621; dinners hosted by,
  335; at Levy Gallery exhibition,
  474; at Miró dinner party, 541;
  painting donated to Museum of
  Modern Art by, 360; paintings
  purchased by, 284, 286, 288, 313,
  480

Seitz, William C., 437, 569, 570, 572,
  693*n*, 701*n*
Seliger, Charles, 482
Seligman, Kurt, 380, 386, 696*n*
Seljuks, 12
Senate, U.S., 367
Sert, José Luis, 541
Seurat, Georges, 296, 361, 521, 657*n*,
  667*n*
Shaghoian, Nazlu, 99
Shagoyan, Levon Pasha, 58, 99
Shahn, Ben, 256
Shakespeare, William, 49, 546
Shane, Myrtle O., 646*n*
Shaw, Charles, 263
Siamanto (poet), 139–40
Sinan (Armenian architect), 101
Sisley, Alfred, 122
Sistine Chapel, 155
Skon, Sigurd, 127
Slobodkina, Esphyr, 676*n*
Smith Act (1940), 367
Smith, David, 170, 174, 207, 221, 256,
  278, 392, 670*n*
Smith, Hazel, 673*n*
Snapper, Else Oak, 325
Soby, James Thrall, 380, 476, 515,
  541, 573
Social Realism, 215, 258, 260
Société Anonyme, 216, 670*n*, 698*n*
Society of the Black Cross, 637*n*
Solman, Joseph, 159, 260
Soutine, Chaim, 368
Soyer, Moses, 296
Soyer, Raphael, 129, 180, 197, 228,
  296–97, 301, 312, 375, 510,
  559–60
Soyer, Rebecca, 296
Spender, Matthew, 638*n*, 653*n*, 655*n*,
  659*n*, 663*n*
Stackpole, Ralph, 347, 349
Stalin, Joseph, 192, 310, 311, 354,
  394, 546, 602, 706
Stalingrad, battle of, 312
Stalinism, 172, 256, 260
Steel, Bob, 208

Stein, Gertrude, 550
Steinberg, Saul, 527, 705n
Stella, Joseph, 207
Stergis, Stergis M., 127–29, 131, 133–34, 136–37, 142
Still, Clyfford, 388
Stoehr, Taylor, 672n
Stone, Allan, 455, 625
Stone, Grace Zaring, 463
Stravinsky, Igor, 447
Suleyman the Magnificent, Sultan, 101
Surrealists, 4, 163, 183, 218, 308, 334, 344, 351, 430–32, 520, 536–38, 557, 580, 585, 667n; affairs and divorces among, 540, 608–9; ambiguity of, 436; American Abstract Artists' bias against, 262; C shape icon of, 186; Cubism and, 192, 271, 279, 629, 693n; decline of, 539; excommunication and reinstatement of Matta by, 623; exhibition in Paris of, 531; exile in New York of, 379–88; free association techniques of, 381; games of, 499, 508; Graham and, 178, 179, 662n; hostility of critics to, 478, 479; Lautréamont and, 419; Léger and, 403; Levy and, 210, 244, 463, 664n, 696n; magazines published by, 382, 384, 477, 483, 701n; Manifesto of, 379; Museum of Modern Art exhibition of, 380; psychic automatism of, 189–90, 425; Reynal on, 444; sexual themes of, 424, 570; taking objects out of context by, 226; theory of titles of, 465; see also specific artists and writers
Svenningsen, Herluf, 145
Sweeny, James Johnson, 263, 302, 421, 438–39, 457, 476
Swinden, Albert, 260, 265, 673n, 678n

Tahsin Pasha, 48
Talaat Pasha, 24, 56

Tamayo, Rufino, 482
Tanguy, Yves, 380, 386, 388, 483, 496–97, 508, 520, 525–26, 536, 583, 591, 593, 614, 696n, 702n
Tanning, Dorothea, 308, 540, 585
Tartars, 12, 94
Tate Gallery (London), 397, 398, 432, 434
Taylor, Mary, 420, 452, 699n
Taylor, Richard, 676n
Taylor, Thomas, 420, 452, 699n
Tchelitchew, Pavel, 696n
Ten, The, 259–60
Terlemezian, Panos, 134
Thompson, Fred, 337, 344
Tintoretto, Jacopo Robusti, 242; mural in Scuola di San Rocco, 268
Tiridates III, King of Armenia, 12
Titian, 214, 667n
Tobey, Mark, 527
Tolegian, Manuel, 350
Tolstoy, Leo, 79
Toulouse-Lautrec, Henri de, 441, 667n
Toumanian, Hovhannes, 32, 34, 40–41, 79, 698n
Town and Country magazine, 391, 464
Traphagen School of Fashion, 239
Trdat of Ani, 101
Treasury Relief Art Project (TAP), 671n
Treasury Section of Painting and Sculpture, 671n
Tredick, Anne, 521
Trotskyism, 260
Trumbull, R. D., 676n
Turks, 9, 10, 12–15, 22, 32, 34, 38, 50, 52, 55–56, 95, 249, 292; Armenian insurrection against, 66–76, 80; censorship by, 54; counteroffensive of, 83–84; Kemalist, 99; Kurdish violence encouraged by, 14; massacres of Armenians by, 15–17, 23–25, 56–71, 80, 85, 94, 119, 367, 372; women, clothing of, 48

Turner, J.M.W., 667n
Twachtman, John, 122

U.S. Immigration Office, 102
Uccello, Paolo, 178, 217, 262, 361,
    521, 667n, 681n; *The Profanation
    of the Host*, 227; *The Rout of San
    Romano*, 157, 573
Union of Salvation, 637n
United China Relief Agency, 367, 374
Urartian kings, 12, 47–48
Ussher, Clarence D., 14, 23, 24, 49,
    53, 56–58, 61–63, 69, 71–75,
    78–80, 83–87, 90, 639–41nn,
    646–48nn
Ussher, Elizabeth (née Barrows), 49,
    61, 64, 66, 70, 72–73, 76, 78, 80,
    99
Ussher, Neville, 69

Valentine, Kurt, 427
Valentine Gallery (New York), 175,
    210, 211, 276, 308, 663n
Vandercook, Jane (now Jane Gunther),
    374
Vandercook, John, 374
Van Dyck, Anthony, 133, 652n
Vanzetti, Bartolomeo, 256
Varda, Jean, 344
Vardanian, Miriam (also called Maro),
    172, 406
Vasilieff, Alexander, 198
Velázquez, Diego Rodriguez de Silva,
    Rokeby Venus, 162
Venice Biennale, 626
Vermeer, Jan, 149, 156
Verve, 667n
View magazine, 382
Vogue magazine, 520, 704n
Vollard, Ambroise, 188
Vorontsov-Dashkov, Count, 91
Vramian (Dashnak leader), 62
VVV magazine, 382, 384, 477, 701n
Vytlacil, Vaclav, 156, 262, 676n

Wadsworth Atheneum, 664n; *Newer
    Super-Realism*, 696n
Walinska, Anna, 222–24
Walker & Pratt Stove Company, 108
Walkowitz, Abraham, 666n
War Department, U.S., 271
War Services Division, Graphic Sec-
    tion of, 688n
*Waterbury Sunday Republican Maga-
    zine*, 577–79
Weber, Max, 216, 221, 306, 688n
Weiss, Harry, 236, 510–11, 517, 546,
    592–93, 597, 601–5, 607, 621
Wells College, 219
West, Corinne Michael, 239–46, 258,
    331, 363, 516, 673n
West, Faith, 241, 245–46
Weyhe, Erhard, 212–13
Wheeler, Monroe, 391, 712n
Whitney, Gertrude Vanderbilt, 128
Whitney Museum of American Art,
    178, 223, 225, 261, 290, 302, 498,
    671n, 706n; *Abstract Painting in
    America* exhibition, 216, 221, 669n;
    Annuals, 277, 285, 334, 358, 360,
    428, 531, 566, 692n, 703n, 707n;
    centennial exhibition of, 632; group
    shows at, 562; retrospective at,
    626–28; self-portrait of Gorky in,
    151, 153, 155, 658n, 659n
Whitney Studio Club, 128
Wildenstein Gallery (New York), 137,
    655n
Wilfred, Thomas, 454
Wilmington Society of Fine Arts, 219
Wilson, Susanna, 540
Winser, Beatrice, 267
Wood, Grant, 324
Works Progress Administration (WPA),
    178, 238, 256, 258, 259, 302,
    304–7, 339, 359, 681n, 682n,
    688n; *see also* Federal Art Project
World War I, 22, 57–94, 117, 644n;
    Armenian genocide during,
    57–66, 80, 85, 94, 119, 372,
    646–47nn

World War II, 271, 310–12, 367–70, 372, 379, 688n, 693n

Xenophon, *Anabasis*, 49
Xercon, Jean, 687n

Yale University Art Gallery, 670n
Yarrow, Ernest A., 54, 61–62, 65, 72, 74, 80, 89, 90, 647n, 648n

Yarrow, Jane, 80, 90, 645n
Yezidis, 86
Yeznig, Bishop, 60, 63, 67
Young Turks, 24, 640n
Yphantis, George, 131

Zadkine, Ossip, 696n
Zarifian, Hovhannes, 32
Zervos, Christian, 137
Zogbaum, Wilfred, 259, 676n
Zurbarán, Francisco de, 396

Art Acknowledgments

Page 1 Photo by Gjon Mil: courtesy Hulten Archive/TimePix.

Page 7 *Boy with Head on Mother's Lap*, c. 1938–39. Pen and ink on paper. Collection Gorky/Mooradian Archive, Eastern Diocese of the Armenian Church. Photo courtesy Knoedler Gallery.

Page 45 *Self-Portrait*, study for *The Artist and His Mother*, c. 1936. Pen and ink wash on paper, 11 × 8½". Private collection. Photo courtesy Gagosian Gallery.

Page 81 Photo taken from *Armenia*.

Page 105 Photo courtesy Maro and Natasha Gorky and Matthew Spender.

Page 125 Photos courtesy the Hirshhorn Museum and Sculpture Garden Archives, Smithsonian Institute, gift of Abraham Grabar, 1978. Reproduced by Lee Stalsworth.

Page 196 Photo by Wyatt Davis. Courtesy Maro and Natasha Gorky and Matthew Spender.

Page 253 Photo courtesy The Newark Museum.

Page 319 Photo courtesy The Newark Museum.

Page 377 Photo courtesy Maro and Natasha Gorky and Matthew Spender.

Page 411 Photo courtesy Agnes Fielding.

Page 467 Photo by Elisa Breton. Courtesy Maro and Natasha Gorky and Matthew Spender.

Page 491 Photo courtesy Maro and Natasha Gorky and Matthew Spender.

Page 533 Photo courtesy Maro and Natasha Gorky and Matthew Spender.

Page 553 Photo by Ben Schnall: courtesy Hulten Archive/TimePix.

Fig. 1. *Staten Island*, 1927–28. Oil on canvas, 32 × 34". Collection Richard Estes, New York. Photo courtesy Abbeville Press.

Fig. 2. *Pears, Peaches, Pitcher*, c. 1926–27. Oil on canvas, 17¼ × 23⅝". Private collection. Photo courtesy Lennon, Weinberg Gallery.

Fig. 3. *Still Life*, c. 1928. Oil on canvas, 20⅛ × 24". Private collection. Photo courtesy Lennon, Weinberg Gallery.

Fig. 4. *The Artist and His Mother*, c. 1926–36. Oil on canvas, 60 × 50". Collection Whitney Museum of American Art. Gift of Julien Levy for Maro and Natasha Gorky in memory of their father. Photo courtesy Whitney Museum of American Art.

Fig. 5. *The Artist and His Mother*, c. 1926–42. Oil on canvas, 60 × 50". Collection National Gallery of Art, Washington, DC, Ailsa Mellon Bruce Fund. Photo courtesy Abbeville Press.

Fig. 6. Pablo Picasso, *Self-Portrait*, 1906. Oil on canvas, 36 × 28". Philadelphia Museum of Art, A. E. Gallatin Collection. Photo courtesy Art Resource, N.Y. © 2002 Estate of Pablo Picasso/Artists Rights Society (ARS), New York.

Fig. 7. *Portrait of the Artist and His Mother*, c. 1936. Pencil on paper, 29 × 19". Collection National Gallery of Art, Washington, DC, Ailsa Mellon Bruce Fund, 1979. Photo courtesy Abbeville Press.

Fig. 8. *Composition with Vegetables,* c. 1928–29. Oil on canvas, 28¹⁄₁₆ × 36¹⁄₁₆". Jack S. Blanton Museum of Art, The Michener Collection, The University of Texas at Austin. Photo courtesy Agnes Fielding.

Fig. 9. *Still Life,* 1929. Oil on canvas, 47 × 60". Private collection. Photo courtesy Gagosian Gallery.

Fig. 10. Pablo Picasso, *Musical Instrument,* 1923. Oil on canvas, 38 × 51". Collection unknown. Photo courtesy Art Resource, N.Y. © 2002 Estate of Pablo Picasso/Artists Rights Society (ARS), New York.

Fig. 11. *Still Life,* 1929. Oil on canvas, 36¼ × 48½". Private collection. Photo courtesy Gagosian Gallery.

Fig. 12. *Still Life with Palette,* c. 1930. Oil on canvas, 28 × 36". Whereabouts unknown. Photo courtesy Whitney Museum of American Art.

Fig. 13. *Still Life (Harmony),* c. 1931. Oil on canvas, 22 × 27". Collection Gorky/Mooradian Archive, Eastern Diocese of the Armenian Church of America.

Fig. 14. *Still Life,* c. 1930–31. Oil on canvas, 38½ × 50⅜". Collection, The Chrysler Museum of Art, Norfolk, Virginia. Photo courtesy The Chrysler Museum of Art.

Fig. 15. *Blue Figure in Chair,* c. 1931. Oil on canvas, 48 × 38". Private collection. Photo courtesy Gagosian Gallery.

Fig. 16. *Organization,* 1933–36. Oil on canvas, 50¼ × 60¼". Collection National Gallery of Art, Washington, DC, Ailsa Mellon Bruce Fund. Photo courtesy Lennon, Weinberg Gallery.

Fig. 17. Pablo Picasso, *Painter and Model,* 1928. Oil on canvas, 51⅛ × 64¼". Collection The Museum of Modern Art, The Sidney and Harriet Janis Collection (fractional gift). Photo courtesy Art Resource, N.Y. © 2002 Estate of Pablo Picasso/Artists Rights Society (ARS), New York.

Fig. 18. Photo by Wyatt Davis. Photo courtesy Joan Davis.

Fig. 19. *Still Life on Table,* c. 1936–37. Oil on canvas, 54 × 64". Private collection. Photo courtesy Gagosian Gallery.

Fig. 20. *Painting,* 1936–37. Oil on canvas, 38 × 48". Collection Whitney Museum of American Art. Photo courtesy Whitney Museum of American Art.

Fig. 21. *Composition,* 1936–37. Oil on canvas, 36 × 48". Collection Mr. and Mrs. I. Donald Grossman. Photo courtesy Abbeville Press.

Fig. 22. *Organization No. 2,* 1936–37. Oil on canvas, 28 × 36". Private collection. Photo courtesy Gagosian Gallery.

Fig. 23. *Portrait of Myself and My Imaginary Wife,* 1933–34. Oil on cardboard, 8½ × 14½". Collection Hirshhorn Museum and Sculpture Garden, Smithsonian Institution. Gift of the Joseph H. Hirshhorn Foundation, 1966. Photo courtesy Hirshhorn Museum.

Fig. 24. *Portrait of Ahko,* c. 1937. Oil on canvas, 19½ × 15". Private collection. Photo courtesy Lennon, Weinberg Gallery.

Fig. 25. *Portrait of Vartoosh,* 1933–36. Oil on canvas, 20 × 15". Collection Hirshhorn Museum and Sculpture Garden, Smithsonian Institution. Gift of the Joseph H. Hirshhorn Foundation, 1966. Photo courtesy Hirshhorn Museum.

Fig. 26. Photo taken from Karlen Mooradian, *Arshile Gorky Adoian.*

Fig. 27. *Self-Portrait,* c. 1937. Oil on canvas, 55½ × 34". Private collection. Photo courtesy Lennon, Weinberg Gallery.

Fig. 28. *Self-Portrait*, c. 1936–37. Pencil on paper, 24½ × 19". Collection unknown. Photo courtesy Knoedler Gallery.

Fig. 29. *Mechanics of Flying*, Newark Airport, left panel, 1936. Oil on canvas, 110 × 133". Collection The Newark International Airport Art Collection, The Port Authority of New York/New Jersey. Photo courtesy Newark Museum.

Fig. 30. Pablo Picasso, *Three Musicians*, 1921. Oil on canvas, 6' 7" × 7' 3 3/4". Collection The Museum of Modern Art, Mrs. Simon Guggenheim Fund. Photo courtesy Art Resource, N.Y. © 2002 Estate of Pablo Picasso/Artists Rights Society (ARS), New York.

Fig. 31. *Image in Khorkom*, c. 1934–36. Oil on canvas, 33 × 43". Private collection. Photo courtesy Lennon, Weinberg Gallery.

Fig. 32. *Image in Khorkom*, 1936. Oil on canvas mounted on panel, 36 × 48". Collection Albright-Knox Art Gallery, Buffalo. Photo courtesy Anderson Gallery.

Fig. 33. *Khorkom*, c. 1937–38. Oil on canvas, 40 × 52". Private collection. Photo courtesy Lennon, Weinberg Gallery.

Fig. 34. *After Khorkom*, c. 1937. Oil on canvas, 36 × 48". Collection The Art Institute of Chicago. Gift of Mr. and Mrs. Howard Wise. Photo courtesy Art Institute of Chicago.

Fig. 35. *Enigmatic Combat*, c. 1937. Oil on canvas, 35¾ × 48". Collection San Francisco Museum of Art. Gift of Jeanne Reynal. Photo courtesy Abbeville Press.

Fig. 36. *Summer in Sochi, Black Sea*, 1936. Oil on canvas, 24⅛ × 34 ⅛". Private collection. Photo courtesy Jason McCoy Inc.

Fig. 37. *Apricots*, c. 1938. Oil on canvas, 22 × 25". Private collection. Photo courtesy Agnes Fielding.

Fig. 38. *Untitled (Women Dancing)*, mid-1930s. Pen and ink on paper, 9 × 12". Collection Allan Stone Gallery, New York. Photo from Guggenheim Museum, Arshile Gorky, exhibition catalog 1981.

Fig. 39. *Argula*, 1938. Oil on canvas, 15 × 24". Collection The Museum of Modern Art, New York. Gift of Bernard Davis. Photo courtesy Art Resource, N.Y.

Fig. 40. *Untitled*, c. 1939–40. Oil with pencil on cardboard, 8½ × 12½". Private collection. Photo courtesy Newark Museum.

Fig. 41. *Composition*, c. 1939–41. Oil on canvas, 18½ × 20". Whereabouts unknown. Photo taken from Julien Levy, *Arshile Gorky*.

Fig. 42. *Garden in Sochi*, c. 1941. Oil on canvas, 25 × 29". Whereabouts unknown. Photo by Eric Pollitzer, courtesy Knoedler Gallery.

Fig. 43. Joan Miró, *Personages Attracted by the Form of a Mountain*, 1936. Tempera with graphite underdrawing on Masonite, 13 × 19¾". Collection The Baltimore Museum of Art, Bequest of Saidie A. May BMA 1951.338. Photo courtesy Baltimore Museum. Succession Miró/Artists Rights Society (ARS), New York/ADAGP, Paris.

Fig. 44. Photo courtesy Agnes Fielding.

Fig. 45. Photo courtesy Matthew Spender.

Fig. 46. Photo taken from *Armenian Art*.

Fig. 47. Photo courtesy Lennon, Weinberg Gallery.

Fig. 48. Photo taken from Karlen Mooradian, *Arshile Gorky Adoian.*

Fig. 49. *The Artist's Mother,* 1938. Charcoal on paper, 24 × 18½". The Art Institute of Chicago: 1965.510, The Worcester Sketch Collection. Photo courtesy Art Institute of Chicago.

Fig. 50. Photo taken from *Illustration armenienne: 1901–1906,* Keghouni, Venice, St. Lazars.

Fig. 51. Photo taken from *Van.*

Fig. 52. Armenian manuscript. T'oros Roslin, canon table page, from the *Zeyt'un Gospels,* 1256, fol. 8. Collection The J. Paul Getty Museum, Los Angeles.

Fig. 53. Photo taken from Clarence D. Ussher, *An American Physician in Turkey.*

Fig. 54. Photo taken from Henry Morgenthau, *Ambassador Morgenthau's Story.*

Fig. 55. Photo taken from *The Defense of Van.*

Fig. 56. Photo taken from Karlen Mooradian, *Arshile Gorky Adoian.*

Fig. 57. Photo taken from Karlen Mooradian, *Arshile Gorky Adoian.*

Fig. 58. Photo taken from Karlen Mooradian, *Arshile Gorky Adoian.*

Fig. 59. Photo courtesy Gorky/Mooradian Archive, Eastern Diocese of the Armenian Church of America.

Fig. 60. Photo courtesy Maro and Natasha Gorky and Matthew Spender.

Fig. 61. Photo courtesy the Whitney Museum of American Art.

Fig. 62. *Park Street Church,* 1924. Oil on canvas-board, 16 × 12". Collection Lowell Art Association, Lowell, Massachusetts. Gift of Katherine O'Donell Murphy. Whistler House Museum of Art. Photo courtesy Jim Jordan.

Fig. 63. Photo courtesy The Newark Museum.

Fig. 64. Photo courtesy The Newark Museum.

Fig. 65. Photo courtesy Maro Gorky and Matthew Spender.

Fig. 66. *Nude (After Rodin)* also called *The Poet and the Model,* 1925–26. Whereabouts unknown. Photo taken from Grand Central School of Art brochure for 1925–26. Courtesy the Whitney Museum of American Art.

Fig. 67. *Self-Portrait,* 1923–24. Oil on canvas-board, 16 × 12". Collection James Corcoran, Los Angeles. Photo courtesy Jim Jordan.

Fig. 68. *Self-Portrait,* 1926–27. Oil on canvas, 20 × 15". Collection Mr. and Mrs. Edwin A. Bergman. Photo courtesy Jim Jordan.

Fig. 69. *Self-Portrait at the Age of Nine, 1913,* 1927. Oil on canvas, 12 × 10½". Metropolitan Museum. Photo courtesy Abbeville Press.

Fig. 70. *Self-Portrait,* c. 1928. Oil on canvas, 24 × 16". Los Angeles County Museum of Art. Gift of Mr. and Mrs. Hans Burkhardt. Photo courtesy Los Angeles County Museum of Art.

Fig. 71. *Self-Portrait,* 1928. Oil on canvas, 20 × 16". Collection Solomon R. Guggenheim Museum. Gift of David McCulloch. Photo courtesy Abbeville Press.

Fig. 72. Henri Matisse, *Self-Portrait,* 1906. Oil on canvas, 21⅝ × 18⅛". Statens Museum for Kunst, J. Rump Collection, Copenhagen. Photo courtesy Art Resource, N.Y. Succession H. Matisse, Paris/Artists Rights Society (ARS), New York.

Fig. 73. *Self-Portrait,* 1928. Pen and ink on paper. Size and collection unknown. Photo courtesy Knoedler Gallery.

Fig. 74. *Self-Portrait*, c. 1928. Pastel and graphite on paper, 14½ × 11¼". Collection Harry W. and Mary Margaret Anderson. Photo courtesy Gagosian Gallery.

Fig. 75. *Self-Portrait*, 1933–34. Oil on canvas, 10 × 8". Private collection, New York. Photo courtesy Gagosian Gallery.

Fig. 76. *Still Life with Skull*, c. 1927–28. Oil on canvas, 33 × 26¼". Private collection. Photo courtesy Jim Jordan.

Fig. 77. *Still Life with Horse*, 1928. Oil on canvas, 21 × 21". Collection unknown. Photo courtesy Jim Jordan.

Fig. 78. *Still Life with Pears*, 1928. Oil on canvas, 16 × 24". Collection Allan Stone. Photo courtesy Jim Jordan.

Fig. 79. Georges Braque, *Basket of Fruit*, 1922. Gouache on gessoed panel, 6 × 11½". Philadelphia Museum of Art, A. E. Gallatin Collection. Photo courtesy Philadelphia Museum. © 2002 Artists Rights Society (ARS), New York/ADAGP, Paris.

Fig. 80. Photo courtesy Maro and Natasha Gorky and Matthew Spender

Fig. 81. *Reclining Nude*, c. 1929. Oil on canvas, 34¼ × 44⅛". Private collection. Photo courtesy Knoedler Gallery.

Fig. 82. Photo by Ann Dickey. Courtesy Ann Dickey.

Fig. 83. Photo by Ann Dickey. Courtesy Ann Dickey.

Fig. 84. *Cubist Standing Figure*, c. 1931–32. Pen and ink on drawing board, 28⅞ × 23". Private collection. Photo courtesy Stephen Mazoh.

Fig. 85. *Ecorché*, c. 1931. Graphite on paper, 25¼ × 18". Private collection. Photo courtesy Melvin Lader.

Fig. 86. *Nighttime, Enigma, and Nostalgia*, c. 1931–33. Graphite on heavy wove paper, 21½ × 29⅞". Private collection. Photo courtesy Stephen Mazoh.

Fig. 87. *Nighttime, Enigma, and Nostalgia*, c. 1931–33. Pen, brush, ink, and graphite on paper, 22¾ × 29". Private collection. Photo courtesy Stephen Mazoh.

Fig. 88. Giorgio de Chirico, *The Fatal Temple*, 1913. Oil on canvas, 12¾ × 15½". Philadelphia Museum of Art, A. E. Gallatin Collection. Photo courtesy Philadelphia Museum.

Fig. 89. *Untitled* (related to *Nighttime, Enigma, and Nostalgia*), c. 1933–36. Brush, pen, ink, and wash on heavy wove paper, 22⅝ × 30¾". Private collection. Photo courtesy Gagosian Gallery.

Fig. 90. *Khorkom*, c. 1933–36. Graphite with some stumping on chain-laid paper, 19⅛ × 24⅞". Private collection. Photo courtesy Stephen Mazoh.

Fig. 91. André Masson, *Cock Fight*, 1930. Oil on canvas, 8½ × 10¼". Philadelphia Museum of Art, A. E. Gallatin Collection. Photo courtesy Philadelphia Museum. © 2002 Artists Rights Society (ARS), New York/ADAGP, Paris.

Fig. 92. Photo courtesy Jim Jordan.

Fig. 93. Study for *Mural*, c. 1933–34. Pen, brush, and ink on paper, 9¾ × 29". Private collection. Photo courtesy Gagosian Gallery.

Fig. 94. Paolo Uccello, *The Miracle of the Host*, c. 1467–68. Tempera, 17 × 138½". Galleria Nazionale della Marche, Palazzo Ducale, Urbino. Copyright Alinari/Art Resource, N.Y.

Fig. 95. Photo courtesy Christopher Busa.

Fig. 96. Photo courtesy The Newark Museum.

Fig. 97. *Portrait of Jacob Kainen,* c. 1934–37. Oil on canvas, 22 × 18". Private collection. Photo courtesy Gagosian Gallery.

Fig. 98. Photo courtesy Whitney Museum of American Art.

Fig. 99. Photo courtesy Smithsonian Institution, John D. Graham Papers, Archives of American Art.

Fig. 100. Photo taken by Leo Seltzer for the WPA. Photo courtesy Smithsonian Institution, Washington, DC.

Fig. 101. *Self-Portrait,* c. 1936. Pencil, 9⅞ × 8¼". Collection Brenda Webster, Berkeley, CA. Photo courtesy Gagosian Gallery.

Fig. 102. Corinne Michael West, c. 1930. Photo by Jon Boris. Photo courtesy Stuart and Roberta Friedman, Granite Springs, New York.

Fig. 103. Sketch of *Activities on the Field* (left side), north wall of model for Gorky's murals at Newark Airport (lost), 1936. Photographed by the WPA Federal Art Project. Photo courtesy The Newark Museum.

Fig. 104. Fernand Léger, *The City,* 1919. 91 × 117½". Oil on canvas. Philadelphia Museum of Art, A. E. Gallatin Collection. Photo courtesy Philadelphia Museum. © 2002 Artists Rights Society (ARS), New York/ADAGP, Paris.

Fig. 105. Photo courtesy Joan Davis.

Fig. 106. Photo courtesy Whitney Museum of American Art.

Fig. 107. Portrait of Leonore Portnoff, c. 1938–39. Crayon on paper, 13½ × 10¼". Private collection Joel Shàpiro and Ellen Phelan. Photo courtesy Joel Shapiro and Ellen Phelan.

Fig. 108. *Man's Conquest of the Air,* 1939. Oil on canvas mural, Aviation Building, New York World's Fair, dimensions unknown (destroyed). The mural is known only through a postcard in the file of the New York Public Library. Photo courtesy Abbeville Press.

Fig. 109. Sketch for Ben Marden's Riviera Club murals, 1940–41. Gouache on cardboard, 8⅞ × 16¼". Private collection. Photo courtesy CDS Gallery.

Fig. 110. Photo courtesy Maro and Natasha Gorky and Matthew Spender.

Fig. 111. *Portrait of Mougouch,* c. 1941. Pencil on paper, 24¾ × 19". Private collection. Photo courtesy Gagosian Gallery.

Fig. 112. Photo courtesy Maro and Natasha Gorky and Matthew Spender.

Fig. 113. Photos courtesy Maro and Natasha Gorky and Matthew Spender.

Fig. 114. *Bull in the Sun,* 1942. Gouache on paper, 18½ × 24¾". Collection The Museum of Modern Art/Licensed by Scala/Art Resource, N.Y. Photo courtesy Abbeville Press.

Fig. 115. *Flowers in a Vase on Red Cloth,* 1942. Oil on canvas, 16 × 12". Private collection. Photo courtesy Lennon, Weinberg Gallery.

Fig. 116. *The Pirate I,* 1942–43. Oil on canvas, 29¼ × 40⅛". Estate of Julien Levy. Photo courtesy Abbeville Press.

Fig. 117. Roberto Matta Echaurren, *Inscape (Psychological Morphology No. 104),* 1939. Oil on canvas, 28⅛ × 36⅜". Private collection, courtesy Cavanero Fine Arts, New York. Photo courtesy Sotheby's Inc. © 2002 Artists Rights Society (ARS), New York/ADAGP, Paris.

Fig. 118. *Portrait of Mougouch, Pregnant,* 1943. Pen and dark-brown and black ink, brush, and light-brown and gray wash on paper, 13¾ × 9⅝". Collection The Baltimore Museum of Art. Gift of Mr. and Mrs. I. W. Burnham II, for the Thomas E. Benesch Memorial Collection BMA 1963.110. Photo courtesy Baltimore Museum.

Fig. 119. Photo courtesy Maro and Natasha Gorky and Matthew Spender.

Fig. 120. Photo courtesy Maro and Natasha Gorky and Matthew Spender.

Fig. 121. Photo courtesy Maro and Natasha Gorky and Matthew Spender.

Fig. 122. Photo courtesy Maro and Natasha Gorky and Matthew Spender.

Fig. 123. Photo courtesy Maro and Natasha Gorky and Matthew Spender.

Fig. 124. *Portrait of Captain John Magruder*, c. 1943–44. Pencil on paper, 12½ × 9½". Private collection. Photo courtesy Gagosian Gallery.

Fig. 125. *Composition II*, 1943. Pencil and crayon on paper, 22¾ × 29". Collection Barbara and Donald Jonas. Photo courtesy Lennon, Weinberg Gallery.

Fig. 126. *Untitled*, 1944. Pencil and crayon on paper, 19 × 25". Collection Christopher Schwabacher. Photo courtesy Lennon, Weinberg Gallery.

Fig. 127. Photo by Mina Metzger. Courtesy David McCulloch.

Fig. 128. Photo courtesy V. V. Rankine.

Fig. 129. Photo courtesy Agnes Fielding.

Fig. 130. Photo taken from Guggenheim exhibition catalog, *Arshile Gorky*, 1981.

Fig. 131. *Diary of a Seducer*, 1945. Oil on canvas, 50 × 62". Collection Mr. and Mrs. William A. M. Burden, New York. Photo courtesy Jim Jordan.

Fig. 132. *From a High Place*, 1944. Oil on canvas, 22 × 28". Collection Mr. and Mrs. Donald M. Weisberger. Photo courtesy Lennon, Weinberg Gallery.

Fig. 133. *From a High Place II*, 1946. Oil on canvas, 17 × 24". Private collection. Photo courtesy Lennon, Weinberg Gallery.

Fig. 134. Photo by Irving Penn. Courtesy Whitney Museum of American Art.

Fig. 135. Photo by Gjon Mili. Courtesy Maro and Natasha Gorky and Matthew Spender.

Fig. 136. *Fireplace in Virginia*, 1946. Ink and crayon, 8½ × 10⅞". Private collection. Photo courtesy Knoedler Gallery.

Fig. 137. *Fireplace in Virginia*, 1946. Pencil and crayon on paper, 21¾ × 29½". Collection Mr. and Mrs. Stanley R. Gumberg. Photo courtesy Lennon, Weinberg Gallery.

Fig. 138. *Drawing*, 1946. Pencil on paper, 18⅞ × 24⅞". Collection Yale University Art Gallery. Photo courtesy Abbeville Press.

Fig. 139. Photo courtesy Maro and Natasha Gorky and Matthew Spender.

Fig. 140. Photo courtesy Maro and Natasha Gorky and Matthew Spender.

Fig. 141. *The Calendars*, 1946–47. Oil on canvas, 50 × 60". Formerly Collection Nelson A. Rockefeller, destroyed by fire, 1961. Photo courtesy Jim Jordan.

Fig. 142. *The Orators*, 1947. Oil on canvas, 60 × 72". Collection Mr. and Mrs. William C. Janss, Thousand Oaks, California. Photo courtesy Jim Jordan.

Fig. 143. Photo courtesy Enrico Donati.

Fig. 144. Photo by Ben Schnall/Hulton Archive/TimePix.

Fig. 145. Photo by Ben Schnall/Hulton Archive/TimePix.

Fig. 146. Photo courtesy Maro and Natasha Gorky and Matthew Spender.

Fig. 147. *Dialogue of the Edge*, c. 1947–48. Oil on canvas, 31½ × 40⅜". Jack S. Blanton Museum of Art, The University of Texas at Austin. Gift of Mari and James A. Michener, 1991. Photo courtesy Jim Jordan.

Fig. 148. Photo by Wifredo Lam. Courtesy Eskil Lam. © Wifredo Lam, Photo Wifredo Lam.

Fig. 149. *Garden in Sochi*, 1941. Oil on canvas, 44¼ × 62¼". Collection The Museum of Modern Art. Purchase Fund and Gift of Mr. and Mrs. Wolfgang S. Schwabacher (by exchange). Photo courtesy Art Resource, N.Y.

Fig. 150. *Garden in Sochi*, c. 1943–47. Oil on canvas, 31 × 39". Collection The Museum of Modern Art. Acquired through the Lillie P. Bliss Bequest. Photo courtesy Art Resource, N.Y.

Fig. 151. *Waterfall*, 1942–43. Oil on canvas, 60½ × 44½". Collection The Tate Gallery, London. Photo courtesy Art Resource, N.Y. Copyright Tate Gallery, London/Art Resource, N.Y.

Fig. 152. *Golden Brown Painting*, 1943–44. Oil on canvas, 43¹³⁄₁₆ × 55⁹⁄₁₆". Washington University Gallery of Art, St. Louis. University purchase, Bixby Fund, 1953.

Fig. 153. *Drawing*, 1943. Pencil and crayon on paper, 22¾ × 29". Private collection. Photo courtesy Lennon, Weinberg Gallery.

Fig. 154. *Untitled*, c. 1943–44. Oil on canvas, 34⅛× 46". The Art Institute of Chicago: The Worcester Sketch Collection. Photo Courtesy Art Institute of Chicago.

Fig. 155. *To Project, to Conjure*, 1944. Oil on canvas, 35½ × 46½". Collection Stephen and Nan Swid, New York. Photo courtesy Lennon, Weinberg Gallery.

Fig. 156. *One Year the Milkweed*, 1944. Oil on canvas, 37 × 47". Collection National Gallery of Art, Washington, DC, Ailsa Mellon Bruce Fund. Photo courtesy Lennon, Weinberg Gallery.

Fig. 157. *How My Mother's Embroidered Apron Unfolds in My Life*, 1944. Oil on canvas, 40 × 45". Collection Seattle Art Museum. Gift of Mr. and Mrs. Bagley Wright. Photo courtesy Seattle Art Museum.

Fig. 158. *The Liver Is the Cock's Comb*, 1944. Oil on canvas, 73¼ × 98⅜". Collection Albright-Knox Art Gallery, Buffalo. Gift of Seymour H. Knox. Photo courtesy Albright-Knox Art Gallery.

Fig. 159. Study for *The Liver Is the Cock's Comb*, 1943. Ink, pencil, and crayon on paper, 19 × 25½". Collection Frederick Weisman Family. Photo courtesy Melvin Lader.

Fig. 160. *Water of the Flowery Mill*, 1944. Oil on canvas, 42½ × 48¾". Collection The Metropolitan Museum of Art, George A. Hearn Fund, 1956. (56.205.1) Photo © 1984 The Metropolitan Museum of Art.

Fig. 161. *Good Afternoon, Mrs. Lincoln*, 1944. Oil on canvas, 30 × 38". Collection Barney A. Ebsworth, Missouri. Photo courtesy Knoedler Gallery.

Fig. 162. *They Will Take My Island*, 1944. Oil on canvas, 38 × 38". Collection Art Gallery of Ontario, Toronto. Purchased with assistance from the Volunteer Committee Fund, 1980. Photo courtesy Art Gallery of Ontario.

Fig. 163. *Painting*, 1944. Oil on canvas, 65¾ × 70³⁄₁₆". The Solomon R. Guggenheim Foundation, New York, Peggy Guggenheim Collection, 1976 76.2553.152. Photo courtesy Abbeville Press.

Fig. 164. *Good Hope Road II* (also called *Pastoral* or *Hugging*), 1945. Oil on canvas, 25½ × 32⅝". Collection Fundación Colección Thyssen-Bornemisza. Photo courtesy Agnes Fielding.

Fig. 165. *Landscape Table*, 1945. Oil on canvas, 36 × 48". Collection Musée National d'Art Moderne, Centre Georges Pompidou, Paris. Photo courtesy CNAC/MNAM/Dist. Réunion des Musées Nationaux/Art Resource, N.Y.

Fig. 166. *Charred Beloved I*, 1946. Oil on canvas, 53⅝ × 39¾". Collection David Geffen, Los Angeles. Photo courtesy David Geffen.

Fig. 167. *Charred Beloved III*, 1946. Oil on canvas, 50 × 38⅛". Collection Jason McCoy Inc., New York. Photo courtesy Jason McCoy Inc.

Fig. 168. *The Plough and the Song*, 1947. Oil on canvas, 52⅛ × 64¼". Collection Milton A. Gordon. Photo courtesy Abbeville Press.

Fig. 169. Study for *The Plough and the Song*, 1944. Pencil and crayon on paper, 19 × 25½". Allen Memorial Art Museum, Oberlin College, Oberlin, Ohio, Friends of Art Fund 56.1. Photo courtesy Allen Memorial Art Museum.

Fig. 170. *The Betrothal II*, 1947. Oil on canvas, 50¾ × 38". Collection Whitney Museum of American Art. Photo courtesy Whitney Museum of American Art.

Fig. 171. *Pastoral*, 1947. Oil on canvas, 44 × 56¾". Private collection. Photo courtesy Lennon, Weinberg Gallery.

Fig. 172. Study for *Pastoral*, 1946. Pencil and crayon on paper, 18⅞ × 24⅝". Whereabouts unknown. Photo courtesy Lennon, Weinberg Gallery.

Fig. 173. *The Limit*, 1947. Oil on paper on canvas, 50¾ × 62½". Private collection. Photo courtesy Abbeville Press.

Fig. 174. Study for *The Limit*, 1946. Pencil and wax crayon, 19 × 25". Collection Galleria Galatea, Turin. Photo courtesy Whitney Museum of American Art.

Fig. 175. *Agony*, 1947. Oil on canvas, 40 × 50½". Collection The Museum of Modern Art, A. Conger Goodyear Fund. Photo courtesy Art Resource, N.Y.

Fig. 176. Study for *Agony I*, 1946–47. Pencil, crayon, and wash on paper, 21¾ × 29½". Collection Edward Minskoff, New York. Photo courtesy Agnes Fielding.

Fig. 177. *Dark Green Painting*, c. 1948. Oil on canvas, 43¾ × 55½". Collection Philadelphia Museum of Art. Gift (by exchange) of Mr. and Mrs. Rodolphe Meyer de Schauensee and Mr. and Mrs. R. Sturgis Ingersoll. Photo courtesy Philadelphia Museum.

Fig. 178. Study for *Dark Green Painting*, 1946. Pencil and crayon on paper, 19 × 24". Private collection. Photo courtesy Lennon, Weinberg Gallery.

Fig. 179. *Painting* (unfinished), c. 1947–48. Oil on hemp canvas, 44 × 54". Private collection. Photo courtesy Lennon, Weinberg Gallery.

Fig. 180. *Last Painting*, 1948. Oil on canvas, 30¾ × 39¾". Collection Fundación Colección Thyssen-Bornemisza. Photo courtesy Lennon, Weinberg Gallery.